P9-ARJ-230

Hydrology in Mountainous Regions. II

Artificial Reservoirs

Water and Slopes

TITLES RECENTLY PUBLISHED BY IAHS

Drainage Basin Sediment Delivery. Proceedings of the Albuquerque Symposium, August 1986
Publ.no.159 (1986), price $45

Hydrologic Applications of Space Technology. Proceedings of the Cocoa Beach Workshop, August 1985
Publ.no.160 (1986), price $45

Karst Water Resources. Proceedings of the Ankara Symposium, July 1985
Publ.no.161 (1986), price $45

Avalanche Formation, Movement and Effects. Proceedings of the Davos Symposium, September 1986
Publ.no.162 (1987), price $50

Developments in the Analysis of Groundwater Flow Systems. Report prepared by a Working Group of the IAHS International Commission on Groundwater
Publ.no.163 (1986), price $35

Water for the Future: Hydrology in Perspective
Proceedings of the Rome Symposium, April 1987
Publ.no.164 (1987), price $50

Erosion and Sedimentation in the Pacific Rim. Proceedings of the Corvallis Symposium, August 1987
Publ.no.165 (1987), price $55

Proceedings of the symposia held during the IUGG Assembly, Vancouver, August 1987:

Large Scale Effects of Seasonal Snow Cover
Publ.no.166 (1987), price $42

Forest Hydrology and Watershed Management
Publ.no.167 (1987), price $55

The Influence of Climate Change and Climatic Variability on the Hydrologic Regime and Water Resources
Publ.no.168 (1987), price $55

Irrigation and Water Allocation
Publ.no.169 (1987), price $32

The Physical Basis of Ice Sheet Modelling
Publ.no.170 (1987), price $40

Hydrology 2000. Report of the IAHS Hydrology 2000 Working Group
Publ.no.171 (1987), price $22

Side Effects of Water Resources Management. Report prepared by an IHP-III Working Group
Publ.no.172 (1988), price $40

Groundwater Monitoring and Management. Proceedings of the Dresden Symposium, March 1987
Publ.no.173 (1990), price $55

Sediment Budgets. Proceedings of the Porto Alegre Symposium, December 1988
Publ.no.174 (1988), price $60

Consequences of Spatial Variability in Aquifer Properties and Data Limitations for Groundwater Modelling Practice. Report prepared by a Working Group of the International Commission on Groundwater
Publ.no.175 (1988), price $45

Karst Hydrogeology and Karst Environment Protection. Proceedings of the IAH/IAHS Guilin Symposium, October 1988
Publ.no.176 (1988), price $55

Estimation of Areal Evapotranspiration. Proceedings of a workshop held during the IUGG Assembly, Vancouver, August 1987
Publ.no.177 (1989), price $45

Remote Data Transmission. Proceedings of a workshop held during the IUGG Assembly, Vancouver, August 1987
Publ.no.178 (1989), price $30

Proceedings of symposia held during the Third IAHS Scientific Assembly, Baltimore, Maryland, May 1989:

Atmospheric Deposition
Publ.no.179 (1989), price $45

Systems Analysis for Water Resources Management: Closing the Gap Between Theory and Practice
Publ.no.180 (1989), price $45

Surface Water Modeling: New Directions for Hydrologic Prediction
Publ.no.181 (1989), price $50

Regional Characterization of Water Quality
Publ.no.182 (1989), price $45

Snow Cover and Glacier Variations
Publ.no.183 (1989), price $30

Sediment and the Environment
Publ.no.184 (1989), price $40

Groundwater Contamination
Publ.no.185 (1989), price $40

Remote Sensing and Large-Scale Global Processes
Publ.no.186 (1989), price $40

FRIENDS in Hydrology. Proceedings of the Bolkesjø Symposium, April 1989
Publ.no.187 (1989), price $50

Groundwater Management: Quantity and Quality Proceedings of the Benidorm Symposium, October 1989
Publ.no.188 (1989), price $60

Erosion, Transport and Deposition Processes. Proceedings of the Jerusalem Workshop, March-April 1987
Publ.no.189 (1990), price $40

Hydrology of Mountainous Areas. Proceedings of the Strbske Pleso Workshop, Czechoslovakia, June 1988
Publ.no.190 (1990), price $45

Regionalization in Hydrology. Proceedings of the Ljubljana Symposium, April 1990
Publ.no.191 (1990), price $45

Research Needs and Applications to Reduce Erosion and Sedimentation in Tropical Steeplands. Proceedings of the Suva, Fiji, Symposium, June 1990
Publ.no.192 (1990), price $50

Hydrology in Mountainous Regions. I - Hydrological Measurements; the Water Cycle. Proceedings of two Lausanne Symposia, August 1990
Publ.no.193 (1990)

Hydrology in Mountainous Regions. II - Artificial Reservoirs; Water and Slopes. Proceedings of two Lausanne Symposia, August 1990
Publ.no.194 (1990)

First of New Series!

Hydrological Phenomena in Geosphere-Biosphere Interactions: Outlooks to Past, Present and Future
by Mälin Falkenmark
Monograph no.1 (1989), price $15

Available only from IAHS Press, Wallingford

PLEASE SEND ORDERS AND/OR ENQUIRIES TO:

Office of the Treasurer IAHS, 2000 Florida Avenue NW, Washington, DC 20009, USA
[telephone: +1 202 462 6900; telex: 7108229300; fax: +1 202 328 0566]

IAHS Press, Institute of Hydrology, Wallingford, Oxfordshire OX10 8BB, UK
[telephone: +44 (0)491 38800; telex: 849365 hydrol g; fax: +44 (0)491 32256]

Please send credit card orders (VISA, ACCESS, MASTERCARD, EUROCARD) and IAHS Membership orders to the Wallingford address only. A catalogue of publications may be obtained free of charge from either address.

Hydrology in

Mountainous Regions II

ARTIFICIAL RESERVOIRS

WATER AND SLOPES

Edited by

Richard O. SINNIGER
Federal Institute of Technology, GR Ecublens,
CH-1015 Lausanne, Switzerland

Michel MONBARON
Institut de Géographie, Pérolles 1700,
CH-1700 Fribourg, Switzerland

Proceedings of two international symposia,
the Symposium on the Impact of Artificial
Reservoirs on Hydrological Equilibrium (S3)
and the Symposium on the Role of Water
in the Morphological Evolution of Slopes
(S4), held at Lausanne, Switzerland, 27
August–1 September 1990. The symposia
were part of the International Conference
on Water Resources in Mountainous
Regions jointly convened by the
International Association of Hydrological
Sciences (IAHS)and the International
Association of Hydrogeologists (IAH).

IAHS Publication No. 194

Published by the International Association of
Hydrological Sciences 1990.

IAHS Press, Institute of Hydrology, Wallingford, Oxfordshire
OX10 8BB, UK.

IAHS Publication No. 194.

ISBN 0-947571-62-0.

The designations employed and the presentation of material throughout the
publication do not imply the expression of any opinion whatsoever on the part of
IAHS concerning the legal status of any country, territory, city or area or of its
authorities, or concerning the delimitation of its frontiers or boundaries.

The use of trade, firm, or corporate names in the publication is for the
information and convenience of the reader.   Such use does not constitute
an official endorsement or approval by IAHS of any product or service
to the exclusion of others that may be suitable.

The camera-ready copy for the papers was prepared by the authors and
assembled/finished at IAHS Press.

Printed in The Netherlands by Krips Repro Meppel.

PREFACE

Mountainous regions may not only offer considerable quantities of water running in rivers or entering into the hydrogeological system but due to the relief, surface water presents also the potential for hydropower generation. As one of the best known renewable forms of energy, large use of hydropower generation is therefore made in mountainous regions.

For many communities in the mountains, hydropower is still today the only source of regular revenue. This fact together with the creation of work places, better access roads and modern infrastructure helps to reduce emigration from the mountainous regions.

Water running from the high mountains is to a large extend the result of the snow- and ice melt in summer. For that reason hydropower would mainly be produced in summer if the water could not be partially accumulated in artificial reservoirs to be used in winter when the energy demand is considerably higher and when the river powerplants in the flatter regions produce less.

The creation of artificial reservoirs has therefore two main consequences:

-   water is partially stored in the warm season and the natural flow in the rivers downstream of the reservoir is reduced;
-   water used in winter for electricity generation flows in galleries and enters the river downstream of the power house.

This change in the flow regime entails considerable modifications to the river runoff. Some aspects of these modifications will be discussed under the topics of Symposium 3.

An important consequence of artificial reservoirs is their capability to control floods and thus to reduce flood risks in the downstream area. Statistical analysis made by Zeller for a number of measuring stations in Switzerland proved this fact and showed in the same time that this effect decreases with increasing distance from the reservoir.

But not only water and flood peaks are stored in the artificial reservoirs. According to the morphological characteristics of the catchment, more or less bed load is transported to the reservoir. The bed load may either remain, thereby continuously reducing the reservoir capacity, or it may be partially released by scouring.

Changes in the flow regime of water and in the bed load also have their consequences for the riverbeds downstream of the reservoirs. Due to the generally reduced water flow, and to the modified flood peaks in particular, the downstream beds risk to lose their capacity if regular flushings do not occur.

However, by all these artificial interventions, the former or the new biological character of the rivers should not be considerably changed. This condition implies a knowledge in fields other than hydrology, geology or hydraulics. Fundamental knowledge extends even to legal aspects, as today almost all interventions by men are regulated by laws. The total absence of contributions concerning legal aspects show, however, that the discussion between engineers, scientists and lawyers has not yet started, at least not in a way that constructive solutions to long pending problems could be found.

It is my general impression that the unsatisfactory behaviour of constructions is often due to a lack of awareness in other fields. I hope therefore that the contributions to this conference may lead to a better understanding between scientists and engineers.

Richard O. Sinniger

PREFACE

Le symposium 4 propose un thème de convergence et donc, par essence, pluri-disciplinaire: géologues, géomorphologues et pédologues se joignent aux hydrologues et hydrodynamiciens pour fournir des éléments d'appréciation de la situation aux aménagistes et gestionnaires de l'espace. Ce symposium aurait d'ailleurs fort bien pu s'intituler ainsi:

"Eaux sauvages et maîtrise de l'eau sur les versants montagnards naturels et anthropisés".

En montagne alpine plus qu'ailleurs, paysages naturels et paysages anthropisés se côtoyent et s'imbriquent étroitement. La pression humaine s'accentue chaque jour, du fait du développement touristique et des activités de loisirs, ce qui a pour conséquence un recul constant et inexorable des milieux encore intacts. Dans un tel cadre, la gestion de l'eau et de ses effets, tant sur la nature que sur l'homme et ses infrastructures, est un problème sans cesse réactualisé.

Les thèmes 4A et 4B sont consacrés aux aspects et phénomènes naturels liés au cycle de l'eau en milieu montagnard. Dans le thème 4A, les mécanismes de façonnage des versants sont examinés du point de vue de l'incidence du ruissellement diffus sur les interfluves, et de la concentration progressive de l'eau dans les lits des cours d'eau. Ces phénomènes ont une influence capitale, non seulement sur le modelé des versants, mais également sur le pouvoir d'infiltration de l'eau, sur la capacité de rétention en eau des sols, sur la conservation des formations superficielles meubles, sur la préservation de la couverture végétale et, en définitive, sur une gestion harmonieuse des versants. Nous retrouvons ainsi, à ce stade, les préoccupations "aménagistes" déjà évoquées plus haut!

Le thème 4B s'intéresse plutôt aux effets brutaux et dévastateurs des crues exceptionnelles en bassin-versant montagnard. Les conséquences de ces crues sont apparemment (et dans un premier temps) limités aux thalwegs et aux cônes d'alluvions. Mais l'influence des déséquilibres brutalement créés par de tels événements se fait sentir à long terme sur l'ensemble du territoire (tout se tient dans la nature) et appelle à des réajustements jusqu'aux confins les plus éloignés des bassins-versants affectés. Au phénomène instantané, brutal, se superposent donc des incidences de longue durée qu'il est intéressant de prendre en compte, et qui font référence à l'aspect prospectif de l'aménagement du territoire.

Bien entendu, les crues exceptionnelles qui se sont produites dans les Alpes suisses en été 1987 sont un sujet de choix, qui a fourni matière à plusieurs présentations. La récurrence possible de tels événements hante les esprits des autorités et des populations locales et "habite" les médias. Bien connaître les mécanismes et les signes avant-coureurs de telles catastrophes et en tirer parti est le but avoué des études de grande envergure entreprises en Suisse à la suite de ces événements. L'aménagement des rivières et de leurs abords va, plus que jamais, être inspiré par un souci d'efficacité et de pragmatisme, afin de parer aux risques de répétition de ces catastrophes. Mais l'aspect naturel des paysages montagnards ne fera-t-il pas trop les frais de ces interventions humaines?

Le sujet proposé pour le thème 4C concernait précisément et explicitement l'intervention de l'homme sur les processus naturels de façonnage des versants. C'est là un thème vaste et difficile à cerner. Il touche de très près au "Global Change" dont se préoccupent désormais de larges cercles de la communauté scientifique internationale. La sorte d'"inflation informative" que l'on constate en ce domaine est-elle paradoxalement à l'origine du désintérêt (apparent) constaté? Ce thème C n'a suscité que peu de communications. Mais qu'on ne s'y trompe pas: la prise en compte de l'influence humaine est très présente, en filigrane, dans les préoccupations des chercheurs des quatre thèmes du symposium. Il apparaît dès lors superflu d'en faire état explicitement, tant cela semble aller de soi: l'homme, en tirant parti trop agressivement de son milieu naturel, le fragilise et semble préparer la voie aux dérèglements et accidents de parcours, notamment ceux évoqués par le thème 4B.

Il faut certes aménager judicieusement le cadre montagnard et tirer avantageusement parti des techniques de dépistage et de prévention des risques naturels, parmi lesquels les crues et les mouvements gravitaires occupent une place prééminente. C'est ce que propose le thème 4D, qui met en exergue le rôle-clef de la cartographie, outil privilégié en main des aménagistes. La Suisse, pays-hôte de ce Congrès, vient de rendre obligatoire les études d'impact sur l'environnement (EIE) lors de toute implantation d'ouvrage important. Dans de telles opérations de grande envergure, il est primordial de pouvoir faire appel aux techniques les plus performantes d'introspection du milieu. L'emploi des méthodes probabilistes en matière d'évaluation des risques, la modélisation sont, avec la cartographie, des instrument de travail performants dont la mise en oeuvre s'avèrera certainement payante en zone de montagne.

En recherchant dans le proche ou le lointain passé de la Terre les traces d'événements hydrologiques et morphologiques générateurs de déséquilibre (ou

d'équilibre!),   l'hydrogéomorphologue   (nous   osons   ce
néologisme!) peut s'imposer tel un détective attentif et
perspicace. Il   est   à   même   de   fournir   les   clefs   de
compréhension des processus prodigieusement complexes qui
gèrent l'évolution des versants. Au seuil d'un temps dont
on nous prédit qu'ils sera caractérisé par une modification
sensible   des   conditions   climatiques,   l'approche
"globalisante" des problème doit être encouragée.   La
pertinence d'études pluri-disciplinaires, "généralistes",
telles que celles qui sont proposées dans ce symposium 4,
s'imposera alors sans difficulté.

      Michel MONBARON

CONTENTS

TOPIC C: CONSEQUENCES OF MODIFIED FLOW REGIME DOWNSTREAM OF RESERVOIRS

TOPIC D: ECOLOGICAL EFFECTS AND FISHERY PROBLEMS RELATED TO RESERVOIRS

TOPIC F: GENERAL PAPERS

Symposium on the Role of Water in the Morphological Evolution of Slopes

TOPIC A:
FLOOD CONTROL BY ARTIFICIAL RESERVOIRS

Hydrology in Mountainous Regions. II - Artificial Reservoirs; Water and Slopes
(Proceedings of two Lausanne Symposia, August 1990). IAHS Publ. no. 194, 1990.

The contribution of hydropower reservoirs to flood control in the Austrian Alps

W. PIRCHER
Tiroler Wasserkraftwerke Aktiengesellschaft (TIWAG)
Landhausplatz 2, A-6o2o Innsbruck, Austria

ABSTRACT A considerable improvement to flood control is a
significant - and free - additional utility accruing to the
general public from the construction of hydropower storage
reservoirs. By way of illustration, the author presents a
comparative study on the basis of a number of flood events
in valleys influenced by storage power plants.

INTRODUCTION

Austria has approximately thirty major storage reservoirs built by hydropower companies and operated on a seasonal basis. Since they tend
to be located at high altitudes, total stored energy from a combined
active storage of 1.3oo hm^3 is over 3.5oo GWh for winter and peak power
generation, and this forms the backbone of electricity generation in
Austria. Taking into account also the smaller reservoirs for daily and
weekly storage, approximately 31% of the country's present annual total
hydroelectric generation of 34.ooo GWh is controlled by reservoir storage, with the high degree of control and flexibility this offers.
   The primary goal in the construction of all storage power schemes
in Austria, and the only source of subsequent earnings for the hydropower companies, is of course electricity generation, but such schemes
also involve a whole series of additional utilities that accrue to the
general public free of charge. As a rule, significant improvements in
flood control are the most important of these spin-offs, although benefits to the local infrastructure and tourism as well as a markable
increase of flow during the winter period are not to be underestimated,
either.

SOME BASIC CONSIDERATIONS AND STATISTICAL DATA

The fact that the retention capacity of a reservoir is a significant
flood-risk reducing factor for downstream areas is obvious enough and
is appreciated by the people who directly benefit there, but this function has not yet been given due recognition by a wider public in their
frequently unfavourable judgment on further hydropower development
schemes. At any station along a river downstream of a dam, the degree
of improvement in flood control is determined by two parameters:

   a) the ratio between the storage volume available for retention at
      the time of a flood and that part of the flood which contributes
      to peak outflow, and
   b) the percentage of total catchment area which is controlled by
      the reservoir (decrease in flood control capacity with increa-

3

sing distance from the dam).

Criticism is frequently made of the apparently contradictory strategies of providing either for a full energy reservoir or for empty
flood storage. Theoretical studies and long-term operating records,
however, show that for conditions common with seasonal storage reservoirs in the Austrian Alps, firstly, even a relatively small retention
volume can drastically reduce a flood, and secondly, such a retention
volume will in all probality be available at the time of extreme floods.

Available retention volume is determined by the volume between actual and retention water level, plus an additional flood surcharge
above the latter, i.e. above the crest of the usual free overflow
spillway. This flood surcharge volume would also be available in the
case of flood discharge into a full reservoir, but that is an extremely unlikely event given the normal filling cycles of Austria's seasonal storage reservoirs. Extreme flood events, and especially the
biggest occuring in July and August, in all probality do not coincide
with maximum storage in the reservoirs, whose filling, as a rule, is
not completed until September or October, so that only heavy rains in
September can still pose a hazard to a certain extent. In any case,
statistics show that maximum reservoir level is only reached once
every five years on average, and that this condition is maintained
for only a few days so as to avoid seepage losses (Lauffer 1975).

Given the considerable size of Austria's seasonal storage reservoirs relative to the runoff from their catchment areas, even an available retention capacity of only a few percent of reservoir capacity
is sufficient to effectively reduce peak discharge. For example, with
only 5% of its active storage capacity of 138 hm^3 left, i.e. only
2,8o m below retention level, the Gepatsch reservoir (fig. 4) could
completely impound a more than 1oo-year flood with peak inflow of
232 m^3 s^{-1}. An analysis of data taken from decades of operating experience with over thirty Austrian reservoirs (Widmann 1974 and 1988,
Ganahl & Widmann 198o) leads to the prediction that the spillways of
reservoirs with an active storage equal to at least 4o% (6o%) of annual inflow will be activated only by floods with return periods of
more than 1o (25) years. No side valley in Austria that is controlled
by a seasonal storage reservoir upstream has ever sufferred flood damage since the construction of the reservoir, and peak flows in the
main valleys have been significantly reduced since then as well.

The following two sections give a number of specific examples of
the flood protection function of reservoirs in Austria.

FLOOD CONTROL EXPERIENCE IN THE VICINITY OF STORAGE POWER PLANTS

In the Kaprun Valley (fig. 1) the Wasserfallboden and Mooserboden seasonal reservoirs, with total active storage of 168 hm^3, control 57% of
the catchment area at the Kaprun gauge. The construction of the power
plants has artificially increased floods with short return periods because the 36 m^3 s^{-1} design discharge of the Kaprun power house in itself corresponds to a natural two-year flood, while the increase in
discharge capacity of the Kapruner Ache to 7o m^3 s^{-1}, achieved by some river bed regulation, permits plant operation to continue unre-
stricted even under minor flood discharge conditions. On the other
hand, there has been a significant decrease in major flood events,

and the peak discharge of a natural ten-year flood (before construction) corresponds to a 75-year flood under present operating conditions, while the peak discharge of a natural fifty-year flood (before
construction) corresponds now to a 2.5oo-year flood, which means that
the Kaprun area now has practically total flood protection (Ganahl &
Widmann 198o, Widmann 1988).

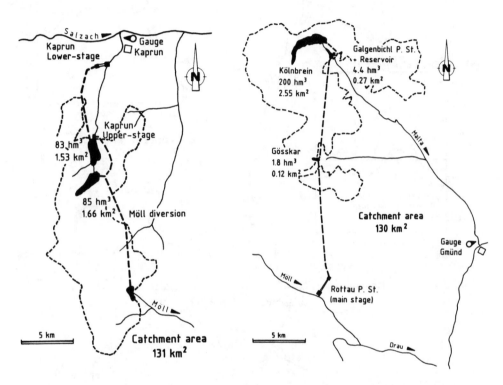

FIG.1 Glockner-Kaprun scheme.   FIG.2 Malta scheme.

In the second example (fig.2), extremely heavy precipitation centred
on the Malta Valley led to extremely high runoff, which - as subsequent calculations showed - would have reached the level of a hundred-
year flood at Gmünd and would have led to greater damage throughout
the valley than that caused by the catastrophic 1965 September flood
or the 1966 August flood. Through the appropriate use of the hydropower plant facilities, however, i.e. pumping at the upper stage and
turbining into the Möll river at the main stage, plus utilization of
available retention capacity in the Samerboden-Kölnbrein seasonal storage reservoir and the Galgenbichl and Gösskar compensation basins, it
was possible to reduce peak discharge at the Sandriesen gauge near
Gmünd, upstream of the confluence with the Lieser, from a theoretical
figure without the Malta hydropower plant of 3oo m^3 s^{-1} (i.e. a hundred-year flood, as derived from subsequent calculations) by no less
than 45% to a recorded figure of 165 m^3 s^{-1}, i.e. the equivalent of only a fifty-year flood prior to the construction of the scheme (Kugi &
Weissel 1986).

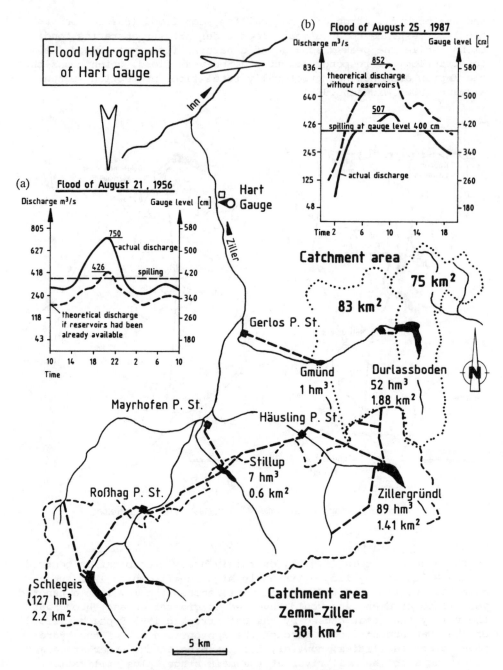

FIG.3 Zemm-Ziller and Gerlos power schemes:
3a Flood hydrographs of August 21, 1956;
3b Flood hydrographs of August 25, 1987.

Prior to construction of the seasonal storage schemes in the Ziller Valley (fig.3), adjoining fields and meadows used to be flooded every two to three years, and major flood events would inundate the local communities with up to a metre of water, as on 21 August 1956, when peak discharge reached 75o m^3 s^{-1}. With today's hydropower plants (fig. 3a), this figure could have been reduced to 426 m^3 s^{-1} (Gmeinhart 1988).

Since first filling of the seasonal storage reservoir at Durlassboden (1966), Schlegeis (1971) and Zillergründl (1987), and also of the weekly storage reservoirs at Gmünd (rebuilt in 1964) and Stillup (1969), inundation from the Ziller has been greatly reduced or altogether prevented.

Peak discharge of the major flood events of the last 15 years has been reduced by 25-4o% compared with the theoretical figures calculated for the same flood conditions without storage reservoirs. Peak discharge for the 3oo-year flood on 25 August 1987, for example, would have been 852 m^3 s^{-1} - and the damage correspondingly great - instead of the recorded figure of only 5o7 m^3 s^{-1}, which involved only some isolated overflow (fig. 3b).

These data relate to the Ziller gauge at Hart near Fügen, with a 1o95 km^2 catchment area which is 12% directly controlled by seasonal storage and 12% indirectly controlled via diversions, while the hydropower plants influence a total of 53% catchment. Not only was power generation discontinued pursuant to regulations at a predetermined highwater mark on the Hart gauge (34o cm, fig. 3b), but also standby procedures within the Austrian and south German grids permitted power to be made available to pump water from diversions back into the Schlegeis and Zillergründl reservoirs. As a result, water retention during this flood totalled 14 million m^3 (Gmeinhart 1988).

Also on 25 August 1987, the Ötz Valley was heavily damaged by floodwater, while the Stubai Valley suffered its worst damage on 19 July 1987. On these two days the Kauner Valley (fig. 4), which is located only 1o-12 miles to the west of the Ötz Valley and also runs parallel to it, suffered no damage at all - thanks to the effects of the Gepatsch reservoir. The gauge at Platz near Feichten, with a 189 km^2 catchment area which is 54% directly controlled by the Gepatsch reservoir and 25% indirectly via diversions, recorded peak discharge of only 5 m^3 s^{-1} on both days, which is a normal figure for summer discharge. Without the reservoir, peak discharge would have been 62 and 5o m^3 s^{-1} respectively for 19 July and 25 August 1987 (fig. 6), figures that correspond to a more than hundred-year flood and would certainly have been higher than peak discharge for the 196o flood, whose devastating effects have not yet been forgotten by the people of the Kauner Valley. At all events, the result would have been flooding across the full width of the valley in the flatter sections where most people live. In fact, however, the Fagge river has not once burst its banks during any flood event since the opening of the Kauner Valley hydropower plant in 1964 (Tschada & Moschen 1988).

The Montafon in Vorarlberg similarly enjoys almost total flood protection from the hydropower plants built by the Illwerke company. For the Gaschurn gauge, for example, with a 145 km^2 catchment area which is 44% controlled by reservoirs, the theoretical greatest flood discharge peaks calculated without storage reservoirs for the last 33 years have been reduced by 26 - 82%.

In addition, a marked reduction of flood flows has been observed also downstream of mere water intakes. Depending on their design capacity, this effect relates above all to minor and medium floods. Thus, the diversion from the upper Pitz Valley to the Gepatsch reservoir reduced the peak discharge at the gauge in St. Leonhard during the 1965 flood from 54 to 36 m^3 s^{-1} (fig.4), with the result that the Pitz Valley

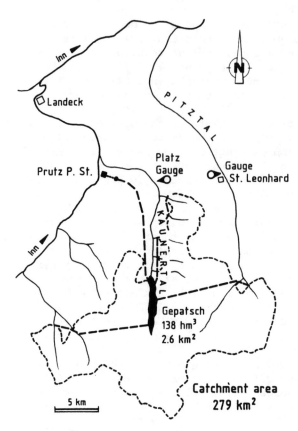

FIG.4 Kaunertal scheme.

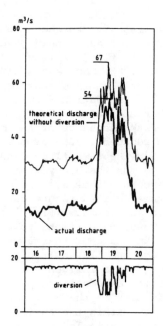

FIG.5 Flood hydrographs
at St. Leonhard gauge of
July 19, 1987.

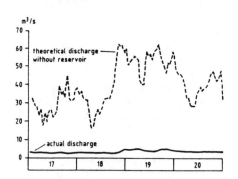

FIG.6 Flood hydrographs at
Platz gauge of July 1987.

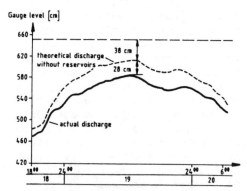

FIG.7 Flood hydrographs at
Innsbruck gauge of July 1987.

- unlike neighbouring valleys without hydropower structures - suffered no flooding at all (Lauffer 1975). On 19 July 1987 the same diversion reduced peak discharge from 67 to 54 m^3 s^{-1} (fig.5), thereby
reducing an approximately eighty-year flood to the magnitude of a
thirty-year event.

  Even short-term storage reservoirs, in spite of their limited active storage relative to flood discharge, can significantly reduce
discharge peaks. A case in point is the Klaus reservoir on the Steyr

river, which is normally kept at maximum storage level so as to ensure maximum head for the run-off-river power plant. However, when the transmitted figures for precipitation in the 539 km^2 catchment area exceed a given threshold, a flood forecast is calculated and continuously updated with the help of the flow figures transmitted from the feeder waterways, and if necessary generating is stepped up to achieve deliberate drawdown and thus create a flexible retention capacity of up to 7,8 million m^3. This permitted the two floods experienced since the plant opened in 1975 to be reduced by 3o and 42% respectively (Widmann 1988).

In general, bed load management and the related effects of hydropower plant construction is a highly complex subject. In this context, suffice it to say that decades of continuous monitoring of the desilting chambers of numerous water intakes has made the biggest contribution to date to our knowledge of bed load yield, and that the torrent control measures financed in whole or in part by power companies as part of all hydropower generating projects in mountain locations in Austria do not merely prevent any exacerbation of bed load problems but in most cases represent a clear improvement (Lauffer 1975, Sommer 198o, Tschada 1975).

REMOTE RESERVOIR EFFECTS ON FLOOD DISCHARGE IN THE MAIN RIVER

In the Alpine region there are many examples showing how seasonal storage reservoirs located on the side streams have a beneficial effect on winter runoff in the main river, which in turn benefits its biology and purity and improves the operating efficiency of run-of-river power plant.

The 5794,3 km^2 catchment area of the River Inn at the Innsbruck gauge, for example, is influenced by three seasonal storage reservoirs, whose total active storage of 362 hm^3 accounts for approximately 32% of natural winter runoff volume. 68 km further downstream, the 9313,3 km^2 catchment area at the Kirchbichl gauge is influenced by eight reservoirs, whose total active storage of 717 hm^3 again accounts for about 31% of natural winter runoff volume. Hence, the resulting increase in flow in winter is almost one third, and over half in the coldest months, while the 1o% average retention in summer is hardly even noticed (Moschen & Lauffer 1977).

Such significant changes to natural flow patterns and the fact that more than 1o% of total catchment is directly controlled by seasonal storage reservoirs for both gauging stations, would lead one to expect significant reductions in flood discharge too, and this aspect was therefore analysed in an actual case at the Innsbruck gauge (fig. 7).

Of the two 1987 flood events discussed in the previous section, it was the flood on 19 July that led to highest peak discharge in the Inn. Backanalysis of the retention effect of the hydropower reservoirs and the natural peak discharge in the Inn that would have occurred without them must carefully take due account of the timing of peak discharges from the side valleys and their superimposition in the Inn, because such factors as overflow and the activation of retention capacities are influenced by relatively slight changes in flow and water level. Careful calibration of the mathematical flow model on the basis of numerous gauge records is therefore essential. An analysis of the flood on 19 July 1987, conducted with such care and precision, showed that peak discharge at the Innsbruck gauge decreased from 125o to 113o m^{3}s^{-1}, with 7o

m^{3}s^{-1} of this reduction deriving from the Gepatsch reservoir alone.
During this flood, a total of 13,4 m^3 was retained in the reservoirs
of Livigno (Switzerland/Italy), Gepatsch, Finstertal and Längental or
diverted to the reservoirs of the Vorarlberger Illwerke company.

Consequently, a 2oo-year flood was reduced to the magnitude of a
natural forty-year flood (without storage reservoirs), and the Innsbruck city precincts were saved from partial flooding (fig. 7). It was
sufficient to restrict generating for just the few critical hours of
peak discharge (Tschada & Moschen 1988).

On the basis of these encouraging results, the decision was taken
to institutionalise contacts which had hitherto been ad hoc and sometimes improvised - but successful for all that - between the meteorological and hydrographic services, civil defence organizations, water-
way authorities and power companies, in the form of a fully coordina-
ted flood management system with the backing of mathematical flow models and forecasts.

CONCLUSION

Storage hydropower plants not only meet 23% of Austria's electricpower
generation requirements but also make a major contribution to flood
control. The considerable significance of this protective function today is the result of developments that go back over a number of decades.
And it has been achieved without imposing direct charges on either the
beneficiaries or public funds. To that extent it is a low-profile function, and that explains the regrettable inability of the general public to recognize its importance. The time has therefore come to focus
more attention on the flood control function of hydropower plants in
public discussions of both existing installations and new projects so
as to attain a greater degree of objectivity.

REFERENCES

Ganahl, P. & Widmann, R. (198o) Speichereinfluß auf Hochwässer. Inter-
    praevent, Bad Ischl, Vol. 2, 2o9-22o.
Kugi, W. & Weissel, G. (1986) Das Augusthochwasser 1985 im Maltatal.
    Carinthia II, Klagenfurt, S. 311-319.
Lauffer, H. (1975) Die Auswirkungen der Speicherkraftwerke auf die Um-
    welt. Österr. Wasserwirtschaft, Wien, 1977 (5/6), 1o1-118.
Moschen, H. & Lauffer, H. (1977) Der Einfluß der Speicher und Überlei-
    tungen auf die Wasserführung des Inn in Tirol. Österr. Wasserwirt-
    schaft, Wien, 1977 (5/6) 88-95.
Sommer, N. (198o) Untersuchungen über die Geschiebe- und Schwebstoff-
    fürhung und den Transport von gelösten Stoffen in Gebirgsbächen.
    Interpraevent, Bad Ischl, Vol. 2, 69-94.
Tschada, H. & Moschen, H. (1988) Die Hochwasserschutzfunktion der Spei-
    cherkraftwerke der TIWAG. Österr. Zeitschrift für Elektrizitäts-
    wirtschaft, Wien, 1988 (8), 256-265.
Widmann, R. (1974) Erfahrungen mit Hochwasserentlastungsanlagen öster-
    reichischer Talsperren. Österr. Wasserwirtschaft, Wien, 1974 (5/6),
    116-12o.
Widmann, R. (1988) Influence of alpine reservoirs on flood discharge.
    ICOLD-Congress San Francisco 1988, Vol. IV, Report 85, 1471-1483.

Hydrology in Mountainous Regions. II - Artificial Reservoirs; Water and Slopes
(Proceedings of two Lausanne Symposia, August 1990). IAHS Publ. no. 194, 1990.

Stochastic streamflow modelling for reservoir planning and management

V. P. SINGH & J. F. CRUISE
Department of Civil Engineering, Louisiana State University
Baton Rouge, Louisiana 70803, USA

ABSTRACT

Reservoirs are used for a multitude of purposes. Their planning and management require knowledge of various streamflow characteristics. For example, design and operation of a flood control reservoir are based on peak flow, flood volume and time interval between floods (or interarrival times). If the reservoir is to be used as a water supply source, then its design and operation may be based on minimum flows, duration of minimum flow and interarrival times of such flows.

The streamflow characteristics above certain threshold values can be considered as random variables, and a stochastic model can therefore be constructed for the streamflow series. Certain "textbook" stochastic processes have often been used for this purpose. Popular models have been based on the representation of streamflow series by Markov or Poisson processes. However, the data must sometimes be manipulated in order for these models to be applicable. If a stochastic model of streamflow could be constructed which was not based on these classical approaches, it would have many advantages. This would involve the derivation of the probability distributions of the associated flood variables, taking into account their mutual dependence.

Probability distributions of flood peaks have been derived in umpteen ways. Using the peak discharge-duration joint distribution, we derive the probability distribution of the associated flood volumes. The distribution of interarrival times of flood peaks is derived using cross-entropy with fractile constraints. A major advantage of this approach is that a model derived in this way would be applicable at lower thresholds than most current models. Based on the distributions derived in this way, a risk methodology is suggested to assist with real-time operation of reservoirs for flood control, hydropower and water supply.

INTRODUCTION

Reservoirs are used for a multitude of purposes. Water supply for irrigation, domestic and industrial use, and recreational facilities, hydropower generation, flood control, navigation, fish and wildlife enhancement, water quality improvement, low flow augmentation, and log driving are some of the reservoir uses.

Planning, design, operation and management of reservoirs require knowledge of various streamflow characteristics. For example, design and operation of a flood control reservoir are based on peak flow, flood volume and time interval between floods (or interarrival time). If the reservoir is to be used as a water supply source, then its design and operation may be based on minimum flow, duration of minimum flow, and interarrival time between such flows. Streamflow forecasting can be used for planning, design and operation of multipurpose reservoir systems. Streamflow forecasts allow time for better decision making in reservoir operation, increasing energy output and reliability by raising turbine hydraulic head and minimizing spillage, mitigating drought repercussions by augmenting dependable water supply, and reducing flood damages by avoiding excessive releases. In fact, streamflow forecasting can be used with a variety of reservoir control schemes and optimal operating rules can therefore be derived.

In real time reservoir operation, the reservoir operator frequently faces important decisions which must be made quickly and with little available information for various purposes. As an example, these decisions include setting release schedules during flood events and prereleasing to accommodate incoming floods of unexpected large magnitudes. Because of limited data, the decisions to be made sometimes do not fully account for the risks involved to the downstream areas. The actual releases may not necessarily coincide with those derived from optimal operating rules. The objective of this paper is to present a stochastic streamflow model and its application to reservoir design, operation and management.

A SHORT REVIEW OF RESERVOIR MODELS

Two broad classes of reservoir models can be distinguished: (1) design models and (2) operation and management models. The latter class of models can also be employed, with some modification, for reservoir planning.

Design Models

The hydrologic deign of a reservoir system involves determination of reservoir sizing, reservoir lifetime, and probability of failure. The design models can be distinguished as empirical, stochastic and optimization types. Many of the design procedures currently used are empirical in nature. For instance, storages in water supply reservoirs are frequently based on mass curves (Fair, et al., 1971) or the sequent-peak procedure (Thomas and Fiering, 1962). This procedure has been modified by Loucks (1976) to incorporate the calculation of storages for different levels of reliability. Design discharges and heads for hydropower projects are frequently based on empirical flow duration curves for the stream under investigation. These procedures lack the advantages which can be obtained from parametric analysis.

Recently, Singh and Durgunoglu (1989, 1990) presented a mathematical model for economic reservoir design and storage conservation by reduced sedimentation. The model estimates the design storage capacity of a reservoir by using the expected water demand, watershed area and regional K-values where K is a constant defining the average annual stream sediment yield in a region. Storage capacities of 82 water supply reservoirs, located in Illinois, were estimated. The model could be employed to analyze the remaining useful life of an existing water supply reservoir, selecting sites for prospective reservoirs, and determining the economic viability of incorporating alternative design measures.

Stochastic models are either based on storage theory, streamflow generation, or hydrologic processes. Some of these models have been developed to derive the reservoir storage distribution, subject to natural inflows and pre-determined outflows. One of the main objectives of these methods has been to quantify the risk that for combination of inflows and outflows the reservoir would run dry, or the actual release of water would have to be reduced below what the reservoir was supposed to deliver during its lifetime. The amount of this risk indicates the performance reliability of the reservoir. Some of the methods quantifying this uncertainty use either observed data on reservoir depletion or synthetic streamflow sequences.

The stochastic theory of reservoir storage is based on the probabilistic structure of inflow to the reservoir from which it is then possible to derive the probability distribution of reservoir storage. An excellent discussion of reservoir theory has been presented by Klemes (1981), and McMahon and Mein (1986).

Stochastic models of streamflow generation are used to generate stochastic streamflow sequences. A number of models are available for generating such sequences. A good discussion of such models is given in Salas, et al. (1982). Savic (1989) compared four streamflow generation models for reservoir capacity-yield analysis: (1) log-one autoregressive (AR-1) model (Thomas and Fiering, 1962), (2) proration of annual streamflow, (3) method of fragments, and (4) modified Valencia-Schaake model (Valencia and Schaake, 1973). The latter three models are the disaggregation models. Several criteria have been employed to evaluate adequacy of streamflow models in sizing reservoirs. One of the criteria is to compare statistics from the generated streamflow sequences to the corresponding values for the historical data. Included in these statistics are means, standard deviations, and serial correlation coefficients up to some specified lag. Askew, et al. (1971) compared statistics of the critical drought period computed from the generated data with those of the historical drought record. Jettmar and Young (1975) used statistical criteria and an economic criterion to select the model that provided the greatest net benefits from a reservoir simulation model. Hirsch (1979) used the method of support techniques to determine the ability of the historical data to support hypotheses obtained from generated data. Savic, et al. (1989) used statistical criteria and the relationship between storage volume required based on the historical record and the volume based on the generated data. They found that the modified Valencia-Schaake model was a superior streamflow generating model for sizing reservoirs. The reservoir capacity is controlled by the critical flow period in the inflow sequence. It is possible for a model to adequately reproduce the historical moments but be inadequate to reproduce critical flow periods.

Gani and Yakowitz (1989) developed a probabilistic model to estimate the life of a reservoir and the probability of failure by considering rainfall-runoff process, sedimentation process, sediment transport process, and reservoir storage and release. Probabilistic models were derived for the component processes based on concepts established in the hydrologic literature. They showed that for a certain assembly of process components, the sedimentation process was Poissonian, with parameters interpretable in terms of physical variables. No verification of the model was however undertaken.

Optimization models, based on different approximations, have been used to size reservoir systems. One important class of such models includes implicitly stochastic models taking into account uncertainty in the inflows by considering a large set of equally likely inflow sequences. According to Stedinger, et al. (1983), the basic drawback of such models is that the resulting size of the constraint set is proportional to the number of inflow sequences considered, which may become prohibitively large due to small time interval especially in flood control cases. This drawback is alleviated by using only the average inflow sequence (Dorfman, 1962), critical periods (Hall, et al., 1969), or yield models (Loucks, et al., 1981). Kelman, et al. (1989), using the theoretical results of Marien (1984), discussed a method to dramatically reduce the number of constraints of a stochastic model without any approximation. They defined the objective function by the minimum of penalties associated with providing flood protection. A set of probability constraints on occurrence of floods were explicitly considered. The method was applied to determine the flood control volumes to be provided in a hydropower system of eight reservoirs on the Parana River in Brazil.

Operation and Management Models

The reservoir operation and management models can be classified as optimization models, and stochastic models. In the past 3 decades or so, there has been a phenomenal surge in development and application of optimization techniques in planning, design, operation and management of complex water resources systems in general and reservoir systems in particular. Yeh (1982, 1985) reported a comprehensive state-of-the-art review of reservoir operation and management models. He classified these models into four categories: (1) linear programming (LP) including chance-constrained LP, stochastic LP, and stochastic programming with recourse; (2) dynamic programming (DP) including incremental DP, discrete differential DP, incremental DP and successive approximations, stochastic DP, reliability constrained DP, differential DP, and the progressive optimality algorithms; (3) nonlinear programming; and (4) simulation. Combinations of these models have also been reported in the literature. Yeh provided a much needed critique and analysis of these models. The merits and limitations of each of the models were also assessed.

The stochastic models are based on stochastic streamflow forecasting. Streamflow generation models, discussed earlier, can also be used for streamflow forecasting (Frevert, et al., 1989). The value of streamflow forecasting in reservoir operation has been discussed by Georgakakos (1989). Streamflow forecasting models (Rodriguez-Iturbe, et al., 1979; Kitanidis and Bras, 1978) have been coupled with reservoir control systems (Yeh, et al., 1976, 1979; Bras, et al., 1983; Wasimi and Kitanidis, 1983; Stedinger, et al., 1984; Loaiciga and Marino, 1985; Georgakakos and Marks, 1987), with the emphasis on the performance of the forecast-control models. Georgakakos (1989) evaluated the benefit of streamflow forecasting in the Savannah River system, the High Aswan Dam, and the Equatorial Lake system, using extended linear quadratic Gaussian control methodology. This methodology is capable of handling effectively reliability storage constraints.

Kojiri, et al. (1989) formulated a methodology to derive reservoir operating rules in terms of fuzz inference theory. The methodology consists of four parts: (1) prediction of the required step-ahead discharge with short computational time even if it is of low accuracy using linear regression (Hino, et al., 1982); (2) prediction of discharge with enough accuracy even if it takes long computational time (Kimura, 1966); (3) determination of release rule using fuzz theory with information on current inflow, current storage volume, predicted inflow hydrograph, predicted total mass volume of inflow and field experiences; and (4) monitoring of the controlled results, observing meteorological and hydrological conditions until the discharge level becomes lower than the critical level.

STOCHASTIC STREAMFLOW MODEL

The streamflow variables of interest to reservoir design and operation are: peak flow, volume, duration, and time interval between events of high or low discharges. A schematic conceptualization of a streamflow time series is shown in Figure 1. A stochastic model capable of handling all of these variables will be developed and applied to the Amite River watershed in Louisiana, USA.

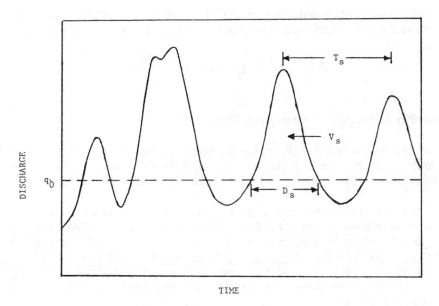

FIG. 1 A typical streamflow time series.

The model is based on the conceptualization of streamflow above a certain threshold as a stochastic process. Consequently, its characteristics of interest can be described by their probability distributions.

Probability Distributions of Flood peak and Duration

The probability distributions of flood peak and flood duration were determined using the power transformation (Box and Cox, 1964). This transformation renders the data to be normally distributed. If x is a flood variable (peak or duration) and y is its transformed value, then

$$y = \frac{x^{\lambda} - 1}{\lambda} , \lambda \neq 0 \tag{1}$$

and

$$y = \log x, \lambda = 0 \tag{2}$$

where λ is a constant of transformation. In general, the value of λ varies from -1 to +1. The value of λ for a particular flood series is estimated by trial and error such that the coefficients of skewness and kurtosis of the transformed series are nearly zero and 3.0, respectively. Thus, in the transformed domain, the probability distribution of the flood variable (peak or duration) will be approximately normal, with its probability density function (pdf) expressed as

$$f(y) = \frac{1}{s\sqrt{2\pi}} \exp [\frac{- (y - \bar{y})^2}{2s^2}], \ y \geq 0 \tag{3}$$

in which s is the standard deviation of y, and $\bar{y}$ is the mean of y, and f(y) is pdf of y. The cumulative distribution function (cdf) or nonexceedance probability, F(y), is

$$F(y) = \frac{1}{s\sqrt{2\pi}} \int_0^\infty \exp [- \frac{(y - \bar{y})^2}{2s^2}] \ dy \tag{4}$$

Probability Distribution of Interarrival Time

The probability distribution of interarrival time between high or low discharges is determined using the method of relative entropy with fractile constraints (REF) due to Lind and Solana (1988). This method can be briefly summarized as follows.

Let T denote the interarrival time and t its specific value. A set of independent distinct observations of T, denoted as S, is available on the interval domain $I = (t_0, t_{r+1})$. These observations are arranged in ascending order, $S = \{x_1, x_2, ..., x_r\}$. Let $F = F(t) = F(t|t_1, t_2, ..., t_r)$ and $f = f(t) = f(t|t_1, t_2, ..., t_r)$ be the probability distribution function and the corresponding probability density function of T which are estimated from the sample data S. According to the sample rule, the fractiles at the points $T = t_j$ are the set of fractile-pair constraints

$$(t, F(t|t_1, t_2, ..., t_r) = (t_j, \frac{j}{r+1}), \ j = 0, 1, 2, ..., r+1) \tag{5}$$

The domain $I = (t_0, t_{r+1})$ of the random variable T is partitioned by the sample elements into r+1 subintervals $I_j = (t_j, t_{j+1})$, j = 0, 1, 2, ..., r. A reference probability distribution function $G = G(t) = G(t; a_0, a_1, ...)$ are assumed on I, where $a_0, a_1, ...$ are parameters. The value of G(t) at fractile point $t = t_j$ is denoted as G_j. The reference probability of the event $T \in I_j$ can be expressed as $g_j = G_{j+1} - G_j$.

The REF method selects the probability distribution function $F(t|t_1, t_2, ..., t_r)$ that satisfies the fractile-pair constraints in equation (5) and minimizes the Kullback-Leibler relative entropy functional

$$H(f, g) = \int_I f \log (\frac{f}{g}) \ dt \tag{6}$$

Using the method of Lagrange multipliers, the probability density function can be written (Lind and Solana, 1988) as

$$f(t) = g(t) \ u(t) \tag{7}$$

where u(t) is a stepwise function dependent on Lagrange multipliers. Equation (7) shows that $f(t)$ is a piecewise linear transformation of the reference distribution $g(t)$, scaled over each subinterval I_j by the factor u_j. Or

$$f_j = g_j u_j, \ g_j = G(t_{j+1}) - G(t_j), \ j = 0, 1, ..., r \quad (8)$$

or

$$u_j = \frac{f_j}{g_j} = (1+r)^{-1} g_j^{-1}, \ j = 0, 1, ..., r \quad (9)$$

The probability distribution function can be written as

$$F(t) = \frac{j}{r+1} + u_j [G(t) - G_j], \ t \in I_j, \ j = 0, 1, ..., r \quad (10)$$

or

$$F(t) = Q_j + u_j [G(t) - G_j], \ t \in I_j, \ j = 0, 1, ..., r \quad (11)$$

Lind and Hong (1990) proposed a tail entropy approximation for modeling hydrologic extremes. For design of flood control reservoirs our interest is focused on the extreme left tail of the probability distribution of interarrival time. The lower tail may be defined as the portion below the lowest observed value x_1. In the lower tail, the probability density function $f(x)$ is a constant multiple, F_1/G_1, of the reference probability density function $g(x)$. Considering just the total probability constraint and the first fractile $F(x_1) = 1/(r+1)$, the multiplier $u = r/[(r+1)G_1]$ is obtained which is to be applied to $f(t)$ and $F(t)$ outside of the lower tail. Therefore, the following is obtained:

$$u^- = \frac{1}{(r+1)P_1}, \ t < t_1 \quad (12)$$

$$u^+ = \frac{r}{[(r+1)P_1]}, \ t > t_1 \quad (13)$$

$$f(t) = u^- g(t), \ t < t_1 \quad (14)$$

$$f(t) = g^+ g(t), \ t > t_1 \quad (15)$$

$$F(t) = u^+ G(t), \ t > t_1 \quad (16)$$

$$F(t) = u^- G(t), \ t < t_1 \quad (17)$$

Joint Probability Distribution of Flood Peak Q and Duration D

In the transformed domain, marginal probability distributions of flood peak and flood duration are normal. Their joint probability distribution is a bi-variate normal distribution expressed as

$$f(Q_S, D_S) = \frac{1}{2\pi\, s_{Q_S} s_{D_S} \sqrt{1-\rho^2}} \exp(-w) \tag{18}$$

where

$$w = \frac{1}{2(1-\rho^2)} \left[\frac{(Q_S - \overline{Q_2})^2}{s_{Q_S}^2} - \rho\,(Q_S - \overline{Q_S}) \frac{(D_S - \overline{D_S})}{s_{Q_S} s_{D_S}} + \frac{(D_S - \overline{D_S})^2}{s_{D_S}^2} \right],\ Q_S \geq 0,\ D_S \geq 0$$

where ρ is coefficient of correlation between Q_S and D_S, D_S is mean of transformed D, D_S, and s_{Ds} is standard deviation of D_S. The joint probability distribution of Q_S and D_S is

$$F(Q_S, D_S) = \int_0^{Q_S} \int_0^{D_S} f(Q_S, D_S)\, dQ_S\, dD_S \tag{19}$$

The conditional probability distribution $F(Q_S|D_S)$ can then be expressed using Bayes' theorem as

$$F(Q_S|D_S) = \frac{F(Q_S, D_S)}{F(D_S)} \tag{20}$$

where $F(D_S)$ is given by equation (4) applied to D_S instead of y, and $F(Q_S, D_S)$ is given by equation (19).

Probability Distribution of Flood Volume

The flood hydrograph is assumed to be a triangular hydrograph (Soil Conservation Service, 1975). This implies that the flood duration is correlated with the flood peak and flood volume. If this is so, the volume under the hydrograph is given by and the probability density function would be approximated by

$$V_S = \frac{Q_S D_S}{2} \tag{21}$$

and the probability density function would be approximated by

$$f(V_S) = f(Q_S, D_S)$$

where $f(Q_S, D_S)$ is the joint distribution of peak and duration and is given by equation (18).

For flood hydrographs above a high base level, the triangular representation has been found satisfactory by Ashkar and Rousselle (1981). This assumption obviates the need for directly computing the probability distribution of flood volumes from observed data which may be difficult and tedious to compute.

APPLICATION

The model was applied to the Amite River at Darlington, Louisiana. This river presents one of the most persistent flooding problems of any Louisiana stream. Thirteen major flood events have occurred on this stream in the past 50 years, with four occurring in the last 15 years alone. These four events have caused an average flood damage worth $64.8 million. A long-term stream gage is operated by the U.S. Geological Survey at Darlington, and has 36 years of record. In all, 52 flood events were analyzed in this study. The pertinent data with regard to this flood series are summarized in Table 1.

TABLE 1 Pertinent flood characteristics of the data used.

	Peak (cfs)	Duration (days)	Interarrival Time (days)
Mean	0.269×10^5	2.200	0.234×10^3
Standard Deviation	0.153×10^5	1.060	0.301×10^3
Coefficient of Variation	0.571	0.481	1.29
Coefficient of Skewness	1.25	0.072	2.58
Kurtosis	4.01	2.950	11.80

The correlation coefficient beween flood characteristics was found to be: 0.861 between peak and volume, 0.725 between peak and duration, and -0.06 between peak and interarrival time.

In order to mitigate flooding in the Amite River basin, the Louisiana Department of Transportation and Development (LDOTD) is planning to construct a flood control reservoir near the Darlington site.

Goodness-of-Fit Characteristics

To evaluate the adequacy of distributions fitted to the data, the following goodness-of-fit characteristics were used:

$$BIAS = \frac{x_c - x_0}{x_0} \tag{22}$$

$$SE = \frac{s(x_c)}{x} \tag{23}$$

$$RMSE = \frac{E[(x_c - x_0)^2]^{1/2}}{x_0} \tag{24}$$

in which x_0 is observed value of a variable, x_c is computed value of the variable, $s(x_c)$ is standard deviation of the computed values, BIAS is standardized bias, SE is standard error, and RMSE is root mean square. Also computed was the correlation coefficient between observed and computed probability distributions.

Marginal Distributions

The series of flood peaks, durations, and interarrival times were obtained for all the events above a base level of 283 m^3/s at the Darlington gage. This base level was recommended by Cruise and Arora (1990). Observed values of flood peaks and flood durations were transformed using the power transformation.

The data were arranged in ascending order and assigned the rank of one to the smallest value, two to the second smallest value, and so on. The plotting position of each observed value was obtained from the Gringorton plotting position formula expressed as

$$P(x) = \frac{m - 0.44}{N + 0.12} \qquad (25)$$

where m is the rank assigned to the value x.

The normal distribution was then fitted to the observed values of flood peaks and durations. The goodness-of-fit statistics for the fitted distributions are given in Tables 2 and 3. The statistics show that the normal distribution adequately represents flood peak and flood duration at the Darlington site.

The probability distribution of interarrival time was obtained by the REF method. The reference distribution was chosen to be an exponential distribution. The goodness-of-fit statistics for the fitted distribution are shown in Table 4. The REF method was an adequate model for describing the probability distribution of interarrival time.

TABLE 2 Goodness-of-fit characteristics for probability distribution of flood peak.

Nonexceedance Probability	Peak (cfs)		BIAS	SE	RMSE
	Observed	Computed			
0.95	62,700	58,900	-0.061	0.228	0.044
0.90	46,500	51,600	0.110	0.307	0.059
0.80	41,550	38,600	-0.071	0.344	0.066
0.60	25,400	28,300	0.1142	0.562	0.108
0.40	18,500	21,100	0.141	0.772	0.148
0.10	12,500	12,500	0.000	1.137	0.218

Correlation coefficient between observed and computer probability distribution = 0.984.

TABLE 3 Goodness-of-fit characteristics for probability distribution of flood duration.

Nonexceedance Probability	Peak (cfs)		BIAS	SE	RMSE
	Observed	Computed			
0.95	3.968	4.202	-.0555	0.240	0.0325
0.90	3.574	3.534	.0111	0.285	0.0386
0.80	3.091	2.867	.0780	0.351	0.0476
0.60	2.460	2.511	-.0204	0.401	0.0544
0.40	1.919	2.000	-.0407	0.504	0.0682
0.10	0.812	0.731	.111	1.378	0.187

Correlation coefficient between observed and computed flood volume = 0.994.

TABLE 4 Goodness-of-fit statistics for probability distribution of interarrival time.

Nonexceedance Probability	Peak (cfs)		BIAS	SE	RMSE
	Observed	Computed			
0.95	789.30	789.30	0.000	0.307	0.081
0.90	632.55	579.75	-0.083	0.383	0.101
0.80	389.75	389.75	0.000	0.621	0.164
0.60	189.00	189.00	0.000	1.281	0.338
0.40	65.20	119.35	0.831	3.713	0.780
0.10	14.20	25.70	0.810	17.048	4.50

Correlation coefficient between observed and computed probability distributions = 0.986.

Joint and Conditional Distributions of Flood Peak and Duration

Based on the adequacy of the normal distribution representing the probability distributions of flood peak and volume in the transformed space, the joint probabilities of the observed values of these variables for each flood event were computed using equation (19). Of course, inherent in the computations is that the bivariate normal distribution is an adequate model of the bivariate probability distribution of flood peak and duration in the transformed space.

The validity of this method was checked by computing the conditional probability distribution of flood peak for given flood duration and comparing it with that based on observed data. The observed data were divided into two groups based on the flood duration: (1) from 0 to 2 days, and (2) from 2 to 4.7 days. In each group twenty-six data points (or flood events) were available. The normal distribution was then fitted to the flood peak data of each group, which is the conditional probability distribution of flood peak for the duration of that group. The goodness-of-fit statistics were again computed to evaluate the adequacy of fit and are given in Tables 5 and 6. It is clear that the bivariate normal distribution was an adequate model.

Reservoir Operation

In real time reservoir operation, it is helpful to know the probabilities of sequences of streamflow events. For instance, if a flood occurs which fills part of the flood control storage, it would be useful to know the probability that another flood of

TABLE 5 Goodness-of-fit statistics for probability distribution of flood peak conditioned on flood volume (0 to 2 days).

Nonexceedance Probability	Peak (cfs)		BIAS	SE	RMSE
	Observed	Computed			
0.95	26,377	28,189	-.0643	.190	.0464
0.90	24,051	26,774	-.102	.200	.0489
0.80	20,803	20,499	.0148	.261	.0639
0.60	17,352	16,853	.0297	.317	.0777
0.40	14,871	14,117	.0534	.378	.0927
0.10	10,895	10,691	.0191	.500	.122

Correlation coefficient between observed and computed distributions = 0.991.

TABLE 6 Goodness-of-fit statistics for probability distribution of flood peak conditioned on flood volume (2 to 4.7 days).

Nonexceedance Probability	Peak (cfs)		BIAS	SE	RMSE
	Observed	Computed			
0.95	67,641	64,662	.0461	.242	.0343
0.90	56,675	59,847	-.0530	.262	.0370
0.80	46,127	45,236	.0197	.346	.0490
0.60	35,129	39,177	-.103	.400	.0566
0.40	27,554	24,754	.113	.634	.0895
0.10	16,878	16,093	.0488	.974	.138

Correlation coefficient between observed and computed distributions = 0.990.

sufficient magnitude to exceed the remaining storage volume would occur before the reservoir is emptied. Another scenario might be applicable to water supply reservoirs. One might be interested in a sequence of drought events interspersed with small runoff events whose volumes would not be sufficient to replenish the demand placed upon the reservoir storage. The stochastic model developed here can easily be adapted for this purpose.

For instance, suppose a flood has occurred which has filled part of a flood control reservoir. The available storage remaining after the flood will be known. The probability that an event of sufficient volume to exceed that which is available would occur within a given time frame can be calculated from the distribution of volumes and interarrival times. I this way, the reservoir operator can make informed decisions about the rapidity with which the reservoir must be emptied. Likewise, the conditional distributions of peaks and durations can be used in conjunction with the interarrival time distribution to construct sequences of droughts and runoff events. Specific examples will be given in a later section of this paper.

Reservoir Design

The stochastic model developed here can also be useful in the planning and design of multipurpose reservoirs. For instance in the planning of a hydropower or water supply reservoir, one must plan for the maximum time span during which the inflow to the reservoir may be below the demand volume. This can be calculated by placing the base level at the demand discharge and calculating the maximum time span corresponding to desired exceedance probabilities. Note that in this model, the base level to define the series may be set as low as desired because no assumptions as to mutual independence are made. This is in contrast to most textbook counting process models.

The model may also be used to estimate design peak discharge and volumes for flood control reservoirs. Since the joint and conditional distribution of both variables are approximated the necessity of calculating design volumes by deterministic watershed models or by other methods is obviated. For planning purposes, a sequence of flood events can be constructed corresponding to any desired annual exceedance probability. For instance, in economic analyses, it may be useful to know the probabilities of multiple events occurring in any given year. This type of information may prove very useful in estimating future flood control benefits associated with the project. Again, as in the case of reservoir operation, specific examples are given later.

EXAMPLE APPLICATIONS

In this section, the use of the stochastic model in reservoir operation, planning and design is demonstrated. We will use the Amite River Reservoir data base previously discussed. We will demonstrate the sequencing of hydrologic events in order to aid in real time reservoir operation and design. This will be accomplished using the reservoir rule curves shown in Figure 2. The marginal distribution function (cdf) of the annual flood peak series for the Amite data is shown and labeled on the figure. The cdf of the flood volumes is determined from the joint distribution of flood peaks and durations. This curve is also shown on the figure and was determined as the best fit line through the computed probability points. The points would scatter on the figure because there is not a perfect correlation between flood peaks and durations. Likewise, the transformed peaks corresponding to these points are also plotted and labeled. These values can be converted to real space using $\lambda = .0172$.

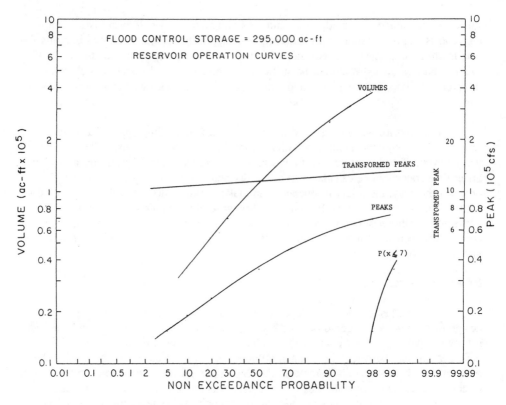

FIG. 2 Reservoir operation curves.

Also shown on the figure is a graphical representation of the probability of interarrival times less than seven days for threshold values ranging from 10,000 to 35,000 cfs. This curve was derived using the interarrival time distributions computed as previously described based upon the series of events above base levels of 10,000, 15,000, 20,000, 30,000 and 35,000 cfs. The probability that T ≤ 7 days was computed from each marginal distribution and plotted against its corresponding base level in order to derive the curve. Thus,we are determining sequences of events with probabilities of occurring within one week of each other. The seven days value was chosen arbitrarily; any convenient value would suffice.

According to information obtained from the Louisiana Department of Transportation and Development, the proposed Darlington Reservoir will contain 295,000 acre-feet of flood control storage including surcharge. Now suppose a flood of recurrence interval 5 years occurred above the reservoir site. Our marginal peak distribution curve shows that this flood would have a peak discharge of about 50,000 cfs. This corresponds to a transformed peak of 11.890. In order to determine the volume of this hydrograph, we must determine the nonexceedance probability of this peak from the joint distribution function (curve 2, Figure 2). From this curve, we determine this probability to also be approximately .20. From the volume curve, we find that the volume corresponding to this nonexceedance probability is approximately 204,000 ac-ft. Using this value, the reservoir operator can determine a release schedule such that the optimum amount of storage remains in the reservoir.

For instance, suppose he desires to store the entire hydrograph. Then, 91,000 ac-ft of storage would remain in the reservoir. This storage corresponds to a nonexceedance probability of .60 from the volume curve. The joint probability curve shows that this hydrograph would have a transformed peak of about 11.4 which corresponds to a value in real space of 33,000 cfs. The interarrival time distribution curve shows that the probability of occurrence of a flood of this magnitude within one week of a previous flood above that value would be only .008. The operator might find this degree of risk acceptable if he can drain the flood control storage within the alloted time.

Now, suppose for economic analysis purposes the planner wishes to know the probability of multiple events above the reservoir site. For instance, he may wish to know the probability that two 2-year flood events may occur within one year. Our model can also be used to answer this question. From the marginal curve, we see that the 2-year event corresponds to a magnitude of about 35,000 cfs. So, we need to know the probability that two events above that magnitude will occur within 365 days of each other. From our interarrival time distribution above a base level of 35,000 cfs, we find that the probability that two events above that level would occur in less than 365 days is .35. This information may be useful in forecasting expected benefits to accrue to the proposed project.

CONCLUSIONS

A stochastic streamflow model has been developed and used to generate sequences of streamflow events to assist in reservoir management and operation. The model can be utilized to derive reservoir rule curves which can be used by operators to estimate the risk associated with their actions. Since the model is based upon transformations to univariate and bivariate normal distributions, it should be generally applicable to most streamflow series. Specific examples shown are based upon Louisiana (USA) streamflow records. This model complements and enhances the previously developed reservoir models discussed in this paper.

REFERENCES

Askew, A. J., Yeh, W. W.-G., and Hall, W. A., 1971. A comparative study of critical drought simulation. Water Resources Research, Vol. 7, pp. 52-62.

Box, G. E. P. and Cox, D. R., 1964. An analysis of transformation. Journal of the Royal Statistical Society, Vol. B26, pp. 211-252.

Bras, R., Buchanan, R. and Curry, K., 1983. Real-time adaptive closed-loop control of reservoir with the High Aswan Dam as a case study. Water Resources Research, Vol. 19, No. 1, pp. 33.

Corradini, C., Melone, F. and Singh, V. P., 1987. On the structure of a semi-distributed adaptive model for flood forecasting. Hydrological Sciences Journal, Vol. 32, No. (2/6), pp. 227-242.

Cruise, J. F. and Arora, K., 1990. A hydroclimatic application of the Poisson partial duration flood model. Water Resources Bulletin, in press.

Fair, G. M., Geyer, J. C. and Okum, D. A., 1971. Elements of Water Supply and Wastewater Disposal. John Wiley and Sons, New York.

Frevert, D. K., Cowan, M. S. and Lane, W. L., 1989. Use of stochastic hydrology in reservoir operation. Journal of Irrigation and Drainage Engineering, Vol. 155, No. 3, pp. 334-343.

Gani, J. and Yakowitz, S., 1989. A probabilistic sedimentation analysis for predicting reservoir lifetime. Water Resources Management, Vol. 3, pp. 191-203.

Georgakakos, A. P. and Marks, D. H., 1987. A new method for the real time operation of reservoir systems. Water Resources Research, Vol. 23, No. 7, pp. 1376-1390.

Georgakakos, A. P., 1989. The value of streamflow forecasting in reservoir operation. Water Resources Bulletin, Vol. 25, No. 4, pp. 789-800.

Hall, W. A., Askew, A. J. and Yeh, W. W.-G., 1969. Use of critical period in reservoir analysis. Water Resources Research, Vol. 5, No. 6, pp. 12-5=1215.

Hirsch, R. M., 1979. Synthetic hydrology and water supply reliability. Water Resource Research, Vol. 15, pp. 1605-1615.

Jettmar, R. U. and Young, G. K., 1975. Hydrologic estimation and economic regret. Water Resources Research, Vol. 11, pp. 648-656.

Kelman, J., Damazio, J. M., Marien, J. L. and DaCosta, J. P., 1989. The determination of flood control volumes in a multireservoir system. Water Resources Research, Vol. 25, No. 3, pp. 337-344.

Kimura, T., 1962. The storage function method (II). Tech. Rep. in Civil Engng., 41-51, Gifu Univ., Japan.

Kitanidis, P. K. and Bras, R. L., 1978. Real-time forecasting of river flows. Technical Report No. 235, R. M. Parsons Laboratory for Hydrodynamics and Water Resources, Massachusetts Institute of Technology, Cambridge, Massachusetts.

Klemes, V., 1981. Applied stochastic theory of storage in evolution. Advances in Hydroscience, edited by U. T. Chow, Vol. 12, pp. 79-141, Academic Press, New York.

Kojiri, T., Ikebuchi, S. and Yamada, H., 1989. Basin wide flood control system by combining prediction and reservoir operation. Stochastic Hydrology and Hydraulics, Vol. 3, pp. 31-49.

Lind, N. C. and Solana, V., 1988. Cross-entropy estimation of random variables with fractile constraints. Paper No. 11, Institute for Risk Research, University of Waterloo, Waterloo, Ontario, Canada.

Lind, N. C. and Hong, H. P., 1990. Entropy estimation of hydrological extremes. Stochastic Hydrology and Hydraulics, in press.

Loaiciga, H. A. and Marino, M. A., 1985. An approach to parameter estimation and stochastic control in water resources with an application to reservoir operation. Water Resources Research, Vol. 21, No. 11, pp. 1575-1584.

Loucks, D. P., 1976. Surface water quantity management models. in: Systems Approach to Water Management, edited by A. K. Biswas, pp. 167-170, McGraw-Hill Book Company, New York.

Loucks, D. P., Stedinger, J. and Haith, D. A., 1981. Water Resource Systems Planning and Analysis. Prentice-Hall, Inc., Englewood Cliffs, New Jersey.

Marien, J. L., 1984. Controllability conditions for reservoir flood control systems with applications. Water Resources Research, Vol. 20, No. 11, pp. 1477-1488.

McMahon, T. A. and Mein, R. G., 1986. River and Reservoir Yield. Water Resources Publiations, Littleton, Colorado.

Rassam, J. C., 1987. Flood management of the Ottawa River system under uncertainties. Water Resources Management, Vol. 1, pp. 143-154.

Rippl, W., 1883. The capacity for storage reservoirs for water supply. Proceedings, Institution of Civil Engineers, Vol. 71, pp. 270-278.

Rodriguez-Iturbe, I., Valdes, J. B. and Velasquez, J. M., 1978. Applications of Kalman Filter in rainfall-runoff studies. Proceedings, AGU Chapman Conference on Applications of Kalman Filter to Hydrology, Hydraulics and Water Resources, Pittsburgh, Pennsylvania.

Salas, J. D., Delleur, J. W. Yevjevich and Lane, W. L., 1980. Applied Modeling of Hydrologic Time Series. Water Resources Publications, Littleton, Colorado.

Savic, D. A., Burn, D. H. and Zrinji, Z., 1989. A comparison of streamflow generation models for reservoir capacity-yield analysis. Water Resources Bulletin, Vol. 25, No. 5, pp. 977-983.

Singh, K. P. and Durgunoglu, A., 1989. A new method for estimating future reservoir storage capacities. Water Resources Bulletin, Vol. 25, No. 2, pp. 263-274.

Singh, K. P. and Durgunoglu, A., 1990. Economic reservoir design and storage conservation by reduced sedimentation. Journal of Water Resources Planning and Management, ASCE, Vol. 116, No. 1, pp. 85-98.

Stedinger, J. R., Sule, B. F. and Pei, D., 1983. Multiple reservoir system screening models. Water Resources Research, Vol. 19, No. 6, pp. 1383-1393.

Stedinger, J. Sule, B. and Loucks, D., 1984. Stochastic dynamic programming models for reservoir operation optimization. Water Resources Research, Vol. 20, No. 11, pp. 499-1504.

Thomas, H. A. and Fiering, M. B., 1962. Mathematical synthesis of streamflow sequences for the analysis of river basins by simulation. In: A. Mass, et al. (editors), Design of Water Resources Systems, Harvard University Press, Cambridge, Massachusetts.

Valencia, R. and Schaake, Jr., J. C., 1973. Disaggregation processes in stochastic hydrology. Water Resources Research, Vol. 9, pp. 580-585.

Wasimi, S. and Kitanidis, P. K., 1983. Real-time forecasting and daily operation of a multireservoir system during floods by linear quadratic Gaussian control. Water Resources Research, Vol. 19, No. 6, pp. 1511-1522.

Yeh, W. W.-G., Becker, L., Fults, D., Sparks, D. and Logan, G., 1976. Optimization of real-time daily operation of multiple reservoir system. Engineering Report No. 7628, University of California, Los Angeles, California.

Yeh, W. W.-G., Beck, L. and Chu, W. S., 1979. Real-time hourly reservoir operation. Journal of Water Resources Planning and Management Division, ASCE, Vol. __, pp. 187-203.

Yeh, W. W.-G., 1982. State of the art review: Theories and applications of systems analysis techniques to the optimal management and operation of a reservoir system. Report UCLA-ENG-82-52, 149 p., School of Engineering and Applied Science, University of California at Los Angeles, California.

Yeh, W., 1985. Reservoir management and operation models: A state of the art review. Water Resources Research, Vol. 21, NO. 12, pp. 1797-1818.

Topic B:
Sediment Transport Prediction, Sediment Deposit Formation and Problems Related to Flushing

Hydrology in Mountainous Regions.   II - Artificial Reservoirs; Water and Slopes
(Proceedings of two Lausanne Symposia, August 1990). IAHS Publ. no. 194, 1990.

Evaluating Williams' runoff factor for some Sicilian watersheds

V. BAGARELLO
Dipartimento di Idrotecnica, Università degli Studi del Molise, Campobasso, Italy
V. FERRO
Istituto di Genio Rurale, Università degli Studi di Reggio Calabria, Gallina di Reggio Calabria, Italy
G. GIORDANO
Dipartimento E.I.T.A., Università degli Studi di Palermo, Palermo, Italy

ABSTRACT Some modifications of the USLE were proposed to apply this equation to sediment yield prediction. Williams proposed a "modified" USLE in which a runoff factor replaces the rainfall erosivity factor. In this paper the Authors preliminarly control the existence of a correlation between the measurements of suspended sediment transport and Williams' runoff factor. Then, by using the hydrological data of ten river gauges, for each watershed the Authors propose an equation which estimates the annual runoff factor by hydrological data published by Italian Hydrographic Service. At the end a relationship between the mean annual value of Williams' runoff factor and a morphological variable is proposed.

GENERALITIES

For predicting sediment yield at the outlet of a watershed many mathematical models can be used. Some models, called "phisically based", are based on the fundamental concept that sediment yield is determined by either the amount of sediment made available by detachment processes or by the transport capacity of the runoff.

These models are generally complex because include equations for detachment by raindrop impact, detachment by flow, transport by flow and deposition by flow. These procedures need also information about detachment rate, transport rate and properties of the sediment being eroded, transported and deposited.

Sediment yield can also be evaluated by using soil loss models.

A procedure for computing sediment yield from a watershed based on a soil loss model needs yet the estimate of the sediment delivery ratio SDR (Roehl, 1962), (Renfro, 1975). The Universal Soil Loss Equation (USLE) is the most known and applied soil loss prediction procedure. The USLE is very useful for predicting field soil loss because the equation was developed by using data from small plots. When the equation is used for computing sediment yield from watersheds, all factors, except the rainfall factor, must be modified (Williams & Berndt, 1972). In a watershed the susceptibility to erosion varies widely; therefore the prediction procedure has to consider the influence of different soils, of a variable morphology, land use, treatment and erosion control practices on watershed sediment yield.

Late researches, continuing Wischmeier's studies, have been carried out in order to simplify the computation procedure of the mean annual value of the rainfall factor R. Several Authors proposed correlations between the R-factor and other rainfall parameters which need very little input data and can easily be calculated (Ateshian, 1974), (Arnoldus, 1980).Other modifications attempted to obtain R values more applicable to regional conditions (Mc Cool et al., 1974).

Other models, called "direct", are based on a different definition of the climatic factor. Williams (1975) proposed a modified Universal Soil Loss Equation (MUSLE) in which a runoff factor R_d replaces the rainfall erosivity factor R.

R_d can be evaluated by runoff data (peak flow, runoff volume). Williams' prediction procedure is convincing from a physical point of view, since R_d is representative of the influence of runoff on sediment transport. However the evaluation of R_d needs a river gauge at the outlet of the watershed.

In this paper the Authors preliminarly control the existence of a correlation between suspended sediment transport and Williams' runoff factor by using sediment and hydrological data of four sicilian river gauges. Then the Authors, by using the hydrological data of ten sicilian river gauges, develop an equation which allows to estimate the annual runoff factor for each watershed. At the end, for each sicilian river watershed, the mean annual value, R_d, of the runoff factor is calculated and a relationship between R_d and some morphological variables, holding in Sicilian region, is proposed.

THE UNIVERSAL SOIL LOSS EQUATION AND WILLIAMS' MODEL

The universal soil loss equation is one of the most widely used methods for predicting soil loss. The USLE is a multiple factor equation in which four non dimensional parameters (L S C P) are used to modify a potential soil loss equal to the product of two dimensional parameters which respectively represent the erosivity of rainfall (R) and the erodibility of a particular soil (K). As it is known, the USLE has the following form (Wischmeier & Smith, 1972):

$$A_s = R K L S C P \tag{1}$$

where A_s is the soil loss (t/ha), R is the rainfall erosivity factor (t/ha per unit of K), K the soil erodibility factor, L and S are the topographic factors, C the crop management factor and P the erosion control practice factor.

Next researches restricted the "universality" of the USLE an account of difficulties for applying this equation to situations for which factor values are not yet determined (land use conditions, cropping systems, conservation practices different from the american ones). Another limit to the USLE's applicability is the workload needful for calculating some factors.

In Sicily the USLE was applied in its full form (1) only for some small areas (Santoro, 1974), (Dazzi & Santoro, 1983) in order to verify its applicability and to adapt the equation to a very different situation from the american one. For Sicily the rainfall erosivity map was also compiled (D'Asaro & Santoro, 1984).

The applicability of eq. (1) for evaluating sediment yield from a watershed needs the estimate of SDR; nevertheless the SDR data, known from literature, show a high variability of the mean value of this coefficient. The researches carried out in order to evaluate the mean value of SDR showed that SDR generally depends on watershed morphological parameters (drainage area of the watershed, lenght and slope of the main channel, etc.) (Roehl, 1962), (Renfro, 1975).

Williams (1975) proposed to evaluate sediment yield Y_s (t/ha) from a watershed by using a modified USLE equation (MUSLE)

$$Y_s = R_d K L S C P \tag{2}$$

in which the runoff factor R_d replaces R. Williams, by using field data of 18 small american watersheds, defined for each flood event i the runoff factor $R_{d,i}$ as following

$$R_{d,i} = 0.8776 \, (Q_i \, V_i)^{0.56} \tag{3}$$

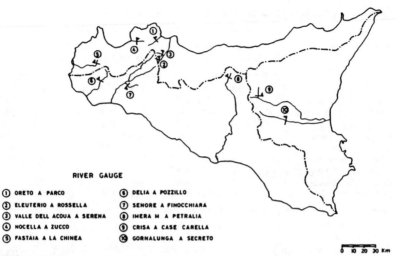

RIVER GAUGE

① ORETO A PARCO   ⑥ DELIA A POZZILLO
② ELEUTERIO A ROSSELLA   ⑦ SENORE A FINOCCHIARA
③ VALLE DELL ACOUA A SERENA ⑧ IMERA M A PETRALIA
④ NOCELLA A ZUCCO   ⑨ CRISA A CASE CARELLA
⑤ FASTAIA A LA CHINEA   ⑩ GORNALUNGA A SECRETO

FIG. 1 River gauges used in this research.

in which $R_{d,i}$ is the event runoff factor (t/unit of K with K (t h/kg m²)), Q_i is the peak flow rate of the flood event (m³/s) and V_i is the runoff volume (m³). The annual value per unit of drainage area $R_{d,j}$ (t/ha per unit of K) is

$$R_{d,j} = \sum_{i=1}^{n} R_{d,i}/S_w \qquad (4)$$

in which n is the number of flood events in the year j and S_w (ha) is the watershed drainage area. The runoff factor R_d is the annual mean value:

$$R_d = \sum_{j=1}^{N} R_{d,j}/N \qquad (5)$$

in which N is the number of years.

DATA USED IN THIS RESEARCH AND RESULTS

In this paper the Authors use the sediment transport data of four river gauges ("Fastaia a La Chinea", "Delia a Pozzillo", "Gornalunga a Secreto", Imera Meridionale a Petralia") and the hydrological data of ten river gauges. Fig. 1 represent the map of Sicily with the river gauges used in this research. In Table 1, for each river gauge, the following characteristic data are listed: the sample lenght N, the measurement period, the watershed drainage area S_w, the watershed perimeter P, the lenght of the main channel L, the total channel lenght L_c, the mean altitude H_m, the mean annual rainfall A, the mean annual runoff D and the mean annual number of rainy days NRD. Initially, by using sediment and hydrological data of four river gauges, the Authors control the existence of a correlation between monthly measurements of suspended sediment transport (t/km²) and monthly runoff factor values (Bagarello et al., 1987). The controls show that, although in some cases the scatter of experimental data is noticeable, a correlation between the two considered variables exists. In Table 2 the values of the r correlation coefficient and of the mean square error MSE, for a linear correlation between the two variables, are listed. From a statistical point of view the results made worse by using the monthly runoff as independent variable (lower values of r and higher values of MSE). After all the correlation between the sediment transport measurements and the runoff factor values seems to confirm the applicability of eq. (3) in Sicily. This statistical result has also a physical meaning; in fact in Sicily the watercourses are generally streams and runoff and sediment

TABLE 1 Characteristic data of the river gauges.

RIVER GAUGE	N	Measurement period	Sw [km]	P [km]	L [km]	Lc [km]	Hm [m]	A [mm]	D [mm]	NRD
ORETO a Parco	20	1951 - 1970	75.6	49.7	11.4	86.0	608	1034	496	73
ELEUTERIO a Rossella	5	1952 - 1956	10.5	12.8	4.8	14.6	670	833	399	82
VALLE DELL'ACQUA a Serena	10	1971 - 1981	21.7	26.9	10.0	31.0	638	920	243	71
NOCELLA a Zucco	10	1971 - 1981	56.6	36.0	12.0	92.0	540	941	199	92
FASTAIA a La Chinea	15	1962 - 1978	32.5	22.4	7.5	37.3	313	672	175	82
DELIA a Pozzillo	12	1959 - 1970	138.7	52.4	21.6	138.7	259	681	150	72
SENORE a Finocchiara	12	1961 - 1972	76.8	41.8	21.7	151.4	422	640	200	81
IMERA MERIDIONALE a Petralia	11	1971 - 1982	27.9	22.2	8.0	49.7	1231	843	661	83
CRISA a Case Carella	13	1959 - 1980	46.9	31.4	15.0	87.2	597	686	195	80
GORNALUNGA a Secreto	10	1957 - 1966	232.1	81.4	42.2	358.2	389	601	85	59

TABLE 2 Values of r and MSE for a linear correlation between suspended sediment transport and R_d.

FASTAIA a La Chinea			DELIA a Pozzillo			IMERA a Petralia			GORNALUNGA a Secreto		
year	r	MSE	year	r	MSE	year	r	MSE	year	r	MSE
1962	0.918	3.2	1962	0.923	36.3	1971	0.600	58.3	1962	0.903	63.2
1964	0.822	97.4	1963	0.858	10.2	1972	0.902	103.2	1964	0.865	420.0
1965	0.843	8.8	1964	0.674	10.2	1974	0.984	48.6	1965	0.721	18.6
1967	0.978	0.4	1965	0.939	23.6	1975	0.588	27.9	1966	0.869	111.3
1968	0.883	7.5	1966	0.521	10.1	1977	0.847	13.9			
1969	0.910	13.9	1967	0.842	6.3	1978	0.699	401.3			
1970	0.970	0.7	1968	0.739	1.9	1979	0.646	847.7			
			1969	0.703	15.6	1980	0.922	78.2			

transport are considerable only during flood events (Cannarozzo & Ferro, 1985, 1988). For this reason the R_d index, which depends on peak flow rate and runoff volume, is convenient for evaluating sediment yield.

In Fig. 2, for "Oreto a Parco" and "Crisa a Case Carella" river gauges, the annual $R_{d,j}$ values versus time are plotted; these figures show a remarkable temporal variability of the runoff factor.

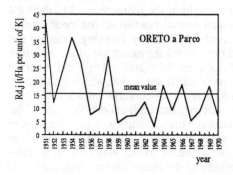
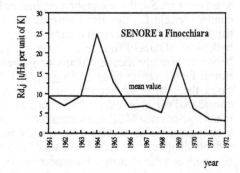

FIG. 2 Annual values of the runoff factor.

In order to obtain a simplified computation procedure of $R_{d,j}$ a regression analysis was carried out by using hydrological data published by the Italian Hydrographic Service. Particularly, for each year, the maximum rainfall intensity i_t (mm/hr) of given duration t (t = 1, 3, 6, 12, 24 hr), the rainfall amount A (mm), the runoff D (mm) and the intensity index A/NRD (mm/days) were considered. For the sicilian region, due to the different characteristics of watersheds (morphology, geology, etc.), only a weak correlation between $R_{d,j}$ and each of the above mentioned variables was found. Then data were analyzed in order to determine a relationship having the same functional form for each watershed. Under this hypothesis the regression analysis showed that the best results are obtained by correlating the $R_{d,j}$ runoff factor to the annual runoff D_j. This occurence could seem to be easily predictable; nevertheless the control needs since $R_{d,j}$ is calculated by using runoff volume and peak flow rate of each event while D_j is an annual value.

TABLE 3 b_0, b_1, r coefficients and MSE for eq. (6).

RIVER GAUGE	bo	b1	r	MSE
ORETO a Parco	- 14.97	0.0615	0.761	56.1
ELEUTERIO a Rossella	4.53	0.0405	0.956	4.7
VALLE DELL'ACQUA a Serena	- 4.66	0.0886	0.979	7.7
NOCELLA a Zucco	- 5.88	0.0839	0.767	26.1
FASTAIA a La Chinea	- 3.70	0.1098	0.908	19.8
DELIA a Pozzillo	- 0.23	0.0638	0.907	5.7
SENORE a Finocchiara	- 6.07	0.0833	0.973	2.3
IMERA MERIDIONALE a Petralia	- 42.72	0.1043	0.944	71.2
CRISA a Case Carella	- 0.84	0.1103	0.875	44.4
GORNALUNGA a Secreto	- 6.60	0.2123	0.970	12.2

In Table 3, for each river gauge, the b_0 and b_1 coefficients of the equation

$$R_{d,j} = b_0 + b_1 \, D_j \qquad\qquad (6)$$

the r correlation coefficient and the mean square error MSE are listed. For some river gauges the scatter of values estimated by eq. (6) is noticeable. In order to improve the estimate of $R_{d,j}$, the best regression equation was researched for each river gauge. In Table 4 the following results of this analysis are listed: the variables which appear in the multiple regression equation

$$y = b_0 + b_1 \, x_1 + b_2 \, x_2 \qquad\qquad (7)$$

the value of the b_0, b_1 and b_2 coefficients, the r correlation coefficient and the mean square error MSE. In Fig. 3 either the relationships between $R_{d,j}$ factor and hydrological data or the comparisons between the calculated $R_{d,j}$ values and those estimated by the developed regression equations (7) are shown. In order to avoid an overfitting the maximum number of independent variables was equal to two. For seven river gauges a "rainfall intensity" index, together with runoff, is best correlated to the runoff factor. This occurence confirms the influence of rainfall intensity on the phenomenon as previously recognized by other Authors which observed a strong correlation between the Sicilian values of the rainfall erosivity factor and rainfall intensities of given duration and return period (D'Asaro & Santoro, 1984).

In order to provide an equation useful for estimating the mean annual value of the runoff factor in Sicily, another multiple regression analysis between R_d values, calculated for each river gauge, and some hydrological and morphological variables was carried out (Table 5). R_d is less correlated to the hydrological variables, although significantly from a statistical point of view, than to the morphological ones. Among the hydrological

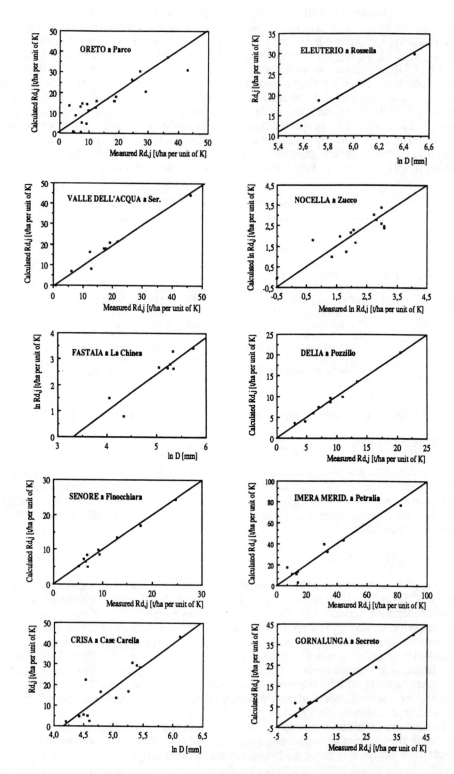

FIG. 3 Comparison between measured R$_{d,j}$ values and eq. (7).

TABLE 4 Multiple regression analysis results.

RIVER GAUGE	y	x1	x2	bo	b1	b2	r	MSE
ORETO a Parco	Rd,j	D	i24	- 18.79	0.04	5.75	0.873	33.70
ELEUTERIO a Rossella	Rd,j	ln D		- 87.20	18.17		0.977	2.55
VALLE DELL'ACQUA a Serena	Rd,j	D	i1	- 6.17	0.08	0.12	0.982	7.63
NOCELLA a Zucco	ln Rd,j	ln D	ln A/NRD	- 12.76	2.22	1.35	0.863	38.20
FASTAIA a La Chinea	ln Rd,j	D		- 4.76	1.43		0.911	21.60
DELIA a Pozzillo	Rd,j	D	i6	- 8.86	0.07	1.19	0.994	0.45
SENORE a Finocchiara	Rd,j	D	i12	- 8.65	0.08	0.66	0.986	1.41
IMERA MERIDIONALE a Petralia	Rd,j	D	A/NRD	- 59.20	0.10	1.91	0.965	53.70
CRISA a Case Carella	Rd,j	ln D		- 90.19	21.71		0.898	36.50
GORNALUNGA a Secreto	Rd,j	D	ln i6	- 12.48	0.20	3.01	0.977	10.80

TABLE 5 Relationships between R_d and some
, morphological and hydrological variables.

EQUATIONS	r	MSE
Rd = 19.36 - 0.0526 S	0.622	22.3
Rd = 20.49 - 0.3183 L	0.614	22.7
Rd = 22.69 - 0.1887 P	0.658	20.6
Rd = 19.06 - 0.0333 Lc	0.584	24.0
Rd = 5.58 + 0.0176 Hm	0.848	10.2
Rd = 9.55 + 0.1043 Hm/L	0.920	5.6
Rd = 3.54 + 0.0153 A	0.400	30.5
Rd = 8.73 + 0.0244 D	0.776	14.5
Rd = 8.01 + 0.0972 NRD	0.152	35.5
Rd = 7.01 + 0.8436 A/NRD	0.299	33.1
Rd = 7.39 + 23.816 D/A	0.792	13.5

variables the runoff coefficient is the best correlated to R_d.
    The best relationship for estimating R_d is the following (Fig. 4):

$$R_d = 9,5524 + 0,1043 \ H_m/L \tag{8}$$

The attempt of finding a multiple regression equation failed since r coefficient was slightly higher while MSE was higher too. The developed eq. (8) has also a physical meaning; in fact the H_m/L ratio is a "watershed slope" index. Since the runoff velocity increases when the slope steepness increases too, the detachment and transport flow capacity increases when H_m/L increases too.

CONCLUSIONS

For evaluating watershed sediment yield Williams proposed a modified universal soil loss equation in which a runoff factor replaces the rainfall erosivity factor. In this paper the Authors have recognized the existence of a correlation between suspended transport measurements and Williams' runoff factor for some sicilian river gauges. This result seems to confirm that the proposed runoff factor holds in Sicily. In order to obtain a simplified computation procedure of the annual runoff factor the Authors carried out a regression analysis by using hydrological data published by the Italian Hydrographic Service. They developed for each river gauge an equation which allows a simple estimate of the annual runoff factor. At the end a relationship, holding in Sicilian region, between the

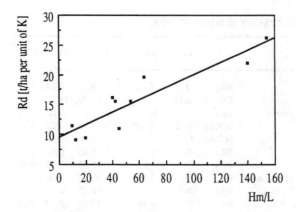

FIG. 4 Relationship between R_d and the morphological variable H_m/L.

annual mean value of Williams' runoff factor and a morphological variable having a physical meaning was proposed.

REFERENCES

Arnoldus, H.M.J. (1980) An approximation of the rainfall factor in the universal soil loss equation. In: Assessment of erosion , M. De Boodt, D. Gabriels Eds., J. Wiley & Sons, New York.

Ateshian, J.K.H. (1974) Estimation of rainfall erosion index. Proc. ASCE, IR3.

Bagarello, V., Ferro, V., Giordano, G. (1987) Considerazioni sul legame tra produzio nedi sedimenti e dati idrologici per alcuni bacini idrografici siciliani. Proc. of First International Congress of Geohydrology - Antropization and Degradation of the Physical Environment, Firenze.

Cannarozzo, M., Ferro, V. (1985) Un semplice modello regionale per la valutazione del trasporto solido in sospensione nei corsi d'acqua siciliani. Atti Acc. Naz. Sc. Lett. e Arti di Palermo, Serie V, Vol. V, Parte I.

Cannarozzo, M., Ferro, V. (1988) Il problema dell'interrimento dei serbatoi artificiali - Un diverso approccio di risoluzione alla luce dei precedenti studi. Idrotecnica, 5.

D'Asaro, F., Santoro, M. (1984) Aggressività della pioggia nello studio dell'erosione idrica del territorio siciliano. Progetto finalizzato "Conservazione del Suolo", Sotto progetto Dinamica dei Versanti , Pubbl. n. 130.

Mc Cool, D.K., Wischmeier, W.H., Johnson, L.C. (1974) Adapting the universal soil loss equation to the Pacific Northwest, unpublished paper n 74 - 2523, ASAE, Michigan.

Renfro, W.J. (1975) Use of erosion equations and sediment delivery ratios for predicting sediment yield. Present and prospective techonology for predicting sediment yield and sources, Agricultural Researche Service, U.S. Department of Agriculture.

Roehl, J.W. (1962) Sediment sources areas, delivery ratios and influencing morphologi cal factors. International Association of Scientific Hydrology , Pubbl. 59.

Santoro, M. (1974) L'erosione idrica nell'area sperimentale di Sparacia: studio sperimen tale ad una indagine di pieno campo. Bollettino dell'Ordine degli Ingegneri della Provincia di Palermo, 1.

Santoro, M., Dazzi, C. (1983) Modello di studio integrato del territorio (Ficuzza, Pa- lermo), Nota 8, Deduzione dell'erosione potenziale. Quaderni di Agronomia, 10.

Williams, J.R. (1975) Sediment yield prediction with universal equation using runoff energy factor. Present and prospective techonology for predicting sediment yield and sources, Agricultural Researche Service, U.S. Department of Agriculture.

Williams, J.R., Berndt H.D. (1972) Sediment yield computed with universal equation. Proc. ASCE, Vol. 98, HY12.

Hydrology in Mountainous Regions. II - Artificial Reservoirs; Water and Slopes
(Proceedings of two Lausanne Symposia, August 1990). IAHS Publ. no. 194, 1990.

Stochastic elements of bed load transport in a step-pool mountain river

P. ERGENZINGER
K.-H. SCHMIDT
Institut für Physische Geographie, Freie Universität Berlin, 1000 Berlin 33, West-Germany

ABSTRACT The study of step length and travel length of cobbles in a step-pool alpine river reveals that the best description of the distribution of the material is given by an e-function or a Poisson distribution. The deposition of the material is strongly influenced by the changing gradient of the step-pool longitudinal profile. Only a small amount of particles can be deposited in step reaches, by far more material rests in the pool areas.

INTRODUCTION

The conditions of transport of coarse material in steep channels are difficult to observe and to measure both in the laboratory and in nature. Here we refer to measurements in nature in the Lainbach catchment close to Benediktbeuern in Upper Bavaria (fig. 1). The river has a typical alpine regime and a pronounced step - pool longitudinal profile (Ergenzinger & Stüve 1989). The investigations are part of a special program dealing with processes in fluvial geomorphology funded by the German National Science Association (Deutsche Forschungsgemeinschaft).

For the development of a Lagrangian model of bed load transport the following questions must be solved:

- How long are the step lengths and the rest periods during different floods?
- How long are the travel lengths (or accumulated step lengths) of coarse material for
.   different floods?
- How are transport lengths influenced by weight and/or form of the coarse material?
- How is the deposition of the transported material affected by the step-pool profile of the river?
- What are the favoured storage positions in the step and pool areas of the river?

In this paper not all of these questions will be handled in detail; we will concentrate especially on the first four questions.

Refined techniques are needed to get new data sets for the old questions. Coarse bedload material was tracered using magnets (Magnetic Tracer Technique = **MATT**) or iron bolts (Ferruginuos Tracer Technique = **FETT**) and by transmitters (Pebble Transmitter System = **PETSY**) implanted into various cobbles. In this presentation these techniques can be treated only in a very concise manner.

STEP LENGTHS AND REST TIMES OF COBBLES DURING FLOODS OF DIFFERENT MAGNITUDES

First measurements of step lengths, transport velocities and the lengths of rest periods were done with cobbles tracered by transmitters (PETSY). The new technique was developed independently by two research groups at the same time on both sides of the Atlantic (Chacho, Burrows &

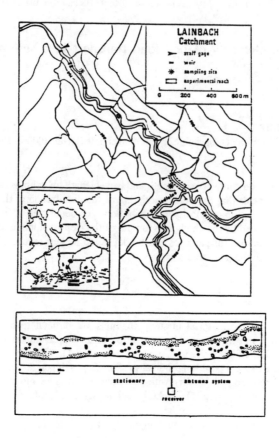

FIG. 1 Measuring site and the PETSY antenna system.

Emmett, 1989 and Ergenzinger, Schmidt & Busskamp 1989). One of its possible uses is to check the assumptions of Einstein (1950).

PETSY consists of a transmitter, an antenna system, a receiver and a data logger. The transmitters are combined with a battery to a pack of 60 mm length and 20 mm in diameter, they are installed into holes drilled into cobbles and operate at a frequency close to 150 MHz, which can be received inside and outside the water. By the stationary antenna system, which is installed along the observation reach of 150 m, the movement of the selected cobbles can be monitored with about 2 m of resolution. Furthermore, the transmitter signals change when the cobble turns, movement by gliding and by rolling can be differentiated.

In summer 1988 and 1989 during six floods movements of the tracered cobbles occured. Depending on the discharge conditions there were travel lengths during one single flood of up to 800 m. On each occasion the transport was discontinuous (fig.2). The first flood was rather low and the movement of the cobble was interrupted several times by long rest periods, whereas in the second case during a steeply rising flood the cobble needed only half the time for approximately the same travel distance. This experience proves that the travel lengths and the rest periods during the phases of transport can be measured as proposed by Einstein (1937). The question is whether the probability-function of Einstein delivers a good description. Table 1 shows the properties of the tracered cobbles.

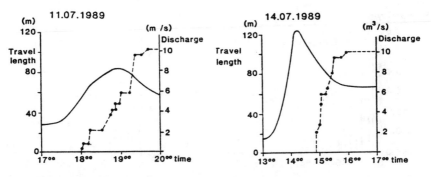

FIG. 2 Typical time/travel diagrams for two cobbles.

TABLE 1 Properties of the tracered cobbles (PETSY).

Volume	(cm³)	400	877	325	740	1200	340	130
Weight	(g)	1079	2238	878	1934	3205	880	345
a-axes	(mm)	108	141	125	152	158	116	81
b-axes	(mm)	85	122	90	112	130	93	60
c-axes	(mm)	83	96	58	83	115	62	49

Figure 3 shows the frequencies of all measured single step lengths for the cobbles. The distribution can be described by an e-function, the average step length is about 23 m. But for different hydraulic conditions there are remarkable changes in the length of individual steps.

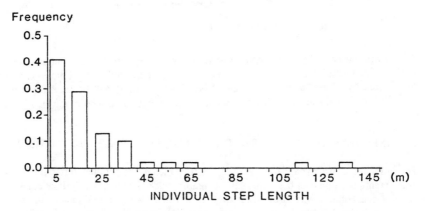

FIG. 3 Frequencies of individual step lengths.

If the dataset of the Lainbach is split into two classes of floods with maximum discharges below or above 7.7 m³/s there are great differences in the distributions and in the average travel lengths of the cobbles (Fig. 4). The average step lengths for the different classes are 13.7 m and 26.2 m. Since the individual steps are not independent of the flow conditions, the best statistical description of this distribution is according to Einstein (1939,27) the Poisson distribution. For higher flows the average step length is more than 200 times the grain diameter. As was shown first by Einstein (1939), the frequency distribution of the duration of rest periods after each individual step can again be described by the same type of function (fig.5).

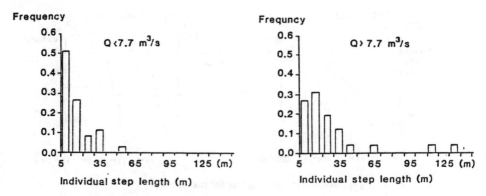

FIG. 4 Frequencies of individual step lengths during floods with more than or less than 7.7 m³/s discharge.

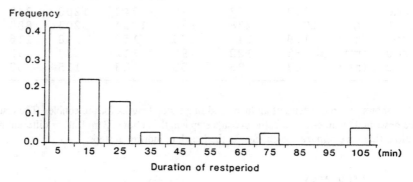

FIG. 5 Frequencies of rest times.

The dataset obtained by measurements with the PETSY system in the Lainbach demonstrates that it offers rich possibilities for detailed studies of coarse material bed load movement. The proposals of Einstein for a stochastic description of bed load transport will be used for a new attempt at modelling bed load transport. What's needed are more data on transport during high floods.

THE INFLUENCE OF WEIGHT AND FORM ON THE TRAVEL LENGTHS OF COBBLES

The influence of weight and/or form on the travel length of cobbles during individual floods was experimentally studied in the Lainbach. In summer 1988 the so called "yellow collection" of coarse pebbles and cobbles was inserted into the river (mean weight: 1330 g, minimum weight: 330 g, maximum weight: 5020 g.) All stones were tracered by artificial iron cores implanted into drilled holes and by yellow paint. The main results of these attempts are shown in figure 6 and 7.

The relationship between the weight of these particles and the travel length is rather obscure. There is a cloud of dots and only a weak tendency for shorter travel lengths of the heavier particles. The correlation coefficient ($r = -0.536$) is significant at the 0.01-level, but only one third of the variance of travel distance is explained by weight alone. The same is true if this dataset is used for the relationship between grain size (b-axes) and travel lengths (fig.7). There is a comparable amount of scatter in this distribution and the correlation is also very poor ($r = -0.558$) (cf. SCHMIDT et al. 1989).

In order to investigate the influence of form on the travel length a "coloured collection" of artificial cement stones was created in summer 1989. The weight of all stones is between 950 and 1000 g and

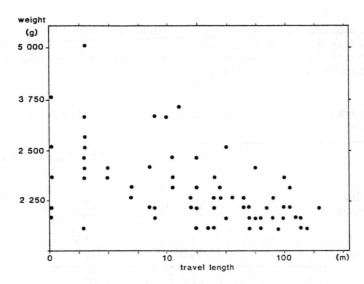

FIG. 6 Weight versus travel length of the "yellow collection".

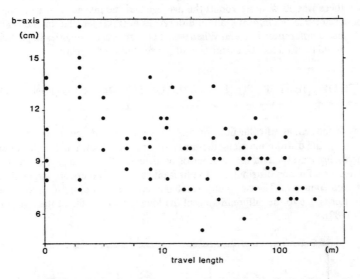

FIG. 7 Grain size versus travel length of the "yellow collection".

all cobbles are tagged by magnets and numbers. There are four times 120 particles with four different colours, which are indicative for different positions in the river bed (step, pool, gravel bar, bars upstream from large blocks). The forms of the artificial cobbles are quite distinctive. and in each of the four river bed positions 30 specimens of the four different forms were placed.

TABLE 2 Geometrical properties of the "coloured collection".

	a-axis mm	b-axis mm	c-axis mm	stoss area m²
ball	12	9.5	6.2	0.0058
ellipsoid	16	10	4.8	0.0060
disk	16	13.5	3.8	0.0061
rod	23	6	5.7	0.0131

During the observation time of summer 1989 there were only two floods. The first flood occured on July 11th with a peak discharge of 8 m^3/s, the second flood was only three days later with a maximum discharge of 12 m^3/s. The average and maximum travel length of the different forms of the coloured collection are included in table 3.

Table 3 Average and maximum travel lengths of the different forms of the cobbles of the "coloured collection".

	rods	balls	ellipsoids	disks
	m	m	m	m
11.7.1989:				
average travel	38	33	28	13
maxim. travel	170	175	164	71
14.7.1889:				
average travel	76	61	66	19
maxim. travel	430	345	400	133

The differences between the rods with an extreme stoss area and the disks are three- to fourfold. Between the ellipsoids and the balls there are no big differences in travel length. It is also worth noticing that when there was 50 % more runoff the average and the maximum travel lengths were doubled. A lot of the noise in the information on differences in travel lengths for the same weight class of cobbles is due to differences in form. Whenever there are great diversities in particle forms, correction factors should be used for the calculation of the related travel lengths.

THE INFLUENCE OF THE STEP - POOL PROFILE ON THE DISTRIBUTION OF TRAVEL LENGTHS

The travel lengths of the "coloured collection" of cobbles were mapped and measured in summer 1989. In figure 8 the spatial distribution along the measuring reach is shown in 2-meter intervals. In principle with increasing travel length the number of particles declines, which is described rather well by an e-function or a Poisson distribution. The fit is much better if there are larger classes with intervals of 10 or even 20 meters. The two meter resolution creates a lot of noise. According to our experience this scatter is due to the differentiation of the longitudinal profile of the river into steps and pools (CHIN 1989).

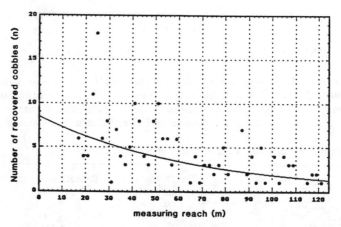

FIG. 8 The distribution of travel lengths of the "coloured collection" after two floods in July 1989 with the calculated e-function.

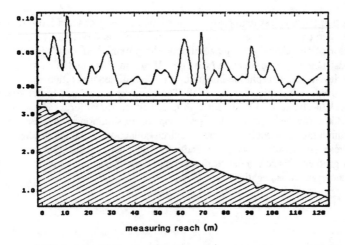

FIG. 9 Longitudinal profile of the Lainbach at the measuring site .

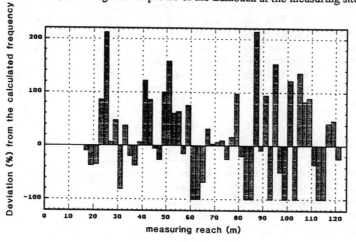

FIG. 10 The percentage of relative deviation from the calculated distribution of travel lengths for the "coloured collection".

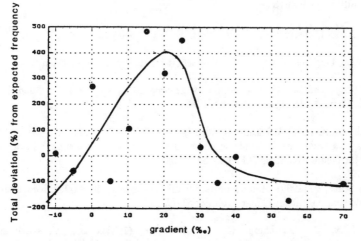

FIG. 11 The relationship between the deviation (%) from the expected frequency and the gradient of the channel .

The assumption is that there is less temporary sedimentation in the steps and more sedimentation in the pool reaches. The changing gradient along the river bottom is shown in figure 9. In order to overcome the impact of the changing slope conditions the potential "normal" distribution of the travel lengths is constructed by an e-function (see fig.8). If the numbers on the curve are defined as 100%, the relative deviation by surplus sedimentation or lack of sedimentation can be calculated. The result of this procedure is depicted in figure 10. These figures are related to the gradient along the river bottom and the balance of sedimentation is calculated for different classes of gradients (fig.11). By this result it can be predicted that according to the situation in the step - pool system there is surplus sedimentation of cobbles of the "coloured collection" when the gradient is between 0 and 30 o/oo. These are simultaneously the limits for the pool reaches. On parts of the river bottom with higher gradients there is a deficit in sedimentation. The same is true for the upper side of the pools when the gradient is negative.

FUTURE WORK

The investigations on bed load transport in the Lainbach catchment were concentrated on the analysis of the distribution of travel lengths and step lengths during different floods. According to our results the best fit for the step lengths, the related rest periods, and the travel lengths are Poisson distributions. This was theoretically predicted by Einstein in 1937 for situations when there is no unit step length. More measurements are needed for different particle weights and different flood volumes. By the combination of a deterministic description of erosion and a stochastic description of transport a new bed load function will be developed. In order to overcome the restrictions of Eulerian predictions for the transport through a river section more Lagrangian models are needed.

ACKNOWLEDGMENTS

We thank the German National Science Association for the financial support. The results could not have been obtained without the help and the enthusiasm of our co-workers Dr. Kasimierz Banasik, Dagmar Bley, Ralf Busskamp, Dorothea Gintz and Dr. Peter Stüve.

REFERENCES

Chacho, E.F., Burrows, R.L., Emmett, W.W. (1989) Detection of coarse sediment movement using radio transmitters. - Manuscript.

Chin, A. (1989) Step pools in stream channels. - Progress in physical geography: 391-407.

Einstein, H. A. (1937) Der Geschiebetrieb als Wahrscheinlichkeitsproblem. - Zürich.

Einstein, H. A. (1950) The Bed-Load Function for Sediment Transportation in Open Channel Flow. - U.S. Dept. Agric., Techn. Bull. no. 1026.

Ergenzinger,P. Schmidt,K.-H. & Busskamp,R. (1989) The Pebble Transmitter System (PETS): first results of a technique for studying coarse material erosion, transport and deposition Zeitschrift für Geomorphologie N.F. 33: 4:503 - 508.

Ergenzinger, P. & Stüve, P. (1989) Räumliche und zeitliche Variabilität der Fließwiderstände in einem Wildbach. - Göttinger Geogr. Abh. 86: 61-79.

Schmidt, K.-H., Bley, D., Busskamp, R. & Gintz, D. (1989) Die Verwendung von Trübungsmessung, Eisentracern, Magnettracern und Radiogeschieben bei der Erfassung des Feststofftransports im Lainbach, Oberbayern. - Göttinger Geogr. Abh. 86: 123-135.

Expériences concernant les vidanges et curages des bassins de retenue

RUDOLF GARTMANN
Chef de l'office de la protection de l'environnement du
Canton des Grisons, 7001 Coire, Suisse

RESUME: Les vidanges et curages, rendus nécessaires par
l'exploitation, peuvent amener à une crue artificielle
avec transport élevé de matières de charriage et de suspensions, à des dépôts de boues indésirables, ainsi qu'à
une atteinte de la flore et de la faune. Dans les Grisons,
les vidanges et curages des bassins de retenue sont projetés systématiquement et surveillés par les autorités.
Les expériences faites ont permis d'établir des directives
dont le respect strict évite les dégâts dans l'exutoire et
son entourage. En s'appuyant sur quelques exemples con-
crets, cet exposé montre les expériences et les conclusions qu'on a tirées concernant la protection des eaux, la
pêche et la police des eaux.

MISE EN VALEUR DES PROBLEMES

De nombreux cours d'eau suisses, et parmi eux également des cours
d'eau grisons, sont modifiés considérablement dans leur équilibre, en
particulier par les barrages artificiels. A cause de la vitesse réduite des affluents, des matières anorganiques surtout, transportées
par charriage de fond ou en suspension, mais aussi des matières provenant de la pollution organique se déposent et produisent ainsi une
sédimentation qui diminue le volume d'eau utilisable. La sécurité du
dispositif de vidange et celle d'autres parties des installations se
trouvent également réduites. Si un barrage est situé en aval d'une
agglomération, l'affluent est chargé d'eaux usées dont les matières
polluantes se sédimentent. Ceci se produit surtout lorsque les eaux
usées ne sont pas ou que partiellement traitées dans des stations
d'épuration.

La sécurité des barrages impose des contrôles périodiques des différentes installations de vidange, et éventuellement des réparations
de celles-ci. Pour cette raison, les vidanges des bassins d'accumulation sont indispensables. Les sédimentations dans les bassins rendent
nécessaires les curages périodiques, particulièrement lorsqu'il s'agit
de bassins de compensation relativement petits. Les vidanges et les
curages peuvent tous deux provoquer une crue artificielle dans l'exutoire, avec un transport très élevé de matériaux charriés et en suspension. C'est le cas surtout lorsque ces mesures sont prises arbitraire-
ment. De plus, des dépôts peu esthétiques de boue dans le lit des
ruisseaux et des rivières ainsi qu'aux emplacements de frai peuvent se
produire. Cela peut provoquer la mort des poissons et occasioner des
dégâts à la flore et la faune aquatiques en aval du barrage. Les vidanges et les curages causent donc des problèmes touchant à la protection des eaux, à la pêche et à la police des eaux. Pour maintenir

de telles servitudes sur l'environnement à un niveau aussi bas que possible, il convient d'adapter les changements artificiels du régime de l'écoulement aux processus naturels des eaux.

Dans les Grisons, depuis environ 10 ans, les vidanges et les curages nécessaires des bassins sont projetés systématiquement par les propriétaires des usines hydro-electriques et annoncés aux autorités compétentes, qui en surveillent la réalisation. Les expériences faites ont permis d'établir les conditions à respecter pour les vidanges et les curages et de fixer des directives. Grâce à l'observation stricte de ces directives, on peut éviter désormais des dégâts dans l'exutoire et dans son entourage, ainsi que l'atteinte portée à la flore et à la faune.

LES VIDANGES DE BASSINS

Le bassin d'accumulation de Zervreila, situé dans la vallée supérieure de Vals, avec une capacité utile en eau de 100 mio m^3 et un niveau maximum atteignant 1862 m s/m, a dû être vidangé pour la première fois le 12 mars 1981 soit après 24 ans d'exploitation. Dans une première phase, l'abaissement partiel du lac a été effectué à travers les pertuis des turbines de la centrale située au pied du barrage et par la galerie à écoulement libre menant à la vallée de Safien. Dans une deuxième phase, le lac a été vidé complètement par la vidange de fond directement dans l'exutoire, c'est-à-dire dans le Rhin de Vals. A cette occasion on a enregistré, pendant 3 heures, un débit d'environ 50 m^3/s à la station hydrométrique située à 6,5 km en aval, près du village de Vals. Ce débit correspond à une crue qui ne se produit jamais spontanément au mois de mars. Il représente un écoulement spécifique de 780 l/s km^2 près du barrage ou de 390 l/s km^2 près de la station hydrométrique. En mars, le débit moyen, avant la construction du barrage, s'élevait à 1,2 m^3/s et l'écoulement maximum à 4,4 m^3/s. Comme conséquence de cette vidange, on a constaté la présence de bois provenant d'avalanches, des zones de nutrition des poissons recouvertes par la sédimentation ainsi qu'une forte régression du nombre des jeunes poissons.

Des mesures adéquates ont été proposées à la suite de ces expériences négatives et, lors de toutes les vidanges de barrages ultérieures effectuées dans le canton des Grisons, celles-ci ont été appliquées avec succès. Aujourd'hui, les directives, respectivement les règles suivantes sont en vigueur pour la vidange d'un barrage:
(a) La première vidange devrait avoir lieu déjà après quelques années d'exploitation. On évite ainsi le dépôt de trop grandes quantités de matériaux solides devant les barrages et leurs organes de vidange.
(b) Chaque vidange est à organiser individuellement en tenant compte des conditions locales. Elle doit être coordonnée au préalable avec les autorités compétentes.
(c) Avant chaque vidange, l'exutoire doit être inspecté. Les dépôts éventuels dans le lit du cours d'eau, provoqués par des avalanches et des éboulis, sont à éliminer.
(d) Lors de la vidange, le débit dans l'exutoire doit être augmenté lentement et régulièrement; ceci est valable surtout pour les cours d'eau sans débit résiduel. Des pointes de débit maximum sont à éviter.

(e) Afin de protéger les poissons et leurs zones de nutrition, les
    vidanges doivent être effectuées avec le maximum de précautions.
(f) Afin de limiter les dégâts aux pêcheries par des mesures à prendre
    dans le bassin et dans l'exutoire, les vidanges projetées doivent
    être annoncées officiellement 3 ans à l'avance.
(g) Normalement, les vidanges doivent être effectuées hors de la pério-
    de de frai des poissons, c'est-à-dire au plus tard à fin juillet.
    Les exceptions sont à motiver.

LES CURAGES DE BASSINS D'ACCUMULATION ET DE COMPENSATION

Le curage de retenues - précédé d'une vidange - conduit nécessairement
à une charge de l'exutoire par les matériaux charriés et transportés
en suspension. Cette charge ne doit cependant pas dépasser certaines
limites. La concentration en matières solides représente le critère
décisif pour l'exutoire. De ce fait, les échantillons d'eau chargée
pris dans l'exutoire servent de base pour l'estimation et le règlement
des curages. On peut ainsi déterminer le débit minimum nécessaire dans
l'exutoire et adapter en conséquence l'écoulement évacué par la vidange de fond, c'est-à-dire diriger avec une certaine précision les travaux (mécaniques) d'évacuation des matières déposées dans le bassin.
Ces directives basées sur la détermination de la concentration en
matières solides ne sont valables que si les valeurs du mesurage sont
établies à court terme. Nos expériences montrent qu'après 30 minutes
une sédimentation relativement stationnaire est généralement atteinte
dans l'entonnoir d'Imhof.
    Pour arriver à des normes qui devraient être respectées lors de
curages de bassins, nous avons déterminé, à titre de comparaison, la
concentration des matières solides dans divers cours d'eau quand il y
a une augmentation naturelle du débit, comme par exemple pendant les
orages, la fonte des neiges ou lors de crues moyennes. A cette fin,
nous avons pris de nombreux échantillons dans divers fleuves et rivières lors de crues et déterminé la concentration des matières solides après une sédimentation de 30 minutes. Il s'est avéré que les
cours d'eau naturels présentent à débit élevé des concentrations de
suspensions semblables à celles atteintes pendant les curages. Nous
avons constaté également que les zones de nutrition des poissons sont
détruites ou recouvertes de matériau. Les concentrations établies
dépendent des conditions marginales, par exemple du bassin de réception des affluents, des conditions géologiques, du contenu en minéraux
des matières en suspension. Ces concentrations varient entre 0,4 et 6
ml/l. Quelques valeurs extrêmes ont atteint 30 ml/l. Ces normes déter-
minées dans les écoulements naturels peuvent être respectées, comme
nous l'avons vu lors de nombreux curages.
    Par exemple, le bassin de compensation de Bergün, avec une capa-
cité exploitable de 35'000 m^3, a été vidangé le 18 août 1981, après 4
ans d'exploitation (fig. 1). Le nettoyage, respectivement le curage,
du matériau fin déposé dans le bassin a été effectué avec une quantité
d'eau de curage de $Q_c \hat{=} 5$ m^3/s en utilisant des moyens mécaniques. La
concentration en matières solides dans l'exutoire Albula, qui n'a
qu'un faible volume d'eau, a atteint une valeur maximum de 10 ml/l à
l'endroit de prélèvement A à 50 m en aval de la restitution d'eau dans
l'Albula, respectivement 1,5 ml/l seulement à l'endroit B à 3,5 km en
aval. Cette diminution est causée par le débit liquide supérieur de la

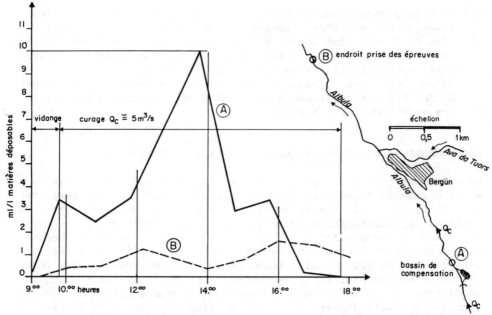

FIG.1 Curage bassin de compensation Bergün 18 août 1981.

rivière à ce dernier endroit. Après avoir terminé le curage d'environ 8 heures, on pouvait observer dans le lit de l'Albula des bancs de sable fin.

Dans les Grisons, il est aujourd'hui de règle que, lors d'un curage, on mesure la concentration de matériaux fins dans l'exutoire à un ou plusieurs endroits adéquats. Les normes de 10 - 20 ml/l après un trajet de mélange de 50 - 100 m en aval de la restitution de l'eau doivent être respectées si possible et ceci pendant tout le processus. De plus, les conditions mentionnées dans l'alinéa précédent concernant les vidanges sont aussi valables pour les curages. L'annonce d'un curage projeté pour des bassins relativement petits doit être faite au plus tard jusqu'à fin mars, ceci par égard pour la pêcherie. Les curages doivent être effectués la même année, avant la fin juillet, s'il n'y a pas d'exceptions motivées.

CONCLUSIONS

Les règles appliquées aujourd'hui dans les Grisons se sont avérées judicieuses lors de vidanges et de curages de bassins d'accumulation et de compensation. Elles tiennent compte des exigences posées par l'environnement, sans toutefois être exagérées pour les exploitants d'usines électriques. Des évènements semblables à ceux constatés dans la vallée de Vals ne se sont pas reproduits. Il est indispensable cependant que les vidanges et les curages de chaque bassin soient adaptés aux conditions locales et aux installations particulières. Si tel est le cas, des conséquences défavorables ne devraient pas être attendues, tant en ce qui concerne l'aménagement des cours d'eau que la protection qualitative des eaux et de la pêche.

Les règles valables dans les Grisons entreront effectivement en vigueur par la nouvelle loi fédérale sur la protection des eaux.

Hydrology in Mountainous Regions. II - Artificial Reservoirs; Water and Slopes
(Proceedings of two Lausanne Symposia, August 1990). IAHS Publ. no. 194, 1990.

Calculation of sediment deposition in the Katse reservoir, Lesotho

P. JEHANNO, C. LAVOREL, P. MEILLAND (Engineers)
J.P. HURAUT (Project Manager)
SOGREAH Consulting Engineers, GRENOBLE, France

ABSTRACT The projected Katse dam, in Lesotho, will be equipped with a water intake, in order to divert water to the Vaal catchment in South Africa. Estimation of the risk of sedimentation in front of the water intake (and sand entrainment through it) was carried out using the Char2 mathematical model of movable beds, developed by SOGREAH, taking into account the main characteristics of the sediment and hydraulics conditions of the river entering the reservoir.

Deposition in the reservoir over a long period (50 years) was calculated, as well as the displacement of the deposits by flood action. Because of the uncertainty surrounding sediment characteristics and specific degradation of the catchment area, several scenarios were contemplated. As a conclusion, this study confirms the proposed location of the water intake, which would not be affected by siltation for a long period. Only a combination of extreme rare events would cause deposits to reach the intake.

INTRODUCTION

The Lesotho Highlands Water Project is a multipurpose project, planned to develop the water resources of the highlands region of Lesotho. The first phase of the project includes an arch dam (Katse dam) creating the main storage reservoir of the whole project. A first transfer tunnel conveys water from Katse reservoir to a power plant (Muela). Downstream of Muela power plant, a gravity dam is projected. A delivery tunnel links this reservoir to the Ash river valley in the Republic of South Africa. As the catchment area of Katse dam is subject to erosion, examination of siltation in the water intake was carried out with the help of a mathematical model simulating movable beds.

DESCRIPTION OF THE PROJECT

The Lesotho Highlands Water Project (LHWP) is a multipurpose project to develop in successive phases the water resources of the highlands region of Lesotho by a series of dams, tunnels, pumping stations and hydroelectric works.

The primary objectives of the project are:
(a) to redirect some of the water which presently flows in a south-westerly direction out of Lesotho to the north towards the population centres in the Republic of South Africa,

51

(b)   to generate hydroelectric power in Lesotho utilising the re-directed water flow,
(c)   to provide water supply, irrigation and regional development in Lesotho.

The project will be built in four main phases to be completed in year 2020 with the first phase subdivided into phases 1A and 1B.

Phase 1A consists of the following main structures to be carried out concurrently after completion of the access roads and infrastructure works so as to complete the whole of phase 1A at the same time:
(a)   access roads and infrastructure works presently under construction,
(b)   Katse dam (concrete arch, $h = 180$ m, concrete volume = 2 100 000 m³) which will create the main storage reservoir for the whole project; the dam is located on the Malibamatso river,
(c)   the first Transfer Tunnel (length = 45 km) from the Katse reservoir to Muela power plant and the first Muela power plant,
(d)   Muela dam (concrete curved gravity dam) (height = 60 m; concrete volume = 90 000 m³),
(e)   the first Delivery Tunnel (length = 35 km, 4,2 m diameter) from the Muela reservoir to the Ash river valley in the Republic of South Africa,
(f)   the terminal structures for Transfer Tunnels of phases 1B and 2.

Phase 1B will include the Mohale dam and transfer tunnel from the Mohale reservoir to the Katse reservoir, and a diversion weir on the Matseku river together with a transfer tunnel from the Matseku river to the Katse reservoir.

Phases 2, 3 and 4 will include the construction of dams on the Senqu river, downstream of the Katse dam, together with transfer tunnels and pumping stations to direct water northwards into the Katse reservoir.

THE MATHEMATICAL MODEL

The mathematical model (CHAR2) developed by SOGREAH, solves a set of non-linear differential equations of river flow and sediment movement using Preissmann's semi implicit finite difference scheme. The following assumptions are made:
(a)   flow is one dimensional in accordance with the De Saint-Venant hypothesis,
(b)   liquid wave celerities are high compared to bottom perturbation celerities, which justifies the assumption of constant discharge all along a reach of river,
(c)   flow resistance is described using the Manning formula with the Manning coefficient constant in time,
(d)   bed material is homogeneous or can be represented by a specific diameter of sediment.

The above assumptions lead to the following system of differential equations:

$$\frac{\delta}{\delta x} \left[\frac{Q^2}{2A^2} + gy \right] + \frac{g \; Q|Q|}{D^2} = 0$$

$$(1-n)\frac{\delta z}{\delta t} + \frac{1}{b}\frac{\delta G}{\delta x} = 0$$

$$G = F(y, z, Q, d, ...)$$

Where:

$y(x,t)$	= water stage	$A(y,z)$	= wetted area
$z(x,t)$	= river bed elevation	d	= sediment diameter
$G(x,t)$	= sediment discharge	$Q(x,t)$	= liquid discharge
D	= conveyance		
x	= longitudinal coordinate	t	= time
n	= porosity of deposited sediment		
$b(y,x)$	= width of river bed affected by the solid transport		

CONSTRUCTION OF THE MODEL AND CALCULATION HYPOTHESES

The model represents about 43 km of the Malibamatso river of which 34.9 km is upstream of the intake site and 8.7 km downstream (the water intake is located 26 km upstream of Katse dam). The average river bed slope is about 2.6 m/km and the river bed elevation is in the range of 1960-2080 m.

The topography is represented by 25 cross sections taking into account in-situ measurements. The study considered sediment diameters between 0.1 and 2 mm, and, according to this range of sediment sizes, the Engelund-Hansen formula was adopted for calculation of the solid transport.

The density of deposits was calculated with the help of Miller's equation, with leads to a density of 1.35 t/m³.

A calculation scenario analysis attempts to evaluate the probability of sedimentation in Katse reservoir interfering with the operation of the tunnel water intake. The probability is assessed by modelling various scenarios of inflow over the sediment delta that is formed in the upstream reach of Katse reservoir combined with various operating levels in the reservoir.

The following ranges of parameters have been considered:

(a) Specific basin degradation is estimated to be between 200t/km²/year and 800t/km²/year. With a catchment area of 1273 km², and allowing for the reservoir side slope degradation as a result of fluctuating water levels, the yield of sediment entering the reservoir over 50 years is estimated as $15 \; 10^6$ t for 200 t/km²/year (and $53.2 \; 10^6$ t for 800 t/km²/year).

(b) Sediment is deposited with the reservoir at mean operating level. Floods occurring when the reservoir level is low would scour part of the deposited sediment and redeposit it further downstream.

(c) The flood peak discharges and reservoir levels are as
     follows :

Table 1

PEAK DISCHARGES AND RESERVOIR LEVELS			
Return period (years)	Frequence of Exceedance	Peak (m3/s)	Level (m)
2	0.50	465	-
10	0.10	988	2016.8
20	0.05	-	2006.0
50	0.02	1706	1996.5

CONSTRUCTION OF A 50 YEAR DEPOSIT

It was decided to study the influence of floods occurring after
50 years of sediment deposit.

The 50 year deposit was formed by running a constant
discharge of 500 m³/s through the model with some 2 t/s of
sediment transported by the flow (500 m³/s is sufficient to
transport 2 t/s of sediment with a size range between 0.1 and 2 mm
in the reach of river where the reservoir has no influence, and
500 m³/s represents a discharge higher than the 2-year peak flow).
This flow rate was maintained sufficiently long to transport a
volume corresponding to a specific degradation of 800 t/km²/year
over 50 years. The reservoir level was maintained at 2040 m (the
average reservoir operating level).

Figure 3 shows a 50 year deposit obtained for a specific
catchment degradation of 800 t/km²/year and an average particle
size of 0.5 mm. The downstream toe of the deposit is about 10 km
upstream of the water intake site (Figure 4 shows a 50 year
deposit for a catchment degradation of 800 t/km²/year and an
average particle size of 0.1 mm).

DISPLACEMENT OF THE 50 YEAR DEPOSIT BY FLOODS

A simulation of the displacement of the 50 year deposit was
performed with the following assumptions:
(a) Specific degradation of catchment: 800 t/km²/year
(b) Sediment diameter: 0.5 mm
(c) 50 year recurrence interval flood
(d) Reservoir level: 1996,5 (2% frequency of occurrence) at the
beginning of the flood.

Inflow into the reservoir was increased from 100 m³/s to
1700 m³/s (50 year return period flood) while the reservoir level
rose. Flow into the reservoir was then decreased down to 100 m³/s.

Figure 5 shows the final deposition pattern. The frequency of
occurrence of the event would be about 0.0004 (recurrence interval
about 2500 years). From figure 5 it is clear that with a very high
catchment degradation rate (800 t/km²/year) and a mean sediment
diameter of 0.5 mm the downstream toe of the deposit stops about
2 km upstream of the water intake.

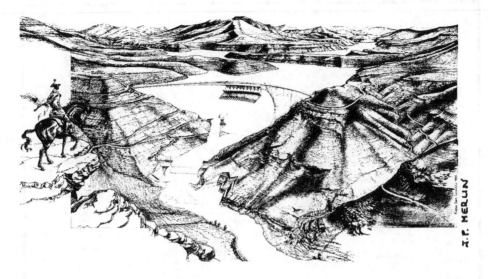

FIG. 1 Katse dam.

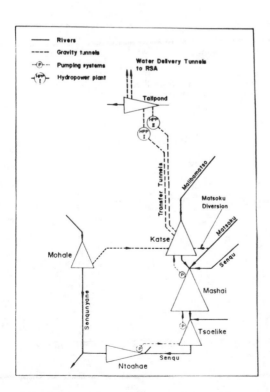

FIG. 2 Schematic diagram of the reservoir system.

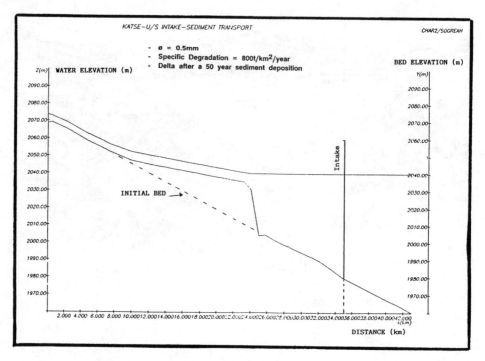

FIG. 3

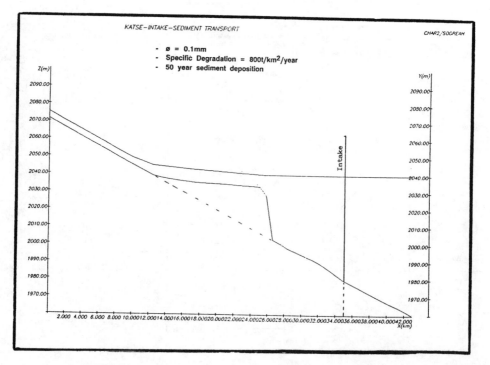

FIG. 4

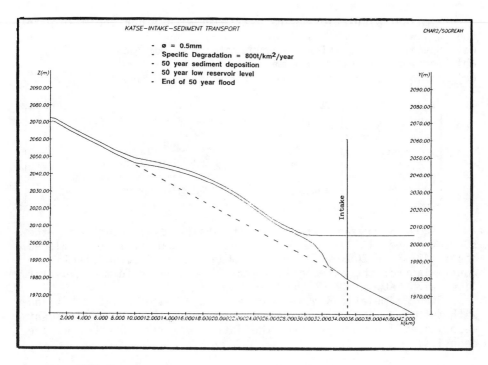

FIG. 5

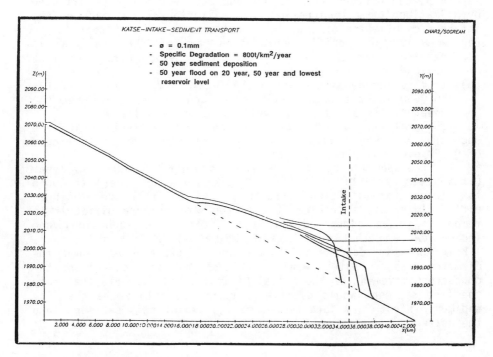

FIG. 6

Similar calculations were performed with finer sediment with the following assumptions:
(a)   Specific degradation of catchment: 800 t/km²/year
(b)   Sediment diameter: 0.1 mm
(c)   Various flood and reservoir starting conditions as follows:

Frequency event	Flood	Reservoir level at the beginning of the flood
0.001	50 year	2006 (5% frequency)
0.0004	50 year	1996.5 (2% frequency)
0.00001	50 year	1989 (minimum operating level)
0.0087	average year	1996.5 (2% frequency)

Figure 6 presents the deposit shapes calculated with the 50 year flood. It is clear that a water intake sill level placed above elevation 2005 will not be subject to siltation within the constraints of the calculations that have been performed thus far (i.e. with between 99.9% and 99.99% assurance).

Other simulations were made with a 50 year flood occurring with a 50 year low reservoir level and after 14 years of sediment deposition. They showed that the intake was not affected by the deposits.

CONCLUSIONS

From the various scenarios presented above it appears that a water intake placed between levels 2000 and 2005 would not be affected by siltation for a long period. For siltation to encroach on the intake a combination of extreme (rare) events are required:
(a)   a very high specific degradation rate of 800 t/km²/year is
      required over at least 50 years, all sediment must be fine
      grained,
(b)   to move the deposit down to the intake a flood of at least a
      50 year recurrence interval must occur at at time when the
      reservoir level is low (level 1996.5 or below).
The combined probabilities of the above extreme events are such that the probability of assurance of operation is in excess of 99.9% over the first 50 years.

If the specific degradation rate is lower than 800 t/km²/year (it may very well be as low as 400 t/km²/year or lower) it would take longer for sufficient silt to accumulate in the reservoir to ultimately create a problem. Coarse sediment is more difficult to remobilise than fine sediment (if there is no cohesion) and indications are that more coarse sediment than fine sediment is likely on this catchment. A mixture of grain sizes with the diameter range tested would lead to a restriction on the downstream movement of the delta. Ultimately, it appears that only the fine sediment would eventually reach the intake. As the fine sediment is not very abrasive, some ingress of this sediment into the delivery tunnels could be tolerated.

Hydrology in Mountainous Regions. II - Artificial Reservoirs; Water and Slopes
(Proceedings of two Lausanne Symposia, August 1990). IAHS Publ. no. 194, 1990.

Sediment transport in mountain streams

F. B. KHOSROWSHAHI
Faculty of Civil Engineering
K. N. Toosi University of Technology, Tehran, Iran

ABSTRACT the problem of sediment transport in mountain streams was investigated using information gathered from suspended sediment concentration records and results of reservoir surveyings at Jajroud River Basin. The aim was especially focused on the possibility of quantitative overall catchment erosion evaluation and bed load suspended load configuration. Results of evaluations clarify notable discrepancies between surveyed sediment, settled at the reservoir, and that appraised from historical suspended concentration records, adjusted for the bed load. Applying appropriate transport formulas, for steep slope morphology, it has been shown that such discrepancies can mainly be attributed to underestimations of bed load. This implies that, for sedimentation predictions in mountain streams, it would be logical to evaluate bed load using transport formulas rather than estimating solely from suspended load of the respective river.

INTRODUCTION

River engineering practices and morphological inspections are mostly encountered with various features of erosion and sedimentation processes. Although the governing hydrodynamical principles are basically the same, because of existing complexities, results obtained from a river study may disclose wide range of scatterness, depending on the applied procedures and imposed scientific view points. This originates from limitations and uncertainties inherent of sediment transport formulas. Many of these equations are based on flume studies and do not accord fairly with natural field conditions. In this respect more divergences may be expected for mountain streams than alluvial rivers of plain areas. In the latter case uniformity of grains and their individual movement usually prevail. In mountainous rivers, however, one is faced with possible massive movement of soil layers, wide ranges of grain sizes, step pools, frequent floodings, and occasional severe basin-wide erosion caused by sudden intens bursts. Despit of such constraints, there have been continuous researches and struggles in the hope of better improvements and accurate appraisals. Schoklitsch(1934), Ackers & White(1973),

Ashida & Egashira (1989), Meyer-Peter & Muller(1948), and other scientists have presented various transport equations applicable for mountain rivers. Few of such proposed equations were applied on Jajroud River and the amount of load was evaluated. Fig. 1 shows details of Jajroud catchment, location of Latian Dam Reservoir, and main hydrometry stations including the domain of studied area which approximates 691 km^2.

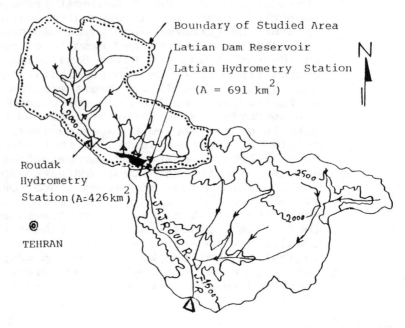

Boundary of Studied Area

Latian Dam Reservoir

Latian Hydrometry Station

(A = 691 km^2)

N

Roudak
Hydrometry
Station (A=426km^2)

TEHRAN

Darvazeh Hydrometry

Station (A = 1774 km^2)

FIG. 1 Jajroud River Basin map (Scale 1/500000).

SEDIMENT EVALUATION FROM HISTORICAL DATA AND LAKE SURVEYINGS

Since the impoundment in 1976 several lake surveyings were conducted at Latian Dam Reservoir. The results are shown in Table 1. Such periodical soundings are useful for effective storage evaluation and appraisal of reservoir loss rates. In 1981, with the lake hydrography, samples of deposited material were also taken and analysed for grain size distributions and other solid properties. Figure 2 illustrates gradation curves of pertinent samples inside the reservoir and up to 35 km far from the dam. On this figure, the curve marked with (d) demonstrates suspended sediment gradation at Roudak hydrometry Station (see Fig. 1 for the station location), for a flow rate of 10 m sec, approximately. Also curves titled (a), (b), and (c),

illustrate bed material size distribution for samples taken
from three different river cross sections along the Jajroud
River Course. From the point of view of sediment
classification, on Fig. 2 the portion of particles with
diameter less than 0.065 mm can be classified as wash load
and the remainig coarser ones specify bed material load.
By definitions curve (e) symbolyses bed material carried by
the river and settled in the reservoir. this curve fairly
coincides with the river bed material gradation
distribution, represented by curves (a), (b), and (c). The
total volume of surveyed sediment in Table 1 also includes
that portion passed the dam. This outwashed sediment volume
was evaluated from trap efficiencies appraised by classical
Brune's curves (1953).

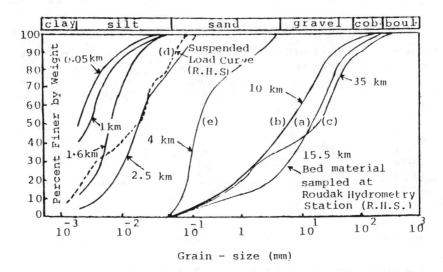

Grain - size (mm)

FIG. 2 Grain size distribution in Latian Dam Reservoir and
gradation variation along Jajroud River Course (curves (a),
(b), and (c)).

For comparision purposes and reliability tests on
sedimentation predictions, transported sediment was also
evaluated using recorded concentrations. For Jajroud River,
suspended load concentrations are available from main and
some tributary streams.
     Using sediment rating curve procedure, transported
sediment was evaluated and is shown in Table 1. In this
evaluation bed load was assumed to comprise about 20% of
suspended load based on concepts introduced by
Linsley et. al (1972). It should be mentioned that for
converting sediment weight into volume the specific weight
(dry) of settled material was assumed to be in order of
1140 kg m , according to notions given by Bondraunt (1985).
     The results of surveyings and volumes obtained from
data processing clarify some notable differences

(see Table 1 for comparison).
For a duration of 15 year, the table discloses a
volumetric divergency of 8 m. c. m. between actual surveyed
sediment and the appraised values based on guaged suspended
solid concentrations. From sedimentation prediction view
point such discrepancy cannot be neglected and the cause
should be investigated.
In the meantime there is an interesting point in Table 1.
For the first five years of reservoir operation the two
sediment volumes are almost equal. This is because of
exceptionally rainy year of 1967-1968 during which more
than 3 million tons of sediment were transported.

TABLE 1 Calculated and surveyed sediment at Jajroud River.

Year	Operation Duration (Year)	Surveyed Sediment Volume (m. c. m)	Calculated Sediment Volume (m. c. m)	Sediment Volume Difference (m. c. m)
1971	5	3.66	3.71	-0.05
1974	7	7.87	4.67	3.2
1979	13	11.59	5.35	6.24
1981	15	13.7	5.72	7.98

CALCULATION OF BED LOAD DISCHARGE

Like many other cases, there exist no measured bed load
values for Jajroud River system. It is, therefore,
necessary to evaluate bed load discharge and clarify its
practical importance in aggradation degradation
predictions. Appropriate formulas for mountain streams may
be applied and potential sediment discharge calculated
accordingly. The following equations were selected for this
purpose :

The bed load equation of Schoklitsch (1962):

$$q_{sb} = \frac{2.5}{\rho_s/\rho} \, s^{3/2} \, (q - q_c) \tag{1}$$

where the amount of q_c is :

$$q_c = 0.26 \, (\rho_s/\rho - 1)^{5/3} \, \frac{D_{40}^{3/2}}{s^{7/6}} \tag{2}$$

The bed load equation of Meyer - Peter & Muller (M.P.M.) (1948):

$$\frac{q_{sb}}{(g \; (\rho_s/\rho -1) \; D^3)^{1/2}} = 8 \; (\; (k_s/ k_r \;)^{3/2} \tau_* - 0.047)^{3/2} \qquad (3)$$

The bed load equation of Smart (1984):

$$\frac{q_{sb}}{(g \; (\rho_s/\rho - 1) \; D^3)^{1/2}} = 4((\frac{D_{90}}{D_{30}})^{0.2} \, s^{0.6} \, \frac{U}{U_*} \, \tau_*^{0.5}(\tau_* - \tau_{*c})) \quad (4)$$

where:

q_{sb} : volumetric bed load discharge ($m^3 \; s^{-1}/ \; m$);
s : channel slope (m/m);
q : river discharge ($m^3 \; s^{-1}/ \; m$);
q_c : critical discharge ($m^3 \; s^{-1}/ \; m$);
D : mean diameter of bed material (m);
k_s/k_r : correction factor for bed form roughness;
ρ_s/ρ : specific gravity of grains assumed to be equal 2.65;
U, U_* : mean flow velocity and shear velocity, respectively ($m \; s^{-1}$);
τ_*, τ_{*c} : shear stress (dimensionless);
D_{40}, D_{90}, D_{30} : bed material grain sizes (m);

Using three foregoing methods bed load discharge was evaluated for selected floods (Fig. 3) of Jajroud River at Roudak hydrometry station. Grain size distribution of bed material used in these computed bed load and its comparison with observed suspended material load are shown in Table 2. According to that table bed load varies from 7 to more than 160% of suspended sediment. This scatterness is illustrated also in Fig. 4. It is evident from Fig. 4 that generally for high flows the portion of bed load is lower than suspended sediment, while for low flows the situation is reversed rather markedly. In the meantime, low quantities belong to Schoklitsch, highests come from Smart and M.P.M.'s values lie in between.

CONCLUSIONS

This inspection reveals some useful aspects of sediment transport phenomena in mountain streams, summarized as follows:
(a) appraisal of total sediment discharge based on suspended load concentration records cannot be a reliable procedure in sedimentation prediction practices for mountain streams. It seems, therefore, necessary to evaluate each portion of total load separately and combine them together.
(b) precise and detailed understanding of sediment

TABLE 2 Comparison of calculated bed load and observed
suspended load.

Flood Event	Suspended Load (t)	Calculated Bed load (t)			Ratio of bed load to Suspended load (%)		
		Sch.	Smart	M.P.M.	Sch.	Smart	M.P.M.
A	49052	6313	16704	12188	12.9	34	24.8
B	18180	1281	4747	4441	7	26	24.42
C	946	1517	3128	3435	160	331	--

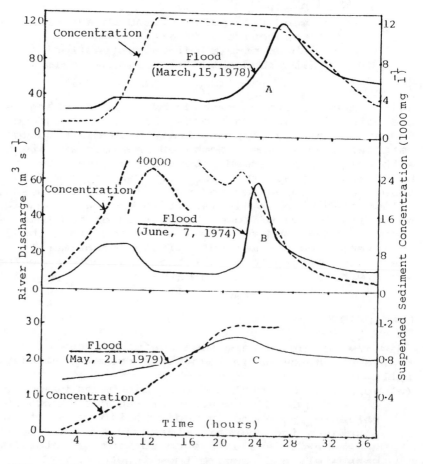

FIG. 3 Flood hydrographs at Jajroud River (R.H.S.)

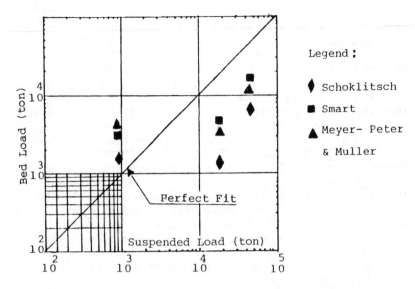

FIG. 4 Comparison of bed load and suspended load.

transport problems undoubtedly require both
mathematical and physical model studies. This will
enable sound evaluations and fundamental equation
developments for mountain streams.
(c) it is an urgent necessity to establish well
instrumented stations for sediment gauging and
visualization of various sediment transport features.
Using such actual field data and observations, model
calibration and extension of theoretical notions are
practically possible.

ACKNOWLEDGEMENTS This project was sponsored by K.N.Toosi
University of Technology for promoting research activities
in river engineering problems which I hereby express my
appreciations to the university authorities.
I am also grateful to Mr.K.Ashida, professor ,and
Mr.S.Egashira, Associate Professor, at Kyoto University,
for their valuable discussions and notions presented during
a three month training course at that university in 1989.
Special thanks to Mr.Ashabi for prepairing drawings and
Mr.Ghaemmaghami for typing the paper.
Required data were obtained from the Ministry of Power
(Surfae Water Department and Institute for Water Resources
Investigations,). I submit my gratitudes to them herewith.

REFERENCES

Schoklitsch, A. (1934) Geschiebetrieb und die
    Geschiebefracht. Wasserkraft und Wasserwirtschaft, J99.
    39, Heft 4.

Ackers, P.& White, W.R. (1973) Sediment transport: new
    approach and analysis. proc. ASCE, 99, HY 11, Paper
    10167, 2041-2060.
Meyer-Peter, E. & Muller. R. (1984) Formulas for bed load
    transport. In proc. 2nd Congr. IAHR, Stockholm, Vol 2,
    paper 2, pp. 39-64
Ashida, K.& Egashira, S.   (1989) The mechanism of sediment
    transport and control in mountain streams. Proc. of the
    Japan-Taipei Joint Seminar on Natural Hazard Mitigation
    Keyoto, Japan.
Brune, G.M. (1953) Trap efficiency of reservoirs, Trans.,
    AM. Geophes. Union, Vol. 34, pp. 407-418.
Ray K. Linsley & Joseph B. Franzini (1972) Waterresources
    engineering. Mc. Graw-Hill Book Company, New York.
Bondrant,D.C. (1958) Sedimentation studies at Conchas
    Reservoir in New Mexico. Transaction, ASCE, Vol. 116,
    pp. 1283-1295.
Schoclitsch, A. (1964) and smart (1984) Tests of bed load
    equations.
    in: Sediment transport in gravel bed rivers, C.R. Thorn
    J.C. Buthrust, & R.D. Hey, John Wiley & Sons Ltd.
    England.

Hydrology in Mountainous Regions. II - Artificial Reservoirs; Water and Slopes
(Proceedings of two Lausanne Symposia, August 1990). IAHS Publ. no. 194, 1990.

Estimation of soil erosion from a lower Alpine catchment

E. KLAGHOFER
Institute for Land and Water Management Research
A-3252 Petzenkirchen, Austria
W. SUMMER
Institute for Water Management, Hydrology and Hydraulic
Engineering, Univ. f. Bodenkultur
A-1180 Vienna, Austria

ABSTRACT A three dimensional digital terrain model
(3D-DTM) is used in coordination with a geographic information system (GIS/ARC-INFO) to assemble and retrieve
the physical parameters to estimate the rate of soil
erosion from a lower alpine catchment by the deterministic soil erosion model EPIC (Erosion Productivity
Impact Calculator). This combination, applied to a
section of the Ybbs-river catchment situated in the
northern region of the eastern part of the austrian alps
(Fig. 1), makes it possible to produce a detailed map of
different erosion risks.

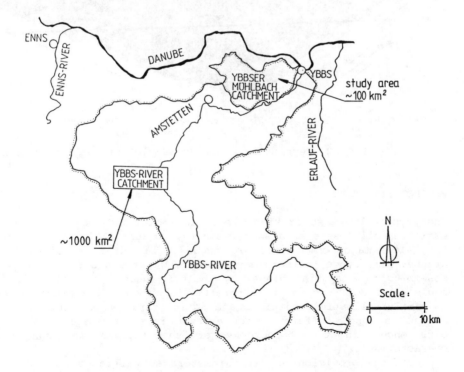

FIG. 1 Location of the study area.

INTRODUCTION

One of the major problems in modern agricultural management is the loss of soil due to surface runoff. The pollution in runoff, seepage or perculation from these management activities has besides agricultural deficiencies, major impact on the water quality. Pollutant sources or areas with a high risk of erosion are not readily identifiable in a watershed. In order to solve this task in a manner of reasonable resolution a 3D-DTM was set up in conjunction with a GIS. The DTM of a part of the Ybbs-river catchment sized at approximately 100 km^2 (Fig. 2) is based on the available rectangular altitude grid which covers almost all of Austria. The grid distance varies from 30 to 50 m, and each node is given in Gauss-Krueger coordinates. The GIS was then used to determine and assemble physical catchment parameters, which are required in estimating the soil erosion risk in each grid element of the watershed.

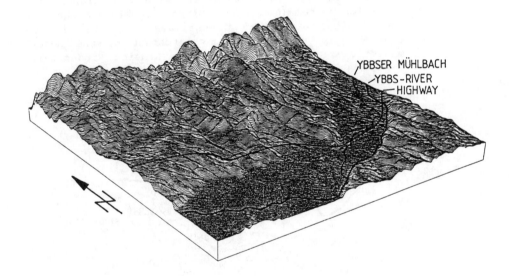

FIG. 2 Vertically extended 3D-plot of the subcatchment.

PROJECT STRUCTURE

The physically based erosion prediction model EPIC can be used to estimate soil losses at a specific site. To run EPIC, information in the EPIC's major components are needed. This data including topography, soil types, climate data, cropping pattern and tillage were assembled in a spatial manner by the GIS. Under the assumption of neglectable soil erosion from forests, urban and water areas as well as similar climatic conditions and agricultural management on areas of arable land, different soil erosion rates basically depend on differences in the topography of the terrain and the soil characteristics.

With the provision of all parameters as well as a soil erosion matrix, considering several possibilities of different gradients and soil types, it is possible to run EPIC. Overlaying 4 maps with the

topic of land use, topography or gradient, erosive slope length and
soil type, the resulting map distinguishes areas of different soil
erosion conditions. Assigning the data of the soil erosion matrix to
it,a detailed map showing the distribution of the erosion rate in
the catchment could be produced (Fig. 3).

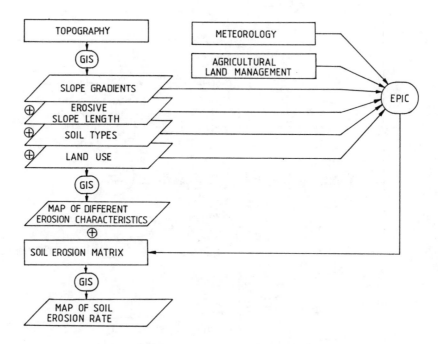

FIG. 3 Schematic of the project.

MODEL DESCRIPTION, PARAMETERS AND ASSUMPTIONS

EPIC can be considered as a deterministic model that predicts besides the soil erosion, the transfer of nutrients and its influences
on the agricultural productivity (Williams et al., 1983). Based on
daily information, EPIC shows these changes over such a short period
of time as well as over a period of many years. It presents a model
intensive in computation where the output of one calculation step is
used as input for the next.
        EPIC provides a so called "weather" subroutine which can be
used to generate daily weather characteristics by the input of statistical long term weather parameters such as standard deviation and
skewness of single precipitations. The daily data like precipitation, radiation, temperature, humidity and wind are used to estimate
the surface and subsurface runoff.
        The surface runoff is simulated by the Stanford Watershed Model
(Crawford and Linsley, 1966), where its calculation is based on the
SCS-curve method, considering besides the daily weather conditions,
the soil water content at the beginning of the simulation period
(Fig. 4).

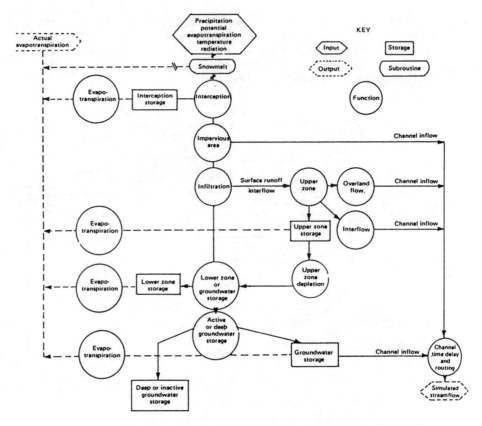

FIG. 4   Flowchart of the Stanford Watershed Model
(Shaw, 1984).

The parameters controlling the soil erosion process are strongly
related to the USLE, Universal Soil Loss Equation (Wischmeier and
Smith, 1978), but its application is partly extended in EPIC due to
new theoretical regressions and equations which are not empirically
proved yet.

   With the assistance of the GIS the gradient of the terrain
could be calculated in each grid box, from the DTM. The results were
classified into 6 groups ranging from 0 to 19 % slope gradient. Each
class having the mean value, 0.2 %, 0.9 %, 2.7 %, 6.5 %, 11 % and
16 %. The 7th group contains those greater than 19 % with a mean
value of 20 %.

   For the arable land, typical erosive slope lengths of 50 and
100 m were assumed. This parameter determines the sediment transport
distance of an inclinated surface and is therefore shorter than the
actual slope.

   The required soil characteristics can be determined from carto-
graphic maps. In the study area which is mainly under intensive
agricultural use, 64 different soil types were found. These soil
types were summarized into 9 main soil groups, which convey the soil
conditions sufficiently (Fig. 5). They are distinguished by chemical
and soil physical parameters such as grainsize distribution, content

of organic carbon as well as calcium carbonate and the pH-value.

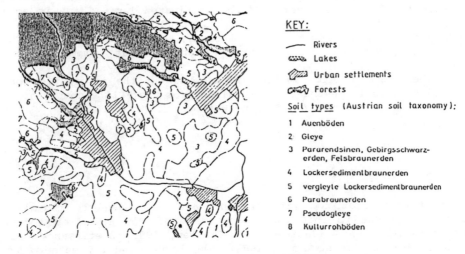

FIG. 5   Soil types of a section of the subcatchment.

Daily meteorological parameters such as rainfall, maximal and minimal temperatures, mean relative humidity and the sum of the total
radiation were taken from a nearby station south of the catchment.
This data was available over a ten year period from 1963 to 1972.
Over this timelap a maximal average rainfall duration of 0,5 hours
is assumed in the same way as a value of 6 hours (Fig. 6).

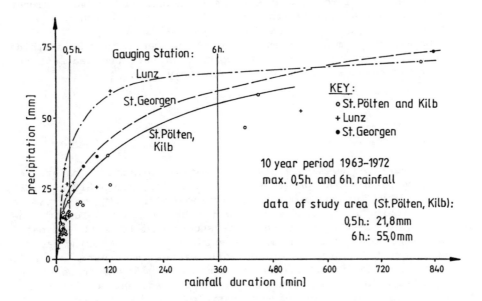

FIG. 6   Measured functions of precipitation rates.

From the watershed all areas were eliminated which did not contribute to the soil erosion process. Such areas are forests, urban
settlements, lakes and rivers. Of the cultivated land, which is not
used as grassland, 57 % grain, 33 % corn and 10 % potatoes, sugar
beet, fodder beat, beans, peas, oil seeds, clover etc. is grown. A
typical crop rotation for this area is summer wheat, summer barley
and corn.

The actual tillage method was adopted but the information on
agricultural soil treatment was attained from the EPIC's components,
which are based on american farming methods.

RESULTS

A long term simulation period of ten years was chosen to minimize
model errors due to inaccurate assessment of single and/or short
term rainfall events (Jamieson and Clausen, 1988; Svetlosanov and
Knisel, 1982; Williams et al., 1983). The input of daily meteorological data had much influence on the improvement of the results of
EPIC.

The calculated soil erosion rates vary between 0,5 and 54
t/ha/year depending on the gradient, erosive slope length and soil
type. The gradient dominates the influence on the results. The increase of the mean gradient from 0,2 to 20 % leads to an amplified
annual erosion rate which is then between 50 and 100 times greater.

In comparison to 50 m, an erosive slope length of 100 m only
produces a significant difference in the soil erosion process at
steep gradients. The soil erosion rate then increases by approximately 40 % (Table 1).

Hydromorphical soil types show approximately 15 to 40 % higher
annual erosion rates than lithomorphical soil types which are built
up of quartz and have a clay content less than 30 %.

Detailed sediment concentration measurements in the draining
river of the catchment lead to the conclusion that the sediment delivery ratio reaches a value of approximately 1 %.

DISCUSSION AND CONCLUSION

A 3D-DTM overlayed by maps containing spatial information on erosion
controlling parameters, provides in coordination with a GIS/ARC-INFO
efficient data for the erosion prediction model EPIC, to estimate
the soil erosion rates of the catchment with a high resolution. The
draining water discharge of the watershed could be well estimated
and sediment concentration measurements show that during actual
rainstorm events 1 % of the eroded soil reaches the river.

The installation of a grid version which makes it possible to
set up mass balance calculations of water, sediment and nutrients
for each grid element was not yet possible. But only the solution to
this step would provide a complete tool for integrated land management tasks.

TABLE 1   Soil erosion matrix - soil erosion weight in pounds/ha/year.

Soil types	slope gradient classes (%)													
	< 0,4		0,4-1,4		1,4-4		4-9		9-13		13-19		≥ 19	
	mean gradient of the class (%)													
	0,2		0,9		2,7		6,5		11		16		20	
	erosive slope length (m)													
	50	100	50	100	50	100	50	100	50	100	50	100	50	100
Auenböden	0,5	0,5	0,5	0,5	1,5	1,5	4,0	6,0	9,0	12,5	16,0	22,5	23,0	32,0
Gleye	0,5	1,0	1,0	1,0	2,0	3,0	7,0	10,0	15,0	21,0	27,0	38,0	39,0	54,0
Pararendsinen, Gebirgsschwarzerden, Felsbraunerden	0,5	0,5	0,5	0,5	1,5	1,5	4,5	6,0	9,5	13,0	17,0	23,5	24,0	33,5
Lockersediment- braunerden	0,5	0,5	1,0	1,0	2,0	2,0	5,5	8,0	12,0	17,0	22,0	30,5	31,0	43,5
vergleyte Locker- sedimentbraunerden	0,5	0,5	1,0	1,0	2,0	2,5	6,0	8,0	12,5	17,5	22,5	31,0	32,0	44,5
Parabraunerden	0,5	0,5	1,0	1,0	2,0	2,5	6,5	9,5	14,5	20,0	26,0	36,5	37,0	51,5
Pseudogleye	0,5	0,5	1,0	1,0	2,0	2,5	6,0	8,0	12,5	17,5	23,0	32,0	32,5	45,5
Kulturrohböden	0,5	0,5	1,0	1,0	2,0	2,5	6,0	8,5	12,5	18,0	23,0	32,0	33,0	46,0
Ranker	0,5	0,5	0,5	1,0	1,5	2,0	5,0	7,0	10,5	14,5	19,0	26,5	27,0	37,5

REFERENCES

Crawford, N. H., Linsley, R. K. (1966) Digital Simulation in Hydrology. Stanford Watershed Model IV. TR.39, Dept. of Civil Eng. Stanford.

Jamieson, C. A., Clausen, J. C. (1988) Tests of the Creams Model on Agricultural Fields in Vermont. Water Resources Bulletin, Vol. 24, No. 6, p. 1219 - 1226.

Shaw, E. M. (1984) Hydrology in Practice. Van Nostrand Reinhold Co. Ltd., UK.

Svetlosanov, V., Knisel, W. G., Editors (1982) European and United States Case Studies in Application of the Creams Model. International Institute for Applied Systems Analysis, Laxenburg, Austria.

Williams, J. R., Dyke, P. T., Jones, C. A. (1983) EPIC - A Model for Assessing the Effects of Erosion on Soil Productivity. Analysis of Ecological Systems: State-of-the-Art in Ecological Modeling. Developments in Environmental Modeling, 5, p. 553 -572. Elsevier Scientific Publishing Company, Amsterdam - Oxford - New York.

Williams, J. R., Jones, C. A., Dyke, P. T. (1984) A Modeling Approach to Determining the Relationship between Erosion and Soil Productivity. <u>Transactions of ASAE</u>, p. 129 - 144.

Wischmeier, W. H., Smith, D. D. (1978) Predicting Rainfall Erosion Losses, a Guide to Conservation Planning. USDA Agric. Handbook No. 537.

Hydrology in Mountainous Regions. II - Artificial Reservoirs; Water and Slopes
(Proceedings of two Lausanne Symposia, August 1990). IAHS Publ. no. 194, 1990.

Lake Wohlen near Berne: sediment deposits, protection of shores and of the environment

H.L. KNUSEL
Bernische Kraftwerke AG (Berne Power Company), Construction Division, Viktoriaplatz 2, 3000 Berne 25, Switzerland

ABSTRACT This paper is concerned with lake Wohlen near Berne which was created around 1920 by constructing a concrete dam and power station at Mühleberg across the Aare river valley. It describes the observed sediment deposits and the countermeasures taken against the loss of transport force resp. scouring.

INTRODUCTION

The lake of Wohlen is situated northwest of Berne, the Capital of Switzerland. It was created around 1920, when the Berne Power Co. started impounding the Aare valley after having constructed a dam and a powerstation. This valley consists of a fairly flat bottom, containing a meandering river and of steep slopes of sandstone being some 50-70 m high. The impounded length is about 15 km and the lake width extends from 50 m to 500 m. The water level is at 481 m above sea level and is being kept there constantly (+0 / -0.5 m).

FIG. 1 Situation: dam and powerstation near Mühleberg. Areas of counter-measures at Wohlei-Talmatt resp. at Eymatt-Gäbelbach.

By today the lake and its shores have become a fairly important recreational area of Berne's citizens. Apart from using camping grounds, parks and boat jetties people like to explore nature at the many little reserves along the shores, which are accessible by a number of footpaths.

SEDIMENTATION

Impounding the valley meant automatically increasing the cross section
of the flow or otherwise a substantial loss in speed and sediment
transport capacity. Immediately thereafter began the formation of sediment deposits, starting at the upper end of the lake and continueing
towards the barrage. The imported quantity of roughly 100 000 m3 per
year was observed and measured every 10 years. It will lift the upper
part of the river and it will fill up the present lake within about
250 years by which time we'll have a river valley again.

FIG. 2 Aquatic plants form considerable carpets due to a
high content of organic materials in the water.

Within the catchment area of this lake we count a population of
approximately 400 000. The larger sewage plants have taken up operation only after 1968. This is the reason why sediments did not consist
only of gravel, sand and silt, but also of organic materials. The deposits being mainly at the shallow inner side (1 -2 m deep) of river
bends brought a certain decrease of the flow cross-section, but also
an unacceptable odour as soon as the deposits started being exposed to
air (decomposition/decay). Still today the lake contains very much
organic material. Aquatic plants grow fast and the access lanes to
boat jetties require frequent mowing and clearing.

STUDIES

To counteract unwanted conditions there were six single untertakings
at particular spots from 1942-1967. In 1968 the Swiss Federal Institute of Technology, Department of Water Affairs, issued a study con-

sidering the sedimentation problem of this reservoir over the whole
period of its lifetime. The main statements cover:
(a) a prognosis of the future river bed as envisaged by nature;
(b) proposals for measures to upkeep the transport force of the river
    flow (reducing the river cross-section to the future river bed by
    depositing materials onto the shallow inner side of bends, thus
    creating little islands 20 cm above the water level);
(c) proposals for protecting the outer side of bends from erosion;
(d) biological engineering techniques and construction phases which
    allow an easy adapation of nature.
This report caused a 10-year work programme out of which some basic
ideas are shown in the next figures.

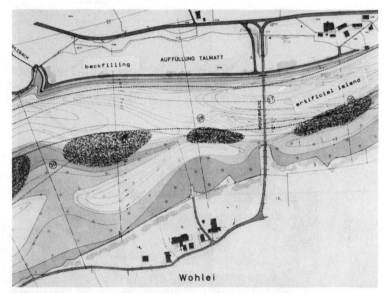

FIG. 3 Typical work of the 10-year programme.

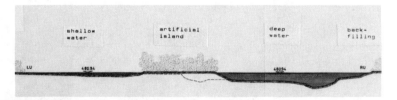

FIG. 4 Typical cross-section.

PROJECT WOHLEI-TALMATT (1972-1974)

This area is placed 200 m upstream to 500 m downstream of the Wohlei-
bridge in a slight river bend. About 50% of the water has a depth of
less than 2 m. The lake is 200 - 300 m wide (deep water 80 m only) and
the stonebridge has a steel framework center span of some 30 m.

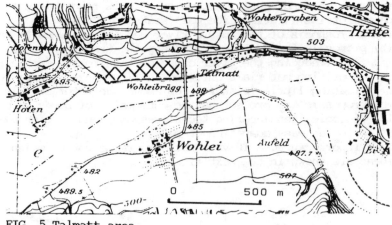

FIG. 5 Talmatt area.

The slim right bank bay was backfilled to form a straight shoreline.
The left bank received directional units (one island, two reed noses)
with a humid surface being some 20 cm above the water level.

FIG. 6 Construction of the cofferdam before backfilling.

FIG. 7 Artificial island 15 years after construction.

Both areas required the formation of stable cofferdams that were able
to withstand earthpressure from the wet backfilling as well as erosion
from wind or from boat traffic. Various soiltests established to what
extent the areas to be backfilled were influencing the bridge pier
foundation. The source of backfill was defined nearby, to provide some
140 000 m3 sand and gravel. Construction work started at the cofferdams, excavating the gravel by backhoe into a barge. The footing had
to be secured by heavy blocks or palisades. Lateron the backfilling
was excavated by a grab but then pumped through a floating pipeline.
After natural draining the right bank was rented out to interested
farmers, and the left bank areas were planted with bushes.
Today after 15 years both right and left bank look as if they always
had been that way. One serves farming or leisure and the other one is
undisturbed nature. The odour is gone, the fillings keep in place and
the amount of sedimentation is slightly smaller than predicted.

PROJECT EYMATT-GÄBELBACH (1991-1993)

This area stretches from 200 m upstream of the Kappelen-bridge to 300m
downstream where the Gäbelbach meets the Aare river. The bridge crosses the river in one span. There the Aare is 150m wide at the deep water section and on the left 50-100m wide being less than 2m deep. It
is a stretch of transition from river valley to lake. On the left bank
upstream of the bridge we find a large recreational park with a camping area and a small jetty for boats. Just downstream of the bridge
follow the family gardens. The area ends at the entry of the Gäbelbach, a little brook that some times brings a lot of bedload and wood.

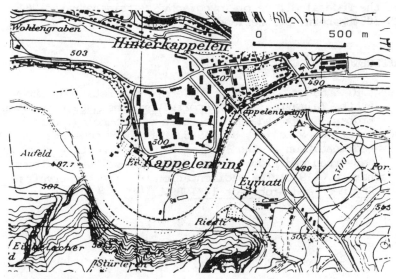

FIG. 8 Eymatt area.

Here again the left bank fillings intend to push the Aare back to
where it would run anyway in the far future. The bank upstream of the
bridge will get a new car park and a complete boat harbour, whilst the

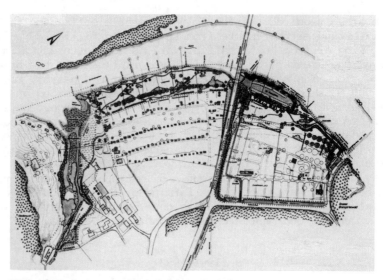

FIG. 9 Leisure area project Eymatt.

downstream bank contains mainly pedestrian walks, gardens and nature reserves at the Gäbelbach estuary. Five partners have agreed to the detail planning. They expect the decision of the authorities for this year and are looking forward for the execution to take place in 1991 to 1993.

AKNOWLEDGEMENTS This manuscript benefits from the copyright for maps of the Federal Office of Topography, Seftigenstrasse 264, CH-3084 Wabern, Switzerland as from 13.2.1990.

REFERENCES

Lang, H. & Huder, J. (1969) Mühleberg powerstation, Study of backfills at the Talmatten area, Reports Versuchsanstalt für Wasserbau und Erdbau, Swiss Federal Institute of Technology Zürich.

Schnitter, G. & Zeller, J. (1968) Mühleberg powerstation, Study of sedimentation at the lake of Wohlen. Reports Versuchsanstalt für Wasserbau und Erdbau, Swiss Federal Institute of Technology Zürich.

Vischer, D. (1980) The sedimentation of river reservoirs. The Swiss Engineer and Architect 14/1980.

Hydrology in Mountainous Regions. II - Artificial Reservoirs; Water and Slopes
(Proceedings of two Lausanne Symposia, August 1990). IAHS Publ. no. 194, 1990.

Approche de l'étude d'érosion sur microbassin versant en zone semi-aride

L. LAAJILI GHEZAL
Assistante à l'Ecole Supérieure Agricole de
Mograne,Tunisie
M. SLIMANI
Assistant au Département de Génie Rural de
l'INAT, Tunis
N. ENNABLI
Professeur. Directeur du Département de Génie
Rural, INAT-TUNIS

RESUME   Dans le cadre d'un projet de coopéra-
tion TUNISIE-US portant sur les systèmes de
production, une étude d'évaluation de l'érosion et de l'érosivité a été menée dans une
zone du semi-aride tunisien.
Nous avons pu mettre en évidence que l'érosion varie linéairement avec la lame ruisselée pour des faibles valeurs de celle-ci.
Elle est conditionnée par la pluie totale
et le débit maximum de ruissellement. Quant
à l'érosivité, elle semble être liée à la
pluie totale, aux états de surface du sol
(battance, labour) et à la végétation.

INTRODUCTION

En Tunisie, on assiste à une dégradation progressive
du patrimoine sol, tant sur les plans quantitatif
que qualitatif, entraînant un appauvrissement des
terres fertiles et un envasement accéléré des bar-
rages.Malgré l'importance de l'érosion et l'ampleur
qu'elle prend sous l'effet de pratiques culturales
inadéquates, d'une mécanisation irrationnelle et d'un
défrichement intense des forêts, ce phénomène est
encore mal connu. C'est ainsi que dans le but d'évaluer l'érosion au niveau d'un microbassin versant
(2550 mètres carré) dans le semi-aride tunisien ,le
choix a porté sur la zone d'étude Mazreg-Echems,
située à l'amont du barrage Siliana (70 10^6 m^3) et
dont le sol est exposé à des phénomènes érosifs
assez intenses. Dans cette note, nous nous proposons
de quantifier et d'identifier certains paramètres
explicatifs de l'érosion et de l'érosivité au
niveau du microbassin.

MATERIELS ET METHODES
Caractéristiques physiques et pluviométriques du microbassin versant

Localisé sur le versant gauche de l'oued Sanhajia,
au niveau du cours moyen de l'oued Siliana, le
microbassin versant d'étude a une superficie de
2550 m^2, un indice de compacité de 1.21 et une pente

moyenne de 10 %. Il est caractérisé par un sol calcima-
gnésique argilo-limoneux à faible teneur en matière
organique (0.7%) et une forte teneur en calcaire total
(60 %). Sa perméabilité est de 3 cm/h. La zone est à
vocation agricole (céréaliculture en sec). Le régime
pluviométrique est irrégulier et torrentiel. Le total
pluviométrique annuel observé pour l'année hydrologique
1986-1987 s'élève à 534,6 mm (valeur décennale). Le
maximum journalier annuel est de 35 mm, correspondant
à la médiane observée dans la région. Les intensités
maximales, calculées pour un pas de temps de cinq minutes et observées durant la campagne de mesure, varient
de 3.3 mm/h à 108 mm/h.

LE DISPOSITIF DE MESURE

Description et limites

Le dispositif expérimental consiste en une station cli-
matologique, et en une fosse à sédiments équipée d'un
limnigraphe (OTTX) et d'une échelle limnimétrique. Lors
des crues, le volume d'eau s'évacue par l'intermédiaire
d'un déversoir triangulaire à paroi mince métallique. A
l'aval de la fosse, un orifice de vidange permet l'évacuation des eaux à la fin des mesures. Grâce à ce dispositif, on peut mesurer d'une part le ruissellement et
d'autre part le transport solide en suspension et le
charriage. Toutefois, il est à noter que ces mesures
ne sont valables que pour l'érosion en nappe et en
rigole, représentant l'essentiel de l'érosion agricole.

Technique de mesure du transport solide

Au cours du passage de la crue, on fait des prélèvements
d'eau à l'entrée de la fosse à sédiments, d'une façon
continue et bien répartie dans le temps. Après passage
de la crue, des prélèvements d'échantillons sont effectués à différentes profondeurs après agitation et homo-
généisation des eaux turbides. Après décantation, on
procède au séchage et puis à la pesée. Connaissant le
poids de matière solide et le volume des eaux turbides,
on en déduit celui des matériaux qui ont été déposés
dans la fosse.

RESULTATS ET DISCUSSION

Durant la période de mesures s'étalant entre février et
octobre 1987, quatorze averses ont été enregistrées,
dont six seulement ont donné au ruissellement. Les deux
premiers ruissellements ont été tellement rapprochés
que la fosse n'a pas pu être vidée, par conséquent les
quantités de terres érodées ont été cumulées. Les principaux paramètres mesurés ou calculés sont, les suivants :

   (a) Es :érosion spécifique en kg/ha
   (b) E :érosivité en kg/mm
   (c) Lr :lame ruisselée en mm
   (d) IPA:indice des précipitations antérieures en mm

(e) $I_{max\ 5}$: intensité maximale calculée sur un pas de
          temps de cinq minutes en mm/h.
(f) R_{USA} : indice d'agrèssivité climatique de
          WISCHMEIER
(g) Q_{max} : débit maximum de ruissellement en l/s.

L'analyse des résultats a montré que l'érosion est pro-
portionnelle à la lame ruisselée (Fig.1) et qu'elle
varie dans le même sens que le débit maximum.

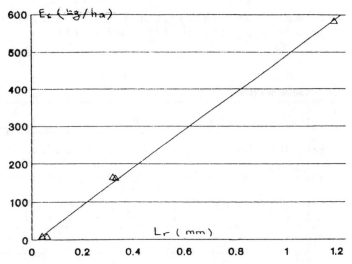

FIG.1 Variation de l'érosion spécifique en
fonction de la lame ruisselée.

La quantité de terre totale érodée durant cette campagne
s'élève à 235 kg, ce qui correspond à une érosion spécifique de 0.92 t/ha (la tolérence de perte de terre varie
entre 2.3 et 11.3 selon H.M.J. Arnoldus, 1977).
En exprimant l'érosion par la perte de couche arable
du sol en millimètres, on trouve une valeur de 0.061 mm.
Le ruissellement du 06-07/10/87 a enlevé à lui seul
0.039 mm ce qui correspond à 64 % de la valeur totale.
Quand à l'érosivité qui correspond à la quantité de
matières solides que peut arracher et transporter un mm
d'eau ruisselée, elle croît avec cette dernière puis
tend vers une valeur limite de 125 kg/mm. Ceci est dû
essentiellement à l'état de surface du sol. En effet,
les ruissellements du 30/03 et du 01/04/87 sont survenus
juste après le labour, sur un sol pulvérulant sans
couverture végétale importante, ce qui a facilité le
transport des particules de terre. Au fur et à mesure
que le sol se tasse et que la végétation se développe,
l'eau trouve plus de difficultés à détacher les particules et par conséquent sa capacité de transport diminue.

Pour l'identification des paramètres explicatifs de
l'érosion et de l'érosivité, les méthodes de régressions
simple, multiple et pas à pas ont été utilisées. C'est
ainsi que, l'érosion spécifique est liée à la lame ruisselée (Lr) par la relation :

$$E_s = 4.0 \; Lr - 11.5 \qquad R = 0.99 \qquad (1)$$

Ce qui s ppose une augmentation indéfinie et dans les
mêmes r ortions de l'érosion, d'où le choix de cette
équation :

$$E_s = 15.6 \; (1 - e^{-0.032 \; Lr}) \; R = 0.99 \qquad (2)$$

La figure 2 représente la variation de l'érosion spécifique calculée à partir de l'équation (2).

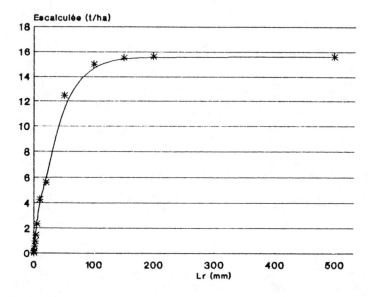

FIG.2 Variation de l'érosion spécifique calculée
à partir du modèle exponentiel.

Ainsi, on remarque que la relation entre l'érosion et
la lame ruisselée est linéaire pour des faibles valeurs
de celle-ci. Mais le poids de matières transportées
croît de moins en moins vite pour des lames ruisselées
importantes (THEBE, 1987).
Quant aux caractéristiques de la pluie, l'érosion spécifique et l'érosivité varient paraboliquement avec
l'intensité maximale et l'indice d'agrèssivité climatique de WISCHMEIER.
Pour le débit maximum de ruissellement, les modèles suivants ont été retenus :

$$E_s = -86.0 \, Q_{max}^2 + 475.4 \, Q_{max} - 14.0 \qquad R=0.98 \qquad (3)$$

$$E = 116.4 \, Q_{max} 0.3 \qquad\qquad R=0.78 \qquad (4)$$

Ces équations ne traduisent pas la cinétique du transport solide qui est mise en évidence par la figure 3 qui
montre que le débit solide varie rapidement avec le
débit liquide pendant la montée de la crue, puis chute
pendant la décrue, ce qui pourrait correspondre à une
phase de tarissement.

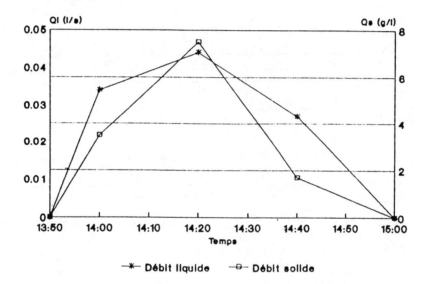

FIG.3 Evolution des débits solide et liquide
pour le ruissellement du 14/04/87.

Cette approche d'étude de l'érosion, fait intervenir
les différents paramètres comme s'ils agissaient indé-
pendemment les uns des autres. Or le phénomène est plus
complexe et il existe une intéraction entre les caractéristiques physiques du microbassin versant, de l'averse
et celles du ruissellement. C'est ainsi que plusieurs
formules ont été établies dans ce sens, dont la plus
connue est celle de WISCHMEIER, qui lie les transports
solides à l'importance relative des différents facteurs
mesurables et s'exprime par :

$$E = R. \ K. \ SL. \ C.P$$

C'est ainsi qu'il a été procédé à une analyse des résultats obtenus, en cherchant à faire ressortir la part des
caractéristiques de l'averse (P_{tot}, I_{max5} et R_{USA}), des

caractéristiques du sol (IPA) et celles du ruissellement (Lr et Q_{max}) dans le phénomène de l'érosion.

Le tableau (1), regroupe les différents modèles retenus pour l'érosion spécifique et l'érosivité.

TABLEAU 1 Modélisation de l'érosion et de l'érosivité en fonction des caractéristiques du sol de l'averse et du ruissellement.

Variable expliquée	Variables explicatives	Modèle Retenu	
Erosion spécifique en kg.ha-1	L_r, R_{USA}, IPA	$E_s = 595.0\ Lr^{1.4}$	$R^2 = 0.98$ (5)
	P_{tot}, IPA, Q_{max}	$E_s = 8.1\ P_{tot}^{1.20} Q_{max}^{0.5}$	$R^2 = 0.99$ (6)
	R_{USA}, P_{tot}, Q_{max}	$E_s = 102.3\ R_{USA}^{0.7}$	$R^2 = 0.98$ (7)
	Lr, R_{USA}, IPA	$E = 365.1\ R_{USA}^{0.2}$	$R^2 = 0.87$ (8)
Erosivité en km mm-1	P_{tot}, I_{max}, IPA		
	P_{tot}, I_{max}, Q_{max}	$E = 81.6\ P_{tot}^{0.6}$	$R^2 = 0.95$ (9)
	P_{tot}, I_{max}, R_{USA}		
	Lr, I_{max}, Q_{max}	$E = 594.9\ Lr^{0.4}$	$R^2 = 0.85$ (10)

On remarque à partir de ces relations que :

(a) dans le cas de l'érosion :

(i)   Ce sont les caractéristiques de l'averse (P_{tot}, R_{USA}) et du ruissellement (Lr et Q_{max}) qui conditionnent ce phénomène. L'IPA étant rejeté pour l'ensemble des modèles.

(ii)   la lame ruisselée semble être le facteur conditionnant le plus ce phénomène, puisque le R_{USA} est rejeté. Par conséquent, c'est le processus de ruissellement qui prédomine, faisant ainsi intervenir la pente et sa longueur en plus de la rugosité du sol.

(iii) le R_{USA} se place en second lieu, comme facteur explicatif de l'érosion, puisqu'il explique à lui seul 96 % de l'érosion en présence de la P_{tot} et du Q_{max}.

(iiii) par analogie avec la formule de WISCHMEIER, la constante de l'équation (7) pourrait intégrer l'effet de pente, de la végétation, des pratiques culturales et de l'érodabilité du sol. L'introduction d'un indice de végétation pourrait améliorer les relations trouvées.

(b) dans le cas de l'érosivité , c'est la pluie totale

qui semble être le principal facteur conditionnant ce phénomène, l'indice R_{USA} se plaçant en second lieu.

Les quantités de terres érodées, calculées à partir de la formule de WISCHMEIER s'élèvent à 265 kg, ce qui correspond à une surestimation de 11.3 % par rapport à la valeur observée .

CONCLUSION

L'étude qui a été menée dans une zone du semi-aride tunisien et qui est basée sur des mesures classiques de ruissellement et d'érosion, nous à permis de montrer que :

(a) l'érosion varie linéairement avec la lame ruisselée pour des faibles valeurs de celle-ci. Pour des lames ruisselées importantes, le poids de matières trans-portées tend vers une valeur limite de 15.6 t/ha.

(b) l'érosivité semble être liée à la pluie totale, aux états de surface (battance, labour) et à la végéta-tion.

(c) par analogie avec la formule de WISCHMEIER, plu-sieurs formules ont été établies. Elles font inter-venir soit la lame ruisselée, soit le R_{USA}, soit la P_{tot} et le Q_{max}. Cette dernière semble être la plus compléte puisqu'elle fait intervenir d'une part la pluie totale responsable du processus de désagré-gation du sol, d'autre part le débit maximum reflè-tant l'importance du ruissellement et par conséquent du transport sur le plan pratique. La formule qui fait intervenir la lame ruisselée pourrait être retenue.

(d) le maximum d'érosion est enregistrée en automne, gé-néralement sur sol nu et suite à des pluies torren-tielles.

REFERENCES

Arnoldus, H.M.J. (1977) Prédiction des pertes de terres par érosion en nappe et en griffe. Aménagement des bassins versants , bulletin FAO, p.121-149.

Babeau, M.C. (1983) la pluie et son agrèssivité en tant que facteur de l'érosion.

Claude , J. et Chartier, R. (1977) Mesure de l'enva-sement dans les retenues de six barrages en Tunisie, campagne de 1975. Cahiers O.R.S.T.O.M. ser. Hyd. Vol.XIV, n°1, 1977, p. 3-35.

Masson, J.M. (1971) l'érosion des sols par l'eau en cli-mat méditerranéen. Méthodes expérimentales pour l'étude des quantités érodées à l'échelle du champ.

Montibert, A. (1983) Recherches en milieu méditerranéen semi-aride. Microbassin de Boufaroua. Analyse des principaux facteurs du ruissellement et de l'érosion (période 1976-1982).

Roose, E. (1977) Erosion et ruissellement en Afrique de l'ouest, vingt années de mesures en petites parcelles expérimentales. Travaux et documents de l'O.R.S.T.O.M. n°78.

Thébé (1987) Hydrodynamique de quelques sols du Nord-Cameroun, bassin versant de Mouda. Contribution à l'étude des transferts d'échelle. Thèse, universitë des sciences et techniques du Languedoc.

Wischmeier, W.H. (1959) Un index d'érosion hydrique pour une équation universelle de perte en terre, soil science society of America proceedings, vol 23, n°3 Mai-Juin 1959 p . 246-249. Traduit par A.J. Vignes, ingénieur des travaux agricoles.

Wischmeier, W.H. (1962) Erosion rates and contributing factors in semi-arid regions. International seminar on water and soil utilisation, Brookings, South Dakota, july 18 - August 10, 1962.

Hydrology in Mountainous Regions. II - Artificial Reservoirs; Water and Slopes
(Proceedings of two Lausanne Symposia, August 1990). IAHS Publ. no. 194, 1990.

Sediment by-pass structure for high sediment loads

A. PETER LARSEN
Institut für Wasserbau und Kulturtechnik mit dem Theodor Rehbock
Laboratorium, Universität Karlsruhe, D-7500 Karlsruhe, FRG

ABSTRACT An experimental investigation of sediment transport through
a short, rectangular conduit yielded information on the mechanics of high
rates of sediment transport as bedload. Functional relationships between
the flow of water and that of sediment, derived in the study, form the
basis for design rules for by-pass structures that transport coarse
sediments at high volume rates.

INTRODUCTION

High loads of coarse sediments in steep mountain streams cause substantial problems to
the designer of water intakes. The intake water should be free of sediment whereas the
sediment must be transported past the intake structures. A case in point is the
Marsyangdi hydropower project on the Marsyangdi river in Nepal. To aid the design
of intake and adjacent structures model tests were carried out at the Theodor Rehbock
Laboratory. The severity of the sediment transport is clearly indicated by the test
conditions: the model tests were to simulate sediment transport rates of 100 to
60 000 m^3/day.
    A review of published material showed that the available design information was
inadequate for good design. Hence, plans were made for a systematic experimental
study to develop useful design criteria. This research was part of a larger project
"Investigation of the transport mechanisms in sediment discharge structures based on
physical model studies". Some of the results are reported herein.

TEST FACILITIES

Two significant criteria were adopted during the planning of the test facilities:
(a) the Reynolds number based on the grain size was to be high enough that the flow
    would be in the fully rough regime;
(b) the sediment was to be recirculated in such a way that its transport rate could be
    measured accurately.
The minimum grain size to obtain fully developed turbulence was determined from the
Shields criterion for incipient motion, and it was found to be 2 mm. The sieve analyses
for gravel used in the study are shown in Fig. 1.
    The sediment separated from the water immediately downstream of the test conduit
and was transported by conveyor belts to the inflow section of the test channel. A
hopper provided intermediate storage and supplied the gravel to a variable speed
conveyor belt from which it was dropped on to a magnetically vibrated distributor. It
was then fed into the water in the approach flow box where it formed a cone with a
slope equal to its angle-of-repose, Fig. 2. The pressure conduit was 15 by 15 cm in
cross section and two lengths, 1.25 m and 2.50 m were used. The sediment flowed
directly from the cone into the conduit.
    The rate of sediment discharge was controlled by the speed of the belt and the
height of the slot through which it left the hopper. The rate was established as a
function of belt speed by weighing volumes of sediment collected in measured time
intervals.
    Water discharge was measured by a magnetic flow meter. The discharge could be
controlled at the entrance to the test stand. At the downstream end of the test conduit

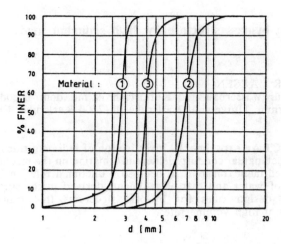

FIG. 1 Sieve curves of material used in tests.

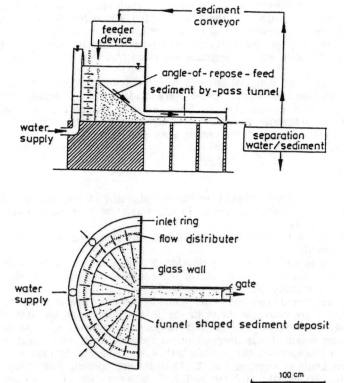

FIG. 2 Test apparatus, principle.

a vertical gate was provided by which the pressure level could be adjusted.

Pressure taps were placed along the conduit, and a Prandtl tube was employed for velocity measurements. Fig. 3 is a photograph of the test facilities.

FIG. 3 Test apparatus, over-all view.

MEASUREMENTS

In addition to the water and sediment discharge rates, the static pressure was measured at various points along the test conduit. At various sections the velocity distribution and the height of the free flowing section were measured. Thus the variable thickness of the sediments deposited on the bottom of the channel was also determined. The velocity of sediment grains was estimated from photographs with various exposure times. The thickness of the moving sediment layer was measured as well as the thickness of the layer after it was abruptly brought to a stand still.

The water discharge could be varied from 0 to 40 l/s, and the sediment discharge from 0 to and 2 kg/s. Sediment volume concentrations were as high as 20 %, and typical water velocities in the conduit were between 1 and 2,5 m/s.

DESCRIPTION OF THE FLOW

Sediment transport is normally studied in long conduits so as to have fully developed flow. In this study, however, the conduit was comparatively short. Consequently the flow was developing, and only in the longer of the two conduits, was the flow fully developed over part of the length.

For all rates of water and sediment discharge, the sediment moved as bedload. The thickness of the moving layer of sediment was nearly constant along the length of the conduit. In contrast, the thickness of the deposited material increased in the direction of flow, i.e., the height of the flow section decreased, and consequently the mean velocity increased in the downstream direction. These conditions prevailed within the length of conduit in which the flow established itself. The reason for the velocity increase in the section of flow establishment is as follows. The shear required to transport a certain rate of bedload is constant along the length of conduit. At the entrance to the conduit the velocity distribution is approximately rectangular, i.e., the velocity gradient is steep near the boundary. As the boundary layer develops the velocity gradient becomes less steep. Thus a higher mean velocity is required to produce the necessary shear. The depth of flow section and hence the depth of deposited sediments automatically adjust so that this condition is fulfilled. Fig. 4 is a longitudinal section that shows the velocity distributions and layers of sediment deposits.

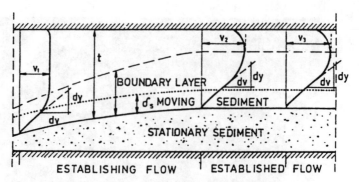

FIG. 4 Section through test conduit, principle.

The thickness of the moving layer, which appeared to be constant along the conduit, changed with the rate of sediment discharge. Its thickness varied between zero and about 3 cm. The movement of the grains was a vigorous performance with grains at the top moving at high speeds ($\sim$80 % of the water velocity) and frequently colliding with considerable noise. The particles at the bottom of the moving layer merely vibrated. When the layer was brought to rest (quick shut-down of the flow) the sediment layer collapsed to about half its thickness when moving, a ratio that was independent of rate of sediment discharge.

THEORETICAL CONSIDERATIONS

The high transport rates are characterized by a moving layer of sediment with a thickness of several grain diameters. Within this layer the shear stress is partly a fluid stress, partly an inter-granular shear stress. The existence of inter-granular normal and shear stresses was demonstrated in the classical experiments by Bagnold (1955). Hence,

$$\tau_o = \tau_f + \tau_s = \tau_f + \sigma_s' \tan \varphi' \tag{1}$$

where τ_o is bottom shear stress, τ_f fluid shear stress, τ_s inter-granular shear stress, σ_s' inter-granular normal stress and φ' dynamic friction angle. Measurements have shown (Shook et al, 1982) that the concentration within the moving layer decreases approximately linearly with elevation. This concentration distribution was measured employing various methods in tests with coarse particles such that no suspended load existed above the layer in motion.

It can be expected, that the density of the uppermost stationary layers of sediment approaches that of a dense packing, c_d . The motion and scrambling of particles in layers just above would provide compaction.

The inter-granular normal stress at any level must be in equilibrium with the submerged weight of the grains above that level. Based on these statements the normal stress distribution can be computed within the moving layer. The distribution of inter-granular shear stress can then be computed if a coefficient of friction is adopted. At the bottom of the moving layer, the friction factor would be that of the sediment at rest (tan of angle of repose). At this level the fluid shear stress is negligible, so that the shear is entirely granular friction.

$$\tau_o = \tfrac{1}{2} g \left(\rho_s - \rho\right) c_d \tan \varphi \, \delta_s \tag{2}$$

with g acceleration of gravity, ρ_s and ρ density of sediment and water, respectively, and δ_s is the thickness of the moving layer.

RESULTS AND THEIR USE IN DESIGN

The measured layer thickness, δ_s , was plotted as a function of rate of sediment transport. It was found that a unique relationship existed, which was independent of grain size. The plotted data could be approximated with an expression of the form

$$\delta_s = c\,g_s^{2/3} \tag{3}$$

where c is a constant and g_s the mass rate of sediment transport per unit width of conduit. The combination of eqn. 2 and 3 gives the sediment transport rate as a function of shear stress. With values of $C_d = 0{,}6$, the measured value of the density of densely packed sediment, and $\tan\varphi = 0{,}32$ (Bagnold's value), the following equation is obtained

$$g_* = 10\,\tau_*\quad,\quad \tau_* > 0{.}1 \tag{4}$$

in which g_* is the nondimensional transport rate per unit width and τ_* the nondimensional shear stress, i.e.,

$$g_* \equiv g_s\,/\rho_s v_* d \quad and \quad \tau_* \equiv \tau_o/(\rho_s-\rho)gd$$

where $v_* = (\tau_o/\rho)^{1/2}$ is shear velocity and d is grain diameter.
   Eq. 4 is comparable with established bedload transport equations. Fig. 5 shows such a comparison from which is apparent, that for high shear stresses the slope of eq. 4 approaches those of the Meyer-Peter and the Einstein equations and that the values are slightly lower.
   Not only did the tests show a unique relationship between sediment transport rate and layer thickness that was independent of grain size, they also showed that the velocity distribution could be expressed as a function of layer thickness. In accordance with the condition of turbulent flow over rough surfaces, the velocity distribution is

$$v/v_* = 2.5\,ln\left(\frac{30}{\delta_s/6}\,y\right) \tag{5}$$

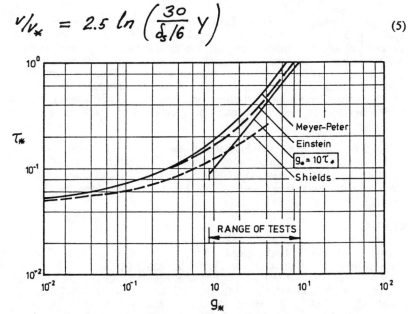

FIG. 5 Sediment discharge as a function of shear stress - comparison with established functions.

where y is distance from a fictive origin at mid depth of the moving layer. From eq. 5 the equivalent roughness height equals one sixth of the layer thickness (by comparison with the equation describing the velocity distribution at a rough, solid surface).

More important for the design of sediment by-pass conduits is the pressure loss. For the region of conduit where the flow was uniform, the pressure gradient is shown in Fig. 6 as a function of sediment concentration. The concentration is given as the ratio of volume of sediment to volume of sediment plus water. Also the pressure loss was found to be independent of grain size, i.e., it depended only on rates of sediment and water discharge.

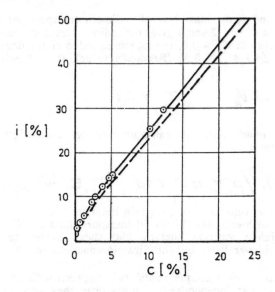

FIG. 6 Pressure gradient vs sediment volume concentration. Dotted line represents computation disregarding sidewall effect, full line represents measurements.

The information derived from the experimental study enabled design rules for sediment by-pass structures to be worked out. For a given rate of sediment to be by-passed and known length of conduit (determined by the geometric conditions) required water discharge and pressure drop can be computed for different ratios of conduit width to depth. For different sediment transport rates - which in turn depend on river and take-off discharges - this computation helps to establish a strategy.

Once the dimensions of the by-pass have been fixed, similar computations establish operating rules for varying conditions. Further details are contained in Kley (1988).

ACKNOWLEDGEMENTS This paper is based on a Ph.D. thesis by Dr.-Ing. G. M. Kley: "Zur Bemessung von Geschiebeabzügen". The research carried out at the Theodor Rehbock Laboratory was financed by the German Research Foundation, DFG. The conversion of the author's Swenglish into English was done by Prof. J. McNown.

REFERENCES

Bagnold, R.A. (1955) Experiments on a gravity-free dispersion of large solid spheres in Newtonian fluid under shear. Royal Society London, A 225.
Kley, G.M. (1988) Zur Bemessung von Geschiebeabzügen. Mitteilungen No. 177, Institut für Wasserbau und Kulturtechnik, Universität Karlsruhe, FRG.
Shook, C.A., Gillies, R., Haas, D.B., Husband, W.H.W. & Small, M. (1982) Flow of coarse and fine sand slurries in pipelines. Journal of Pipelines, Elsevier vol. 3, 13-21.

Quelques problèmes concernant l'alluvionnement de la retenue de Luzzone

OTTAVIO MARTINI
Officine Idroelettriche di Blenio SA, CH-6600 Locarno

Les eaux de la "Valle di Blenio",une vallée alpine du Canton du Tessin (CH), ont été valorisées par la construction,en 1956-64,d'un aménagement hydroélectrique (Forces Motrice de Blenio SA) en trois paliers ayant une production d'énergie moyenne de 930 GWh par année.
La retenue de Luzzone, qui a un bassin versant direct de 36.5 km2, permet l'accumulation d'environ 90 millions de m3 d'eau provenant en grande partie d'autres vallées (Val Lucomagno, Val Camadra, Val Carassina)grâce aux galeries d'adduction.
Le barrage-voûte a une hauteur de 208 m, un couronnement de 530 m de longueur et un volume de béton de $1.35x10^6$ m3.
Le bassin versant direct est formé essentiellement par des schistes avec quelques intrusions de trias. Le rocher est en bonne partie fracturé et disloqué. Dans l'ensemble,les versants sont donc très friables et facilement érodibles par les écoulements d'eau.
De la mise en eau du barrage en 1963 jusqu'en 1981 l'alluvionnement de la retenue de Luzzone a été très faible et n'a pas posé de problèmes.
Au Sud des Alpes,le mois de septembre 1981 a été caractérisé par des précipitations extraordinaires; l'Observatoire météorologique de Locarno-Monti a mesuré 710 l/m2 de pluie contre une moyenne pluriannuelle de 195 l/m2. La région de Luzzone a été particulièrement touchée par l'intensité des orages entre le 22 et le 28.9.
Deux ans plus tard, le 10.9.83, une vraie tempête a de nouveau touché la vallée en amenant 175 l d'eau par m2 en moins de 24 heures.
Aux cours des deux évènements cités,le bassin versant de Luzzone a été fortement érodé et les matériaux solides ont été transportés en grande quantité dans la retenue.
Suite à cet ensablement la vidange de fond s'est trouvée sous une couche de sédiments de 20 m d'épaisseur et la prise d'eau de la centrale a été obstruée sur un bon tiers de sa hauteur (voir Fig. 1)
Un essai de pompage des sédiments déposés devant la prise d'eau b) afin de remettre en état de fonctionnement le drainage c) a été exécuté en 1983 sans aboutir au résultat attendu.
En effet, si d'une part le dévasage de 17'000 m3 de matériau à une profondeur d'environ 200 m a réussi, il n'a pas été possible d'autre part de dégager le puits du drainage (vraisemblablement engorgé de bois).
La seule solution possible pour rétablir une situation normale, à savoir: une retenue avec vidange de fond dégagée (facteur sécurité) et une prise d'eau n'étant plus menacée d'obturation (exploitation sûre) consistait à vider le bassin et purger les sédiments à travers la vidange de fond.
L'autorisation d'exécuter la purge des sédiments fût accordée par les autorités compétentes en 1985 aux conditions suivantes:

- capture des poissons par pêche électrique entre le
  barrage et Olivone (13 km)

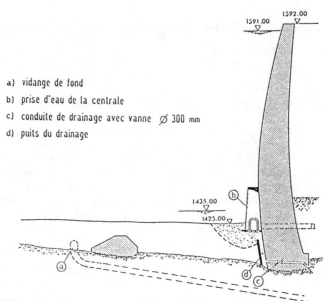

a) vidange de fond
b) prise d'eau de la centrale
c) conduite de drainage avec vanne ∅ 300 mm
d) puits du drainage

FIG. 1

- période de purge: avril-mai 1985

- dilution du mélange matériel-eau

 ≤ 3‰ à Olivone (km 13)

 ≤0.7‰ après la confluence avec le fleuve Tessin
   à Biasca (km 38).

Les débits auxquels l'on pouvait s'attendre à l'époque de la purge,
d'après la moyenne pluriannuelle, étaient les suivants (voir Fig.
2):

Débit de purge = Q_p		2.5 m3/s
Débit de dilution	3.7 m3/s	
R1 = Brenno Greina	3.7 m3/s	
R2 = Ri Carassino	1.4 m3/s	
R3 = Brenno Lucomagno	2.9 m3/s	8.0 m3/s

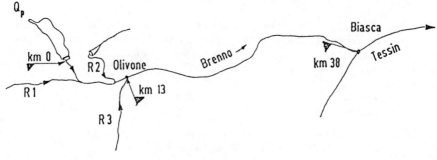

FIG. 2

Les limites de turbidité imposées par l'autorité étaient très sévères,
surtout à Olivone où le rapport débit de dilution/débit de purge
est très petit ($\dfrac{\sum_1^3 R_x}{Q_p}$ = 3.2)

Comme information il faut dire qu'effectivement au moment de la purge
les débits furent nettement inférieurs à la moyenne. Ce fait n'a
pas beaucoup changé le rapport $\dfrac{\sum_1^3 R_x}{Q_p}$ mais a peut-être compliqué

ultérieurement le problème d'ouverture de la vanne, comme on le verra
ci-après.

La Fig. 3 montre les caractéristiques de la vidange de fond de Luzzone:
un puits incliné juste après la prise d'eau dans la retenue suivi
par une longue galerie à faible pente; des vannes à glissières instal-
lées à 220 m de la prise; une galerie de restitution de 270 m de
longueur. Brièvement: une situation très défavorable pour une purge
de matériaux solides (bois y compris). Si en plus on ajoute les limitations de la turbidité données ci-dessus (qui amènent à une ouverture
réduite de la vanne), on voit que les possibilités de réussite de
l'opération étaient dès le début très précaires.
Au début de l'opération de purge, on a constaté que l'ouverture prudente
de la vanne à 35 cm (30%) était trop faible pour permettre l'évacuation
des troncs et des pierres qui se trouvaient mêlés à la boue,
mais en même temps trop grande pour la turbidité de l'eau!
Après deux jours, la première obturation de la vidange de fond a eu
lieu (voir Fig. 4). Il fallut laisser monter le niveau du lac pendant
deux jours avant de pouvoir déboucher la vidange de fond et continuer
la purge.
L'ouverture de la vanne fut réduite à 10% en moyenne (10÷15 cm!).
Après trois semaines de purge totalement inefficace, l'autorité se

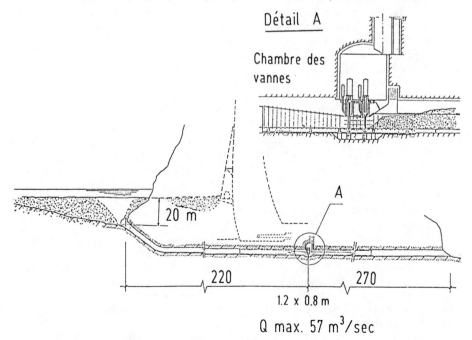

FIG. 3 Bassin de Luzzone: vidange de fond.

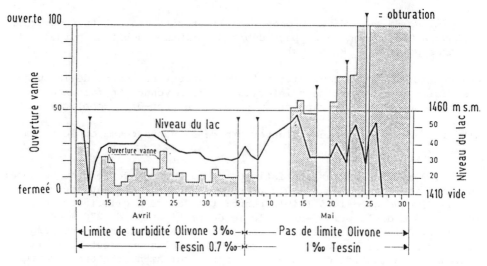

FIG. 4 Bassin de Luzzone: purge 1985.

décida finalement à supprimer la limitation de turbidité dans la
rivière Brenno (voir Fig. 2 et 4), se bornant à contrôler la nouvelle
limite de dilution à Biasca sur la rivière Tessin (admis 1‰).
A partir de ce moment, après quelques obturations initiales dues
au remplissage de la galerie de la vidange de fond (voir Fig. 3
Détail), le degré d'ouverture de la vanne fut augmenté et l'opération
continua avec la vidange complète du lac et la purge de 300'000 m3
de matériau alluvionnaire, de pierres et de racines d'arbre.
Pendant la purge, la vanne d'exercice de la vidange de fond et les
glissières ont été endommagées dans leur partie inférieure, de même
que le revêtement en tôle d'acier à l'aval des vannes. Sur une
longueur de quelques mètres, la tôle du radier a été érodée complètement et une partie du béton armé également.
Le matériau alluvionnaire purgé, composé en grande partie de limon et
de sable, s'est déposé un peu partout le long du Brenno et aussi du
Tessin, jusqu'au Lac Majeur, en formant des bancs de sable sur les
rives et en bouchant les interstices du lit de la rivière.
Il a fallu attendre une grande crue pour déplacer ce matériau.
D'un point de vue général, on peut affirmer qu'après la suppression
des limites de turbidité dans le Brenno, on n'a pas observé de poissons morts même si les 30‰ de concentration en matériau ont été
dépassés régulièrement. Il faut tout de même dire que le sable a
couvert une bonne partie des micro-organismes qui forment la nourriture des poissons et que le limon a, dans une certaine mesure, dérangé
les organes respiratoires des poissons en se déposant sur les
branchies.
Des contrôles des micro-organismes en 4 différents points du Brenno,
éxecutés par l'Institut Fédéral pour la protection des eaux, ont démontré que déjà deux ans après la purge, dans la partie supérieure
du Brenno (la plus raide), la situation était satisfaisante et qu'il
ne fallait plus s'attendre à une amélioration.
Dans la partie basse du Brenno (plus plane), le sable couvrait encore
une certaine partie des interstices.
La crue de septembre 87 a déplacé le sable et même provoqué de forts
dégâts!

Hydrology in Mountainous Regions. II - Artificial Reservoirs; Water and Slopes
(Proceedings of two Lausanne Symposia, August 1990). IAHS Publ. no. 194, 1990.

Removal of sediment deposits in reservoirs by means of flushing

H. SCHEUERLEIN
Obernach Hydraulics Laboratory, Oskar von Miller-Institut,
Technical University Munich, F. R. Germany

ABSTRACT Removal of sediment deposits from reservoirs by
means of flushing is a widely used method to regain
storage volume. However, its efficiency is very often
overestimated. The importance of supporting auxilliary
measures as water level drawdown is not always recognized
to sufficient extent. Estimation of flushing efficiency by
means of theoretical approach is problematic. The
mechanism is complex and verification of the parameters
involved is difficult. In the paper a straightforward
approach starting from extreme simplifications is
presented. The method allows for a rough estimate on the
prospect of flushing including information on the
necessary drawdown to produce a desired effect. By means
of two graphs the limits and the effictivity of flushing
activities can be judged quickly. The procedure is
demonstrated by means of examples.

INTRODUCTION

Sedimentation of man-made reservoirs is one of the major problems
hydraulic engineers will have to face in future. In spite of the
various methods which can be taken to minimize sediment yield from the
watershed, the intrusion and the deposition of sediment in reservoirs
can never be avoided completely. Sediment enters the reservoir either
as bedload or as suspended load. Usually the amount of sediment
carried in suspension exceeds the bed load transport by a factor of
5 to 10. The sediment deposits in a reservoir are composed accord-
dingly. First the coarse material transported close to the bed settles
down forming a delta at the reservoir entrance. Material in suspension
is carried further and deposited more or less uniformly all over the
reservoir.

REMOVAL OF SEDIMENT FROM RESERVOIRS BY MEANS OF FLUSHING

In principle, the mechanism described above takes place similarly in
any reservoir. However, the magnitude of the depositions, the pace of
the deposition process, and the importance of the depositions for the
operation of the reservoir may vary considerably.

In mountain reservoirs, usually the uniformly distributed fine
deposits are of minor importance. It is the gravel and sand settling
at the entrance of the reservoir that causes problems, such as

- occupation of the most active (upper) part of the reservoir,
- raise of water level in the river upstream of the reservoir
  (backwater effect),
- degradation of the river bed downstream of the dam due to trapping
  of coarse material in the reservoir.

With respect to the reasons listed above, it is desirable to remove
particularly the deposits of coarse material at the reservoir entrance,
preferably by passing it downstream where it is needed to avoid
degradation.

An elegant method to solve the problem is to take advantage of the
transport capacity of the flow itself without using external energy.
This technique which commonly is called "flushing" is used throughout
the world, however, not always with the desired success. The
efficiency of flushing depends significantly on the water level in the
reservoir during the measure (ACKERS et al, SCHEUERLEIN, 1987, WHITE
et al). Flushing can be carried out very effectively when the water
level in the reservoir can be kept low for some time while the flow
rate is high. As this, on the other hand, means a substantial loss of
water, effective flushing must be oriented towards minimization of
water level drawdown and flushing time.

Theoretical treatment of reservoir sedimentation and flushing is
difficult for various reasons. The mechanism is complex and the
verification of the parameters involved is problematic due to the
stochastic character of the water and sediment afflux. For any
analysis extensive simplifications are unavoidable.

SIMPLIFIED METHOD TO ESTIMATE FLUSHING EFFICIENCY

With respect to the limited possibilities to describe and to verify
reservoir sedimentation and flushing activities analytically,
sophisticated theoretical treatment seems hardly justified. A
simplified approach has been tried by SCHEUERLEIN, 1989, however, the
procedure presented there proved to be still somewhat troublesome and
unhandy by incorporating the energy gradient of the flow through the
reservoir. On the other hand, the lateral mixing of the incoming flow
on the way through the reservoir was left out of consideration.

In the following another simple method to estimate the possibility
and the limit of eventual flushing activities will be presented. Using
the notations of Fig. 1, and the assumptions
- simplified prismatic shape of the reservoir,
- inflow equal outflow during flushing,
- onedimensional analysis,

the continuity equation close to the dam site at a hypothetical
drawdown water level DWL can be written as

$$Q_D = v_D \; \frac{B_D + B_A}{2} \; h_D \tag{1}$$

For geometrical reasons,

$$\frac{h_D}{B_D - B_A} = \frac{H_o}{B_o - B_A} \tag{2}$$

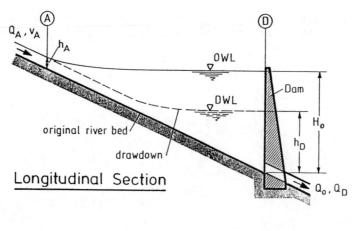

Longitudinal Section

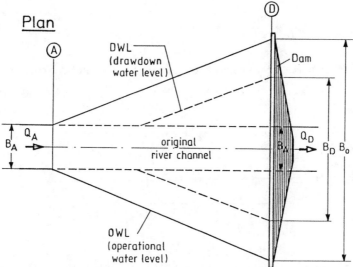

FIG. 1   Flow through a reservoir - definition sketch.

or,

$$B_D = B_A + \frac{h_D}{H_o} (B_o - B_A) \tag{3}$$

substituted in (1),

$$Q_D = v_D (B_A + \frac{h_D}{H_o} \frac{B_o - B_A}{2}) \ h_D \tag{4}$$

According to the definition that the discharge is to be considered constant during flushing, the flow velocity starts to decrease as soon as the backwater influence of the dam becomes effective, and reaches its minimum close to the dam.

As velocity of flow and sediment motion are closely related, for each grain size a threshold or critical velocity for incipient motion can be difined (HJULSTROM in ASCE 1977). Hence, the minimum flow

velocity close to the dam can also be interpreted as the governing
factor for the efficiency of any flushing activity. Considering

$$v_D = v_{Dc} \tag{5}$$

with

$$v_{Dc} = f(d) \qquad \text{(f.i. after HJULSTROM)} \tag{6}$$

and

$$Q_D = Q_A \qquad \text{(per definition)} \tag{7}$$

equation (4) changes to

$$Q_A = v_{Dc} \ (B_A + \frac{h_D}{H_o} \frac{B_o - B_A}{2}) \ h_D \tag{8}$$

which after some transformation and with the substitution

$$q_A = \frac{Q_A}{B_A} \tag{9}$$

finally reads

$$\frac{h_D}{H_o} = \frac{\sqrt{\dfrac{2 \ q_A}{v_{Dc} \ H_o} \ \dfrac{B_o}{B_A} (\dfrac{B_o}{B_A} - 1) + 1} \ -1}{\dfrac{B_o}{B_A} - 1} \tag{10}$$

Fig. 2 shows the graphic verification of equation (10). For easier
handling the HJUSSTROM function (6) has been incorporated in the
auxilliary graphs given in Fig. 3.
With Fig. 2 and 3 a direct and straightforward determination of the
drawdown water level corresponding with a desired flushing effect,
f. i. sluicing of a certain defined grain size is possible. Furthermore it is possible to check the limits of flushing at extraordinary
conditions.
    The presented primitive method to estimate the margins within
which flushing activities will necessarily have to stay might help to
develop a more realistic feeling of what might be possible and what
even under favourable conditions must be impossible. It is neither
meant nor capable to describe the flushing process realistically. It
rather serves the purpose to bring unjustified expectations towards
the effictivity of flushing (particularly at partly filled reservoirs)
back to the ground.

EXAMPLES

Example 1: Small reservoir at a run-of-river power plant in the Alps

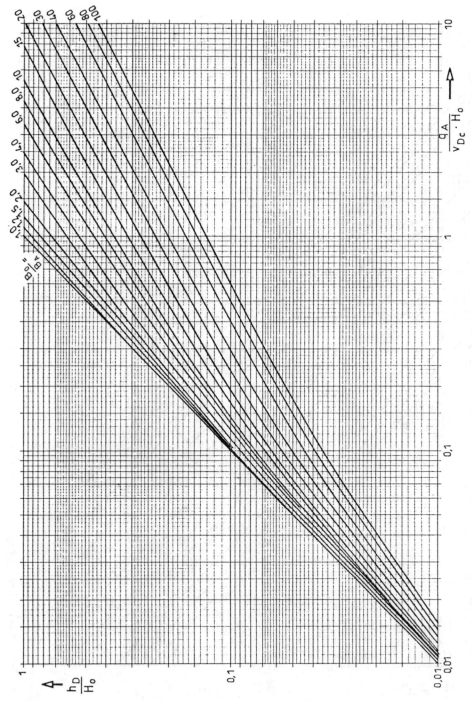

FIG. 2 Simplified determination of required water level drawdown for flushing.

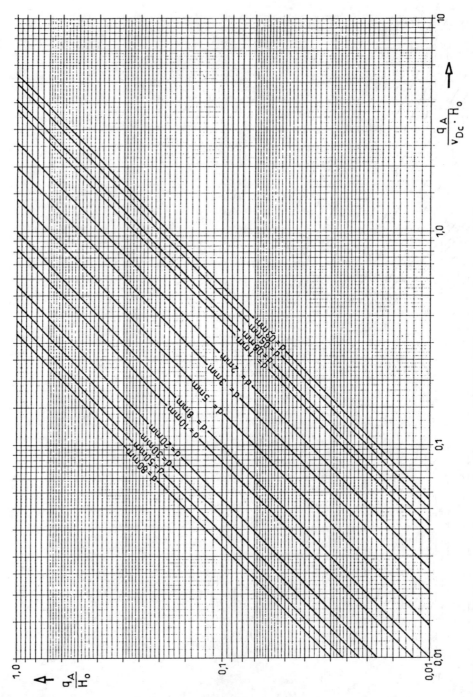

FIG. 3 Auxilliary graphs on the basis of HJULSTROM function v = f(d).

Given:

$$Q_A = Q_D = 400 \ m^3/s$$

$$B_A = B_o = 60 \ m$$

$$H_o = 7 \ m$$

Question:
   Necessary drawdown to guarantee flushing of coarse gravel
   (d = 30 mm)?

Procedure:

$$q_A = \frac{Q_A}{B_A} = \frac{400}{60} = 6,67 \quad \left[m^3/s/m\right]$$

$$\frac{q_A}{H_o} = \frac{6,67}{7} = 0,95$$

From Fig. 3 for $\frac{q_A}{H_o} = 0,95$ and   d = 30 mm

$$\frac{q_A}{v_{Dc} \ H_o} = 0,44$$

From Fig. 2 for $\frac{q_A}{v_{Dc} \ H_o} = 0,44$ and $\frac{B_o}{B_A} = 1,0$

$$\frac{h_D}{H_o} = 0,44$$

$$h_D = 0,44 \cdot 7 = 3,10 \quad \left[m\right]$$

Flushing of coarse gravel would require a drawdown of

$$\Delta H = H_o - h_D = 7 - 3,10 = 3,90 \quad \left[m\right]$$

Example 2: Large reservoir in the Middle East

Given:

$$Q_A = Q_D = 1000 \ m^3/s$$

$$B_A = 140 \ m$$

$$B_o = 420 \ m$$

$$H_o = 90 \ m \quad \text{(operational water level)}$$

Question:
   Up to which grain size will flushing be effective when the
   drawdown shall not drop more than 60 m below operational water
   level?

Procedure:

$$h_D = H_o - 60 = 90 - 60 = 30 \quad [\text{m}]$$

$$\frac{h_D}{H_o} = \frac{30}{90} = 0,33$$

From Fig. 2 for $\quad \dfrac{h_D}{H_o} = 0,33 \quad$ and $\quad \dfrac{D_o}{B_A} = \dfrac{420}{140} = 3$

$$\frac{q_A}{v_{Dc} \, H_o} = 0,42$$

From Fig. 3 for $\quad \dfrac{q_A}{v_{Dc} \, H_o} = 0,42 \quad$ and $\quad \dfrac{q_A}{H_o} = \dfrac{1000}{140 \cdot 90} = 0,08$

$\quad$ d = 0,3 mm

Even with a water level drawdown of 60 m flushing efficiency would be very poor.

Additional question:
$\quad$ Necessary drawdown when flushing of coarse sand (d = 2 mm) shall be guaranteed?

Procedure:

From Fig. 3 for $\quad \dfrac{q_A}{H_o} = 0,08 \quad$ and $\quad$ d = 2 mm

$$\frac{q_A}{v_{Dc} \, H_o} = 0,21$$

From Fig. 2 for $\quad \dfrac{q_A}{v_{Dc} \, H_o} = 0,21 \quad$ and $\quad \dfrac{B_o}{B_A} = 3$

$$\frac{h_D}{H_o} = 0,18 \quad \rightarrow \quad h_D = 0,18 \cdot 90 = 16,2 \quad [\text{m}]$$

Necessary drawdown $\quad H_o - h_D = 90 - 16,2 = 73,8$ m

REFERENCES

ACKERS, P., THOMPSON, G. (1987) Reservoir sedimentation and influence of flushing. In: Sediment Transport in Gravel-bed Rivers. J. Wiley & Sons, London, 845–868.

ASCE (1977) Sedimentation Engineering. ASCE Manuals and Reports on Engineering Practice No. 54, New York.

SCHEUERLEIN, H. (1987) Sedimentation of reservoirs - methods of prevention, techniques of rehabilitation. In: First Iranian Symposium on Dam Engineering. Tehran.

SCHEUERLEIN, H. (1989) Sediment sluicing in mountain reservoirs. In: International Workshop on Fluvial Hydraulics of Mountain Regions. Trent, B 77 - B 88.

WHITE, W., BETTESS, R. (1984) The feasibility of flushing sediments through reservoirs. In: Challenges in African Hydrology and Water Resources (Proceedings of the Harare Symposium). IAHR Publ. No. 144, 577–587.

Hydrology in Mountainous Regions. II - Artificial Reservoirs; Water and Slopes
(Proceedings of two Lausanne Symposia, August 1990). IAHS Publ. no. 194, 1990.

Transportation and deposition of sediment in the reservoir of the Altenwoerth hydropower plant on the Danube

W. SUMMER
Institut fuer Wasserwirtschaft, Hydrologie und konstruktiven Wasserbau, Universitaet fuer Bodenkultur, Gregor Mendel Strasse 33, A-1180 Vienna, Austria

ABSTRACT Human interaction on the Danube such as setting up of hydropower plants, strongly influences its sediment regime. In order to get an impression on the processes of sedimentation and erosion in such a reservoir, a one dimensional model to simulate these processes has been developed and tested on the Danube's reservoir of the hydropower plant Altenwoerth.

INTRODUCTION

The environmental impacts due to the erection of the hydropower scheme Altenwoerth, which is situated on the Austrian part of the Danube 60 km upstream of Vienna, were analysed within the UNESCO's Man and Biosphere Program (Hary et al., 1989). One of the study aspects is focused on the morphological changes of the river bed, providing information to assess the benthic symbiosis and/or the accumulation of heavy metal concentration refering to the grainsize fraction less than 0.02 mm (Nachtnebel et al., 1989).

Altenwoerth which is the largest power plant on the Austrian Danube has a capacity of 328 MW. This is 13% of the total installed capacity on the stream. The energy output of the power plant is 1950 GWh per year (DOKW, 1987). It went into operation in 1976. Since then the sedimentation in the reservoir was monitored annually. During periods of high flow, scour of the river bed was also observed. These processes were analysed and a one dimensional transportation model was developed to simulate the quantitative accumulation of the sediment in the reservoir.

DATABASE

The head of the Altenwoerth reservoir is more than 34 km upstream of the power plant which is located at stream-km 1980.4. The rise in the water level required the construction of dams on both sides of the Danube along its river banks in the reservoir. Its cross sections became similar and the flow velocity was reduced. The flow velocity near the power plant was changed from 1.4 - 2.7 m/s before its errection to 0.1 - 1.1 m/s after it was built. It can be said that over a long section of the reservoir the median of the velocity distribution was reduced from 1.85 m/s to 0.35 m/s (Hary et al., 1989).

Since 1976 the change of the reservoir's river bed is monitored once a year to determine the sedimentation rate along the longitudinal profile of the reservoir. Parameters such as water depth, flow velocity and slope were calculated for the range of discharges between 500 and 10000 m^3/s, in steps of 500 m^3/s (Godina, 1987) by applying upstream of the dam, a hydraulic model to a 20 km long river section.

The grainsize distribution of the sediment load transported into the reservoir can be summarized as being sandy and silty material (Fig. 1). Cores taken along the riverbed (Müller et al., 1987) show that coarse material sediments upstream location km 2000, while downstream the reservoir's bed is built up by suspended material, such as sand and silt (Fig. 3).

At different locations on the Austrian Danube Gruber (1973) determined exponentional relations between the concentration of suspended material c [g/m³] and the discharge Q [m³/s]. Based on these sediment rating curves the input of suspended load into the Altenwoerth reservoir could be estimated:

for $Q \leq 4350 \ m^3/s$ ... $c = 2.244 \ 10^{-06} \ Q^{2.162}$ $\qquad$ (1)
for $Q > 4350 \ m^3/s$ ... $c = 6.385 \ 10^{-10} \ Q^{3.137}$ $\qquad$ (2)

But in comparison the daily concentration measurements show a high spread. It also can be said, that during the early summer period the concentration of suspended material in the Danube is approximately 3 times as high as during the rest of the year (Summer, 1989).

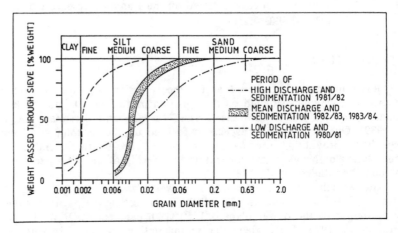

FIG. 1 Measured and estimated grainsize distribution of the Danube's suspended load (Summer, 1989).

SEDIMENTATION MODEL

The model simulating the sedimentation and degradation process in the 20 km long section upstream of the dam is based on the Unit Stream Power Concept (Bagnold, 1966). This theory hypothesizes that for steady uniform open channel flow the product of shear stress along the bed and average flow velocity which has the dimension of power per unit bed area, can be related to the sediment load.

A comparison is made of the transport capacities in subsequent cross sections with a distance of 1 km. The applied total load equation was that by Engelund and Hansen (1967):

$$Fr_* = \tau_0[(\mathcal{g}_s - \mathcal{g}_w)d]^{-1} \qquad (3)$$

$$\phi = 0.1 Fr_*^{2.5} v^2 (2gSD)^{-1} \qquad (4)$$

$$q_t = \phi[(\mathcal{g}_s - \mathcal{g}_w)gd^3(\mathcal{g}_w)^{-1}]^{0.5} \qquad (5)$$

D ... water depth [m], d ... mean particle diameter [m], Fr* ... Froude number of the grain, g ... gravitation [m/s^2], q_t ... discharge of sediment per unit width of the channel [kg/s/m], S ... Slope [m/m], u_* ... shear velocity [m/s], v ... mean flow velocity [m/s], ν ... kinematic viscosity [m^2/s], ρ_s and ρ_w ... density of the sediment grains and of the water [kg/m^3], ϕ ... transport parameter, τ_0 ... shear stress along the bed [kg/m^2]

The hydraulic conditions expressed by the Reynolds number Re$_*$ and the Froude number Fr$_*$ of the particle determine it being subject to erosion and sedimentation, shown in Figure 2 (Müller, 1985).

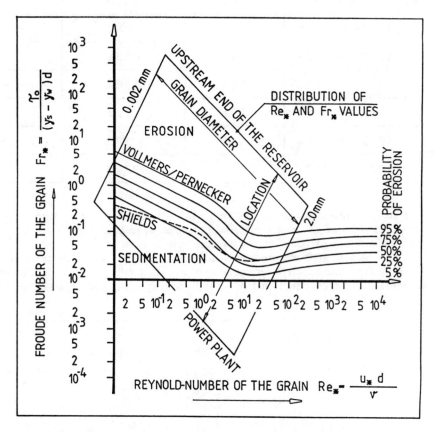

FIG. 2 Extended diagram by Shields (Summer et al., 1989).

For a specific diameter and a given discharge the sedimentation or erosion rate is obtained from the change in the transport capacity multiplied by the probability of sedimentation.

RESULTS

The model was used to estimate the aggradation in the reservoir of the hydropower plant Altenwoerth during the flow period 1976 to 1984. The procedure was applied to a daily discharge hydrograph and to several characteristic grain size distributions of the transported sediments, inorder to obtain the total sedimentation rate in this nine year period. The comparison with the actual data showed a good agreement (Table 1).

TABLE 1 Comparison of calculated and measured sums of sedimentation (Summer, 1989).

Period	Volume of sedimentation		Difference
	Measured	Calculated	
	10^3 m^3		%
05.1976–08.1979	1365	1100	– 19
08.1979–05.1980	317	288	– 9
05.1980–05.1981	235	231	– 2
05.1981–05.1982	1353	1280	– 5
05.1982–05.1983	301	303	+ 1
05.1983–06.1984	340	327	– 4
05.1976–06.1984	3920	3740	– 5

The analyses revealed that in the long run 25% of the sediment load remains in the reservoir; 100% of the coarse material deposites whereas almost all of the fraction less than 0.006 mm is carried through the reservoir.

The natural grainsize distribution of the river bed along the examined section, resulting from the selective sedimentation process, could also be well simulated by the model (Fig. 3), even assuming a mean bulk density for the accumulated material.

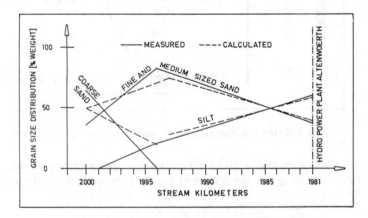

FIG. 3 Calculated and measured profile of the grainsize distribution in the reservoir in the period 1976/84 (Summer et al., 1989).

The sediment analysis showed in some areas high density of the upper bed layer, which leads to the conclusion that there is a low risk of erodibility even during hydraulic conditions indicating scour. Nevertheless during heavy floods the reservoir sections of erosion could be well determined by the model.

DISCUSSION AND CONCLUSION

The sedimentation process in the Altenwoerth resevoir has been monitored over more than 9 years. The average annual sedimentation rate is approximately $0.39 \cdot 10^3 m^3$. The maximum value was observed in the period 1981/82 with $1.28 \cdot 10^3 m^3$. The assumed mean grainsize distribution of the carried sediment load resulted from measurements along the Danube and from sediment samples taken from the reservoir's bed. No data about short term changes were available, only mean distributions of the sediment load over the research period.

A one dimensional model has been developed to estimate the sedimentation rate in several sections of the reservoir of the hydropower plant Altenwoerth, assuming a daily discharge hydrograph and different characteristic diameters of the transported grains. The model makes also the assumption that scour and deposition are reversible processes. However, laboratory investigations were in good agreement with this assumption (Müller, 1985).

The results of the applied selective sedimentation model, which predicts the longterm changes of the reservoir's river bed, fitted well with the observations. But it could be seen that over a short period the application of the model is not appropriate because there is a very high uncertainty in the daily concentration and gradation of the carried sediments.

The analysis showed that 25% of the sediments transported into the Altenwoerth reservoir remain there. During periods of high flow the river bed gets locally eroded.

REFERENCES

Bagnold, R. A. (1966) An Approach to the Sediment Transport Problem from General Physics. U.S. Geological Survey Professional Paper 422-I.

DOKW (1987) Strom aus dem Strom. Pressereferat der österreichischen Donaukraftwerke AG. Wien.

Engelund, F., Hansen, E. (1959) A Monograph on Sediment Transport in Alluvial Streams. 62 p. Teknish Forlag. Copenhagen. Denmark.

Godina, R. (1987) Analyse der Oberflächengewässer im Stauraum Altenwörth. Bericht der Arbeitsgruppe Hydrologie. Institut für Wasserwirtschaft, Hydrologie und konstruktiven Wasserbau. Universität für Bodenkultur. Wien.

Gruber, O. (1973) Schwebstoffmessungen, ihre Auswertung und Interpretation im Bereich der österreichischen Donau. Hydrologie-Fortbildungskurs. Wiener Mitteilungen. Band 14. Institut für Wasserwirtschaft, Hydrologie und konstruktiven Wasserbau. Universität für Bodenkultur. Wien.

Hary, N., Nachtnebel, H. P. (1989) Ökosystemstudie Donaustau Altenwörth - Veränderungen durch das Donaukraftwerk Altenwörth. Veröffentlichungen des österreichischen MaB-Programms. Band 14. Universitätsverlag Wagner. Innsbruck.

Müller, H., Kuderna, P., Ottner, F., Schwaighofer, B. (1987) Sedimentologische Untersuchung der Stauseesedimente - Ökosystemstudie Donaustau Altenwoerth. Institut für Bodenforschung und Baugeologie. Universität für Bodenkultur. Wien.

Müller, P. (1985) Transport und selektive Sedimentation von Schwebstoffen bei gestautem Abfluß. Mitteilung des Institutes für Wasserbau. Heft 56. Universität Stuttgart. Stuttgart.

Nachtnebel, H. P., Summer, W., Müller, H., Schwaighofer, B. (1989) Sedimentation in the Reservoir of the Hydropower Plant Altenwoerth. International Conference on Water Pollution Control in the Basin of the River Danube. WPCRD, Novi Sad, Yugoslavia.

Summer, W. (1989) Umfassende Betrachtung der Erosions- und Sedimentationsproblematik. Wiener Mitteilungen. Band 86. Institut für Wasserwirtschaft, Hydrologie und konstruktiven Wasserbau. Universität für

Bodenkultur. Wien.

Summer, W., Nachtnebel, H. P. (1989) Erosionsvorgänge und Ablagerungen: Fallstudie Donaustau Altenwörth. Symposium: Hydraulik offener Gerinne. <u>Wiener Mitteilungen.</u> <u>Band 79.</u> Institut für Wasserwirtschaft, Hydrologie und konstruktiven Wasserbau. Universität für Bodenkultur. Wien.

Hydrology in Mountainous Regions. II - Artificial Reservoirs; Water and Slopes
(Proceedings of two Lausanne Symposia, August 1990). IAHS Publ. no. 194, 1990.

Evaluation of sediment deposition in Sicilian artificial reservoirs*

V. TAMBURINO
Agricultural Engineering Institute, University of Reggio Calabria, Italy
S. BARBAGALLO, P. VELLA
Agricultural Hydraulic Institute, University of Catania, Italy

ABSTRACT The application of some available models for predicting sediment deposit in Sicilian reservoirs evidences considerable differences between surveyed sediment deposit data and computed data. Some simple models for Sicilian conditions have been developed through regression analyses. The results have evidenced the presence of linear regressions between annual sediment load for unit area and depth of intense rainfall (one day long). Intense precipitations appear to influence the sediment deposit in reservoirs more than other parameters.

INTRODUCTION

Understanding reservoir sedimentation involves consideration of erosion, transportation and deposition of the soil material. It is not possible to study these complex processes only through deterministic models; for this reason various statistical models have been developed. In such models the entity of sediment deposit is evaluated on the basis of the characteristics of the drainage basin (climate, soil type, geology, topography, land use, etc.) together with the reservoir capacity and age.

The evaluation of sediment deposit is particularly important in Sicilian artificial reservoirs as the rate of soil erosion and transportation is fairly high, mainly because of adverse hydrological conditions (long periods of aridity, intense rainfalls). An approximate evaluation of the amount of expected sediment deposit could supply designers with indications concerning the reservoir capacity, the characteristics of outlet works and the conservation structures.

---

* This paper has been carried out with equal participation by authors.

In Sicily 26 artificial reservoirs with storage capacity over
1.10^6 m^3 are in operation. The total useful capacity of Sicilian
reservoirs is about 650.10^6 m^3; stored water volumes represent
about 1/5 of used water resources in the whole Island.

AIMS AND METHODS

The aim of the present investigation is to evaluate those parameters
which are more effective in determining the sediment deposit in
Sicilian reservoirs. Some available models have been tested and some
simple models have been developed using multiple regression analysis.

First, reliable data of sediment deposit in 11 reservoirs have
been collected thanks to a research on the 19 reservoirs which have
now been operating for over 15 years (Tamburino, Barbagallo, Vella,
1989). The sediment deposit volumes have been evaluated on the basis
of topographic surveys carried out after a long period of operation.
The total sediment load has been evaluated by taking into account the
sediment deposit in the reservoirs and the solids in the flushing
water.

The Sicilian sediment deposit data have been used to test some
models developed through regression analyses in different
environmental conditions : Witzig (1944), Gottschalk (1964), Dendy-
Bolton (1976), Bazzoffi (1987) and Gervasoni (1987).

Regression analyses have been carried out by considering the
sediment load as dependent variable and the characteristics of
precipitations, reservoirs and drainage basins as independent
variables. The statistical analysis has been carried out of the data
of 10 homogeneous reservoirs characterized by a ratio of capacity to
mean annual water inflow which is superior to 0.4; a reservoir showing
a ratio value inferior to 0.01 has been neglected because the trap
efficiency was expected to be far less than 1.

The number of reservoirs examined, although limited, is sufficient
for the development of an evaluation model due to the homogeneity of
reservoir characteristics. As a matter of fact, all reservoirs are
localized in the same geographic area and they are managed according
to similar procedures (nearly all reservoirs are emptied almost every
year).

RESULTS

Sediment deposit in Sicilian reservoirs

Some characteristics of the 11 Sicilian reservoirs are listed in Tab.
1; in this table sediment deposit volume and average annual sediment
load for unit area are reported. For the Ancipa, Pozzillo and

Gammauta reservoirs the average annual sediment load for unit area comprises sediment volumes present in flushing water (in the other reservoirs they are negligible). Sediment losses through overflows and water releases have been neglected because of the high trap efficiency of reservoirs (with the exception of Gammauta) due to the high capacity/mean annual water inflow ratio.

TABLE 1 Sediment deposit in Sicilian artificial reservoirs.

Reservoirs	S (Km^2)	C $(m^3.10^6)$	N (years)	Vd $(m^3.10^6)$	T (mm/year)
ANCIPA	99.4	22.0	29	1.50	1.422
DISUERI	238.8	12.0	11	5.86	2.231
GAMMAUTA	69	1.0	43	1.37	0.497
NICOLETTI	49.5	17.3	11	1.50	2.755
OGLIASTRO	170.5	108.0	21	2.40	0.670
PIANA ALBANESI	41.4	32.8	60	3.02	1.216
POMA	163.6	67.3	18	1.45	0.492
POZZILLO	577.0	140.5	25	25.96	2.016
PRIZZI	20.1	9.2	40	0.80	0.995
RAGOLETO	117.5	21.1	17	1.28	0.641
TRINITA'	190.0	17.5	22	6.11	1.462

S = drainage area; C = initial capacity; N = deposit period; Vd = sediment deposit volume; T = average annual sediment load for unit area.

Results of available models in evaluating sediment deposit in Sicilian reservoirs

Some available models have been tested in evaluating sediment deposit in 10 Sicilian reservoirs. The sediment deposit data observed and computed have been compared in order to evaluate the approximation of the predicted values. The results of this comparison (Tab. 2) indicate that sediment deposit data of Sicilian reservoirs are not adequately explained through prediction models developed in different regions.

Witzig and Gottschalk models are easy to use because of the limited number of parameters; Dendy-Bolton model has been tested only in 6 reservoirs where mean annual runoff data were available. Bazzoffi model is difficult to use because of the great number of parameters required (7 independent variables). The survey of some of these variables, such as erodible area, average basin slope and drainage density, is subjective and uncertain.

TABLE 2 Results of the application of some available models in 10 Sicilian reservoirs.

Model	Dependent variable	Independent variables	I=mean of absolute values of relative residuals	Number of reservoirs with absolute value of relative residuals	
				< 0.2	0.2÷0.4
Witzig	V/S	C	0.69	0	2
Gottschalk	V	C, S, N	0.67	2	2
Dendy-Bol.*	T	S, D	0.39	3	0
Bazzoffi	T	C, i, d gP, R, Se	1.09	3	1
Gervasoni	T	C, t, Ss	0.99	2	1

* Tested only 6 reservoirs

V = total sediment load; D = average annual runoff; i = average basin slope; d = drainage density; gP = average number of rainy days; R = circularity coefficient; Se = erodible area; t = detention time; Ss = arable area
(for the other symbols see Tab. 1)

Models for Sicilian reservoirs

Precipitations (in particular intense precipitations) are important parameters which influence soil erosion and transportation in Sicily. Different parameters related to intense precipitations have been defined and tested in order to find significant regressions in relation to surveyed sediment data. The parameters taken into account are: average annual precipitation; maximum precipitation in 12 hours, 1, 2 and 5 days; the mean value of maximum annual precipitation in 12 hours, 1, 2 and 5 days; total precipitation in 1 day when there are precipitation superior to 30, 40 and 50 mm; average precipitation in 1 day when there are depths superior to 30, 40 and 50 mm; number of events with daily depths of precipitation superior to 50 and 100 mm; average number of rainy days.

In order to evaluate the influence of the characteristics of drainage basins the following parameters have been taken into account:

drainage area, length of the main stream, mean slope of the main
stream, elevation difference between basin head and local base level,
drainage density and some land use parameters. Other parameters
(numbers of years of deposition, reservoir capacity, etc.) have been
taken into account in order to evaluate the influence of other factors
(for instance the process of sediment consolidation in reservoirs).

Table 3 gives the results of linear regression analyses in the 10
reservoirs (regressions of the 2nd order do not give much better
results). In this table the independent variables with a high degree
of correlation are reported. They are: the mean value of maximum
annual precipitation in 1 day (H), years of deposition (N), drainage
area (S). The parameter "mean of maximum annual precipitation in 2
days" is correlated to the sediment load even if this correlation is
less meaningful than H. All the other parameters (in particular
parameters characterizing the basins and the channel systems) are not
worthwhile correlated to the average annual sediment load per unit
area (the regressions have values of correlation coefficients less
than 0.3).

In order to evaluate the accuracy of the predicted values, in
addition to correlation coefficients, the relative residuals
(difference between computed and observed data divided by observed
data) for each regression and reservoir have been calculated. For each
regression Table 3 gives average of relative residuals in absolute
value and number of reservoirs with relative residual inferior to 0.2
or between 0.2 and 0.4.

The results reported in Table 3 indicate the suitability, as a
dependent variable, of the parameter "sediment load for unit area"
(V/S) or "average annual sediment load for unit area" (T) instead of
"total sediment load" (V). The linear regression between total
sediment load and drainage area shows a high value of correlation
coefficient (r=0.94). However, a detailed analysis on the basis of the
values of relative residuals shows a limited relevance of the
regression; as a matter of fact, the high value of the correlation
coefficient is mainly influenced by the non normality of the
distribution of the variables (in particular, values of Pozzillo
reservoir are much higher than others).

The best fit of data with two independent variables is given by
the following linear regression:

V/S = - 22.4 + 1.21 N + 0.48 H   r = 0.88 I = 0.40
with V/S e H in mm, N in years

Considering the relative residuals instead of residuals the best fit
of linear regression by weighted least squares method is:

V/S = - 36.7 + 1.23 N + 0.534 H
with V/S and H in mm, N in years

This regression shows the lowest I index (I = 0.31) and allows us to evaluate the volume of sediment deposit with an error factor of 20% in 5 reservoirs out of 10 examined and an error factor between 20 and 40% in other 2 reservoirs.

The best linear regression for only one dependent variable was found between T and H. This regression has been obtained by weighted least squares method giving the following result:

T = - 0.450 + 0.0235 H   I = 0.33
with T in mm/year and H in mm

TABLE 3 Results of the linear regression analysis in the 10 Sicilian reservoirs.

Dependent variable	Independent variables	r	I= Mean of absolute values of relative residuals	Number of reservoirs with absolute value of relative residuals	
				< 0.2	0.2 ÷ 0.4
V	S	0.94	1.23	2	0
	H	0.26	1.86	1	1
	N	0.03	1.82	2	1
	S, N	0.97	0.86	3	3
	S, N, H	0.97	0.73	3	1
V/S	H	0.41	0.71	1	4
	N	0.80	0.55	4	2
	N, H	0.88	0.40	3	4
	N, H (*)		0.31	5	2
T	H	0.68	0.44	2	3
	H (*)		0.33	4	2
	N	0.28	0.61	3	3
	log N	0.40	0.61	4	2
	H, N	0.76	0.42	4	3
	H, N (*)		0.33	4	1
	H, log N	0.75	0.43	4	3

(*) Developed minimizing the sum of squares of relative residuals (instead of residuals)

CONCLUSION

The results of the investigation have indicated the relevant amount of sediment deposit in Sicilian reservoirs. It is therefore important to develop models for an approximate evaluation of sediment deposit in reservoirs.

The results of the application of available models for evaluating sediment deposit show considerable differences between observed and computed data. Furthermore, when some models were applied, it was difficult to obtain an objective quantification of some parameters characterizing drainage basins because of the lack of standard measurement procedures or the changes in the parameter value during the deposition period. Owing to these factors a statistical analysis was carried out in order to define relevant parameters (and related regressions) influencing sediment deposit in Sicilian reservoirs.

The results of the regression analysis show that intense precipitations influence the sediment deposit more than other hydrological parameters and other peculiar characteristics of drainage basins. Such an influence could be explained by considering that soil erosion and transportation is mainly related to high runoff flows due to intense precipitations. The best fit of the observed data is given by regressions between the average annual sediment load for unit area and the mean value of maximum annual precipitation for one day in the deposit period.

A noteworthy influence between deposit period and average annual sediment load for unit area has not been found. In other environmental conditions annual sediment deposit for unit area appears to reduce as years go by due to several factors, such as the slow consolidation of submerged sediment. Such an influence may be negligible in Sicily because almost all reservoirs are emptied every year and so the sediment consolidates fast. This hypothesis has not been tested because of the lack of sediment deposit data related to the same reservoir in different periods. The influence of other factors (such as the characteristics of drainage basins and streams) has not emerged perhaps because of the homogeneity of the examined basins.

The sediment deposit in reservoirs is influenced by various factors. It is difficult to quantify many of these factors; therefore, no model could completely explain the differences in sediment deposit for unit area among the different reservoirs, since only that part of deposit influenced by examined parameters can be explained. The prediction of sediment deposit by means of statistical models can be carried out provided that rather large confidence intervals are accepted; a more accurate prediction can be made by thorough investigation into the specific basin performed by an expert.

REFERENCES

Bazzoffi P. (1987) Previsione dell'Interrimento nei Serbatoi Artificiali Italiani, Modello P.I.S.A. Idrotecnica no.1.

Dendy F.E., Bolton G.C. (1976) Sediment yield-runoff-drainage area relationships in the United States. Journal of Soil and Water Conservation, no.3.

Gervasoni S. (1987) Interrimento dei serbatoi artificiali. Dissertazione finale, Dottorato di Ricerca tra le sedi di Ferrara, Firenze, Parma, Pavia, Perugia, Siena.

Gottschalk L.C. (1964) Reservoir sedimentation. In: Handbook of Applied Hydrology, V.T. Chow Editor, MacGraw-Hill, New York.

Tamburino V., Barbagallo S., Vella P. (1989) Indagine sullo interrimento dei serbatoi artificiali siciliani, Rivista di Ingegneria Agraria no. 3.

Witzig B.J. (1944) Sedimentation in reservoirs. Transactions of American Society of Civil Engineers, paper no. 2227, vol. 109.

Hydrology in Mountainous Regions. II - Artificial Reservoirs; Water and Slopes
(Proceedings of two Lausanne Symposia, August 1990). IAHS Publ. no. 194, 1990.

Total solids load from the catchment area of the Kaunertal hydroelectric power station: the results of 25 years of operation

H. TSCHADA & B. HOFER
Tiroler Wasserkraftwerke AG, Innsbruck, Austria

ABSTRACT   25 years of monitoring on the intakes to the Kaunertal hydroelectric plant have produced accurate bed load and suspended load records for a 279 m2 catchment area, from which the following results have been calculated:

mean annual bed load yield	25.7oo m^3y^{-1}
	92 m^3 $km^{-2}y^{-1}$
mean annual suspended load yield	86.6oo m^3y^{-1}
	31o m^3 $km^{-2}y^{-1}$
mean reservoir deposits	88.ooo m^3 y^{-1}
mean annual suspended load in the turbine water	11.ooo m^3 y^{-1}

In-depth research work has demonstrated that water diversion systems have only minimal effects, if any, on biocenosis upstream and downstream of the intakes.

INTRODUCTION

The Kaunertal Hydropower plant built by TIWAG in 1961 - 1964 is located in the west of the Tyrol at the confluence of the Faggenbach with the River Inn. Pondage for the plant is provided by the Gepatsch seasonal reservoir, which has a storage capacity of 14o million m^3. The power conduits comprise a 13 km pressure tunnel and a 1,9 km pressure shaft leading to the powerhouse in Prutz, where the water is discharged into the Inn, making a gross head of 87o m. At a design discharge of 48 m^3s^{-1}, the power plant has a max. power generating capacity of 392 MW, and annual energy production is 62o GWh. (Fig. 1)

The Gepatsch reservoir receives the natural runoff from a catchment area measuring 1o7 km^2. Three diversion systems channel additional runoff from a further 172 km^2 from the upper reaches of the Pitz Valley, the Radurschl Valley and the eastern catchment area of the Kauner Valley. These diversion systems comprise a total of ten intakes with a design capacity of between o,8 and 12,1 m^3 s^{-1}. Nine of the intakes, all bottom type designs ("Tyrolean Weir"), feature an automatic hydraulic sluicing system for the desilting chamber which is activated whenever the deposits in the chamber reach a preset level. Given the total number of flushings, it is possible to calculate the volume of transported bed load cleared. Suspended load was determined photometrically on the basis of a large number of individual samples.
(Hofer 1987; Tschada 1975, 1979; Lauffer 1982)

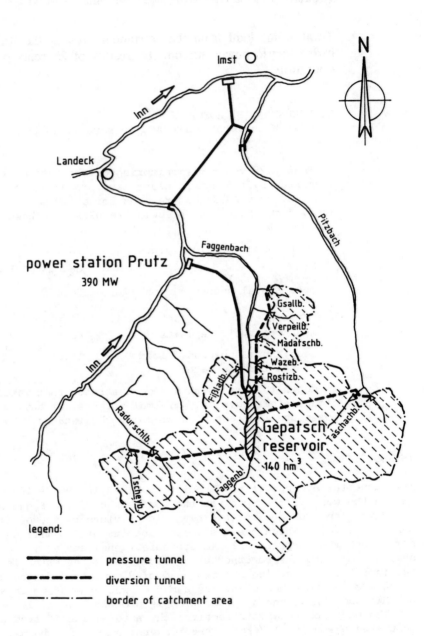

FIG.1 TIWAG Kaunertal Hydroelectric Power Scheme.

With regard to their geology, the Faggenbach and the diverted streams
are located in the crystalline basement of the Ötztal massif, which
is made up of schistous gneisses, and granite and hornblende gneisses.
The catchment area is located at an altitude of approx. 1.800 -
3.600 m and has up to 60% glacier cover. The streams utilized for the
diversion systems mainly pass through moraine and scree zones with
steep gradients, except for short stretches of pasture and woodland.

TOTAL SOLIDS LOAD

Bed load

From an evaluation of desilting chamber flushings for each intake and
the addition of the totals deriving from mechanical diggings and mud
loads, total bed loads were calculated for the individual streams.
(Table 1)

TABLE 1 Bed load of the brooks, diverted to the Gepatsch reservoir.

water intake		Gsall	Verpeil	Madatsch	Waze	Rostiz	Fißlad	Pitzbach	Taschach	Radurschl	Tschey
catchment area (km²)		3.9	12.3	4.0	6.7	4.8	11.3	26.8	60.6	24.5	16.5
flushed bed load in the years 1965–1989 (m³)		3658	2961	2574	3940	2609	3293	101959	49712	12947	17797
diggings and mud loads 1965–1989 (m³)		digging 1972: 1000	digging 1974–89: 20700	digging 1969,72 a. 89: 6900	0	0	0	mud load 87 a. digging 88 a. 89: 101950	0	0	0
total bed load transport 1965–1989	(m³)	4658	23661	9474	3940	2609	3293	203909	49712	12947	17797
	(m³ year⁻¹)	186	946	379	158	104	132	8156	1988	518	712
	(m³ km⁻² year⁻¹)	47.8	76.9	94.7	23.5	21.7	11.7	304.3	32.8	21.1	43.1

Bed load yields differ significantly between the individual streams,
with a minimum of approx. 1o m^3 $km^{-2}y^{-1}$ and a maximum of approx.
3oo m^3 $km^{-2}y^{-1}$. By relating the catchment areas to the relevant bed
load parameters of the terrain, e.g. glacier cover, moraine area,
pasture and woodland, however, it is possible to draw up a more systematic classification, as shown in Table 2.

TABLE 2 Characteristics of catchment area and bed load transport.

characteristics of the area	brooks	annual bed load transport (m³ km⁻² year⁻¹)
little glacier percentage, high percentage of wood and alps	Waze-, Rostiz-, Fißlad-, Tschey-, and Radurschlbach	~ 10–40
medium glacier percentage, little percentage of wood and alps	Gsall-, Verpeil-, Madatsch-, and Taschachbach	~ 40–100
high glacier percentage, almost no woods and alps	Pitzbach	~ 300

The only stream in the catchment area of the Kaunertal hydropower
plant without a sediment measuring station is the Faggenbach, the natural inflow into the Gepatsch reservoir, with a catchment area of
1o7 km^2. Some parts of this catchment area resemble that of the Pitzbach while others resemble that of the Taschachbach, so that it was
possible to estimate bed load for the Faggenbach as an average of the
results for these two streams, i.e. approx. 116 m^3 $km^{-2}y^{-1}$. Thus, bed
load yield for the Faggenbach is 116 x 1o7 = approx. 12.41o m^3y^{-1}.

Suspended load

Suspended load was carefully monitored for three streams within the overall catchment area, namely the Radurschlbach, which has minimum glacier cover, the Taschachbach, which has moderate cover, and the Pitzbach, which has extensive glacier cover (Lauffer 1982). Plotting annual suspended load against the degree of glacier cover shows a clear increase in suspended loads with increasing glacier cover (fig. 2).

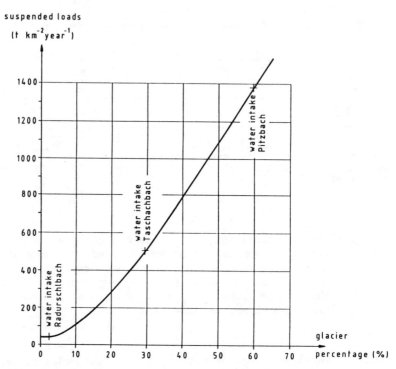

FIG. 2   Suspended loads versus glacier percentage of three typical brooks.

This relationship was used to estimate suspended loads and annual yields for all the other streams without resorting to individual monitoring (Table 3).

TABLE 3 Annual suspended loads of the diverted brooks.

brook		Gsall	Verpeil	Madatsch	Waze	Rostiz	Fißlad	Pitzbach	Taschach	Radurschl	Tschey
glacier percentage (%)		10.3	9.9	12.5	11.6	1.7	3.1	59.5	29.5	2.4	0
catchment area (km^2)		3.9	12.3	4.0	6.7	4.8	11.3	26.8	60.6	24.5	16.5
suspended load	(t km^{-2}year^{-1})	120	110	150	130	41	41	1380	504	41	41
	(t year^{-1})	470	1350	600	870	200	460	36980	30540	1000	680
	(m^3 year^{-1})	260	750	330	490	110	260	20550	16970	560	380

Based on the results of thorough sampling a compactness factor of 1.8 t m-3 was established and used to convert suspended load mass to volume (Hofer 1987).

As in the case of bed load, suspended load in the Faggenbach, the natural inflow to the Gepatsch reservoir, was estimated by taking an average of the suspended loads in the Faggenbach and the Pitzbach, i.e. approx. 429 m^3 $km^{-2}y^{-1}$, which makes an annual yield for suspended solids of 429 x 1o7 = approx. 45.93o m^3 y^{-1}.

Suspended load transported from the Gepatsch reservoir was determined by measuring the concentrations of suspended solids in the turbine water at the Kaunertal hydropower plant and calculating the mean monthly totals.

TABLE 4 Average suspended sediment concentrations in the turbine water of the Kaunertal power station.

month	I	II	III	IV	V	VI	VII	VIII	IX	X	XI	XII
average suspended sediment concentration (g m^{-3})	35	27	25	38	58	37	87	120	120	60	40	38

In November 1986 samples were taken from the reservoir itself to determine suspended load, and the results showed an increase in suspended solid concentrations at increasing depths (from approx. 35 to approx. 5o mg 1^{-1}). These results are consistent with the concentrations for November given in Table 4.

On the basis of the average monthly turbine water volumes and the mean monthly concentrations of suspended solids in the turbine water in Table 4, the annual mean concentration of suspended solids in the turbine water was calculated as 66 mg 1^{-1}. At an annual average turbine water volume of 3o3 million m3, this gives an average annual suspended load in the turbine water of 11.11o m^3y^{-1}.

Total solids load

With desilting chambers preventing sediment input into the Gepatsch reservoir from the diverted streams, the only source of sediment input to the reservoir is the Faggenbach which carries a mean annual bed load of approx. 12.41o m^3y^{-1}.

Out of a total suspended load from the diverted streams plus the Faggenbach of 4o.66o + 45.93o = approx. 86.59o m^3y^{-1}, an annual suspended load of 11.11o m^3y^{-1} is discharged from the Gepatsch reservoir via the turbine water, leaving annual average deposits of suspended solids in the reservoir of 75.48o m^3y^{-1}.

Combined average annual deposits of sediment and suspended solids in the reservoir therefore come to 12.41o + 75.48o = 87.89o m^3y^{-1}. Bed load and suspended load deposits over the 25 years of operation of the Kaunertal hydropower station therefore total 25 x 87.89o = approx. 2.2 million m3 (fig. 3).

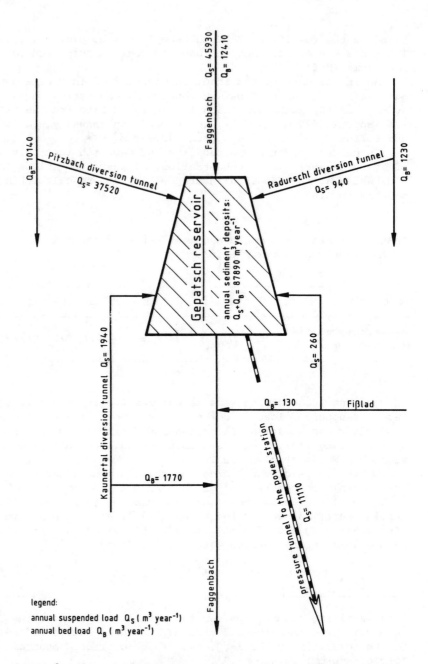

FIG. 3 Balance of debris transports - principal scheme.

In order to confirm the estimates for bed load and suspended load and check the validity of the readings, which are always a potential source of error, further calculations were conducted to test for any decrease in reservoir storage capacity. The last significant drawdown was in the spring of 1987, involving emptying of the area of the reservoir upstream of the lower part of the reservoir where a sedimentation basin formed naturally prior to impounding, i.e. the "Mandar-

fenboden", which is located at 1685 - 171o m above sea level. Storage
level at midnight on 25 March 1987 was at EL 171o,33, and the lowest
level - at EL 1682,o9 - was reached at midnight on 4 May 1987. Water
inflow into the reservoir during the two dates was 8,43 million m^3,
while the turbine water discharge volume was 29,43 million m^3. The
difference between these figures represents the volume of water between the two storage levels observed in the spring of 1987, namely
21 million m^3. On the basis of the storage diagram surveyed at first
filling, water storage between the two recorded storage levels should
be 22,93 million m^3. Storage capacity therefore decreased by 1,93 million m^3 between 1965 and the spring of 1987. Extrapolated for the 25-
year operating period, the loss in storage capacity is 2,19 million
m^3, which is very close to the figure of 2,2 million m^3 calculated for
total sediment deposits. The check therefore verifies the results from
the readings and estimates.

OPERATING EXPERIENCE WITH THE INTAKES AND THE RESERVOIR BOTTOM OUTLET

The bed load flushed out of the intake desilting chambers is deposited in the bed of the streams and transported further by the action
of the sluicing water and the overflow from flood discharge. Operating experience shows that, in spite of the low downstream flow volumes, bed load capacity - although considerably reduced - was still
sufficient to transport the flushed bed load in most cases, with mechanical clearance of the stream bed required only very occasionally.
    During the 25-year operating period, the outfall for the Gepatsch
reservoir, i.e. the Faggenbach, has lost almost 3o% of its flood discharge capacity as a result of scarcely visible sediment deposits and
vegetation growth. This finding was made when the bottom outlet had to
be used for reservoir drawdown in 1983, a process that lasted about
two months. The sluicing effect of the drawdown seems to have eroded
the armour coat in the stream bed, and this has resulted in bed degradation.

EFFECTS OF BED LOAD FLUSHING ON BIOCENOSIS

Upstream from the intakes, 25 years of stream diversion without residual discharge has had no effect on biosenosis at all. Even rare species that are found only in Alpine biotopes have survived, declining
neither in terms of variety nor of populations, as comparative studies of virgin streams in the same massif clearly demonstrate.
    Downstream from the intakes, the biotope has been reduced in size.
On the other hand, water diversion means that the natural enemies of
biocenosis have been diverted, too. For the most part, the water is
slightly warmer and clearer, and certain species of algae do better
there and in turn form the nutrient basis for higher biocenosis. Immediately downstream from the intakes there is a shift in the composition of the species found, but only 1oo m further downstream, with
increased residual discharge, the original spectrum is gradually re-
established.
    Bed load flushing from the desilting chambers has hardly any ef-
fect on biocenosis, as the insects in particular are protected by
their natural flight mechanismus and the sluicing process is of limi-

ted duration (Jäger et al 1985; Margreiter & Perhofer 1982, Margreiter et al 1984; Margreiter 199o).

REFERENCES

Hofer B., Der Feststofftransport von Hochgebirgsbächen am Beispiel des Pitzbaches, Österr. Wasserwirtschaft, Jg. 39, H. 1-2, S. 3o ff., 1987.

Jäger P., Kawecka B., Margreiter-Kownacka M., Zur Methodik der Untersuchungen der Auswirkung des Wasserentzuges in Restwasserstrecken auf die Benthosbiozönosen, Fallbeispiel Radurschlbach, in Österr. Wasserwirtschaft 37, H. 7/8, S. 19o-2o2, 1985.

Lauffer H., Sommer N., Studies on Sediment Transport in Mountain Streams of the Eastern Alps, Q. 54, R. 28, ICOLD, Rio de Janeiro 1982.

Margreiter M., Perhofer H., Die Auswirkungen von Nutzwasserentzug auf das Makrozoobenthos dreier Gebirgsbäche in den Zentralalpen Tirols (Österreich), in Ber. nat. med. Ver. Innsbruck, H. 69, S. 29-51, 1982.

Margreiter-Kownacka M., Pechlaner R., Ritter M., Saxl R., Die Bodenfauna als Indikator für den Saprobizitätsgrad von Fließgewässern in Tirol, in Ber. nat. med. Ver. Innsbruck, H. 71, S. 119-135, 1984.

Margreiter M., Einfluß der Gletscherbachfassungen auf die Biozönosen der unmittelbar anschließenden Entnahmestrecke (Fallbeispiel: Pitzbach und Taschachbach), Österr. Wasserwirtschaft, Jg. 42, H. 3, 199o.

Tschada H., Beobachtungen über die Geschiebefracht von Hochgebirgsbächen, "Interpraevent 1975", S. 1o9 ff.

Tschada H., Betriebserfahrungen mit den Bachfassungen des Kaunertalkraftwerkes, Österr. Wasserwirtschaft, Jg. 31, H. 5-6, S. 21o ff., 1979.

Hydrology in Mountainous Regions. II - Artificial Reservoirs; Water and Slopes
(Proceedings of two Lausanne Symposia, August 1990). IAHS Publ. no. 194, 1990.

Reservoir sedimentation and flushing

W. R. WHITE
Head of River Engineering, Hydraulics Research,
Wallingford, UK

ABSTRACT This paper is concerned with the engineering
assessment of the deposition and re-erosion of sediments
in reservoirs. This deposition and re-erosion can be
assessed by methods which vary in their complexity.
Historically, simple empirical methods have been used
which require only a limited amount of data and analysis.
More recently, however, computer models have been
developed which can simulate the mechanics of sediment
movement within the reservoir as flows and levels change.
These are used to predict sedimentation patterns and also
to look at the possibility of the strategic flushing of
sediments through the dam in order to extend the useful
life of the scheme.

An assessment of catchment sediment yield is a
prerequisite to any consideration of sediment problems in
reservoirs and this has been shown to be difficult and
often imprecise. Sediment yields vary with climate, the
geology of the catchment and land-use practices.

INTRODUCTION

Reservoir sedimentation and the consequent loss of valuable water
storage is becoming increasingly important in tropical countries.
High sediment yields are natural in the tropics and are balanced by
the high rates of erosion and soil production. When this balance is
disturbed by man's activities then the sediment yield is dramatically
increased at the expense of soil renewal. The steady rise in soil
erosion in tropical countries due to increased cultivation has
endangered reservoir projects and caused doubts about the viability of
existing and future schemes. The impoundment of water for potable and
irrigation supplies, hydro-power, and flood control is a necessary
step towards improved national incomes. Untimely sedimentation may
reduce the benefits and, if it is ignored, remedial measures may
become prohibitively expensive.

ASSESSMENT OF RESERVOIR SEDIMENTATION

The assessment of the deposition of sediments can be made using simple
empirical desk calculation techniques or more sophisticated numerical
modelling. In the case of existing reservoirs these estimates can be
improved by measuring sedimentation during the early life of the

129

reservoir and using these base-line data to help with predictions of future deposition.

Survey and computation of reservoir sedimentation

Figure 1 shows sediment yields derived from recent reservoir surveys carried out by Hydraulics Research in Indonesia, the Philippines and East Africa. The order of magnitude difference in annual sediment yield is due to the large differences in soil erosion between the sites in the humid, steeply sloping drainage basins of south east Asia and those in the drier, less steep areas of central Kenya. In addition sediment yields fluctuate annually due to variations in rainfall intensity and distribution, and over longer time periods due to changes in land use and runoff. The important point to note is that all the sediment yields measured by means of these reservoir surveys (after allowing for errors in survey and computation) are several times higher than the figures used during the design of the dams. In the absence of reliable sediment transport data and sediment yield estimates from tropical areas, designers have had to use data from temperate regions.

Reservoir	Country	Drainage Area km^2	Annual Sediment Yield tonnes/km^2	Survey Period
Karangkates	Indonesia	2050	4200	1973 - 77
"	"	2050	1550	1977 - 82
Selorejo	"	238	4660	1970 - 77
"	"	238	1370	1977 - 82
Tokol	"	180	4200	1975 - 77
Kindaruma	Kenya	10000	460	1968 - 81
Kamburu	"	9520	430	1968 - 74
"	"	9520	770	1974 - 78
"	"	9520	280	1978 - 81
Magat	Philippines	4123	3800	1982 - 84

FIG. 1 Sediment yields based on recent HR reservoir surveys.

However, not all the variation in sediment yield can be explained as a change in rainfall and runoff. The accuracy of the result depends upon the detail of previous basin surveys. The volume of deposited sediment is generally obtained as the difference between the total reservoir capacity at the time of survey and the capacity at some time in the past (usually pre-impoundment). In this way the result is obtained by taking the difference of two, large, approximately equal numbers. A small error in the calculated reservoir capacity may give rise to an error up to two orders of magnitude different from the calculated volume of deposited sediment.

Research at Hydraulics Research has focused on examining suitable methods for surveying and computing deposited volumes. The aim has been to provide information on the most appropriate method for the accuracy of result required.

Survey techniques   There are numerous ways of surveying a
reservoir to determine the elevation of the bed and hence the total
storage and sediment volume; and the method and equipment chosen
should reflect the nature of the reservoir project. The method of
data processing and volume calculation should be decided first since
this will constrain the choice of equipment. In many cases estimation
of design capacity is based upon small-scale mapping, whereas later
range line surveys give more detailed information. Combination of
these two types of data, particularly when pre-impoundment data are
sparse, can lead to poor estimates of sediment volume.

Traditionally survey data are collected along pre-determined range
lines which can be re-surveyed so that the changes of sectional shape
can be noted directly. Depth measurement is obtained by using an
echo-sounder (sonar) with a chart or digital readout. From our
experience, more discrepancies in cross-section data can be attributed
to errors in the initial triangulation than any other source.

Computational techniques   The literature contains details of a
variety of techniques for computing the volume of deposited sediment
but gives little guidance on their relative merits. Reservoir
managers with limited financial and skill resources need to know how
the choice of method will affect the accuracy of the results. Studies
undertaken by HR have gone some way in identifying suitable methods.
These are categorised into three groups :
• End-area methods (based on range line surveys)
• Contour methods (based on contour information)
• Combined methods (based on range line and pre-impoundment contour
  information)

Terrain models (see Figure 2)   The use of Digital Terrain
Models (DTMs) has increased dramatically over the last few years.
They are used to model ground surfaces and can be used in processing
reservoir survey data and in calculating the volume of deposited
sediment.

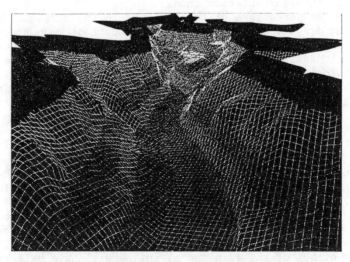

FIG. 2 Three-dimensional representation of DTM, Manjirenji
reservoir, Zimbabwe.

Use of DTMs necessitates investment in expensive surveying
equipment with integrated data collection in a form which is readily
transferable to a computer for processing. The high cost of DTMs
means that their use for reservoir surveys in the developing world
will for some time be limited to specialist survey companies. The
advantages of DTMs are the improved accuracy, speed of computation,
and reduction of preparatory work (setting up range line beacons).
The accuracy of the results depends heavily on the adequacy of the
surveys, in particular the pre-impoundment survey.

EMPIRICAL METHODS OF PREDICTING SEDIMENTATION

Until recently reservoir sedimentation could only be assessed using
simple, empirical methods. To estimate the volume of deposited
material the notion of trapping efficiency was introduced. The
trapping efficiency of a reservoir is defined as a ratio of the
quantity of deposited sediment to the total sediment inflow.

Gottschalk (1948), Churchill (1948) and Brune (1953) provided
simple graphical means to determine trapping efficiency and these have
been used extensively. Since, however, the trapping efficiency must
depend upon the sediment size, the flow through the reservoir, the
distribution of flows into the reservoir and the way that the
reservoir is operated, it follows that such estimates of trapping
efficiency can only provide approximate values which may, on
occasions, be seriously in error.

After analysing several reservoirs in the USA, Churchill came to
the conclusion that along with the retention time, the transit
velocity, ie, the velocity with which the water flows in the
reservoir, governs the trap efficiency. If the water held in the
reservoir is moving fairly rapidly in the reservoir, very little
sedimentation will occur because the turbulence associated with the
higher velocity hinders settling, even though the retention time may
be high. He introduced a parameter known as sedimentation index which
is the ratio of the period of retention to the mean transit velocity.
The trap efficiency of the reservoirs was found to increase with
increase in the sedimentation index.

If a large percentage of the sediment in the stream is moving in
the form of density currents, then the concept of mean transit
velocity introduced by Churchill is questionable. In such a case, the
velocity of density currents may be very different from the mean
transit velocity of the flow.

Brune analysed the records of 44 different reservoirs in the USA
(41 of which were normal ponded reservoirs) and found that the
capacity to inflow ratio gives better correlation with trap efficiency
than the capacity to watershed area ratio. Figure 3 shows Brune's
plot of the trap efficiency against capacity to inflow ratio.

Pitt and Thompson (1984) developed the methodology proposed by
Brune and used the concept of "reservoir half life" (ie, the time
taken to fill 50 percent of the reservoir storage with sediment).
Figure 4, based on Brune's curve, shows that reservoir half life
varies roughly in proportion to reservoir size and the inverse of the
sediment concentration. Assuming an average sediment inflow
concentration in the range 1000-4000ppm, most reservoirs with storages
in excess of 50% of the mean annual inflow will have half lives

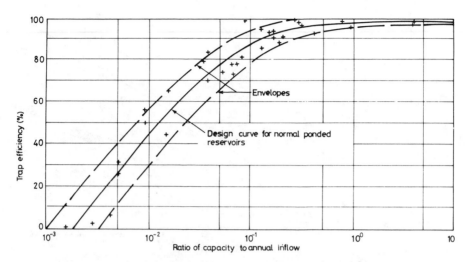

FIG. 3 Trap efficiency of reservoirs after Brune (1953).

measured in hundreds of years. For storages in the range 5-50% of the
mean annual inflow, half lives will be measured in decades whilst for
the smaller reservoirs the half life may be less than 20 years.

Kabell (1984) presented a similar methodology based on
observations of sedimentation in reservoirs in Zimbabwe. Figure 5
shows how the reservoir half life depends on the initial storage rates
and the concentration of fine sediments entering the reservoir.
Kabell used the curves given in Figure 5 and suggested that all
reservoirs with an initial storage ratio of less than 0.10 are
uneconomic. Furthermore, in areas of poor land use practices, a
minimum economic initial storage ratio of 0.25 is likely to apply.

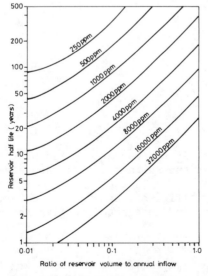

Fig. 4 Reservoir half life as a function of the average
sediment concentration of the inflow, reservoir volume and
mean annual flow after Pitt & Thompson (1984).

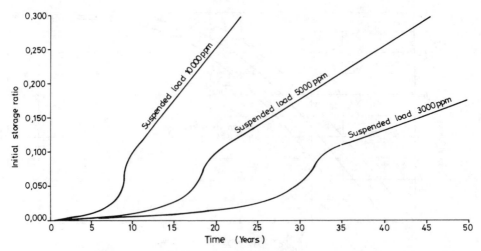

FIG. 5 The influence of the initial storage ratio and the
mean sediment concentration of the reservoir inflow on
reservoir half life after Kabell (1978).

HR has recently carried out work to provide a method of estimating
reservoir sedimentation which was simple to apply but took account of
the size and shape of the reservoir, the nature of the sediment and
the hydraulics of the flow.

Rather than consider trapping efficiency to be a yearly average an
instantaneous trapping efficiency was defined. By dimensional
analysis it was concluded that the instantaneous trapping efficiency
was a function of three non-dimensional variables

$$Z_1 = \frac{bdw}{Q}$$

$$Z_2 = \frac{b}{L}$$

$$Z_3 = \frac{d}{L}$$

where

b = mean width
d = mean depth
L = length
w = fall velocity
Q = discharge

By using a numerical reservoir sedimentation, see next section,
the variation of trapping efficiency with these variables was
determined.

The instantaneous trapping efficiency can then be determined for
different times during the year and integrated to give the annual
trapping efficiency.

NUMERICAL MODELS FOR PREDICTING SEDIMENTATION

Recently, with the availability of computers, it has been possible to
develop numerical models of reservoir sedimentation. These models

calculate the water flow and sediment movement throughout the
reservoir and can provide a reliable and detailed estimate of the
impact of sedimentation.

Reservoir sedimentation results from a complex interaction of a
number of physical phenomena. While water flow can be satisfactorily
described our understanding of the movement, settlement and
consolidation of sediment is not complete. Despite this, it is
certainly possible to improve on how these processes are described in
existing numerical models.

Most numerical reservoir models are time-stepping models. For
given initial conditions, the equations are used to predict what
happens in the reservoir over a short time-step. The process is then
repeated a number of times over the required time period. The
time-step used depends upon the size and nature of the reservoir but
is typically of the order of a day. Once the geometry of the
reservoir and incoming river, and the nature of the flow and sediment
are specified, three modelling stages can be carried out : firstly of
the reservoir's storage, secondly of its flow and thirdly of the
sediment transport within it.

Modelling reservoir storage

When flow enters a reservoir, its velocity drops dramatically and it
is no longer capable of transporting the coarser sediment fractions.
If the water level in the reservoir is near full supply level the
sediment will be deposited near the head of the reservoir. If the
reservoir is partially full then deposition will occur further into
the reservoir basin and at a lower elevation. It is thus important to
model the reservoir water level. The finer sediment will be carried
further into the reservoir where its deposition is controlled by the
opposing effects of particle weight and turbulence. To predict the
reservoir water level a storage sub-model is used. The sub-model uses
a continuity equation to relate the inflow of water into the reservoir
to any outflows plus the change in storage in the reservoir.

Modelling of flow

The water flow in the reservoir and the upstream river is determined
using a backwater calculation. The water level predicted in the
reservoir storage simulation, described above, is used as an initial
downstream boundary condition at the dam to enable the backwater
calculation to proceed upstream. This calculation provides water
depths, velocities and slopes at each cross section along the length
of the reservoir and up the incoming river.

Modelling sediment transport

In modelling sediment movement the primary concern is deposition. The
trapping efficiency and the location of the deposition depend on the
volume of water stored in the reservoir. Since, however, the water
level in the reservoir fluctuates and the inflowing discharge varies,
sediment that has previously been deposited may be subsequently
eroded. It is necessary, therefore, to be able to model both the

deposition and erosion of sediment. In performing such calculations, which are of a volumetric nature, due allowance is made both for initial density, and for subsequently increased density due to compaction by overlying deposition. From the calculated velocities, depths and slopes, the sediment concentrations at each section may be calculated, but when modelling the sedimentation process it is necessary to treat the sand and silt fractions separately. This is because sand movement depends only upon local hydraulic conditions, whereas silt movement is also influenced by preceding flow history.

Sand movement   The transported sand sizes at each section are calculating using one of the many established sediment transport theories for non-cohesive materials, eg, Ackers and White (1973). The movement is dependent upon the sediment diameter. For sediments which do not contain too broad a range of different sizes a representative sediment diameter, D_{35} is often used. For widely graded sediments the range of sediment sizes is divided into a number of classes each with a representative diameter.

Silt movement   The concentrations of the silt fractions entering the reservoir depend on the drainage basin's sediment yield and total annual runoff. The silt is convected with the flow but its concentration reduces as some of the material settles out of suspension onto the bed. The rate of settling is dependent upon the fall velocity which in turn is dependent on concentration and flow conditions. The calculation of the silt concentrations requires more closely spaced sections than for flow. The resulting transport rates of the silt fractions at each section are added to the sand transport rates to obtain the total sediment transport rate. The change in bed level at each section due to the variations in sediment transport rate along the reach can then be determined.

At the head of a reservoir different sediment sizes are sorted according to the ability of the flow to transport the material. Studies at HR have shown that to represent conditions in this region it is best to use a number of representative sand and silt sizes.

Predicting reservoir sedimentation using numerical modelling offers a significant improvement over other methods based on simple estimates of trapping efficiency. The method can readily take account of :
• variable flows
• variable water levels
• sediment size
• reservoir geometry
• reservoir operating rules
and can provide :
• volume, location and compaction of sediment deposited over a specified time period
• annual stage-storage curves
• longitudinal profile of the reservoir at any given time
• effectiveness of using sediment flushing to maintain storage capacity

FLUSHING SEDIMENTS THROUGH RESERVOIRS

Sediment flushing refers to the method of hydraulically clearing
accumulated sediments from a reservoir, usually by releasing flow
through low-level outlets at the dam.

As the low-level outlets are first opened in a reservoir with a
high retention level, the local concentration of flow entrains the
fine material deposits close to the outlet. This gives a false
impression to a lay observer of extensive desilting of the reservoir.
As soon as the local deposits are removed, this action stops. The
velocity of flow away from the outlet decreases very quickly so that,
in a relatively short distance, the velocity becomes too small even to
move the fine material.

Sediment flushing is not effective unless the reservoir is drawn
down to an extent that flow velocities over large areas of the
deposited material are sufficient to create high sediment transport
rates. Even then these hydraulic conditions have to be maintained for
a significant period of time in order to remove the high volumes of
sediments which will have been deposited over the previous months or
years.

In practice this means that reservoirs have to be drawn down to a
relatively low level for an extended period of time and for this
reason the trend in recent years has been towards larger and larger
low-level outlets. The proposed dam at Kalabagh on the River Indus,
for example, has low-level outlets with a capacity of more than
4000m³/s.

Whether sediment flushing is a practicable, economic proposition
at particular reservoir sites depends on may factors:-
(a) The ratio of the annual run-off to the reservoir volume must be
    high in order to provide the "extra" water required for flushing
(b) A climate with distinct wet and dry seasons is an advantage
    because flushing can take place early in the wet season and the

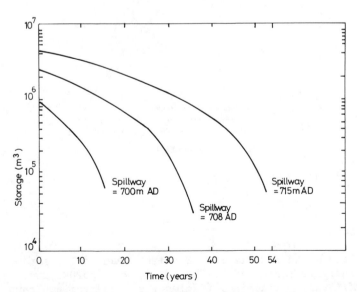

FIG. 6 Decrease in storage volume with time, Kamativi,
Zimbabwe.

reservoir can be refilled to supply water through the following
dry season
(c) Flushing is more likely to be an economic proposition for water
supply schemes than for hydro-electric schemes because the need to
draw down the reservoir for extended periods can have a major
impact on power output

Hydraulics Research's numerical reservoir sedimentation model was
recently used (White and Bettess (1984)) to investigate whether the
net annual water requirement ($1.1 \times 10^6 m^3$) of the Kamativi Mine in
Zimbabwe could be obtained by constructing a dam on the adjacent Gwai
river. A range of heights for the proposed dam were considered, but
all suffered from significant deposition.

The loss in storage against time for various proposed dam heights
is shown in Figure 6. The large ratio of annual flow ($580 \times 10^6 m^3$) to
storage requirement and the fact that the workings of the mine would
tolerate an interuption to the water supply led to a study of using
sediment flushing through large low-level outlets to maintain the
storage required. This study identified under what conditions
flushing is a practical means of maintaining reservoir storage, and in
the case of Kamativi dam, showed that storage could be maintained for
a considerable period of time, Figure 7.

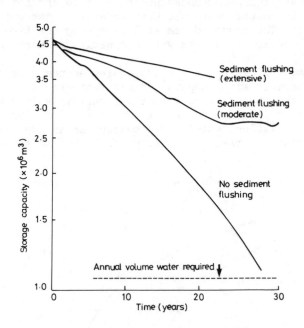

FIG. 7 Effect of flushing on storage, Kamativi, Zimbabwe.

REFERENCES

Ackers, P. and White, W. R. (1973)   Sediment transport : a new approach
    and analysis. Proc ASCE, 99, HY 11, Nov, pp2041-2060.
Brune, G. M. (1953)   Trapping efficiency of reservoirs. Trans AGU,
    Vol 34, No 3.
Churchill, M. A. (1948)   Discussion to Gottschalk (1948).

Gottschalk, L. C. (1948)   Analysis and use of reservoir sedimentation
    data. Proc FIASC, USDA (Washington).
Kabell, T. C. (1978)   Sediment storage requirements for reservoirs.
    IAHS Publication No 144 (Proc IAHS Symposium, Harare).
Pitt, J. D. and Thompson, G. (1984)   The impact of sedimentation on
    reservoir life. IAHS Publication No 144 (Proc IAHS Symposium,
    Harare).
White, W. R. and Bettess, R. (1984)   The feasibility of flushing sediments
    through reservoirs. IAHS Publication No 144 (Proc IAHS Symposium,
    Harare).

Hydrology in Mountainous Regions. II - Artificial Reservoirs; Water and Slopes
(Proceedings of two Lausanne Symposia, August 1990). IAHS Publ. no. 194, 1990.

Numerical simulation of bed evolution along the downstream channel of a reservoir

JINN-CHUANG YANG, Associate Professor
KUAN-PING CHIU, Graduate Student
Department of Civil Engineering
National Chiao Tung University
Hsinchu, Taiwan, R.O.C.
MING-YANG WU, Director
Environmental Protection Administration
Taipei, Taiwan, R.O.C.

ABSTRACT This article introduces a sediment
transport model which is especially suitable for
simulating the bed evolution along the
downstream channel of reservoir in Taiwan under
the peaky flood condition. The governing
equations used for this model consist of a set
of three partial differential equations — the
sediment continuity equation and equations of
continuity and motion for sediment-laden flow.
These equations where transformed into three
pairs of characteristic and compatibility
equations. The method of characteristics with
the fixed time-space grid system is used to
solve these equations. Since the fixed grid
system is used, the interpolation for the
solution is always inevitable. In this article,
instead of the commonly-used linear
interpolation, the cubic interpolation technique
is used. In addition, the reach-back scheme is
used for the bed wave characteristics, which is
expected to give the better results.

INTRODUCTION

The construction of a dam at the upstream of stream can
always induce a progressive change of the channel bed
elevation. This bed-level change, or
degradation/aggradation will cause numerous environmental
and structural problems including potential undermining of
bank protection works and bridge foundations, and reduce
efficiency of water intake works etc. For performing the
future planning for the river system development and
management, it is necessary to predict the future course
of bed-level change affected by the build-up of a dam. For
Taiwan's rivers, the construction of a dam has also caused
the river stability problems. The major cause for the
river bed change in Taiwan's river is not the sediment
cutoff by the dam, but the large amount of sediment

141

evacuated from the reservoir. In Taiwan, most streams carry very little water except the floods occurring two or three times in a year. The sediment evacuation is conducted during the flood period to use the large amount of water to flush the deposited sediment out of the reservoir. Nevertheless, the large amount of sediment carried by the flood transmitting to the downstream channel can cause serious change of the river pattern. The prediction of such impact caused by the sediment evacuation from the reservoir to the downstream channel has become an important issue to be investigated in Taiwan. In order to be able to accurately simulate the movement of the sediment carried by the peaky flood for most of Taiwan's streams with a steep slope, a sediment transport model has been developed. This model is expected to be capable of simulating the sediment movement along the downstream channel of reservoir under the unsteady condition. The characteristics method is tentatively used for this model to simultaneously solve the three governing equations consisting of water continuity and momentum equations and the sediment continuity equation. The set of governing equations will be transformed into a set of characteristics equations, three distinct characteristics are obtained. Two of the characteristics represent the propagation of hydrodynamic waves which in fact are similar to the case of unsteady water flow computation, and the third represents the propagation of bed deformation. For solving these three characteristic equations, one can apply the method of characteristics with specific time intervals(MOC) in combination with linear spatial interpolation at the present time level(Chang & Wang, 1972; Wu, 1973). However, with the use of this kind of model, the time step is severely limited by the courant constraint, and the coupling of hydrodynamic and transport processes is not so effective due to the great disparity between the speeds of surface and bed-deformation waves. Lai(1988) has proposed a multimode scheme which can simultaneously solve unknowns by the implicit mode along the rapidly traveling hydrodynamic characteristics, as well as by temporal of spatial reachback scheme along the slowly moving bed-deformation characteristics. However, for these methods mentioned above the interpolation is always needed since the fixed grid system is used. Usually, the linear interpolation technique is used, which can cause a tremendous extent of errors to the solution. This may overwhelm the benefit from the multimode technique. In this article, the cubic interpolation technique is used to incorporate with the characteristics method to tentatively reduce the errors induced by the interpolation. This article will introduce the mathematical formulations for this new method for the mobile bed modeling. The expected difficulties and problems are also stated. This model will be applied to the study of bed evolution along the downstream channel of reservoir in Taiwan.

GOVERNING EQUATIONS

For sediment-laden flow in a unit width of cross section of an alluvial channel, the governing equations can be written as follows [Lai, 1988]:

$$\frac{\partial h}{\partial t} + \frac{\partial uh}{\partial x} + \frac{\partial z}{\partial t} = 0 \tag{1}$$

$$\frac{\partial hC}{\partial t} + \frac{\partial uhC}{\partial x} + (1-P)\frac{\partial z}{\partial t} = 0 \tag{2}$$

$$\frac{\partial u}{\partial t} + u\frac{\partial u}{\partial x} + g\frac{\partial h}{\partial x} + g\frac{\partial z}{\partial x} + [\frac{\gamma_s - \gamma_w}{\gamma_m}]\frac{gh}{2}\frac{\partial C}{\partial x}$$

$$- \frac{[(1-P)\gamma_s + P\gamma_w]}{\gamma_m}\frac{u}{h}\frac{\partial z}{\partial t} = g(S_o - S_f) \tag{3}$$

in which P = porosity; g = gravitational acceleration; u = flow velocity; C = sediment concentration; h = flow depth; z = active sediment layer; γ_s = sediment specific gravity; γ_w = water specific gravity; γ_m = specific weight of sediment-laden water; S_o = bed slope; S_f = energy slope; t = time; x = distance. In the above equations, Eq. (1) is the sediment-laden flow continuity; Eq. (2) is the sediment continuity; Eq. (3) is the momentum equation for sediment-laden flow.

With the use of a simple power relation, $C = ku^a h^b$ for the sediment transport capacity, appearing in Eqs (2) & (3), the system of Eqs (1) to (3) can be reduced to three unknowns (u,h,z).

The characteristic equation and compatibility equation for the above equations have been derived by Lai [1988], which can be restated as follows:

$$\lambda_i = [\frac{dx}{dt}]_i = y_i + \frac{2}{3}u \tag{4}$$

$$i = 1,2,3$$

$$L_i = S_i\frac{Dh}{Dt} + T_i\frac{Du}{Dt} + P_i\frac{Dz}{Dt} + F_i = 0 \tag{5}$$

in which

$$S_i = \mu_i + \phi; \quad T_i = \omega h + \nu_i;$$

$$P_i = \mu_i + (1-P) \quad ; F_i = \nu_i g(S_t - S_o);$$

$$\phi = \frac{\partial C}{\partial h}; \quad \omega = \frac{\partial C}{\partial u} \quad ;$$

$$\mu_i = [\frac{\phi}{\mu}]\lambda_i - \phi \quad ; \quad \nu_i = [\frac{\phi}{g}]\lambda_i[\frac{\lambda_i}{\mu} - 1];$$

$$p = \phi - (1-P); \quad y_1 = 2\sqrt{-P/3}\cos\theta/3;$$

$$y_{2,3} = -2\sqrt{-P/3} \cos\frac{\theta + \tau_1}{3} \ ; \ \theta = \cos^{-1}[\frac{-q}{2\sqrt{-(P/3)^3}}]$$

Lai and Chang [1987] have indicated that $\lambda_1\lambda_2\lambda_3 < 0$. This result leads to that there must be an odd number of negative-valued characteristic roots. For subcritical flow, it is known that $\lambda_1 \approx \mu+c > 0$ and $\lambda_2 \approx \mu-c < 0$, in which $c = \sqrt{gh}$. Therefore, for a subcritical flow λ_3 must be positive, $\lambda_3 > 0$; and for a supercritical flow $\lambda_3 < 0$. The characteristic direction for these water wave propagation and bed deformation can be shown in the following schematic space-time figures, Figs.1 & 2.

REVIEW OF MULTIMODE SCHEME

In order to better handle the great disparity between the magnitudes of λ_3 and λ_1 , λ_2 in maintaining a coupled computational algorithm, Lai [1988] has proposed the multimode scheme which combines the implicit & reachback schemes together. The schematic diagrams for the characteristics trajectories of this scheme are shown in Figs. 3 & 4.

As shown in Fig. 3, the characteristics λ_1 & λ_2 intersect the adjacent time line at 1 & 2 within the present time step. To interpolate quantities at 1 & 2 from adjacent grid points, involves additional unknowns at points S and Q. Therefore this scheme is usually referred to as implicit scheme.

The value for λ_3 is always small. Therefore, the characteristics may be projected back beyond the present time level for temporal interpolation at the adjacent time tine, as shown in Fig. 3. This is so called temporal reachback scheme.

However, for mobile problem, λ_3 is so small that it always needs a very large reachback time steps to apply the temporal reachback scheme. In order to present the number of reachback time steps from growing too large, a limit can be set for λ_3 at which a spatial interpolation can be used instead of temporal interpolation, as shown in Fig. 4.

Lai has combined the aforementioned three schemes, with the classical scheme as a special case, into one scheme for affording better coupling of hydrodynamic and bed-deformation waves.

For the above-mentioned computational scheme, Eqs. (4) & (5) can be converted to the corresponding finite-difference expressions:

$$x_p - x_i = \lambda_{ip}(t_p - t_i) \tag{6}$$

$$S_{ip}(h_p - h_i) + T_{ip}(u_p - u_i) +$$

$$P_{ip}(z_p - z_i) + F_{ip}(t_p - t_i) = 0 \tag{7}$$

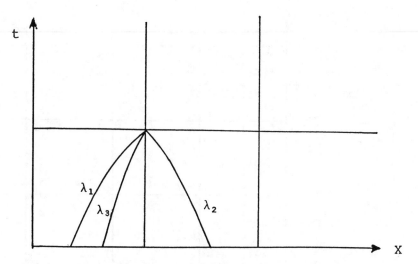

FIG. 1   Characteristics for subcritical flow.

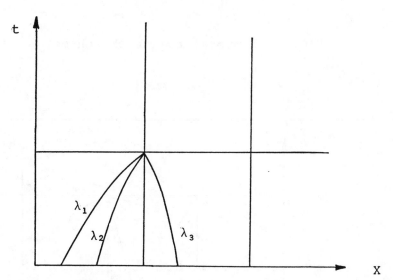

FIG. 2   Characteristics for supercritical flow.

Lai   used   the   time/space   linear   interpolation
technique to solve the variables $\phi = (h, u, z)$.

$$\phi_1 = \xi_1 \phi_{j-1}^{k} + \xi_1' \phi_{j-1}^{k+1}; \qquad \phi_2 = \xi_2 \phi_{j+1}^{k} + \xi_2' \phi_{j+1}^{k+1};$$

$$\phi_3 = \xi_3 \phi_{j-1}^{k-m} + \xi_3' \phi_{j-1}^{k+1-m}; \qquad \phi_4 = \xi_4 \phi_{j-1}^{k+1-m} + \xi_4' \phi_{j}^{k+1-m};$$

$$(8)$$

The factors ξ_1 , ξ_2 , and ξ_3 or ξ_4 can be calculated   from
Eq.(6) as :

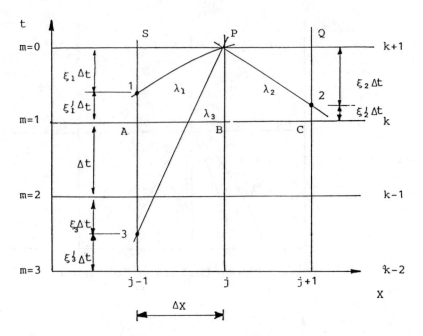

FIG. 3   Temporal reachback scheme.

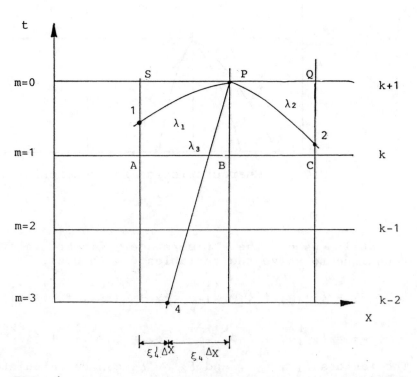

FIG. 4   Spatial reachback scheme.

$$\xi_1 = [\frac{\Delta x_j}{\Delta t}]/[\frac{dx}{dt}]_{1p} = \frac{r_j}{\lambda_{1p}}$$

$$\xi_2 = - [\frac{\Delta x_{j+1}}{\Delta t}]/[\frac{dx}{dt}]_{2p} = \frac{-r_{j+1}}{\lambda_2}$$

$$m_3 + \xi_3 = [\frac{\Delta x_j}{\Delta t}]/[\frac{dx}{dt}]_{3p} = \frac{r_j}{\lambda_{3p}}$$

(9)

$$\xi_4 = [\frac{M\Delta t}{\Delta x_j}]/[\frac{dx}{dt}]_{4p} = \frac{M\lambda_{4p}}{r_j}$$

in which M is the maximum reach-back number; $r = \Delta x/\Delta t$
The compatibility equations along the characteristics C_i
can be written from Eq. (7) with h_i , u_i , and ξ_i replaced
by the corresponding expressions given in Eq. (8).

With two upstream boundary conditions and one
downstream boundary condition, one can close the system of
equations to construct a matrix equation of the form $AZ = B$. Here A is the coefficient matrix, Z is the column
unknown vector, and B is the column known quantities. This
can be solved by any matrix solution technique.

CUBIC INTERPOLATION TECHNIQUE

However, it is known that the linear interpolation can
cause a great numerical damping and phase errors. In this
paper, instead of the linear interpolation technique
described above the cubic interpolation technique is used
to compute the variables ϕ_i . In fact, the cubic
interpolation technique has been used to solve the
dispersion equation which was proposed by Holly &
Preissmann [1977].

The key of Holly-Preissmann method is to use the
dependent variables and its derivatives at the adjacent
two points as the parameters to construct the
interpolation polynomials. When the cubic interpolation is
used, Eq. (8) has to be written as follows:

$$\phi_1 = a_{11}\phi_{j-1}^{k} + a_{12}\phi T_{j-1}^{k} + a_{13}\phi_{j-1}^{k+1} + a_{14}\phi T_{j-i}^{k+1}$$

$$\phi_2 = a_{21}\phi_{j+1}^{k} + a_{22}\phi T_{j+1}^{k} + a_{23}\phi_{j+1}^{k+1} + a_{24}\phi T_{j+1}^{k+1}$$

(10)

$$\phi_3 = a_{31}\phi_{j-1}^{k-m} + a_{32}\phi T_{j-1}^{k-m} + a_{33}\phi_{j-1}^{k+1-m} + a_{34}\phi T_{j-1}^{k+1-m}$$

$$\phi_4 = a_{41}\phi_{j-1}^{k+1-m} + a_{42}\phi X_{j-1}^{k+1-m} + a_{43}\phi_{j}^{k+1-m} + a_{44}\phi X_{j}^{k+1-m}$$

in which a_{11} , a_{12} , $....$, a_{44} are the coefficients which
can be derived by following Holly & Preissmann's
idea[1977] ; ϕT is the time derivative of ϕ, $\frac{\partial \phi}{\partial t}$; ϕX is
the space derivative of ϕ, $\frac{\partial \phi}{\partial X}$.

The use of Holly-Preissmann's method introduces uT, hT, zx or zT as new dependent variables. Therefore, four additional equations are required to evaluate ux, hx and zx or zT. These four equations can be obtained by taking the derivation of Eq. (7) with respect to x or t.

This method may have the potential to improve the accuracy over that of the linear interpolation method but the complexity of the mathematical formulation and the additional variables may cause program coding problem and some other difficulties which are described in the following section.

DIFFICULTIES EXPECTED

Several difficulties in practical use of this method can be identified at the outset. The first problem is in the treatment of boundary values of ux, hx, zx or zT. The evaluation of these boundary values is very difficult since no analytical values are available. The error induced at the boundary point for the mobile bed problem can retain for a very long time and propagate downstream due to the fact of the slow bed wave motion. Hence, the unsuitable evaluation for these derivatives of dependent variables may make the accuracy of computation rather poor.

The second problem is in the approximate integration of the characteristic equations. First-order integration is easy and commonly used but not adequate for accurate computation. When the strong nonlinearity appears, faithful integration along the trajectory is especially important. However, accurate integration of the energy term seems extremely difficult, which may make it difficult to achieve good accuracy in computed values of uT, hT, zx or zT.

The third problem is in the coding of program. Since the reachback technique is used for the bed deformation equation, one needs to determine the values of reachback number for each computation point at time step. In addition, the program has to be so designed to memorize the values of dependent variables at the reach-back time level.

CONCLUSION

The evacuation of sediment from reservoir during the flood period, which occurs very often for Taiwan's reservoirs, has caused severe change of channel pattern. In order to study how the downstream channel of the reservoir is affected by the sediment carried by a peaky flood flow, a numerical model has been tentatively developed. The multimode scheme which has been verified by Lai to be the most suitable method for the highly unsteady sediment transport problem, is used for this model. In addition, for the purpose of avoiding the exessive error induced by the interpolation procedure used for the fixed grid characteristics method, the cubic interpolation technique is used. This article briefly introduces the mathematical formulations of this newly-developed model. By the time of writing this paper, no solid results has been obtained yet. Therefore, no analysis can be presented in this paper. However, in principle, it is expected that the better results should be able to be obtained with the use of cubic interpolation technique.

ACKNOWLEDGEMENTS

The writers would like to express their appreciations to Dr. C.T. Lai who provided his papers related to this article, and gave many valuable suggestions.

REFERENCES

Chang, F.F.M. and Wang, T.W., "Scour and Fill in the Missouri River as related to the Water Resources Planning", Completion Rep. for Proj. No.B-008-SDAK, South Dakota State Univ., Brookings, S.D., 1972.

Lai, C.T., "Numerical Modeling of Unsteady Alluvial-Channel Flow Using the Multimode Method of Characteristics", 14th Southeastern Conference on Theoretical and Applied Mechanics, Biloxi, Mississippi, 1988.

Holly, F.M. Jr. and Preissmann, A., "Accurate Calculation of Transport in Two Dimensions", JHYD, ASCE, Vol.103, No. HY11, PP.1259-1277,1977.

Wu, C.M., "Unsteady Flow in Open Channel With Movable Bed", Proc. Int. Symp. River Mechanics, IAHR, Bangkok, Thailand, 3,447-488, 1973.

TOPIC C:
CONSEQUENCES OF MODIFIED FLOW REGIME DOWNSTREAM OF RESERVOIRS

Hydrology in Mountainous Regions. II - Artificial Reservoirs; Water and Slopes
(Proceedings of two Lausanne Symposia, August 1990). IAHS Publ. no. 194, 1990.

The influence of a dam on the downstream degradation of a
river bed: case study of the Tigris River

Thair M.AL-Taiee
Assistant Lecturer, Saddam Dam Research Center,
Mosul University, Mosul, Iraq

ABSTRACT Changes in Tigris river bed profiles
at Mosul station for different period during
the years 1985, 1986, 1987 and 1988 after Mosul
dam construction, in addition to the measurements of suspended sediment concentration from
the downstream river were used to study the
effect of water storage in Mosul dam on the
degradation processes occurred in the downstream Tigris river's bed due to the high velocity
and tractive force of the released clear water
from the reservoir.
    From the comparison of Tigris river profi-
les, surface water levels of the river associated with the analysis of grain size distribution of the bed load material and water temperature variation it was concluded that Mosul dam
effect on the degradation of Tigris river bed
was clear due to its retaining percent of 95.5
of suspended sediment load in the reservoir.Al-
so it was observed that about twenty five centimeters in an average was degraded from Tigris
river bed in addition to the increment of the
(D_{50}) of river bed material from 8 mm.to 17mm.
after four years of Mosul dam construction.

INTRODUCTION

There are many negative side effects of the dam construction on the downstream river's regime and on its hydraulic
structures.Before dam construction the river was in a state
of equilibrium characterized by a clear low water and a
flood was loaded with suspended matter.As the water stores
behind a constructed dam, it looses most of the material
suspended in it. The increased water velocity of pure water
in front of the dam starts to degrade the bottom and the
banks of the downstream river to compensate for the loss of
the material deposited in the reservoir. Minor degradation
below dams is somtimes desirable and beneficial since it
increases channel capacity and improves drainage of
adjoining lands.
    Tremendous quantities of bed materials have been removed
from the channel below Hoover dam.Measurements reported by
Borland and Miller,(1964) indicated that about 11,559,320
cubic metres have been removed from the channel for a dist-

ance of 148 kilometers miles below the dam during the period 1935 to 1951. Observation made at lake Mead indicated
that when the clarified water was released from the dam on
the Rio grand, the flow was carried away from the bed more
fine materials than coarse particles (lane, 1953). Several
modern dams in India of relatively low height have failed
as a result of erosion at the toe of the structure due to
the sediment carried away from the bed by the clarified
water (Jogtekar,1951).

The rate of degradation below reservoirs depends upon
the type of material in the channel and the hydraulic characteristics of the outflow.These degradation processes will
eventually reduce the water level and increase the hydraulic pressure on the structures located downstream of the dam
such as bridges.

The present case study for the above mentioned problem
was applied to observe the effect of Mosul dam on the
degradation of Tigris river bed. The dam was located on
Tigris river 60 kilometers north of Mosul city, (Fig 1).
The dam construction completed in 1985 and started to store
water behind in the beginning of 1985.

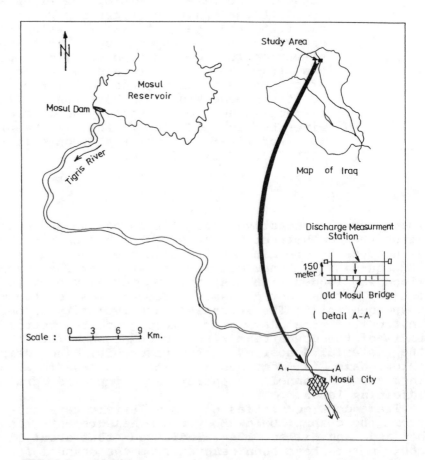

FIG. 1 Location map.

METHODOLOGY

A Tigris river profile in the entrance of Mosul city was selected in the present work as a case study of the present problem.
This river profile was located within Mosul discharge measurement station which was installed 150 metres upstream of an old Mosul bridge.
The field estimates of degradation are based on observations of drops in the bed level of the studied river profile and the decreases in water levels. Field suspended sediment measurements, discharge measurements, measurements of surface water slope and cross section profiles are periodically carried out after dam construction for the years 1985 till the end of the year 1988 by the ministry of Irrigation (1988). Sediment samples from the Tigris river bed at Mosul station were analyzed for grain size distribution by Nedeco (1976),Najib (1980) and Hayawi (1987). Water temperatures from the upstream and downstream of Mosul dam were measured and recorded too.

RESULTS AND DISCUSSION

It is natural that such a complex scheme like a dam should have some effects. Some of those are positive whilst others are negative.An important one of those negative effects are the degradation processes which are the by-product of flowing clear water from the dam to the downstream river. This clear water has trapped its suspended sediment material in the upstream reservoir before releasing from the dam. The above mentioned problem was applied on Mosul dam trying to study its effect on the downstream Tigris river specially near one of the oldest hydraulic construction in Mosul city (old Mosul bridge).
Three important factors and indications were used in the present work to satisfy and discuss the effect of releasing clear water from Mosul dam on downstream river. One of those indications was the sediment concentration measurements in downstream river for the periods before and after Mosul dam construction.The other two factors were the cross section profiles of Tigris river for different periods and the water temperature differences between the upstream and downstream behaviour of erosion and deposition processes. For the sediment concentration, the mean annual suspended load transported by Tigris river prior to construction of the dam have been amounted to about 20500 tons. The maximum observed sediment concentration prior to construction of Mosul dam was 6725 ppm. whilst the minimum was 29 ppm. giving the ratio of (230 - 1), (ministry of Irr. 1988). After the construction of the dam, the mean monthly concentration of suspended sediment in the downstream river dropped to a range between 85 ppm. and 38 ppm. It is clear from the above mentioned numbers that since construction of the dam (1985),95.5% of the total suspended sediment load carried by flood was deposited in Mosul reservoir. This

siltation process in the reservoir brought into clear degradation downstream river of the dam due to the releasing of
clear water with high tractive force and high resistance.
Average monthly records of suspended sediment concentration
befor and after dam construction were shown in Table (1).

TABLE 1 Average Monthly Sediment concentration (ppm) in
        Tigris River at Mosul station Before and After Dam
        Construction.

Period/year	J	F	M	A	M	J	J	A	S	O	N	D
1959 - 1975	1163	2052	2427	1346	1063	903	964	807	661	516	518	785
1986 - 1988	60	65	70	81	85	62	48	42	38	40	51	70

Variation of Grain Size Bed Material

Bed material size in the downstream reach from Mosul dam
exerts considerable influence on the nature, degree, rate
and extent of degradation. Decrease in peak discharges and
its sediment concentration after dam closure due to flood
storage, reduces the ability of the river to transport the
coarsest fractions of the bed material. However, reduced
sediment loads downstream from the dam allows the regulated
flows to erode fine material from the bed and banks. This
leads to progressive coarsening of the bed material and the
development of surface armour layers which protect the subsurface layers from erosion.
The analysis of the field measurements and observations
made on the Tigris river indicated that when the treated
water released from Mosul dam to the river the flow carry
away from the bed more fine particles than coarse
particles.Figure (2) shows the increase in the size of the
Tigris river bed material at Mosul station for different
periods before and after dam construction.
    One of the important indications of the river degradat-
ion is the water surface slope and the water surface
elevation of the river at certain site. It was found that
the water surface slope at Mosul river station for the
periods before and after the dam construction (1980, 1987)
was 4.7×10^{-4} and 4.85×10^{-4} m/m respectively. (Figure 3)
shows the discharge rating curve at Mosul station before
and after dam construction ,(Ministry of Irrigation,1988) .
It was clear from the figure that the average water level
drop in the river after Mosul dam construction was about
twenty five centimeters which gave an indication that a
river bed degradation occurred.
    Number of Tigris river profiles at Mosul station were
dependant as the second factor in the observation of river
degradation. These river profiles represent different

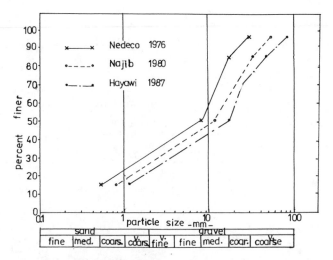

FIG. 2 Grain-size distribution of Tigris river bed material
at Mosul station.

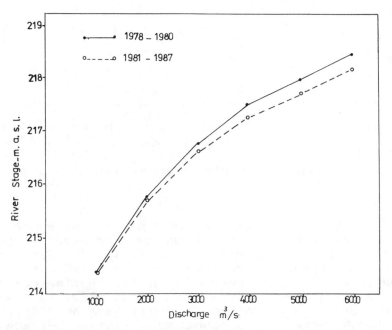

FIG. 3 Tigris River rating curve at Mosul station.

discharges and period after dam construction,(Figure 4). An
observation of the Tigris river profiles for the years 1985
and 1988, the effect of sediment absence in the downstream
river due to Mosul dam construction was clear . During the
year 1985 , the maximum degradation occurred was forty to
fifty centimeters when the river discharge increased from
285 m³/s during December 1984 to 2044 m³/s during March
1985.While during the year 1988(the abnormal flood season),

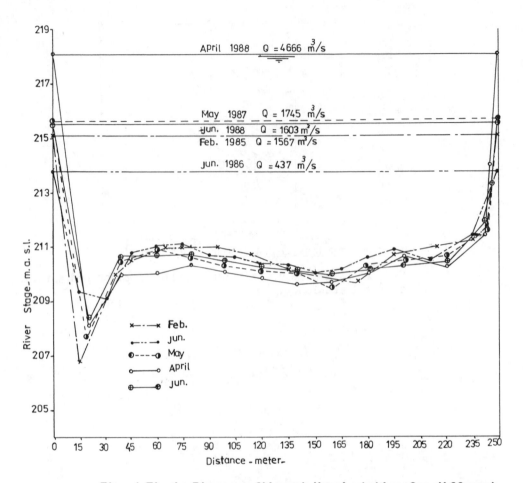

Fig. 4 Tigris River profiles at Mosul station for different
periods.

the degradation depth reached ninety to one hundred centimeters when the river discharge increased from 530 m³/s
druing Feb. to 4666 m³/s during April. The same degradation
process occurred during the year 1987 in which the
degradation depth reached thrity centimeters when the
discharge increased from 450 to 1600 m³/s. These observations of the degradation processes gave an indication that
although there is a proportional relation between degradation depth and discharge, there is also an inverse relation
with the sediment concentration.

Figure (5)shows clearly that Tigris river bed was degraded and refilled during the years 1985,1987 and 1988 after
dam construction due to subsequent high and low flood crest
as clearly shown through the river profiles at April and
June 1988. These degradation and deposition processes were
extended and continued around the piers of the old Mosul
bridge. These processes show that some engineering protection around the piers of the bridge may be required such as
<u>filling</u> the degraded cavities around the foundation of the

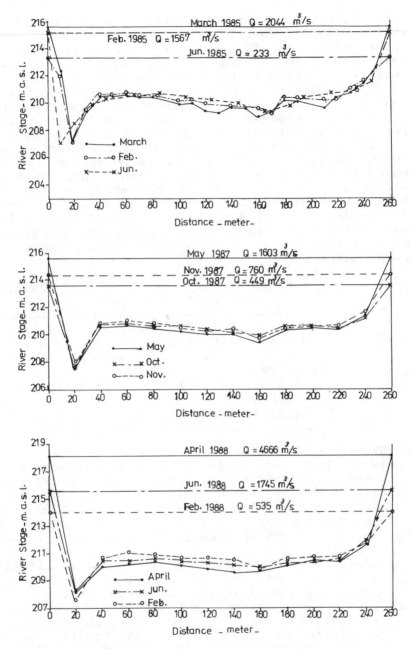

FIG. 5 Tigris River profiles at Mosul station for the years 1985, 1987 and 1988.

piers with large size rock riprap which gives more stabliz-
ation to the piers and push away the vortices formed there.

Water Temperature Effects

It has been noted that the movement of bed material in movable bed can be affected by the temperature of the water, (Walter, 1963). That is to say the change in viscosity of water affect the fall velocity of a particle of sediment. This fall velocity essentially determines or controls the ability of water to put into suspension or motion certain sizes and quantities of sediment. A preliminary analysis to some of the laboratory experiments showed an increase in the energy gradient with a decrease in water temperature for the same rate of bed movement,(Walter 1963).

It is known that the stored water behind a dam,releases to the downstream river from a large depths in reservoir in which it keeps water in a cool temperature. This cool water will aid in the degradation processes of the river bed. Water temperature differences between the upstream and downstream of Mosul dam was observed,(Table 2). This decrease in the water temperature downstream of the dam added a significant factor to the mentioned reasons for Tigris river degradation.

TABLE 2 Water Temperature in C^{o} of Tigris River For Different Periods.

Period	Oct. 1987	Nov. 1987	Jan. 1988	Feb. 1988	Mar. 1988	May. 1988	June. 1988
upstream of dam	27	25	18	15.5	10	14	24
downstream of dam	22	19	13	9	9	12	17

REFERENCES

Borland, W.M and Miller, C.R. (1964) Degradation below reservoir. Handbook of Applied Hydrology, V.T. Chow.

Hayawi,G.A.M.(1987)A hydraulic model to study and train Tigris river between Ninavah bridge and AL-Hurriya bridge at Mosul city. Thesis presented to the University of Mosul at Mosul.College of Engineering, Irrigation Department.

Jogtekar, D.V. and Wadelar, G.T.(1951) The effect of weirs and Dams on the regime of rivers. International Association of Hydraulic Research. Bombay.

Lane, E.W and Borland, W.M.(1953) River bed scour during floods. American Society of Civil Engineers, Journal of Hydraulic Division . Vol. 5. Ministry of Irrigation (1988).Seasonal Reports,Mosul Irrigation Office,Iraq.

Najib, Y.E.(1980) Characteristics of Tigris river at Mosul. Thesis presented to the University of Mosul at Mosul, College of Engineering , Irrigation Department.

Nedeco (1976) Navigation study Tigris river, Mosul-Baghdad Reach, Republic of Iraq, Planning report.

Walter C.Carey (1963) Effect of Water temperature on the river bed configuration. Paper No. 31 In The Proceeding of the Federal Inter-Agency of Sediment Conference.Miscellaneous Publication No.970. Agricultural Research Service.

Hydrology in Mountainous Regions. II - Artificial Reservoirs; Water and Slopes
(Proceedings of two Lausanne Symposia, August 1990). IAHS Publ. no. 194, 1990.

Transformation d'une ancienne digue sur le cours de la rivière l'Arve

L. DELEY
Ingénieur au service du lac et des cours d'eau du Département des travaux publics du canton de Genève, SUISSE

RESUME Etude sur un modèle hydraulique de la transformation d'une ancienne digue en rivière détruite par des crues. Formation d'importantes érosions avec mise en péril d'ouvrages divers. But de l'étude : maîtriser l'emplacement des érosions et assurer la stabilité des ouvrages.

HISTORIQUE

L'Arve est la seule rivière traversant le canton de Genève à caractère glaciaire et torrentiel. Elle prend sa source dans le massif français du Mont-Blanc et se jette dans le fleuve le Rhône à Genève. Son bassin versant représente 1976 km^2 dont 121 km^2 de glacier et on peut estimer son débit de crue spécifique à 0,44 m^{3}s^{-1}km^2.

Un certain nombre d'ouvrages de captage et/ou d'accumulation ont été construits au cours des dernières décennies sur son cours inférieur et sur certains de ces affluents, qui ont eu pour effet de modifier sensiblement le régime des apports, tant liquides que solides, des cours d'eau. La modification la plus importante résulte de la modification de l'aménagement d'Emosson (mise en service en 1973) qui, en dérivant une partie des eaux du bassin versant vers un autre bassin (en direction du Rhône à Martigny, Suisse), a, d'une part, engendré une diminution non-négligeable du débit moyen annuel de l'Arve et, d'autre part, créé une situation totalement nouvelle en ce qui concerne les conditions de transport des sédiments en provenance, notamment, des glaciers d'Argentière et du Mont-Blanc situés en aval. L'influence de ces modifications s'est fait sentir et se sent encore dans le tronçon inférieur genevois de l'Arve, où l'état d'épuisement du lit du cours d'eau ne s'est pas encore rétabli.

Il faut noter également que l'Arve, dans la période du 19ème siècle et du 20ème siècle, a été utilisée à des fins industrielles. Soit pour l'exploitation de son gravier, abondonnée depuis en raison des approfondissements non contrôlés du fond du lit et par conséquent du risque de pollution de la nappe phréatique, soit pour la production d'énergie pour des machines hydrauliques, remplacées aujourd'hui par des machines électriques. De ce fait l'Arve a conservé les vestiges de ces activités passées par le maintien d'une série de digues, redonnant un nouveau profil d'équilibre à la rivière. Le dernier tronçon de l'Arve avant q'elle se jette dans le Rhône se situe dans un milieu urbain et les constructeurs ont utilisé les ouvrages dans le lit de la rivière pour concevoir des ouvrages tels que les ponts, les murs de quai, voire une traversée électrique enterrée qui fait partie d'une boucle assurant l'alimentation principale pour la ville.

Il va de soi qu'il est très difficile actuellement de modifier le profil en long de la rivière sans remettre en cause la stabilité de nombreux ouvrages. Or, en 1981, la digue de la Fontenette, construite au 19ème siècle, d'une conception ancienne (entassement de petits blocs d'enrochements de 500 kg, rideau amont en bois et dalle béton sur la surface) qui servait à capter un certain débit pour la production d'énergie, fut détruite partiellement par une série de trois crues rapprochées estimées d'un temps de retour de 5 ans pour la plus forte (débit 1er jour = 650 m^{3}s^{-1}; débit 2ème jour = 410 m^{3}s^{-1}; débit 3ème jour = 630 m^{3}s^{-1}).

Malheureusement, la brèche ouverte dans la digue eut pour effet de concentrer le flux principal contre les piles d'un pont routier se trouvant 50 mètres en aval. L'impossibilité de boucher la brèche a conduit à la destruction complète de cette digue pour sauvegarder le pont. L'élimination de la digue provoqua rapidemment la mise en mouvement du profil en long et une érosion régressive remonta sur 150 mètres, mettant à nu une traversée électrique de câbles haute tension (130kV et 18kV).

Une solution provisoire

Les services industriels de Genève (SIG), responsables de ces câbles ont dû procéder à une intervention urgente, sans avoir le recul nécessaire sur les conditions hydrauliques et sur l'importance a priori des travaux à exécuter. Leur solution a constitué à couler une dalle sur les câbles, la protéger en amont par une paroi constituée de palplanches et en aval, par des blocs d'enrochements en calcaire de l'ordre de 2000 kg disposés selon une pente de 1:2.5, maintenus par des rails fichés et tenus en tête par des moises soudées. Une année après, une nouvelle intervention a dû avoir lieu pour rajouter des enrochements (1000 tonnes), dont une partie avaient été arrachées par le courant.

Premier bilan

L'ouvrage provisoire ainsi réalisé n'a pas représenté un état stable et des dommages apparents (arrachements de blocs lors des crues) ont pu être constatés. D'autre part sa géométrie, en biais par rapport à la section normale de la rivière, formant un angle de 55 degrés par rapport à la berge, dirige les filets d'eau contre la rive droite, risquant de provoquer à la longue des érosions inacceptables.
Si, par calcul, il est possible de déterminer un certain nombre d'effet, comme le calcul du poids des enrochements nécessaires, les approfondissements prévisibles maximaux, voire d'une certaine manière la pente idéale de la protection aval, l'intégration de ces données pour réaliser un ouvrage se révèle difficile et peu sûre. D'autant que des questions tell que la conservation de l'ouvrage existant, le redressement des lignes de courants et le maintien des piles du pont en aval nécessitent des réponses précises tenant compte de phénomènes d'érosions générales et locales. Dans ce but, la solution d'essais sur modèle s'avère indispensable.
C'est le Laboratoire de recherches hydrauliques, hydrologiques et glaciologique de l'Ecole polytechnique fédérale de Zürich qui a dirigé l'étude.
Cette dernière se fit en deux étapes. Premièrement, des essais à réaliser dans un canal à deux dimensions, modèle à l'échelle 1:35 qui permet d'obtenir rapidemment des renseignements sur les éléments principaux de dimensionnement du seuil provisoire (ci-après, seuil SIG). Deuxièment, des essais à réaliser dans un canal à trois dimensions (largeur 1 mètre, longueur 10 mètres), modèle à l'échelle 1:80, qui permet de déterminer si le seuil SIG peut engendrer des affouillements locaux, non décelés dans la première étude, de déterminer si le seuil SIG doit être renforcé ou doublé. Outre la stabilisation du lit de l'Arve, une répartition optimale de l'écoulement dans les trois passes du pont routier et une sollicitation acceptable des berges en aval a dû être prise en considération.

NATURE GEOLOGIQUE DU SOL

L'ensemble du lit de l'Arve dans cette région est creusé dans de l'alluvion ancienne, gravier moyen à grossier, sablo-limoneux compact, localement cimenté par du carbonate de chaux. Cette unité graveleuse est aussi le réservoir d'une nappe phréatique importante et la zone considérée est le siège d'échanges continus rivière-nappe. La destruction de la digue de la Fontenette a augmenté les résurgences de la nappe, mais ces pertes gardent cependant une valeur tolérable avec le seuil SIG.

L'étude en laboratoire s'est faite avec des matériaux légèrement différents, c'est-à-dire à partir de prélèvements antérieurs, constitués d'une couche sablo-limoneuse semi-consolidée de retrait glaciaire. Malgré cette différence de terrain, l'incidence n'est pas fondamentale pour les essais, car les érosions se produiront de toute façon. Ce qui va changer, ce sont les pentes des talus des surcreusements. Concernant ces surcreusements, de l'ordre de 4 à 5 mètre ils ne sont pas bénéfiques pour la couche de transition de la nappe, si l'on tient compte d'un risque de remplissage après les crues de sédiments fins, ayant une teneur non négligeable en matière organique. Heureusement, ces inconvénients peuvent être minimisés par le phénomène de tourbillons créés par le remou en aval du seuil, emportant une grande partie des ces éléments fins.

RESULTATS DES ETUDES

L'expérimentation a permis d'abord d'examiner les conditions critiques. Par exemple, le débit à prendre à considération. Il s'est révélé qu'un débit , $Q = 460$ m^{3}s^{-1} (par comparaison, le débit d'un temps de retour de 100 ans est de 1000 m^{3}s^{-1}), remplissait les sollicitations presque maximum: le surcreusement et l'arrachement des blocs, avec la possibilité de voir apparaître une faille à l'aval de la dalle en béton et par conséquent le risque d'avoir des érosions locales sous la dalle. Si l'action des plus grands débits n'est plus déterminante, c'est à cause de la réduction de la différence de niveaux d'eau engendré par le seuil.

Un autre exemple est celui des matériaux de construction. Compte tenu de la possibilité d'approvisionement de la région et surtout du poids des blocs (1000 à 2000 kg), il a pu être démontré qu'il fallait plusieurs couches de blocs pour assurer une stabilité. D'autre part l'emploi d'un filtre (100 à 400kg) a été déconseillé. En effet, lors de crues importantes, le filtre disposé en tapis sous les blocs peut subir des sous-pressions et l'ouvrage pourrait se mettre en mouvement. Si nous partons de l'hypothèse qu'un filtre sert à économiser la quantité de gros blocs, puisque les essais ont montré que l'arrachement des blocs pouvait se produire et que seuls plusieurs couches, de deux à trois, permettaient de rendre insignifiant la perte de quelques blocs, alors cette épaisseur peut remplacer avantageusement la couche d'un filtre. Une remarque : un seuil en enrochements est un ouvrage à surveiller périodiquement, car il risque de ne pas être stable, par le mouvements des blocs qui le compose.

Après plusieurs variantes de positionnement d'un seuil, une solution a pu être trouvée, répondant à tous les buts fixés (Fig. 1). Il s'agit de conserver le seuil SIG et de le compléter par un nouveau seuil rattaché celui qui existe. En plan cela correspond à un seuil arrondi (rayon de courbure de 55 mètres depuis la crête du seuil),

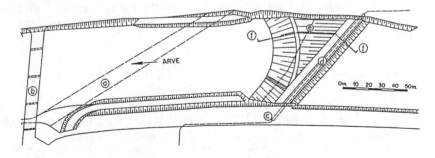

FIG. 1 Situation en plan
a) Ancienne digue de la Fontenette   d) Dalle en béton
b) Pont routier   e) Ancien seuil SIG
c) Câbles 130kV et 18kV   f) Profil type du seuil

placé de telle manière que la crête du seuil SIG forme une tangente avec le nouveau seuil. La partie gauche du seuil SIG a pu de ce fait être intégré dans l'ouvrage définitif. La pente aval du seuil est de 1:6 et mesure en plan 18 mètres (Fig. 2).

Avec cette forme, la tendance à l'affouillement se concentre au milieu de l'Arve et il se crée trois chenaux principaux, pouvant atteindre théoriquement 5 mètres de profondeur. L'écoulement à l'aval du seuil est totalement contrôlé et est parfaitement parallèle aux berges. De plus, il n'y a pas besoin de rideau (palplanches ou rails fichés) à l'aval car l'ouvrage est "tenu" par le niveau d'eau déterminé par une autre digue qui provoque une courbe de remous remontant jusqu'au pied du seuil définitif. Cette hauteur minimum permet la formation d'un bassin amortisseur naturel.

Le pont routier subit aussi les influences du contrôle des remous. En principe, à l'aval des cuvettes de surcreusement, les matériaux emportés par les crues se déposent plus loin. Dans notre cas, on peut estimer ce trajet à environ 100 mètres. Il y a par conséquent formation d'une barre transversale, empêchant toute érosion régressive pouvant menacer les piles du pont.

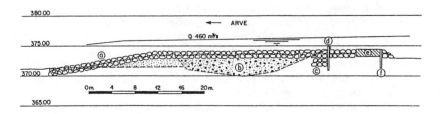

FIG. 2 Profil type du seuil définitif
a) Enrochements
b) Remblai
c) Ancien seuil SIG
d) Rails fichés
e) Dalle béton
f) Rideau de palplanches

CONCLUSION

Les crues peuvent amener d'importantes modifications dans le lit d'une rivière graveleuse et provoquer des réactions en chaîne tant sur le profil en long du fond que sur la stabilité des ouvrages. Lorsqu'on se trouve dans une zone fortement construite, comprenant tout particulièrement des murs, un pont et une traversée souterraine, il est conseillé d'avoir recours pratiquement à des modèles hydrauliques. Ceux-ci permettent une prévision assez précise des phénomènes d'érosions générales et locales. C'est à ce prix qu'une réparation ou la construction d'un nouveau seuil peut être défini tant pour la stabilité des ouvrages que pour le contrôle des érosions prévisibles du fond de la rivière.

REFERENCES

Laboratoire de recherches hydrauliques, hydrologiques et glaciologiques de l'Ecole polytechnique fédérale de Zürich (1983) Rapport sur les essais sur modèle effectués à l'échelle 1:35 . L'Arve, aménagement km 2,56 à 3,00 .

Laboratoire de recherches hydrauliques, hydrologiques et glaciologiques de l'Ecole polytechnique fédérale de Zürich (1984) Rapport concernant les essais sur modèle effectués à l'échelle 1:80. L'Arve, aménagement km 2,56 à 3,00 .

G. Amberger (1985) Aménagement de l'Arve km 2,530 à 2,990 lieu dit : La Fontenette. Rapport du service cantonal de géologie du canton de Genève .

Hydrology in Mountainous Regions. II - Artificial Reservoirs; Water and Slopes
(Proceedings of two Lausanne Symposia, August 1990). IAHS Publ. no. 194, 1990.

The geomorphological impact of modified river discharge and sediment transport regimes downstream of hydropower scheme meltwater intake structures

A.M. GURNELL, M.J. CLARK & C.T. HILL
GeoData Institute and Department of Geography,University of Southampton,
Southampton S09 5NH, England

ABSTRACT   The Grande Dixence hydro-power scheme diverts meltwater from 35 glacier basins in southern Switzerland. Meltwater intake structures in the contributing glacier basins divert virtually all of the meltwater in the proglacial streams into tunnel systems through which the water is transported to a large reservoir for storage. The intake structures include sedimentation basins which settle out the bedload and a part of the suspended load of the streams. These basins are periodically emptied by allowing the meltwater to flow through the basins and along its natural course for short periods of time. This paper describes the changed discharge and sediment regimes downstream of the meltwater intake structures, and assesses the morphological response of river channels to the changed downstream discharge and sediment regimes in the Val d'Arolla and Val de Ferpècle, by examining field evidence of changes in channel size, shape and pattern and by assessing the morphological impact of a flood.

INTRODUCTION

Many studies have demonstrated the fluvial geomorphological adjustments to human modifications of river flow and sediment regimes. The direction, magnitude and rates of these adjustments vary widely and are dependent on the nature of the human influence and the existing physical environment, though the actual change may exhibit a complex response (Schumm, 1973). Despite an extensive literature on the nature of proglacial fluvial processes (Gurnell and Clark, 1987), there are few specific references to changes induced by meltwater intake structures.

The present paper considers the adjustment of river channels to changes in the sediment transport and discharge regime downstream of meltwater intake structures associated with the Grande Dixence hydro-power scheme, southern Switzerland. The influence of these structures will be evaluated using field information collected in the Val d'Arolla and the Val de Ferpècle (tributary valleys of the Val d'Hérens, southern Switzerland): firstly, by comparing the upstream and downstream sediment and discharge regimes; secondly, by describing changes in channel size and pattern in response to the changes in fluvial processes; and thirdly by assessing the significance and the impact of a high-magnitude discharge event on the downstream channel system.

THE GRANDE DIXENCE HYDRO-POWER SCHEME: MELTWATER INTAKE STRUCTURES AND THEIR INFLUENCE ON FLUVIAL PROCESSES

The Grande Dixence hydro-power scheme diverts meltwater from 35 glacier basins in the valleys of St Nicolas and Hérens in southern Switzerland. Details of the glacier basins, their hydrology and their contribution to the hydro-power scheme are provided in Bezinge (1987). In summary, the meltwater diverted from the 35 basins is stored in a large reservoir, the Lac des Dix, before being released to generate hydro-electricity. Meltwater intake structures in the contributing glacier basins divert virtually all of the meltwater in the proglacial streams into tunnel systems through which the water is transported to the Lac des Dix for storage. Thus, the intake structures act as small dams in reducing the downstream river flow. The structures include sedimentation basins which settle out the bedload and a part of the suspended load of the proglacial streams. These basins are periodically emptied by allowing the meltwater to flow through the basins and along the natural river channels for short periods of time. Thus, the operation of these structures translates the upstream diurnal and seasonal rhythm of the meltwater regime into downstream low and consistent flows interrupted by small and frequent 'flood' events associated with the purging or cleaning of the meltwater intake sediment traps.

Bezinge *et al.* (1989) describe the operation of the meltwater intake structures and provide information on the implications of these structures for upstream and downstream fluvial processes in the Val d'Arolla and the Val de Ferpècle (Val d'Hérens). Above the structures, proglacial streams have a discharge and sediment transport regime that is heavily influenced by glacier ablation. Discharge is low throughout the winter, but during the summer the diurnal rhythm of glacier ablation is reflected in diurnal cycles in discharge and sediment transport, whose amplitude reflects recent hydrometeorological conditions. Alpine glacier basins have a typically high discharge and sediment yield per unit area (Gurnell, 1987). Studies of the intake structure on the Glacier de Tsidjiore Nouve, Val d'Arolla, indicate an average annual sediment yield (suspended load and bedload) in the period 1977 to 1987 in excess of 12000 tonnes and an average suspended sediment concentration of 1260 mg l^{-1} from a catchment area of less than 5 km^2 (Bezinge *et al.*, 1989).

In the Val d'Arolla the meltwater intake structures have negligible impact on winter river flows but in the summer, and particularly in July and August, they cause an enormous reduction in discharge in the downstream river channels. Above the meltwater intakes, discharge during July and August in the Tsidjiore Nouve, Bas Arolla and Haut Arolla catchments, Val d'Arolla (based on the active catchment areas currently draining to the meltwater intakes) is typically of the order of 150 l s^{-1} km^{-2} and often exceeds 200 l s^{-1} km^{-2}. River flows below the structures at La Gouille gauging station (5.5 km downstream of the Bas Arolla intake structure) rarely exceed 60 l s^{-1} km^{-2}, which is similar to spring and late autumn flows in nearby unregulated proglacial streams. The high and diurnally-varying, upstream, proglacial suspended sediment and bedload transport regime is replaced downstream by short (less than one hour), small (less than bankfull) floods of water that are highly charged with sediment as a result of the purging of the meltwater intake sediment traps. Bezinge *et al.* (1989) list the average number of purges from the 18 meltwater intakes in the Val d'Arolla and Val de Ferpècle; in total the annual average is over 500, of which over 80% occur in the Val d'Arolla, affecting flows at the La Gouille gauging station.

CHANNEL ADJUSTMENT IN RESPONSE TO WATER ABSTRACTION

The degree and nature of channel adjustment to the changed discharge and sediment regime below the meltwater intake structures can be assessed in relation to evidence on channel size, channel pattern, and response to a high discharge event.

Channel size adjustment

The adjustment in channel size can be established by comparing the dimensions of channels that are affected to various degrees by the hydro-power scheme. 'Unaffected' channels upstream of the meltwater intakes can be related to the catchment area supplying discharge to them. 'Reconstructed' channels (relict features created by the fluvial regime prior to the establishment of the hydro-power scheme) downstream of the meltwater intakes can be related to the current topographic catchment area, since this would have supplied discharge to the channels when they were active. 'Affected' channels are currently active channels downstream of meltwater intakes. They can be related to their currently active catchment area, which is the catchment area below the intakes that is currently draining to these channel reaches. They can also be related to the topographic catchment area which would supply the river discharge in the absence of the hydro-power scheme. An analysis of the capacity, width and depth of 'unaffected', 'reconstructed' and 'affected' channel reaches in the Val d'Arolla and Val d'Ferpècle was undertaken by Gurnell (1983). Several river sections were surveyed along short channel reaches to estimate average reach channel dimensions which were related to their topographic catchment areas and, in the case of 'affected' channels, to their currently active catchment areas, in order to assess the degree to which 'unaffected' or 'reconstructed' channels differed in their dimensions from 'affected' channels. Estimated regression relationships between channel dimensions and catchment area are presented in Table 1. The active catchment area relationships are most informative for the 'affected' channels because these remove the effect of the highly variable proportions of the natural catchments which are located above intake structures for each of the 'affected' reaches. The coefficients of the relationships between the 'unaffected' and 'reconstructed' channels and topographic catchment area and the 'affected' channels and active catchment area are similar for each of the channel dimensions investigated. Differences in the power terms give an indication of the nature of the adjustment. It appears that the 'affected' channels are smaller for the same catchment area (all power terms are smaller, coefficients are slightly smaller for capacity and width and slightly larger for depth), that they increase in size less rapidly for an increase in catchment area, and that the reduction in capacity has probably been achieved by a reduction in channel width (although the width relationship slope coefficient is not significantly different from zero).

TABLE 1. Relationships between channel capacity, mean depth and width and catchment area.

Channel reach sample	Relationship	n*	R	Significance of slope (ho:β=0)
Unaffected + reconstructed	$Cc = 1.562\ Ca^{0.769}$	9	0.949	P<0.001
Affected	$Cc = 0.172\ Ca^{0.824}$	12	0.750	P<0.01
Affected	$Cc = 1.252\ CA^{0.552}$	12	0.752	P<0.01
Unaffected + reconstructed	$\bar{d} = 0.275\ Ca^{0.258}$	9	0.731	P<0.05
Affected	$\bar{d} = 0.241\ Ca^{0.125}$	12	0.231	NS
Affected	$\bar{d} = 0.287\ CA^{0.161}$	12	0.445	NS
Unaffected + reconstructed	$w = 5.403\ Ca^{0.435}$	9	0.870	P<0.01
Affected	$w = 1.283\ Ca^{0.502}$	12	0.792	P<0.04
Affected	$w = 5.299\ CA^{0.204}$	12	0.484	NS

Cc = channel capacity (m²)   Ca = natural catchment area (km²)
$\bar{d}$ = mean channel depth (m)   CA = active catchment area (km²)
w = channel width (m)   (i.e. catchment area below H.E.P. intakes)

Channel pattern adjustment
There is evidence from relict channel patterns that the reduction in channel size has been achieved by a change from a braided to a single thread, wandering, channel pattern (Mosley, 1987). The upstream, proglacial channel patterns vary from a single-thread pattern at low flow to an increasingly complex braided pattern during high flows in July and August (Fenn and Gurnell, 1987; Warburton, 1989). Thus, the downstream single-thread pattern is consistent with the upstream low flow pattern. Figure 1 maps two downstream river reaches (La Monta and Satarma, 3 km and 4.5 km downstream of the Bas Arolla intake) where relict channel patterns are particularly well preserved. These channels have become vegetated. In the case of the Satarma reach, the relict channels have been colonised by shrubs which have been assessed through dendrochronological evidence to post-date the development of the Grande Dixence scheme. Thus, it would appear that the channels were active prior to the implementation of the scheme.

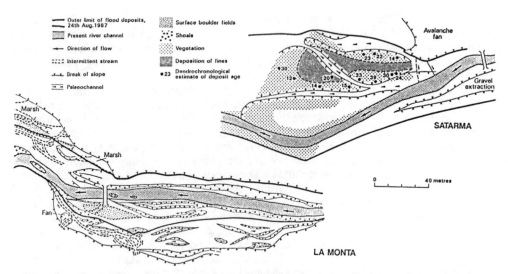

FIG. 1   Currently active and relict channel patterns at La Monta (left) and Satarma (right) mapped in 1983. The La Monta map also shows the limits of erosion and deposition of sediments as a result of the 24 August 1987 flood.

A high-magnitude event

Further evidence of the reduction in channel size and the change in channel pattern is provided by the impact of a precipitation induced flood event on 24 August 1987. This event was created by the release of the total proglacial stream discharge through the meltwater intake structures in the Val d'Arolla because the tunnel systems were already full from draining the glacier basins of the St. Nicolas valley. Thus, the flows during this event were representative of natural high flows prior to the implementation of the hydro-power scheme. The peak discharge, estimated as 13-15 m^3 s^{-1} at La Gouille, was twice the previous recorded maximum flow in the 18 years since the intakes had been operational (Grande Dixence, 1988). The significance of the magnitude of this flood can be assessed by comparing it with typical high flows from the basins of the Glacier de Tsidjiore Nouve, Bas Glacier d'Arolla and Haut Glacier d'Arolla (the three largest of the ten basins contributing to the hydro-power scheme in the Val d'Arolla) which typically have annual flood flows which exceed 2, 5 and 6 m^3 s^{-1}, respectively; a major proportion of the estimated flood peak flow. Thus, although the 1987 event may be rare in the context of the present, regulated, flow regime, it was probably not a large return period event prior to the implementation of the scheme. It thus permits comparison to be made between pre- and post-Grande Dixence flow conditions and channel geomorphology and illustrates the degree to which downstream channels have changed since the implementation of the hydro-power scheme.

Morphological mapping of the channel adjustment to the flood and evidence of flood level was made ten days after the flood. The flood impact consisted of damage to installations, morphological channel changes and debris deposition. Damage in the Arolla Valley included exposed pipes and cables, eroded bridge foundations which have been inventoried by Grand Dixence (1988). Morphological evidence included sediment deposition on vegetated banks and mid-channel bars, undercutting of the pre-flood channel banks and local bank collapse. Debris carried in the flood produced scarring of shrubs, deposition on the flood channel margins and within shrubs bordering the channel, providing further evidence of the areal extent of the flood. Changes were evident in channel geometry and planform. Palaeobraids were reoccupied, as evidenced by sediment and debris deposition, and at least in the upper reaches new braids were cut.

CONCLUSIONS AND IMPLICATIONS

It has been demonstrated that a comparison of sediment and discharge regimes upstream and downstream of hydro-power water intakes provides an effective basis for estimating the downstream geomorphological impacts of such structures in an alpine area. These impact estimates have been assessed against the evidence provided by a restoration of 'pre-intake' hydrological conditions which occurred in August 1987 in the form of closure of the intakes to by-pass storm-generated flood flows. The 'pre-intake' flows that were simulated on this occasion re-activated palaeo-channels and entrained palaeo-sediments in a manner which suggested that relict forms and sediments can be used as an acceptably reliable indicator of likely geomorphological activity under high-intensity flood conditions. This represents an advance in the discussion of hydro-power impacts on the environment. Most such studies have necessarily been either speculative or retrospective, and theoretical debate has concentrated on forecasting the cumulative impact of a change on an environment; an approach which is well exemplified for the Grande Dixence scheme by Aegerter and Messerli (1983). This paper extends this approach by recognising that climatic change may occasionally disrupt or reverse the cumulative impact, thus restoring pre-disturbance conditions. The future planning of areas adjacent to channels downstream of hydro-power water intakes should incorporate this possibility.

ACKNOWLEDGEMENTS The Grande Dixence S.A. is gratefully acknowledged for logistical support and for provision of discharge data.

REFERENCES

Aegerter, S. & Messerli, P. (1983) The impact of hydroelectric power plants on a mountainous environment: a technique for addressing environmental impacts, Mountain Research and Development, 3, 157-175.
Bezinge, A. (1987) Glacial meltwater streams, hydrology and sediment transport: the case of the Grande Dixence hydroelectricity scheme. In A.M. Gurnell & M.J. Clark (Eds) Glacio-fluvial Sediment Transfer: An Alpine Perspective, John Wiley and Sons, Chichester, 473-498.
Bezinge, A., Clark, M.J.; Gurnell, A.M. & Warburton, J. (1989) The management of sediment transported by glacial melt-water streams and its significance for the estimation of sediment yield. Annals of Glaciology, 13, 1-5.
Fenn, C.R. & Gurnell, A.M. (1987) Proglacial channel processes. In A.M. Gurnell & M.J. Clark (Eds) Glacio-fluvial Sediment Transfer: An Alpine Perspective, John Wiley and Sons, Chichester, 423-472.
Grande Dixence (1988) Analyse des crues exceptionnelles de l'été, 1987. (Dayer, D. & Rey, G.) Grand Dixence.
Gurnell, A.M. (1983) Downstream channel adjustments in response to water abstraction for hydro-electric power generation from alpine glacial melt-water streams. The Geographical Journal, 149, 342-354.
Gurnell, A.M. (1987) Suspended sediment. In A.M. Gurnell & M.J. Clark (Eds) Glacio-fluvial Sediment Transfer: An Alpine Perspective, John Wiley & Sons, Chichester, 305-354.
Gurnell, A.M. & Clark, M.J., (eds) (1987) Glacio-Fluvial Sediment Tranfer; An Alpine Perspective, John Wiley and Sons, Chichester.
Gurnell, A.M., Warburton, J. & Clark, M.J. (1988) A comparison of the sediment transport and yield characteristics of two adjacent glacier basins, Val d'Hérens, Switzerland. In Sediment Budgets (Proc. Porto Alegre Symp.) IAHS Publ. 174, 431-441.
Mosley, M.P. (1987) The classification and characterization of rivers. In K.S. Richards (Ed) River Channels: Environment and Process, Basil Blackwell, Oxford, 295-320.
Schumm, S.A. (1973) Geomorphic Thresholds and Complex response of Drainage Systems.

In Morisawa, M. (ed). Fluvial Geomorphology, George Allen and Unwin. London (published 1981). 299-310.

Warburton, J. (1989) Alpine Proglacial Fluvial Sediment Transfer. Unpublished PhD Thesis, University of Southampton.

The flow regime downstream of dams in arid areas: development and effects of channel stability

M. NOUH
Professor of Civil Engineering, Department of Civil Engineering, Sultan Qaboos University, P. O. Box 32483 Al-Khod, Muscat, Sultanate of Oman

ABSTRACT   Data collected from 3 ephemeral straight channels in the south-west region of Saudi Arabia were used to investigate the variation in flow parameters and its effects on channel stability downstream annual storage dams. Mean concentration of suspended sediment is less, sediment sizes are finer, stable bed slope of channel is smaller, stable width is smaller, stable depth is larger, and stable depth to width ratio of channel is larger in the downstream of dams than in the upstream of the dams. The difference in these parameters between upstream and downstream of dams decreases with the increase in the downstream distance from the dams, and becomes negligible at a downstream distance which depends upon flow and sediment characteristics.

INTRODUCTION

Ephemeral channels (which carry water during storms only) are normally characterized by steep slopes (Nouh, 1988a). In these channels, the suspended sediment, especially transported during flash flood events, is of high concentrations and is larger in amount than that transported as bed load (Nouh, 1988b, 1988c). Generally, in ephemeral streams, velocity increases downstream at a faster rate than in perennial streams (Leopold and Maddock, 1953). This results in transporting sediment in the former streams with a rate larger than that in the later streams (Nouh, 1988c). Because natural channels often adjust their dimension and pattern to maintain certain balance between sediment and hydraulic conditions, the stable dimension and pattern of ephemeral channels having a certain discharge capacity are found (Nouh, 1988a) different from those of perennial channels having the same discharge capacity. Unlike perennial channels whose stable dimensions (width, depth, and bed slope) can be expressed as functions of the discharge, Nouh (1988a) found that these stable dimensions for ephemeral channels can be best expressed as functions of discharge parameters (annual mean flood flowrate, and annual peak flood flowrate for a return period of 50 years) and suspended sediment characteristics (median grain size diameter and mean concentration of suspended sediment). This study extends the above previous studies on the stability of ephemeral channels to include the behaviour of flow regime downstream of dams in arid areas, and the effects of such flow on the stability of ephemeral channels.

Generally, water and sediment flow characteristics upstream of a dam are different from those downstream of the dam. Upstream of a dam on an ephemeral channel of an arid area, large amounts of sediment (mainly as suspended load) transport with flash floods, and a large percentage of these amounts is normally trapped in the reservoir of the dam. Downstream of the dam, the flow of water is controllable according to the reservoir operations technique, and the sediment released from the reservoir is much less in amounts than and different in grain size composition from the sediment supplied with flash floods to the reservoir (Nouh, 1986, 1989). Since a channel adjusts its dimension to maintain certain balance between sediment and hydraulic conditions, it is expected that the stable dimensions of the channel downstream of a dam to be different from the stable dimensions of the channel upstream of the dam. In a previous study (Nouh, 1988a), formulas have been developed to identify the stable width, depth, and bed slope of an ephemeral straight channel. The present study is directed to identify the variation in these dimensions and in sediment properties downstream of annual storage dams constructed across typical ephemeral of arid areas. To

171

achieve these objectives, real data from 3 ephemeral straight channels in the southwest region of Saudi Arabia were used.

THE STUDY REGION

The investigated 3 ephemeral channels are located in the southwest region of Saudi Arabia, between latitudes 16o 30 00 N and 22o 00 00 N and longitudes 39o 30 00 E and 46o 00 00 E. The climate of this region is classified as arid to semi-arid (Nouh and Jamjoom, 1981), and its characteristics cover a wide range. Temperature ranges from 2oC to 53oC (yearly mean is about 37oC). The three annual storage dams on these channels, which considered in this study, are built for the purpose of flood control. Their storage capacity is in the range between 6.2 to 71.0 million cubic meters, and their capacity-inflow ratio ranges between 0.73 to 1.50.

Upstream of the investigated dams in this region, runoff are characterized by spates which generally last on average 12 hours from start to finish. Runoff hydrographs are characterized by steep rise and rapid recession. The period of total hydrograph rise, i.e. up to the start of recession, varies from 45 min to 5 h. The average total sediment transport rate to the reservoirs is about 1600 gm/s/m, the average reservoir deposition rate is 120, 000 m^3/km^2 of drainage basin, and the average trap efficiency of the reservoirs is 0.86. The average percentages of clay, silt, and sand in the reservoirs deposits are approximately 25%, 35%, and 40%, respectively.

The operations strategy of the dams is to provide, when water is available in the reservoirs, a constant amount of water supply downstream. However, the reservoirs and their channels are normally dry during a yearly period which varies between 4 and 6 months. During the remaining period (referred to as the wet period) the suspended sediments observed just downstream of the dams generally consists of clay (about 70%) and silts (about 30%). The mean concentration of such suspended sediment varies between 8.2 and 12.5 gpl.

MEASUREMENTS TECHNIQUES

As it has been mentioned before, three dams in the southwest region of Saudi Arabia were selected for the study. These particular dams were selected because each of the dimensions (i.e. depth, width, and bed slope) of their downstream channels, while fluctuate from year to year around a mean value, does not vary significantly with time. At selected distances downstream from the dams, measurements of channel and flow parameters were made. These include mean suspended sediment concentration, particle size, specific gravity of suspended sediment, temperature of the water-sediment mixture, water discharge, distribution of flow in the stream cross section, bed materials, and water surface elevation measurements. Sediment concentrations were determined from pump samples collected from nozzles fixed to two masts and positioned at various heights above the stream bed. The concentrations of sediment determined by this method were compared with those determined using calibrated automatic sampling equipment at selected verticals. The comparison resulted in a correction factor which should be applied to the concentrations from the pump samples to obtain corrected concentrations for the samples. Water discharge and flow distribution in the cross section were determined from velocity and depth observations at properly spaced stream verticals. Data on particle-size distribution were obtained from samples selected to be representative of a range of sediment discharge and runoff conditions. The average bed material size grading was derived from nine surface layer samples collected near the bed. Previously reported most accurate methods for estimating the transported rate of suspended sediment (Nouh, 1988b) and bed load (Nouh, 1988c) were used.

RESULTS AND DISCUSSIONS

The width "B", depth "D", and bed slope "S" of an infinite straight stable ephemeral channel, having certain water and sediment flow characteristics, were estimated from previously developed relationships (Nouh, 1988a) as

$$B = 28.30 \ (Q_{p50}/Q)^{0.83} + 0.018 \ (1+d)^{0.93} \ C^{1.25} \tag{1}$$

$$D = 1.29 \ (Q_{p50}/Q)^{0.65} - 0.01 \ (1+d)^{0.98} \ C^{0.46} \tag{2}$$

$$S = 18.25 \ (Q_{p50}/Q)^{-0.35} - 0.88 \ (1+d)^{1.13} \ C^{0.36} \tag{3}$$

in which Q_{p50} is the annual peak flowrate for a return period of 50 years in hundreds of m^3/s, Q is the annual mean flood flowrate in hundreds of m^3/s, d is the median size diameter of suspended sediment in mm, and C is the mean concentration of suspended sediment in kg/m.

The dimensions of stable straight ephemeral channels, estimated from the above relationships (Eqs. 1 to 3), have been taken as baselines for studying the variation in the channel dimensions downstream of the investigated dams. The sediment collected at selected locations downstream of the dams were used to study the variation in transported sediment characteristics downstream of dams. The average value of mean concentration of suspended sediment and that of percentage of clay, silt, and sand in the transported suspended sediment are plotted against distance downstream from dam, and shown in Fig. 1.

Inspection of Fig. 1 indicates that:

[1]   Mean concentration of suspended sediment increases as distance downstream from dam increases. This may be explained by the fact that a large amount of sediment is deposited in the reservoir, resulting in water with relatively low concentration of sediment released from the dam. The amount of sediment is released with the stream is much less than the transport capacity of the stream. As a result, the stream erodes the channel bed and banks to supply this deficiency and to maintain between water and sediment flows. As the distance downstream from dams increases the amount of sediment eroded from the channel bed and banks increases, resulting in increasing the mean concentration of the transported suspended sediment.

[2]   The rate of increase in mean suspended sediment concentration decreases as distance downstream from dams increases. This indicates that the rate of sedi-

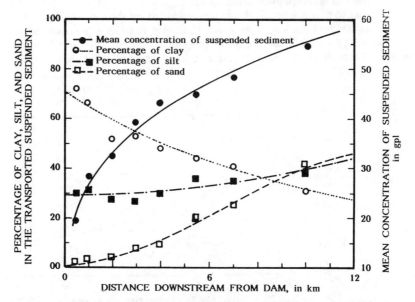

FIG. 1   Average variation of transported suspended sediment composition and concentration with distance downstream from dam.

ment supplied to the stream from channel bed and banks erosion decreases with increase in the distance downstream from the dams. Such rate of sediment supply becomes negligible at a certain distance downstream from the dams, where the amount of transported sediment satisfies the stream carrying capacity.

[3]   The percentage of finer grain sizes in the transported suspended sediment decreases as distance downstream from dam increases. Just downstream from the dams, the transported suspended sediment consisted of only clay and silt. As the stream moved downstream, large grain sizes (such as sand, cobbles, etc.) are eroded from channel bed and banks, and then transported as suspended load under the condition of high velocity and turbulence. When the stream reached its balanced state, at a certain distance downstream from dam, the suspended sediment was found to consist of only clay, silt, and sand. Generally, the percentage of clay decreases, but those of silt and sand in the suspended sediment increase as distance downstream from dam increases. However, the rate of decrease in the clay percentage, followed by the rate of increase in the sand percentage, is larger than the rate of increase in the silt percentage.

The average rate of sediment transported as suspended load and that transported as bed load observed at different cross sections along the distances downstream from the dams are shown in Fig. 2. It can be seen that the rate of transported suspended sediment increases, but that of bed sediment decreases, as distance downstream from dam increases. In addition, the transport rate of bed load is larger than that of suspended load towards the dams, but smaller than that of suspended load far away from the dams. Due to the low concentration of suspended sediment just downstream from dams, the capability of the stream to erode channel bed and banks is too high, resulting in large amount of eroded coarse grain sizes of sediment transported as bed load under the condition of high velocity and turbulence. Far away from the dams, the turbulence level decreases. In addition, the channel adjusts its dimension to accommodate the flow, resulting in velocities having magnitude much less than the velocities just downstream from the dams. Moreover, the capability of the stream to erode the channel bed and banks becomes too low as a result of having high suspended sediment concentration. For these reasons, considerable percentage of the bed load, observed in the reach followed immediately the dams, is deposited on the channel bed. This reduces the bed load transport rate, which was found to have a value far away from the dams smaller than that observed towards the dams.

Due to the variation in the sediment load along the distance downstream of dams, the channel adjusts its dimension, as previously mentioned, to maintain a certain balance between water and sediment flows. The stable channel bed slope, width, depth, and depth to width ratio were measured at selected distances downstream from the dams, and then averaged. These average

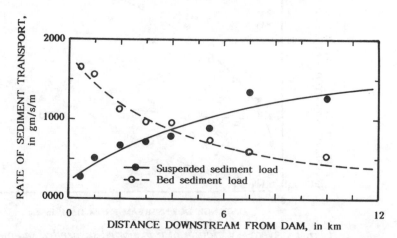

FIG. 2   Average variation of transported sediment rates with distance downstream from dam.

dimensions were divided by the corresponding dimensions of stable infinite straight channels (computed from Eqs. 1 to 3) to yield relative dimensions of stable channels. The relative dimensions of stable channels were plotted against distance downstream from dam, and are shown in Fig. 3.

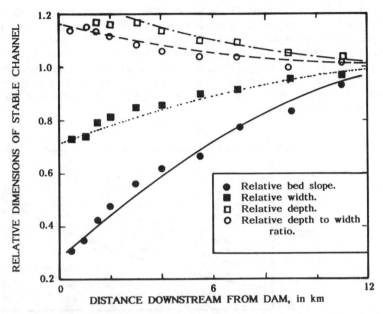

FIG. 3 *Average variation of relative dimensions of stable channels with distance downstream from dam.*

It is apparent from Fig. 3 that:

[1]   The stable bed slope of channel is small in the zone followed immediately the dams, and increases as distance downstream from dam increases. This may be explained by the fact that the large amount of sediment eroded from the channel bed by the relatively pure water released from the dams. As distance downstream from dam increases the eroded sediment from channel bed decreases, resulting in increasing the bed slope. It can be seen that the bed slope approaches the value of the stable slope of infinite straight ephemeral channel at a certain distance downstream from dam. At this distance (referred to as stable distance) the carrying capacity of the stream is satisfied.

[2]   The depth of stable channel is large in the zone followed immediately the dams, and decreases as distance downstream from dam increases. This can be explained by the large rate of channel bed erosion which takes place in this zone, and by the decrease in such erosion along the downstream distance. Again, such stable depth approaches that of stable infinite straight ephemeral channel at the stable distance mentioned above.

[3]   The width of the stable channel increases as distance downstream from dam increases, and approaches the value of the width of stable infinite straight ephemeral channel at the stable distance. This natural adjustment of the channel is due to the variation in the channel depth along the distance, and to maintain balance between flow (including its area) and sediment conditions.

[4]   The depth to width ratio decreases as distance downstream from dam increases. However, such decreases seem not to be significant after a downstream distance in the order of 4.0 km.

From the above results, it is apparent that both water and sediment flow conditions as well as stable channel dimensions, while vary from one cross section to another along the distance downstream from dam, become almost invariant after the stable distance downstream from dam. In the following investigation, a trial has been made to identify such stable distance as a function of flow and sediment characteristics.

Previous investigations (Nouh, 1988b, 1988c, 1989) have indicated that the parameter $(\Delta h/\Delta t)(1/u_*)$ can explain the variation between observed sediment transported during unsteady flow condition and predicted sediment calculated for an equivalent steady flow condition. In this parameter, Δh is the depth variation of a hydrograph over a time interval Δt, and u_* is the shear velocity. Based on the results, and since the stable dimensions of an ephemeral channel vary with water and sediment flow characteristics, one may argue that these stable dimensions, and the stable distance accordingly, depends on this parameter. Fig. 4 shows the variation of this parameter with distance downstream from dam.

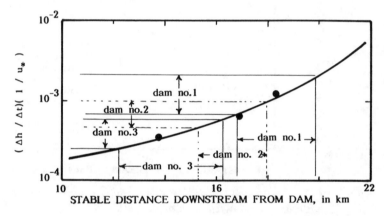

FIG. 4 *Variation of (sh/st) with distance downstream from dam.*

The solid line in Fig. 1 is plotted using data from 17 dams in the southwest region of Saudi Arabia. The range of data collected from each of the investigated dams is also shown in the figure. The range of the stable distances for each dam covers the distance downstream from the dam after which both channel dimensions and flow (water and sediment) characteristics become invariant with the downstream distance. The solid circle represents the average of the data set for the respective dam. Inspection of Fig. 4 indicates that as average depth of hydrograph increases, and/or as the average duration of hydrograph decreases, the stable distance downstream from dam increases.

CONCLUSIONS

Data collected from 3 ephemeral channels were used to investigate the variation in flow parameters and its effects on channel stability downstream annual storage dams. From the results obtained, the following conclusions are made:

[1]   Mean concentration of suspended sediment increases, transport rate of suspended sediment increases, and transport rate of bed sediment decreases as distance downstream from dam increases up to a certain stable distance, after which these sediment parameters become invariant with distance.

[2]   Released sediment from dams consists only of fine particles, which become coarser as distance downstream from dam increases.

[3]   Stable channel width, depth, and bed slope vary with distance downstream from dam up to a certain stable distance, after which these dimensions become invariant with time.

[4]   The stable distance downstream from dam, after which all flow characteristics and
         stable dimensions of channel become invariant with distance, can be related to a
         parameter describing the flow and sediment characteristics.

ACKNOWLEDGEMENTS   This study was supported by King Abdul-Aziz City for Science
and Technology, Saudi Arabian National Water Research Project Numbers AR-2-17 and AR-5-62.

REFERENCES

Leopold, L. B. and Maddock, T. (1953) The hydraulic geometry of stream channels and some
     physiographic implications. Professional Paper No. 252, U.S.G.S.
Nouh, M. and Jamjoom, T. (1981) Transport of sediment in wadis in Saudi Arabia. Final Techni-
     cal Report Prepared for the Saudi Arabian National Center for Science and Technology,
     Riyadh, Saudi Arabia, 113p.
Nouh, M. (1986) Reservoir sedimentation in arid areas. In: River Sedimentation edited by S.Wang,
     H.Shen, and L.Ding (Proc. 3rd International Symp. on River Sedimentation, University of
     Mississippi, USA, April 1986) 1346-1356. UNESCO/University of Mississippi.
Nouh, M. (1988a) Regime channels of an extremely arid zone. In: River Regime edited by
     W.White (Proc. International Conf. on River Regime, Wallingford, England, May 1988), paper
     B2, 55-66. John Wiley & Sons Ltd.
Nouh, M. (1988b) Transport of suspended sediment in ephemeral channels. In: Sediment Budgets
     (Proc. Porto Alegre Symp., December 1988), 97-106. International Association of Hydrologi-
     cal Sciences Publ. no. 174.
Nouh, M. (1988c) Methods of estimating bed load transport rates applied to ephemeral streams.
     In: Sediment Budgets (Proc. Porto Alegre Symp., December 1988), 107-115. International
     Association of Hydrological Sciences Publ. no. 174.
Nouh, M. (1989) Erosion control measures: implementation and effects on processes of reservoir
     sedimentation in arid areas. Proc. 4th International Symp. on River Sedimentation, June
     1989, Beijing, China. IWRA/ International Research and Training Center on Erosion and
     Sedimentation.

The effect of large mountain and Piedmont reservoirs on
the water resources of USSR rivers

V. S. VUGLINSKY
State Hydrological Institute, 199053 Leningrad,
USSR

ABSTRACT Operation of big mountain and piedmont reservoirs with volumes exceeding 1 bln m^3
leads to general water resources changes in
the rivers where these reservoirs are made.
These changes are subdivided into temporary
(observed during the period of reservoir filling and during the first years of its operation) and permanent (observed during the whole
period of reservoir operation). The main types
of temporary water resources changes are runoff losses for filling the permanent pool and
for ground water recharge in bottom and coastal zones. Permanent changes in river runoff
are due to additional water losses for evaporation from the flooded areas and from the
areas around the reservoir where ground water
table tends to rise and due to some water resources compensation at the reach downstream
the reservoir, because of reducing the flooded
areas in case of runoff control. These water
losses are determined for a number of large
mountain and piedmont reservoirs of the USSR
on the basis of the proposed methodological
approaches.

A reservoir as a new water body made in a river basin
affects the water resources of the river, introducing
changes into relationships between water balance components in that portion of the basin which is affected
by the reservoir.
    It has been established that the greatest water re-
sources changes occur when large reservoirs are made in
plain rivers and large adjacent areas are flooded. If a
reservoir is built by producing backwater effect in a
lake in the plain, the water resources changes are insignificant and may be neglected (Anon., 1983; Shiklomanov, 1979). This is valid relative to mountain and piedmont reservoirs as well, though the scales of water
resources changes will be less at the construction of
such reservoirs, which will be shown below. Piedmont
reservoirs are those reservoirs where the mark of the

normal backwater level (NBL) exceeds 200 m above mean
sea level, while mountain reservoirs are those where the
NBL mark exceeds 600 m above mean sea level.

There are temporary and permanent water resources
changes caused by the construction and operation of reservoirs. Temporary changes are observed during particular periods of reservoir construction and operation.
They include runoff losses for filling the permanent
pool of the reservoir and ground water recharge. Permanent water resources changes are those associated with
the additional water losses for evaporation from the
zone of flooding and from the areas around the reservoir
where the rise of ground water table is observed, as well
as those caused by the disturbed natural conditions of
water availability in the channel, floodplain and delta
below the dam in case of runoff control. In the latter
case some water losses are compensated due to lower
evaporation losses from the specified river reaches
because of reducing the flooded areas if compared with
natural conditions.

Most significant compensation occurs due to reduced
flooded areas in the deltas of southern large rivers
affected by reservoirs. In this case the type of the
reservoir does not matter, it may be plain, and piedmont
or mountain reservoir. The nature of runoff control and
the location of the reservoir in the river are most important there. The estimates made show that this compensation ranges within 2 and 3 km^3/year for the Amu Darya
river (normal runoff being 73 km3/year), while it is
about 1.5 km3/year for the Volga river (normal runoff
is 254 km3/year). This value is much lower for the other
large southern rivers with deltas.

The amount of temporary losses for filling the permanent pools of reservoirs depends on the basin morphology and on the elevation mark of the permanent pool
level (PPL), specified from runoff control problems.
The evaluation of water losses for filling permanent
pools of reservoirs may be easily made if we have a
curve of volumes and the data on mean water levels at
the beginning and at the end of the design period. These
estimates made for large piedmont reservoirs of the USSR
of the river type with high-backwater dams (e.g., more
than 70-100 m high) show that the filling of the permanent pools of reservoirs may require 100 and even more
per cent of mean annual river runoff at the site of the
dam. Since such reservoirs operate in the USSR mainly
on the rivers of Siberia and Far East where man's impact
on river runoff is insignificant, the permanent pools
filling may use only 10-20% of the total annual runoff
(for large plain reservoirs this factor does not usually
exceed 1-5%). The filling of the permanent pools of
such reservoirs will be during 5-7 years respectively
(Bratskoje, Viliuyskoje, Zeiskoje, and Ust-Ilimskoje
reservoirs). Large mountain reservoirs with high dams

are mainly built in the south of the USSR in upstream
river reaches; river runoff of such streams, after leaving mountains, is intensively used for irrigation. In
these conditions the filling of permanent pools would
require no more than 1-5% of mean annual runoff every
year. Taking into account that the permanent pools filling usually requires 30-50%, if compared with the volume
of mean annual runoff at the dam gauging site, the period
of this filling may be as long as 10 years and even longer. This is proved by the Nurekskoje reservoir in the
Vakhsh river and Toktogulskoje reservoir in the Naryn
river. As to piedmont reservoirs with dams lower than
50 m, the filling of the permanent pools of such reservoirs would require no more than 5% of mean annual river
runoff.

As mentioned above, temporary water losses connected
with the ground water recharge, include filtration losses
for saturation of the bottom and shores of reservoirs.
Water losses for saturating the reservoir bottom occur
during   the reservoir filling and they are over
soon after (some days or weeks) the filling. These losses
may be computed from the following equation:

$$U_g = F_{PPL}\, H_g\, \mu_g \tag{1}$$

Where: F_{PPL} – the area of the reservoir at PPL; H_g –
mean depth of the aeration zone of the reservoir bottom
before the construction; μ_g – deficit of ground saturation (coefficient of water yield).

Computations made by this formula for the Bratskoje
reservoir (total volume = 169.3 km^3, water surface area
= 5500 km^2) show that water losses for saturation the
bottom are 2.5 km^3 (about 3% of mean annual discharge
of the Angara river at Bratskaya hydroelectric power
plant).

Water losses for filtration into the shores of the
reservoir are significant since the moment of reservoir
filling up to the time when the ground water regime is
steady. The duration of this period for large piedmont
reservoirs may be up to 10 years, in some cases it may
be longer (Razumov, 1984; Anon., 1975). To compute
water losses filtrating into the shores, V.S.Vuglinsky
and S.V.Zavileisky (1989)have developed methodology
based on the use of geofiltration modeling results at
the electric analogue modeling installation with RC-grid.
First developed for large plain reservoirs, this methodology was also a success to evaluate filtration losses
into the shore of reservoirs in the piedmont zone.

To evaluate the position of the depression surface
of the aquifer in the coastal zone of the reservoir
the following equation was applied as the basic design
dependence:

$$\Delta h_1 = \Delta H \left[\sqrt{(\frac{h_p}{\Delta H})^2 + \sqrt{(2L - 1)} \; 1/L - h_p/\Delta H} \right] \quad (2)$$

where: Δh_1 – difference in the marks of ground water levels at the distance of 1 from the water edge in the reservoir (h_1) and at the water edge (h_p); ΔH – difference of ground water level marks at the watershed-divide (H) and at the edge of the reservoir (h_p); L – distance from the reservoir edge up to the watershed-divide. The values of dimensionless coefficient ($\sqrt{}$) in equation (2) are determined for every design reach from the following equation:

$$\sqrt{} = 1 + 2 \; h_p/\Delta H \quad (3)$$

A schematic diagram of the zone for ground water accumulation in the coastal reservoir zone is shown in Fig. 1.

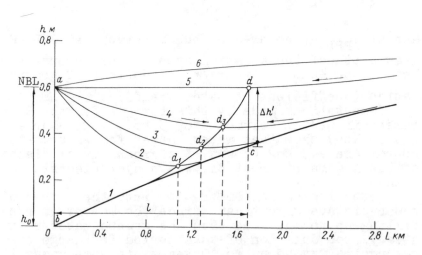

FIG. 1 Diagram for the zone formation of ground water accumulation in the coastal reservoir zone. 1 – position of ground water table (depression curve) before the construction of reservoir; 2,3,4,5 – positions of ground water table at various stages of filling the depression cone; 6 – position of ground water table when filtration from the reservoir is over; d_1, d_2, d_3, d – minimal marks of the depression cone surface; l – width of the zone of ground flow penetration into the reservoir shores.

On the basis of the obtained theoretical dependences and the results of geofiltration modeling the universal graphs were plotted, which made it possible to compute the period during which the recharge of ground water occurred and to compute the projections of the ground water accumulation zone in the coastal zone of the reservoir (for various time intervals) onto a vertical plane f_i. The computation is made by individual cross sections into which the coastal zone is divided.

To obtain data on water volumes flowing into the reservoir shores, the coastal area is divided into a number of blocks covering the areas from the water edge to the watershed-divide. Areas similar by their geohydrological features are taken as individual blocks. The blocks are separated on the basis of the assumption that the first aquifer without head, the nearest one to the surface, is hydraulically connected with the reservoir along the whole coastal line.

The volume of filtration losses is determined for every design i-th block from the following formula:

$$U_i = f_i \, B_i \, \mathcal{M}_i \tag{4}$$

where f_i – area of the projection of the ground water accumulation zone onto a vertical plane; B_i – block width; $\mathcal{M}_i$ – parameter of the gravitational capacity of rocks.

The developed methodology was applied to evaluate water losses for saturating the shores of large piedmont reservoirs with the volumes exceeding 1 km^3. The results of computation are given in Table 1. It is seen in the table that filtration losses usually do not exceed 5% of mean annual runoff of the river at the dam.

Permanent changes of the river water resources after the construction of the reservoir are connected with the change of ratios between the water exchange components in reservoir – river basin system.

To evaluate water losses from the zone flooded by the reservoir (U_f, km^3) for any time interval the following formulas are applied (Vuglinsky, 1981):

$$U_f = 10^{-6} \, (z_w - x + y_f) f d - q f_{p.c.} + c f \quad , \text{ km}^3 \tag{5}$$

$$U_f = 10^{-6} \, (z_w - z_1 - b) f d - q f_{p.c.} + c f \quad , \text{ km}^3 \tag{6}$$

where x – precipitation, mm; z_w and z_1 – evaporation from water surface and from land flooded by reservoir, mm; y_f – runoff which might be formed within the land area flooded by reservoir, mm; f – reservoir surface, km^2; q – water storage changes in the channel network, mm; b – parameter characterizing water changes on the

TABLE 1   Water Losses for Saturation of Shores in Some
          Large Reservoirs of the USSR in Piedmont Zone.

Reservoir	Total volume km^3	NBL mark by the Baltic system	Water losses into reservoir shores	
			volume km^3	in % of mean annual runoff at the dam
Bratskoje	169.3	402.00	4.85	5
Zeiskoje	68.4	315.00	1.60	5
Iriklinskoje	3.3	245.00	0.02	1
Irkutskoje	2.1	457.00	0.15	1
Kapchagaiskoje	28.1	485.00	0.38	2
Chardarinskoje	5.7	252.00	0.33	2

river basin surface and in the zone of aeration within
the reservoir, mm; c – changes in the water volume of
the reservoir due to runoff control, mm; $f_{p.c.}$ –area of
water surface of the river, km^2; α – coefficient of
flooding equaled $\alpha = f_f/f$, where f_f – land area flooded
by reservoir, km^2.
     Relative to a one-year interval for reservoirs,
where the change of water volume cf = 0, equations (5)
and (6) are simplified and characterise river runoff
reduction due to additional evaporation from reservoir
surface (water losses for additional evaporation (Vuglinsky, 1981; Shiklomanov, 1979):

$$U_f = 10^{-6}(z_w - x + y_f)f\alpha ,km^3 \tag{7}$$

$$U_f = 10^{-6}(z_w - z_1)f\alpha \qquad ,km^3 \tag{8}$$

During computations of annual water losses from the
flooded mountain and piedmont reservoirs for which water
balances were made for a long period of time equation
(7) was used. In the rest cases the preference was given
to equation (8) which was more simple than equation (7)
and the number of unknown terms was less.
     Additional water losses from the area around the re-
servoir where ground water table rose (U_{gr}, km^3) were
computed from :

$$U_{gr} = 0.9 \cdot 10^{-6} z_w f_{gr}, \quad km^3 \tag{9}$$

where f_{gr} – area around reservoir where ground water
table rose, km^2.
     The coastal areas of reservoirs around with the
water table of 1 m deep were considered as the zones

where ground water table rose. During the detailed computations of water losses the boundaries of these zones
were determined from the same blocks used for filtration
losses computation into the coastal zone of reservoirs.
To evaluate the distance X from the reservoir edge to
the boundary of the zone with shallow water table the
following equation was used:

$$X = \frac{L^2 + \triangle H \triangle H'}{L (\triangle H' - \triangle H)} \qquad (10)$$

All the parameters in equation (10) are shown in Fig. 2.

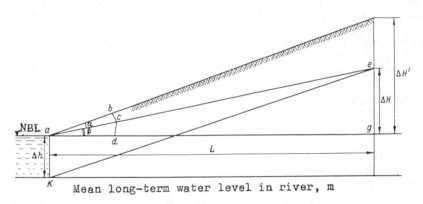

Mean long-term water level in river, m

FIG. 2 Scheme applied to derive equation (10)
to determine the boundaries of the zone with
shallow ground water table.

Section ab is the unknown distance X. Lines ke and ae
characterise the position of ground water tables before
and after reservoir filling. The areas with the shallow
water tables for individual design blocks were determined
with the account of the obtained distances to the boundaries of the zones with shallow water table.
    When computations were made by the simplified scheme,
the area of the zone with shallow water table was determined from the graph of dependence upon the reservoir
water surface at NBL. On the basis of the above methodology mean annual losses of river runoff for additional
evaporation from the flooded areas and from the areas
around with shallow water table of large piedmont and
mountain reservoirs of the USSR were computed. The results of these computations are given in Table 2.

TABLE 2   Water Losses for Evaporation from Flooded Areas
           and from Zones around with Shallow Water Table
           of Large Piedmont and Mountain USSR Reservoirs.

Reservoir	NBL mark by B.S.	f_f km^2	f_{gr} km^2	U_f km^3/yr	U_{gr} km^3/yr	Total losses km^3/yr
Andizhanskoje	808	53	48	0.04	0.03	0.07
Araksinskoje	778	140	60	0.09	0.03	0.12
Bratskoje	402	4100	610	0.29	0.03	0.32
Viliuyskoje	244	1520	890	0.17	0.10	0.27
Zeiskoje	315	2130	180	0.23	0.01	0.24
Iriklinskoje	345	250	160	0.09	0.04	0.13
Kairakkumskoje	347	520	440	0.18	0.11	0.29
Kapchagaiskoje	486	1750	170	1.56	0.13	1.69
Krasnoyarskoje	243	1500	940	0.61	0.32	0.93
Nurekskoje	910	95	10	0.11	0.01	0.12
Sayano-Shushenskoje	540	590	60	0.19	0.02	0.21
Toktogulskoje	905	270	30	0.20	0.02	0.22
Tyuyamuyunskoje	1110	740	620	0.78	0.58	1.36
Ust-Ilimskoje	296	1830	200	0.18	0.01	0.19
Chardarinskoje	252	860	250	0.86	0.22	1.08
Charvakskoje	890	38	4	0.02	–	0.02

REFERENCES

Anon. (1975) Filtratsia iz vodokhranilishch i prudov
    (Filtration from reservoirs and ponds) ed.by N.N.
    Verigin. Kolos, Moscow, USSR.
Anon. (1983) Rukovodstvo po gidrologicheskim raschetam
    pri proektirovanii vodokhranilishch (Guide for hydro-
    logical computation of reservoir projects). Gidro-
    meteoizdat, Leningrad, USSR.
Razumov, G.A. (1984) Pod'em urovnia podzemnykh vod v
    pribrezhnoi zone vodokhranilishch (Rise of ground
    water table in the coastal reservoir zone). Vodnye
    resursy(6), 41–47.
Shiklomanov, I.A. (1979) Antropogennye izmenenia vodnosti
    rek (Anthropogenic changes in water availability of
    rivers). Gidrometeoizdat, Leningrad, USSR.
Vuglinsky, V.S. (1981) K voprosu o metodike ucheta vlia-
    nia vodokhranilishch na rechnoi stok (On methodology
    of inventory reservoirs effect on river runoff).
    Trudy GGI, (274), 73–85.
Vuglinsky, V.S., Zavileisky, S.V. (1989) Metodika otsen-
    ki filtratsyonnykh poter v beregovuyu zonu vodokhra-
    nilishch (Methodology for evaluation of filtration
    losses into the coastal reservoir zone). Meteorolo-
    gia i gidrologia, (6), 95–102.

Hydrology in Mountainous Regions. II - Artificial Reservoirs; Water and Slopes
(Proceedings of two Lausanne Symposia, August 1990). IAHS Publ. no. 194, 1990.

Downstream hydrological effects of reservoirs built in mountainous areas and their environmental influences

XU JIONGXIN
Institute of Geography, Chinese Academy of
Sciences, Beijing 100012, China

ABSTRACT This paper deals with the changes in
the hydrological characteristics of plain
rivers after the construction of reservoirs in
upstream mountainous areas of the Haihe River,
China. These changes not only result in the
change in river channel shape, but also
influence the plain environment as a whole,
including the influences on sediment accumulation rate in the plain, on groundwater regime
and salt balance in soils and on the ecological
environment of rivers and lakes.

INTRODUCTION

The construction of reservoirs in a mountainous area
changes the input of the rivers running from the mountains
into the plain. This leads to changes not only in the
rivers themselves, but also in the environment of the
plain as a whole. In fact these changes reflect the process
in which the plain physico-geographical system adjusts its
sub-systems to a new balance after interfered by human
activities. In this study, an attempt has been made to
deal with such a process, with the Haihe River as an
example. The sudy area is shown in Fig. 1.

CHANGES IN THE HYDROLOGICAL REGIME OF THE RIVERS

The Haihe-Luanhe River basin has an area of 318162 km^2, of
which 189722 km^2 are located in mountainous areas. Up to
1982, 134 large- and moderate-scale reservoirs have been
constructed in the mountainous areas of the river basin,
with the total capacity of 2.34 X 10^{10} m^3, 1.117 times as
much as the mean annual total runoff from the mountainous
part of the river basin. Obviously the river's hydrological regime will be regulated by these reservoirs to a
great degree. Most of the reservoirs were built in the
late 1950s or early 1960s. From the construction of the
reservoirs to the late 1960s, the regulation of the river's
hydrological regime in the plain by the reservoirs can be
characterized as reducing peak flow, increasing low water
discharge and therefore making the runoff distribution

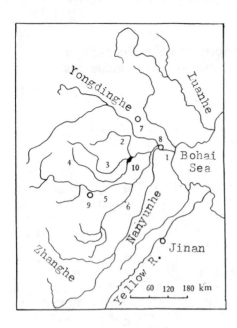

Fig. 1 Location map of
      study area
1. Haihe R. 2. Daqinghe
R. 3. Dasha-Zhulonghe R.
4. Tanghe R. 5. Hutuohe
R. 6. Fuyanghe R.
7. Beijing 8. Tianjin
9. Shijiazhuang
10. Baiyangdian Lake
    Sometimes the Haihe
River basin and the
Luanhe River basin are
taken as one drainage
basin called the
Haihe-Luanhe River basin.

Fig. 1 location map of study area.

uniform. For example, after the construction of the Guanting Reservoir on the upper Yongding River,the runoff
percentage of the high water months (from June to September) for the downstream river reaches was reduced from
65.7 % in the pre-dam period to 57.1 %, but the runoff
percentage of the low water months (from October to May)
increased from 34.3 % to 42.9 %, and the variation coefficient of monthly runoff decreased from 1.01 to 0.67. Since
the early 1970s, with the development of agriculture and
industry, the water consumption has been increasing sharply, causing an increasingly serious water shortage. As a
result the natural hydrological process of rivers in the
Haihe River alluvial plain has been altered thoroughly,
and these rivers dry up in most days of a year (up to
200-300 days per year for many rivers) and the originally
permanent rivers become temperary ones.

One of the most serious effects of human activities
upon rivers in the Haihe River plain is the sharp reduction
in river runoff. We introduce the index R_r to express the
relative reduction of the runoff, which is defined as
$(R_n-R_m)/R_n$ where R_n and R_m are the natural runoff and
measured runoff respectively. Based on the data from the
Hutuohe River at Huangbizhuang station just downstream the
Huangbizhuang Reservoir, the index R_r has been plotted
against time in Fig.2, which shows that after the construction of the reservoir in 1959 the R_r value increases
continuously.

The reduction of the plain rivers' runoff can be
attributed to three factors, namely, the increase in the

net water consumption by irrigation in mountainous areas, the decrease in runoff yield from the plain and the water loss in reservoirs through evaporation. Among the three factors the last is the least one. According to the measurements from 14 reservoirs, the mean annual evaporation loss is 1.2 × 10^8 m^3 totally, making 2.24 % of the outflow from these reservoirs (Gong and Xu, 1987).

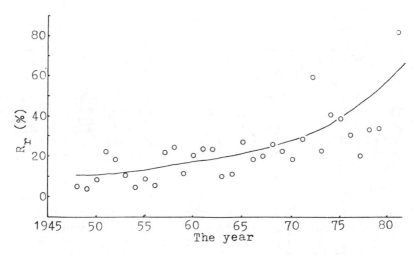

Fig. 2 Temporal variation in the relative reduction of runoff (R_r) at Huangbizhuan station of the Hutuohe River.

Fig. 3 shows how rapidly the net water consumption by irrigation in the mountainous areas increases after the construction of the reservoirs. From the early 1960s to early 1970s, this amount increased by 60 % and in general it makes 11.5 % of the total runoff from the mountainous part of the Haihe River basin. But for dry years this percentage can be very high.

Due to the construction of reservoirs in mountainous areas, the groundwater stage in the plain declines continuously, -- the reason for this will be discussed later, -- leading to a greatly increased infiltration and therefore a sharp reduction of runoff from the plain. So it is very difficult for the river to get water supply from plain areas. The temporal variation in the runoff coefficient of the plain drainage area between Huangbizhuang and Beizhongshan stations of the Hutuohe River has been plotted in Fig. 4, showing a marked decline after the reservoir construction. For instance, the annual precipitation in 1977 was 723 mm, but the runoff yield from this plain area was only 28.6 mm and the runoff coefficient was as low as 0.04 (Liu et al., 1989).

Because the reservoirs intercept the runoff from mountainous areas and the runoff yield from plain areas

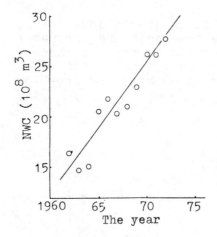

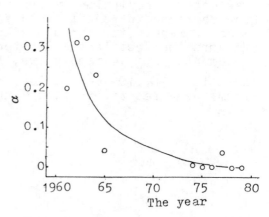

Fig. 3 Temporal variation in the net water consumption by irrigation in mountainous areas (NWC) of the Haihe-Luanhe River.

Fig. 4 Temporal variation in the runoff coefficient (α) of the Hutuohe River between Huangbizhuang and Beizhong-shan stations.

decreases markedly and water consumption by human activities increases continuously, the river runoff poured into the sea will inevitably decline. We express the relative amount of runoff poured into the sea as $R_s = V_s/P$ where V_s is the river runoff poured into the sea and P the annual precipitation, and plot R_s against time in Fig. 5. Although the data points are rather scattered, a mild tendency towards decreasing can be discerned.

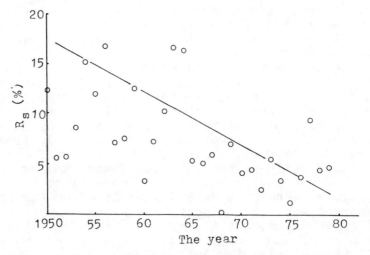

Fig. 5 Temporal variation in the relative runoff poured into the sea based on the Haihe-Luanhe River.

CHANGES IN SEDIMENT ACCUMULATION IN THE PLAIN

Before the reservoir construction the sediment accumulation
rate of the Haihe River alluvial plain was rather high,
because most of the tributaries of the Haihe River were
heavily sediment laden rivers (e.g. the Yongdinghe River's
mean annual suspended sediment concentration at Guanting
station was 60.8 kg/m^3). After the reservoir construction
most of the sediment supplied by the mountainous areas has
been trapped by reservoirs and therefore the material
available for plain building is reduced markedly, leading
to a much lower plain building rate than before. According
to the measurements from 16 large-scale reservoirs, up to
1983, 1.25 X 10^9 m^3 sediment has been deposited in these
reservoirs. Assuming that the average operation time for
them is 25 years and 80 % of the sediment carried by the
river was deposited in the river bed or on the plain
before the reservoir construction, the result of calculation shows that the sediment trapping of reservoirs has
reduced the plain building rate by 0.54 mm/yr. Additionally
the material deposited on the flood-plain becomes coarser
and contains much less nutrient-rich fine sediments (e.g.
analysis shows that one tonne loessic sediment in this area
contains nitrogen 1.0 kg, phosphorus 1.5 kg and potassium
20 kg), and as a result the soil fertility of flood-plain
declines.
    The sediment trapping of reservoirs also influences
the lakes in the plain. Take the Baiyangdian Lake as an
example.According to the measurements made in the reservoirs built in the upper part of the lake's drainage basin,
the total sediment volume deposited in the reservoirs up to
1983 is 1.3 X 10^8 m^3, almostly the same as the lake's capacity at normal water stage which is 1.26 x 10^8 m^3. It is
thus evident that the reservoirs greatly slow down the
sediment accumulation rate in the Baiyangdian Lake and
thereby prolong the lake's lifetime. But on the other hand,
the reservoirs reduce sharply the water quantity poured
into the lake, leading to some infavourable effects on the
lake's ecological environment.

CHANGES IN RIVER CHANNEL PROCESS AND **THE** CONSEQUENCY

From 1950s to 1960s, clear water was released from reservoirs with an approximately constant discharge, and thereby
the channels of plain rivers were cut down. Since 1970s,
however, most of the plain rivers dry up for a longer or
shorter time in a year, and therefore the major channel-
forming force has turned from permanent streamflow to
temporary water flow and wind. Accordingly, the dominant
channel process has been turned from downcutting of channel
to within-channel deposition. Due to a marked transmission
loss of water, the flood released from the reservoir tends
to increase its sediment concentration and eventually

deposition occurs. Due to a coarser composition of material
and a poorer vegetation cover on flood-plain than before,
the along-river zones are more easy to be eroded by wind
during winter and spring months which is perpendicular to
river channels. So huge quantities of sands are carried
by wind from bars and flood-plain to the river channel and
deposit there. Since 1970s, climate in the river basin is
a little bit drier than 1960s and the runoff is highly
regulated by reservoirs, so the opportunities for flood
occurrence in plain rivers become much fewer. As a result
the land of flood-plain and point-bars has been brought
under cultivation and tree-planting, and even used for
construction of new villages. For these purposes, new dikes
have been built along the river, making the channel much
narrower. All these increase greatly the roughness of the
river channel and reduce its cross-sectional area at a
given water level, giving rise to a marked reduction in
the river's flood-releasing capacity. According to the
investigation made in 1985, of the totally 3040 km long
plain river reaches of the Haihe River and its tributaries,
48.6 % can no longer meet the designed flood-protection
standards which were once met after the river channel
training in the early 1960s. If climate in the river basin
turns to a wetter cycle, the potential of flood threat
will be very high. So measures are urgently needed to take
in the Haihe plain to solve such problems.

CHANGES IN GROUNDWATER STAGE AND THE CONSEQUENCY

Due to the sharply reduced water discharge of plain rivers
and their drying-up, the pre-existing hydraulic links and
balance between streamflow and groundwater are broken down.
Studies show that during the period 1962-1972, 60.2×10^8
m^3 water was annually supplied by rivers for groundwater
through water seepage, making 31.6 % of the yearly total
runoff of plain rivers. After the rivers dry up, this
amount will be reduced to a great extent. But the most
important factor responsible for groundwater stage lowering
is the man's pumping of groundwater in this plain, which
reaches the magnitude of 100×10^8 m^3 per year. As a result
many depressions form on the groundwater surface, with a
total area of 27800 km^2 which makes 18.5 % the Haihe
plain's area.

Take the groundwater surface depression near Shijiazhuang as an example. The formation of the depression has
been studied in relation with human activities, and the
following empirical equation has been obtained:
$$H = 67.99 - 0.0005156 Q_p - 0.008816 Q_r$$
where H is the yearly average groundwater stage at the
center of the depression in m above sea level, Q_p the
yearly groudwater quantity pumped in $10^4 m^3$ and Q_r the
cumulative reduction in the Hutuohe River's runoff at
Huangbizhuang station since the reservoir construction,

which is defined as the cumulative value of the difference
between the yearly natural runoff and the measured runoff
at the gaging station, in 10^4 m^3. The equation is based on
the data during the period 1965-1975, with a multiple
regression coefficient of 0.99.

On one hand, the lowered groundwater stage makes a
poorer vegetation cover which is not able to protect the
land surface from wind erosion, so soils alongside the
river become more sandy, with the land productivity
decreased. The area of the land susceptable to wind erosion tends to increase. On the other hand, it has been
found that the lowered groundwater stage suppresses the
process of soil salinization in the plain to a great
degree. In the early 1960s, the salinized land in the
Haihe plain was 163100 ha, but in the early 1980s, the
salinized land was reduced to 339000 ha, 79.2 % less than
that in the former case. This is mainly because that after
the construction of reservoirs the groundwater level in most
areas of the plain has been lowered below the critical level
at which salinization occurs. For instance, the groundwater
stage near the Yongdinghe River is 2-4 m, near the Daging-
he River is 4-6 m and near the Hutuohe River is 3-8 m
below the land surface. Consequently, the salt accumulation process has been substituted by a process of salt
leaching. As mentioned earlier, due to the lowered
groundwater stage, rainfall infiltration has been greatly
enhanced, leading to a dominant tendency of downward
migration of salts, which is conducive to desalinization
in this plain.

However, when we deal with the same problem from a
macroscopic viewpoint, we should point out a significant
salt accumulation tendency concerning the salt balance in
this plain as a whole. The sharply decreased river runoff
poured into the sea has weakened the horizontal migration
of salts to a marked extent. According to the data from
the Hebei province, the river runoff poured into the sea
during the period 1952-1965 was 2.10 x 10^{10} m^3 per year,
but during the period 1966-1979 it was only 1.01 x 10^{10} m^3
per year. Since the mean annual salt concentration of
river water poured into the sea is 545 mg/l, this reduction
means that compared with the former case, the salt accumulation in this plain is 5940000 t/yr more. This also means
that the salt accumulation in the latter case is 68
t/km /yr more than that in the former case. Obviously, this
is a potential environmental problem which should not be
ignored.

CHANGES IN ECOLOGICAL ENVIRONMENT OF RIVERS AND LAKES

Since the reservoir construction in mountainous areas leads
to a pronounced reduction in the runoff of plain rivers,
and in the mean time the sewage poured into rivers increases
rapidly with the development of agriculture and industry,
the river water quality has been deteriorating increasingly.

The sewage poured into the Haihe and Luanhe Rivers and
their tributaries is 3.67 x 10⁹ m³ per year, which makes
12.5 % of the annual total river runoff. During the months
when the plain rivers dry up, they become the channel for
sewage entirely. According to the investigation in 1979,
the organically-polluted river reaches of the Haihe and
Luanhe Rivers made 79 % of the total river length evaluated, and the poison-polluted river reaches made 54% of
the total length, and among them the seriously polluted
reaches made 39 % of the total length.

Consequently the ecological environment   has been
affected to a great degree. On one hand, the reduced water
storage of the lake makes the "living space" for aquatic
living things much smaller; on the other, the increasing
pollutants poison their living conditions. Take the
Baiyangdian Lake. After the reservoir construction the
mean annual incoming water of the lake has been reduced
from 2.065 x 10⁹ m³ to 7.2 x 10⁸ m³, the average water
storage reduced from 3.452 x 10⁸ m³ to 1.44 x 10⁸ m³, and
the water surface area of the lake reduced from 277.3 km²
to 160.5 km². After the reservoir construction the lake
has dried up for 6 times. The sewage poured into the lake
is 1.16 x 10⁸ t/yr. As a result, the fishes in the lake
have reduced from 16 families and 54 species to 12 families
and 35 species, and the planktons reduced from 129 species
to 29 species. The fishery yield of the lake also declines
sharply. During the period 1949-1965, the mean annual
fishery yield of the lake was 5325 t, but during the
period 1965-1978, it declined to 436 t, 79.5 % lower than
that in the former period.

REFERENCES

Gong, G. Y. and Xu, J. X. (1987) Environmental effects of
    human activities on rivers in the Huanghe-Huaihe-Haihe
    Plain, China. Geografisca Annaler 69A (1), 181-188.
Liu, C. M. et al. (1989) Agricultural Hydrology and Water
    Resources in the North China Plain. Science Press,
    Beijing, 236 pages (in Chinese).

TOPIC D:
ECOLOGICAL EFFECTS AND FISHERY PROBLEMS RELATED TO RESERVOIRS

Water flow regime as the driving force for the formation of habitats and biological communities in Alpine rivers

U. BUNDI, E. EICHENBERGER & A. PETER, Swiss Federal Institute for Water Resources and Water Pollution Control (EAWAG), CH-8600 Dübendorf

ABSTRACT The ecological consequences of water diversion were studied in three Swiss rivers. River habitat and biology were strongly altered, primarily because of moderated highwater discharges and reduced low water flow. To fulfill the ecological objectives of Switzerland's Water Protection Law the typical characteristics of the water flow regime should be maintained. The capactiy of water diversion has to be limited to some Q_{100} and minimal water flow shall not be lower than Q_{300} (except in dry periods).

INTRODUCTION

Hydropower generation may cause various types of interferences with rivers and creates manyfold physical and chemical alterations relevant to the biology of the rivers (table 1). This poses the following questions:

(a) What are the consequences of altering the river conditions on the biological communities?

(b) In which way should the interferences with the rivers be adapted to ensure minimal ecological damage?

TABLE 1 Activities in hydropower generation and their physical and chemical effects on running waters.
A Primary effects
B Secondary effects (as a consequence of primary effects).

Physical and chemical effects of activity	Type of activity				
	Water diversions	Grit remover operation	Water return	Water storage	Hydraulic constructions
Change of flow regime	A	(A)	A		
Change of flow Conditions	B		B		A
Change of solids transport regime	B	A	B	A	(B)
Alteration of chemistry and temperature of water and sediments	B		B	A	
Size reduction and/or structural change of habitat	B	B	B		B

The above questions were studied in 1987/88 in the threee Swiss rivers Töss (Canton Zurich), Schächenbach(Canton Uri) and Niemet (Canton Graubünden). From all these rivers water is diverted for hydroelectric power generation. Biological, physical and chemical investigations were carried out above (= reference section) and below (= minimal flow section) the water diversions (see Bundi & Eichenberger, 1989). Table 2 shows some characteristics of the study objects.

    This paper concentrates on the ecological consequences of water abstraction. The other types of activities like water return or grit removal operation, also they may strongly influence the river biocenosis, will not be treated.

TABLE 2 Characteristics of the investigated rivers .

Discharge Values m³/s	Toess		Schaechen		Niemet	
	Reference section	Minimal flow section	Minimal flow section		Reference section	Minimal flow section
			Natural discharge	Actual discharge values		
Average flow MQ	4.2	2.5	3.7	1.2	0.5[1)]	unknown
Q_{300}	1.0	0.35	1.0	0.4		
Q_{347}	0.6	0.0	0.8	0.4	0.05[1)]	unknown
Altitude of water intake point (m)	500		987		1950	
Max. water-diversion m³/s	4.5		5.75		unknown	
Water dosage to minimal flow section m³/s	practically 0		0		0	
Area of river basin km²	150		60		10	
Special characteristics of the minimal water flow section	Zero discharge during 20-30 days per year		Is being fed just below the water intake point by constant inflows from groundwater		Is being fed below the water intake point by small tributaries	

[1)] Discharges in the Niemet river are not known and therefore estimated.

RIVER-HABITAT CHARACTERISTICS AND THEIR DEPENDENCE ON FLOW REGIME

The living space of the water organisms in alpine rivers is characterized by four main factors:

(a)   physical structure of the river such as course, slope, character of the river bed;
(b)   flow regime (variation of discharge in time);
(c)   chemical conditions in water and sediments;
(d)   temperature (variations in time and along the river).

The more one of these factors is extreme the more it will play a dominant role for the development of the biocenosis. This is for instance the case in polluted water for the chemical conditions . The flow regime plays a key role since it strongly influences the other factors and thus the variations of the living conditions such as structure of river bed, sedimentation of fine particles, chemical conditions at the sediment-water-interface, flow conditions, temperature, etc.

The river beds consist of one or several elements like blank rock, big boulders, coarse gravel, fine gravel, sand, mud, algae colonies and colonies of macrophytes. The relative presence of the different elements makes out the specific habitat-character at a given place in a given time. The lower the flow-velocity is and the less often highwaters occur, the more fine material is deposited and the more algae and macrophytes are likely to grow. This is why an artificial moderation of the discharge dynamics will result in changes of the river-habitat and as a consequence in changes of the biocenosis depending on this habitat.

LIFE IN ALPINE RIVERS AND ITS DEPENDENCE ON FLOW REGIME

The main groups of river-organism

The variety of organisms living in alpine rivers may, in a simplified manner, be divided into the following four main groups:

(a)   Heterotrophic microorganisms such as bacteria, lower fungi and protozoa which grow on the river bottom and play an important role in modifying the chemical substrates, especially in mineralizing the organic substances in the river water. They are mainly responsible for the so-called self-purification of rivers.

(b)   Algae, primitive plants, usually growing on stones, as thin and crusty layers or as filamentous more or less floating formations.

(c)   The so-called macroinvertebrates, mainly insects, whose larval stages live in the water. As winged insects they leave the water and mate in the air. They deposit their eggs again in the water.

(d)   Fish, which are feeding to a large extent on macroinvertebrates (and in summer also on terrestrial insects dropped into the water).

The occurrence and the development of these diverse organisms are regulated by the living conditions in the river and the complex interdependence between the organisms.

Algae and macroinvertebrates

In alpine rivers the main animal biomass consists in general of invertebrates, that is worms, small crustaceae and insects. Most insects in fast flowing water are in their larval stage. After a development time lasting according to species from a few months up to 3 years the larvae metamorphose to winged adults who mate and then lay their eggs into the water. Therefore the immediate terrestrial environment is essential for aquatic life.

The animals of alpine rivers show a large number of adaptations in morphology and behaviour to current. The feeding behaviour for example is highly specialized; some eat only small algae forming a thin crust on stones, others can feed on filaments of larger algae and on mosses, some catch with various filter mechanisms small organic particles such as algae and detritus. In addition there are the hunters or predators who feed on other invertebrates. Changes in food supply have serious consequences. For example an excessive supply in fine particles will clog up the filter mechanisms, the spread of filamentous algae will disloge the small crustose algae thus destroying the food basis for whole groups of animals

The modification of the flow regime will affect the aquatic invertebrates in many ways. Foremost are the changes of habitat as for instance the reduction of frequency and intensity of highwater events, the smoothing of the flow velocities, the reduction of habitat size, the erosion of fine material, the depletion of oxygen in the sediments and seasonal changes of water temperature.

The observed scarcity of the vegetation in mountain rivers is in general not the consequence of a low nutrient content, but results from the scouring action of floods. For this reason any regulation of the discharge resulting in the suppression of the scouring action of the water will give algae the opportunity to grow according to nutrient, temperature and light conditions. The better the conditions for the growth of algae, the deeper the change in the composition of the invertebrate fauna to be expected.

Life-cycle of brown trout as an example of specific flow requirements of an alpine river organism (see table 3)

Spawning and incubation are the most sensitive stages for population survival. Females deposit their eggs in pockets that they have excavated in clean gravel (October-December). Preferred gravel size is between 6 and 76 mm.

TABLE 3 Life-cycle of brown trout.

	Life stage
Spawning, fertilization and incubation (October-December) prior to spawning flushing flows are needed	Fertilized egg ↓
Incubated in gravel	Embryo ↓
Hatching between February and April (high oxygen demand)	Alevin ↓
Emergence from gravel, beginning of feeding, territorial behaviour accompanied by high mortality rates (April-May)	Fry ↓
Yolk sac is absorbed, living in juvenile habitats (riffles) early summer /.summer	Parr ↓
Growth, movement to deeper areas	Juvenile trout ↓
Males ripe at 2 years, females ripe at 3 years, migration to spawning grounds	Reproductive trout

Deposited fine sediment can adversely affect trout rearing habitat. Fine sediment (< 5 mm) should not exceed 20-25% of total substrate (during spawning, incubation and emergence). Flushing flows remove fines from spawning grounds. Eggs and alevins need a high concentration of dissolved oxygen (for newly hatched fish: > 7 mg O_2/l) and good permeability of the gravel bed. Hatching occurs between February and April. Newly-hatched fish (alevins) remain in the gravel and depend on their yolk sac. After depletion of the yolk sac (March-May) trout emerge from the gravel, start to feed and display strong territorial behaviour. They are still dependent on clean gravel-substrate.

After growing for a few weeks, in order to avoid competition by larger fish, trout segregate to riffles (shallow, fast flowing areas), which are often restricted by flow reductions. But the most obvious reduction by minimal water flow is observed for adult habitat areas and pools. Larger trout depend highly on cover and show preference for deeper areas (pools). Cover for adult fish is often reduced in the minimal water flow section. Several works showed that salmonid abundance declined when cover was reduced (Boussu 1954, Elser 1968). Nickelson and Reisenbichler (1977) and Nickelson (1976) suggested that a definite relationship exists between cover area and carrying capacity for fish.

Flow regime has to be variable and adjusted to the requirements of different life-stages of fish. Increased flow is especially necessary in spring and early summer when fish are emerging and moving to juvenile habitats.

Impact of minimal water stream flow situations on fish

Lowering stream flow affects trout populations in different ways. Dams and places from which water is diverted create physical barriers to the movement of adult and juvenile fish. River regulation will often interrupt the stream continuum. Reductions of water flow can have significant adverse effects on fish and their habitat (decrease of total habitat area, destruction of certain habitat types). All habitat components can be concerned: spawning grounds, nursery and rearing areas, food supply areas and migration sections. In order to complete their life-cycle trout depend on all of these habitat components.

The main macrohabitat parameters for trout are flow, temperature, water quality and channel structure. Due to reduction of flow an increase of stream temperature occurs especially in late spring, summer and early fall. Trout prefer a narrow temperature range and growth can be highly affected by increased temperatures.

As a result of a decrease in transport capacity of the river in the minimal water flow sections, algae and organic depositions cover the stream bed and reduce water exchange. One can assume that water chemistry in the substrate is changed by this organic layer. To prevent a negative impact on spawning grounds and incubation areas, flushing flows have to be released prior to spawning in order to remove fine sediments and algae from downstream spawning habitats.

Dramatical changes of the microhabitat components (depth, velocity, substrate and cover) by water diversion may have severe consequences for fish populations. Habitat degradation is followed by a decrease in fish numbers and often by a loss of natural reproduction. Destroyed spawning grounds may prevent completion of the trout's life cycle. However, from the population genetics' point of view stocking of young trout is no substitute for any natural trout population.

STUDY RESULTS

In our study the following impacts were observed (see table 4):
(a)   Temperature: In the minimal stream flow section of the Toess River an increase of temperature of more than 3°C between May and September was observed. In the

TABLE 4 Effects of water diversion on water organism in fall.

	Toess		Schaechen		Niemet	
	Reference section	Min. flow section	Reference section	Min. flow section	Reference section	Min. flow section
Sampling date for invertebrates and plant cover	21.9.87		26.10.87		15.9.87	
Average discharge (m^3/s) during the 10 days prior to sampling	1.0	0.50	0.9[1]	0.50	0.5[2]	0.06[2]
plant cover	Gravel bed almost completely covered with algae and detritus. Coverage in minimum water flow section clearly greater		Coverage of the stone blocks in % of their total surface		Coverage of the river bed with algae in % of total surface of river bed	
			5-25%	75-100%	25-50%	almost 100%
Macro-invertebrates[4]						
- number of individuals/m^2	13'732	2'659	1'067	1'910	-	-
- number of individuals/sample	-	-	-	-	67	445
- proportion of the different groups in % of the total number of individuals						
noninsects	1	2	1	1	3	7
ephemeroptera	11	6	41	8	72	11
plecoptera	5	4	22	8	16	5
coleoptera	3	3	0	0	0	0
diptera	80	84	29	80	9	77
trichoptera	0	1	7	3	0	0
total	100	100	100	100	100	100
Fish						
- density in kg/100 m river length	15.1	8.1	2.8 [3]	2.4 [3]	5.3	2.2
in kg/ha	19.4	62.3	29.9	38.1	64.7	55.2

[1] The reference section is situated in the "Vorder Schaechen" (upper Schaechen), whose discharge is less than half the discharge of the Schaechen. The 0.9 m^3/s on the Vorder Schaechen would correspond to about 2m^3/s in the minimal water flow section if there was no water diversion.

[2] Discharge at the time of sampling.

[3] The fish populations in the Schaechen are not comparable; trout (Salmo gairdneri) in the reference section, brown trout (Salmo truta) in the minimum water flow section.

[4] Macroinvertebrates in the gravel bed.

Schaechen River the reference and the minimal water flow sections showed a totally different temperature regime. The water in the minimal water flow section originated mainly from groundwater below the water diversion.

(b)   Water chemistry: No relevant modification in the free water of the minimal stream flow sections was measured. However, water chemistry was not analyzed in the gravel bed, where macroinvertebrates live and trout eggs are incubated. If one takes into consideration the increased density of algae, a modification of water chemistry in the gravel bed of the minimal stream flow section may be expected.

(c)   Habitat: In all of the three minimal stream flow sections an increase of small size substrate (< 30 mm) was observed. This is mainly a function of the decreased transport capacity. In Niemet River total cover area for adult trout was reduced by 4 times, in Toess River by about 3 times. All riffle habitats (mainly used by young of the year trout to avoid competition by adults trout) disappeared. To survive in the minimal flow section young trout were forced to use the same cover types as adult fish (pool civer). In Toess River there has been no flow at all for about 20-30 days per year.

(d)   Impacts on organism communities: During fall and after periods with no flood all sections with minimal water flow showed an increase in the density of algae. Parallel to the shift in algal growth there were, at some periods of the year, changes in the composition of the macroinvertebrate fauna. In fall, for example, in Schaechen and Niemet River a basic change in the composition of invertebrate fauna occurred. The dominating families (stoneflies - Plecoptera and mayflies - Ephemeroptera) were scarce below the water diversion. They were replaced by midges (Chironomidae), which are adapted to live in algal mats. Moreover, in Toess River even these midges could not tolerate the very dense sludge being built up in the minimal water flow section, and midges-density decreased to about 20% (to that in the reference section).

As fish communities in the study sections of Schaechen River were managed with different species, they could not be compared. For the two other rivers an obvious decrease of trout biomass was detected in the minimal stream flow sections. In Niemet River trout biomass was reduced 2.4 times (from 5.3 kg per 100 m stream-length to 2.2 kg per 100 m) and in Toess River 1.9 times (from 15.1 kg per 100 m to 8.1 kg per 100 m). Reproduction, one of the major phases in the trout life cycle, was endangered or even impossible in minimal stream flow sections. Reproductive success generally declined clearly with increasing amounts of fines that were observed in our minimal water flow sections.

CONCLUSIONS: ECOLOGICAL REQUIREMENTS FOR WATER FLOW REGIME

Ecological objectives

To what degree will we allow a river biocenosis to be altered as a consequence of the modification of the water flow regime? To be able to answer this most difficult question one has to refer to clear ecological objectives. Such are given by the Water Protection Law of Switzerland (in the Ordinance for Waste Water Discharge). These uncontestable objectives, originally formulated for water pollution control, are generally valid and have thus to be applied for the case of water diversion too. They state that:

(a)   No excessive and unnatural growth of algae and aquatic macrophytes shall occur.

(b)   The animal biota of the river shall present the typical composition observed under the natural conditions of a given river.

(c)   The naturally occurring fish populations shall be able to exist. Their natural reproduction is to be guaranteed. The age-structure of the fish populations shall not be altered and the fish density not substantially be reduced.

Minimal Flow Requirements

In order to meet the ecological objectives the typical characteristics of the water flow regime are to be maintained. First of all this means that highwater events shall not substantially be reduced, neither in frequency nor in intensity of the singular events. This is the basic conclusion resulting from the studies presented here.

An adequate minimal water flow has always to be maintained except in periods with natural low flow. This minimal flow shall guarantee that the basic habitat needs of the water organism be fulfilled. Thus, the minimal water flow requirement has to be of the order of that natural discharge which is occurring most often during a year. In Switzerland the "most likely discharge" usually lies somewhere around Q_{300}.

In addition higher discharges are necessary in spring and early summer. In this period natural high discharges occur which are most important for the development of juvenile fish and to which water biocenosis in general is adapted. As already mentioned, additional highwater events (flush flows) during all the year are necessary to clean the river bottom from fines and plant cover built up in low water flow periods.

Ecologically adequate highwater conditions can best be achieved by limiting the capacity of water diversion to some Q_{100}.

REFERENCES

Boussu, M.F. (1954)Relationship between trout populations and cover on a small stream. J. Wildl. Management 18, 277-239.

Bundi, U. &. Eichenberger, E. (1989) Wasserentnahme aus Fliessgewässern: Gewässerökologische Anforderungen an die Restwasserführung. Schriftenreihe Umweltschutz Nr. 110, Bundesamt für Umwelt, Wald und Landschaft, Bern, 50 p.

Elser, A. (1968) Fish populations of a trout stream in relation to major habitat zones and channel alterations. Trans. Am. Fish. Soc. 97, 389-397.

Nickelson, T. (1976) Development of methodologies for evaluating instream flowneeds for Salmonid rearing, 588-596. In: Osborn, J.F. & C.H. Allmann, editors. Instream Flow Needs, vol. II, Am. Fish. Soc., Spec. Publ.

Nickelson, T.E. & Reisenbichler, R.R. (1977) Stream flow requirements of salmonids. Prog. Rep. Oreg. Dep. Fish and Wildl. AFS-62, Portland.

Hydrology in Mountainous Regions. II - Artificial Reservoirs; Water and Slopes
(Proceedings of two Lausanne Symposia, August 1990). IAHS Publ. no. 194, 1990.

Démographie du Hotu *(Chondrostoma nasus nasus)* en relation avec la gestion d'une usine hydro-électrique

MICHEL DEDUAL
Institut de Zoologie, Université de Fribourg, Pérolles, 1700 Fribourg,
Suisse

RESUME L'étude de la biologie et des problèmes de dynamique de
population de C.n.nasus dans la Petite Sarine nous indiquent quelles sont
les principales incidences de la gestion de l'usine hydro-électrique
d'Hauterive. La brutalité des déversements provenant de l'hypolimnion du
Lac de la Gruyère durant la période de reproduction ainsi que le débit
réservé dans la Petite Sarine constituent les principaux aléas auxquels le
Hotu est exposé. Ces incidences sont décrites et plusieurs alternatives
visant à une amélioration sont présentées.

INTRODUCTION

Le Hotu est une espèce piscicole rhéophile non-exploitée. Les conditions fondamentales
pour qu'une telle espèce se maintienne, sont : la qualité physico-chimique de l'eau
adéquate, la réussite de la reproduction qui a lieu au début mai et la suffisance de
nourriture laquelle dérive plus ou moins de la qualité physico-chimique de l'eau. Ces
conditions dépendent dans une large mesure de la gestion de l'usine hydro-électrique
d'Hauterive puisque c'est elle qui dicte les débits et dans une moindre mesure les
températures de l'eau qui est injectée dans la Petite Sarine. Le fait que cette rivière coule
entre deux barrages et que le Hotu ne soit pas exploité par la pêche nous a donné
l'opportunité d'étudier comment le poisson s'adapte à ces conditions environnantes
modifiées par l'homme.

SITE DES TRAVAUX

La Petite Sarine est un tronçon de la
Sarine confiné entre le Barrage de
Rossens et l'usine hydro-électrique
d'Hauterive. Son cours s'étire sur
une quinzaine de kilomètres avant
de rencontrer celui de la Sarine. Le
système est limité en aval par le Lac
de Pérolles et le Barrage de la
Maigrauge. Avant l'édification des
barrages le débit de la rivière était
d'environ 30m^3/sec. Le débit
réservé actuel est de 1m^3/sec (Fig.
1).

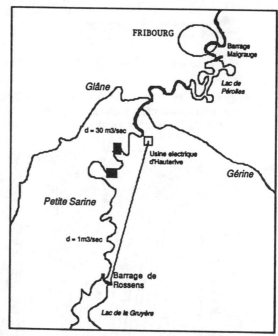

FIG. 1   Description du site d'étude.

REGIME DES DEBITS ET DES TEMPERATURES DE L'EAU

Graph. 1 Débits de la Petite Sarine de 1968 à 1988

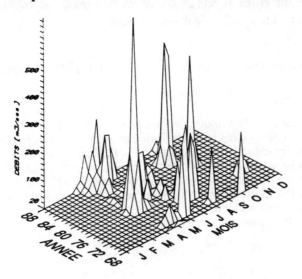

Graph. 2 Température de l'eau de la Petite Sarine.

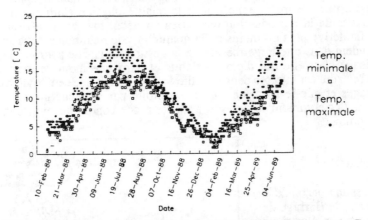

Graph. 3 Echelle verticale des températures de l'eau du Lac de la Gruyère. Les ordonnées représentent les profondeurs en mètres, l'alimentation de la Petite Sarine provient habituellement d'une vanne située au pied du barrage.

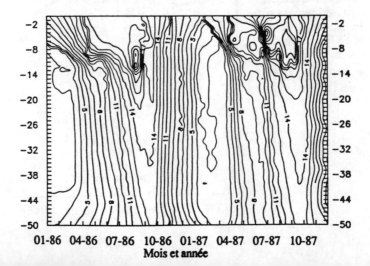

CONDITIONS DE REPRODUCTION

Le Hotu est un poisson qui éjecte ses oeufs sur et dans le gravier (Fig. 2). Lors des périodes de reproduction 1986-1989 il a été possible d'observer qu'à part la mortalité naturelle il existe une mortalité supplémentaire causée par l'augmentation de courant issue des déversements du Barrage de Rossens. Si le courant varie de

(a) 1 à 20 m^3/sec il n'emporte pas les oeufs pondus

(b) 20 à 100 m^3/sec il arrache la partie des oeufs flottante, ce qui signifie une perte de 10 % des oeufs

(c) 100 à 200 m^3/sec il entraîne la partie des oeufs collés aux pierres causant 15 % de mortalité supplémentaire

(d) > 200 m^3/sec, il provoque un déplacement du lit de la rivière et le roulement des pierres entraîne l'écrasement des oeufs dans le gravier et 100 % de mortalité.

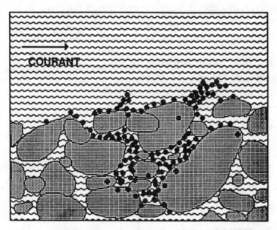

FIG. 2 Disposition des oeufs sur et dans le substrat.

Pour quantifier cet impact, nous avons construit un modèle déterministe qui nous permet de suivre la démographie de l'espèce. Le modèle est du type Leslie (1945, 1948), il permet la prévision de la structure d'une population au temps t + 1 à partir de la structure au temps t :

$$\underline{n}_{t+1} = A\underline{n}_t$$

La structure étant donnée par le vecteur $\underline{n}_t = \begin{array}{c} n_{t,1} \\ n_{t,2} \\ n_{t,k} \end{array}$

où, pour $1 < i < k$; $n_{t,i}$ désigne l'effectif de la classe d'âge i à l'époque t

L'effectif total de la population au moment t est donné par :

$$N_t = \sum_{i=1}^{k} n_{t,i}$$

où k est le nombre de classes d'âge.

A est une matrice carrée (k x k) indépendante du temps

$$A = \begin{array}{ccccc} f_1 & f_2 & \dots & f_{k-1} & f_k \\ p_1 & 0 & \dots & \dots & \dots \\ 0 & p_2 & \dots & \dots & \dots \\ \dots & \dots & \dots & \dots & \dots \\ 0 & 0 & \dots & p_{k-1} & 0 \end{array}$$

fi représente la fécondité d'une femelle de la classe d'âge i

p_i = taux de survie d'une femelle dans le passage de la classe d'âge i à i+1.

Dans notre matrice $p_1 = h(d)*B(Q_t)$

où h(d) = taux de survie des oeufs (h) en fonction du débit (d)

B = taux de survie du type Beverton et Holt (1957)

Nous avons inclus dans notre modèle la relation de Beverton et Holt avec une valeur arbitraire pour éviter une explosion de la population due à la non-linéarité du modèle causée par la densité-dépendance. Cette densité-dépendance peut être en première approximation, concentrée sur la survie de la première classe d'âge (Ginzburg et al. 1982). En ce qui concerne le recrutement, nous considérons :

Q_t = nombre d'oeufs produits par toutes les classes d'âge en t.

Remarque : Nous avons choisi de faire agir l'effet du débit avant celui de densité, ce qui signifie que nous admettons que les déversements ont lieu juste après la ponte et que c'est sur les oeufs restants que l'effet de densité agit. Cette situation est optimiste car il serait également possible de considérer les déversements en fin d'incubation avec un effet de densité qui a opéré pendant toute la période précédant les déversements. Dans ce cas il est clair que p_1 diminuerait. Ce point sera étudié de façon plus détaillée dans un prochain travail.

A partir de ces observations, nous avons construit la fonction reliant le débit au taux de mortalité supplémentaire h(d) (graph. 4). Cette relation nous évite de reconstruire une nouvelle matrice de Leslie pour chaque année considérée.

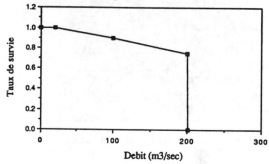

Graph. 4 h(d)

h(d) = 1 pour 1< d< 20 m^3/sec

h(d) = - 0.15*d/80 + 415/400 pour 20< d< 200 m^3/sec

h(d) = 0 pour d> 200 m^3/sec

La fécondité selon l'âge a été déterminée d'après un échantillon de 52 femelles âgées de 8-18 ans. Les taux de survie ont été calculés en suivant l'abondance relative moyenne (année 1971-1976) des groupes d'âge 1+ à 17+ d'une cohorte de Hotus étudiée par Philippart (1981). L'équation de régression de l'abondance relative en fonction de l'âge permet de calculer la valeur moyenne du coefficient instantané de mortalité et les taux de survie p_i correspondant.

Les variations de la fécondité et du taux de survie dans le temps, dues à la qualité stochastique de l'environnement, ne sont ni exclues ni mesurables. Certains auteurs (Ginzburg et al., 1984; Tuljapurkar et Orzack, 1980; Cohen, 1979; Deriso et Parma, 1988) introduisent ces effets stochastiques sur la dynamique des modèles, en termes de moyennes et de variance de la taille d'une population, de prédiction du temps d'extinction, etc.

Dans notre étude, nous voulons déterminer uniquement quelle proportion d' oeufs est perdue à cause du courant. Cette proportion n'est d'ailleurs pas influencée par les variations du taux de survie ou de fécondité. En disposant des débits qui ont existé durant les vingt dernières années (graph. 1) et en considérant les fécondités et taux de survie stables, nous testons le comportement démographique d'une population standardisée afin de montrer l'impact d'une telle gestion. Notre modèle est optimiste puisque nous admettons que les poissons fraient chaque année, ce qui n'est pas évident du tout.

APPLICATION DU MODELE

Nos simulations s'étendent sur une période de 20 ans. Nous considérons premièrement le cas où aucun déversement néfaste n'est effectué, c'est-à-dire que le débit varie de 1 à 20 m^3/sec. Dans une deuxième simulation nous testerons le comportement de la population si durant les 20 ans des déversements de 100 m^3/sec ont lieu juste après la ponte. Enfin nous soumettrons la population aux conditions qui ont effectivement existé ces 20 dernières années (graph. 1). Les résultats sont présentés sur le tableau 1.

TABLEAU 1 Modifications de la démographie d'une population de Nases standardisée dans diverses conditions de reproduction.

Classe d'âge	né en	Situation initiale	Situation finale pour :		
			Débit constant de 1m3/sec.	Débit constant de 100 m3/sec.	Débits effectifs de 1972 à 1988
1	1988	38000	37834	33965	30824
2	1987	2199	2270	2037	1849
3	1986	1534	1657	1487	1349
4	1985	1113	1209	1085	984
5	1984	842	883	792	0
6	1983	637	644	578	525
7	1982	350	470	422	383
8	1981	322	343	308	279
9	1980	322	250	225	204
10	1979	225	183	164	149
11	1978	120	133	119	108
12	1977	97	97	87	79
13	1976	58	71	63	57
14	1975	71	51	46	0
15	1974	71	37	34	30
16	1973	41	27	24	22
17	1972	30	20	18	16

La sensibilité de notre modèle est limitée par d'autres paramètres, mais il montre clairement le comportement d'une cohorte de Nases dépendante des conditions de reproduction hasardeuses. Nous constatons qu'une période de 17 ans avec des débits supérieurs à 200 m^3/sec lors de l'incubation des oeufs suffit à détruire totalement la population. Nous observons également que les conditions qui ont effectivement existé sont les moins bonnes. La structure de la population présente certaines classes d'âge avec aucun individu correspondant à une année de ponte où des déversements supérieurs à 200 m^3/sec ont été pratiqué. Pour les autres espèces piscicoles qui fraient à la même période et qui pondent d'une manière similaire, mais dont l'âge maximal n'atteint pas celui du Hotu, la période d'extinction diminue.

TAUX DE CROISSANCE

Dans ce paragraphe, nous voulons comparer les années de croissance qui vont de 1967 à 1984 en utilisant la méthode décrite par Kempe (1962).

Nous calculons l'accroissement linéaire moyen aux âges I, II, III, ... XVIII des poissons nés entre 1967 et 1984.

Ces valeurs servent de standard et prennent la valeur 100 %. La croissance de chaque classe d'âge à chaque année de croissance est ensuite calculée comme pourcentage du standard correspondant .

Le taux de croissance moyen de chaque année peut ensuite être calculé comme une moyenne de ces pourcentages pour chaque groupe d'âge.

Les taux de croissance moyens annuels sont mis en relation avec la quantité d'eau injectée annuellement dans la Petite Sarine (cf. graph. 5).

Graph. 5 Taux de croissance relative en fonction de la quantité d'eau injectée dans la Petite Sarine.

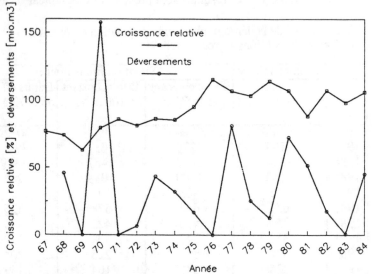

Cette méthode ne permet pas de mettre en évidence de subtiles différences entre chaque année. Néanmoins, si l'on considère la période 67-76, nous constatons :
(a)   Les taux de croissance sont nettement plus faibles que durant les années suivantes
      (test du $\chi^2 = 3{,}172$ entre la moyenne 67-75 et 76-84). L'année 1976 correspond à
      la donnation de 1m^3/sec d'eau dans la Petite Sarine par l'exploitation
      hydroélectrique d'Hauterive. Auparavant, les conditions hydrologiques et
      chimiques de l'eau (N-NO3 : 0.45-1.3 mg/l, P-PO4 : 0.01-0.21 mg/l)
      devaient favoriser une croissance algologique luxuriante surtout représentée
      par quelques espèces d'algues vertes comme *Cladophora sp.* au détriment des
      Diatomées qui constituent la nourriture principale des Hotus, si bien que la
      croissance de ces derniers était ralentie.
(b)   Cette situation d'eutrophisation montre un "peak" en 1969, année sans aucune
      injection d'eau dans la Petite Sarine hormis quelques petits affluents comme les
      ruisseaux d'Arconciel qui drainaient les égouts des villages et les terrains agricoles.
(c)   La croissance est maximale en 1976, année correspondant à l'instauration d'un
      débit réservé de 1m3/sec. Cette année a également été déterminée comme excellente
      pour la croissance du Gardon dans le Lac de Sarnen (Müller et Meng, 1986).
(d)   La chute du taux de croissance observable en 1981 reste inexpliquée mais il est
      possible que les forts déversements effectués en 1980 conjugués avec la mauvaise

qualité de cette année-là (Müller et Meng, 1986) se soient répercutés sur la croissance en 1981.

(e)   Les très forts déversements comme en 1970 ont eu un effet stimulant sur la croissance.

(f)   La variation de croissance durant la première année est importante. La première année de croissance va influencer toutes les autres. La croissance étant corrélée avec la quantité de nourriture à disposition, il semble que les Diatomées consommées par les Nases, aient besoin d'eau courante pour ne pas être remplacées par d'autres espèces d'algues impropres à la consommation du Hotu. La capacité maximale en Hotus que la rivière peut supporter est donc dépendante de la superficie des facies lotiques. Celle-ci est bien évidemment dépendante du débit.

DISCUSSION ET CONCLUSIONS

Nous avons vu que le régime des débits dans la Petite Sarine affecte la démographie du Hotu de deux façons différentes. Le succès de la reproduction n'est pas garanti à cause des forts déversements durant la période de frai. Ce problème a déjà été soulevé par maints auteurs qui ont étudié l'impact des régulations de cours d'eau (Heggberget, 1984; Aass, 1984; Saltveit et Styrvold,1984). La croissance et la capacité de la rivière diminuent avec un faible débit réservé car les conditions : faible débit, faible turbidité, haute température et fortes concentrations en $N-NO_3$ et $P-PO_4$ favorisent une croissance luxuriante d'algues vertes, qui se fait aux dépens des Diatomées constituant la nourriture principale des Hotus. Ce processus d'eutrophisation des effluents de réservoirs a également été observé par Skulberg (1984).

La conjonction des deux effets néfastes du régime de débit constitue pour l'espèce un réel danger qui va encore augmenter dans le futur si nous ne prenons pas de mesure appropriée. Ce genre de considérations doit être pris en compte lors des études d'impact.

Actuellement la majorité de ces études effectuées en Suisse émanent de bureaux privés et il est important que leurs responsables disposent d'outils simples à l'utilisation. A ce niveau-là les modèles peuvent s'avérer d'excellents outils. C'est le rôle des scientifiques d'élaborer de tels modèles. Pour ce qui est du concensus avec les politiciens et les économistes, il est absolument nécessaire de pouvoir présenter des résultats clairs et compréhensibles pour qu'une quelconque amélioration puisse avoir lieu.

Plus globalement nous devons nous demander, à part l'énergie, ce que nous voulons réellement quand nous projetons la construction d'un réservoir : veut-on un lac de retenue qui ressemble le plus possible à un lac naturel ou veut-on un effluent qui ressemble le plus possible à l'affluent ?

Pour avoir un réservoir naturel il faut que l'eau sorte de la surface du lac, que les variations de niveau de l'eau soient faibles ou les inondations des berges de courtes durées.

L'effluent ressemble le plus à l'affluent si leurs débits sont proportionnels et si la qualité physico-chimique de leurs eaux est semblable.

Nous remarquons que la première alternative a pour désavantage de modifier complètement l'effluent. Il apparaît donc plus sage d'opter pour la seconde. Théoriquement et techniquement, il est possible dans une large mesure de satisfaire ce choix. Dans le cas de la Petite Sarine nous disposons de toutes les mesures et données nécessaires nous permettant de comprendre comment le système hydrologique de la Petite Sarine fonctionne. Sur la base de ces indications il devient possible de choisir quelle proportion du débit de l'affluent doit avoir l'effluent, ou au moins quel est le débit réservé minimal acceptable, et à quelle profondeur il convient de pomper l'eau pour qu'elle ait les principales caractéristiques de l'affluent. Un système siphon avec prises d'eau à différentes profondeurs ferait très bien l'affaire.

Même si les aléas de la météo ne permettent pas d'avoir un plan de relargage strict il convient d'apporter certaines modifications au mode de gestion actuel car pour l'instant nous n'avons ni un réservoir naturel ni un effluent semblable à l'affluent. Parmi les espèces piscicoles qui souffrent le plus de cette situation nous pouvons citer le Hotu mais également l'Ombre Thymallus thymallus. Il est à noter que d'autres espèces ont profité de ces nouvelles conditions, le Chevaine Leuciscus cephalus ou le Vairon Phoxinus phoxinus, et dans une mesure plus nuancée la Truite Salmo trutta fario. Elle profite des débits stables et de l'eau relativement chaude pendant le frai mais ses alevins sont très facilement prisonniers dans les mares formées lors des crues.

La résolution du problème des sédiments nécessite également une convention entre économistes, écologistes et scientifiques et les futures travaux devraient aller dans ce sens.

REMERCIEMENTS J'aimerais exprimer ma sincère reconnaissance au Professeur J.-P. Gabriel et au Dr C. Mazza de l'Institut de Mathématiques de l'Université de Fribourg pour leur aide à la résolution mathématique et la programmation du modèle utilisé.

REFERENCES

Aass, P. (1984) Age, growth and yield of Brown Trout Salmo trutta in the River Hallingdalselv, eastern Norway. Chapter 4 in : Regulated Rivers.Edited by A. Lillehammer & S.J. Saltveit. Universitetsforlaget.

Beverton, R. J. H. & Holt, S. J. (1957) On the dynamics of exploited fish populations. U. K. Minist. Agric. Fish. Food Fish. Invest. (Ser. 2) 19, 533p.

Cohen, J. E. (1979) Comparative statics and stochastic dynamics of age-structured populations. Theor. Pop. Biol. 16, 159-171.

Deriso, R. B. & Parma, A. M. (1988) Dynamics of age and size for a stochastic population model. Can. J. Fish. Aquat. Sci. 45, 1054-1068.

Heggberget, T. G. (1984) Populations of presmolt Atlantic salmon and Brown trout before and after hydroelectric development and building of weirs in the River Skjoma, North Norway. Chapter 4 in : Regulated Rivers.Edited by A. Lillehammer & S.J. Saltveit. Universitetsforlaget.

Ginzburg, L. R., Slobodkin, L. B., Johnson, K. & Bindman, A. G. (1982) Quasiextinction probabilities as a measure of impact on population growth. Risk Analysis.3, 171-181.

Ginzburg, L. R., Johnson, K., Pugliese, A. & Gladden, J. (1984) Ecological risk assessment based on stochastic age-structured models of population growth. Special Technical Testing Publ. 845, 31-45.

Kempe, O. (1962) The growth of roach Leuciscus rutilus L. in some Swedish Lakes. Rep. Inst. Freshwat. Res. Drottningholm. 44, 42-104.

Leslie, P. H. (1945) On the use of matrices in certain population mathematics. Biometrika. 33, 183-212.

Leslie, P. H. (1948) Some further notes on the use of matrices in population mathematics. Biometrika. 35, 213-245.

Müller, R. & Meng, H. J. (1986) Factors governing the growth rate of roach Rutilus rutilus (L.) in pre-alpine Lake Sarnen. Schweiz. Z. Hydrol. 48 (2), 135-144.

Philippart, J. C. (1981) Démographie du Hotu Chondrostoma nasus dans l'Ourthe. Annales Soc. r. Zool. Belg. 3-4, 199-219.

Saltveit S. J. & Styrvold J. O. (1984) Density of juvenile Atlantic salmon and Brown trout in two Norwegian regulated rives. Chapter 4 in : Regulated Rivers.Edited by A. Lillehammer & S.J. Saltveit. Universitetsforlaget.

Skulberg O. (1984) Effect of stream regulation on algal vegetation. Chapter 2 in : Regulated Rivers.Edited by A. Lillehammer & S.J. Saltveit. Universitetsforlaget.

Thierrin, J. (1990) Contribution à la connaissance des eaux souterraines situées entre les Préalpes Fribourgeoises et le Lac de Neuchâtel. Thèse Université Neuchâtel.

Tuljapurkar, S. D. & Orzack, S. H. (1980) Population dynamics in variable environment, I. Long-run growth rates and extinction. Theor. Pop. Biol. 18, 314-342.

Hydrology in Mountainous Regions. II - Artificial Reservoirs; Water and Slopes
(Proceedings of two Lausanne Symposia, August 1990). IAHS Publ. no. 194, 1990.

Problèmes piscicoles liés à la réalisation de la retenue de Petit-Saut

C. SISSAKIAN
Division Sites-Projets et Environnement,
Centre National d'Equipement Hydraulique,
Services du CIG MARSEILLE, Electricité de France
140, avenue Viton, 13009 MARSEILLE, FRANCE

RESUME La réalisation de l'aménagement
hydroélectrique de PETIT-SAUT en GUYANE française
crée un plan d'eau qui va recouvrir 310 km^2
environ de forêt tropicale non déboisée. Cet
aménagement va avoir de nombreux effets sur
l'environnement, le plus important est la
modification de la qualité de l'eau et donc de la
vie piscicole. En parallèle aux études
entreprises sur la biologie des poissons de cette
région, Electricité de France a retenu des
dispositions constructives et une gestion de
l'aménagement qui assurent, le plus rapidement
possible un retour à une vie piscicole normale.

INTRODUCTION

La production d'énergie électrique de la GUYANE qui était
de 67 GWH en 1976 a atteint 270 GWh en 1988. Compte tenu
des projets connus en GUYANE et de l'évolution prévisible
de la consommation, cette production pourrait atteindre
370 GWH en 1990.
    Pour faire face à ce développement, Electricité de
France (EDF) a entrepris l'étude d'un aménagement
hydroélectrique permettant d'éviter, dans des conditions
économiques particulièrement interessantes, le recours à
des combustibles fossiles importés. Après inventaire
général il apparait que le site le mieux approprié pour des
raisons économiques et pour sa situation privilégiée, le
plus proche des centres de consommation, est situé sur le
SINNAMARY au lieu-dit PETIT-SAUT.
    Mais si l'objectif premier de ce barrage est la
production d'énergie, cet ouvrage s'inscrit dans un
environnement humain et économique et un patrimoine naturel
d'autant plus important qu'il s'agit de la forêt
amazonienne dont beaucoup d'aspects sont encore inconnus.
C'est de plus le premier aménagement de ce type réalisé par
EDF en région équatoriale. Aussi, dans le cadre de la
législation en vigueur et d'une Convention EDF/Ministère
chargé de l'Environnement/Ministère de l'industrie, de
nombreuses actions et études ont été entreprises. De plus
devant la sensibilité de l'écosystème Guyanais et la
modification des conditions de pénétration en forêt liée

à la création de la route d'accès et de la retenue, EDF
participe à une réflexion et à une action à plus long terme
en matière de protection de la nature avec tous les
compétences locales et nationales existantes. Le présent
exposé s'attachera à montrer les dispositions prises pour
assurer le maintien d'une vie piscicole dans la retenue et
à l'aval de celle-ci.

PRESENTATION DU SITE (Fig. 1)

Le relief de la GUYANE française se présente comme une
topographie essentiellement collinaire, typique des très
vieux boucliers de la planète, c'est-à-dire de pénéplaine ;
celle-ci est cependant assortie de volumes résiduels,
cloisonnés, éparpillés, voire complètement isolés, de
formes diverses mais qui, par contraste, font figure de
"montagnes" et sont ainsi nommés dans la tradition créole.
   Le site de PETIT-SAUT, situé sur le fleuve SINNAMARY,
se trouve à 35 km à vol d'oiseau de la ville de SINNAMARY,
proche de l'embouchure du fleuve. Le SINNAMARY prend sa
source en plein centre de la GUYANE au pied de la montagne
CONTINENT qui culmine à 600 m environ. Il s'écoule en
direction du Nord vers l'Atlantique. La longueur de son
cours est de 200 km. Au site du barrage, le SINNAMARY a un
bassin versant de forme allongée qui recouvre 5930 km^2 de
forêt. La retenue de PETIT-SAUT va recouvrir 80 km du cours
du fleuve sur une surface non déboisée d'environ 310 km^2.
<u>Caractéristiques de l'aménagement</u> (Fig. 2)
Barrage en béton compacté au rouleau
   crête à la cote : 37 m
   hauteur maximale s/fondation : 44 m
   longueur totale : 750 m
   débit d'équipement : 430 m^3/s
   4 turbines de type KAPLAN
   puissance installée : 111 MW
   productible annuel moyen : 560 GWH
<u>Retenue non déboisée de 310 km^2</u>
   volume total 3,5 millions de m^3
   volume utile 1   millions de m^3
   cote de retenue normale 35 m
   cote de retenue minimale 31,50 m

PEUPLEMENT PISCICOLE D'ORIGINE

Les pêches d'inventaires effectuées par l'INRA GUYANE
(Institut National de Recherche Agronomique) ont permis de
dénombrer près d'une centaine d'espèces dans la zone de la
future retenue. Neuf d'entre elles représentent 90 % de la
biomasse capturée. Cette faune ne semble comporter ni
espèce endémique*, ni espère rare. Les piranhas et les
Tucunarés*, carnassiers typiques des fleuves d'Amazonie,
sont absents ici. Aucun déplacement massif de poissons n'a
pu être observé. Cet inventaire qui a porté plutôt sur une

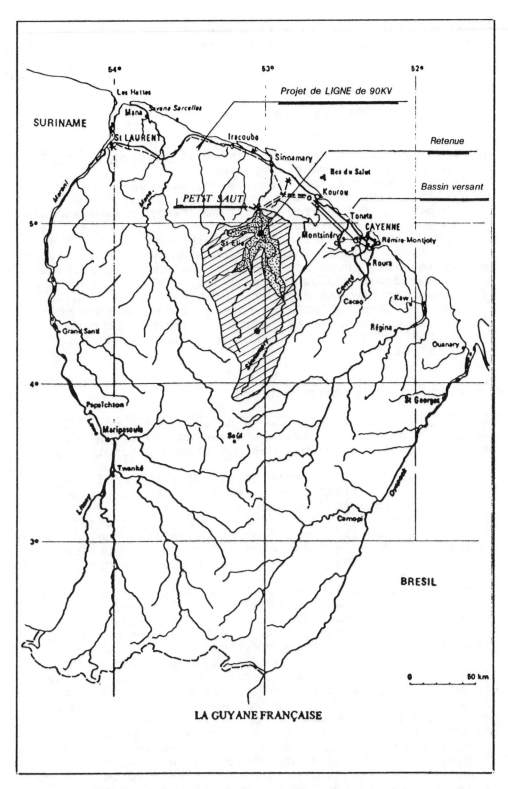

FIG. 1

étude qualitative, va être complété par une étude quantitative d'ici la fin de l'année 1990.

QUALITE DE L'EAU DU SINNAMARY

L'eau du SINNAMARY est caractérisée par les données suivantes :

(a) poids peu élevé des matières en suspension, 20 mg/l, formées de fins débris végétaux.

(b) profondeur de disparition de SECCHI : 80 à 100 cm (atteint 150 cm dans les criques)

(c) pH moyen : 6,5. Varie de 5,4 (fortes pluies===>acides humiques) à 6,8 (étiage).

(d) conductivité électrique très faible en amont (11 à 23 $\mu S/cm$) à faible dans le cours moyen (35 $\mu S/cm$).

(e) milieu oligotrophe (pauvre en substances nutritives et matière organique végétale).

(f) teneur en oxygène dissous : 8 mg/l à 25 °C.
Par ses caractéristiques physiques, édaphiques et biotiques le SINNAMARY peut se rattacher au type "CLEAR WATER RIVERS" de la classification du Dr H. SIOLI.

EVOLUTION DE LA QUALITE DE L'EAU

La mise en eau de la retenue va noyer 310 km^2 de forêt. La décomposition de cette matière organique va entrainer une modification très sensible des différents paramètres de la qualité des eaux.

Le bilan global de cette décomposition produira du méthane en phase finale, mais aussi de l'hydrogène sulfuré, du gaz carbonique et de l'ammoniac.
La première phase consécutive à la mise en eau sera caractérisée par la dégradation de la matière organique par l'oxygène dissous de l'eau conduisant à la production de CO_2, d'H_2S et de NH_3 (acidification pouvant descendre jusqu'à un pH de l'ordre de 5).
Après consommation totale de l'O_2 dissous existant le pH remontera probablement vers une valeur de l'ordre de 6 et se stabilisera pendant une période assez longue qui correspond à la méthanisation du milieu, possible sur une plage de pH proche de la neutralité.

EDF a étudié plus particulièrement l'évolution de l'oxygène dissous car c'est le paramètre fondamental de la vie aquatique et a développé un modèle mathématique de simulation de l'évolution de la teneur en oxygène dissous.
Le modèle a mis en évidence les tendances suivantes :

(a) dans la retenue : chute rapide de la teneur en O_2 durant les 6 premiers mois (0mg/l dans les couches profondes). Par la suite alors que la couche supérieure (épilimnion) rapidement renouvelée retrouvera sur environ 5 m des valeurs correctes, les

couches profondes pourraient rester en conditions
anaérobies plusieurs années.
(b) à l'aval : la teneur en O_2 peut ponctuellement être
inférieure à 2mg/l à l'aval sur les 10 premiers
kilomètres les 2 premières années qui suivent la mise
en eau. A 45 km, au niveau de la prise d'eau potable de
Pointe Combi, la concentration en oxygène est toujours
supérieure à 4 mg/l.

CONSEQUENCES SUR LA VIE PISCICOLE

Le bouleversement de l'habitat lotique* dû à l'édification
du barrage : bi-partition du bassin hydrographique,
création d'un milieu lentique*, modification du régime des
débits en aval, ne peut manquer d'influer sur le peuplement
piscicole d'origine. De plus durant les premières années
suivant la mise en eau, on a vu qu'il allait y avoir une
altération marquée de la qualité chimique de l'eau avec
notamment donc une désoxygénation importante du milieu.
    On a actuellement assez peu de renseignements sur la
biologie des poissons sud-américains et si un taux
de 4 mg/l d'O_2 correspond à une vie piscicole normale on
peut penser qu'un taux de 2 mg/l suffit à la survie de la
plupart des espèces. Aussi c'est ce taux que l'on essaie de
maintenir, à minima, à l'aval immédiat du barrage. De plus,
il existe des zones "refuge" où la survie et surtout la
reproduction de certains espèces seront toujours possibles
notamment dans les 40 criques perennes recensées en aval du
site.
    En ce qui concerne la retenue l'expérience acquise lors
des études menées sur certains grands lacs artificiels
édifiés en zone tropicale montre un développement explosif
d'un petit nombre d'espèces et simultanément la disparition
de nombreuses autres. On peut penser que, pendant la phase
de remplissage, par suite notamment du déficit en oxygène
de l'hypolimnion*, il y aura disparition de poissons
benthiques* y compris certaines espèces dotées d'une
respiration aérienne qui ne trouveront plus les petits
invertébrés dont elles se nourrissaient. Le développement
explosif de certaines espèces observé par ailleurs (les
Tucunarés* dans la retenue de TUCURUI au Brésil) pourrait
porter sur des espèces phytophages ou herbivores.
L'introduction de carnassiers de choix, absents du
SINNAMARY, pourrait être envisagée ainsi que celle
éventuelle de planctonophages. Une seule condition est
absolument impérative : les espèces à introduire ne doivent
provenir que de la zone zoogéographique correspondante pour
éviter des pertubations écologiques majeures et
imprévisibles. Actuellement, à la demande d'EDF, l'INRA
Guyane poursuit des études sur la recherche d'espèces
susceptibles de se développer dans la future retenue, sur
la biologie des espèces essentielles et, comme on l'a déjà
dit, sur la détermination d'indices d'abondance.

MESURES PRISES À PETIT-SAUT

En parallèle aux études entreprises, des mesures
particulières ont été prises à PETIT-SAUT afin de tout
mettre en oeuvre pour garantir le maintien d'une teneur
minimale en oxygène dissous, paramètre fondamental vis-à-
vis des critères de possibilité de vie aquatique, à l'aval
de l'aménagement tout en essayant de ne pas pénaliser trop
longtemps l'eau de la retenue.
        Ces mesures ont donc été décidées en fonction des
tendances données par le modèle mathématique de simulation
de l'évolution de la teneur en O_2 dissous et les éléments
connus actuellement relatifs à la biologie des poissons.
Elles sont de 2 sortes : dispositions constructives et
gestion de la retenue.

Dispositions constructives (Fig. 2)
Ce sont les suivantes :
(a) Pertuis de fond (3 pertuis, dimensions : 7 x 7 m)
    Pendant le remplissage de la retenue ils seront équipés
    de batardeaux afin de créer une chute permettant la
    réoxygénation de l'eau lors du passage du débit réservé
    de mise en eau (100 m^3/s). Le gain d'oxygène est estimé
    à 1,5 mg/l pour une chute d'environ 4 m.
(b) Digue à l'amont des prises d'eau
    Il s'agit d'une digue en enrochements, dont la crête
    est fixée à la cote +20,00 m. Placée à l'amont des
    prises d'eau elle permettra de turbiner en priorité et
    donc évacuer à l'aval l'eau de surface de meilleure
    qualité. Son bon fonctionnement a été vérifié sur
    modèle réduit au Laboratoire National d'Hydraulique
    d'EDF à CHATOU.
(c) Clapet de surface (10 m de longueur sur 4,5 m de
    hauteur)
    Il permettra la réoxygénation de l'aval par déversement
    des eaux de surface.
(d) Déversoir de surface (crête à la cote 35,00 m)
    Le coursier en béton armé est équipé de marches
    destinées à dissiper l'énergie de la lame déversante.
    Ces marches contribueront aussi à la réoxygénation des
    eaux déversées.

Gestion de la retenue
Les principales mesures sont les suivantes :
(a) Débit réservé
    Pendant le remplissage de la retenue, un débit réservé
    de 100 m^3/s sera assuré de façon permanente soit par
    l'intermédiaire des pertuis de fond munis de batardeaux
    (voir plus haut) soit par l'intermédiaire d'une turbine
    dès que la cote 25 m sera atteinte. Par la suite le
    débit minimal laissé à l'aval est fixé à 80 m^3/s.
(b) Dispositif de surveillance
    Un dispositif de surveillance de la qualité de l'eau du
    SINNAMARY et plus particulièrment de la teneur en O_2
    dissous sera installé à l'aval de l'aménagement.

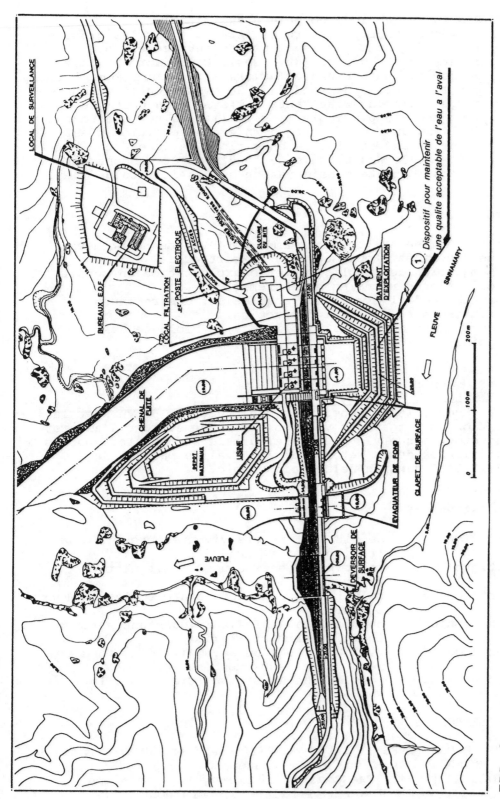

FIG. 2

(c) Gestion en période normale d'exploitation
   L'évacuation prioritaire se fera soit par les groupes
   (turbinés) soit par le clapet de surface et le
   déversoir de surface (déversés). Cependant une partie
   du débit non turbinable (déversés) pourra être évacuée
   par les pertuis de fond dans la mesure où la teneur en
   oxygène dissous résultante à l'aval sera compatible
   avec une vie piscicole (possibilité de renouvellement
   de l'eau du fond). Cette dernière disposition n'est
   bien sûr pas applicable en période de crues où
   l'ouverture des pertuis de fond peut être nécessaire en
   dehors de toute considération sur la qualité de l'eau.

ETUDES

D'ici la mise en eau programmée en 1994, de nombreuses
études vont être poursuivies, en particulier :
- simulation de remplissage et d'exploitation en conditions
  climatiques normales et extrêmes,
- synthèse de l'expérience acquise sur des retenues
  réalisées en milieu intertropical,
- conditions d'oxygénation liées à la biologie des
  poissons.

CONCLUSION

Les études, les dispositions constructives prévues et la
gestion envisagée des volumes d'eau permettront d'assurer
un retour à une vie piscicole normale et dans les couches
supérieures de la retenue et à l'aval du barrage de
PETIT-SAUT dans un délai raisonnable.

GLOSSAIRE (*)

Endémique :   se dit des espèces vivantes propres à un
                  territoire bien délimité
Lotique   :   relatif aux eaux douces à circulation
                  rapide
Lentique :   relatif aux eaux douces à circulation lente
                  ou nulle
Hypolimnion :   couche d'eau inférieure dans une retenue
                  thermiquement stratifiée
Benthique :   vivant au fond ou à proximité du fond des
                  mers ou des eaux douces
Tucunaré :   poisson sud-américain (Cichla ocellaris)

REFERENCES

EDF DR DOM (1986)   Chute de PETIT-SAUT en GUYANE française
    Etude d'impact sur l'environnement.
SIOLI H. (1984)   The Amazon. Limnology and landscape
    ecology. Dr W. Junk. Publishers, Dordrecht.

TOPIC F:

GENERAL PAPERS

Hydrology in Mountainous Regions. II - Artificial Reservoirs; Water and Slopes
(Proceedings of two Lausanne Symposia, August 1990). IAHS Publ. no. 194, 1990.

Impact of artificial reservoirs on hydrological equilibrium

J. J. CASSIDY
Bechtel Corporation, Hydraulics/Hydrology Group,
45 Fremont,San Francisco, California 94119, USA

ABSTRACT The operation of reservoirs as a function of their design purpose and mode of operation is discusssed and a listing and summary of impacts produced as a result of the reservoir are given. Particular considerations are given to flood control, sediment deposition and the problems involved in flushing sediment past a dam, consequences of downstream flow modification, ecological problems produced including those for fisheries, and the legal aspects related to development of reservoirs.

INTRODUCTION

Reservoirs have been constructed since antiquity for the purpose of conservation of water. The Iranian Committee on Large Dams (Iran 1990) has assembled a description of many dams which were constructed in Iran up to more than 1000 years ago. Many others existed and some hve been described by Biswas (Biswas 1967). It is obvious that these old dams were developed because of the benefit or expected benefit which accrued to those who used the water. It is entirely logical that such dams first were constructed in arid or semi-arid areas where rainfall was seasonal and agriculture and society in general benefited from the storage and subsequent use of water from the reservoir. The first dams to be constructed in mountainous areas were most likely constructed to develop power for mills, initially mechanical, and as a result were constructed at the mill site. One had the choice of building the dam at the best dam site or at the best mill site, a possible conflict in choices. With the discovery of electricity and the means of generating it from water and transmitting it to other sites, it became possible to build dams farther up in the mountains where the site conditions were more favorable for the dam and still supply electricity for distant needs. This is the pattern today.

Early cities developed along the rivers and streams because of the need for a water supply and because trade could be carried on using river transportation; the same pattern exists today. Frequent flooding undoubtedly proved to be an inconvenience and a danger particularly in regions subject to rapidly rising river crests. As a result, the concept of flood control was developed and levees were constructed to protect life and property. When the concept of building dams for storage of flood waters began is not precisely known, but serious flood-control planning using dams and reservoirs in the USA began after a disastrous 1913 flood with the creation of the Miami

Conservancy District in 1914 which was organized to develop a flood-protection system for the the Miami River valley in Ohio (Woodward 1920). That report stated that two flood-retention reservoirs had been constructed on the Loire River in France in 1711 and that they had flood-storage capacities of 100 and 108 million m³ respectively.

Benefits Derived From Reservoirs

The benefits which are obtained from reservoirs are numerous and well known. They include: flood control downstream; establishment of a dependable water supply for municipal, agricultural, and industrial uses; generation of electricity; improvement of navigation; and recreation. For large reservoirs the benefits accrue to a broad array of people and, thus, those projects are usually constructed and operated by public or quasi-public agencies. Other smaller dams often have as their primary benefit the storage of water for private irrigation use or the generation of electrical energy and are usually constructed and operated by private companies or by special-purpose associations. Direct benefits from these special-purpose dams usually go only to stockholders of the company or to members of the association.

OPERATION OF RESERVOIRS AND HYDROLOGICAL IMPACT

The operation of reservoirs varies with the purpose for which the reservoir was constructed. For reservoirs with the soul purpose of providing downstream flood protection through storage of flood runoff, retention of the flood waters is short and the flood waters are released at a flow rate which does not exceed the downstream channel capacity. Impact of such reservoirs on the hydrological equilibrium is usually small since only the large peak flows are modified and flow into the reservoir is quickly released as long as it does not exceed the channel capacity. The hydrological equilibrium is only slightly altered as a result of the reservoir. For larger reservoirs the retention time is longer (frequently part of the storage is for conservation) and impact is greater. The most obvious impact usually appears downstream where use of the flood plain increases as a result of reduced flooding. The stream is usually confined to a smaller channel and often wetlands are modified as a result of streamside development.

Reservoirs that have been constructed for conservation storage include those whose purpose is hydroelectric development as well as storage for downstream use by irrigators, municipalities, and industries. The operation of such reservoirs requires that flow in excess of some minimum value be stored for later use. Thus, these reservoirs are storing water during the rainy and snow-melt periods and releasing at flow rates less than the inflow rates. The reservoir operation serves to smooth out irrratic inflow patterns and provide release rates more nearly equal to the average annual flow rate of the river. However, the extent to which the river flows can be limited to the average annual value is dependent upon the reservoir storage volume and the variance of the river flows. In general it is impossible to store all of the reservoir inflow since unusually large inflows always occur during which the reservoir must spill. Depending upon the design of the dam and its spillways and outlet works, more or less of the annual inflow can be stored. The larger the reservoir storage volume, the more the hydrological regime will be changed by storage and the reservoir operation.

The impacts of artificial reservoirs on hydrological equilibrium is profound in many cases and predominantly involves enviornmntal issues. The current major activities in the field of dam engineering today is primarily associated with means to mitigate those imnpacts. In the case off new dams, concern over these impacts has greatly increased the length of time required to obtain legal permits to construct dams as well as the uncertainty of sucess in obtaining those pemits. For existing dams the impacts have been identified and current activity is primarily associated with attempting to mitigate those impacts through modification of the dams and/or the operational policies of the reservoirs. For many old dams the mitigation is required in order to renew legal permits to own and operate the dam.

Impacts of large reservoirs

Introduction of storage on a stream alters the natural hydrological regime by reducing the flood peaks and releasing a streamflow which is more nearly equal to the average annual flow unless the reservoir provides for diversion either to another drainage basin or to a point further downstream. In the latter two cases the streamflow in the river downstream can be greatly reduced. In the United States before approximately 1960, it was often allowable to reduce the stream flow to zero. In any event the hydrological equilibrium is drastically changed downstream. Following is a list of impacts which are produced:

1. Interuption of Sediment: Sediment is stored in the reservoir with the coarsest part stored in the upstream reaches and the fine material stored further down. The flow released to the stream contains, on the average smaller concentrations of sediment. As a result, the river downstream of the dam degrades if the bed of the river is erodible. Even if it is erodible, degradation of the bed is often limited because of armoring of the bed occurs as erosion takes place and the river carries away the small material which its velocity is capable transporting. The character of the bed material changes becoming more coarse with a resultant impact on the aquatic life. Sediment stored in the reservoir often fills at least a portion of the live storage reducing the beneficial storage and the potential benefits of the reservoir as well. Problems of aggradation can occur downstream of the dam because sediment entering from downstream contributory channels will have reduced flow to transport the sediment; the peak flood flows, which normally transport the majority of the sediment, may no longer occur in suficient frequency and magnitude to move all sediment entering from tributaries downstream.

2. Altered Flow Regime: The downstream flow regime will be changed by operation of the reservoir. The sediment concentration in released flow is usually much less than that which occurred without the reservoir (for large reservoirs the water released may be essentially

clear). As a result the channel downstream has a slope which produces velocities large enough to have transport capacity greater than the concentration of the outflow. Degradation occurs near the dam and some distance downstream as a result of the imbalance between the transport capacity and concentration of the released flow. Eventually, as degradation proceeds, the channel will armor effectively stopping the erosion; or the channel slope will be reduced until equilibrium is reached.

However, the armoring of the channel bottom is followed by more aggressive erosion of the banks and as a result the stream will become wider and may tend to meander. Sediment eroded from the banks and that brought in by the tributaries may produce a sediment load that is greater than the transport capacity of the releases. Since peak flows released from the reservoir are reduced in both magnitude and frequency from that which provided flushing prior to construction of the reservoir the downstream peak flows no longer occur in sufficient number and magnitude to carry away the downstream sediment load. As a result aggradation of the channel occurs at some distance downstream from the dam may further tending to reduce the gradient of the river.

Interstices in gravel substrate used for spawning by the riparian fish population sometimes become clogged as a result of sediment deposition. As a result the eggs laid in the gravel by the spawning fish often have insufficient oxygen for survival. To reduce this impact it is necessary to release peak flows of a desired magnitude and duration from the reservoir. The establishment of the required magnitude and durationof this flushing flow is difficult at best and is highly dependent upon the type of bed material contained in the river. Without the release of flushing flows, it is possible for biocenosis to occur where nearly all the native aquatic plants and animals are eliminated or at least seriously impacted.

The reduction of downstream peak flows also allows more vegetation to grow in the main channel; as a result the resistance to flow is increased and the capacity of the channel is reduced; higher flood stages occur for a given flow than occurred prior to construction of the reservoir.

At the upstream end of the reservoir the hydrogical regime of the river is also changed. Coarser sediment deposits at the upper end of the reservoir and form a delta there which impacts the active storage. If the reservoir is a storage reservoir the surface level will drop as storage is released and the upstream deposited delta becomes exposed. The river then cuts a channel through the delta. The slope of the river channel becomes flatter than it was prior to construction of the dam and, as a result, the flow capacity of the channel is reduced below that of the channel prior to development of the reservoir.

3. Altered Water Quality: If the dam is high, the reservoir contents will usually stratify with the result that flow released from the lower portions of the reservoir will often be in the order 3 to 5 $^\circ$C. If this temperature is significantly colder than the original stream temperatures the downstream resident fishery will change drastically. At reservoirs on the White River in Missouri and Arkansas the resident Black Bass fishery (wearm water species) was completely lost after the dams were

closed and a thriving Rainbow Trout popualtion (a cold water species) developed (Smith 1973).

Because the surface area of the reservoir is larger than the surface area of the original stream and is often warmer there may also be an increase in evaporation volume which reduces the amount of downstream flow below that experienced before the reservoir was built.

Water quality effects produced by artificial reservoirs are frequently created by temperature stratification of the reservoir and decomposition of organic material in the reservoir. For high dams the oxidation of organic materials reduces the dissolved oxygen of the water stored in the lower parts of the reservoir. Releases made in the fall or winter after a summer of stratification and decomposition of bottom material frequently results in the release of water having zero or very low dissolved-oxygen content. Often hydrogen-sulfide gas is released as a result of decomposition of vegetation. These releases are frequently a serious problem for the resident aquatic colony below the dam. The Tucurui dam is probably the most famous of the recent examples of water quality problems that can occur as a result of construction of a reservoir (Canali et.al. 1988).

4. Interruption of Migrant Fish: Both high and low dams will interrupt free passage of fish. Although some species of riparian fish do not move far from their resident habitat others migrate during spawning periods. Both the Atlantic and Pacific Salmon migrate between the oceans and fresh-water rivers where they spawn. In the western part of the United States the Steelhead Trout also migrates between salt and fresh water, but like the Atlantic Salmon returns to the sea after spawning. Reservoirs in the eastern and western United States and Canada and in the Scandinavian countries have interupted the spawning of these anadromous fish to the extent that in some places entire runs of Atlantic Salmon have been lost and have been replaced by Salmon raised in hatcheries.

Efforts in the United States began about 10 years ago to restore runs of Atlantic Salmon to streams in the northeast and have been expensive and only moderately succesful to date (Rogers 1989). In Australia some species of fish exist that spawn in the sea and the young return to live in rivers; efforts there are now considering means to allow for passage of these fish. Fish ladders for the passage of downstream migrants have now been provided for some low dams but accomodation of upstream migration of juveniles is in the early stages of consideration (ANCOLD 1990). The passage of Atlantic Salmon using fish ladders and locks have been allowed for in Ireland and Scotland for many decades but there appears to be little data to assess the success of all of the measures used (Aitkin 1980).

SOME EXAMPLES OF PROBLEMS

The topic sessions which follow this plenary session all contain papers which describe examples of problems or solutions to problems which have been briefly covered in the preceding parts of this paper. The following examples supplement those papers and provide some additional insights to the problems. Unfortunately problems seem to be more prevalent and easier to identify than solutions. Hopefully, the results of this conference will produce some ideas for solutions which will make the use of artificial reservoirs even more beneficial in the future by eliminating or at least reducing the impact of changes in hydrological equilibrium produced by artificial reservoirs.

COWLITZ FALLS HYDROELECTRIC DAM

The Cowlitz Falls project is to be constructed on the Lewis River in the southwestern corner of the State of Washington in the USA. The dam will be 35 m tall and will impound a reservoir about 32 km long. The drainage area above the dam is 2868 km^2 and produces an annual average flow of 123 m^3 s^{-1} . The drainage area is mountainous and includes two volcanos, Mt. Ranier with a height of 4270 m and Mt. St. Helens which, after its May 1989 eruption, has a height of only 2700 m. The dam will house two hydroelectric units with a total capacity of 36 mw. At one time the river hosted a substantial run of Chinook Salmon and Steelhead Trout, but two dams downstream, one of which is a 172 m high arch dam, stopped the run of anadromous fish in 1968. The controlling agency for permits for the dam is the Federal Energy Regulatory Commission which overseas all hydroelectric dams in the United States. In granting the license for construction of the dam two restrictions relating to the hydrological equilibrium were made a part of the license. First, the dam and its operation had to be designed so that the presence of the dam would not increase flooding at the town of Randal at the the upper limits of the reservoir. This restriction meant that sediment could not be allowed to deposit to depths upstream that would increase flooding and secondly that the reservoir would need to be lowered during floods exceeding that magnitude beyond which the backwater curve from the dam would reach the critical zone on the river.

Sediment characteristics were obtained from a limited number of suspended sediment measurements, from samples taken from the delta in the downstream reservoir, and from bars deposited along the river. Samples of bed material were collected to estimate bed-load sizes. As is common for mountain drainages the river has a gravel bottom and the sediment conveyed has a median size ranging from 0.5 to 0.8 mm. Bed load was found to be about 5% of the total load. The U.S. Army Corps of Engineers computer program HEC-6, Erosion and Deposition in Rivers and Reservoirs, (U.S. Army 1977) was used to perform sediment routing using a 50-year record of daily average flows. Hydraulic analysis of long-term sediment deposition depths and resulting water-surface profiles during floods showed that even though the dam will be only 35 m tall, long-term aggradation of the channel in the upper reaches of the reservoir could not be prevented unless the reservoir water-surface is lowered by 6.1 m from its normal maximum whenever the flow exceeds 767 m^3 s^{-1}. Lowering the reservoir increases velocities in the reservoir and, thus, increases transport capacity. , Since

HEC-6 is a one-dimensional simulation, it could not be used to study effects of sediment deposition near the dam. Instead a 1:46 scale model, which was used to verify hydraulic design, was used to study the effectiveness of the two 3.6 m x 4.9 m sluices located beneath the spillway bay on the left side of the dam. Using plastic pellets, 1.71 mm diameter by 3.21 mm long, with a specific gravity of 1.02 to represent the sediment, the model showed that the sluices would indeed sluice away material which reached the front of the dam. In this case the sluices will be effective because of their large flow capacity (568 m /s), because the reservoir would be lowered to increase the velocity in the reservoir, and because the diversion channel in the bottom of the river will be left in place to trap sediment and divert it toward the sluices. For most dams the sluices are not effective in passing sediment for significant distances upstream from the dam unless strong density currents are developed by the sediment and/or the reservoir surface is lowered during passage of large flows.

The second restriction attached to the project license required that the construction of the dam not prevent the trapping of downstream migrating anadromous fish since the State of Washington was considering the re-establishment of a Chinook Salmon fishery in the river upstream of the dam. Because of the large dam downstream it would be necessary to trap adult fish downstream of the dams and transport them to the river upstream of Cowlitz Falls Dam for release. It would likewise be necessary to trap downstream migrating juveniles at the Cowlitz Falls dam and transport them to a point downstream of the dams from which they could continue their migtration to the sea. It would be necessary to trap downstream migrants at Cowlitz Falls Dam because earlier tests had shown that, because of the very small velocities in this large reservoir, the downstream migrating juveniles could not find their way through the large reservoir which is immediately downstream of Cowlitz Falls. A screening concept was designed which would intercept downstream-migrating juveniles at the turbine intakes and direct them to a holding tank for later transport downstream of the dams by truck. The design would screen only the top 1/3 to 1/2 of the intake area since field studies of migrating juvenile Salmon
have shown that most swim in the upper 15 to 20% of the approaching flow. The ultimate design of the screens would be based on field studies of actual migrating fish once the dam is in place and planting of the fish upstream has been accomplished.

SEDIMENT FLUSHING AND/OR REMOVAL

Probably the most serious and most common impact of reservoirs on hydrological equilibrium is that of sediment interruption. The resulting sediment deposits have seriously reduced the capacity of reservoirs in all parts of the world (ICOLD 1989). The reduction in capacity decreases the benefits of the reservoir and, if not corrected, can render the project useless. Problems for reservoirs on the Yellow River in China are probably among the most famous because of that river's extremely large suspended load; as a result a means of sluicing must be developed such as that planned for the Xiaolangdi reservoir, which without effective sluicing would be essentially filled with sediment in 5 years or less (Hsu 1988).

The effectiveness of passing sediment through dams is not always good and, if the dam is not initially designed for passing sediment, it may become prohibitively expensive to modify the dam and outlet works to do so later. It appears that for most dams the predicted amount of sediment entering the reservoir each year is very uncertain at best. Plotted on a log-log scale data on sediment concentrations versus discharge normally scatter over more than two cycles for a particular discharge illustrating the uncertainty inherrent in sediment-load prediction. However, the prediction of the volume of sediment inflow that will be experienced is very important. If the predicted inflow volume proves to be smaller than what actually occurs, no problems will occur and the life of the reservoir is extended beyond that anticipated. However, if the annual amount of deposition is underestimated, the reservoir may be rapidly filled, frequent operation problems can occur, and the project will fail to realize its expected economic worth. For the Shihmen Reservoir in Taiwan the annual prediction was 800,000 m^3 year-1 when the dam was designed in 1955 but in 1964 alone the actual input was 19.5 million m^3 . After the years of operating experience the annual input is now estimated to be 0.862 m^3 (Hsu et.al.1988). When sediment deposition reached the power intake structure at Shihmen Dam it became necessary to institute a dredging program in order to maintain hydropower operations.

The Public Works Department of Los Angeles County in the State of California in the USA constructed three reservoirs on the San Gabriel River in the San Gabriel Mountains for flood protection of cities in the Los Angeles Basin. The dams are San Gabriel, Cogswell, and Morris and were constructed in the early 1930's. These dams, although constructed for flood control, are actually operated for conservation as well. Since rainfall in California is very seasonal it is possible to store water in the reservoirs at the end of the flood season and release it for downstream recharge of groundwater aquifers later during the dry season. Table 1 shows the reservoir storage capacity when constructed and as they are in 1990(Coale 1989):

TABLE 1 Reservoir Characteristics, San Gabriel Reservoirs.

Reservoir	Year Constructed	Drainage Area (km2)	Original Capacity (10^6 m3)	1990 Capacity (10^6 m3)
Cogswell	1935	111	15.17	10.92
SanGabriel	1938	518	65,74	53.91
Morris	1935	562	39.84	27.49

The reservoirs are in a series on the San Gabriel River. The area in the upper part of the basin beyond San Gabriel is a pristine forested mountain area. Sediment entering the reservoir is typical of mountain streams and ranges in size from silt and fine sands to gravels. A scenic popular Trout-fishing area has developed on the river downstream from Cogswell Dam. About 2 million m³ of sediment had been removed from San Gabriel in 1979 using conventional earth moving equipment with the reservoir drawn about 30 m. The removed sediment was placed in an engineered fill in a ravine about 2 km upstream from San Gabriel reservoir. The County of Los Angeles decided that sediment again needed to be removed from the reservoirs in 1987 because, at the rate of sedimentation experienced, the reservoirs would no longer be able to contain the design flood (100-year) by 1990. The urban area downstream from Morris dam is a highly developed residential, commercial, and industrial development which makes flood control upstream a vital concern. However, for environmental reasons, the U.S. Forest Service, which is the owner of the land around the reservoirs, decided that placing removed sediment on forest land would no longer be acceptable and refused to issue the necessary permits. The County was therefore forced to locate another disposal site and chose a number of large unused gravel quarries downstream from Morris dam. Attempts had been made to use the low-level outlets to slluice sediment from Cogswell reservoir in 1978 and had resulted in a serious citation from the State of California Department of Fish and Game for destruction of fish habitat since the silts sluiced from the reservoir had covered substantial amounts of aquatic habitat in the popular fishing stream.

The scenarios for removal of the sediment considered: wet removal using a cutter-head dredge, dry removal using conventional earth-moving equipment, and transportation of the removed sediment by slurry pipeline, trucks, conveyor belt, railway, or aerial tramway. The final scheme selected on the basis of economics utilized a 1000 m³ hour^{-1} floating dredge and a 45 cm diameter slurry pipeline. The slurry is to have a concentration of 30% by weight. Capital cost for the project is estimated at $US 30 million and operational costs will be $US 4.15 per m³. The project is just beginning and will remove about 20 million m³ initially. This sediment removal project is one of very few to be carried to completion in the United States and was economically feasible only because of the very serious consequences of not providing satisfactory flood protection to the downstream area.

LEGAL ASPECTS

The legal aspects of the impacts of artificial reservoirs on hydrological equilibrium are primarily related to environmental concerns. In the United States these concerns began to be raised in the early 1960's. The concerns were primarily related to the loss of fish habitat, the inundation of land, and the loss of scenic rivers. In actuality these concerns actually were initially raised in the early 1900's when the City of San Francisco began plans to build the Hetch hetchy reservoir on the Tuolome River which inundated a scenic valley in Yosemite National Park. However, it was not until about 1965 that the Environmental Protection Agency was created and the the National Environmental Protection Act was passed by the Congress. That act was quite broad and led to a large number of environmental protection policies at the federal level. Many of these policies impacted the individual States strongly. The act essentially requires that any project to be constructed in the United States must be studied for its environmental effect which requires an Enviornmental Impact Report. That Enviornmental Impact Report must identify all impacts that construction of the project will cause and must be reviewed by all Federal and State agencies concerned with the any of the potential impacts. Any private person may also review and comment on the enviornmental report. Public hearings are usually held, and may be required to inform the public about the proposed project.   If the potential impact is judged to be significant, an Enviornmental Impact Statement may be required. The Enviornmental Impact Statement references the Enviornmental Impact Report and must develop mitigation measures which will be undertaken to mitigate the identified enviornmental impacts. For the case of dams and reservoirs detailed field studies are frequently required. These field studies usually include some studies that are normally required for design such as reservoir surveys and sediment surveys but usually include many other studies such as a survey of riparian types of fish and their numbers and the extent of use of the river and the general area for recreation. This Enviornmental Impact Statement will be widely reviewed by Local, State, and Federal agencies as well as environmental activist groups and individuals.   For a new dam the process takes several years and may result in legal action by enviornmental activist groups or concerned citizens who wish to stop the project and believe that the environmental impact of the project outweighs the economic benefit.

For storage dams without power facilities the enviornmental permits are issued by the relevant State Agencies and also by the pertinent federal agency which is usually the U.S. Army Corps of Engineers. For a dam which is to include hydroelectric power, the Federal Energy Regulatory Commission is the responsible federal agency under authority of the Electricity Consumers Protection Act. However, they cannot grant a construction license unless the required permits are granted by the pertinent State and Federal agencies.

Most developed countries have enviornmental laws which are similar to but not as broadly restrictive as those of the United States. Many developing countries, where most of the dam building is required, do not have such restrictive policies or environmental laws. If the necessary money is available, the project can go ahead. However, it is in obtaining the necessary capital that the environmental restrictions show up. The World Bank and other international lending institutions normally have developed a set of environmental considerations that must be met before they will agree to grant construction loans. They in effect require the preparation of an equivalent to an environmental impact report and its review and acceptance before they will agree to fund the project.

Almost no one would question that the US environmental laws have improved the environment or that protection of the environment must have a high priority. However, any one connected with the process of obtaining a permit is frustrated by the very long time required to pursue purely administrative requirements to obtain the necessary permits. The entire process has increased the cost of engineering and planning by at least 100% and often more for large complex projects. Most of the increase in cost occurs as a result of administrative delays and not because of technical additions. Those who are planning projects feel that the entire process can and should be shortened, that they should not need to wait for months and years after preparing an Environmental Impact Statement to receive a decision as to whether or not they are going to be allowed to build their project. Whether or not such a streamlining process can and will be achieved remains to be seen. One thing that is certain is that the entire environmental process in the USA has produced several new professions the largest, most active, and most wealthy of which may the Environmental Attorney.

REFERENCES

Aitkin, P. (1980) Salmon and Dams in Scotland, Water Power and Dam Engineering, Vol 32, No 10, October.

Australian Committee on Large Dams (1990) Dams in Australia, Hydroelectric Commission, Hobart, Tasmania, 7001, Australia.

Biswas, A. (1967) Hydrologic Engineering Prior to 600 B.C., J. Hydraul. Div. ASCE, Vol. 93, HY5, September.

Canali, G, H. Munoz, & M. Schwab (1988) Hydro in Brazil: Resolving Enviornmental Conflicts, Water Power and Dam Engineering, Vol.40, No. 4. April.

Coale, R. & J. Brezack (1989). Debris Removal from San Gabriel Watershed Reservoirs, Proc. 16th ASCE Conf. on Water Resources, Sacramento, California, USA.

Hsu, R., & M. Hsu (1988) Dredging Program for Shihmen Reservoir, 6th Congresss Asia and Pacific Regional Division IAHR, Kyoto, Japan.

Hsu, S. (1988) Headloss Characteriatics of Closely Spaced Orifices for Energy Dissipation, Proc. Symposium on Hydraulics for High Dams, Beizing, Republic of China.

International Commission on Large Dams (1989) Sedimentation Control of Reservoirs, Bulletin 67, Paris, France.

Iran Committee on Large Dams (1990) Ancient Dams of Iran, Ministry of Energy, Tehran, Iran.

Smith, H. (1973) Detrimental Effects of Dams on Environment, Transactions, Vol. 5, 11th ICOLD Congress, Madrid, Spain.

Rogers, W. (1989) The Enviornmental Benefits of Further US Hydro Development, Water Power and Dam Engineering, Vol. 41, No. 8, August.

U.S. Army Corps of Engineers (1977) HEC-6 Sour and Deposition in Rivers and Reservoirs, Hydrologic Engineering Center, Davis, California, USA.

Wodward, S. (1920) Hydraulics of the Miami Flood Control Project, Technical Report Part VII, Miami Conservancy District, Dayton, Ohio.

Hydrology in Mountainous Regions. II - Artificial Reservoirs; Water and Slopes
(Proceedings of two Lausanne Symposia, August 1990). IAHS Publ. no. 194, 1990.

Une bibliographie internationale: les impacts des actions anthropiques sur les hydrosystèmes alpins

(Réseau Européen Monde Alpin)

H. VIVIAN
Laboratoire de la Montagne Alpine, URA 344,
17 rue Maurice Gignoux, 38031 Grenoble, France

RESUME   Née en 1987, dans un groupe de travail du Réseau Européen Monde Alpin, l'idée de constituer un fond documentaire susceptible de servir de base à une action scientifique portant sur les changements subis par les eaux alpines, leurs vallées et les écosystèmes qui leurs sont liés, a abouti à la rédaction d'une bibliographie dont le fond et la forme sont décrits ici.

INTRODUCTION

L'Arc Alpin, depuis que l'homme a pénétré dans ses vallées et a peu à peu conquis ses versants, a largement utilisé une ressource semblant inépuisable et inaltérable : l'eau. De cette ressource dite renouvelable, il a été fait grand usage : usage traditionnel de l'alimentation des populations et de l'agriculture irriguée, usage énergétique et industriel né avec la seconde moitié du XIX° s. et considérablement développé au XX° s. Il ne semblait pas, jusqu'à ces dernières décennies, que des problèmes liés à cette utilisation vitale puissent apparaître. Le thème même de cette conférence internationale montre le souci présent, actuellement, dans l'esprit de tous, de connaître mieux la portée des diverses utilisations des eaux montagnardes afin de mieux les gérer et les protéger.

Ce souci a été dès 1987, celui d'un des groupes thématiques du Réseau Monde Alpin qui avait défini lors d'une réunion tenue à Zermatt, les termes d'une première action effectuée en collaboration entre les 5 pays alpins : produire une bibliographie donnant une image concrète des impacts subis par les hydrosystèmes alpins du fait d'actions humaines. Cette bibliographie, outil de travail et de réflexion et qui devrait entrainer d'autres actions, est aujourd'hui terminée.

Il a semblé opportun que sa présentation soit effectuée à l'occasion de cette conférence.

LE THEME - SES LIMITES

Le titre, donné un peu comme un défi, "la nouvelle hydrologie alpine" recouvre deux préoccupations essentielles :

   - dresser un premier inventaire des transformations subies par les eaux alpines et leurs biotopes afin de donner une image actualisée de l'hydrologie "anthropisée" du XX° siècle et la juxtaposer au schéma classique de description, d'où l'homme est exclu ;

   - mettre l'accent sur les problèmes essentiels et divers, inhérents à l'apparition de nouvelles conditions d'alimentation et d'écoulement, donc de nouveaux fonctionnements des hydrosystèmes ou même à la genèse de systèmes dérivés. La notion d'hydrosystème est prise dans son acception la plus large possible afin que soient inventoriés, du bassin versant montagnard à la vallée fluviale, les problèmes de l'évolution des paramètres du flux liquide et solide, du flux lui même, de sa dynamique et des communautés aquatiques (végétales et animales) qui sont associées à la présence de l'eau.

Préciser la limite spatiale de l'aire géographique à explorer a été une de nos préoccupations premières. Nous avons préféré opter pour la solution de l'extension spatiale maximum de l'Arc Alpin, extension portée jusqu'aux cours des quatre grands fleuves qui le bordent et qui, dans leur régime hydrologique et ceux de leurs affluents, sont marqués par l'empreinte montagnarde fort loin à l'aval. Ont pu être abordés ainsi la plus grande gamme possible d'impacts liés aux diverses formes d'utilisation des eaux, du torrent glaciaire au fleuve.

LA CONSTITUTION DU FOND DOCUMENTAIRE

Elle n'a porté que sur la documentation appartenant au domaine public, publiée ou consultable aisément et elle s'est faite en plusieurs étapes.

1. Constitution d'une équipe de travail

Dans chacun des pays alpins des correspondants ont bien voulu se charger de la collecte des références bibliographiques et de leur mise en forme provisoire. L'équipe technique qui a donné sa forme finale à la bibliographie a été celle du centre de documentation du Laboratoire de la Montagne Alpine (responsable : A. Claudel). S'y est adjoint un comité scientifique composé de cinq responsables nationaux :

- Allemagne et Suisse : Ch. Leibundgut - Institut für Physische Geographie - Freiburg i. B et Geographisches Institut - Bern.

- Autriche : H.P. Nachtnebel : Universität für Bodenkultur - Institut für Wasserwirtschaft - Wien.

- France : H. Vivian - Université de Grenoble I. - CNRS - Laboratoire de la Montagne Alpine - Grenoble. (coordonnateur)

- Italie : G. Braga - Università degli studi - Dipartimento di Ingegneria del Territorio. Pavia

- Yougoslavie : I. Bleiweis - Vodnogospodarski Institut p.o. Water Management Institut - Ljubljana

avec la colloboration de F. Vigny - Ingénieur d'Etudes CNRS (Biologie Végétale - Grenoble)

2. La banque de données centralisée à Grenoble a été alimentée de plusieurs façons :

 - réception, mise en forme, tri éventuel, traduction des références reçues des différents pays ;
 - dépouillement complémentaire de revues et ouvrages existant dans diverses bibliothèques ;
 - interrogation directe de fichiers documentaires nationaux et européens : EDF, ENEL, SCAD, ECHOS jus, ETH Zurich, Lausanne, ECOTHEK, CNRS, RESAGRI etc...

3. La forme des références bibliographiques correspond à un souci d'ouverture internationale. C'est ainsi que chaque référence est répertoriée avec son titre dans la langue

d'origine auquel est adjointe la traduction française. Il en est de même, chaque fois que cela a été possible, pour le résumé.

Les mots clefs, permettant les repérages faciles par thèmes abordés et également les interrogations directes du fichier RESALP, sont donnés en français, italien, allemand et anglais. Sont ainsi répertoriées 846 références. La France quant à elle seule en compte 381. Des travaux antérieurs avaient été entrepris au sein de RESALP - Grenoble et nous avons pu en bénéficier. Il n'en était pas de même pour les quatre autres pays alpins.

LE PLAN DE CLASSEMENT

Il a été dicté par la logique en tenant compte du fichier disponible. Quatre grandes parties sensiblement égales ont été distinguées.

1. Eaux et aménagements (180 références).

Cette partie est, de toutes, peut être la moins homogène puisqu'elle regroupe plusieurs sous-thèmes et se présente en fait comme une partie plus générale que les trois autres. Ont été classées ici des références se rapportant à des ouvrages généraux et méthodologiques sur la notion d'impact, d'environnement, l'étude des hydrosystèmes etc..., à des études dites de synthèse faites pour une action donnée et qui traitent de façon globale de toutes les répercussions possibles. Il ne s'agit parfois que d'hypothèses, justifiées certes, mais émises avant l'aménagement et pas toujours vérifiées après l'entrée en fonctionnement de celui-ci. Il en est ainsi des études dites "études d'impact" rendues peu à peu obligatoires. Par contre figurent également ici les synthèses de type universitaire, parfois pluridisciplinaires, centrées sur un cours d'eau et s'intégrant dans un programme scientifique.

Les trois parties suivantes se rapportent à des études plus pointues et plus localisées dans l'espace alpin.

2. Les hydrosystèmes alpins perturbés : les flux et leur dynamique (173 références).

Figurent ici des études consacrées à la ressource en eau, à son utilisation et aux répercussions conséquentes sur le volume, le régime, sur les charges solides transportées, sur le lit fluvial. Dans cette partie comme dans les autres, figurent aussi les signalements des études portant sur les eaux souterraines.

3. Les qualités physico-chimiques et biologiques des eaux (259 références).

Il semblerait que l'intérêt pour la qualité des eaux et les problèmes de pollution soit majeur dans toutes les Alpes. Trois sous-parties se rapportent respectivement à l'évolution des eaux courantes superficielles, à la pollution des eaux lacustres et à l'eutrophisation accélérée, à la pollution des eaux souterraines.

4. Les transformations des communautés aquatiques et des franges humides (164 références) constituent la matière de la dernière partie, avec trois grands volets se rapportant à l'écologie des eaux continentales (études de synthèse) à l'écologie végétale et à la zoologie.

Dans une partie de conclusion nous avons regroupé des références portant sur quelques aspects les plus récents de la législation de l'eau qui nous sont parvenues ; mais nous n'avons pas fait sur ce thème une exploration systématique. Le signalement de quelques ouvrages donnant des directives sur l'évaluation des débits réservés ou reflétant les diverses conceptions environnementalistes des pays alpins et leurs politiques respectives, n'a pas paru inutile.

LE CONTENU DE LA BIBLIOGRAPHIE - COMMENTAIRE

1. <u>Le poids des actions anthropiques sur les hydrosystèmes alpins et son extension spatiale</u>.

A travers cette bibliographie qui ne constitue qu'un premier sondage, il est aisé de constater que dans tout l'Arc alpin, à toutes les altitudes, des problèmes ont été posés, se posent encore ou ont été parfois solutionnés après des actions "réparatrices". De façon générale, tous les grands systèmes fluviaux sont "anthropisés", parfois même complétement artificialisés et il en est de même pour la plupart de leurs grands affluents (Durance, Isère, Arve, Aar, Reuss, Isar, Lech, Inn, Enns, Adda, Tessin...).
   Les problèmes d'eutrophisation lacustre et de pollution chimique se retrouvent aussi partout au niveau des lacs alpins et préalpins mais surtout en Italie (lac Majeur, de Garde, Orta, Varese...) France (Le Bourget, Annecy) Yougoslavie (Bled) et autour du lac Léman.
   Les études sur les paysages végétaux des systèmes fluviaux et des franges lacustres sont presqu'exclusivement autrichiennes (l'écosystème Danube), Suisses (les lacs) et françaises (lacs et Rhône supérieur). Il en est de même pour les signalements de travaux sur les changements observés dans les populations animales.

2. <u>Des lacunes documentaires à combler</u>

Parmi les "faiblesses" de la bibliographie, notons la participation inégale, selon les thèmes, des différents pays et, à l'intérieur des thèmes mêmes, un nombre de références dont l'insuffisance n'est pas à imputer à l'absence de problèmes...
   C'est ainsi que la partie consacrée aux <u>communautés aquatiques</u> est plus légère que les trois autres. Le sujet de ce type de recherche en est peut être lui même le responsable. Les perturbations apportées à l'écologie végétale comme à la faune sont des impacts au second degré demandant un certain délai avant même d'être perçus et confirmés dans un état temporaire ou définitif. Domaine encore peu exploré par la communauté scientifique, sous cet aspect évolutif du moins ? La réponse ne pourra être donnée qu'à l'issue d'une investigation auprès d'autres laboratoires que ceux qui jusqu'ici ont bien voulu collaborer.
   La raison de la faiblesse numérique des études concernant <u>les perturbations subies par les flux</u> (1ère partie) n'est peut être pas du même ordre. 38 % des signalements portent sur les changements subis par l'hydrographie et l'hydrologie alpine mais seulement 1O % sur des études précises d'abondance et de régime hydrologique... Les difficultés rencontrées trop souvent pour connaître les <u>débits réels</u> des cours d'eau en sont probablement la cause essentielle.
   Actuellement, seule la Suisse a produit pour l'ensemble de son territoire et sous forme cartographique des études de comparaison entre les débits des cours d'eau "naturels" et ces mêmes cours d'eau "influencés". (carte dressée par l'Office Fédéral des Eaux dès 1968). Une telle cartographie donnant dans l'Arc Alpin <u>les espaces</u> occupés par une hydrologie "anthropisée" et ceux où celle-ci reste pas ou peu touchée par l'homme, donnant également <u>les types d'impact</u> et <u>le poids des perturbations</u> observées, mesurées, constitue le prochain projet de travail du Réseau Européen Monde Alpin.

3. <u>Impact des retenues artificielles sur l'équilibre hydrologique</u>

Tel est le thème d'un des symposiums de la conférence. En conclusion nous avons voulu présenter la part qu'elles occupent dans notre documentation globale en tant que cause évidente de pertubations. Nous n'avons pu les distinguer des autres aménagements mis en cause que dans la mesure ou la présence d'une retenue ou d'un barrage réservoir était clairement énoncée ; d'où sans doute une sous-estimation de cette présence lorsque l'auteur parle d'un aménagement hydroélectrique, sans plus de précision (titre et résumé).

Malgré cette possible sous-estimation, le rôle des retenues est indéniable puisqu'il est évoqué dans la moitié des références se rapportant aux impacts des aménagements divers et aux impacts sur les flux et leur dynamique, ainsi que pour le quart dans les causes pertubatrices des communautés aquatiques. (Tableau 1).

TABLEAU 1

Chapitres du plan	Nombre total de références	% portant sur le rôle des retenues
1. Eaux et aménagements		
- les eaux alpines et l'hydroélectricité	43	63 %
- les impacts conjugués d'aménagements divers	33	27 %
2. Les hydrosystèmes		
- impacts sur les ressources en eau	90	53 %
- dynamique fuviale	60	43 %
3. Qualités physico-chimiques et biologiques (études de cas)	200	7 %
4. Les transformations des communautés aquatiques	168	25 %

Toutefois si la présence des ces retenues (hydroélectriques ou pour l'irrigation) en marquant le paysage alpin amène à penser qu'elles jouent un impact majeur dans les changements subis par l'environnement, d'autres aménagements contribuent aussi fortement à des transformations parfois mineures et remédiables, parfois irréversibles. Les dérivations et court circuitages de cours d'eau (liés aux retenues), les endiguements, le calibrage des lits et une surpopulation touristique sont autant de responsables de l'apparition d'une "nouvelle hydrologie alpine".

Topic A:
Runoff Processes and Slope Development

Hydrology in Mountainous Regions. II - Artificial Reservoirs; Water and Slopes
(Proceedings of two Lausanne Symposia, August 1990). IAHS Publ. no. 194, 1990.

Envasement du barrage Mohamed Ben Abdelkrim Al Khattabi et lutte anti-érosive du bassin versant montagneux situé à l'amont

ABDELHADI LAHLOU
Administration de l'Hydraulique, Avenue Hassan BEN Chekroune, RABAT, MAROC

RESUME Le bassin versant,situé au Nord-Est du Maroc est l'objet d'une forte dégradation moyenne annuelle de l'ordre de 6000t/km^2/an. A cet égard,un schéma directeur de lutte contre l'érosion et de conservation des sols,a été établi,comportant des actions mécaniques devant freiner au maximum,à court et moyen terme,les transports solides en suspension(correction des ravins,protection des berges, des terres cultivées et aménagement de confluences.par la réalisation de digues ,et des actions biologiques devant permettre,à long terme,de parvenir au contrôle des processus de l'érosion,à leur origine même.

INTRODUCTION

L'alluvionnement du barrage Mohamed Ben Abdelkrim Al Khattabi,réduit la durée de vie de ce réservoir.L'étude montre que l'envasement moyen annuel de ce lac est de 2,7 10^6m^3,pour une capacité de 43.10^6m^3 (à la cote normale)et correspondant à un pourcentage de perte annuelle du volume utile de la retenue de 6,3 % (soit 12 fois supérieure à la perte moyenne annuelle de 0,5 % obtenue pour les grands barrages du Maroc) . Par ailleurs la dégradation moyenne annuelle du bassin versant du Nekor est de 5900t/Km^2/an,l'une des plus élevées au monde.Des mesures importantes de traitement anti-érosif du bassin versant ont été effectuées consistant,particulièrement,en la reforestation et conservation des sols,et présentant des avantages indubitables à moyen et long termes. Ces travaux biologiques ont été complétés par d'autres mécaniques.

CARACTERISTIQUES DU BASSIN VERSANT

1.1. Localisation géographique
Le bassin versant du Nekor, localisé dans le Nord-Est du Maroc et dans la partie orientale des montagnes du Rif(entre les latitudes 35° 43' et 35° 6' Nord et entre les longitudes 3°36' et 4°0),s'ouvre à la Mer Méditerranée par une large plaine alluviale à l'Est de la ville d'Al Hoceima.

1.2. Courbes hypsométriques,pentes et sections longitudinales
Le bassin versant du Nekor présente des montagnes de 1000m d'altitude et la plupart dépassent 1500m.Le relief le plus accusé se trouve à l'Est du bassin versant à Azrou Akechou (2009m l'altitude).

TABLEAU 1   Altitudes moyennes et de fréquence 50 %.

AFFLUENTS	Baiou	Aissa	Malou	Chekrane
ALTITUDES MOYENNES (m)	1.318	1.052	1.207	1.154
ALTITUDES DE FREQUENCES 50%(m)	1.300	1.010	1.210	1.160

Les courbes hypsométriques établies pour les affluents du Nekor,mon-
trent que le relief est accusé:55% de la surface du bassin versant
dépassent 1000m, occasionnant des pentes élevées.
L'index global de pente est de 20,7m/km dans tout le bassin versant.
Cet index est plus élevé dans les berges de la rive gauche que pour
celles de la rive droite.
Les sections longitudinales montrent que les pentes progressent d'une
façon sensible, de l'aval à l'amont.

1.3. Caractéristiques climatiques
Le bassin versant du Nekor est localisé dans une zone aride de climat
méditerranéen(250mm de précipitation).
Le graphique n°1 montre que les précipitations moyennes annuelles des
pluviomètres,ci-haut mentionnés,varient entre 260 et 425mm.
Les précipitations sont mesurées par 2 pluviomètres présentant une
assez longue période d'observation et qui sont représentatifs de tout
le bassin versant:le premier est celui d'Imzoren(altitude 20m,implanté
dans les environs d'Al Hoceima),et le deuxième est celui de TIZI OUZLI
(altitude 1300m,situé à la limite Sud-Est du bassin versant).

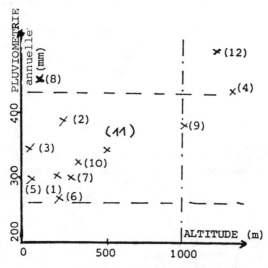

FIG. 1   Caractéristiques des pluviomètres.

Chaque numéro représente un pluviomètre

TABLEAU 2   PLUVIOMETRIE MENSUELLE,ET ANNUELLE P en mm,AUX STATIONS
             PLUVIOMETRIQUES IMZOREN ET TIZI OUZLI.

MOIS	S	O	N	D	J	F	M	A	M	J	J	A	P(mm)
IMZOREN	10	26	28	44	38	31	38	46	32	12	0	0	306
TIZI OUSLI	23	37	36	40	46	43	56	66	28	19	5	10	419

TABLEAU 3   NOMBRE DE JOURS DE PLUIE MENSUEL,ET ANNUEL N,AUX 2 STATIONS
             PLUVIOMETRIQUES PRINCIPALES.

MOIS	S	O	N	D	J	F	M	A	M	J	J	A	N'
IMZOREN	1,7	3,4	4,7	5,9	5,2	4,9	5,3	4,9	3,5	3,0	0,4	1,5	42
TIZI OUSLI	3,2	5,2	4,7	6,0	5,2	5,3	6,5	6,3	3,5	3,0	0,4	1,5	51

Il y a, par an, 42 jours de pluie à Imzoren et 51 Tizi Ousli.

Intensité de la pluie et agressivité climatique :

Le coefficient d'agressivité de FOURNIER est donné par : $C = P^2 / \bar{P}$ (où
P est la précipitation du mois le plus humide et $\bar{P}$ est la précipitation
moyenne annuelle)
Le tableau n°4 indique la comparaison entre le coefficient C calculé
dans le bassin versant du LOUKKOS(côté atlantique du RIF), et dans le
bassin versant du Nekor (Coté Est du Nekor).

TABLEAU 4   COEFFICIENTS D'AGRESSIVITE CLIMATIQUE.

BASSIN VERSANT DU NEKOR		BASSIN VERSANT DU LOUKKOS		
IMZOREN	TIZI OUSLI	S.EL KOLLA	OUEZZANE	ZOUMI
33	34	124	81	134

Au Maroc, les données des précipitations mensuelles dûment contrôlées
de 112 pluviomètres, sont disponibles. La relation log-log suivante
trouvée dans les pays de l'Est Africain, a été appliquée, à bon escient,

au Maroc et vérifiée par les 112 stations précitées :

$$R = 1,735 \times 10(1,5 \quad \log \sum_{1}^{12} \frac{P^2}{\bar{P}} - 0,8188)$$ (1)

avec P : précipitation du mois le plus humide
$\bar{P}$: précipitation moyenne
annuelle

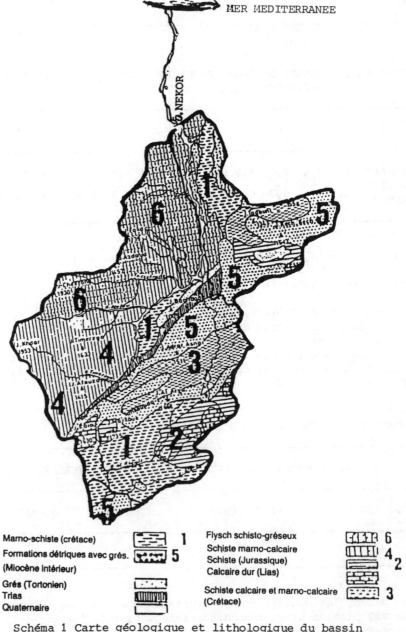

Marno-schiste (crétace)	1
Formations détriques avec grés. (Miocène intérieur)	5
Grés (Tortonien) Trias Quaternaire	

Flysch schisto-gréseux	6
Schiste marno-calcaire Schiste (Jurassique) Calcaire dur (Lias)	4 2
Schiste calcaire et marno-calcaire (Crétace)	3

Schéma 1 Carte géologique et lithologique du bassin versant du Nekor.

1.4. Géologie et géomorphologie
La géomorphologie du Nekor est définie par un ancien géosynclinal,
tous les faciès présentent une faible résistance à la météorisation
(voir schéma 1)

1.5. Apports à la station hydromètrique de Tamellaht
La station hydrologique de Tamellaht,couvrant une superficie de
bassin versant de 685km^2 (eu égard à celle de 780 Km^2 au barrage), a
permis, avant la construction du barrage,de déterminer,par corrélation
hydropluviométrique(entre les apports à la station hydrologique et le
barrage),et par reconstitution statistique d'une période de 30 ans
(de 1932 à 1977), l'apport moyen annuel au site de la retenue qui
était alors de 93.10^{6}m^3,correspondant à un débit moyen annuel de 2,95
m^3/s, débit   un peu plus élevé que celui établi sur 38 ans (de
1947 à 1985),vu que les dernières années ont été l'objet d'une sécheresse aigüe.

1.6. Caractéristiques de l'Oued Nekor au site du barrage Mohamed Ben
Abdelkrim Al Khattabi.
- La surface du bassin versant du fleuve au barrage est de : 780 km^2
- L'apport moyen annuel au barrage (jusqu'à 1985)est de:89.10^6 m^3,
  correspondant à un débit moyen annuel au barrage de : 2,54 m^3/s.
- La pluviomètrie moyenne annuelle (à fin 1985),est de 340 mm.
- La nature lithologique dominante du bassin versant est constituée
  par des marnes, des flyschs, des calcaires et des grès.
- La dégradation moyenne est de : 5900 t/Km^2 /an.

- Le transport solide par charriage de l'Oued Nekor, représente 20 à

  30 % du transport solide en suspension.

1.7. Transports solides de l'Oued Nekor
Les différents types d'érosions observées au bassin versant sont :
rigoles,ravines,glissements des berges.Les concentrations des matériaux
solides mesurées à la station hydrométrique de TAMELLAHT, ont fourni
les volumes solides transportés annuellement à cette station,ainsi que
les dégradations spécifiques moyennes annuelles indiquées dans le
tableau 5 .

* Les transports solides indiqués par l'astérix (*) sont fournis par
M.C. Balau en 1974 dans le cadre du schéma d'aménagement du bassin
versant du Nekor.
+ Les transports solides indiqués par l'indicatif(+)sont fournis par
le rapport établi en 1982 par la Division des Ressources en Eau et
intitulé : "Elaboration des débits liquides et solides de l'Oued Nekor
à la station Tamellaht".

Les 2 tableaux suivants montrent respectivement la grande variabilité
des apports liquides et solides,d'une année à l'autre,à la station
hydrométrique principale de Tamellaht,conséquence: du climat méditerranéen : c'est ainsi que les apports d'eau à la station peuvent varier
de 7.10^{6}m^3/an (1984/85) à 208.10^{6}m^3/an (1955/56), d'une année trop
sèche à une année trop humide. De même on remarque que les apports
solides annuels accusent des variations de 0,28 10^{6}m^3/an (1971/72) à
19,4 10^{6}m^3/an (1967/68).

TABLEAU 4   Années trop sèches, sèches, moyennes, humides et   trop
humides: (apports moyens annuels et nombre de ces années),au barrage
Mohamed Ben Abdelkrim AL Khattabi.

Caractéristiques des années	Probabilité f %	Limites des apports par types d'an- nées(en $10^6 m^3$)	nombre d'années	%par rapport au nombre total d'années
Trop sèches(TS)	f>90	41>A> 7	3	8
Sèches (S)	90>f>65	65>A>41	10	26
Moyennes (M)	65>f>35	104>A>65	29	
Humides (H)	35>10	145>A>104	10	26
Trop humides(TH)	f<10	208>A>145		
		Total	n-38	100 %

Années(TH) : 1955/56, 1967/68, 1954/55 et 1952/53.
Années(H)   : 1947/48, 1962/63, 1975/76, 1969/70, 1961/62, 1968/69,
              1959/60, 1951/52 et 1956/57, 1953/54.
Années (M) : 1964/65, 1973/74, 1950/51, 1971/72, 1970/71, 1974/75
              1958/59, 1965/66, 1948/49 et 1960/61, 1977/78.
Années (S)   1949/50, 1966/67, 1957/58, 1976/77, 1980/81, 1963/64,
              1979/80, 1978/79 et 1981/82, 1972/73.
Années(TS) : 1949/50, 1983/84, 1982/83 et 1984/85.

TABLEAU 5   Transport solide et dégradations moyennes annuelles à la
station de Tamellaht.

Années	Transports solides $10^6 m^3$			Degradation spéci- moyenne annuelle D en t/km2./an
	*T	+T	*D	+D
1965/66	2,7		3.400	
1966/67	2,8		3.600	
1967/68	19,4	8,4	25.000	12.300
1968/69	13,3		17.000	
1969/70	4,8		6.200	
1970/71	5,4	1,26	7.000	1.900
1971/72	0,8	0,28	1.000	400
1972/73	2,3	1,54	3.000	2.300
1973/74	4,1	1,71	5.300	2.500
1974/75		2,24		3.300
1975/76		0,82		1.200
1976/77		0,64		940
1977/78		1,03		1.500
1978/79		0,5		730
1979/80		0,24		350

1.8. <u>Expicitation des différences élevées des dégradations spécifiques</u>
<u>moyennes annuelles observées à la station hydrologique Tamallaht</u>

Parmi les causes des écarts élevés constatés entre les valeurs des érosions spécifiques annuelles, on peut citer entre autres :

- Les fortes variations annuelles des apports liquides transitant ces suspensions .

Comme toutes les régions arides à semi-arides,la moyenne des précipitations est sujette à des fluctuations relativement grandes d'une année à l'autre, avec des périodes sèches ou humides de 2 à 5 années consécutives (exemple:sècheresse des 5 années successives de 1980 à 1985 dans tous le MAROC). La valeur des dégradations annuelles liées à ces fluctuations pluviométriques subit,par conséquent,des variations corrélativement aussi élevées .

- Les fortes variations annuelles d'agressivité climatique d'une année à l'autre, dues aux intensités pluviométriques maximales instantanées : Certes plusieurs formules ont été présentées telles que celle de HMJ.ARNOLDUS établie à partir des observations relevées sur 112 pluviomètres (en AFRIQUE), fournissant le coefficient d'agressivité R en fonction du rapport $\dfrac{P^2}{\overline{P}}$ (P : précipitation du mois le plus humide et $\overline{P}$ précipitation moyenne annuelle, en mm)

$$R = 17,3 \left(1,5 \log \sum_{1}^{12} \frac{P^2}{\overline{P}} - 0,8188 \right)$$

Au Maroc l'érosion par saturation est la plus élevée,comparativement à l'érosion non moins importante dûe aux pluies intenses (ont été observés des intensités maximales de 30', de période de retour 10 ans,de 1 mm/mn à 2,5 mm/mn). Comme les apports liquides élevés se situent entre Novembre et Février, c'est dans cette période que sont observées des variations élevées de dégradations spécifiques moyennes annuelles.

TRAITEMENTS ANTI-EROSIFS REALISES DANS LE BASSIN VERSANT MONTAGNEUX AMONT

Par ailleurs, les traitements mécaniques des bassins versants, à court et moyen termes : (protection des berges et des terrasses alluviales, construction de seuils et d'épis guide-eau aux confluences),et les interventions biologiques à long terme,sont des aménagements déterminants,réduisant l'érosion à sa source, donc le transport solide et l'envasement des barrages,en plus d'une politique adéquate de gestion des grands ouvrages hydrauliques. Ci-après les photos n° 1 et n° 2 fournissent quelques exemples de seuils de sédimentation en gabions et en pierres sèches,réalisés dans le bassin versant du Nekor,en vue de réduire la torrentialité du réseau hydrographique par la réalisation d'un nombre déterminé de ces ouvrages sur le même affluent (c'est ainsi que 12 grands seuils type photo n°1 ont été réalisés sur les grands affluents, et 800 petits seuils, de type photo n° 2 , ont été réalisés, répartis comme suit : seuils en pièrre sèche 130, gabions 254 et seuils métalliques : 4160. Remarquons que la protection biologique a consisté, à ce jour, en la réalisation de reboisements de protection de 3200 ha dans 3 provinces situées en montagne (AL HUCEIMA, NADOR et TAZA) et en plantations fruitières : banquettes sur 355 ha.

Dans le schéma directeur du bassin versant du Nekor,il est prévu des traitements anti-érosifs agro-sylvo-pastoraux de 59.000 ha sur les 78.000 ha du bassin versant et la réalisation d'une grande quantité de seuils de sédimentation supplémentaires (12.000 petits en pierres sèches type photo n°2 et 5 grands améliorés type photo n°1) .

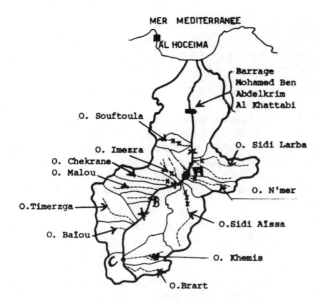

Localisation des 3 stations hydrologiques du bassin versant du Nekor :

A : station Tamellaht

B : station Takenfoust

C : station d'Ajdir

Seule la station hydrologique de Tamellaht a servi à la présente étude,vue la série plus étendue des apports liquides et solides qui y sont observés.

Schéma 2 : Implantation des 12 seuils réalisés à ce jour
(représentés par des croix   x   ).

Photo 1 : Type de seuil de sedimentation réalisé sur
l'oued BRART.

CONCLUSION

Cette étude, récapitulant les analyses d'érosion, de débit liquide et de la suspension de l'Oued Nekor et de ses affluents, ainsi que l'envasement du barrage Sidi Mohamed Ben Abdelkrim Al Khattabi, en tenant compte de la lithologie de la surface de la pluviométrie du bassin versant , permet :
- l'évaluation du transport solide moyen annuel en vue de la déter-

Photo 2 : Type de seuil (en pierres sèches) de correction
torrentielle hydrographique.

mination des seuils à réaliser à moyen terme (de 1988 à 1990), et à
long terme, qui sont prévus dans le plan directeur de traitement
anti-érosif du bassin versant.
-l'envasement moyen annuel du barrage Sidi Mohamed Ben Abdelkrim Al
Khattabi (2,7 $10^6 m^3$ par an), à partir des méthodes précitées a été
complété,en 1985   , par des travaux bathymétriques ,ayant abouti à
un envasement total de la retenue de 4,9 $10^6 m^3$ à la cote 140 m ,depuis
Janvier 1981, date de mise en service et Mai 1985) soit 11 % du volume initial ou 1,2 $10^6 m^3$ par an : mais cette valeur trop faible, est
justifiée par la sécheresse vécue par cette région depuis 1981,et ne
représente pas une valeur moyenne.

Recommandations
- Il est intéressant, en vue de parfaire l'analyse précédente,
d'augmenter la fréquence de travaux d'envasement des barrages exis-
tants,au vu de l'importance de leurs taux annuels d'alluvionnement
(la fréquence sera d'autant plus élevée que la sédimentation est
importante et que la capacité est réduite). Une fréquence de 2 ans
et,même annuelle,de mesures d'atterrissements aux barrages (par
bathymétrie , topographie, etc...)est à réaliser; il est à remarquer
que ces travaux doivent être réalisés juste après une crue importante
en vue de rétablir la nouvelle courbe de capacité (en fonction de la
hauteur).
- Il est recommandé d'analyser tous les facteurs intervenant dans le
phénomène de l'érosion:exemple couvert végétal, superficies cultivées
pluviométrie avec toutes ses fréquences (maximale de 24 h, de 30',
etc...): apports de crues, pentes,etc.. une série de formules,basées
sur ces données, reste à établir.
- Une analyse détaillée de la suspension et du charriage reste à faire
à cet égard, des mesures de concentrations sont à réaliser à plusieurs
niveaux de l'Oued Nekor et de ses affluents, en vue de parfaire la
connaissance de ces transports, de leur évolution dans le temps et
l'espace.
- Les traitements mécaniques décrits précédemment(construction de
seuils de sédimentation), sont à réaliser dans le temps prévu,car
tout retard dans la réalisation du programme du plan directeur aura
un impact sur la réduction de l'érosion souhaitée.
-Les interventions biologiques annuelles,en vue de réduire l'érosion
à son origine,seront 10 fois plus importantes que celles précédemment
réalisés;pour cette raison,un intérêt particulier est à imposer dans
divers domaines : financier, technique, moyens personnels. Il est

nécessaire, par conséquent, de respecter les travaux précisés dans le plan directeur.

- Dans le but de réduire l'envasement du barrage Sidi Med Ben Abdelkrim Al Khattabi,plusieurs solutions ont été étudiées, les premières à l'aide d'un modèle mathématique et ensuite à l'aide d'un modèle hydraulique développé dans le laboratoire hydraulique de Zurich.

REFERENCES

M.LAHLOU Abdelhadi : "Erosion et dégradation du substratum des bassins versants au Maroc, Communication personnelle présentée dans le cadre de l'International Symposium on Erosion and sedimentation, UNESCO PARIS (from 4 to 8 July 1977).

Mediterranean conference : " L'Erosion et l'aménagement des bassins versants dans les pays méditerranéens", 11-15 Sépt.1978.Publié par le Comité National MAB du Maroc avec la contribution de l'UNESCO dans le n°30 de Jan-Fév. 1979 de la revue : "Hommes,terres et eaux' de l'ANAFID.

M.LAHLOU Abdelhadi : Conférence "dévasage des barrages" Tunis, 1980 communication : "Envasement des barrages du Maroc" CEFIGRE.

M.LAHLOU Abdelhadi : First national conference of hydrology in Irak (Baghdad) the paper presented is : "Envasement des barrages au Maroc" (1981).

M.LAHLOU Abdelhadi :"La dégradation spécifique moyenne annuelle des bassins versants et son impact sur l'envasement des barrages",in the first international conference of AISH intituled : " Recent developments in the Explanat nation and prediction of erosion and sediment yield" (Proceeding of the Exeter Symposium,in England , July 1982, IAHS publication n°137, pp.163-169).

M.LAHLOU Abdelhadi : "Etude actualisée de l'envasement des barrages au Maroc", texte présenté dans "les technologies appropriées pour l'eau et l'assainissement en zones arides", organisé par l'OMS,le PNUD et l'Ecole Mohammadia d'Ingéniers p.p. 61 à 78 du rapport de l'OMS, 9184.

Proceedings vth world congress on water resources AIRE Brussels volume 3, supplements 8-15 June 1985. Water Resources For Rural Areas and their communities Paper number 391 aspect number 4. " Etude actualisée de l'envasement des retenues des barrages du Maroc "par M.LAHLOU Abdelhadi, pp. 1419 à 1430.

Groupement d'intérêt scientifique pour les sciences de l'eau. vol.6, n°3, 1987 Trimestriel n°ISSN 0298-8663.LAVOISIER ABONNEMENT PARIS. "Etude actualisée de l'envasement des barrages du Maroc" par M.LAHLOU Abdelhadi, pp. 337 à 356.

M.LAHLOU ABDELHADI : "Silting-up of Moroccan dams" la communication présentée dans le cadre du 1ier Colloque international en Afrique sur la simulation numérique et les Ressources en Eau,sponsorisé pour l'Administration de l'Hydraulique et l'EMI, et tenu à l'Ecole Mohammadia d'Ingénieurs du 14 au 24 Mars 1988 à Rabat

M.LAHLOU ABDELHADI:Présentation d'une communication personnelle intitulée "Silting-up of Moroccan dams" dans le cadre de l'international symposium on sediment budgets,organisé par les 2 institutions brésiliennes:IRH,URFGS et AISH,11-15 Déc.1988 p.71 à 77 (PORTO ALLEGRE) BRESIL.

Hydrology in Mountainous Regions.   II - Artificial Reservoirs; Water and Slopes
(Proceedings of two Lausanne Symposia, August 1990). IAHS Publ. no. 194, 1990.

Relations entre les pertes de terre mensuelles et les conditions climatiques sur une parcelle défrichée du massif des Maures, France

C. MARTIN
U.R.A. 903 du C.N.R.S., 29 Avenue Robert Schuman,
F 13621 Aix-en-Provence Cedex, France

RESUME   Les recherches portent sur une parcelle défrichée
non labourée.   Elles conduisent à établir un indice
d'érosivité climatique adapté à l'étude de l'érosion
pluviale des sols sableux.

INTRODUCTION

Le massif des Maures subit périodiquement des incendies de forêt
catastrophiques.   L'exploitation, à la station de Lambert, d'une
parcelle expérimentale défrichée, permet d'aborder le problème des
relations entre les conditions climatiques et l'érosion pluviale en
l'absence de couvert végétal.

MESURES

Située au coeur du massif (Fig. 1), à 550 m d'altitude, la station
connaît un climat de type méditerranéen humide.   La parcelle est
isolée par une bordure en tôles.   Elle présente la forme d'un
parallélogramme de 87.5 m² pour une longueur de 12 m (Fig. 2).   La
pente est de 11°.   Un chenal d'écoulement relie la parcelle à une
batterie de deux cuves réceptrices (1000 l) dont la première sert de
partiteur au 1/9. L'équipement comporte un pluviographe.   Les sols
sont des rankers sur gneiss, très caillouteux et sableux (épaisseur :
< 30 cm ; structure :   particulaire à submotteuse ; refus à 2 mm :
45 % ; fraction 0.05-2 mm :   72 % de la terre fine ;   fraction < 2µm :
10 % ; matière organique :   4.1 %).   Ils peuvent être considérés comme
peu érodibles, leur indice d'érodibilité K de Wischmeier et al. (1971)
avoisinant 0.05.   Ils ne sont jamais binés ni labourés.
  Le Tableau 1 regroupe l'ensemble des observations mensuelles.   De
septembre 1976 à août 1980, sous l'action conjuguée de la saltation
pluviale et du ruissellement diffus, les pertes de terre mensuelles
ont varié de 0 à 5.41 t ha^{-1} (P = 1 à 485 mm) et les exportations
annuelles de 2.00 à 16.09 t ha^{-1} (P = 841 à 1683 mm).   Les pertes de
terre annuelles moyennes se sont élevées à 6.98 t ha^{-1} (P = 1290 mm).
L'érosion a bien sûr manifesté un caractère nettement sélectif, les
produits exportés étant beaucoup plus riches en matière organique et
en particules fines que les sols (Martin, 1986, 1989).

DISCUSSION

Lors du traitement statistique des données, deux mois n'ont pas été

FIG. 1   Localisation de la station expérimentale.

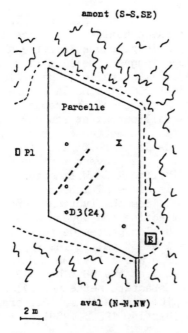

FIG. 2   Présentation de la parcelle défrichée.
∘ : piézomètres. Pl : pluviographe. E : appareil
enregistreur de l'humidité des sols (X : électrodes et
thermosonde en terrain défriché).   --- : principaux
alignements de chicots de gneiss.

TABLEAU 1 Exportations de terre et paramètres hydrologiques.

	S	O	N	D	J	F	M	A	M	J	Jt	At
1976-77												
E	23.1	40.1	8.2	3.0	3.4	0.0	1.2	0.0	14.5	0.0	0.0	47.3
c	20.3	3.3	4.8	7.6	0.5	–	5.0	–	6.2	–	–	7.4
V	1138	12247	1695	396	7242	0.0	250	0.0	2327	0.0	0.0	6385
P	68.6	485	95.0	127	273	78.0	77.8	5.4	273	9.8	21.6	168
i.moy	5.2	7.2	5.0	4.5	4.0	4.0	7.2	0.8	9.9	1.4	3.1	16.5
d	86.3	182	89.2	14.1	106	0.0	23.1	0.0	84.3	0.0	0.0	626
IAPm	5.0	85.3	7.6	8.6	16.9	3.5	6.2	0.0	49.2	0.0	0.0	93.2
1977-78												
E	0.0	0.0	2.5	25.6	0.1	0.01	1.4	0.3	0.7	0.1	0.0	0.0
c	–	0.0	1.9	2.5	0.2	0.1	2.8	1.1	1.1	0.5	–	–
V	0.0	137	1270	10390	925	135	495	275	670	190	0.0	0.0
P	3.6	44.2	94.0	238	287	198	174	107	116	16.4	4.8	1.2
i.moy	0.7	1.8	8.3	8.4	4.8	3.6	8.4	3.4	4.7	2.9	2.1	1.0
d	0.0	5.6	112	366	15.5	2.5	23.8	8.7	27.2	33.6	0.0	0.0
IAPm	0.0	0.3	19.9	58.8	27.0	9.4	33.8	3.3	6.4	0.0	0.0	0.0
1978-79												
E	16.2	0.0	0.0	0.0	0.0	0.5	0.3	0.5	0.0	0.0	0.0	0.0
c	16.2	–	–	0.0	–	2.0	1.3	2.1	–	–	–	–
V	1000	0.0	0.0	50	0.0	226	230	241	0.0	0.0	0.0	0.0
P	62.8	24.4	21.8	126	238	162	127	60.2	8.2	4.2	5.2	1.6
i.moy	24.7	1.0	1.2	2.3	2.6	4.2	3.5	4.2	1.6	1.5	2.2	0.8
d	393	0.0	0.0	0.9	0.0	5.9	6.3	16.8	0.0	0.0	0.0	0.0
IAPm	53.5	0.02	0.05	2.0	6.2	10.2	3.8	3.4	0.0	0.0	0.0	0.0
1979-80												
E	0.1	40.8	1.8	0.0	0.0	0.0	0.4	0.0	3.3	0.0	0.0	9.0
c	0.4	3.5	1.9	0.0	0.0	–	0.8	0.0	1.8	–	–	1.5
V	223	11715	963	308	178	0.0	470	213	1812	0.0	0.0	5950
P	53.8	416	56.8	141	129	6.0	103	75.8	174	23.4	16.6	155
i.moy	2.9	7.4	5.3	4.1	2.6	2.0	4.1	2.0	4.4	5.3	4.4	18.5
d	12.0	208	89.9	9.0	3.6	0.0	18.7	5.6	45.8	0.0	0.0	712
IAPm	0.7	75.9	5.1	9.0	3.0	0.0	6.3	0.9	13.4	0.0	0.0	108

E : exportations (kg). c : charge solide moyenne des eaux écoulées (g l^{-1}). V : volume d'eau écoulé (l). P : précipitations (mm). i.moy : moyenne arithmétique des intensités momentanées de la pluie pondérées par les volumes d'eau précipités (mm h^{-1}). d : indice d [d = (eau ruisselée en l x i.moy en mm h^{-1}) / P en mm ; il correspond approximativement à la moyenne arithmétique des débits instantanés à l'exutoire de la parcelle pondérés par les volumes d'eau écoulés, en l h^{-1}]. IAPm : indice d'agressivité pluviométrique mensuel (voir dans le texte).

pris en considération :
(a) Septembre 1976, pour lequel l'efficacité de l'érosion résulte -
outre de la perturbation des sols provoquée par l'aménagement de la
parcelle - de l'ablation d'un mince horizon superficiel très humifère,
extrêmement sensible à l'action des eaux pluviales du fait de sa
structure finement grenue.
(b) Août 1980, au cours duquel la parcelle s'est trouvée envahie par
des herbes. Celles-ci n'ont pas entravé le ruissellement superficiel,
mais elles ont beaucoup gêné l'érosion mécanique.

Relations entre les variables mesurées

L'étude des régressions linéaires entre les données concernant les
exportations de terre et différents paramètres hydrologiques ou
climatiques (nombre de mois considérés, n = 46 - dont 24 où les pluies
ont provoqué une ablation du sol), fournit les indications suivantes :
    (a) Les coefficients de corrélation (r) entre la concentration
des éléments solides dans les eaux écoulées (0 à 16.2 mg l^{-1}) et
trois variables caractéristiques des intensités de la pluie (i.moy :
voir la légende du Tableau 1 ; i.méd : médiane des intensités
momentanées de la pluie ; iQ$_3$: troisième quartile des intensités
momentanées de la pluie) sont compris entre + 0.842 et + 0.886
(i.moy = 0.7 à 24.7 mm h^{-1} ; i.méd = 0.7 à 36.0 mm h^{-1} ; i.Q$_3$ = 0.9 à
36.0 mm h^{-1}). Ces résultats témoignent de l'influence de l'intensité
des précipitations sur l'érosion pluviale.
    (b) Le coefficient de corrélation entre la concentration des
éléments solides dans les eaux et un indice d représentatif de la
violence de l'écoulement (voir la légende du Tableau 1), s'établit à
+ 0.621, avec d compris entre 2.5 et 603 (Fig. 3). Cette relation
manifeste un caractère assez lâche pour deux raisons principales :
d'une part, l'épaississement de la lame d'eau superficielle gêne la
saltation pluviale lors des averses très violentes et, d'autre part,
des écoulements assez forts se produisent lorsque des précipitations
peu intenses mais extrêmement abondantes amènent les roches altérées
et les sols à saturation. A l'évidence, sur sol humifère à texture
sableuse, le ruissellement diffus ne possède pas, par lui-même, un
grand pouvoir abrasif.
    (c) Le coefficient de corrélation entre les exportations de
terre et les précipitations s'élève à + 0.644. Les relations
apparaissent beaucoup plus étroites avec les volumes d'eau écoulés
(r = + 0.867) et les produits des précipitations par les intensités
i.moy, i.méd et i.Q$_3$ (r = + 0.880 à + 0.901).

Pertes de terre et conditions climatiques

L'indice d'agressivité climatique le plus largement utilisé dans le
monde est celui de Wischmeier (1959). A la station de Lambert, le
coefficient de corrélation entre les pertes de terre mensuelles et
l'indice R de Wischmeier se révèle très décevant : r = + 0.655.
    Une approche par tâtonnements successifs nous a permis de mettre
au point une formule empirique traduisant de façon satisfaisante les
liens entre les exportations de terre mensuelles (E) et les conditions
climatiques (r = + 0.946) :

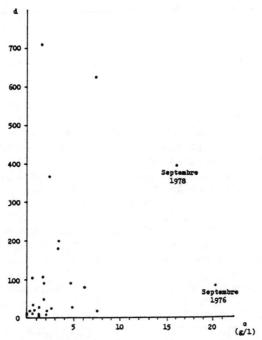

FIG. 3   Relation entre les concentrations moyennes
mensuelles des eaux en produits solides (c) et l'indice d.

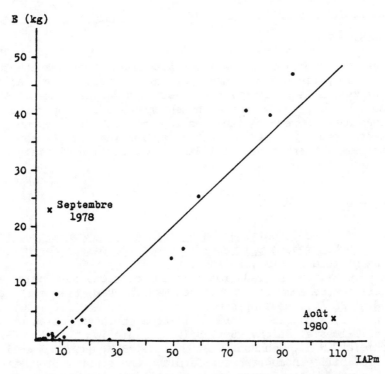

FIG. 4   Relation entre les pertes de terre mensuelles
(E) et l'indice d'agressivité pluviométrique IAPm.

E (t ha⁻¹) = 0.0548 IAPm - 0.35

avec

IAPm (indice d'agressivité pluviométrique mensuel) = (A x F) / 100

où

(a) A = (P - 0.3 ETP) x log (0.95 i.méd + 0.05 i.Q₃)
Les précipitations (P) et l'évapotranspiration potentielle selon la
formule de TURC (ETP) sont exprimées en mm ; i.Q₃, en mm h⁻¹. Le
terme A est grossièrement proportionnel à l'abondance de l'écoulement
lorsque les roches altérées ne sont pas saturées en eau. Sa valeur
est volontairement limitée à celle des précipitations.
(b) F = [(0.89 x log (0.7 i.méd + 0.2 i.Q₃ + 0.1 i.5')) +
      1.214] x (0.9 i.Q₃ + 0.1 i.5')
i.méd, i.Q₃ et i.5' (intensité maximale en cinq minutes) sont
exprimées en mm h⁻¹. Le terme F est représentatif de la violence de
l'action érosive développée par les gouttes de pluie.

Les résultats obtenus par cette méthode sont représentés sur la
Figure 4.
La somme des indices mensuels fournit la valeur des indices
saisonniers (IAPs) et annuels (IAPa). Les coefficients de corrélation
entre les pertes de terre et les indices IAP atteignent + 0.953 pour
les données saisonnières (n = 16) et + 0.928 pour les données
annuelles (n = 4).

CONCLUSION

Toutes les conditions climatiques possibles n'ont pas été observées
pendant la période des mesures, en particulier sur le plan des
intensités de la pluie qui sont restées modérées (intensité maximale
en 30 minutes : 36.0 mm h⁻¹ en septembre 1978 ; contre 88.3 mm h⁻¹,
relevés dans le même secteur, en septembre 1968). Cependant, sauf
peut-être pour quelques cas extrêmes, les indices IAP sont
certainement bien adaptés à l'étude de l'érosion pluviale des sols
sableux.

REFERENCES

Martin, C. (1986) Contribution à l'étude de la dynamique des versants
    en roches métamorphiques ; l'exemple du massif des Maures. Thèse
    de Doctorat d'Etat, Paris I.
Martin, C. (1989) Dégradation d'un sol défriché sur gneiss à la
    station de Lambert (Massif des Maures, Var, France). Rev. Géom.
    dyn. 38 (1), sous presse.
Wischmeier, W.H. (1959) A rainfall erosion index for an universal
    soil-loss equation. Soil Sci. Soc. America J. 23, 246-249.
Wischmeier, W.H., Johnson, C.B. & Cross, B.U. (1971) A soil
    erodibility nomograph for farmland and construction sites. J. of
    Soil and Water Conservation 26 (5), 189-192.

Erosion des terres noires de la Vallée du Buech, Alpes du Sud

J. C. OLIVRY & J. HOORELBECK
ORSTOM, 213 Rue La Fayette, 75010 Paris, France

ABSTRACT   Erosion of black grounds of Buech valley.
Since 1985, a BRGM-ORSTOM program is studying erosion processes
on representative basins of Savournon in Buech valley. Suspended and
bed load, hydrological and climatic parameters, slope microtopography
evolution have been measured. Solid transport budget to outlets allow to
consider a specific degradation mean value in the order of 10 000 t.km^{-2}
year^{-1} and to identifie the productive areas so that nuded or with a
scattered vegetation soils. A model is proposed showing a correlation
these data and the slope mean erosion.

GENERALITES

L'ORSTOM et le BRGM ont réalisé de 1985 à 1988 une étude sur l'estimation des
bilans d'exportation de matières solides en zones sensibles à l'érosion, dans les Alpes
du Sud. Les travaux, localisés aux vallées du Buëch et de la moyenne-Durance, ont
porté notamment sur deux bassins emboîtés (75 et 7,8 ha) suivis à Savournon près de
SERRES.
     La région se caractérise par des formations lithographiques très vulnérables à
l'érosion météorique, marnes ou «Terres Noires» du jurassique supérieur ; les bassins
de Savournon sont creusés dans les horizons marneux du Callovien inférieur et moyen
homogène dans la région (calcite : 14%, fraction argileuse : 60% dont 16% argiles
gonflantes...).
     Cette région des Préalpes du Sud connait un climat méditerranéen et montagnard
marqué par la sécheresse estivale, par l'irrégularité interannuelle des précipitations, par
un fort ensoleillement entrainant de fortes amplitudes thermiques diurnes et un grand
nombre d'alternances gel/dégel et par ses précipitations nivales et ses températures
hivernales (plus de cent jours de gel par an). La normale des précipitations annuelles
(1951 - 80) est de 912 mm à SERRES (Alt. 665 m).
     Les bassins étudiés sont caractérisés par un paysage dominant de roubines (ou
bad-lands) aux terres nues ou à faible couvert végétal. Les ravines y sont actives et
constituent autant de drains de ruissellement et de transport des produits d'érosion. Les
pentes sont très fortes et dépassent souvent 50% en tête de bassin et 35% sur bad-lands.

LES OBSERVATIONS ; MESURES ET PROCESSUS DE L'EROSION

Sur la période d'étude, plus de 74% des précipitations journalières mesurées à Savournon sont inférieures à 10 mm et 14% comprises entre 10 et 20 mm. L'apparition de l'écoulement n'est pas observée pour les averses de moins de 10 mm. Un deuxième seuil est celui de l'intensité de la pluie (20 mm h^{-1}). Peu d'evenements sont susceptibles d'avoir un pouvoir érosif. Les paramètres de la pluie (hauteur, intensité, durée de la pluie utile) en jouant sur le volume de la crue et son maximum ajoutent à leur incidence érosive sur les versants, une incidence déterminante dans la capacité de transport et d'érosivité au niveau du réseau hydrographique. Pour des événements pluviométriques très importants, on observe sur les deux bassins des coefficients d'écoulement pouvant aller jusqu'à 50 et 60%, soit un ruissellement de 80 à 90% sur les terres nues de roubines.

L'étude des suspensions et du charriage montre qu'il n'y a pas de relation nette entre tonnages exportés en suspension et ceux piègés après identification de la part de gros matériaux. A Savournon II (75 ha) la part des «fines», (particules inférieures à 0,5 mm) peut passer de 90 à plus de 95% de la charge solide totale alors que pour Savournon I (7,8 ha), la part de la fraction «charriage» est plus forte. Le transport hydrique est trop court pour détruire toute la cohésion du matériel grossier. Pour les plus fortes averses, la charge en matériau grossier peut atteindre 30 à 40% de la charge totale et on a même pu observer de véritables laves torrentielles.

L'analyse des evenements «pluie-crue-exportation de matière» a montré une grande dispersion des phénomènes à l'échelle d'evenements ponctuels. On a noté les plus fortes crues au printemps et des concentrations très fortes (>400, 500 g^{l-1}) en fin d'été ou en automne (disponibilité du matériau par dessication de la surface d'altération des versants). De fortes pluies étalées dans le temps (>60 mm) ne montrent pas de production notable de sédiment à l'exutoire des bassins, mais ont souvent des effets différés (coulée de boue, glissements).

La plupart des phénomènes et processus d'érosion décrits par les géographes sur ce type de milieu ont été observés sur ces bassins. L'intégration de tous ces processus, plus ou moins aléatoires ou plus ou moins spécifiques aux différentes composantes géomorphologiques, suppose bien que les bilans d'érosion de ces paysages de roubines soient directement mesurés à l'exutoire de bassins d'une taille minimale (10 ha).

Les mécanismes les plus fréquents paraissent s'ordonner suivant le schéma suivant : En début d'averse, l'effet splash mobilise les particules libres à la surface des marnes sèches et par ruissellement apporte à la station la première pointe de concentration. Puis l'imbition des marnes provoque rapidement par gonflement des argiles, la fermeture des fissures et une plus grande cohésion des marnes ; avec la diminution de l'infiltration, le ruissellement s'intensifie et l'érosion qui avait diminué va de nouveau se développer suivant les filets et rigoles des versants en suivant en intensité le hyétogramme de l'averse. Lorsque l'imbition a gagné en profondeur, des mottes de marnes altérées peuvent se détacher du versant ou atteindre leur limite de liquidité et rejoindre le lit du ruisseau. A ce niveau d'ailleurs, l'importance de l'écoulement, en augmentant son pouvoir, va exporter des dépôts précédemment stockés et faciliter l'érosion des bas de versants.

En définitive, l'incidence des différents paramètres sur des pas de temps différents explique que l'analyse du transport solide à partir des caractéristiques des crues soit particulièrement délicate. Il peut y avoir un décalage important dans le temps entre la mobilisation des matériaux et leur exportation. Il paraît donc difficile d'appréhender avec une précision acceptable l'exportation des matières d'un bassin à l'échelle de l'averse même si au niveau du versant ou de la ravine élémentaire des correlations apparaissent. La recherche d'un modèle d'évaluation de la dégradation d'un bassin ou du comblement d'une retenue doit se faire en terme de bilan annuel.

BILAN ANNUEL DES TRANSPORTS SOLIDES, DEGRADATION SPECIFIQUE DES TERRES NOIRES

Le bilan global des exportations de matière sur les deux bassins montre sur les 3 années, une valeur moyenne de la charge en suspension de 460 tonnes/an sur Savournon I et de 2550 tonnes/an pour Savournon II, soit un facteur 5,55 pour un rapport des superficies totales de 9,6 et un rapport des bad-lands productif de 6,66. La moyenne annuelle des exportations totales (suspension et charriage est de 536 tonnes à S I et de 2716 tonnes à S II). Ramenée à la superficie des bassins, la dégradation spécifique moyenne serait de 68 T. ha^{-1} an^{-1} à S I contre 36 T ha^{-1} an^{-1} à S II. On a constaté que les marnes protégées par une végétation de pelouses et de landes n'ont qu'une contribution négligeable dans le bilan total d'érosion. Seules les roubines de Terres Noires dénudées ou à végétation clairsemée sont productives mais dans des proportions bien évidemment différentes.

En ne prenant en compte que ces surfaces inégalement réparties en terres nues (52% à S I, 19% à S II) et en roubines à végétation clairsemée (30% à S I, 38% à S II) et en effectuant un transfert d'échelle entre les deux bassins sur les résultats des bilans annuels, on en a déduit que l'érodabilité des roubines faiblement végétalisées ne représentait que le 1/3 de celle des terres nues.

La dégradation spécifique des terres noires dénudées a varié de 75 T ha^{-1} an^{-1} à 140 T ha^{-1} an^{-1} sur la période d'observation. La relation entre la dégradation spécifique D et la hauteur annuelle de Précipitation P s'écrit D = 0,12 P.

Ainsi Savournon devrait connaître , avec Pmoy = 920 mm, une dégradation interannuelle des roubines dénudées de 113 tonnes par hectare, ce qui correspond à une épaisseur d'ablation des roubines de 8,7 mm par an (avec une densité de l'altérite de 1,3). L'estimation du tonnage interannuel de sédiments (TS) exportés par un cours d'eau de ces terres noires se raménerait à la seule détermination, sur photo aérienne des superficies des bassins occupés respectivement par des bad-lands nus (BLN) ou à végétation clairsemée (VC).

$$TS_{tonne} = 0,12P \, [S.B_{LN} + 1/3 \, S_{VC}] \text{ avec P en mm et S en ha.}$$

MESURES DE L'ABLATION SUR LES VERSANTS ET COMPARAISON AVEC LES BILANS D'EROSION

L'ablation des versants a été mesurée à Savournon I sur plusieurs sites, de pentes, expositions et morphologies variables, suivant une méthodologie et un appareil mis au point par les auteurs. Celui-ci est constitué d'une règle permettant de suivre l'évolution de microprofils topographiques sur les sites retenus d'une manière particulièrement simple et économique. Utilisée avec prudence, la méthodologie donne de bons résultats ; ceux-ci doivent être ramenés à des moyennes statistiques et les différents sites doivent comprendre des profils en tête, milieu et bas de versant ; plusieurs échelles de temps paraissent pouvoir être utilisées, y compris l'épisode journalier pour les très fortes précipitations.

Le tableau ci-après permet de comparer pour différentes périodes de mesures les résultats de l'ablation moyenne des versants obtenue à partir des microprofils, à celle obtenue par les tonnages de matière ayant transité à l'exutoire du bassin S I (dégradation ramenée aux superficies équivalentes Terres nues).

TABLEAU 1   Précipitations et lames érodées correspondantes.

Période	Hauteur de pluie correspondante	Microprofils Lame érodée	Exutoire Dégradation	Lame érodée équivalente	Ecart
	mm	mm	t/ha	mm	%
1 jour le 16/5/88	71	3,0	77,8	6,0	- 50
1 mois Août-Sept 86	78	4,4	46,9	3,6	+ 22
1 an Avril 87-Mars 88	1232	16,0	145	11,1	+ 44
Période de suivi 1985-1988 (2,7 ans)	2536	17,0	301	23,2	- 27

Il est tout à fait net que les résultats sur microprofils ne constituent qu'une approximation ; les différents états hydriques de l'altérite au moment des mesures, les mouvements de masse et reprises de sédiments dans les drains expliquent probablement ces anomalies.

Compte tenu de leur faible coût, ces mesures peuvent toutefois fournir une indication précieuse à terme (plusieurs années) dans les régions à forte érosion des bassins de montagne méditérranéens (en particulier le Maghreb).

Ici, à Savournon, sur l'ensemble de la période, l'approximation par rapport aux mesures faites à l'exutoire dépasse à peine 25%, ce qui nous ramène à l'échelle de l'année moyenne à 8,6 mm pour la lame érodée obtenue à partir des bilans exutoires contre 6,3 mm par la méthode de microprofils.

CONCLUSIONS

Sur d'autres sites des Terres Noires des Alpes du Sud (Laragne, Digne, La Motte du Caire), la dégradation spécifique interannuelle est également de l'ordre de 100 T.ha[-1].

Cette érodabilité formidable des marnes jurassiques de cette région compte parmi les plus fortes valeurs observées dans le monde.

Hydrology in Mountainous Regions. II - Artificial Reservoirs; Water and Slopes
(Proceedings of two Lausanne Symposia, August 1990). IAHS Publ. no. 194, 1990.

Evaluation des forces tractrices critiques de la charge caillouteuse: expériences en flume et observations en rivières naturelles

F. PETIT
Laboratoire de Géographie physique, Université de Liège, 7, Place du 20 Août, B-4000 Liège, Belgique

RESUME Des expériences menées en flume avec des cailloux de taille différente montrent que le critère de Schields s'écarte de la valeur généralement admise, du fait de l'imbrication des particules d'une part, de la saillie relative des plus gros éléments d'autre part. Par ailleurs, les forces tractrices ont été évaluées en rivières naturelles en suivant une méthodologie préalablement testée en flume. Il s'est avéré que les forces tractrices calculées à partir des vitesses de frottement - mais avec un paramètre de rugosité redéfini en fonction de la granulométrie du lit - apparaissent comme le meilleur indicateur des phénomènes d'érosion et de transport de la charge de fond. L'analyse du déplacement des particules dans ces rivières, a permis de mettre en évidence une diminution du critère de Schields lorsque la taille des particules augmente. Ceci est partiellement lié aux caractéristiques des sites : phénomènes de dallage, spécifiques aux seuils, assurant une meilleure résistance à l'érosion, tandis que dans les mouilles, il y a érosion de matériel relativement grossier pour des forces tractrices proportionnellement plus faibles.

NOTATION

A, B, C,	Grand axe, axe intermédiaire et petit axe des particules
D	Diamètre des particules
D_{50}	Diamètre médian
k	Constante de von Karman
Re_*	Nombre de Reynolds étoilé (= $u*$ D/v)
u	Vitesse du courant mesurée à une hauteur y au-dessus du lit
$u*$	Vitesse de frottement
y_0	Hauteur de rugosité intervenant dans l'évaluation des vitesses de frottement
θ_c	Critère adimensionnel de Schields
ρ	Masse volumique du fluide

ν	Viscosité cinématique
τ	Force tractrice évaluée à partir du rayon hydraulique et de la pente de la ligne d'énergie
τ_C	Force tractrice critique
τ'	Force tractrice due à la résistance des grains
τ⋆	Force tractrice calculée à partir des vitesses de frottement

INTRODUCTION

Il devient de plus en plus apparent que la force tractrice doit être considérée comme le critère prépondérant pour l'évaluation du transport de la charge de fond et, d'une façon plus générale, pour l'explication du façonnement des lits fluviatiles en milieu naturel. L'application de cette notion au milieu naturel pose cependant un certain nombre de problèmes spécialement lorsqu'il s'agit de charge caillou-teuse. Tout d'abord, parce que les valeurs des forces trac-trices critiques ne sont pas toujours adaptées étant donné qu'il existe des phénomènes propres au matériel caillouteux (phénomène d'imbrication, de saillie relative, de résistance due à la forme des éléments). Par ailleurs, il existe des problèmes quant à l'évaluation de la force tractrice due à la résistance des grains (la seule qui doit être prise en considération pour le transport des sédiments), en rivières naturelles, spécialement lorsque les formes du lit y sont développées ainsi que la méandration.

Différentes expériences ont été menées en flume afin de préciser les forces tractrices critiques propres à la charge caillouteuse d'une part, afin de tester les méthodes d'évaluation des forces tractrices d'autre part. Ces ex-périences sont menées en complément aux recherches effec-tuées depuis quinze ans dans différentes rivières à charge caillouteuse de Moyenne et de Haute Belgique.

EXPERIENCES EN FLUME

Le flume aimablement mis à notre disposition par l'Univer-sité d'Uppsala (Suède) est un flume rectiligne dont la lon-gueur de travail est de 6 m et la largeur de 0,5 m. Sa pente longitudinale est réglable et peut atteindre 0.035 m.m^{-1}. Des cailloux ont été collés sur le fond du flume; ils forment une couche continue, sans modification sensible des formes du lit, le diamètre médian de ce matériel étant légèrement inférieur à 20 mm. Un lit constitué de matériel caillouteux plus fin (D_{50} = 13 mm) a également été utilisé occasionnel-lement dans certaines expériences.

Une première série d'expériences a tout d'abord porté sur l'évaluation de la force tractrice totale (τ) à partir de la pente de la ligne d'énergie et du rayon hydraulique,

tenant compte de la correction dûe à l'effet de paroi laté-
rale telle que recommandée par Vanoni (1975) et ensuite sur
la détermination de la force tractrice due à la résistance
des grains (τ') en appliquant les différentes méthodes testées préalablement par Singhal et al. (1980), dans un flume
à fond sableux. Il s'est vérifié qu'en l'absence de variations sensibles des formes du fond du lit, τ' représentant
bien la totalité de la force tractrice (τ) (Petit, 1989a).
D'autre part, les forces tractrices ont été évaluées à par-
tir des vitesses de frottement $\tau_* = u_*^2 \rho$ avec $\dfrac{u}{u_*} = \dfrac{1}{k} \ln \dfrac{y}{y_0}$.

La relation qui lie le paramètre de rugosité y_0 avec le
diamètre du matériel du fond a été reconsidérée à partir de
l'analyse des gradients de vitesse à proximité du fond (à
moins de 0,2 la profondeur totale), ceci pour différentes
conditions de pente et de débit. Une valeur moyenne $y_0 =$
1.8 mm a été ainsi mise en évidence, valeur proche de celles
déduite de la relation proposée notamment par Kamphuis
(1974). Il s'est avéré que la relation entre les forces
tractrices dues à la résistance des grains (τ') et celles
évaluées par les vitesses de frottement était fiable et
proche de la ligne d'égalité, de telle sorte qu'il était
possible d'utiliser cette dernière méthode pour cerner les
forces tractrices critiques.

Une deuxième série d'expériences a ainsi été menée avec
des cailloux marqués, dont le diamètre était compris entre
10 et 50 mm. Deux populations différentes de cailloux ont
été utilisées : l'une comprenant des cailloux dont la forme
arrondie est comparable à celle des cailloux constituant le
fond du flume (C/B > 0,6 et B/A > 0,7 dans la classification
de Zingg), l'autre étant composée de cailloux présentant un
aplatissement important (C/B < 0,35), ceci afin de quantifier la résistance à l'érosion provoquée par la seule forme
des éléments.

Les forces tractrices calculées par les vitesses de
frottement ont été mesurées à chaque endroit où se situaient
des cailloux marqués quand il y avait mise en mouvement de
ces derniers mais également lorsque les forces tractrices
étaient insuffisantes pour provoquer la mise en mouvement de
ces particules (fig. 1). De telle sorte que dans les relations entre force tractrice et diamètre des particules, il
s'est individualisé deux droites plus ou moins parallèles,
l'une représentant la limite des forces tractrices au-dessus
desquelles il était certain d'avoir une mise en mouvement du
matériel, la seconde représentant la limite en dessous de
laquelle aucune mise en mouvement ne se présente.
Il s'individualise donc une zone intermédiaire où il faut
envisager une probabilité de mise en mouvement des
particules. Trois types de situation se présentent :

(a) Les forces tractrices nécessaires à la mise en mouvement des particules ayant un diamètre identique à celui du
matériel constituant le lit, sont très proches de celles déduites de la relation $\tau_C = D$, ce qui correspond à un critère
de Shields (θ_C) égal à 0,06.

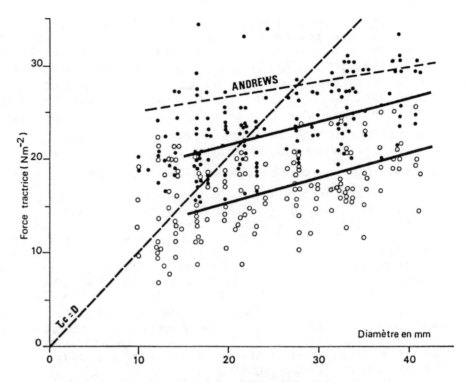

FIG. 1   Valeurs des forces tractrices d'après les
expériences en flume (D_{50} du lit = 20 mm) pour les
éléments arrondis. Les points noirs figurent la
mise en mouvement, les points blancs l'absence de
mise en mouvement.

(b) Pour les éléments plus grossiers, cette relation
n'est plus applicable. Ainsi, par exemple, des forces tractrices de l'ordre de 25 N m^{-2} peuvent provoquer systématiquement la mise en mouvement de particules de 40 mm de
diamètre, ce qui correspond à une valeur de $\theta_C = 0,04$.

(c) En revanche, les éléments dont le diamètre est plus
petit que celui du matériel formant le lit, présentent une
résistance plus grande, les forces tractrices critiques devant être systématiquement plus importantes que celles déduites de l'équation $\tau_C = D$ ($\theta_C = 0,09$).

Un effet d'imbrication des plus petites particules tel
que décrit notamment par Reid & Frostick (1984), est responsable de ce retard de la mise en mouvement. Au contraire,
l'effet de saillie relative mis en évidence par Fenton &
Abott (1977) permet aux particules plus grossières d'être
mises en mouvement par des forces tractrices relativement
faibles.

La combinaison de ces deux effets amène finalement des
résultats proches de ceux d'Andrews (1983) suivant lesquels
des particules qui ont une taille comprise entre 0,3 et 4,2
fois celle du matériel qui constitue le lit peuvent être
mises en mouvement par des forces tractrices quasi similai-

res, ceci étant formulé de la façon suivante :

$\theta_c = 0,083 \ (D/D_{50})^{-0,872}$. Toutefois, les forces tractrices critiques présentées à la fig. 1, sont plus faibles que celles déduites de la relation d'Andrews, ceci résultant du fait que les éléments marqués utilisés dans les expériences sont isolés sur le lit et que, comme démontré par Naden (1987), la possibilité qu'ils soient érodés est alors plus importante.

C'est ainsi que dans une autre série d'expériences, les cailloux marqués ont été disposés avec d'autres cailloux de même taille, de façon à former une couche continue reposant sur la couche sous-jacente du lit. Les résultats présentés à la fig. 2, où chaque point représente en moyenne une vingtaine d'observations, montrent une bonne concordance avec la relation proposée par Andrews.

Les forces tractrices critiques ont également été mesurées pour les cailloux marqués aplatis en vue d'établir une relation similaire à celles proposées ci-dessus. Les droites obtenues sont relativement parallèles montrant que, à des degrés divers , les effets d'imbrication et de saillie jouent aussi pour les éléments plats.

Toutefois, pour ces derniers, θ_c est en moyenne 1,5 fois plus important que pour les éléments arrondis de même diamètre. Ces valeurs ont été confirmées par des observations - composition et structure de dallage résistant

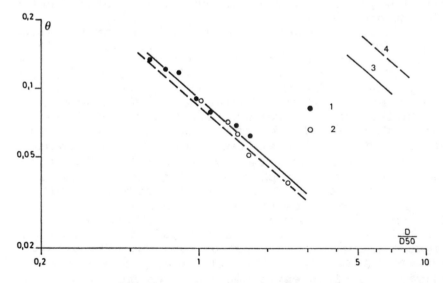

FIG. 2   Relation entre θ_c et le rapport du diamètre des éléments (D_i) et du diamètre médian du matériel constituant le lit (D_{50}) ; (1) lit composé de cailloux avec $D_{50} = 20$ mm; (2) lit composé de cailloux avec $D_{50} = 13$ mm; (3) droite trouvée par régression $\theta_c = 0,09 \ (D_i/D_{50})^{-0,90}$ $(r = 0,98)$; (4) droite déduite de la relation d'Andrews.

à l'érosion - effectuées dans une rivière naturelle où se présentent conjointement des cailloux aplatis et des éléments arrondis (Petit, 1989b).

OBSERVATIONS EN RIVIERES NATURELLES

Les observations ont été principalement effectuées dans une rivière à charge caillouteuse du Sud de l'Ardenne (La Rulles). Cette rivière de dimension modeste (en moyenne 3 m de largeur au niveau du débit à pleins bords), à pente relativement forte (0,012 m.m^{-1}), se caractérise par des systèmes seuil/mouille bien développés en relation avec une méandration marquée. Différents secteurs de rivière ont été équipés afin de pouvoir suivre les modifications géomorphologiques et y mesurer de façon précise les paramètres qui permettent d'évaluer les forces tractrices par les deux approches classiques (Petit, 1984, 1986). Des expériences ont été réalisées avec une gamme de cailloux marqués en place dans différents sites (seuils - mouilles). Par ailleurs, un piège à sédiments a été installé juste en aval des secteurs d'études.

Des relevés complémentaires ont été effectués en suivant une méthodologie identique, dans deux autres rivières, dont l'une se caractérise par une charge sablo-graveleuse (la Rouge Eau). Enfin, des traitements ont été réalisés à partir des mesures faites par Mercenier (1973) dans une petite rivière subrectiligne à forte pente du haut plateau ardennais.

L'évaluation des forces tractrices par les vitesses de frottement a tout d'abord nécessité de redéfinir la relation entre le paramètre de rugosité y_0 et le diamètre du matériel qui constitue le fond du lit de ces rivières. Une analyse des gradients de vitesse à proximité du fond a ainsi été effectuée, principalement dans les différents sites de la Rulles, qui se caractérisent par des différences de taille du matériel (D_{50} de l'ordre de 15 mm sur les seuils, et de 50 mm dans les mouilles). La relation suivante a ainsi pu être mise en évidence : $y_0 = 0,39\ D_{50}^{0.80}$. Ce qui donne des valeurs assez proches de celles déduites de la relation proposée par Hey (1979) pour des rivières graveleuses.

Les forces tractrices évaluées par les vitesses de frottement ont alors été mises en relation avec les forces tractrices totales calculées à partir de la pente de la ligne d'énergie et du rayon hydraulique. Ces dernières sont systématiquement plus importantes mais à des degrés divers, suivant les sites envisagés : le rapport τ_*/τ est proche de 0,5 pour un secteur graveleux sans méandration ni différenciation sensible des formes du lit (la Rouge Eau), il atteint 0,64 pour les seuils de la Rulles généralement situés au point d'inflexion des méandres, mais est inférieur à 0,30 dans les mouilles de cette même rivière, qui sont le plus souvent associées aux boucles des méandres (Petit, 1990).

Par ailleurs, les τ' évaluées dans ces mêmes sites par les méthodes préalablement testées en flume, ne représentent en moyenne que 30 % de la force tractrice totale dans les seuils de la Rulles et le secteur graveleux de la Rouge Eau, et seulement 15 % dans les mouilles de la Rulles. Ces valeurs de τ' semblent donc être sous-estimées et ne pourraient expliquer que très peu de modifications morphologiques. Par contre, comme nous allons le voir ci-dessous, les forces tractrices évaluées par les vitesses de frottement justifient mieux les modifications observées (mise en mouvement des particules, transport, arrêt, absence de mise en mouvement). Ces résultats sont reportés en synthèse à la fig. 3 ainsi que la relation mise en évidence à partir de nos expériences en flume. L'application de cette dernière permet de justifier un certain nombre d'observations telles que l'absence de mise en mouvement sur les seuils, l'érosion dans certaines mouilles - mais non dans toutes - et la mise en mouvement des particules dans une rivière subrectiligne. Elle ne peut cependant pas expliquer le transport des particules tant sur les seuils que dans les mouilles. La disposition des points observés correspond beaucoup mieux avec la relation proposée par Carling (1983) en synthèse d'observations effectuées sur le transport des particules en rivière naturelle. De même, la relation qui prend en compte nos seules valeurs de transport des particules, assez proche de la relation proposée par Carling, justifie un plus grand nombre d'observations et notamment l'arrêt des particules dans les seuils et les mouilles.

A noter que l'absence de mouvement des cailloux qui constituent les seuils, en dépit de forces tractrices relativement élevées, résulte de phénomènes d'imbrication, ces cailloux se présentant sous forme d'un dallage homogène et continu. Par ailleurs, il subsiste un problème dans certaines mouilles où il y a effectivement mise en mouvement de particules assez grossières (D = 50 mm) en présence de forces tractrices relativement faibles ($\theta_C \approx 0.02$). On ne peut, dans de tels cas, faire appel à un effet de saillie relative car ce matériel est de même taille sinon plus petit que celui qui constitue le fond du lit.

Il n'est pas exclu que dans de tels sites, les fluctuations des vitesses instantanées du courant à proximité du fond soient plus importantes. En effet, de telles mesures ont été effectuées au moyen d'une sonde électromagnétique (temps de réponse 0,2 s), dans un flume où des différenciations de formes du fond avaient été créées (alternance de mouilles et de seuils).

Il ressort de ces expériences que les fluctuations des vitesses instantanées sont beaucoup plus importantes dans les mouilles que sur les seuils, avec des pointes de vitesse atteignant respectivement 1,6 et 1,2 fois la vitesse moyenne et des rapports entre maximums et minimums valant respectivement 3,5 et 1,4. Ainsi, l'importance de ces pointes de vitesse, leur succession dans le temps et leur variation différentielle en fonction de la profondeur pourraient favoriser une mise en mouvement préférentielle des particules.

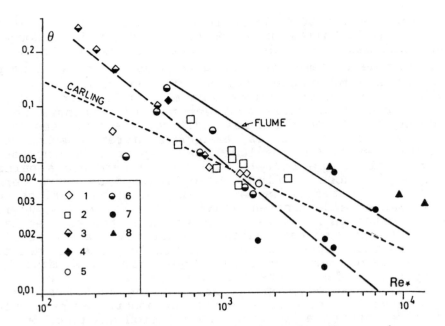

FIG. 3   Relation entre la fonction d'entraînement
de Shields (θ) et R_{e*} ; (1) à (4) seuils de la
Rulles et de la Burdinale : (1) arrêt du transport
des particules, (2) absence de mise en mouvement,
(3) transport, (4) érosion; (5) à (7) mouilles de
la Rulles : (5) arrêt de transport, (6) transport,
(7) érosion, (8) érosion dans une rivière
subrectiligne (Mercenier).

REFERENCES

Andrews, E.D.   1983. Entrainment of gravel from naturally
    sorted riverbed material. Geol. Soc. Am. Bull., 94,
    1225-1231.
Carling, P.A.   1983. Threshold of coarse sediment transport
    in broad and narrow natural streams. Earth Surf.
    Processes and Landforms, 8, 1-18.
Fenton, J.D. & Abott, J.E.   1977. Initial movement of grains
    on a stream bed : the effect of relative protrusion.
    Proc. R. Soc. London, A 352, 523-537.
Hey, R.D., 1979. Flow resistance in gravel bed rivers. Am.
    Soc. Civ. Eng. Hydr. Division, 105, 365-379.
Kamphuis, J.W.   1974. Determination of sand roughness for
    fixed beds. J. Hydr. Res., 12(2), 193-263.
Mercenier, J.   1973. Dynamique fluviale dans un petit bassin
    du rebord méridional du plateau des Tailles. Mém. de
    licence en Sc. Géog., inédit, conservé à l'Univ. de
    Liège, 148 p.
Naden, P.   1987. An erosion criterion for gravel-bed rivers.
    Earth Surf. Processes and Landforms, 12, 83-93.
Petit, F.   1984. Les processus contrôlant l'évolution du
    tracé d'une rivière ardennaise. Zf. Géomorph. Suppl. Bd.

49, 95-109.

Petit, F. 1986. Channel development in two streams of contrasting bed-load and regime. *in* International Geomorphology 1986 Part 1, Gardiner V., Ed. Wiley J. & Sons Ltd, 611-622.

Petit, F. 1989a. The evaluation of grain shear stress from experiments in a pebble - bedded flume. Earth Surf. Processes and Landforms, **14**, 499-508.

Petit, F. 1989b. L'influence de la forme des cailloux en tant que facteur de résistance à l'érosion. Revue de Géographie de Lyon, **64**(4), 231-239.

Petit, F. 1990. Evaluation of grain shear stresses required to initiate movement of particles in natural rivers. Earth Surf. Processes and Landforms, **15**, (in press).

Reid, J. & Frostick, L.E. 1984. Particle interaction and its effect on the thresholds of initial and final bedload motion in coarse alluvial channel *in* Kosher E.M. and Steel, R.J. (Eds.), Sedimentology of gravel and Conglomerates, Canadian Society of Petroleum Geologists Memoir, **10**, 61-68.

Singhal, M.K., Mohan, J. & Agrawal, A.K. 1980. Role of grain shear stress in sediment transport, Irrigation and Power, **37**, 105-108.

Vanoni, V.A. 1975 (Ed.) Sedimentation engineering. Manuals and reports on Engineering practice, n° 54, Am. Soc. Civ. Eng., 745 p.

Hydrology in Mountainous Regions. II - Artificial Reservoirs; Water and Slopes
(Proceedings of two Lausanne Symposia, August 1990). IAHS Publ. no. 194, 1990.

Interaction of bed armouring and slope development

F. SCHÖBERL

Ass.Prof.,Institut für Konstruktiven Wasserbau
und Tunnelbau, Universität Innsbruck, 6020
Innsbruck, Austria

ABSTRACT The widely graded sediment distribution
of mountain streams provides significant
armouring of the bed, strenghtening the erosion
resistance to a certain degree. As evidenced in
laboritory tests, different transition stages of
amour coats exist. The surface coarsening
dominates also bed deformation processes and the
bed stabilization. Stability criteria in
relation to the slope development and the bed
form characteristics are outlined.

INTRODUCTION

Widely graded sediments allow for grain size based
selective erosion and the formation of coarse bed layers.
The coarsening process of surfaces is a well known
characteristic of mountain streams, and an important
feature strengthening the bed resistance to a certain
extent. Beyond that, armouring is also involved in bed
forming actions. Step and pool sequences generated by high
floods in a combined process of self armouring and
antidune formation are a typical bedform of steep reaches.
During long-term intervals, the transported sediment is of
a finer size than the bed material and not adjusted to the
transport capacity, Lauffer & Sommer (1982). Since this
lesser sized load is morphologically inefficient and
without any impact on the surface layer, this condition is
nearly equivalent to totally blocked bed-size sediment
supply, for which different laboratory results are
established, Günter (1971), Little & Mayer (1976),
Proffitt (1980) etc.

ARMOUR COATS IN THE ABSENCE OF BED FORMS AND SEDIMENT
SUPPLY

Without any restrictions in the forming of the channel
profile, such sorting processes are strictly accompanied
by slope adjustments, whereas local bed level fixations
act as abutments for the longitudinal channel development.
In these cases fully developed or mature armour coats

occur, stabilizing at the highest possible slope, Günter (1971). The relation between slope formation and the coarsest mode of armouring is mainly determined by roughness effects, Schöberl (1979).

Restricted to rough turbulent flow conditions, experiments proved a relationship for moderate slopes (S < 2 %) in the form :

$$S = f[\ a_g\ ,\ \varepsilon = d_{mgr}/h,\ F_d{}^2 = v^2/(g' \cdot d_{mgr})\ ]$$

where a_g denotes a composition parameter of the bed material, defined as $a_g = (d_{90}/d_{50})^{1/3} \cdot (d_{mo} \cdot d_{50})^{1/2}$ with d_p as the grain size of the basic material for which p percent is finer and dm_o as the mean diameter of the basic bed mixture, $g' = (\varrho_s - \varrho/\varrho) \cdot g$ with g as the acceleration due to gravity, o the density of the fluid and ϱ_s the density of sediment material, d_{mgr} as the mean effective grain diameter of the armour coat and v as the velocity of the approaching flow. The transformation of the original relationship in terms of dimensionless shear stress provides the stability criterion: $Fr*^2 = (\tau/\varrho)/(g' \cdot d_{mgr}) = 0,41/(a_g \cdot F_d{}^2)$, whereas τ denotes the applied bed shear stress. Fig. 1 illustrates this equation with $Fr*^2$ versus grain Re* number $= \sqrt{\tau/\varrho} \cdot d_{mgr}/v$

Restrictions of slope adjustments lead to different degrees of armour formations, resulting in finer sized

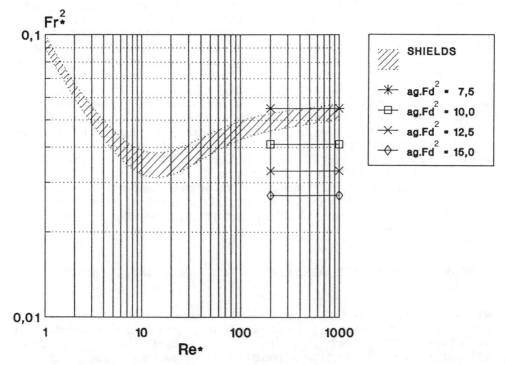

FIG. 1 Stability criterion for fully developed armours in rough turbulent flow.

armours with lower resistance. So the surface composition changes with the actual shear stress. A higher shear stress produces a coarser surface. All cases relate to each other, when standardized by the conditions of the coarsest mode of amour, Schöberl (1990). Approximately the change of the mean grain size of the surface layer can be assessed by the ratio of actual and maximum possible shear stress.

STABILITY OF STEP-POOL SEQUENCES

Armouring also substantially influences the development of deformed beds. In general, the pattern of steep reaches is structured in step and pool sequences emerging from superposing processes of antidune forming and armouring, Whittaker & Jaeggi (1982). In the longitudinal profile, sorting of material leads to a periodical accumulation of coarser elements in accordance with the antidune pattern. The steepness and spacing of the armour-stabilized bed structure tend to maximize the flow resistance. The friction losses are related to the evolving specific

STABILITY OF STEP-POOL SYSTEMS

$$Fr*^2 = Fr*^2_{plane\ bed} + 0,027 \cdot [(ks/d_{mo})-1]^{2/3}$$

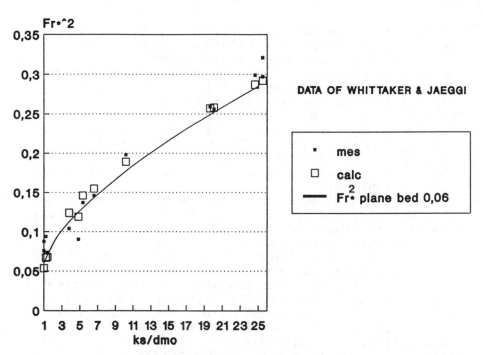

FIG. 2 Increase of the critical dimensionless shear stress $Fr*^2$ in relation to ks/d_{mo}.

geometry and in the same manner the erosion stability is raised by this roughness effect.

To express the combined influence of bed shape and surface roughness a quantity in terms of the equivalent roughness proved to be convenient, Fig.2. Based on the experimental data of Witthaker & Jaeggi, an increase of dimensionless shear stress with the ratio of equivalent sand roughness ks and mean diamter d_{mo} of the original bed material can be demonstrated (In this case areal sample quantities were taken).

Therefore longitudinal grain sorting i.e. armouring of the deformed surface is an important contribution in keeping the bed features stable and raising the friction losses so that only large flood events may disturb the immobile bed.

CONCLUSIONS

In mountain streams armouring processes essentially influence the development of the slope and the bed structure respectively. In the absence of significant bed shaping conditions the upper limit of the possible shear stress is determined by the grading of the basic bed sediment, the relative roughneß and Froude number of the flow. In combination with antidune formations, the friction loss i.e. the equivalent roughness ks of the bed becomes dominant, substantially increasing the critical limits shear stress.

REFERENCES

GÜNTER A. (1971) Die kritische mittlere Sohlenschub-spannung bei Geschiebemischungen unter Berück-sichtigung der Deckschichtbildung und der turbulenzbedingten Sohlenschubspannungsschwankungen (Mitt. No.3 der Versuchsanstalt für Wasserbau, Hydrologie und Glaziologie, ETH Zürich).

LITTLE W.C., Mayer P.G. (1976) Stability of Channel Beds by Armouring (J. Hydraulic. Div. ASCE, No. Hy 11).

LAUFFER H., SOMMER N. (1982) Studies on Sediment Transport in Mountain Streams of Eastern Alps (Comission Intern. des Grands Barrages, Q 54, R28, Rio de Janeiro).

PROFFITT G.T. (1980) Selective Transport and Armouring of Non-Uniform Alluvial Sediments (Research Report 80/22, Department of Civil Engineering, University of Caterbury, Christchurch, New Zealand).

SCHÖBERL F. (1979) Zur Frage der Gefällsausbildung beim Selbststabilisierungsprozeß von erodierenden Fluß-strecken (Dissertation, Institut für Konstruktiven Wasserbau und Tunnelbau, Universität Innsbruck).

SCHÖBERL F. (1990) Upper Limits and Transition Stages of Developing Armour Coats (Conf. on River Flood Hydraulics, Wallingford).

WHITTAKER J.G., JAEGGI M.N.R. (1982) Origin of Step-Pool Systems in Mountain Streams (J. Hydraulic. Div. ASCE, No. Hy 6).

Hydrology in Mountainous Regions. II - Artificial Reservoirs; Water and Slopes
(Proceedings of two Lausanne Symposia, August 1990). IAHS Publ. no. 194, 1990.

Large bed element channels in steep mountain streams

Philippe W. ZGHEIB
Civil and Environmental Engineering, Utah State
University, Logan, Utah 84322, USA

ABSTRACT   The   evolution   of   natural   steep
channels   is   a   function   of   two   factors   in
accordance with the principle of least action:
flow distribution in the channel and terrain
geomorphology.   Large   bed   elements   (LBE)
occurring   in   the   stream   bed   act   on   both
factors. Stream flow in steep natural terrain
occurs   in   two   basic   regimes: hydraulic   and
morphological.   Velocity   head   upstream   of   an
obstacle in the stream is related to the energy
dissipation   mechanism   in   a   simplified   two-
dimensional setting. Simplification holds in
a   localized   manner   and   requires   further   study
to include the entire region around the LBE.

INTRODUCTION

Morphologic changes of natural steep channels result mainly
from two factors: water and sediment flow distribution in
the stream and existing channel geomorphology. Large bed
elements (LBE) in the channel bed interact with both of
them. These two factors, working in concert, modify the
stream flow to comply with the principle of least energy
action   (Leopold,   1960).   In   this   study,   hydro-
geomorphological processes are considered in two parts: 1)
The dynamic processes of channel formation and evolution
according to the theory of least energy and 2) the
hydraulic processes of free surface flow.
    Tumbling flow is the mode of occurrence of most
water flow in steep natural streams, above a thin laminar
sub-layer, due to friction at the stream bed. Mohanty and
Peterson   (Mohanty   and   Peterson,   1959)   have   defined
"tumbling   flow"   as   a   condition   of   flow   dominated   by
scattered   regions   of   alternate   acceleration   and
deceleration through critical flow over large bed elements.
They have linked tumbling flow to the presence of large bed
elements in the stream channel. Thus, tumbling flow appears
to be characterized by a series of localized stationary
hydraulic jumps.
    Internal distortion, skin and spill resistance to
flow characterize mountain steep LBE streams. Bed armoring
of these streams occurs when cobbles or boulders above a
certain size cannot be transported by open water flow. This

277

limiting size depends on stream conditions such as: slope, velocity, shear stress, channel geometry, and flow regime. Bed elements of this size and larger are referred to in this study as large bed elements (LBE).

At the level of the individual LBE, tumbling flow is highly unsteady. Turbulence that accompanies flow around the LBE results in energy dissipation. This energy is quantified as a function of time in two components: the water depth and the velocity head.

LITERATURE REVIEW

Idealized flume experiments of flow in steep, rough, fixed-bed, open channels conducted at Utah State university (Mohanty and Peterson, 1959) have led to the characterization of tumbling flow. For his experimental set-up he proposed three regimes: tranquil, tumbling and rapid. In the tranquil and rapid regimes, flow was dominated by subcritical and super-critical velocities, respectively.

In the tumbling flow regime, roughness elements induced super-critical flow over their crests followed by an overfall back into subcritical flow. Each roughness element acted as an overfall control. The result was alternate acceleration and deceleration from subcritical to super-critical velocities in a cyclical order. Spacing between two successive roughnesses marked the length of one cycle. And hydraulic jumps formed between them. Thus, the stream tended to flow at subcritical velocities between the roughnesses and at super-critical velocities over them.

In steep, rough, open channels, bed roughnesses came to be called "Large Bed Elements" or LBE's. However, it was Engel (Engel, 1960) who first recognized the need for determining the situations in which LBE's were bed roughness elements and those other situations in which LBE's were so large that they became cross-sectional changes in the stream channel. In the first case, Froude numbers could be independent of flow. While in the second case the Froude numbers were associated with the flow such that a deviation of the free surface might result.

As roll waves were observed (Mohanty and Peterson, 1959) at given spacings of roughness elements, excess energy developed by the stream during the tumbling regime would lead to a transition to the rapid regime. At Froude number values exceeding 1.5 the roll waves absorbed the excess stream energy. In an attempt to define the threshold at which the destructive roll waves developed, Mohanty (Mohanty, 1959) stipulated that in nature, where LBE's are variable in size and density they functioned as virtual weirs. However, flow through a virtual weir occurs at minimum specific energy. In such a virtual weir, the crest elevation might be represented by a statistical function describing roughness distribution and density. However, relations proposed didn't account for roughness characteristics.

Virmani (Virmani et al, 1973) developed design methods for the use of LBE's as energy dissipators in steep channels. If they could prevent the formation of roll waves, energy could be safely dissipated in the stream by inducing tumbling flow. For energy dissipation, they considered tumbling flow in terms of discharge, slope, velocity distribution, drag force and boundary geometry. As tumbling flow oscillates around critical flow while it moves down the steep slopes, it keeps dissipating energy. The remaining stream energy is very close to the minimum specific energy for the specific discharge.

As velocity profiles were established (Marchand and Jarrett, 1984) for Colorado streams, water surface elevations were measured by transit stadia surveys twice at each site. Total horizontal distance of the slope measurements was normally about two and a half times the stream width. However, it was difficult to exactly locate the water surface level because of the greatly fluctuating water surface and occasional soft bottom conditions.

Tumbling motion in natural high-gradient streams possesses a single dominant direction with significant turbulent fluxes in directions transverse as well as collinear to this dominant direction of flow. Modelling such turbulence is simpler than for flows with recirculatory motion. A two-dimensional model will reasonably approximate such conditions.

TURBULENCE

According to the statistical theory of turbulence first proposed by Taylor (Taylor, 1938), velocity of fluid is a random continuous function of time and space. It is a random function because mean velocity does not relate to instantaneous velocity. If the instantaneous velocity v_i is considered the sum of a mean velocity v, and a fluctuating velocity v', distribution of the fluctuating component, v' follows a Gaussian normal probability distribution.

High friction loss of turbulent flow is due to the exchange of momentum between fluid particles. If a fluid particle travels between two layers moving at different velocities, a momentum exchange results between the two layers. Slow particles entering the faster layer act as a drag on it. Subsequently, the mixing-length theory defines the mixing length, l as the distance a particle of fluid moves transverse to the mean flow before it loses its identity, and mingles with other particles

The mixing-length theory finds extensive application in turbulent-flow problems where only the temporal mean of flow quantities is known. A knowledge of the fluctuations occurring during tumbling flow around large bed elements would add materially to the understanding of turbulence.

PROBLEM DEFINITION

As water tumbles around an obstacle in the high-gradient stream it is in full turbulence. The presence of the rock in the way of the supercritical flow results in dissipating energy through turbulent eddies. The supercritical velocities immediately upstream of the rock are no longer one-dimensional.

Because of main velocity gradients, turbulence is able to extract energy from mean flow. Thus turbulent motion is self-sustaining. The energy which sustains turbulence is obtained from the mean flow by shearing actions at the expense of additional pressure drop. This energy appears in the form of eddies.

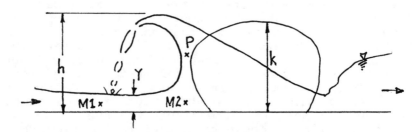

FIG. 1   Side View of the Jet Fan Around the Roughness Element.

Flow regime around the rock is characterized by local flow conditions around the rock. Tumbling flow due to the large bed roughness involves a dissipation mechanism immediately upstream of the large roughness. As supercritical velocities impact the rock, a fan forms upstream. In this region, main flow is no longer longitudinal. It is vertical as well as longitudinal. At the same time, turbulent fluctuations are observed in the longitudinal, vertical and transverse directions.

Direct observation indicates that flow around the rock takes the shape of a jet fan. Experimental procedures isolate the jet impact which causes the main flow to break and deflect in all directions. Main flow occurs in the longitudinal direction of the flume as well as in the vertical direction. At the mid-stream line, flow is reasonably well approximated by a two-dimensional dissipation process. Beyond eddies and turbulence, tumbling flow involves energy mechanisms at the upstream tip of the roughness element best described as:

(a)   Jet fan, or the deflected jet. At the upstream tip of the rock, it results from the impact of the flow on the rock.

(b)   Eddy viscosity. Resulting from turbulence dissipation by eddies, it is directly related to the Reynold's stresses.

The portion of fluid involved in the jet motion is a direct function of the cross-sectional size of the obstacle, and

its frontal slope. Whereas the conditions of occurrence of'
each depends on the height of the obstacle, its width, its
frontal slope, its side slopes, water depth, and water
velocity immediately upstream of the obstacle.

DATA

For five rocks of different sizes, and for six discharges
around each rock, the following measurements were made:
*   Rock height, k.
*   Rock width, w.
*   Discharge, Q.
*   Flow depth, y
*   Jet height, h.
*   Main and turbulent velocities, longitudinal and
        vertical at the tip of the jet fan, at two points
        in each direction, u, v, u', v'.
Rocks used to collect the data are of random shape. They
all display smooth rounded corners. Velocity readings were
obtained in terms of frequency of spinning of a propeller
meter. The diameter of the propeller is 1 cm. Velocity
readings were recorded every second for about one minute
in every situation.

SOLUTION

The two-dimensional model determines the loss in velocity
head as a function of the jet height. The difference
between the velocity head and the potential energy
displayed by the jet height is considered the amount
dissipated at the mid-point of the upstream end of the LBE.
Everywhere else transverse velocities involve three-
dimensional energy mechanisms, which remain beyond the
scope of this paper.

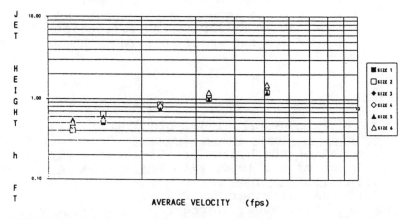

FIG. 2   Log-Log Correlation of the Jet Height
Versus Point Velocity Upstream of the Jet Fan.

Tumbling flow around an LBE is almost always turbulent. Fluid motion is highly random, unsteady, and non-uniform. Problems in free turbulent flow are of a boundary layer nature. The region of space under consideration does not extend far in a transverse direction compared with the main direction of flow, but the transverse gradients may be large. The height of the jet is expressed in terms of the velocity components at the mid-stream line. This height value falls short of the kinetic energy value. The difference quantifies the amount of energy dissipated in deviating the flow upward over and around the obstacle at its middle section.

RESULTS

The two following points result from this study:
(a)   Velocity readings at the upstream edge of the jet fan recorded higher values for the same discharge for a smaller size of the roughness element.
(b)   For all sizes considered in this study, jet height showed a direct exponential correlation with the average values of point velocity recorded upstream of the LBE.

CONCLUSIONS

Respectively, two conclusions can be drawn from this study:
(a)   Velocity profile upstream from the LBE is affected by the LBE size. Pressure waves upstream of LBE resulting from a horizontal pressure gradient slow the flow near the edges of the LBE and accelerate it along the middle line of flow immediately upstream of the fan edge.
(b)   LBE size does not influence energy dissipation since the relationship between jet height and velocity is independent of the size. Velocity head drops between the upstream edge of the jet fan and the LBE. This results from a momentum transfer by turbulent stresses caused by impact and deflection of flow in all directions but mostly upward at the mid-section of the LBE.

REFERENCES

Engel, F. V. A. , et al. 1960. Discussion: Flume Studies of Flow in Steep Rough Channels. Proceedings, ASCE. Journal of the Hydraulics Division. Vol. 86, HY4.
Leopold, Luna, et al. 1960. Flow Resistance in sinuous or Irregular Channels. U. S. Geological Survey Professional Paper No. 282 D.
Marchand, J. P. and Robert Jarrett. 1984. Velocity Profile, Water Surface Slope, and Bed Material Size for Selected Streams in Colorado. U. S. Geological

Survey. Water Resources Division, Lakewood, Colorado. report No. 84-733, 82 p.

Mohanty, Prasanta K. and dean F. Peterson. 1959. <u>Flume Studies of Flow in Steep, Rough Open Channels</u>. ASCE, conference of the Hydraulics Division. Fort Collins, Colorado.

Taylor, G. I. 1938. <u>Proceedings of the Royal Society</u>. 151A:421 London.

Virmani, J.K. et al. 1973. <u>Discharge, Slope Bed Element Relations in Streams</u>. Utah State University, Logan, Utah.

TOPIC B:

EXTREME FLOODS AND THEIR GEOMORPHOLOGICAL EFFECTS

Hydrology in Mountainous Regions. II - Artificial Reservoirs; Water and Slopes
(Proceedings of two Lausanne Symposia, August 1990). IAHS Publ. no. 194, 1990.

Sediment yield in the aftermath of a dambreak flood in a mountain stream

J. C. BATHURST
Natural Environment Research Council, Water Resource
Systems Research Unit, Department of Civil Engineering,
University of Newcastle upon Tyne, NE1 7RU, UK
L. HUBBARD
Department of Geography, Queen Mary College, University
of London, E1 4NS, UK
G. J. L. LEEKS
Institute of Hydrology (Plynlimon), Llanbrynmair, Powys,
SY19 7DB, UK
M. D. NEWSON
Department of Geography, University of Newcastle upon
Tyne, NE1 7RU, UK
C. R. THORNE
Department of Geography, University of Nottingham,
University Park, Nottingham, NG7 2RD, UK

ABSTRACT A six-year study of the sediment transport regime
in the Roaring River, Colorado, following a dambreak flood
has shown that transport rates were massively increased
during the first snowmelt season after the flood. Rates
have subsequently decreased but are still estimated to be
an order of magnitude higher than under pre-flood
conditions. A gradual decrease in transport rates has
been measured at a site remote from out-of-channel
sediment sources, probably as a result of depleted in-
channel supplies. However, at the stream outlet, below a
gorge eroded by the flood, consistently high transport
rates persist, fed by material from the gorge cliffs and
regulated by the action of in-channel shoals. Transport
rates may be additionally boosted by early snowmelt flows
carrying the products of winter erosion processes and by
rainstorms supplying eroded soil directly to the channel
via surface runoff. High sediment yields at the outlet
are likely to continue for the foreseeable future.

INTRODUCTION

The recovery of mountain stream systems from severe flood destruction
takes place within a regime of altered sediment supply relative to
pre-flood conditions. Unstable eroded banks, fans of deposited
material, altered channel geometry, banks denuded of vegetation and
other flood-derived features create a legacy of increased sediment
availability which can affect sediment yield for years after the flood
(e.g. Newson, 1980). The naturally sensitive balance between sediment
supply and transport at the upper end of the river system is altered,
with repercussions potentially extending throughout the whole system

(e.g. Schumm, 1977, p.3; Newson, 1981). However, there has been relatively little research into the long term variation in sediment supply and transport in flood-affected mountain streams. This paper therefore describes the sediment transport characteristics in the Roaring River in the Rocky Mountain National Park, Colorado, USA, during the period 1983-1988 following the ravaging of the stream by the flood wave from the Lawn Lake Dam failure in July 1982. The aim is to show how the sediment transport characteristics have been altered from their pre-flood condition and the extent to which the new conditions have been maintained. The field data were collected in a joint project involving the UK Institute of Hydrology, Colorado State University and Queen Mary College, University of London (Bathurst et al., 1986a, b; Pitlick & Thorne, 1987).

THE LAWN LAKE FLOOD AND ITS IMMEDIATE EFFECTS

The flood wave travelled rapidly along the 7-km length of the Roaring River, from Lawn Lake at an elevation of about 3350 m, to its confluence with the Fall River, at an elevation of about 2620 m. Peak discharges were estimated at 500 m^3 s^{-1} at the dam and 340 m^3 s^{-1} at the Fall River, far in excess of the normal stream discharges which peak at about 5 m^3 s^{-1} during snowmelt events. Details of the wider effects of the flood are given in Jarrett & Costa (1986) and Pitlick & Thorne (1987).

   Before the flood, the Roaring River had a width of around 5-10 m, was bordered by grass and trees and had a generally stable boulder bed. Following the flood, the stream returned to its former width but was left in a 100-m wide swathe of unvegetated debris (grading from sand to boulders) and had a bed of fresh, loose sediment. The flood also produced a series of reaches of alternating scour (typified by eroded gorges with steep sides of compacted glacial material) and deposition (typified by alluvial fans of sand, gravel and boulders). The most spectacular gorge and fan combination occurs immediately upstream of the confluence with the Fall River. The cliffs along the 0.75-km long gorge, up to 30 m high in places, were expected to form an important sediment source for the Roaring River and Fall River and the gorge was therefore the centre of a study into the relationship between sediment supply and transport. The upstream basin area at this point is about 29 km^2.

DATA COLLECTION

Measurements of water and sediment discharge were made just upstream of the gorge at the Ypsilon Lake Trail Bridge and just downstream where the Fall River Road bridge crosses the fan. Water discharge was obtained by current metering, bed load discharge was obtained by Helley Smith sampler and suspended load discharge was obtained with bottle "gulp" samplers (Bathurst et al., 1986b). Usually the measurements were made simultaneously at the two gauging sites. As the techniques were manual, continuous measurements could be kept up for only limited periods, varying from 2½ to 55 hours in length.

   Field data are available for 1984-1988 and the relationship between water and bed load discharge for each site is shown in

Fig. 1. (Suspended load discharge data are not available for 1986–1988.) In this diagram, each region is defined by the average values of the variables for periods of continuous measurement and given flow characteristics (e.g. steady, rising, peak and receding flows).

RESULTS

In order to obtain a meaningful relationship between the water and sediment discharges through time, it is necessary to study changes in chronological order. In this case the transport characteristics can be analyzed according to three successive periods.

1983: general pattern of sediment yield

This was the first snowmelt season following the dambreak and it was expected that the plentiful deposits of sediment along the channel would support a greatly increased sediment yield relative to pre-flood conditions. There were not sufficient resources to mount a full-scale field study in this year but it was nevertheless clear from qualitative observation that, aided by a record snowmelt runoff, sediment transport in the Roaring River was exceptionally high. Gravel and cobbles moving as bed load were observed being propelled out of the flow at waterfalls in the gorge and a high suspended load was apparent from the discolouring of the Roaring River water relative to that of the Fall River. Delivery of large amounts of sand, gravel and cobbles onto the alluvial fan triggered continuous avulsions of the stream channel. Bed material measurements in the Fall River immediately below the confluence similarly showed variations between sand and gravel as pulses of sediment from the Roaring River periodically inundated the otherwise stable cobble bed with a moving carpet of bed load (Pitlick & Thorne, 1987). It is likely that, during this season, a large proportion of the loose sediment deposited along the Roaring River channel by the dambreak flood was either flushed away or else trapped within the bed beneath developing armour layers.

1984–1985: general pattern of sediment yield

Major fieldwork activity was carried out during the periods June–July 1984 and May–June 1985 which, fortuitously, when taken together, illustrate a range of flows and sediment discharge conditions considered typical of a complete snowmelt season. Analyzed as such by Bathurst et al. (1986a) they enable two major sediment supply systems to be identified. The initial snowmelt flows in May–June, peaking at 5 m^3 s^{-1}, carried high bed and suspended loads, composed of material supplied to the channel bed by winter erosion processes. Rapid depletion of these supplies, though, resulted in the sediment loads of later flows being reduced by up to an order of magnitude for a given water discharge. This is apparent for both gauging sites in the shift of the 1985 data bands in Fig. 1, separating the early season yields from the midseason yields. This trend may be reversed in July and August when heavy rainstorms can dramatically increase

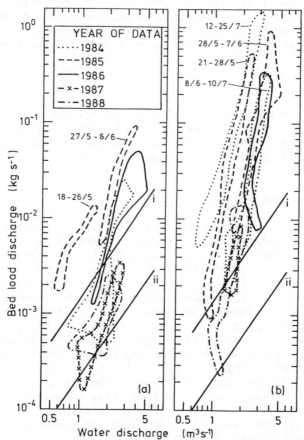

FIG. 1 Variation of bed load discharge with water
discharge at: a) Ypsilon Lake Trail bridge (the upstream
site); b) Fall River Road bridge (the downstream site).
Data bands are segregated by year and, for 1984 and
1985, by day and month. Comparison is made with
Haddock's formula (equation 1) for drainage densities
of: i) 2.17 km km^{-2}; ii) 0.70 km km^{-2}.

cliff erosion and thence sediment transport. Relatively high
transport rates may then persist for several days. In Fig. 1 this
effect is demonstrated for the downstream gauging site by the shift
in the 1984 data bands. The July yields following a series of rainstorms are comparable with those for the early snowmelt flows,
exceeding the midseason yields by an order of magnitude for a given
water discharge. The effect is not apparent for the upstream site
since this does not lie below erodible cliffs feeding sediment
directly to the river. Indeed close examination of the bed load
discharge data suggests that yields there were relatively reduced
following the rainstorms, possibly because the high water flows
further depleted the in-channel sediment supplies.

   Qualitative observation suggests that transport rates were lower
than in 1983. The lower, more average, snowmelt flows of 1984 and

1985 were less able to tap out-of-channel sediment supplies and promote cliff collapses. The 1983 flows, by flushing much of the loose sediment from the channel and stabilising the bed with armour layers, also reduced the in-channel supplies. However, supply effects were still active and a comparison of the transport rates upstream and downstream of the gorge shows the sediment discharge out of the gorge to be between two times and an order of magnitude higher than that entering the gorge. This demonstrates the effect of supply from the gorge cliffs in boosting the sediment yield from the Roaring River.

1986-1988: general pattern of sediment yield

There was a lower scale of fieldwork during this period but bed load discharge data are available for mid/late May to mid/late June in each year. Plotted in Fig. 1a, the results suggest a slight decrease in relative transport rates at the upstream site for 1987 and 1988 compared with the earlier years. This probably reflects the relative remoteness of this site from sediment sources feeding directly to the channel and a further depletion of the in-channel supplies upstream of the site. In addition, snowmelt was below normal in these years, particularly in 1987 and 1988 when the water discharge did not exceed $3 \text{ m}^3 \text{ s}^{-1}$. This further reduced the flow's capability for tapping out-of-channel supplies. By contrast, the pattern for the downstream site (Fig. 1b) remains consistent with that for the earlier years, although the lower water flows produce lower absolute transport rates. This suggests a greater regulation of the sediment yield than is the case for the upstream site, probably as a result of the reservoir effect of in-channel sediment shoals at the downstream end of the gorge and continued supply direct from the cliffs of the gorge itself.

Comparison with pre-flood conditions

No measurements of sediment discharge are available for the Roaring River prior to the dambreak flood. However, two indirect methods give some idea of pre-flood conditions and the subsequent change in yield magnitudes.

The first is a comparison of transport rates in the Roaring River and its main tributary, Ypsilon Creek, which enters the Roaring River about two thirds of the way from Lawn Lake to the Fall River. Ypsilon Creek was unaffected by the flood, its course is closely bordered by trees and grass and it has a bed of dull-looking gravel, cobbles and boulders, clearly not frequently moved. The tributary is therefore considered to be typical of conditions in the Roaring River before the dambreak. By contrast, the bed of the Roaring River at the confluence was composed of loose sand, gravel, cobbles and boulders and was clearly active. Sediment and water discharges were monitored simultaneously in both channels just upstream of the confluence, where the two streams have similar widths, slopes and water discharges. The measurements were made on 6 June 1985, a warm day with a steadily rising snowmelt. Examination of the results (Fig. 2) shows that, although Ypsilon Creek was carrying the higher

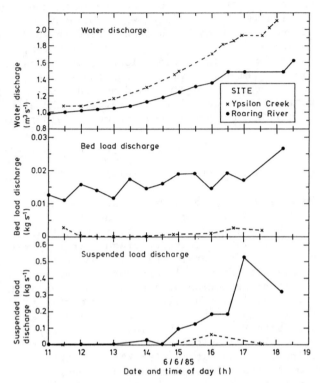

FIG. 2 Comparison of measured sediment discharges for
Ypsilon Creek and the Roaring River immediately above
their confluence.

flow, both bed and suspended load discharges were an order of
magnitude higher in the Roaring River. This difference is significant
relative to any measurement errors and indicates that the Roaring
River was carrying roughly ten times more sediment than would have
been expected in the absence of flood disturbance.

In the second approach, the measured bed load discharges above and
below the Roaring River gorge are compared with the predictions of a
bed load transport equation developed empirically for the nearby Saint
Vrain and Cache la Poudre headwater catchments by Haddock (1978).
This equation accounts for the effect of sediment supply on sediment
discharge through the use of drainage density as a surrogate for bank
erosion. Converted to SI units, the equation is

$$\log Q_S = 1.45 \log Q + 0.563 Dd - 4.07 \qquad (1)$$

where Q_S = bed load discharge (kg s^{-1}); Q = water discharge (m^3 s^{-1});
and Dd = drainage density (km km^{-2}). Knowing the drainage density
this equation can be converted to a sediment discharge rating curve
and compared with the measured data in Fig. 1. However, there are two
complicating factors. First, the typical values of drainage density
used by Haddock (2.17 km km^{-2}) are higher than those measured for the
Roaring River (0.70 km km^{-2}). It is not known whether this reflects
different catchment characteristics or the use of maps with different

scales (1:24 000 in the case of the Roaring River). Lines based on both values are therefore shown in Fig. 1. Second, both the Roaring River and its major tributary, Ypsilon Creek, have lakes in their headwaters which act as sediment traps for material supplied from further upstream. Haddock's stream systems, on the other hand, were not so affected. However, if anything, the presence of lakes should tend to reduce the measured downstream transport rates relative to those predicted by the equation. Figure 1 shows, though, that the opposite is true, at least at the higher flows. Again, therefore, despite the uncertain applicability of Haddock's equation, the suggestion is that the Roaring River is carrying up to ten times more bed load than would have been expected in its pre-flood condition, except possibly at the lower flows.

DISCUSSION AND CONCLUSIONS

The initial impact of the 1982 dambreak flood was a massive increase in the supply of loose material within and along the channel of the Roaring River. Sediment transport in the 1983 snowmelt season was correspondingly high but, with the resulting removal of much of this material, the impact was reduced in the following five years. Nevertheless, the bed load transport rates were still an order of magnitude higher than in the pre-flood channel. The precise characteristics of the transport regime appear to depend on location along the stream relative to sediment sources.

Upstream of the gorge, the impression from Fig. 1a is of a slight decrease in relative transport rates from 1985 to 1988. This pattern is consistent with a gradual depletion of in-channel sediment supplies and little replacement by out-of-channel supplies. However, the picture is complicated by the coincident decrease in snowmelt runoff during this period and the greater scatter in the data, as shown by the widths of the data bands. Downstream of the gorge the pattern is much more consistent, in both the higher and lower transport rate bands (Fig. 1b). There is little shift in the ratings from year to year, indicating that a relatively high sediment yield is being maintained. The data bands are also consistently narrower than for the upstream site. This points to a continuing supply of sediment, presumably fed directly from the gorge cliffs, and a regulating effect by shoals at the downstream end of the gorge. By storing the unsteady injections of cliff material and releasing sediment in accordance with water discharge, these shoals act to reduce some of the larger hysteresis effects usually associated with mountain river sediment transport. Because of the short growing season and harsh winters, the cliff faces remain unvegetated and this pattern is therefore likely to continue for the foreseeable future. In addition transport rates could be boosted to the higher rating band by early snowmelt flows and rainstorms causing erosion of the cliff walls. Thus while locally the sediment transport rate may be slowly decreasing along the channel, high yields continue to be supplied to the Fall River. This supports the findings of other studies which show that catastrophic floods in mountain rivers have significant long term impacts on the sediment yield regime (e.g. Newson, 1980).

Finally the rates of change of sediment discharge with water discharge for the two Roaring River sites are much higher than those associated with lowland rivers. In Fig. 1 the rates of change correlate with both channel slope at the gauging site and sediment supply from upstream. The effect may also depend on the range of sizes making up the bed material. In sand-bed rivers, the range is narrow and most of the sediment starts to move at approximately the same water discharge. In boulder-bed rivers the range is wide and the different sizes come into motion over a range of flows. Thus as the water discharge increases, the increase in transport of each size already in motion is augmented by the transport of new sizes entering motion. The resulting rate of increase of transport is then likely to be higher than for a bed of more uniform material, at least until all sizes in the bed are moving.

ACKNOWLEDGEMENTS Considerable help with the fieldwork was provided by Colorado State University, the United States Geological Survey, the Rocky Mountain National Park and the Institute of Hydrology. Financial support was given by NATO (Collaborative Research Grant 092/ 84) and by the United States National Park Service. The camera-ready manuscript of this paper was carefully typed by Ms Suzanne McLean.

REFERENCES

Bathurst, J.C., Leeks, G.J.L. & Newson, M.D. (1986a) Relationship between sediment supply and sediment transport for the Roaring River, Colorado, USA. In: Drainage Basin Sediment Delivery (Proc. Albuquerque Symp., August 1986), 105-117. IAHS Publ. no. 159.
Bathurst, J.C., Leeks,G.J.L. & Newson, M.D. (1986b) Field measurements for hydraulic and geomorphological studies of sediment transport - the special problems of mountain streams. In: Measuring Techniques in Hydraulic Research (Proc. IAHR Delft Symp., April 1985), 137-151. A.A. Balkema, Rotterdam, The Netherlands.
Haddock, D.R. (1978) Modeling bedload transport in mountain streams of the Colorado Front Range. MS thesis. Colorado State Univ., Fort Collins, Colorado, USA.
Jarrett, R.D., & Costa, J.E. (1986) Hydrology, geomorphology, and dam-break modeling of the July 15, 1982 Lawn Lake Dam and Cascade Lake Dam failures, Larimer County, Colorado. USGS Professional Paper 1369, US Geological Survey, Denver Federal Center, Colorado, USA.
Newson, M. (1980) The erosion of drainage ditches and its effect on bed-load yields in mid-Wales: reconnaissance case studies. Earth Surf. Processes 5, 275-290.
Newson, M.D. (1981) Mountain streams. In: British Rivers (ed. by J. Lewin), 59-89. George Allen & Unwin, London, UK.
Pitlick, J.C. & Thorne, C.R. (1987) Sediment supply, movement and storage in an unstable gravel-bed river. In: Sediment Transport in Gravel-bed Rivers (ed. by C.R. Thorne, J.C. Bathurst & R.D. Hey), 151-178. John Wiley & Sons, Chichester, UK.
Schumm, S.A. (1977) The Fluvial System. John Wiley & Sons, New York, NY, USA.

Hydrology in Mountainous Regions. II - Artificial Reservoirs; Water and Slopes
(Proceedings of two Lausanne Symposia, August 1990). IAHS Publ. no. 194, 1990.

Geomorphological effects of extreme floods (November 1982) in the southern Pyrenees

J. COROMINAS & E. E. ALONSO
Geotechnical Engineering Department,Technical
University of Catalunya, Jordi Girona Salgado 31
08034 Barcelona, E- Spain

ABSTRACT Heavy rains are common in Southeastern
Pyrenees. The geomorphological effects of
November 1982 rains on river bed and their
interaction with civil works are discussed.
Foundation undermining was the main cause of
structural collapse due to the flooding waters.
Landslides triggered by rains are restricted to
specific lithologies and topography.The latter
controls an important parameter : the watershed
area. Influence of river erosion on bank slopes
is also analyzed. It is found that groundwater
table rise is more effective controlling the
slope stability than isolated vertical or lateral
bank erosion although the accumulative effect of
the latter is more dangerous.

INTRODUCTION

Southern Pyrenees have a typical Mediterranean climate.
Heavy rains and consequent floods have been historically
reported several times. In the present century the 1907,
1937, 1940 and 1982 events should be especially mentioned
(Corominas, 1985). These rains are a common occurrence in
the fall season when moist and warm air masses coming from
south Mediterranean sea areas are forced to flow upwards
through the ranges close to the coast. If a cold air front
is located beyond the range, the collision between both
warm and cold air masses provoke a sudden condensation and
a subsequent heavy precipitation. Rainfall records over 300
mm per day are usual in such circumstances and
precipitation over 700 mm per day were recorded during the
1940 events (Novoa 1984).

Pyrenean rivers show a steep channel gradient, so
surface water tend to concentrate quickly. As a result
relatively small watersheds give peak discharges of several
thousand cubic meters per second with relative yields over
2000 l s^{-1} km^{-2}. The November 1982 floods spread over the
entire Eastern Pyrenees reaching maximum rainfall records
of 423 mm and 350 mm in 24hr at La Molina and Puigmal
respectively (fig. 1). Peak discharge attained 3000 m^3 s^{-1}
in the Segre valley at Lleida but the most striking
geomorphological effects were concentrated in the upper
valleys where the relative yields are larger.River levels

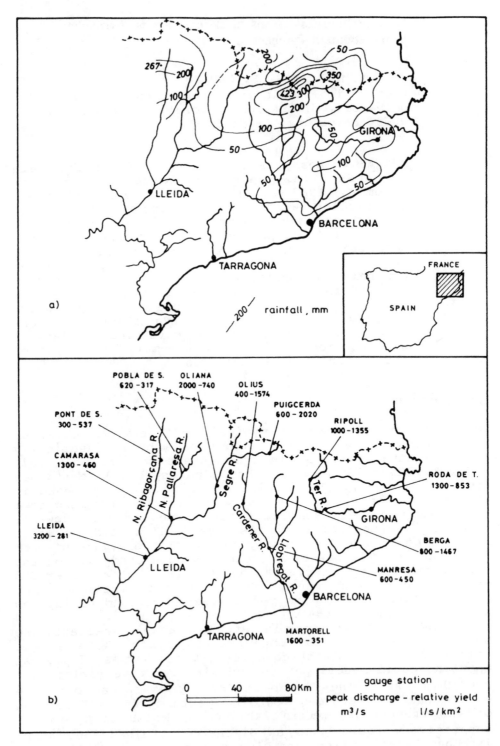

FIG. 1 (a) Rainfall distribution on 7 November 1982.
(b) Maximum peak discharge and relative yield at
several gauging stations on Pyrenean rivers on 7-8
November 1982.

rose up 5 to 8 m in most areas (Banda & Olivera, 1983). At some specific sections such as the gauge stations of Oliana and Organyà at Segre river, water levels rose up to 10.9 and 13.7 m respectively.

Urban growth of the last few decades, spreading over the flood plains was the primary reason for the inflicted damage. 20 lives were lost and more than 400 milion dolars in damage were reported during the November 1982 floods.

In this paper the geomorphological effects associated with the extreme rainfalls will be discussed. They include: river bed modifications, slope instabilities and their effects on civil works.

RIVER BED MODIFICATIONS

Morphological changes and river methamorphosis, are produced if sediment load and discharge are modified (Schumm 1977). Short term channel adjustments occurred during the 1982 floods.The increase in discharge forced the rivers to follow straight paths, steeper in gradient and this led to the scouring of the river bed. Meanders were cut off reducing the sinuosity by generating new channels through the banks of lower terraces. When alluvial plains were well developed the reduction in sinuosity made river channels almost straight. In the Llobregat river at Guardiola, sinuosity reduced from 1.20 to 1.05. In the Segre river at La Seu d'Urgell reduction was from 1.21 to 1.08.

The velocity increase and the solid supply from tributaries and landslides gave an increase in river bed load. As a consequence river channels were enlarged by erosion and retreating bank terraces.Scarp retreat values ranging from 20 to 40 m for the lower terrace bank were usual in Noguera Pallaresa and Llobregat rivers. In the Segre valley the retreat attained 150 to 200 m upstream of La Seu d'Urgell (fig. 2).

Urban areas were badly affected by flooding. Urban development has forced rivers crossing populated areas into narrow channels. Water velocity increases in such sections and scours the gravel-sand bed. Several building foundations were undermined. The subsequent deposition of gravel sediments at the outlet of the channels, at the end of villages, forced the river to bend and to erode the margins. Bank protection walls have sometimes induced the same effect.

Special attention should be paid to brigdes. More than 50% of brigdes in upper Segre valley were destroyed in November 1982.The causes for this destruction are twofold: a)brigde spans were not large enough to allow the free pass of tree trunks which were retained by the structure, damming waters upstream.The increased water head led to either embankment failure of the abutments or the structural collapse of the brigde. b)The scouring and posterior sediment filling had a critical influence on the bridge foundations. The scouring reached more than 3 - 4 m

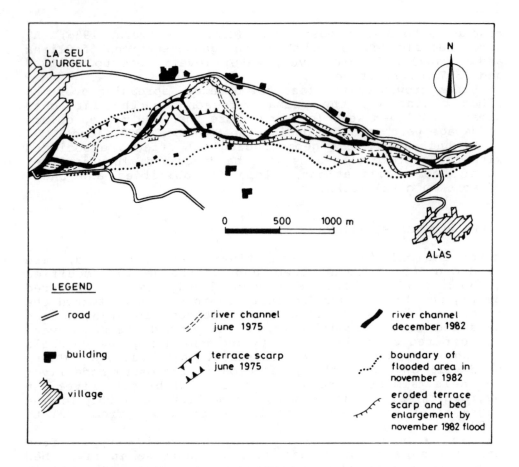

FIG. 2   Bed enlargement of Segre river at la Seu d'Urgell
          by floods of November 1982 (obtained by comparison
          of aerial photographs of June 1975 and December
          1982).

in numerous sections inducing foundation instability due to
differential erosion. Bridges in the Segre and Llobregat
valleys located in la Nou, Organyà, Alàs and Martinet fell
down for this reason. Other unfailed brigdes acted as a
dam, causing upstream sedimentation and downstream bed
scouring and channel enlargement.

SLOPE INSTABILITY

Landslides were triggered by heavy rains in 1982. In a 1250
km^2 area of Llobregat river basin, Gallart and Clotet (1988)
reported more than 1800 movements of all types (shallow
slab slides, debris flows, slumps and rock falls), which
represents a density of 1.5 movements per square kilometer.

The landslide distribution was controlled by lithology and by morphological characteristics of natural slopes. Bedrock was almost unaffected by movements whereas Keuper marls, claystones from late Cretaceous and lower Paleocene ages and recent colluvial and glacial deposits were found in most landslide-prone areas. A first interpretation of data taken from a detailed landslide inventory which is still in progress, shows that failures took place mostly in slope angles ranging from 30 to 40º (fig. 3). Mudflows and debris flows are concentrated in slope angles around 30–35º, slab slides between 35-40º, and rock falls usually occur in steeper slopes over 60º and up to 90º. However no clear distinction is established if only the slope angle is considered.

A relationship has been found between the watershed area above the location of the landslide and its volume (fig. 4). The larger is the watershed area, the bigger is the landslide in terms of mobilized mass. The fit seems to be better for mudflows whereas a lithological influence appears in debris flows and, to a lesser extent, in slab slides. For a given landslide size, colluvium soils need to accumulate more water (larger watershed area) in order to fail than clayey substratums. This behaviour may be explained on the basis of better drainability of colluvial soils if compared with clayey soils.

All the observed movements larger than 200 000 m^3 in mobilized mass showed signs of ancient instability. Old scarps, lateral scars, tilted scree deposits, poorly drained depressions, are typical features easy to recognize in these areas. Geological conditions of the large landslides seem to have a pronounced effect on the onset of instability. In fact not only runoff water but internally fed water from neighbouring watersheds could be suspected in these cases. As an illustration karstic limestone allowed an easy transmission of groundwater towards the ladslide area in La Coma ($0.25 \ 10^6 \ m^3$) Gòsol ($10^6 \ m^3$) and Pont de Bar ($10^7 \ m^3$) movements.

REDUCTION OF SLOPE STABILITY DUE TO EROSIVE ACTION OF RIVERS

Landslides may affect the rivers activity by increasing the bed load. Some debris flows and avalanches may fall down through mountain torrent beds. Conversely river erosion affects slope stability. This erosion is considered in terms of both vertical and lateral undercutting which leads to an increase of shear stresses on the potential failure surfaces.Its influence has been compared with the effect of the groundwater pore pressures increase (Fig. 5).In the example a 20 m high slope is considered which has a friction angle of 30º , a cohesion of 2 T/m^2 and specific weight of 2 T/m^3. The slope is subjected to an increase of slope height (curve a), a lateral erosion including a geometrical change of the foot (curve b), the combined effect of both height increase and lateral erosion (curve

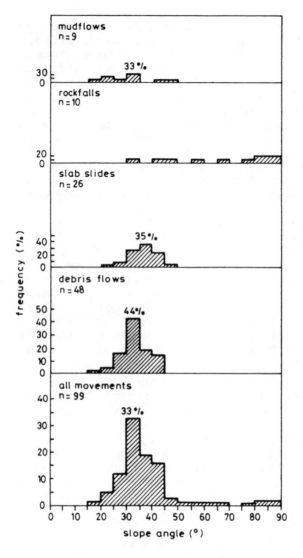

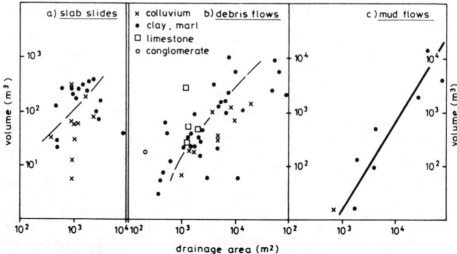

FIG. 3 Relative frequence of landslides for changing slope angles.

FIG. 4 Plot showing the relationship between watershed area and volume of the landslide for different kinds of mass movements induced by 1982 rains. Dashed lines in (a) and (b) provide a rough delimitation of failures in colluvium soils from other lithologies. A relatively good correlation is found for mud flows (c).

c) and increase of groundwater piezometric level (curve d)
The effect is considered in terms of safety factor
reduction using the Bishop simplified method of analysis
with a pore pressure coefficient r_u of 0.25 ($r_u = u/\gamma z$,

 (u) being the pore water pressure, (γ) specific weight of
soil and (z) the depth of failure plane).As can be seen in
fig. 5, pore pressure increase has a pronounced influence
on stability.   The isolated effect of toe or lateral
erosion has a limited influence if the depth of erosion is
made equivalent to the rise in groundwater table.However
the combined erosive action (curve c) is as effective as
groundwater in reducing the F.S. (if height of toe erosion
is compared with height of water table rise).

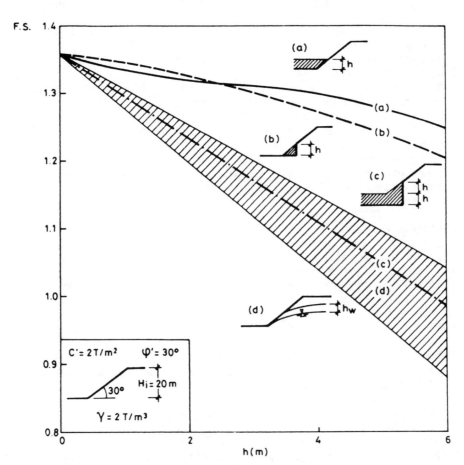

FIG. 5 Relative influence of toe erosion (h) and
increase of pore water pressure (h_w) on safety
factor.
(a) : toe erosion preserving original slope
(b) : lateral erosion maintaining original slope
      height
(c) : combined effect of (a) + (b)
(d) : mean increase in phreatic surface elevation

Nevertheless it should be stressed that the erosive action is an everincreasing phenomenon unlike the pore pressure rise which has a periodic character. Accordingly the effect of toe erosion is perhaps the real triggering effect in many slope instabilities.

CONCLUSIONS

(a) Floods of November 1982 put in evidence that urban growth and engineering works have to consider more realistically river changes during the floods and, specifically, bed load mobility which in this Pyrenean area may imply at least a thickness of 3 to 4 m of alluvial bed. An important number of buildings, walls and brigdes fell by this reason.
(b) More than 50% of the inventored landslides occurred in slope angles ranging from 30 to 40º. There exists a relationship between watershed area and mobilized landslide volume. Failures in clayey soils take place in smaller watershed surfaces than colluvium soils. Large landslides (over $0.25 \cdot 10^6$ m^3) have been found to correspond to the activation of old movements.
(c) A sensitivity analysis of groundwater and river erosion effects on bank slopes shows that the former has a decisive influence on slope stability. Only the combined effect of vertical and lateral erosion may be of the same importance but its cumulative nature make it specially relevant.

ACKNOWLEDGEMENTS

This work has benefited from funds from the Spanish National Research Commission (CICYT) project number PB87-0858. We are also grateful to Ms. C. Baeza for the help provided during field data collection.

REFERENCES

Banda, E. & Olivera, C. (1983) Hidrometria i fenòmens sísmics . In : Efectes geomorfològics dels aiguats del novembre de 1982. Estudis 1, 32-46. Servei Geològic de Catalunya, Barcelona.
Corominas, J. (1985) Els riscos geològics. In : Història Natural dels Països Catalans. Vol. 3, 225-270. Fundació Enciclopèdia Catalana, Barcelona.
Gallart, F. & Clotet, N. (1988) Some aspects of the geomorphic processes triggered by an extreme rainfall event: the November 1982 flood in the Eastern Pyrenees. Catena Suppl. 13, 79-95.
Novoa, M. (1984) Precipitaciones y avenidas extraordinarias en Cataluña. In : Inestabilidad de laderas en el Pirineo, 1.1.1-1.1.15, Universidad Politécnica de Barcelona.
Schumm, S.N. (1977) The fluvial system. John Wiley and Sons, New York.

Hydrology in Mountainous Regions. II - Artificial Reservoirs; Water and Slopes
(Proceedings of two Lausanne Symposia, August 1990). IAHS Publ. no. 194, 1990.

Investigation of 1987 debris flows in the Swiss Alps: general concept and geophysical soundings

W. HAEBERLI, D. RICKENMANN, M. ZIMMERMANN
Versuchsanstalt für Wasserbau, Hydrologie und Glaziologie
ETH Zürich, ETH-Zentrum, 8092 Zürich, Switzerland
U. ROESLI
Ingenieurgeologie, ETH Zürich, ETH-Hönggerberg, 8093
Zürich, Switzerland

ABSTRACT An interdisciplinary study on the causes of debris flows in the Swiss Alps during the catastrophic flood
events of 1987 included qualitative and quantitative air-
photo interpretation, geophysical soundings, geomorphological, glaciological, hydrological and geological assessments, dynamic flow considerations, and historical recon-
structions. Results of geophysical investigations are discussed in detail. Seismic refraction and geoelectrical resistivity soundings were carried out in two catchments
where a considerable number of debris flows had occurred.
Erosion had taken place in thick and extremely loose debris. Neither bedrock nor sedimentary stratification can
be considered as a limiting factor to depth erosion in
these areas. A combination of low P-wave velocities and
high electrical resistivities indicates the existence of
large and probably quite irregular pore spaces: the affected sediments appear to be highly permeable and hydraulically nonhomogeneous. The potential for many more debris
flows still exists in most catchments.

INTRODUCTION

In summer 1987, repeated flood catastrophes occurred in the Swiss Alps
(cf., for instance, Naef et al. 1988, Zeller and Röthlisberger 1988).
On July 18/19 and August 24/25 numerous debris flows in three major
areas (Figure 1) were triggered by intensive rainfall of unusually
long duration, which was superimposed on strong snow and ice melt. Due
to exceptionally high air temperatures, precipitation fell as rain
even in the uppermost parts of the catchments in both cases. First reconnaissance missions using helicopter flights and infrared aerial
photography showed that the periglacial belt had been most severely
affected (Haeberli and Naef 1988, cf. Zimmermann and Haeberli 1989).
Based on the results of the reconnaissance missions, the Federal Government initiated a research programme in order to document and investigate the causes of the 1987 events. The present contribution briefly
explains the general concept of the project and presents the results
of geophysical soundings.

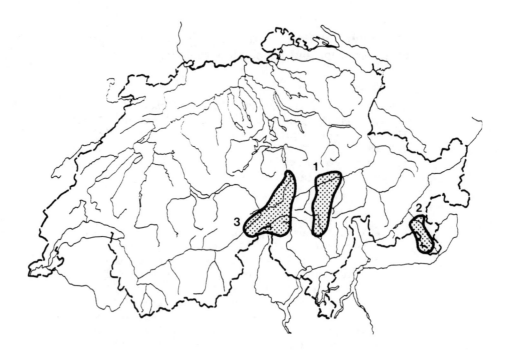

FIG. 1 Most heavily affected areas during the flood catastrophes in the Swiss Alps in summer 1987. 1,2 = July 18/19, 3 = August 24/25.

INVESTIGATION OF 1987 DEBRIS FLOWS IN THE SWISS ALPS

The main goals of the project were (1) to document the distribution pattern of 1987 debris flows in the most severely affected regions, (2) to reconstruct the dynamic behaviour of the most spectacular e-vents (Münster, Varuna, Plaunca, Zavragia), (3) to analyze the factors and combinations of factors which had led to the release of numerous debris flows, (4) to use the collected sample for testing already a-vailable, or deriving new, empirical rules – such as location of starting zones, mass turnover, peak flow rate, run-out distances – in view of assessments concerning debris flow hazards, and (5) to outline perspectives concerning long-term trends and developments, especially in view of observed past and anticipated future atmospheric warming.

The 2-year study was carried out by an interdisciplinary team and mainly involved (a) systematic mapping of 1987 debris flows in select-ed areas from available (in part specially flown infrared) aerial pho-tographs and field investigations, (b) geophysical soundings in two selected catchments, (c) geomorphological and geological inventory of surface phenomena and material characteristics along major debris flow paths, (d) hydraulic/dynamic considerations and modelling, and (e) me-teorological, glaciological and hydrological assessments. The follow-ing discussion concentrates on the geophysical soundings. Other impor-tant parts of the project are being described by Zimmermann (1990: geomorphological aspects), Rickenmann (1990: dynamic considerations) and Rösli and Schindler (geological effects).

GEOPHYSICAL SOUNDINGS

Goals, methods and field work

In order to investigate the thickness, internal layering and the physical properties (state of compaction, water and ice content) of the
affected debris masses, seismic refraction and geoelectrical resistivity soundings were carried out. These two methods have been repeatedly
used in high-altitude quarternary sediments (rock glaciers, debris
cones, moraines) of the Alps for practical reasons (Fisch et al. 1977,
Haeberli and Epifani 1986) as well as for scientific purposes (Barsch
1973, Evin 1983, Evin and Fabre, in press, Haeberli 1975, 1985, Haeberli and Fisch 1984, Hartmann-Brenner 1973, King et al. 1987). Examples of extended soundings in quarternary valley fillings are given by
Aric and Steinhauser (1977) and Scheller (1970). Typical ranges of
geophysical parameters derived from these studies and to be expected
in the investigated materials are compiled in Table 1. Overlapping
ranges and gradual transitions are common. Values outside the given
ranges are also possible in extreme cases: melting permafrost with a
high water content can have P-wave velocities close to groundwater-
values, and thin lenses of dead ice or degrading permafrost are hardly
detectable because of resolution problems. The combination of seismic
and electrical soundings nevertheless enables avoiding grave misinterpretations in most cases.

TABLE 1   Ranges of P-wave velocities (V) and specific electrical resistivities (ρ) for the investigated materials.

material	V (m/s)	ρ (Ωm)
glacier ice,	3300 – 3800	10^7 – $>10^8$
avalanche remains, firn patches	2000 – 3000 ?	10^6 – 10^7
ice-rich permafrost	2000 – 4500	10^4 – 10^6
coarse, dry debris	300 – 600	10^3 – 10^4
moraines, ± consolidated/wet	800 – 2000	10^3 – 10^4
groundwater in debris/moraine	1500 – 2500	$5 \cdot 10^2$ – $2 \cdot 10^3$
rocks (*)	2500 – 4000	higly variable
solid rock	4000 – 6000	higly variable

(*) = according to degree of fissuration

Field work was carried out in August and September 1988 by a geophysical contractor (Geotest, Zollikofen/Bern) and concentrated on two

catchments: the Varuna Valley near Poschiavo where the heaviest damage had occurred, and the Geren Valley in the Gotthard region where a significant variety of debris flow types had been found. In both catchments, the starting zones of the major debris flows are situated in the periglacial belt.

Results and interpretation

Soundings in the **Varuna Valley** were carried out in the scree slope at 2450 to 2700 m a.s.l., where numerous debris flows had started, in a valley section between 1550 and 1700 m a.s.l., where massive erosion had taken place, and on the alluvial fan within the principal valley (1100 - 1200 m a.s.l.).

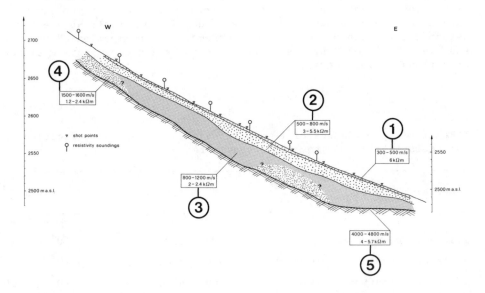

FIG. 2 Geophysical structure of talus slope along starting zone of the main Varuna debris flow: 1 = loose, dry debris, 2 = same material as 1 but slightly more compact and wet, 3 = same material but even more compact/wet, 4 = water-saturated (?) debris, 5 = bedrock.

Figure 2 summarizes results from the starting zone of the main debris flow with an erosional depth of some 5 m. Bedrock surface (V: 4000 - 4800 m/s, ρ: 4 - 6 KΩm) at about 50 m depth is roughly parallel to the slope surface. The very loose and unfrozen scree shows no marked internal layering: V increases rather steadily from 300 - 500 m/s at the surface to 800 - 1200 m/s at depth and ρ correspondingly decreases from 3 - 6 to 2 - 3 KΩm. Unambiguous signs of water saturation (V = 1500 - 1600 m/s, ρ < 1.5 KΩm) can only be detected near the avalanche snow patch at the uppermost end of the slope.

Comparable conditions were encountered in the valley section at 1600 m
a.s.l. A layer with V ≈ 2600 m/s and ρ ≈ 2.3 KΩm at about 40 m depth
was interpreted to be the heavily disintegrated rock visible in the
river course. The bad quality of this rock was largely responsible for
the massive erosion in this reach. Long-distance shots indicated that
sound bedrock with V ⩾ 4000 m/s can only exist at a depth greater than
about 70 m.

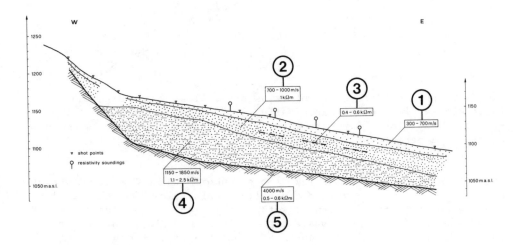

FIG. 3 Geophysical structure of accumulation cone of the main Varuna
debris flow. 1 = loose, dry debris, highly variable resistivity, 2 =
same material as 1 but slightly more compact and wet, 3 = thin layer
enriched in fine material, or aquifer, 4 = more compact/wet debris, 5
= bedrock.

Figure 3 illustrates the longitudinal profile of the cone at valley
bottom. Bedrock with V ≈ 4000 m/s and ρ ≈ 0.5 KΩm (!) is at 60 to 70 m
below surface. This thickness as compared to the thickness of deposits
from the 1987 debris flow (about 0.1 - 1 m) shows that the return period for such events is on the order of decades to centuries. The loose
sediments of the debris flow cone again seem to gradually increase in
V - values from 300 - 600 m/s near the surface to 1100 - 1900 m/s near
bedrock, whereas ρ exhibits a clear minimum of 0.4 - 1.2 KΩm in a
rather distinct layer (concentration of fine material, thin aquifer?)
at about 20 m depth. Signs of extended water saturation are absent.

Low seismic velocities combined with high - in places even extreme -
electrical resistivities are typical in eroded debris of the **Geren
Valley** as well. The example of the main debris flow starting zone at
the locality "Chiebode" is presented in Figure 4. Up to 15 m deep erosion had started at the lower end of a small glacier, 2370 m a.s.l.,
in the immediate vicinity of a modest rock ledge and the local lower
limit of permafrost occurrence (estimated to be at 2400 m a.s.l., cf.
Haeberli 1975). Morainic material from historic/holocene time and

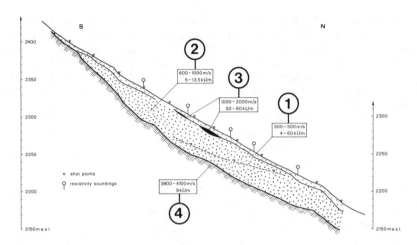

FIG. 4 Geophysical structure of talus slope along starting zone of a large debris flow in the Geren Valley. 1 = loose debris stratified parallel to the slope, 2 = same material but more compact, 3 = remnants of inactive permafrost, 4 = bedrock.

scree is again up to 45 m thick. Above bedrock with V = 4000 - 4100 m/s and $\rho \approx 9$ KΩm, V - values generally remain below 1000 m/s, excluding the possibility of extended water saturation. In two instances, V - values of 1000 - 2000 m/s and ρ - values > 10 KΩm point to the existence of thin permafrost lenses at about 5 - 15 m depth. Other remarkably high ρ - values (10 - 20 KΩm) are related to very low V - values (400 - 800 m/s). This phenomenon is even more pronounced in other profiles of the same study area (350 m/s and up to 30 KΩm) and can most reasonably be explained by the existence of large and quite irregular pore spaces, probably from recently melted underground ice (frozen ground, dead ice, buried avalanche remains).

CONCLUSIONS

The starting zones of 1987 debris flows in the geophysically investigated areas are found in places where saturation of loose debris on steep slopes was possible immediately below local occurrences of bedrock, snow patches/glaciers and permafrost or a combination of them. Erosion had taken place in thick, very loose, in places thaw-destabilized, hydraulically nonhomogenous but generally dry and highly permeable scree and till material. Neither bedrock nor sedimentary stratification were limiting factors for depth erosion, but rather the dynamics of the debris flow process itself. A great potential for many more debris flows from the same as well as other comparable areas undoubtedly exists in the Alps.

ACKNOWLEDGEMENTS

Thanks are due to Prof. Dr. D. Vischer, director of VAW/ETHZ, for his help and encouragement, to the Bundesamt für Wasserwirtschaft, Bern, for funding, and to Prof. Dr. C. Schindler (IGB/ETHZ), Dr. E. Scheller

and P. Holub (Geotest) for critically reading the manuscript. W. Nobs
prepared the drawings and S. Braun edited the English.

REFERENCES

Aric, K. und Steinhauser, P. (1977) Geophysikalische Untersuchung des
    Inntal-Untergrundes bei Thaur, östlich von Innsbruck. Zeitschrift
    für Gletscherkunde und Glazialgeologie XII, 1, p. 37 - 54.

Barsch, D. (1973) Refraktionsseismische Bestimmung der Obergrenze des
    gefrorenen Schuttkörpers in verschiedenen Blockgletschern Graubün-
    dens, Schweizer Alpen. Zeitschrift für Gletscherkunde und Glazial-
    geologie IX, 1 - 2, p. 143 - 167.

Evin, M. (1983) Structure et mouvement des glaciers rocheux des Alpes
    du Sud. Thèse 3e cycle, Université de Grenoble.

Evin, M. and Fabre, D. (in press) The distribution of permafrost in
    rock glaciers of the southern Alps (France). Zeitschrift für Geo-
    morphologie.

Fisch, W. sen., Fisch, W. jun. and Haeberli, W. (1977) Electrical D.C.
    resistivity soundings with long profiles on rock glaciers and mo-
    raines in the Alps of Switzerland. Zeitschrift für Gletscherkunde
    und Glazialgeologie 13, 1/2, p. 239 - 260.

Haeberli, W. (1975) Untersuchungen zur Verbreitung von Permafrost zwi-
    schen Flüelapass und Piz Grialetsch. Mitteilung der Versuchsan-
    stalt für Wasserbau, Hydrologie und Glaziologie ETHZ 17.

Haeberli, W. (1985) Creep of mountain permafrost: Internal structure
    and flow of Alpine rock glaciers. Mitteilung der Versuchsanstalt
    für Wasserbau, Hydrologie und Glaziologie ETHZ 77.

Haeberli, W. and Epifani, F. (1986) Mapping the distribution of buried
    glacier ice - an example from Lago delle Loccie, Monte Rosa, Ital-
    ian Alps. Annals of Glaciology 8, p. 78 - 81.

Haeberli, W. and Fisch, W. (1984) Electrical resistivity soundings of
    glacier beds: A test study on Grubengletscher, Wallis, Swiss Alps.
    Journal of Glaciology 30, 106, p. 373 - 376.

Haeberli, W. und Naef, F. (1988) Murgänge im Hochgebirge - Ereignisse
    1987 im Puschlav und Obergoms. Die Alpen (SAC) 64, 4, p.331 - 343.

Hartmann-Brenner, D.-C. (1973) Ein Beitrag zum Problem der Schutthal-
    denentwicklung an Beispielen des Schweizerischen Nationalparks und
    Spitzbergens. Dissertation Universität Zürich.

King, L., Fisch, W., Haeberli, W. and Waechter, H.P. (1987) Comparison
    of resistivity and radio-echo soundings on rock glacier perma-
    frost. Zeitschrift für Gletscherkunde und Glazialgeologie 23, 1,
    p. 77 - 97.

Naef, F., Haeberli, W., Jäggi, M. und Rickenmann, D. (1988) Morphologische Veränderungen in den Schweizer Alpen als Folge der Unwetter vom Sommer 1987. <u>Oesterreichische Wasserwirtschaft</u> 40, 5/6, p. 134 - 138.

Rickenmann, D. (1990) Debris flows 1987 in Switzerland: Modelling and fluvial sediment transport. International Conference on Water Resources in Mountainous Regions, <u>IAHS Publication</u>, same issue.

Rösli, U. and Schindler, C. (1990) Debris flows 1987 in Switzerland: Geological and hydrogeological aspects. International Conference on Water Resources in Mountainous Regions, <u>IAHS Publication</u>, same issue.

Scheller, E. (1970) Geophysikalische Untersuchungen zum Problem des Taminser Bergsturzes. Dissertation 4560 <u>ETH Zürich</u>.

Zeller, J. und Röthlisberger, G. (1988) Unwetterschäden in der Schweiz im Jahr 1987. <u>Wasser, Energie, Luft</u> 80, 1/2, p. 29 - 42.

Zimmermann, M. (1990) Debris flows 1987 in Switzerland: Geomorphological and meteorological aspects. International Conference on Water Resources in Mountainous Regions, <u>IAHS Publication</u>, same issue.

Zimmermann, M. and Haeberli, W. (1989) Climatic change and debris flow activity in high-mountain areas. Landscape-Ecological Impact of Climatic Change: Discussion Report on Alpine Regions, <u>Universities of Wageningen/Utrecht/Amsterdam</u>, p. 52 - 66.

Hydrology in Mountainous Regions. II - Artificial Reservoirs; Water and Slopes
(Proceedings of two Lausanne Symposia, August 1990). IAHS Publ. no. 194, 1990.

Floods in the high Sierra Nevada, California, USA

RICHARD KATTELMANN
Center for Remote Sensing and Environmental Optics
Computer Systems Lab, 1140 Girvetz Hall
University of California, Santa Barbara, CA 93106, USA

ABSTRACT   A variety of mechanisms generate peak flows in the high
elevation parts of the Sierra Nevada. Snowmelt floods keep discharges
high for several weeks each spring but rarely attain damaging stages much
beyond bankfull. Rain-on-snow events generally account for the highest
peak flows in most rivers. Although summer rainfall is rarely substantial
in the Sierra Nevada, thunderstorms have produced the highest flows on
record in basins where floods produced by other processes are constrained
in magnitude. Lake outbursts generated by impoundment failure or
avalanche displacement of lake water are localized in extent but produce
the largest possible floods. These different types of floods vary in their
potential for geomorphic change, but in combination, they continue to
alter the channel system of the Sierra Nevada.

INTRODUCTION

Rivers originating in the high elevation part of the Sierra Nevada both sustain and
occasionally threaten people and property at lower altitudes. Water flowing from the
Sierra Nevada is a critical resource for California's cities, agriculture, and hydroelectric
generating system. Excessive flows of this mountain water have also created difficulties
for communities and structures since the Gold Rush of the mid-nineteenth century.
Attempts at regulating and redistributing runoff from Sierra Nevada have created a vast
network of dams and diversions along both sides of the range. Considering the extensive
development of water resources in the Sierra Nevada, the basic hydrology of this
mountain range has received surprisingly little study, particularly at higher altitudes.

Most of our hydrologic knowledge of the high Sierra Nevada has come from interest
in water supply forecasting (Miller, 1955), water yield improvement (Anderson, 1963;
Kattelmann & Berg, 1987), or potential effects of acidic deposition (Dozier, et al., 1989).
Little work has been done concerning high-elevation floods and their geomorphic
consequences. This paper was written as part of the background review for a
comprehensive study of the hydrology and hydrochemistry of alpine catchments under
the NASA-Eos program. It discusses the primary mechanisms of flood generation in the
upper Sierra Nevada based on records from the limited set of gaged streams at high
altitude.

Geographic Overview

The Sierra Nevada runs roughly northwest-southeast for more than 600 km and is about
100 km wide, on average. The subalpine forest zone is generally considered to begin
above 2100-2400 m in the northern Sierra Nevada and above 2500-2900 m in the south.
The alpine zone begins above 2800-3000 m in the north and above 3000-3300 m in the
south (Storer & Usinger, 1963). The subalpine zone is about 9000-9500 km^2 in area, and
the alpine zone covers about 2000-2500 km^2. Snow dominates the hydrology of the high
Sierra Nevada, accumulating for six to seven months and then melting for three to four

months. At higher elevations, the snow-free part of the year lasts only from mid-July through mid-October. During four years of a recently-completed study in Sequoia National Park at elevations of 2800-3400 m, more than 90 percent of the precipitation fell as snow. Precipitation is minor and infrequent from May through September. Few stream gages or climate stations exist above 2000 m, but about 100 snow courses and snow sensors are used to monitor the winter snow cover. Most of the Sierra Nevada above 2500 m is reserved from economic use or habitation as National Parks or designated wilderness. Consequently, floods at higher elevations are of little direct concern to society. However, these high-elevation floods obviously contribute to low-altitude floods as well as continue to alter the landscape of the Sierra Nevada.

SNOWMELT

Considering the overwhelming role of snow in the hydrologic cycle of the Sierra Nevada, snowmelt floods are the most obvious source of peak flows. Snowmelt floods are an annual event each spring of sustained high flow, long duration, and large volume. However, they usually do not produce the highest instantaneous peaks. The Sierra Nevada snowpack at the peak of winter accumulation represents an enormous reservoir of potential runoff. The long-term record of snow survey measurements suggests that peak snowpack water equivalence is about 75 to 85 cm, on average, at elevations above 2500 m (Kattelmann & Berg, 1987). In wet years, peak snowpack water equivalence can exceed 200 cm and may persist well into the summer. Differences in snowmelt runoff resulting from differences in snowpack water equivalence may be illustrated by comparing hydrographs from three snowmelt seasons from a small alpine basin in Sequoia National Park (Figure 1).

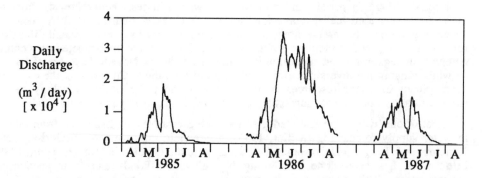

FIG. 1 Peak daily flow during the snowmelt season was almost twice as great in the deep snowpack year of 1986 as in slightly below-average years of 1985 and 1987 in the 1.2 km^2 headwater basin of Emerald Lake. The volume of snowmelt runoff in 1986 was four times larger than in 1985 and three times larger than in 1987.

Snowmelt runoff production from a basin depends on the spatial distribution of both snow and energy available for melt. In the rugged terrain of the alpine Sierra Nevada, snowpack water equivalence is highly variable over large and small spatial scales (Elder, et al., 1989). When snow cover becomes depleted and progressively less of the basin is contributing to runoff, streamflow declines quickly. Snowmelt in the alpine zone generally begins and peaks several weeks later than in the forest zone. In large river basins, snow may have disappeared from the lowest elevations before snowmelt begins at the highest elevations. Such desynchronization of snowmelt contributions helps to reduce peak discharge.

Snowmelt rates also determine the daily and seasonal peak flows. In the Sierra Nevada, net radiation is the dominant influence on snowmelt (Miller, 1955; Aguado, 1985). Widespread cloud cover is infrequent during spring in the Sierra Nevada, and solar radiation input and longwave re-radiation are both high under clear skies. Therefore, the exposure of each slope to solar radiation largely determines the energy balance of the snow cover. Consequently, melt rates may change from 0 on the north side of a ridge to several millimeters per hour on the south side. These drastic differences also diffuse melt water input to streams over time, particularly when snow disappears from south-facing slopes before melt rates peak on north-facing slopes. Melt rates at high altitude are limited by the physics of energy exchange to generally less than 1 cm per hour and 5 cm per day. Daily melt in the alpine zone is highest when several conditions coincide: solar radiation, humidity, and wind are high; snow albedo and nighttime heat loss from the snowpack are low; and the snow cover is nearly continuous with some of it thin enough to allow radiation penetration to the ground. Snowmelt can be rapid once rocks begin to be exposed because re-radiation from the sun-warmed rocks melts snow much faster than does shortwave solar radiation. However, snow covered area must decline simultaneously so the enhancement of streamflow is determined by tradeoffs between higher melt rates and smaller contributing area.

Particularly large snowmelt floods in Sierra Nevada rivers have been documented in 1906, 1938, 1952, 1969, and 1983. In all cases, snow deposition was more than twice average amounts and persisted into April or May. Thus, snow cover was still extensive in late spring when energy available for melt was much greater than in early spring. However, the relative disposition of that energy in 1983, for example, was not particularly different from that in other years with smaller snowpacks that melted earlier (Aguado, 1985). The high rates of snowmelt runoff in the years of late-lying snow cover led to widespread overbank flows, which are generally limited under snowmelt conditions. For example, in 1983 in Sagehen Creek near Lake Tahoe, daily mean discharge exceeded the bankfull level for 45 days and exceeded 230 percent of bankfull discharge for two weeks (Andrews & Erman, 1986). This value of discharge had been equaled or exceeded on only 16 days in 29 years of record before 1983. Compared to more typical snowmelt floods, this event was highly effective in transporting bedload (Andrews & Erman, 1986). In the lowlands, damage from these floods was mostly limited to occupied floodplains and areas drained and converted to agriculture (Stafford, 1956; Dean, 1975).

RAIN-ON-SNOW

Mid-winter rainfall on snow cover has produced all the highest flows in major Sierra Nevada rivers during this century. Rainfall has occurred up to the highest elevations of the Sierra Nevada during winter, but the freezing level of winter storms generally fluctuates between about 1000 m and 2500 m. Even during the warmest storms, snowpacks above 2500 m rarely melt much because temperatures are close to freezing. Snow in the forest zone, particularly at elevations between 1500 m and 2000 m, can dramatically add to floods with melt from convection and condensation processes at temperatures of up to 15°C. The interaction of precipitation amounts, freezing level, energy availability, and basin characteristics determines the relative response of rivers at different elevation zones. For example, a storm in mid-February 1986 produced some of the largest flows of record in major rivers, but it did not produce much of a contribution from areas above the 2000-2300 m rain-snow level. Three weeks later, a storm with much higher freezing level but less precipitation produced some of the highest flows of record in headwater basins, but generally only moderate flows downstream.

In the past 60 years, six large-magnitude floods have occurred in almost all rivers draining the snow zone. Snowmelt from convection and condensation processes was important in all but one of these events when snow was absent. None of these floods was dramatically larger than the others in a majority of rivers, but the relative magnitude depended on storm characteristics and the area-elevation distribution of each basin. These floods at low elevation, which were 4 to 10 times the magnitudes of the mean annual floods, have recurrence intervals of about 10 to 20 years based on the period of record. Large-magnitude warm storms do not seem to occur during spring in the Sierra Nevada. There are only a few moderate rain-on-snow events superimposed on spring snowmelt floods in the streamflow record. The one large flood of this type occurred in April 1982 and ranks in the top ten floods in the annual series in many headwater streams. Storms in April and May generally do not incorporate warm air masses from low latitudes that lead to the warm storms that occasionally occur in the winter months.

In basins that are largely above 2000 m, the highest peaks also tend to be caused by rain-on-snow events, even though almost all the other floods in the annual series are of snowmelt origin. For example, in the Merced River in Yosemite National Park, the four highest floods were caused by rain-on-snow and were 1.5 to 1.8 times greater in discharge than the maximum snowmelt peak of record in May 1983. A hydrograph from a smaller basin in Yosemite, Tenaya Creek, illustrates the contrast between a large snowmelt flood of long duration and a high, but short, rain-on-snow peak (Figure 2). The impact of mid-winter rain-on-snow floods on channel processes may be enhanced by the confining effect of snow along the banks. When present, snow may effectively block overbank spreading of flood water and, thereby increase flow depth and bed shear stress for discharges above bankfull (Erman, et al., 1988).

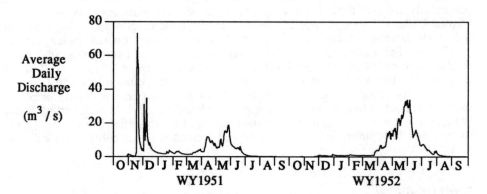

FIG. 2   Peak discharge from a rain-on-snow event in November 1950 was about twice the maximum discharge of one of the largest snowmelt floods on record in 1952. Mean elevation of this 120 km^2 Tenaya Creek basin is about 2000 m.

THUNDERSTORMS

Although the summer and early autumn seasons in the Sierra Nevada tend to be dry, a few minor storms or brief showers occur in most years (Hannaford and Williams, 1967). For example, during the summers of 1985 to 1987, precipitation was measured on 29 days at Emerald Lake at 2800 m (Dozier, et al., 1989). Daily precipitation exceeded 10 mm on only 8 of these days and was in the form of snow on 6 of these 8 days. Intense rainfall, possibly exceeding 20 mm per hour, was noted in the same basin on one day in each of 1984 and 1988 when gages were not present. In general, summer rainfall is much less of a flooding concern in the Sierra Nevada than in the Rocky Mountains (e.g., Jarrett & Costa, 1982).

However, subtropical storms occasionally move into the southern Sierra Nevada in late summer. Intense thundershowers occurring over a period of three or four days can generate local flooding, cause extensive surface erosion, and destabilize hillslopes. Such storms were a common event in the late 1970's and early 1980's when several hikers were killed and bridges were washed out far downstream. These storms may generate the greatest floods in some alpine basins that are sufficiently high to avoid mid-winter rain-on-snow events and are oriented so that snowmelt rates are kept low because of northerly exposure over much of the basin. For example, the four highest floods of Bear Creek (gage near Lake Thomas A. Edison) were generated by summer rainfall. The peak discharge of two of these floods was more than twice that of the largest snowmelt flood in this basin of 136 km^2 with a mean elevation of about 2850 m. Three other summer floods appear in the annual flood series of this stream in 67 years. Widespread summer rainfall has also generated one large flood of approximately 20-year return period in the 640 km^2 upper San Joaquin River. In August 1989, a flood and debris flow generated by a thunderstorm in the 2000 to 3000 m headwaters of Olancha Creek in the southeast part of the Sierra Neavada damaged the Los Angeles Aqueduct several kilometers downstream at 1200 m (Sahagun & Warren, 1989).

LAKE OUTBURSTS

The sudden release of water from storage generates the most extreme floods but occurs under a limited set of conditions in a small fraction of the Sierra Nevada. Although this type of flooding is localized, it may produce flood peaks that are at least several times greater than those caused by any other process and is likely to produce debris flows. Sierra Nevada lakes tend to be stable with little risk of failure of their impoundments of bedrock or broad moraines. Only one failure of a small artificial dam is known to have occurred at high altitude in the Sierra Nevada: North Lake at 2850 m during a summer storm in 1986, although several dam failures have occurred at lower altitudes. The failure of landslide and snow-avalanche dams that temporarily impound streams undoubtedly occurs at a variety of scales in the Sierra Nevada, but large events of this type are not known to have been documented. There is also the possibility of minor outbursts of water stored within the small glaciers of the Sierra Nevada although on a smaller scale than occurs in the Cascades (Richardson, 1968). The greatest potential for this type of flood would be on Big Pine Creek below the Palisade Glacier, but the author is unaware of any reported glacier releases there.

Displacement of lake water by snow avalanches is yet another flood generation process in high elevation streams of the Sierra Nevada. The impact of an avalanche on to the ice cover of a lake can force large volumes of water into the outlet channel. Avalanches are known to generate large flood waves when impacting ice-covered lakes (Schytt, 1965; Jørstad, 1968), but the geomorphic significance of lake water displacement in the absence of dam failure has not been described (e.g., Luckman, 1977). Following the major avalanche cycle of April 1982, the author observed avalanche-induced displacement of lake water in the Virginia Lakes basin where lake ice-cover was piled to several meters depth on the shore near the lake outlet in a manner similar to that described by Jørstad (1968) in Norway. During the Emerald Lake study mentioned above, avalanches occasionally ran on to the lake and displaced water into the gaged outlet stream. In February 1986, a massive avalanche struck the lake and displaced up to 70 percent of the unfrozen water in the lake (about 90,000 m^3) into the outlet stream (Williams & Clow, 1990). The resulting flood removed all snow from the outlet channel for 700 m downstream to the next lake and severely scoured the streambed. Williams and Clow (1990) also observed lake displacement damage in Bishop Creek and Rock Creek on the east side of the crest in 1986. We heard other personal accounts of avalanche-induced outbursts at Corbett Lake in Sequoia National Park and Reds Lake near Mammoth Mountain resulting from the same avalanche cycle. These events may be relatively common and are the only means of generating high flow immediately downstream of lakes, which otherwise tend to attenuate floods. Avalanche-induced outburst floods may also be caused by water supply development where small reservoirs or storage tanks are located in avalanche paths (Oaks & Dexter, 1987). Such a flood almost occurred in Incline Village near Lake Tahoe during the February 1986 avalanche cycle when avalanche debris reached but did not destroy a large water tank.

GEOMORPHIC IMPLICATIONS

These various flood-generation mechanisms modify stream channels to various extents. Although debate continues about the relative effectiveness of common events (e.g., annual snowmelt floods) versus catastrophic events (e.g., rain-on-snow events) in shaping the landscape (e.g., Wolman & Gerson, 1978; Beven, 1981), large floods would seem to be particularly important in mountain streams because of the high proportion of material transported as bedload. In mountain rivers, rare high-magnitude floods are generally required to significantly alter the channel because material comprising the bed and banks tends to be large and resistant to entrainment (Lisle, 1987). However, the sequence of events of different magnitudes also determines the geomorphic effectiveness of particular floods (Beven, 1981). Large floods that destabilize a channel can lead to enhanced sediment transport from low-magnitude events over several decades (Lisle, 1987). Such effects have been documented in the Lake Tahoe basin following extreme rain-on-snow or thunderstorm events (Nolan & Hill, 1987; Glancy, 1988). Similarly, two large rain-on-snow events in 1982 may have created channel conditions favorable for the high bedload transport measured in the snowmelt flood of 1983 (Andrews & Erman, 1986). These interactions of different flood processes may be a critical influence on channel form and sediment transport in the Sierra Nevada.

ACKNOWLEDGEMENTS   Studies contributing to this review of flood processes were supported by the NASA-Eos program, California Air Resources Board, and Pacific Gas and Electric Company.

REFERENCES

Aguado, E. (1985) Radiation balances of melting snow covers at an open site in the central Sierra Nevada, California. Water Resources Research 21 (11), 1649-1654.

Anderson, H. W. (1963) Managing California snow zone lands for water. Research Paper PSW-6, USDA-Forest Service, Pacific Southwest Forest and Range Experiment Station, Berkeley.

Andrews, E. D. & D. C. Erman (1986) Persistence in the size distribution of surficial bed material during an extreme snowmelt flood. Water Resources Research 22 (2), 191-197.

Beven, K. (1981) The effect of ordering on the geomorphic effectiveness of hydrologic events. In: Erosion and Sediment Transport in Pacific Rim Steeplands, International Association of Hydrological Sciences, Publication 132, 510-525.

Dean, W. W. (1975) Snowmelt floods of April-July 1969 in the Buena Vista Lake, Tulare Lake, and San Joaquin river basins In: Summary of Floods in the United States During 1969, Water-Supply Paper 2030, U. S. Geological Survey, Washington, D.C., 77-87.

Dozier, J., J. M. Melack, K. Elder, D. Marks, S. Peterson, & M. Williams (1989) Snow, snowmelt, rain, runoff, and chemistry in a Sierra Nevada watershed. Final report, contract A6-147-32, California Air Resources Board, Sacramento.

Elder, K., J. Dozier, & J. Michaelsen (1989) Spatial and temporal variation of net snow accumulation in a small alpine watershed, Emerald Lake basin, Sierra Nevada, California, U.S.A. Annals of Glaciology 13, 56-63.

Erman, D. C., E. D. Andrews & M. Yoder-Williams (1988) Effects of winter floods on fishes in the Sierra Nevada. Canadian Journal of Fisheries and Aquatic Sciences 45, 2195-2200.

Glancy, P. A. (1988) Streamflow, sediment transport and nutrient transport at Incline Village, Lake Tahoe, Nevada, 1970-73. Water Supply Paper 2313, U. S. Geological Survey, Washington, D.C.

Hannaford, J. F. & M. C. Williams (1967) Summer hydrology of the high Sierra. Proceedings of the Western Snow Conference 35, 73-84.

Jarrett, R. D. & J. E. Costa (1982) Multidisciplinary approach to the flood hydrology of foothill streams in Colorado. In: International Symposium on Hydrometeorology, American Water Resources Association, Bethesda, 565-569.

Jørstad, F. A. (1968) Waves generated by landslides in Norwegian fjords and lakes. Publication 79, Norwegian Geotechnical Institute, Oslo, 13-32.

Kattelmann, R. & N. Berg (1987) Water yields from high elevation basins in California. In: Proceedings, California Watershed Management Conference (R. Z. Callaham and J. J. DeVries, eds.), Report No. 11, University of California Wildland Resources Center, Berkeley, 79-85.

Lisle, T. E. (1987) Overview: channel morphology and sediment transport in steepland streams. In: Erosion and Sedimentation in the Pacific Rim, International Association of Hydrological Sciences, Publication no. 165, 287-297.

Luckman, B. H. (1977) The geomorphic activity of snow avalanches. Geografiska Annaler 59A (1-2), 31-48.

Miller, D. (1955) Snow cover and climate in the Sierra Nevada, California. University of California Press, Berkeley.

Nolan, K. M. & B. R. Hill (1987) Sediment budget and storm effects in a drainage basin tributary to Lake Tahoe. Eos, Transactions American Geophysical Union 68 (16), 305.

Oaks S. D. & L. Dexter (1987) Avalanche hazard zoning in Vail, Colorado: the use of scientific information in the implementation of hazard reduction strategies. Mountain Research and Development 7 (2), 157-168.

Richardson, D. (1968) Glacier outburst floods in the Pacific Northwest. Professional Paper 600-D, U.S. Geological Survey, Washington, D.C., D79-D86.

Sahagun, S. & J. Warren (1989) Storms go on; new aqueduct damage found. Los Angeles Times 109, August 12, 1989, 1 & 22-23.

Schytt, V., (1965) Notes on glaciological activities in Kebnekaise, Sweden during 1964. Geografiska Annaler 47A (1), 65-71.

Stafford, H. M. (1956) Snowmelt flood of 1952 in Kern River, Tulare Lake, and San Joaquin River basins. In: Floods of 1952 in California, Water Supply Paper 1260-D, U.S. Geological Survey, Washington, D.C., 562-573.

Storer, T. L. & R. L. Usinger (1963) Sierra Nevada Natural History. University of California Press, Berkeley.

Williams, M. W. & D. W. Clow (1990-in press) Hydrologic and biologic consequences of an avalanche striking an ice-covered lake. Proceedings of the Western Snow Conference 58.

Wolman, M. G. & R. Gerson (1978) Relative scales of time and effectiveness of climate in watershed geomorphology. Earth Surface Processes 3, 189-208.

Hydrology in Mountainous Regions. II - Artificial Reservoirs; Water and Slopes
(Proceedings of two Lausanne Symposia, August 1990). IAHS Publ. no. 194, 1990.

Crues exceptionnelles et formation des seuils dans les lits naturels sur Flysch

J. KONIAR-SCHAEFER
Ecole Polytechnique de Cracovie, 31-155 Kraków, Pologne
H. WITKOWSKA
Ecole Polytechnique de Cracovie, 31-155 Kraków, Pologne

RESUME L'étude des formes des lits de torrents situés sur le flysch carpatique démontre que leur type dépend de la relation entre la position des couches et la direction du cours d'eau. Les formes comme les seuils, les marmites torrentielles et les faces de réflexion dispersent l'énergie d'écoulement et stabilisent bien le lit, ce qui n'est pas toujours assuré par les constructions hydrotechniques.

INTRODUCTION

Les formes naturelles des lits des torrents de montagne réagissent à l'action des crues et génèrent des mécanismes d'autodéfense. L'action des constructions hydrotechniques ne correspond pas toujours à celle des formes naturelles. Ces installations sont souvent détruites par les crues. L'adaptation à la nature et son imitation pourrait avoir une grande importance et l'étude des formes naturelles présente un grand intérêt. Les recherches consacrées par les géographes (Kaszowski 1970, Klimek 1979, Niemirowski 1974) aux torrents des flyschs carpatiques ont eu surtout un caractère géographique et géomorphologique. Dans les années 1956-1972, J. Koniar-Schaefer a mené des recherches en vue de la régularisation et de la correction des torrents, et les observations des objets choisis ont été poursuivies jusqu'à présent (Koniar-Schaefer 1989).

PRESENTATION ET ANALYSE DES RESULTATS

Le travail présenté est basé sur les longues recherches de J. Koniar-Schaefer dans le terrain. Les formations décrites ont été mesurées et observées sur une longueur de 1700 km de torrents (Tableau 1). De plus, 350 seuils artificiels ont été étudiés et leur action sur les lits analysée. Un certain nombre de ces formes (les séries de seuils, les marmites torrentielles et les faces de réflexion) ont été observées et mesurées après chaque crue exceptionnelle pendant une période de 6 ans.

Le flysch carpatique est caractérisé par un important plissement associé à un réseau de cassures tectoniques; celles-ci sont élargies en crevasses par l'altération.

Les conditions hydrologiques de la région se caractérisent par des crues où les débits de pointe sont 4000 fois plus grands que ceux d'étiage; la hauteur de l'eau sur les seuils en observation varie de 2 à 5 m.

Les objets géomorphologiques observés présentent une grande diversité de formes; on a cependant essayé de trouver certaines régularités et les critères de leur formation sont présentés ci-dessous. On a distingué les segments de torrents composés de séries de seuils, rapides, marmites torrentielles alternant avec les canaux droits et les segments avec méandres composés de seuils, marmites torrentielles et plusieurs faces de réflexion (épis). Leur aspect et leurs dimensions ne dépendent pas seulement de la hauteur et de la vitesse de l'eau, mais aussi de la relation entre la position tectonique des couches (pendage), leur épaisseur, la densité des crevasses (liée à leur épaisseur) et enfin la direction du cours

319

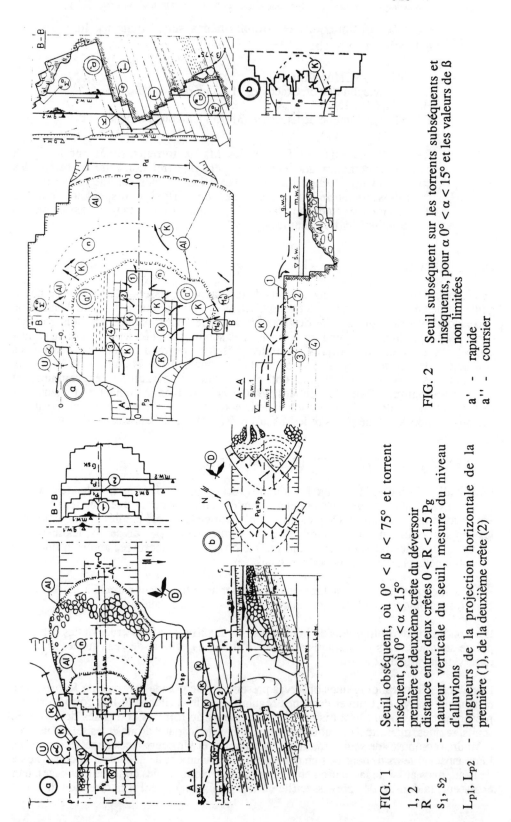

FIG. 1   Seuil obséquent, où 0° < ß < 75° et torrent inséquent, où 0° < α < 15°

1, 2 - première et deuxième crête du déversoir
R - distance entre deux crêtes 0 < R < 1.5 Pg
s_1, s_2 - hauteur verticale du seuil, mesure du niveau d'alluvions
L_{p1}, L_{p2} - longueurs de la projection horizontale de la première (1), de la deuxième crête (2)

FIG. 2   Seuil subséquent sur les torrents subséquents et inséquents, pour α 0° < α < 15° et les valeurs de ß non limitées

a' - - rapide
a'' - - coursier

TABLEAU 1   Les types de seuils observés et mesurés.

Type du seuil		Enrégistrées dans le torrent	nombre	somme Σ	nombre de seuils deformés
nom	Fig.N°				
Obséquent $0° < \beta < 75°$	1	Obséquent	332	426	8
		Inséquent $5° < \alpha < 15°$	94		
Conséquent $0° < \beta < 75°$	(a') 2	Conséquent	105	272	3
		Inséquent $75° < \alpha < 90°$	167		
Subséquent $0° < \beta < 90°$	2	Subséquent $5° < \alpha < 15°$	143	143	2
Inséquent	3	Inséquent $15° < \alpha < 45°$	358	358	--
Rapide (coursier)	(a") 2	(**)	303	303	--
		ΣΣ =	1502	1502	13

(**) - dans les types où l'épaisseur des strates de grès F < 10 cm, avec schistes prédominants, ou dans les torrents 1, 2 3 où 75° < ß < 90°.

LÉGENDE POUR TOUTES LES FIGURES ET LE TABLEAU 1

ß	-	angle de pendage des couches
α	-	angle entre la direction des couches (U) et l'axe du cours d'eau (0 - 0)
Pg, Pd	-	largeur du lit amont (g), aval (d)
Pl	-	largeur des rives
H	-	niveau de l'eau lors d'une crue
G	-	profondeur maximale de la marmite torrentielle
Gsk	-	profondeur de l'eau dans la marmite pendant la crue
GAl	-	épaisseur des alluvions
Al	-	longueur du prisme des alluvions déposées par les crues
Lmw, Lgw	-	longueur de la marmite en étiage (mw) et en crue (gw)
n	-	ligne de niveau

(suite sur la page de la Fig. 3)

d'eau. En outre, la dimension des formes obtenues varie en fonction de la résistance différentielle des affleurement de grès situés à l'aval ainsi que de l'épaisseur de ces bancs. Les seuils observés ont une hauteur S de 0,2 à 8,0 m, les marmites une profondeur G de 0,8 à 12,0 m et les faces de réflexion (épis) Es de 0,5 à 3,0 m (Fig. 1 et 2). Ces formes diverses ont été classifiées en fonction de la position du lit du cours d'eau et de celle des couches rocheuses.

LÉGENDE POUR TOUTES LES FIGURES (SUITE)

a   - vue en plan (torrent à lit étroit) (Pg < 3m)
b   - vue en plan (torrent à lit large) (Pg > 3m)
g.w.   - niveau de la crue
m.w.   - niveau d'étiage
K   - directions de lignes de courants
U   - pendage des couches
T, T'   - surfaces du coursier aval
M_o, M_o - surfaces de réflexion

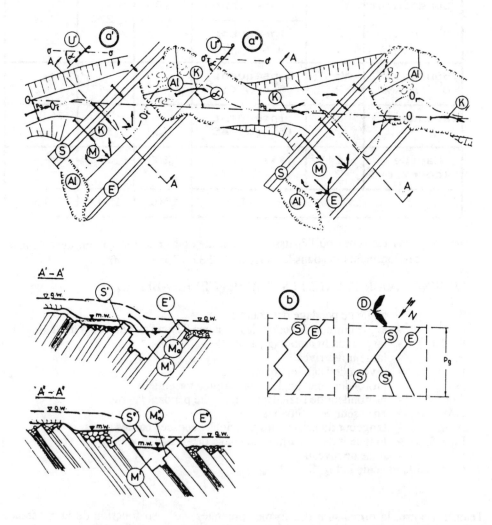

FIG. 3   Seuil inséquent sur les torrents inséquents de 15° < α < 45°, avec une
          série composée d'un seuil (S), d'une marmite (M), d'une face de
          réflexion (E) et deux prismes d'alluvions (AI)
          A-A', A''-A'' - sections verticales pour U' et U''

Dans les torrents obséquents, conséquents et subséquents (Fig. 1 et 2), les seuils sont en principe symétriques à l'axe du cours d'eau, qui peut avoir une pente importante; les marmites sont plus profondes que dans les autres cas.

Dans les torrents inséquents (Fig. 3), les seuils sont en biais par rapport à l'axe et à l'aval de la marmite existent plusieurs faces de réflexion (épis) qui dévient l'eau et créent les méandres. Dans ce cas, la largeur du lit est plus grande, les seuils sont plus bas et les marmites peu profondes.

L'analyse comparative des formes étudiées a démontré que le type dépend aussi de l'angle d'inclinaison des couches (Tableau 1) et de la relation entre la largeur du lit et la hauteur de l'eau sur les seuils (Fig. 1, 2 et 3). Les formes qui apparaissent dans les lits larges sont présentées sur les figures (Fig. 1b, 2b et 3b).

Les formes discutées ci-dessus sont créées pendant les crues par l'action de l'eau sur le flysch fissuré; elles sont bien adaptées au passage de l'eau. La longueur de crête des seuils est en principe plus grande que celle du lit d'un torrent, ce qui provoque la diminution de l'énergie potentielle et le croisement des lignes d'eau (seuils obséquents; Fig. 1), où leur divergence (seuils subséquents; Fig. 2) facilite la dispersion de l'énergie cinétique. En cas de double marche (Fig. 1), l'effet est augmenté. Dans le cas des torrents inséquents, les changements de direction et la réflexion des faces rocheuses dispersent si bien l'énergie que les marmites peuvent être moins profondes.

Pendant les crues exceptionnelles, l'eau est maintenue dans le lit majeur, les sédiments se déplacent dans le lit mineur et les formes du lit s'adaptent aux conditions d'écoulement, ce qui n'est pas toujours le cas pour les constructions hydrotechniques.

La régularisation des torrents de montagnes doit donc s'adapter au pendage des couches. Selon la situation, on doit construire des seuils concaves ou convexes vers l'amont (sur les torrents obséquents, conséquents et subséquents), ou prévoir des coursiers en biais (sur les torrents inséquents). La profondeur et la forme du bassin de tranquilisation doivent imiter les formes naturelles. La longueur de la crête des seuils doit être plus grande que la largeur du lit du torrent.

CONCLUSIONS

(a) Les lits rocheux des torrents situés dans le flysch carpatique plissé et fissuré se défendent contre l'érosion démesurée en produisant des formes adaptées aux conditions naturelles. L'eau des crues exceptionnelles sculpte ces formes en déplaçant les blocs rocheux et le gravier.

(b) Les principales composantes de cette autodéfense sont les brusques variations de tracé d'un cours d'eau, soit verticalement (seuil, marmite), soit horizontalement (seuil en biais, face de réflexion).

(c) L'imitation de ces formes naturelles lors de la construction d'ouvrages hydrotechniques pourrait améliorer les méthodes de régularisation et de correction des torrents.

REFERENCES

Kaszowski, L., Kotarba, A. (1970) Wpływ katastrofalnych wezbrań na przebieg procesów fluwialnych (L'effet des crues exceptionnelles sur les processus fluviaux), Prace geograf. t.B., z-4, Kraków, Pologne.

Klimek, K. (1979) Geomorfologiczne zróżnicowanie koryt karpackich dopływów Wisły (Différentiation géomorphologique des lits d'affluents carpatiques de la Vistule), Folia Geograf. Seria Geograf.-Phys. 12, Kraków, Pologne.

Niemirowski, M. (1974) Dynamika współczesnych koryt potoków gorskich (La dynamique des lits des torrents de montagne), Zeszyty Nauk.U.J. Prace Geogr. z.34, Kraków, Pologne.

Koniar-Schaefer, J. (1989) Funkcja geomorfologicznych form w naturalnych skalnych korytach potoków karpackich w odprowadzaniu wód wezbraniowych (La fonction des formes géomorphologiques dans les lits naturels des torrents carpatiques en régime de crue exceptionnelle), Spraw. z pos.Kom.Geogr.PAN

Hydrology in Mountainous Regions. II - Artificial Reservoirs; Water and Slopes
(Proceedings of two Lausanne Symposia, August 1990). IAHS Publ. no. 194, 1990.

Floods resulting from progressively breached dams

F. MACCHIONE
Department of Soil Defence, University of Calabria,
Cosenza, Italy
B. SIRANGELO
Institute of Civil Engineering, University of Salerno,
Salerno, Italy

ABSTRACT   In the paper the capability of a dam-breach
model to simulate the outflow hydrographs and the breach
characteristics resulting from the progressive erosion of
earth dams is tested. Twenty-four historical dam failures are analyzed and surveyed peak discharges and breach
top widths are compared with model outcomes. The agreement obtained is satisfactory so that the reliability of
the model is verified and therefore it can be usefully
applied for prediction purposes.

INTRODUCTION

One of the most important aspects of the studies concerning the dam
safety is the evaluation of the effects resulting from the potential
collapse of the dam.

In any model developed for the prediction of the damages that
would result in the event of a dam failure, the estimate of the
dam-break outflow hydrograph is a first step that plays a key role in
the overall computation. In fact the reliability of the mapping of
valley areas potentially inundable, obtained by routing the flood
downstream the water course and evaluating the flood plain, strictly
depends on a realistic simulation of the dam-break hydrograph.

In recent years such a problem has led to the development of
several dam-break models. The interest of the researchers has been
mainly focused on earth dams since the graduality of their erosion,
that can follow the failure, makes too conservative the hypothesis,
commonly adopted for concrete arch and gravity dams, of a sudden
removal of a portion or all the embankment.

Therefore, all the suggested models are characterized by a
description of the progressive erosion of the embankment material by
the flow of water either over or through the dam. Such models,
commonly known as dam-breach models, differ mainly in hydrodynamic
description of water flow and in adopted mechanism for representing
the breaching of the embankment.

In the literature can be found approaches in which the breach is
simply considered as a section where flow attains the critical stage.
Breach growing obeys to a predetermined time-depending law or is
computed by means of empirical relations or by well established
sediment transport formulas. An alternative approach describes the
breach as an erodable channel in which water flow is analyzed using
dynamic routing equations. Breach evolution is determined on the

basis of sediment continuity equation.

As a matter of fact the reliability and therefore the practical utility of the various dam-breach models are strongly dependent on their calibration and clearly they can be considered better if agreement with field data is found.

The purpose of this paper is to check the capability of one of these models (Macchione & Sirangelo, 1989) to simulate the main features of dam breach events, namely the peak outflow discharge and the breach top width. This is done comparing the model performances against data of 24 selected historical earth dam failure cases.

DAM-BREACH MODEL

The simulation model of the gradual erosion of an earth embankment used in the present paper was extensively described in previous works (Macchione & Sirangelo, 1988; Macchione & Sirangelo, 1989). Thus only the salient aspects of the model are here summarized in order to explain the bases of breach evolution and outflow hydrograph computation.

The breach is considered as a channel for which progressive erosion widens and deepens the cross sections. The phenomenon continues until the reservoir water is depleted or until the dam resists further erosion. The shape of breach section, according to past earth dam failure observations, is assumed triangular until its bottom reaches the natural ground and then is considered trapezoidal (Fig. 1). The side slope of the breach is kept constant during its formation.

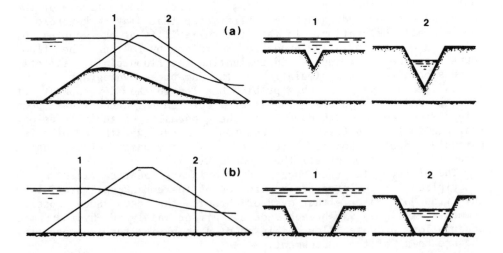

FIG. 1 Schematic representation of the breach geometry assumed in the model: (a) early stage, (b) later stage.

The mathematical description of flow and erosion is based on water continuity and momentum equations and sediment continuity equation. Indicated with x and t, respectively, the spatial and temporal co-ordinates, the equations can be written as (Chen et al., 1975):

$$\frac{\partial Q}{\partial x} + \frac{\partial A}{\partial t} + \frac{\partial A_d}{\partial t} = 0 \tag{1}$$

$$\frac{\partial Q}{\partial t} + \frac{\partial}{\partial x}\left(\frac{Q^2}{A}\right) + g A \left(\frac{\partial Z}{\partial x} + S_f\right) = 0 \tag{2}$$

$$\frac{\partial G_s}{\partial x} + \gamma_s (1-n)\frac{\partial A_d}{\partial t} + \frac{\partial}{\partial t}(A C_s) = 0 \tag{3}$$

where Q is the discharge, A is the cross sectional area of water, A_d is the volume of sediment eroded per unit lenght of channel, Z is the water surface elevation, S_f is the friction slope, G_s is the solid discharge by weight and $C_s = G_s/Q$ while γ_s and n are, respectively, the specific weight and the porosity of the sediment on the bed and g is the acceleration due to gravity. In the first equation the term $\partial A/\partial t$ indicates the temporal variation of A due to water surface elevation changes and the term $\partial A_d/\partial t$ is equal to the temporal variation of A due to bed changes. In the model friction slope and solid discharge were respectively evaluated by means of the Strickler formula and the Meyer-Peter and Mueller formula.

In the upstream reach of the channel, where the flow will be sub-critical, the upstream boundary condition is given by integration of the reservoir water balance equation and the downstream boundary condition is given fixing the critical depth-discharge relationship. The computed values of Q and Z at the last subcritical section will give the two boundary conditions for the downstream supercritical flow. Referring to the sediment, two conditions of nonerodable bed are assumed at the first and at the last section of the channel. Initial conditions are evaluated computing a steady flow profile in a small initial channel breach.

The dam-breach model above described was calibrated using the Teton Dam failure data. As reported in the aforementioned works of Macchione and Sirangelo, such a calibration was performed multiplying the solid discharge given by the Meyer-Peter and Mueller formula by a factor equal to 2.4 in order to obtain the best fitting of the reservoir depletion data surveyed during the Teton Dam failure and the peak discharge estimated by Balloffet and Scheffler (1982). This calibration was adopted in all simulations made in the present paper.

DATA ON EARTH DAM FAILURES

Historical earth dam failure data, collected from various sources, can be found in many papers (MacDonald & Langridge-Monopolis, 1984; Lebreton, 1985; Singh & Scarlatos, 1988; Laginha Serafim & Coutinho-Rodrigues, 1989; etc.) even if, in general, only little information on breaching process of the embankment was reported.

The data here used were selected in order to analyze only the

TABLE 1 Data from selected historical failed dams.

No.	Dam name	Country	Year built/failed	Height (m)	Crest width (m)	Embankment slopes vertical:horizontal upstream/downstream	Storage (hm³)	Time of failure (h)
1	Apishapa	U.S.A.	1920/1933	34	5	1:3/1:2	22.8	2.5
2	Baldwin Hills	U.S.A.	1951/1963	49	19	1:2/1:1.8	1.1	1.3
3	Bradfield	U.K.	1863/1864	29	--	---	3.2	<0.5
4	Coedty	U.K.	1924/1925	11	--	---	0.31	--
5	Eigiau	U.K.	1908/1925	10.5	--	---	4.5	--
6	French Landing	U.S.A.	1925/1925	12	2.5	1:2/1:2.5	--	0.6
7	Frenchman Creek	U.S.A.	1952/1952	12.5	6	1:3/1:2	21.0	--
8	Hatchtown	U.S.A.	1908/1914	19	6	1:2/1:2.5	14.8	3
9	Hell Hole	U.S.A.	1964/1964	67	21	1:1.5/1:1.5	--	5
10	Johnstown	U.S.A.	1853/1889	23	3	1:2/1:1.5	18.9	3.5
11	Kelly Barnes	U.S.A.	1948/1977	11.5	6	1:1/1:1	0.51	0.5
12	Lake Avalon	U.S.A.	1894/1904	14.5	--	---	7.8	2
13	Lake Frances	U.S.A.	1899/1899	15	5	1:3/1:2	0.86	1
14	Lake Latonka	U.S.A.	1965/1966	13	--	---	1.6	3
15	Laurel Run	U.S.A.	--/1977	13	--	---	0.38	--
16	Little Deer Creek	U.S.A.	1962/1963	26	--	---	1.7	0.33
17	Lyman	U.S.A.	1913/1915	20	4	1:2/1:2	49.3	--
18	Machhu II	India	1972/1979	60	6	1:3/1:2	110	2
19	Mammoth	U.S.A.	1916/1917	21	--	---	13.6	3
20	Oros	Brazil	1960/1960	36	--	---	650	--
21	Sheep Creek	U.S.A.	1969/1970	17	6	1:3/1:2	1.4	--
22	Sinker Creek	U.S.A.	1910/1943	21	--	---	3.3	--
23	Teton	U.S.A.	1972/1976	93	10.5	1:3/1:2.5	355	6
24	Wheatland No. 1	U.S.A.	1893/1969	13.5	6	---	11.5	1.5

failures for which the basic hypotheses of the simulation model are verified and the calibration above described can be considered valid. Hence the failed dams analyzed are characterized by:

(a) earthfill or rockfill embankment, so that, besides the obvious exclusion of all the rupture events of concrete arch and gravity dams, it was also descarded the failure of coal waste embankments like the one of Buffalo Creek Dam;

(b) absence of concrete cores or walls or protective concrete surface layers, so that were excluded, for example, the Swift Dam and the Lynde Brook Dam failure events;

(c) height greather than 10 m, with exclusion, thus, of failures like the ones of Frankfurt Dam, Johnston City Dam, Sandy Run Dam, etc.

Moreover, the only events considered were those for which surveys or reliable estimate on the outflow peak discharge or on the breach characteristics are available.

Table 1 is a list of the 24 historical earth dam failure cases that were used in the present paper. The list includes the names and countries of the ruptured dams, the year of construction and failure, the main characteristics of embankment and reservoir and, finally, the maximum breach development time. The surveyed or estimated peak discharges and breach characteristics are reported, respectively, in Table 2 and Table 3.

Concerning the data reported in the literature, it can be noted that, in some cases, they seem unreasonable or, at least, inconsistent. For istance, referring to the failure of the little dam named Goose Creek, the literature (MacDonald & Langridge-Monopolis, 1984) reports a difference between reservoir water surface elevation, at time of failure, and base elevation of the breach of about 1.4 m, a final breach having a top width of about 30 m and a peak rate of outflow approximatively equal to 550 m^3/s. Clearly such a discharge is not consistent with the other data since, even if it is assumed the instantaneous formation of a rectangular breach large 30 m, the peak rate of outflow results only equal to 85 m^3/s.

MODEL APPLICATIONS AND ANALYSIS OF RESULTS

The model was applied using data from the selected dam failure cases in order to check its ability to simulate the main features of the events. Among the observed dam-breach characteristics, peak outflow discharge Q_p and breach top width B_t were chosen for the comparison. Breach development time was not considered because it appears less reliable than the other data. In reality this time was often reported as the time to drain the reservoir, but in such case it could be considerable larger than the actual breach development time and, however, it results extremely dependent from the choice of initial time of reservoir depletion.

Numerical computations were performed integrating the basic equations of the model by means of standard finite difference method. Details can be found in the above mentioned papers on model formulation. However, it should be noted that, at least for the simulation of the cases with the longer time of failure, the spatial and temporal discretization needed for an accurate and stable solution, gives rise to high computing time when programs run on microcomputers.

In the simulation an important role was played by the flow resis-

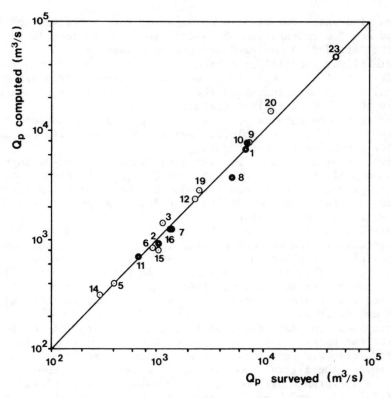

FIG. 2   Surveyed and computed peak outflow discharges.

TABLE 2   Comparison between available dam failure data on peak outflow discharges and simulation results.

No.	Dam name	Peak outflow discharge Q_p (m³/s) surveyed	computed
1	Apishapa	6850	6850
2	Baldwin Hills	950-1150	925
3	Bradfield	1150	1400
5	Eigiau	400	400
6	French Landing	925	850
7	Frenchman Creek	1400	1250
8	Hatchtown	3100-7000	3750
9	Hell Hole	7350	7750
10	Johnstown	5650-8550	7650
11	Kelly Barnes	675	700
12	Lake Avalon	2300	2350
14	Lake Latonka	290	310
15	Laurel Run	1050	800
16	Little Deer Creek	1350	1250
19	Mammoth	2500	2850
20	Oros	9600-13600	15000
23	Teton	48200	48200

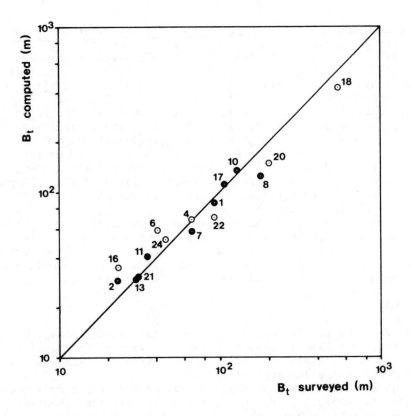

FIG. 3 Surveyed and computed breach top widths.

TABLE 3   Comparison between available dam failure data on breach
characteristics and simulation results.

No.	Dam name	Breach side slope vertical:horizontal	Breach top width B_t (m) surveyed	computed
1	Apishapa	6.7:1 & 2.9:1	92	86
2	Baldwin Hills	2.4:1 & 2.4:1	23	29
4	Coedty	1:2 & 1:2	67	69
6	French Landing	---	41	59
7	Frenchman Creek	3.8:1 & 3.8:1	67	58
8	Hatchtown	1:1 & 1:1	180	120
10	Johnstown	---	128	135
11	Kelly Barnes	1:1 & 2:1	35	41
13	Lake Frances	1.6:1 & 1.6:1	30	30
16	Little Deer Creek	---	23	35
17	Lyman	2:1 & 2:1	107	112
18	Machhu II	---	540	425
20	Oros	---	200	150
21	Sheep Creek	2:1 & 2:1	31	31
22	Sinker Creek	1:1 & 1:1	92	70
24	Wheatland No. 1	5.4:1 & 5.4:1	46	52

tance evaluation. For all the dams analyzed Strickler's K parameter falling in the range 50-60 $m^{1/3}/s$ was used, except for the rockfill embankment of the Hell Hole dam, for which a value of 40 $m^{1/3}/s$ was adopted. Porosity values n=0.30-0.35 were used in the calculations.

The comparison between available surveys on peak outflow discharges and simulation results is shown in Fig. 2 and reported in Table 2. Solid symbols indicate the cases in which all the input data needed by the model were available while light symbols indicate that some data were deduced from general description of the dam or were roughly estimated. Among these data the embankment slopes were assumed equal to 1V:2H or 1V:3H and the breach side slopes were assumed equal to the most frequent observed value 1V:1H (Singh & Scarlatos, 1988). The agreement results very satisfactory over the whole range of peak discharges simulated.

Fig. 3 and Table 3 show the comparison of surveyed versus computed breach top widths for the cases in which surveys were available. The agreement is nearly good as in the case of peak discharges simulation. However, it should be noted that none of historical data on breach top widths were used in the model calibration.

CONCLUSIONS

The computations carried out in the paper have shown that the dam-breach model here used is able to simulate, very satisfactorily, the peak discharge of historical failures of earth dams whose reservoir storages vary in a wide range of values.

Breach top width was also well reproduced and such result broadly indicates the capability of the model to simulate the behaviour of the earth dam erosion process.

All the model performances were obtained adopting a calibration based only on the Teton dam failure data and therefore it can be concluded that the model should be suitable for prediction purposes.

REFERENCES

Balloffet, A. & Scheffler, M.L. (1982) Numerical analysis of the Teton dam failure flood. J. Hydraul. Res. 20 (4), 317-328.
Chen, Y.H., Holly, F.M., Mahmood, K. & Simons, D.B. (1975) Transport of material by unsteady flow. Chapter 8 in: Unsteady Flow in Open Channels, ed. by Mahmood K. & Yevjevich V., Wat. Resour. Publications, Forth Collins, Colorado.
Laginha Serafim, J. & Coutinho-Rodrigues, J.M. (1989) Statistics of dam failures: preliminary report. Water Power and Dam Construction 41 (4), 30-34.
Lebreton, A. (1985) Les ruptures et accidents graves de barrages de 1964 à 1983. La Houille Blanche (6-7), 529-544.
Macchione, F. & Sirangelo, B. (1988) Study of earth dam erosion due to overtopping. Proc. Technical Conf. on Hydrology of Disasters, WMO, Geneva, 212-219.
Macchione, F. & Sirangelo, B. (1989) Aspetti idraulici nel collasso degli sbarramenti in materiali sciolti. Idrotecnica (6), 313-322.
MacDonald, T.C. & Langridge-Monopolis, J. (1984) Breaching character-istics of dam failures. J. Hydraul. Div. ASCE 110 (5), 567-586.
Singh, V.P. & Scarlatos P.D. (1988) Analysis of gradual earth-dam failure. J. Hydraul. Div. ASCE 114 (1), 21-42.

Hydrology in Mountainous Regions. II - Artificial Reservoirs; Water and Slopes
(Proceedings of two Lausanne Symposia, August 1990). IAHS Publ. no. 194, 1990

Dérivation des eaux de crues de l'Aire

J. MOURON
Chef de la division des ponts et des eaux du Département des travaux
publics du canton de Genève, CH-1211 Genève 8, SUISSE

RESUME   La communication présente les problèmes résultant de
l'évolution du régime des crues du bassin versant de l'Aire à Genève
dus à son urbanisation. Les difficultés d'estimation prévisionnelle faute
d'observation in situ sont évoquées ainsi que la méthode de calcul
retenue. Le choix de la dérivation des eaux de crues pour conserver un
secteur de rivière en cours naturel a été déterminé par rapport à
d'autres solutions en fonction de la protection de l'environnement.

INTRODUCTION

Dès le début du XXème siècle, la région du genevois qui totalise environ 800 km² de
bassin versant topographique, dont 280 km² de territoire helvétique du canton de
Genève, a subi une évolution démographique croissante. Il en est résulté une
modification sensible du rapport population rurale / population urbaine due à
l'aménagement de zones d'habitation à forte densité et à la création de zones
industrielles.

Le changement d'affectation des terrains agrestes et agricoles et l'équipement de
nouvelles zones densifiées ont provoqué, en peu de temps, un régime des débits du
cours deau très différent du régime naturel. L'accroissement des crues ayant pour
conséquence de fréquentes inondations, l'érosion des berges et, à l'inverse, les débits
d'étiage plus faibles engendrant une dégradation de la qualité de l'eau et de l'équilibre
biologique.

La rivière l'Aire est un exemple typique des corollaires évoqués; vu l'intérêt
général une étude a été menée afin de rechercher des solutions visant à supprimer les
conséquences dommageables des crues et des étiages.

SYSTEMATIQUE DE L'ETUDE

Les recherches ont été effectuées par un groupe de travail composé de spécialistes de
l'administration cantonale et de mandataires qui ont procédé à une analyse multicritère
selon le schéma suivant :
- Bassin versant   : topographie, géologie, occupation
                                       des sols,
- Hydrologie   : régime hydrologique, inondations, érosions,
- Site   : géographie, écologie,
- Protection contre les inondations et érosions
                                       : débit de projet,
                                       : projets réalisables,
- Environnement   : sauvegarde du site, amélioration de la qualité de
                                       l'eau,
- Synthèse et propositions qui sont résumées ci-après.

DESCRIPTION SUCCINTE DU BASSIN VERSANT

Le mont Salève (altitude max. 1300 m) limite au sud le bassin versant qui reçoit notamment les précipitations apportées par les vents du Sud-ouest considérées comme les plus importantes à part les orages locaux. L'Aire dont le confluent avec l'Arve est à une altitude de 369 m a une pente longitudinale moyenne de 0.41 %.

La superficie totale du bassin est de 100 km², il est subdivisé en deux sous bassins, dont celui qui nous intéresse, totalisant 74 km² comprenant 50,5 km² situés en territoire français et 23,5 km² seulement sur territoire suisse traversé par les 8,9 km du cours inférieur de faible pente.

Le cours d'eau est naturel sur le territoire français, par contre, il est canalisé à ciel ouvert dès son entrée en Suisse, soit 3,6 km (travaux entrepris en fin du 19ème siècle et dans les années 1930) suivi de 3,8 km de cours naturel et de 1,5 km de canal voûté sous route aboutissant à l'Arve.

La nature des sols et sous-sols a été définie sur la base des connaissances existantes et classée selon les critères de perméabilité (moyen, peu, imperméable). On distingue les formations à perméabilité de fissures, les formations à perméabilité d'interstices et les zones urbanisées à régime hydrologique artificiel.

L'occupation des sols a été définie, d'une part pour l'état actuel et, d'autre part, pour l'état futur prévisionnel sur la base du plan directeur de l'aménagement cantonal genevois et des plans d'occupation des sols fournis par la direction française départementale de l'équipement de la Haute-Savoie. La comparaison des deux états a montré que si l'évolution est très limitée sur Suisse, elle est au contraire en forte expansion en France (Fig. 1).

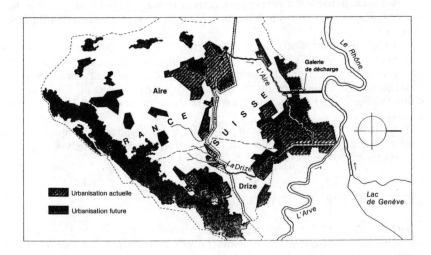

FIG. 1 Bassin versant de l'Aire.

DEBIT DE PROJET

Les éléments indispensables au calcul prévisionnel des débits de crues se sont révélés peu nombreux et peu fiables. Il s'agit d'un pluviographe à enregistrement intermittent à Lully, Genève, et d'une série d'observations limnimétriques jaugées de 1923 à 1931 publiés dans l'annuaire hydrologique de la Suisse.

Afin de compléter au mieux ces données, un limnigraphe a été placé en 1976 sous Confignon et, par chance, plusieurs crues se sont produites dans les 3 ans qui ont suivi son installation.

Pour évaluer l'évolution future de l'occupation des sols pour les 35 ans à venir, la comparaison avec l'état existant basée sur la détermination des surfaces spécifiques pondérées a été calculée par la méthode rationnelle. L'augmentation du débit de crue ainsi obtenue a été estimée entre 10 et 15%. Restait à déterminer la valeur du débit de projet. Après une recherche bibliographique concernant les bassins de faible superficie (moins de 100 km^2) situés sur le plateau suisse, la méthode de Bruschin et Falvey (EPFL 1974) a été retenue car elle est basée sur des éléments régionaux connus qui permettent de calculer la crue moyenne annuelle ($Q_{2,33}$) puis d'introduire ce paramètre dans une relation de type Myer afin d'en déterminer les valeurs pour d'autres temps de retour. La relation s'exprime comme suit :

$$Q_{2,33} = K \ S^{0,84}$$

avec Q = débit de crues en m^3 s^{-1}, K = coefficient régional, S = surface du bassin versant.

Pour le calcul, le coefficient K = 0,8 a été appliqué au bassin versant existant et K = 0,9 au bassin futur.Le débit de projet a été ainsi fixé pour la crue T = 100 à 70 m^3 s^{-1} (débit instantané max.).

LE PARAMETRE ENVIRONNEMENT

L'estimation de la valeur du site riverain des 7,4 km de rivière à ciel ouvert a été appréciée selon une analyse géographique et une approche écologique.

L'analyse géographique a mis en évidence, d'une part la valeur du vallon de l'Aire en tant que pénétrante de verdure dans le site genevois constituant un apport très important à la qualité du paysage et à la qualité de la vie des habitants et, d'autre part, l'importance du maintien de la zone agreste pour la conservation et la reproduction de la faune locale.

Afin d'évaluer les possibilités d'amélioration de la qualité de l'eau fortement dégradée en étiage et d'en tenir compte lors des projets de correction ou d'endiguement, une approche écologique a été entreprise comprenant notamment la prise périodique d'échantillon analysé pendant un cycle complet d'une année.

Basée sur la méthode des indices biotiques mise au point par TUFFERY et VERNAUX, l'étude a conclu, entre autres, qu'un certain pouvoir autoépurateur de l'Aire faisait encore son effet sur les secteurs naturels et que des aménagements permettraient probablement un nouveau peuplement piscicole.

PROJET EXECUTE

Après avoir analysé plusieurs possibilités, soit : bassin de rétention à la frontière nationale, canalisation du cours avec accroissement du gabarit d'écoulement, et déviation des eaux de crue par galerie souterraine. C'est cette dernière solution qui a été choisie avec une prise d'eau située à l'amont du cours naturel, le préservant ainsi de toute intervention vu sa valeur écologique.

La prise d'eau a été dimensionnée de façon à maintenir un débit jusqu'à 15 m^{3}s^{-1} dans le cour naturel afin de lui assurer un écoulement qui ne provoque pas de dommage. Le surplus de 60 m^3 s^{-1} est écoulé en veine libre par la galerie souterraine de 2,1 km, section utile 8 m^2. La prise d'eau et le brise-énergie à l'exutoire au Rhône (vitesse de l'eau à la sortie 7,8 m s^{-1}) ont été conçus après essais

sur modèles hydrauliques sous direction du mandataire; le bureau d'ingénieurs
MOUCHET, DUBOIS, BOISSONNARD S.A.

La galerie reçoit également les eaux de ruissellement d'un collecteur autoroutier
et d'un collecteur local par un puits Vortex, ce qui évite la canalisation d'un ruisseau.

A l'amont de la prise d'eau, un recalibrage et une surélévation des digues ont dû
être entrepris sur 1 km à compter de la frontière nationale.

SUITE DES ETUDES

Les études préléminaires datent de 1975; compte tenu des délais de mise au point du
projet définitif, des démarches administratives pour obtenir le crédit de construction
et de réalisation, 13 années se sont passées jusqu'à la mise en service de la galerie en
1988.

Entre temps les méthodes et les moyens d'estimer la prévision des débits se sont
diversifiés; on dispose entre autre de modèles mathématiques de simulation qui
permettent de reconstituer des crues dans leur globalité et qui fournissent plus
d'informations que le seul débit de pointe.

Le cas du bassin de l'Aire n'étant pas le seul à poser des problèmes sur le
territoire du canton de Genève, une recherche a été entreprise sur le bassin de la
Seymaz, d'une superficie de 38 km², situé en plaine, qui a été équipé d'installations de
mesures des précipitations et des débits. L'Institut du génie rural de l'Ecole
polytechnique fédérale de Lausanne, sur la base des observations in situ, a été chargé
de mettre au point une méthodologie afin d'évaluer les effets de différents scénarios
de modification de l'occupation des sols et du degré d'urbanisation. Le modèle
OTTHYMO mis au point par l'université d'Ottawa a été appliqué; il consiste à calculer
l'hydrogramme de chaque sous-bassin partant d'une pluie observée ou de projet pour
la transformer en ruissellement, simulant la réponse du bassin à la précipitation
excédentaire. L'intégration des hydrogrammes de sous-bassin, après leur
acheminement par la rivière donne l'hydrogramme résultant. Les observations de
pluies et de débits, qui se poursuivent actuellement, permettront de réévaluer la
validité de la méthode, lorsque quelques phénomènes exceptionnels supplémentaires
auront été observés. Partant de ce bassin test, le modèle OTTHYMO a été appliqué
récemment pour évaluer les possibilités de densification de l'urbanisation du bassin de
l'Aire, à l'aval de la prise d'eau de la galerie de décharge, densification qui devrait
s'accroître par rapport aux prévisions de 1975.

Les conclusions sont significatives, à savoir que l'écoulement des nouvelles
surfaces bâties, par un réseau de canalisations directes au cours d'eau générerait, lors
des précipitations intenses de courte durée, des débits qui mettraient en péril le
bénéfice obtenu par la galerie de dérivation en amont.

Afin de résoudre ce nouveau problème, on envisage de mettre en oeuvre un
contrôle des ruissellement par rétention et par des dispositions constructives qui seront
complémentaires à la dérivation des eaux de crues sans, en aucune manière, remettre
en question la validité de ce qui a été entrepris.

Ce principe est également appliqué à la demande des autorités genevoises sur le
territoire français lors d'équipements de surfaces importantes, de façon à rester dans le
cadre des hypothèses de la méthode globale pour le bassin situé à l'amont de la prise
d'eau.

CONCLUSION

Ces ouvrages ont été mis en service en 1988, bien que des crues importantes ne se
soient pas écoulées depuis, ils donnent satisfaction.

Vu les problèmes similaires sur les autres bassins versants du canton, le département des travaux publics s'est doté d'une section spécialisée en hydrologie afin de gérer l'écoulement des eaux de surface. La tâche prioritaire est de mettre sur pied un réseau d'observation in situ,puis de déterminer les moyens de gestion appropriés en vue d'éviter si possible l'accroissement des débits des cours d'eau.

Il est certain que si les éléments suffisant avaient été disponibles pour l'étude de l'Aire, un modèle mathématique plus fiable que la méthode globale, aurait été utilisé pour le dimensionnement des débits, dès 1975. Toutefois, les résultats n'auraient pas modifié le choix de la dérivation, mais y aurait associé un contrôle des ruissellement.

REFERENCES

Bruschin, J., Falvey, T. (1974) Risques relatifs aux crues. Réflexion à propos des résultats d'une analyse concernant la Suisse au nord des Alpes. Bulletin technique de la Suisse romande 21, Suisse.

Turner, L., Perfetta, J., Crozet, B., Lachavanne, J.-B. (1979) Approche écologique de l'Aire. Université de Genève, Suisse.

Mouchet, P.-L., Dubois, C. (1979) Mémoire technique concernant le bassin de l'Aire. Rapport interne au département des travaux publics du canton de Genève, Suisse.

Gloor, R., Jordan, J.-P., Wisner, P. (1983) Etude hydrologique du bassin versant de la Seymaz, Institut du génie rural, Ecole polytechnique fédérale de Lausanne. Publication n° 174, Suisse.

Hydrology in Mountainous Regions. II - Artificial Reservoirs; Water and Slopes
(Proceedings of two Lausanne Symposia, August 1990). IAHS Publ. no. 194, 1990.

Hydrology and morphological consequences of the 1987 flood event in the upper Reuss valley

F. NAEF & G. R. BEZZOLA, Laboratory of Hydraulics, Hydrology and
Glaciology (VAW), 8092 Zurich

ABSTRACT
   In August 1987 after intense precipitation, an extreme flood occured in
the Reuss valley. To understand the processes involved, to assess the
influence of the "Waldsterben" and of the new Gotthard highway on the
discharge and to obtain a base for planning, it was decided to reconstruct
this event, using a model for the simulation of unsteady flow. Statistical
analyses and historical studies were made to establish the frequency of
such an event with a magnitude far greater than all the other events
measured before.
   Since the Gotthard railway was built more than hundred years ago, it
has never been threatened by floods. The riverbed was naturally stabilized
by self armoring, with a top layer containing very coarse boulders. In the
1987 flood, the peak discharge exeeded the threshold value which could
bring this layer into motion. Thus bed and bank erosion could take place.
Widening predominated over bed incision, the active width of the bed was
more than doubled. In addition horizontal oscillations were observed,
reminiscent of the meander formation normally associated with lowland
rivers. Within a few hours the landscape changed dramatically.

INTRODUCTION

The Reuss river has its origin north of the Gotthard pass, and its valley then crosses the canton of Uri in south-north direction. The catchment area at its mouth into the Lake Lucerne is about 800 km^2.

   After heavy precipitation on the 24/25 August 1987, an extreme flood of a magnitude never recorded before, hit the Reuss valley. In a few hours all the traffic connections were interrupted and houses flooded or washed away, leaving damage of several hundred million Swiss Francs. Striking changes in riverbed morphology occured in the 15 km long reach between Göschenen and Amsteg. Here, the active width of the river bed, which had never been seriously threatened by bank erosion in the last 100 years, increased by more than twice the original size.

   The causes of this flood were widley discussed and many people feared that human activities (construction of the highway and other large structures, "Waldsterben" due to air pollution) had changed the runoff process in such a way as to trigger off this dramatic event.

HYDROLOGY

To understand what had happened during these few hours in the Reuss Valley and to provide a base for planning the flood protection work, it was decided to reconstruct the 1987 flood as accurately as possible. But data was scarce: only a few rain gauges were situated within the catchment and from the 5 stream gauges along the 50 km long river, 3 were washed away during the flood and also the records from the other two were not without problems.

A mathematical model served as a tool for the reconstruction, based on the full Saint-Venant equations for gradually varying unsteady flow in open channels (Kuehne and Faeh, 1983), which were integrated using an implicit finite difference scheme. Over a length of 45 km the Reuss was modelled with 400 cross-sections. All available information such as rain and stream gauge recordings, flood traces along the river, eye witness accounts, inflow to storage lakes, radar data for the rainfall distribution, was used to estimate flood hydrographs for the tributaries of the Reuss, which were then used as input to the model. The calibration of the model and the reconstruction of the 1987 event had to be done simultaneously in an interactive process. As the input data was partly inaccurate, inconsistent or even wrong, they had to be interpreted and adapted during the combined model calibration and flood reconstruction procedure, until a consistent picture of the events evolved.

The Reuss Valley consists of several rather different sections. Each of them posed its own problems in modelling. Some of the highest mountains in the catchment are well over 3000 masl. Within a few kilometers, the rivers drop to 1500 masl to join the 10 km long Urseren valley. This relatively flat valley was flooded during the event. Located at the lower end of the Urseren valley is Andermatt where the first working gauging station is situated.

The next section in which the river falls 500 m within 20 km, was mainly affected by erosion. In the last section, before the river enters the lake Lucerne near Seedorf, the Reuss flows between dams. This section is 16 km long with a small slope. The adjoining plains build the most densely populated part of the canton Uri and when the dams along the river broke, the widespread flooding caused serious damage.

With the help of the model and the data, the extent of the zone of the heaviest precipitation and the contributions of the different tributaries could be assessed, so that the evolution of the flood along the river could be reconstructed and a longitudinal profile of the peak discharge of the 1987 flood along the river could be drawn (Fig. 1). The model was also used to analyse specific problems like the influence of two large storage reservoirs, the flooding of the plains or the breaking of the levees on the peak discharge of the flood in 1987 as well as in future events.

The Event

In August 1987, the higher regions of the catchment were still covered with old snow. The weather was warm and dry and intense snow melting occured up to the highest regions, so that the saturation deficits of the slopes was already low at the beginning of the event. At about 10 a.m. of the 24th August, the 3-week period of good weather ended. But the high zero-centigrade line didn't drop and it rained also in the highest part of the Reuss catchment. The intensity of the rainfall with a duration of approximately 12 hours was fairly high, but not extreme in the upper part of the catchment (10 mm/h on the average), as such events are recorded every few years in rain gauges in the area.

Around midnight, a short rain shower of less than one hour occured. The zone of maximum rainfall intensity was located again in the mountainous region of the catchment with a steep gradient to the east and to the north. The rainfall intensity was about 40 mm/h. Such intensities occur on average every ten years, but in 1987, the rain fell on already saturated soils and slopes and the resulting runoff coefficients were very high. As a consequence, the discharge of the Reuss at Andermatt (catchment area 192 km^2), rose from 200 to 340 m^3/s within 90 minutes.

Most of the rain on the 24th August 1987 fell during the period before 11 p.m. If precipitation had ceased at this time, only an average flood would have resulted in the Reuss River and its tributaries. On the other hand, a rain shower of 40 mm alone would have produced only limited runoff. It was the combination of the long snow melting period followed by the lasting rainfall of moderate intensity and the short but intense burst of rain, which led to the extremely high discharge.

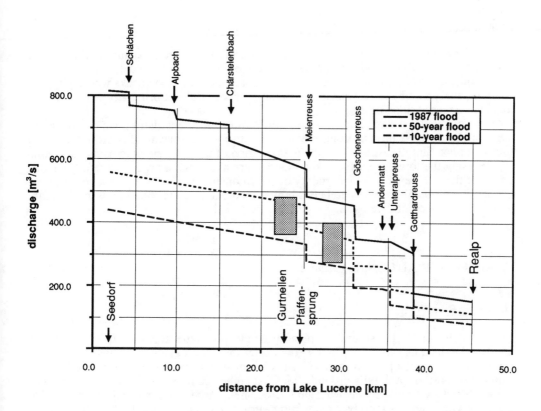

FIG. 1 Longitudinal profile of the peak discharge of the 10-year, 50 -year and 1987- flood along the Reuss River. The shaded rectangles show the range of the computed threshold values for the begin of the erosion (see chapter "threshold of erosion").

Statistics

The 1987 peak discharge of the Reuss before it enters Lake Lucerne, as measured by the stream gauge, was 735 m³/s. With intact levees, the discharge would have reached 800 m³/s.

In the 75 year long discharge record of Seedorf, the 1987 event is a typical outlier, higher than all other recorded events. The return period of the 1987 event with the observed 735 m³/s was estimated by flood frequency analyses to lie between 250 and 700 years; with a discharge of 800 m³/s, the return period would lie between 500 and well over 1000 years.

The uncertainty of the return period can only be diminished with an increased data base. Therefore, based on old maps, cross sections and eye-witness accounts found in different archives, the peaks of the three largest floods between 1780 and 1914 were estimated, extending the period of record of the largest floods to 210 years (Schaub, 1990). Using this data base, the return period of the 1987 event with 800 m³/s shrunk to150 to 300 years.

Conclusions

The 1987 flood was triggered off by a rain with highly irregular spatial and temporal distribution, high above highways, railway and tree line.

The influence of human activities in the catchment on the flood peaks was negligible. Also the analyses of the 75 year long discharge record did not bring any evidence of a trend to increased flood peaks.

A same amount of rainfall as in August 1987 with a different distribution could lead to quite different flood peaks. As no methods exist to assign meaningful probabilities to such complex rainfall distributions, the return period of the 1987 event remains uncertain.

By using the longest discharge records that are available today and carefully reconstructing the 1987 event, the incertainty of the frequency of the 1987 event could be reduced. The probabillity of occurence is higher than one expects, when only the 75 years of the discharge record are used.

MORPHOLOGICAL CONSEQUENCES

The Reuss River Valley

The Reuss River Valley shows a typical, post glacial shape. Between Göschenen and Amsteg the ancient valley, originally formed by the Reuss glacier, is filled with loose materials. The valley bottom therefore mainly consists of morainic material, changing with deposits from rock falls or land slides. At some sections rock outcrops are found. The river's slope varies between 2.5 and 7 %. The riverbed was naturally stabilized by self armouring, with a top layer containing very coarse boulders. These large residual boulders with mean diameters of up to 5 m are typical for the middle reach of the Reuss River. The riverbed remained stable over the last century. River banks were therefore artificially protected only in some shorter reaches.

Morphological Changes in 1987

The Reuss River flood of 1987 changed the river course dramatically within only a few hours. Widening of the riverbed predominated over incision, the active width of the bed was more than doubled. In addition horizontal oscillations were observed, which can be considered as meander formation normally associated with lowland rivers. They were usually triggered off by a natural curve or artificial change in the river's course. At several points the main road through the Reuss valley and the Gotthard railway line were destroyed. At Wassen bank erosion exposed the foundation of one of the Gotthard motorway bridge piers, the whole bridge being in danger of collapse. At Gurtnellen, during the construction of the railway line 100 years ago, a part of a river bend above the village had been cut off and parts of a rock shelf had been removed. This led to the elemination of an assumed, previous fixing of the river's course. As Fig. 2 shows, the extreme discharge caused the reactivation of the existing meanders, combined with their migration downstream. The resulting, severe erosion at the outer banks of the meander bends was the main damage process here.

Threshold of erosion

Despite some notable floods during the last 100 years, the Reuss riverbed remained more or less stable during this period. This fact and the exceptional morphological changes

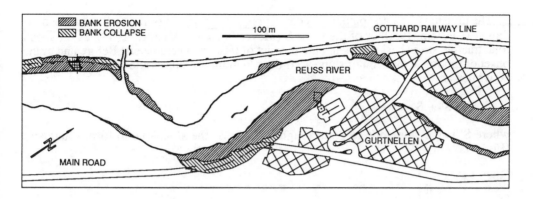

FIG. 2 Situation of the Gurtnellen reach after the flood event, where bank erosion due to meander migration caused major damage.

during the extreme flood in 1987 suggest a high threshold value over which the top layer could be brought in motion. Only discharges exceeding this threshold value would lead to bed and hence to bank erosion. Such a high threshold value contradicts the widespread opinion that a river channel is mainly formed by frequent floods of small magnitudes.

The determination of this threshold value must take special conditions into account which are to be found in a mountain stream like the Reuss river. Form roughness due to the largest particles in the riverbed becomes significant and has to be especially taken into consideration. These large boulders which are hardly set in motion even at extreme discharges have to be considered more as obstacles to flow than as a part of the base material forming the riverbed between the blocks. They disrupt the flow and create wake zones, hence the assumption of a logarithmic velocity profile, for example, seems questionable. However, experiments by Whittaker et al. (1988) indicate that mean velocity and flow depth can be reasonably well predicted by such an approach.

Assuming steady, uniform flow, the mean total tractive stress on the channel boundary (or the resistance of the channel against the flow respectively) is

$$\tau = \rho g R S$$

where ρg is the specific weight of water, R the hydraulic mean radius and S the channel slope.

The mean total tractive stress is not expended completely on individual particles of the base material. A certain amount of the energy of the fluid is dissipated by friction due to irregularities in the channel geometry and obstacles. According to Yalin (1977), the mean total tractive stress on the channel boundary can be divided into three components:

$$\tau = \tau' + \tau'' + \tau'''$$

Among these components, only τ' is excerted on the base material. τ'' and τ''' are "apparent stresses", for they are actually hydrodynamic forces acting on submerged obstacles. τ'' stands for forces acting on residual boulders and channel irregularities, τ''' for forces acting on grains moving in the fluid. Before and at the onset of motion of grains, τ''' is zero.

As only τ' is excerted on the base material directly, the stress excerted on the base material particles in natural channels with bends, bars and large boulders is smaller than τ. τ' has to be used to estimate the beginning of the erosion in such channels.

The division of τ into components corresponds to a division of the hydraulic mean radius R (Einstein, 1950) or of the slope S (Meyer-Peter and Mueller, 1948), as the mean total tractive stress basically being the product of these two parameters. Before and at the onset of motion, a division of slope according to grain roughness and form rougness can be written as

$$S = S' + S''$$

where S' is the slope due to grain roughness and S" the slope due to form roughness (Fig. 3).

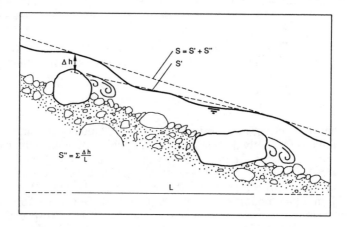

FIG. 3 Schematic presentation of the Reuss riverbed with base material and residual boulders.

Many formulae are available to evaluate resistance to flow in gravel-bed channels. It is outside the scope of this paper to present a review of these approaches; a recent review has been made by Bray (1988). Many of these formulae are applicable to flumes with larger slopes and small relative submergences (i.e. flow depth divided by grain size), as to be found in the Reuss river. Most of the approaches propose corrections on the flow resistance. But usually then the uncorrected slope S is used for the calculation of the stress excerted on the bed particles, and thus the stress acting on these particles is overestimated. A slope reduction may be negligible at smaller slopes or in cases, when form resistance effects are less important.

The reduced friction slope S' can be determined as follows: A resistance law which respects both grain and form resistance is used to calculate the mean velocity and hence the discharge as a function of a given mean flow depth and the channel slope S. If the distance between the boulders is large enough, the flow depth in between can be assumed equal to the overall mean flow dept. In this part, the flow resistance is determined by S' and a friction coefficient of the base material only. By using the continuity equation, the reduced friction slope S' can now be calculated. An example of this approach can be found in Whittaker et al. (1988).

The dimensionless shear stress Θ' excerted on the bed particles is given by

$$\Theta' = \frac{\tau'}{g(\rho_s - \rho)d_m} = \frac{S'}{(s-1)} \cdot \frac{R}{d_m}$$

in which g is the acceleration due to gravity, ρ_s is the density of particle, ρ is the density of water, s is the relative density of bed material ρ_s /ρ and d_m is the mean grain size of the base material. The dimensionless shear stress Θ' then is compared with the critical value Θ_D being the value of the Shields-factor characterizing the breaking of the armour coat. The latter can be estimated from a relation deduced from Guenther's (1971) results:

$$\Theta_D / \Theta_{cr} = (d_{mD}/ d_m)^{0.67}$$

where Θ_{cr} is the critical Shields factor and d_{mD} is the mean grain size of the armour coat. This relation takes into account the increase of the critical shields factor Θ_{cr} for non-uniform material due to self armouring. In the present case Θ_D is about $2\cdot\Theta_{cr}$. Methods of estimating d_{mD} were proposed by Gessler (1965) and Guenther (1971). For a rough estimation it can be set equal to the 90-percentile size of base material, d_{90}. If dimensionless shear stress Θ' exceeds the critical Shields factor of the armour coat Θ_D, the top layer will be set into motion.

Several approaches concerning the resistance to flow developed for comparable conditions as to be found in the Reuss river were examined to estimate the threshold value. Among them, the approaches of Whittaker et al. (1988), Egashira and Ashida (1989), Tsujimoto (1989) and Smart and Jaeggi (1983) shall be mentioned here. The latter authors proposed an explicit equation for the reduced friction slope S'. The consistent application of an approach with a division of flow resistance in components and the introduction of a reduced friction slope S' allows the calculation of threshold values which seem well reasonable. Results from these calculations are shown in Fig. 1. It must be noted, that the calculations which led to these results do not consider further form resistance due to channel geometry in plan alignment and therefore represent a lower limit of the threshold value. The variation of results is due to different approaches used and to locally varying parameters.

As mentioned above, widening predominated over bed incision in 1987. At discharges which exceed the threshold value, smaller boulders are actually set into motion and slide or roll over the bed until settling in zones with lower tractive stresses. But the larger boulders are embeded and shelter the bed material. Hence depth erosion is hindered. Widening takes place until the reduced flow depth and thus the reduced shear stress reaches the value of Θ_D.

River Meandering

During the construction of the railway line, and later of the motorway, embankments were prepared at several points. Due to the narrowness of the valley and its steep flanks, this was necessary to gain space for the traffic lines. These embankments, consisting of finer material could easily be eroded by the river when widening. This caused damage and destruction of these traffic lines and further, led to additional, heavy sediment input in the river. Sediment supply from the riverbed and sediment input resulting from bank erosion favoured the forming of bedforms. The application of the criterion of Jaeggi (1984) shows that the conditions for the formation of alternate bars are given when the active width of the river bed increases. Alternate bars can be considered as beginning of meander formation. Besides the triggering off by natural curves or artificial changes in the river's course, this may be an additional explanation of the horizontal oscillations which were observed in 1987.

Conclusions

The erosion in the Reuss river during the flood of August 1987 began only after a certain discharge had been exceeded. This threshold discharge can be determined using an approach which divides the flow resistance into components due to grain roughness and form roughness and which uses a reduced friction slope S' for the calculation of the shear stress excerted on the bed material. The threshold discharges calculated with this approach are high and can only be exceeded during extreme floods. This explains the stability of the Reuss riverbed during the last 100 years, although several large floods occured in this period. These results were also confirmed in hydraulic model tests (Bezzola et al.,1990) of the river reaches Wassen and Gurtnellen, which suffered major damages in1987.

The fact that only extreme discharges can cause significant riverbed changes contradicts the widespread opinion, that river channels of mountain streams are mainly formed by frequent floods with smaller magnitudes.

REFERENCES

Bezzola, G.R., Kuster, P. & Pellandini, S. (1990) The Reuss River Flood of 1987 - Hydraulic Model Tests and Reconstruction Concepts, Proc. Int. Conference on River Flood Hydraulics, Wallingford, England, in press.

Bray, D.I. (1987) A Review of Flow Resistance in Gravel-Bed Rivers, Seminario Leggi morfologiche e loro verifica di campo, University of Cosenza, Italy, 23-57.

Egashira, S. and Ashida, K. (1989) Flow Resistance and Sediment Transportation in Streams with Step-Pool Bed Morphology, Proc. Int. Workshop on Fluvial Hydraulics of Mountain Regions, IAHR, Trent, Italy, A31-A44.

Einstein, H.A. (1950) The Bedload Function for Sediment Transportation in Open Channel Flows, US Dept. of Agriculture, Techn. Bull. 1026

Faeh, R., Koella, E.& Naef, F.(1990) The flood in the Reuss valley in August 1987: A computer aided reconstruction of a flood in a mountainous region,Proc. Int. Conference on River Flood Hydraulics, Wallingford, England, in press.

Gessler, J. (1965) Der Geschiebetriebbeginn bei Mischungen, Mitt. der Versuchsanstalt für Wasser- und Erdbau, ETH Zürich, Nr. 69.

Guenther, A. (1971) Die kritische mittlere Sohlenschubspannung bei Geschiebemischungen, Mitt. der Versuchsanstalt für Wasserbau, ETH Zürich, Nr. 3

Jaeggi, M.N.R. (1984) Formation and effects of Alternate Bars, Proc. ASCE, J. Hydr. Eng., Vol. 110, No. 2, 142-156.

Kühne, A.& Faeh, R.(1983) Application of a mathematical model to design mesures for flood protection, International conference on the hydraulic aspects of floods and flood control, London, England.

Meyer-Peter, E. and Mueller, R. (1948) Formulas for Bedload Transport, Proc. 2nd Congr. IAHR, Stockholm, 39-64.

Schaub, D., Horat, P. & Naef, F. (1990) Die Hochwasser der Reuss im 18. und 19. Jahrhundert und ihr Einfluss auf die Hochwasserstatistik, Wasser - Energie - Luft, Baden, Switzerland, in press.

Smart, G.M. and Jaeggi, M.N.R. (1983) Sedimenttransport in steilen Rinnen, Mitt. der Versuchsanstalt fnr Wasserbau, Hydrologie und Glaziologie, ETH Zürich, Nr. 64

Tsujimoto, T. (1989) Bed-Load Transport in Steep Channels, Proc. Int. Workshop on Fluvial Hydraulics of Mountain Regions, IAHR, Trent, Italy, A79-A92

Whittaker, J.G., Hickman, W.E. & Croad, R.N. (1988) Riverbed Stabilisation with Placed Blocks, Central Laboratories Report 3-88/3, Central Laboratories, Lower Hutt, New Zealand.

Yalin, M.S. (1977) Mechanics of Sediment Transport, 2nd ed., Pergamon Press, Oxford.

Hydrology in Mountainous Regions. II - Artificial Reservoirs; Water and Slopes
(Proceedings of two Lausanne Symposia, August 1990). IAHS Publ. no. 194, 1990.

Anomalous hydrological behaviour of an Alpine stream (Varuna, Poschiavo, southern Switzerland) and its interpretation in terms of the geology of the catchment

FELIX NAEF & PETER HORAT, Laboratory of Hydraulics, Hydrology
and Glaciology (VAW), 8092 Zürich
ALAN G. MILNES, Geological & Environmental Assessments, (GEA),
8050 Zürich
EDUARD HOEHN, Paul-Scherrer Institut (PSI), 5232 Villigen

ABSTRACT

The Varuna is a steep stream with a small catchment in the Alps of southern Switzerland, which shows an anomalous hydrology: discharge measurements over a period of 30 years do not show a single flood peak. The geology of the catchment is dominated by deep sackung (gravitationally collapsed bedrock). The anomalous runoff characteristics of the Varuna is thought to be due to the rapid infiltration of surface water into this sackung "aquifer". A simple model allows some aspects of this surface/subsurface exchange to be quantified.

In July 1987, a large debris flow was generated in the valley and caused enormous damage in the town of Poschiavo. It is suggested that the anomalous hydrology (lack of floods) and the unusual geology (sackung) were essential causative factors of this event. Thus, for hazard assessment, the lack of flood peaks may be rather a warning signal than a cause of complacency.

INTRODUCTION

Val Varuna is a steep sidearm of the main valley in the Poschiavo area in southern Switzerland (Figure 1). The Varuna stream has a length of only 5.5 km, descending in this distance from 3450 masl to 1020 masl. The total catchment area is 6.2 km². The highest parts are covered by a small glacier, followed by rocks and talus slopes. The lower parts are covered by forest and grassy alps. With the exception of the peaks and cliffs around the glacial source area, rock outcrops are small and discontinuous, but for the deeply incised lower part of the stream (between 1750 and 1200 masl), which is a ca. 50 m deep gorge with rocky walls. Mean annual precipitation over the catchment is around 1800 mm, the 2.33 yearly daily precipitation 80 mm, the 2.33 yearly hourly precipitation 25 mm.

From this brief description, one would assume that the Varuna should be a fairly typical example of an Alpine stream in this size range. However, its hydrological characteristics are highly anomalous: discharge measurements over a period of 30 years do not show a single flood peak. Attention was focussed on this strange behaviour by a recent catastrophic event. On the 18th of July 1987, after intense precipitation, a debris flow of more than 250'000 m³ developed in the Varuna, completely unexpected by the local population (Naef et al., 1989). The main source of the debris was the gorge between 1750 and 1200 msl. Down in the main valley, the debris blocked the river and the village of Poschiavo was flooded, with large masses of debris being deposited in the streets and in the basements. The damage was enormous.

Subsequently, field studies revealed that the geology of the Varuna catchment is unusual in that it is dominated by a particularly large "sackung" (gravitationally collapsed bedrock). The main thrust of the present paper is to show how this unusual geology may be intimately connected with both the anomalous hydrological behaviour and with the generation of the 1987 debris flow.

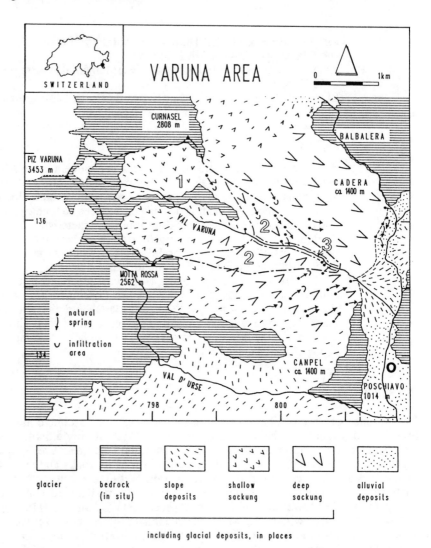

FIG. 1 Overview map of the Varuna area. Indicated are the boundaries of the three subcatchments, which are simulated in the model by three linear reservoirs (see chapter "hydrological model").

ANOMALOUS HYDROLOGY - NO FLOOD PEAKS

Based on commonly used flood estimation formulae, one would expect in the Varuna a peak discharge with a return period of 20 years between 15 and 25 m³/s or even more. Instead, in the gauging station installed 30 years ago, no flood peak at all has been recorded. The largest measured discharge in this long record was 2.5 m^3/s, far below the expected level (the average discharge in June and July is 0.55 m^3/s). Although the stream gauge was not very accurate, there is no doubt that this strange behaviour is real and cannot be attributed to measurement error. Water balance computations over the years showed that no significant amount of water was lost by deep percolation.

In several research projects on flood formation or estimation, which used data from all gauged catchments in Switzerland smaller than 100 km^2, the records from the Varuna were discarded because they looked so unusual. None of the commonly used parameters to describe the runoff process, such as slope, vegetation, land use, soil type, accumulated channel length, etc., gave any hint as to the reason for this behaviour. As we shall show, the Varuna data are actually a serious indication that, under certain conditions, these parameters are not sufficient to describe the runoff process during floods.

As an example, Figure 2 shows the specific discharge of the Varuna in comparison to the Ursé and the Pednal, two streams in adjoining catchments, during a small flood in June 1987, just prior to the 1987 debris flow event. Whereas the Ursé and Pednal react as expected to the heavy rainfall, the discharge of the Varuna, as always in such situations, increases only slightly. We believe that the reason for this anomalous behaviour lies in the geological relations in and around the catchment area.

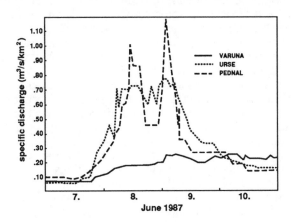

FIG. 2 Specific discharges of the Varuna, Ursé and Pednal, three streams in adjoining catchments, during a small flood in 1987.

GEOLOGY

The bedrock of the Varuna area belongs to the sheared base of the Bernina nappe, a basement-dominated unit of the Lower Austroalpine nappe complex (Staub 1946, Trümpy 1980). The shearing and low-grade metamorphism was heterogeneously overprinted on the pre-Triassic basement rocks during the northward overthrusting of the nappe during the Alpine orogeny, producing sequences of schists, gneisses, mylonites and phyllites surrounding sporadic unsheared remnants of the original granites, diorites, vulkanites, high-grade metamorphites and low-grade metasediments. In this heterogeneous assemblage, marbles are rare, and no carbonate rocks are known from the Varuna area. The bedrock structure, as it is presented in the in-situ outcrops surrounding the Varuna catchment (Fig. 1), is dominated by the penetrative foliation developed during the Alpine shearing, which has a general dip of 20-30 deg. towards the NE.

Varuna sackung

The bedrock outcrops around the source area of the Varuna and in the upper part of the catchment are obviously in-situ. In contrast, the bedrock outcrops in the lower reaches are thought to belong to a large "sackung" complex (Fig. 1), i.e. an area in which the bedrock formations have moved down-slope by a process of slow gravitational collapse, after the main morphogenic phase of the present mountain topography. Sackung is a widespread phenomenon in Alpine areas where retreat of Pleistocene glaciers left over-steepened and unsupported valley walls (e.g. Zischinsky 1969, Forcella 1984, Blanc et al. 1987), but it also occurs in other high-relief situations (e.g. Radbruch-Hall et al. 1976). The collapse mechanisms can be very complex combinations of toppling, sliding and spreading, but the result is typically a slumped mass with coherent internal geologi-cal relations (in contrast to rockslide and landslide debris), i.e. modified but not de-stroyed during the downward movement. Flow is accomplished by sliding on many small planes of weakness within the rock mass (joints, faults, cleavage, bedding planes, etc.) and by small-scale breakage and grinding. This leads to a general dilatancy and the opening of innumerable spaces, pipes and fissures, which remain as partially intercon-nected systems long after the sackung has become inactive. The open spaces and voids make sackung terranes permeable for flowing ground waters. The hydrogeology of sackung areas resembles karst terranes in some respects (cf. White 1988, "tectonic caves" etc.), with the depth of channelling determined by the thickness of the slumped mass. In addition, the disintegration of the bedrock during the collapse processes (which are still locally active today in the Varuna area) can be expected to favour the delivery of large amounts of already comminuted rock debris to stream beds.

That some areas of sackung exist in the Varuna catchment has been known for some time (cf. Staub, 1946). However, it is now clear that geological and morphological fea-tures typical of sackung - broken and deeply fissured, discontinuous rock outcrops; incongruence of structures (foliation, lithological boundaries) in comparison to sur-rounding in-situ bedrock; upward-facing scarps and contour-parallel linear depressions ("Nackentälchen"); irregularly distributed springs, seepages, sinkholes and infiltration zones - are found throughout the drainage basin and its surroundings.

Recent geological and geophysical studies (Haeberli et al., 1990) have revealed that the sackung is not everywhere a relatively superficial phenomenon affecting only the upper few meters or tens of meters of material (shallow sackung, Fig. 1). Over much of the Varuna area, particularly in the lower reaches, the base of the sackung lies much deeper than the level of the Varuna stream, possibly up to 100m below the surface (deep sackung, Fig. 1). In the gorge between 1750 and 1200 masl, the stream bed is not cut in in-situ bedrock but in slumped, fractured and highly weathered rock masses (containing a prominent black phyllite horizon in the lower part which may have played a causative role in the developement of the sackung). In some areas there are good indications that the rock masses lie hundreds of meters lower than their original positions.

Hydrological implications

These relationships suggest that the anomalous hydrology of the Varuna stream is related to the large storage capacity of the underlying sackung "aquifer". Surface waters infiltrate rapidly into it over the whole catchment area. Subsurface waters drain only slowly to the main stream as the reservoir fills up. The following data may be a direct indication of this surface/subsurface exchange in the main stream bed. In June 1987, measurements were made in the gorge to estimate the amount of water infiltrating into the debris from the river bed. At the uppern end of the gorge, a discharge of 1 m^3/s was measured using the salt dilution method.Two kilometer downstreams, at the lower end of the gorge, the discharge at the same time was 1.3 m^3/s. By measuring the concentra-tion of the salt injected at the upper end of the reach at the outflow and comparing it with the measured discharges, the surface/subsurface exchange could be estimated. The results indicated that 0.3 m^3/s of traced water infiltrated, to be replaced by an inflow of 0.6 m^3/s of untraced water. Some of this inflow is contributed by springs along the valley sides (Fig. 1), but a significant inflow comes from the subsurface reservoir. One could conclude from these measurements that there are actually two "streams" flowing downwards, one at the surface and one underground, with an intense exchange between them.

HYDROLOGICAL MODEL OF THE VARUNA

The 1987 debris flow event focussed attention on the Varuna because the planning of measures to prevent similar catastrophes required an understanding of the event and its causes. Apart from the origin and dynamics of the debris flow itself, the study of the peculiar hydrological behaviour became of high interest. Does a relation exist between the fact that no floods occur in the Varuna and the occurrence of the debris flow? Were the underground reservoirs in the catchment saturated by the intense precipitation and snowmelt before the event, so that the heavy rainfall in July could no longer infiltrate, resulting in a flood which triggered the debris flow? When future debris flows are prevented by check dams, what is the amount of the clear water discharge to be expected during floods - 3 m^3/s (as measured up to now), 30 m^3/s (as calculated from flood formulae) or more? Have the runoff characteristics of the Varuna changed due to the fact that 250'000 m^3 porous debris has been washed out of the valley? (This volume could store around 50'000 m^3 water, corresponding in the size to a respectable flood retention basin!). Of more general interest is the question, whether the features which led to the specific runoff behaviour of the Varuna can be found in other catchments and, if so, how they could be parameterised. A simple quantitative model to account for the water input and output of the catchment has been developed and applied to conditions during the July 1987 event to answer some of these questions. The modelling procedure and some results are given in the following.

No discharge records exist for the 1987 debris flow event, since the gauging station was washed away. Therefore, the event had to be reconstructed, based on meteorological measurements, accounts of eye witnesses and traces left in the field by the debris flow and the rainstorm. In a simple model, the reaction of the catchment was simulated by three linear reservoirs, which represented (1) the upper, unvegetated part of the catchment with the deep talus slopes, (2) the lower, forested valley sides and (3) the gorge of the Varuna below 1750 masl. To distinguish between snowfall and rain, the catchment was divided into 11 elevation bands at 200 m intervals. For each interval, snowfall, snow depth, snowmelt and rainfall was computed, using temperature, snow depth and rainfall profiles derived from three meteorological stations at different elevations in the vicinity. The time step for the computations was 1 day, since daily data were readily available. With the slow reaction of the discharge of the Varuna, the hydrograph could be approximated well with this time step.

The summer periods, May to October, from 1977 to 1987 were used to calibrate the model. In 1987, discharge records were available up to July 16th, two days prior to the event.

Results

The results of the simulations for 1987 are shown in Figure 3. In June, the upper parts of the catchment were still covered with snow, which melted only in the first half of July. During the intense precipitation which preceded the debris flow, air temperature was high, so that it rained even in the highest parts of the catchment. As no raingauge is situated in the Varuna catchment, rainfall was estimated. To be on the safe side, the rainfall on July 18th, estimated on the basis of the surrounding stations, was doubled for the model computation. Even so, the computed mean daily discharge of 1.5 m³/s for this day is low, as expected for the Varuna, and gives no indication of the extraordinary events that occurred in the valley. The model reservoir representing the upper part of the catchment contained a maximum of 1.4 Mio m³ water during the debris flow.

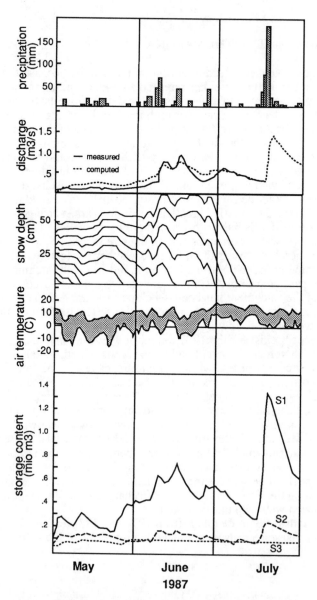

FIG. 3 Model computations for the Varuna from May to July 1987. The debris flow occured on the 18th July.
Snow depth is given for 11 different elevation bands, the range of the air temperature between Poschiavo (1000 masl) and Piz Varuna (3450 masl) is also indicated. S1, S2, S3 show the contents of the linear reservoirs, representing the three subcatchments (see Fig. 1).

This was only the second highest value attained in the period from 1977 to 1987. In July 1977, a slightly higher value was reached without any unusual events taking place in the catchment. A marked difference between the two years is that in 1987 the reservoirs reached this level within a few days, whereas in 1977 the filling occurred over a period of nearly one month.

From this data, it is clear that the amount of the accumulated rain and snowmelt water in the catchment in the period preceding the debris flow was not exceptionally high. One can conclude that the reservoirs in the catchment were not filled to overflowing, that the infiltration rate was not limited, and that the Varuna reacted in a normal way prior to the debris flow. The upper capacity limits of the reservoirs could not yet be assessed. From the depth of the sackung, it might well be that these limits are much higher than the accumulated volumes of July 1987.

The model computations are also supported by observations in the catchment. After the debris flow, no traces of overland flow or of exceptional discharge in the channel network, except in the main channel and in the uppermost parts, could be found. A few minutes prior to the first pulse of the debris flow, it was observed that the capacity of the aperture under the bridge at 1750 masl. was still amply sufficient for the water of the Varuna. From the geometry of this aperture, it can be estimated that the discharge was certainly less than 10 m^3/s at that moment. The debris flow was therefore not triggered by a peak flow of exceptional magnitude (the estimated "discharge " of the flow itself at the exit of the Varuna valley was several 100 m^3/s !), and another mechanism has to be sought (see Zimmermann, 1990). The model results also indicate that even after long and intense precipitation, the Varuna cannot produce substantial flood peaks, due to the large infiltration rates and storage capacities.

The behaviour of reservoir (3), which simulates the gorge reach, is interesting, since this is the main source of the debris. Compared with the reservoirs (1) and (2), which feed it, reservoir (3) was small (about 100 000 m^3). In the years considered in the model, it was practically always full and did not have a retention effect during times of flood. After the 1987 debris flow, with the gorge deeply eroded, this reservoir was removed. However, as it could not influence the peak discharge before, the runoff behaviour of the Varuna can be expected to remain unchanged.

CONCLUSIONS

Combining the hydrological and geological data from the Varuna catchment and applying the hydrological model to the 1987 debris flow event leads to the following conclusions. The "bedrock" of the Varuna catchment is an heterogeneously porous and permeable mass of fissured rock and/or coarse rubble belonging to a large sackung complex. These characteristics facilitate rapid infiltration and provide large storage volumes during periods of high precipitation. This completely dominates the runoff regime of the Varuna and prevents the generation of floods, the maximum discharges during periods of highest precipitation are only a fraction of the expected amount. In addition to this hydrological function, the disintegration of the bedrock during the (still locally active) collapse processes can be expected to favour the delivery of large amounts of already comminuted rock debris to the stream bed. Because of the absence of floods, rubble accumulates, particularly in the floor of the lower part of the valley, and is not regularly washed away. It becomes part of the subsurface storage system until at some point it becomes unstable, and moves downwards as a catastrophic debris flow, as in the 1987 event. The debris cone at the valley exit has been built by many such large but rare events.

In the Varuna and in catchments with similar characteristics, commonly used flood estimation methods are useless. In such catchments, floods might not be a problem, but the anomalously low flood peaks might be an indication of a dangerous potential for debris flows. The Varuna is a salutary example of the intimate coupling of geological, hydrogeological, geomorphological and hydrological phenomena.

ACKNOWLEDGMENTS The research was partly financed by the community of Poschiavo, the Canton of Graubünden and the hydroelectric power company Kraftwerke Brusio AG.

REFERENCES

Blanc, A., Durville, J.-L., Follacci, J.-P., Gaudin, B. & Pincent, B. (1987) Méthodes de surveillance d'un glissement de terrain de très grande ampleur: La Clapière, Alpes Maritimes, France. Bull. Internat. Assoc. Eng. Geol., 35, 37-46.
Forcella, F. (1984) Brevi note sulla tettonica gravitativa di versante nelle Alpi Centrali. Boll. Soc. Geol. Ital., 103, 689-696.
Haeberli, W., Rickenmann, D., Zimmermann, M.& Rösli, U. (1990) Investigation of 1987 debris flows in the Swiss Alps: general concept and geophisical soundings. International Conference on Water Resources in Mountainious Regions, this volume
Naef, F., Haeberli, W.& Jäggi, M. (1989) Morphological changes in the Swiss Alps resulting from the 1987 summer storms. Hydrology of disasters, proceedings of the WMO technical conference, Geneva, November 1988.
Radbruch-Hall, D.H., Varnes, D.J. & Savage, W.Z. (1976) Gravitational spreading of steep-sided ridges ("sackung") in Western United States. Bull. Internat. Assoc. Eng. Geol., 14, 23-35.
Staub, R. (1946) Geologische Karte der Berninagruppe, 1:50 000. Schweiz. Geol. Komm. Spezialkarte 118.
Trümpy, R. (1980) An Outline of the Geology of Switzerland. Wepf, Basel.
White, W.B. (1988) Geomorphology and Hydrology of Karst Terrains. Oxford Univ. Press (New York, etc.).
Zimmermann, M. (1990) Debris flows 1987 in Switzerland: Geomorphological aspects. International Conference on Water Resources in Mountainious Regions, this volume
Zischinsky, U. (1969) Ueber Sackungen. Rock Mech., 1, 30-52.

Hydrology in Mountainous Regions. II - Artificial Reservoirs; Water and Slopes
(Proceedings of two Lausanne Symposia, August 1990). IAHS Publ. no. 194, 1990.

Evolution comparée des conditions hydrologiques et des mouvements du glissement de la Frasse (Alpes suisses occidentales)

F. NOVERRAZ
Centre interdépartemental d'Etude des Terrains Instables
(CETI), Ecole Polytechnique Fédérale de Lausanne,
1015 Lausanne, Suisse
A. PARRIAUX
Ecole Polytechnique Fédérale de Lausanne, Laboratoire de
Géologie (GEOLEP), 1015 Lausanne, Suisse

RESUME: Le glissement de la Frasse, important glissement
du retrait glaciaire situé dans les Alpes suisses
occidentales, a fait l'objet d'études pluridisciplinaires
très poussées, dont est résulté un nombre élevé de
données relatives à l'évolution des mouvements, à
l'hydrogéologie, à l'hydrologie de surface et à la
climatologie. Ces dernières données, et notamment les
mesures de débits de la rivière érodant le pied du
glissement, sont disponibles sur plusieurs dizaines
d'années; l'évolution des mouvements, connue en détail
sur les vingt dernières années, fait l'objet de données
remontant à plus de 200 ans.

La confrontation de ces informations, visant à expliquer les fluctuations de la vitesse des mouvements, et
notamment les crises destructrices périodiques du glissement, a fourni d'intéressants résultats: elle a permis
d'établir qu'aucun paramètre hydrologique pris isolément
ne parvenait à rendre compte de ces fluctuations. Le
déclenchement des crises semble consécutif à une conjonction de conditions défavorables incluant la pluviométrie
antécédente, la pluviométrie à court terme, un état de
charge élevé des eaux souterraines et vraisemblablement
une évolution défavorable du profil en long du
glissement.

INTRODUCTION

Le glissement de terrain de la Frasse, qui représente un volume de 50
millions de mètres cubes, est actif en permanence et provoque
d'importantes déformations de deux routes cantonales, dont l'une est
fréquentée par un trafic intense en saison touristique. Ce glissement
subit en outre de très fortes accélérations temporaires, qui
provoquent la destruction totale de la route inférieure. Trois phases
d'accélérations ont eu lieu au cours de ce siècle, et les deux
dernières (1966 et 1981-82) sont bien connues (Lugeon et al., 1922;
Bersier & Weidmann, 1970; Bonnard & Noverraz, 1986). Cette ultime
crise s'est même produite durant la période d'étude que lui a
consacré le projet de recherche pluridisciplinaire de l'EPFL DUTI
(Détection et Utilisation des Terrains Instables) entre 1980 et 1984.
Ces investigations ont notamment donné lieu à d'importants travaux
géodésiques et photogrammétriques qui ont conduit à une excellente
connaissance de la répartition des mouvements sur le court terme

depuis 1980, sur le moyen terme (tranches de quelques années) depuis 1957 et sur le long terme (tranches de plusieurs décades) depuis 1768 et 1861 (comparaison graphique et numérique de trois états cadastraux notamment) (Engel, 1986). La courbe d'évolution des mouvements qui en résulte peut être directement comparée à celle des données hydrologiques au cours des dernières décennies.

BUT DE LA RECHERCHE

Il était dès lors très intéressant de chercher à établir les relations entre les deux crises de 1966 et 1981-82, au cours desquelles la vitesse du glissement dans sa partie basse passait de quelques dm/an à 2-3 m/mois durant deux à quatre mois.

Des accélérations aussi importantes des mouvements pour un glissement d'une telle ampleur sont rares. Si les fluctuations climatiques sont globalement une cause majeure, il restait à établir quels facteurs avaient joué un rôle dominant.

Les études antérieures sur le glissement de la Frasse lors du projet DUTI avaient mis l'accent sur une caractérisation hydrologique basée sur les conditions à la surface de la masse glissée (Bonnard & Noverraz 1986). Les indicateurs comme la pluie efficace mensuelle n'ont pas permis de corrélation univoque satisfaisante avec la fonction déplacements.

Le but de cette communication est la recherche de paramètres hydrologiques plus explicatifs des mouvements.

Notre choix s'est tourné vers deux facteurs complémentaires qui a priori pourraient avoir un rôle important dans la dynamique de ce glissement (voir fig. 2):

- un indicateur des conditions hydrogéologiques globales dans le massif: le régime de la grande source karstique du Fontaney.
- un indicateur du pouvoir d'érosion du pied de la masse glissée: le régime de la rivière Grande Eau.

Nous avons également cherché quels pas de temps devaient être considérés pour obtenir la meilleure explication du mouvement. D'emblée, nous nous sommes orientés vers la recherche de conjonction de facteurs, non seulement entre paramètres hydrologiques mais également avec les considérations géomécaniques.

CONTEXTE GEOLOGIQUE ET HYDROLOGIQUE

Le glissement de la Frasse s'est développé probablement à la suite du dernier retrait glaciaire dans un synclinal de Flysch ultra-helvétique constitué de roches schisto-marneuses à bancs gréso-calcaires, occupant le coeur d'un grand pli déjeté formé par d'épaisses séries mésozoïques du Trias et du Malm et par des Couches Rouges marno-calcaires de l'Eocène (fig. 1) (Lombard et al, 1974; Gabus & Badoux, 1990). Les calcaires massifs du Malm y dominent et affleurent largement à l'amont du glissement, donnant lieu à un vaste karst superficiel (lapiez) et profond (réseau souterrain de plus d'un kilomètre de développement appelé gouffre du Chevrier). Ce gouffre a été exploré par l'un des auteurs, qui a pu notamment établir qu'il ne s'était plus trouvé noyé (en charge) depuis fort longtemps, même dans sa partie profonde (- 500 m p.s à l'entrée) située près de la tête du glissement (Lutz et al, 1987).

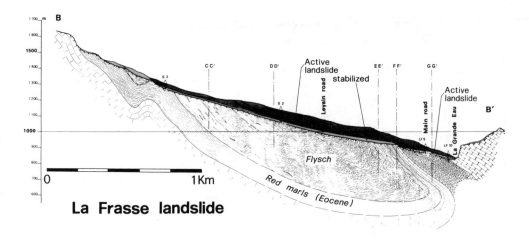

FIG. 1 Profil en long géologique du glissement et de son substratum.

Un essai de traçage à l'uranine a permis d'établir que la majeure partie des eaux circulait très rapidement en direction de la plaine du Rhône (source du Fontaney), et n'avait de ce fait que peu de relations avec le glissement.

La masse glissée, épaisse de plusieurs dizaines de mètres, voire de plus de cent mètres dans certaines zones, est constituée presqu'entièrement de roches du Flysch disloquées et broyées en une masse de fins débris argileux et de blocs de toutes tailles de calcaires marneux, de calcaires gréseux et de grès. Cet ensemble est peu perméable (K 10^{-6} à 10^{-7} m/s). Les dix-huit forages profonds réalisés à ce jour dans le glissement ont montré que les conditions hydrogéologiques différaient beaucoup entre les parties hautes, médianes et basses du glissement. Un aquifère complexe propre à la masse glissée, à zones de potentiels très différents, a été observé. Le substratum rocheux en place présente une faible charge dans le haut du glissement (marnes rouges éocènes), un état artésien dans la partie médiane (Flysch crétacé), et un état de nouveau passablement drainé dans la zone basse (flanc renversé du pli, avec une série amincie de calcaires du Malm et des calcaires dolomitiques et cornieules du Trias).

Long de deux kilomètres environ pour une surface de 1 km^2, le glissement offre une pente moyenne de 11° sur les trois quarts supérieurs, et de 20° pour la zone en glissement plus active du bas (fig. 1). Plusieurs niveaux superposés de glissement ont été identifiés grâce aux inclinomètres et un coussin de matériaux glissés actuellement stabilisés sépare la base du glissement actif de la roche en place; ce niveau plus perméable à potentiel hydraulique faible semble exercer le rôle de drain à la base du glissement dans la plus grande partie de sa moitié inférieure. Le pied du glissement est érodé par la rivière Grande Eau sur une largeur de 600 m; cette érosion est responsable d'une activité permanente sur l'ensemble du glissement. Il a pu être établi que le profil en long de la rivière s'est progressivement élevé au cours des dernières décennies (fig. 2), ce qui démontre que la rivière ne parvient actuellement pas à évacuer la totalité des matériaux amenés par le glissement.

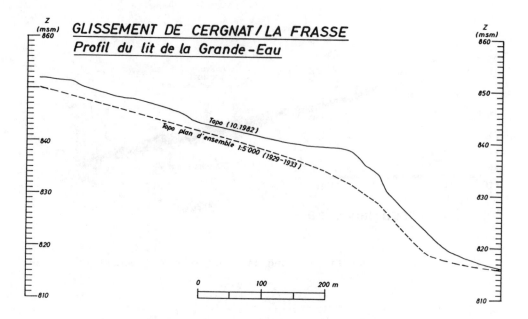

FIG 2   Evolution au cours du temps du profil en long du
lit de la Grande Eau au front du glissement.

DONNEES DISPONIBLES

Les données de déplacement sont connues par quatre procédés:

- La comparaison d'états cadastraux a fourni les déplacements à long
  terme pour les périodes 1768-1861-1981/82 (Miserez et al., 1982;
  Bonnard, 1983; Engel, 1986).
- Les mesures photogrammétriques ont fourni les déplacements à moyen
  terme pour les périodes 1957-1969-1974-1980-1982-1985 (Miserez et
  al., 1982).
- Les mesures géodésiques ont fourni les déplacements à moyen et
  court terme pour la crise de 1966, localement pour la période
  1951-1982, et de manière resserrée pour la période 1981-1985
  (Bonnard & Noverraz, 1985 et 1986).

Données de déplacement

L'ensemble de ces mesures a permis la mise en évidence de variations
considérables de l'activité du glissement entre différentes périodes
d'activité "normale" d'une part, et surtout entre ces périodes
d'activité normale et les périodes de crise d'autre part: la crise de
l'hiver 1966 a provoqué un déplacement de l'ordre de 12 m de la
partie basse du glissement en trois à quatre mois (7-8 m pour la
route), alors que celle de 1981-1982 s'est conclue par un déplacement
de 4 m de la route en trois mois (fig. 3).
     On ne connaît pas avec précision la répartition et l'amplitude des
mouvements durant l'ensemble de la crise de 1966. Les déplacements
totaux sont tirés des mesures pour la période 1957-1969, par
déduction des déplacements moyens à long terme pour les douze années.
     On sait que les mouvements furent très faibles durant la période
1969-1974 et vraisemblablement 1967-1974 (quelques cm/an pour la

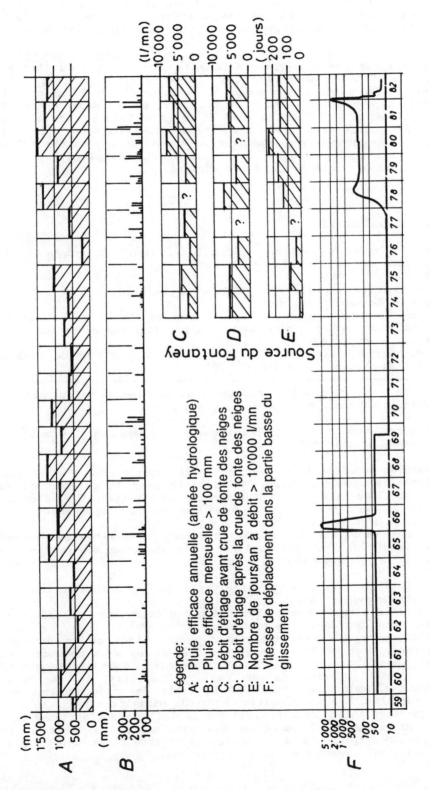

FIG 3   Comparaison des séries temporelles hydrologiques et des vitesses de déplacement du glissement.

partie la plus rapide du glissement), et cela malgré le printemps très humide de 1970, marqué par une fonte rapide d'un tapis neigeux très épais. On sait aussi que les années postérieures à la crise de 1981-1982 furent caractérisées par des mouvements également très faibles

Pour le très long terme, on sait par la comparaison d'états cadastraux que les déplacements dans la partie basse du glissement furent de 45 cm/an de 1768 à 1861 et de 62 cm/an de 1861 à 1982; sachant en outre que le mouvement de la route fut de 22 m entre 1840 et 1867 (Lugeon et al., 1922), on peut évaluer les déplacements à 36 cm/an de 1768 à 1840 (72 ans) et à 65 cm/an de 1840 à 1985 (125 ans), soit une accélération très importante. Les données climatiques manquent cependant pour permettre une corrélation avec ces valeurs. On peut voir par contre dans celles-ci l'explication de la surélévation actuelle du lit de la rivière.

Données hydrologiques

Grâce aux réseaux fédéraux, nous bénéficions de longues séries temporelles sur les paramètres suivants :

- Pluviométrie : pluies journalières à la station Leysin jusqu'en 1976 et Le Sépey depuis 1977.
- Climatologie : mesures de la hauteur de neige, mesures de température de l'air plusieurs fois par jour aux mêmes stations de Leysin et du Sépey.
- Hydrométrie : enregistrement des débits instantanés de la Grande Eau à la station Aigle depuis 1935.

Une autre série temporelle importante a été mise en valeur grâce aux services industriels de la Commune d'Aigle :

- Hydrogéologie : mesures mensuelles du débit de la source du Fontaney depuis 1974.

Les mesures acquises lors du projet DUTI (hydrométrie des ruisseaux, pluviométrie complémentaire, piézométrie dans le glissement) sont plus détaillées mais portent sur des périodes nettement plus réduites (4 ans) et sont moins utiles pour l'étude du comportement à long terme du glissement.

La mise en valeur des données hydrologiques brutes en vue de la comparaison histoire hydrologique - histoire des mouvements a été conçue de la manière suivante (fig. 3):

- Pluviométrie : reprise de l'analyse du projet DUTI avec les pluies efficaces depuis 1960.
- Hydrométrie de la Grande Eau : étude d'événements de crue par le traitement des débits de pointe.
- Hydrogéologie : traitement des hydrogrammes de la source du Fontaney pour en faire ressortir l'état des eaux souterraines à des moments choisis de l'année. Notamment, nous avons cherché à cerner les conditions de part et d'autre de la période potentiellement dangereuse de la fonte des neiges. Nous avons retenu ainsi une décomposition en trois paramètres (fig. 3):
  • caractérisation de l'état de charge des eaux souterraines en fin d'hiver, avant la crue de fonte de neige. Le débit à cette période représente le volume de la réserve d'eau dans le milieu souterrain avant une nouvelle recharge.

- état après la recharge du printemps. Ce débit sert de valeur d'index pour décrire globalement l'efficacité de l'infiltration durant la fonte.
- intensité et durée de la recharge souterraine printanière avec le nombre de jours à débit supérieur à 10'000 l/mn.

CORRELATION ENTRE DONNEES HYDROLOGIQUES ET MOUVEMENTS

En premier lieu nous examinons quelles ont été les conditions hydrologiques avant et pendant chacune des crises importantes d'activité :

- hiver et printemps 1966
- hiver 1981 - 1982

Puis nous verrons d'autre périodes caractérisées par des conditions hydrologiques a priori défavorables mais qui n'ont pas donné lieu à des mouvements importants.

I Crise de 1966

- Pluviométrie: Les précipitations du printemps et de l'été 1965 ont été particulièrement importantes. Celles de novembre et décembre se distinguent par une somme de 518 mm soit 235% des précipitations mensuelles moyennes. Cette grosse couverture neigeuse a été restituée en février 1966, mois au cours duquel les précipitations furent encore de 163 mm; elles furent à nouveau de 147 mm le mois suivant.
- Hydrométrie: Le débit de la Grande Eau a présenté une crue assez importante (39 m^3/s, environ 8 fois le débit annuel moyen) au début de la période d'accélération des mouvements (février).
- Hydrogéologie: en l'absence de mesures à la source du Fontaney, il est difficile de caractériser l'état des eaux souterraines. Il est logique de penser au vu des pluies du printemps et de l'été 1965 que le débit d'étiage durant l'hiver 1965-1966 devait être très élevé.

Les conditions hydrologiques qui semblent avoir régi cet événement sont donc une conjonction pluviométrie (y compris fonte) et état général des eaux souterraines. Les débits maxima de la rivière sont restés relativement bas.

II Crise de 1981 -1982

- Pluviométrie: Dès le début de l'année, 1981 a été très pluvieux, jusque et y compris durant les mois critiques où les précipitations ont atteint 300 mm en octobre (environ 3 fois la valeur moyenne) et 290 mm en décembre (partiellement sous forme de neige, rapidement fondue).
- Hydrométrie: La crue d'octobre dans la Grande Eau a nettement dépassé celle de 1966 avec des débits de pointe supérieurs à 50 m^3/s. Cet événement a cependant été de courte durée et n'a pas agi tout au long des mouvements.

- Hydrogéologie: La figure 3 montre un état élevé des eaux souterraines avant les déplacements, sur la base des hydrogrammes de la source du Fontaney.

Les conditions des mouvements sont ici liées à la conjonction pluviométrie antécédente et par conséquent haut niveau des eaux souterraines avec une nouvelle période très pluvieuse en automne, essentiellement sous forme liquide.

Il convient maintenant d'examiner aussi les cas où des conditions hydrologiques similaires n'ont pas conduit aux mêmes conséquences sur la stabilité des terrains. L'histoire hydrologique récente permet de sélectionner au moins trois événements de hautes eaux:

- Eté 1968: 660 mm d'eau sont tombés de juillet à septembre, soit un total comparable à celui des deux périodes de crise. La pluviométrie efficace est cependant moindre du fait de l'évapotranspiration plus élevée des mois d'été. Les débits de la Grande Eau furent importants avec une pointe de 33 m^3/s en août et surtout une pointe de 77 m^3/s en septembre, correspondant à un débit journalier maximum de 37 m^3/s. En revanche, les précipitations antécédentes furent modérées; il n'y a donc pas lieu de penser que les eaux souterraines étaient dans un état critique. Cet événement correspond par ailleurs lui aussi à la période de faibles mouvements ayant fait suite à la crise majeure de 1966.
- Printemps 1970: Le régime pluviométrique de cette période est très semblable à celui de 1966: fort couvert neigeux, pluie printanière accompagnant la fonte. Les débits de la Grande Eau sont également du même ordre de grandeur, bien que beaucoup plus persistants. Ce qui diffère en revanche, c'est les précipitations antécédentes de l'année avant l'événement. Ces conditions n'ont conduit à aucune accélération des mouvements qui sont restés très bas au cours de toute la période 1969-1976 (voir fig. 3). Il faut chercher les raisons de cette différence d'incidence sur le mouvement notamment dans le fait que les eaux souterraines n'étaient pas dans une situation critique.
- Hiver 1979-1980: 707 mm d'eau sont tombés de novembre 1979 à janvier 1980, et même 870 mm jusqu'à février 1980 ou 1'000 mm jusqu'à mars 1980. Les débits de la Grande Eau furent importants en nombre 1989 (pointe à 36 m^3/s) et février (pointe à 22 m^3/s). Ces précipitations sont cependant tombées en partie sous forme de neige, dont la fonte a été fortement différée et étalée en mai. Les précipitations antécédentes furent importantes; néanmoins l'étiage avant la crue de printemps 1989 de la source du Fontaney avait été particulièrement bas suite à la série d'années sèches qui avaient précédé (tandis que l'étiage d'été 1989 fut moyen).

A côté de ces critères hydrologiques, un autre élément semble pouvoir jouer un rôle: en période d'activité normale du glissement, le profil en long de celui-ci évolue dans le sens d'un "gonflement" de la partie médiane (+ 1 à 1,5 mètre, établi par photogrammétrie entre 1969 et 1980); cette déformation, défavorable à la stabilité, conduirait à une situation de plus en plus critique, jusqu'au moment où la conjonction d'éléments hydrologiques moteurs, non suffisants en d'autres périodes, aboutit à la crise. Cette dernière se traduirait par un profil moins critique du glissement. Celui-ci resterait par conséquent moins sensible aux événements hydrologiques défavorables durant une période de plusieurs années (voire de dix à vingt ans) après la crise, au point que son activité est même réduite à un

niveau bien inférieur à celui de l'activité moyenne à long terme
(période 1967-1974 et depuis 1982). Toutefois, pour mieux étayer
cette thèse, un contrôle de l'état du profil avant les mouvements de
1966 aurait été nécessaire, et celui-ci n'a pu être effectué, faute
de photographies aériennes de qualité adéquate.

SYNTHESE

L'examen des événements étudiés permet de conclure de la manière
suivante :
     Les événements qui ont donné lieu à une accélération des
mouvements montrent une conjonction d'une situation critique des eaux
de pluie et de fonte avec une situation de hautes eaux des réserves
souterraines. La période critique a donc été dans les deux cas
l'hiver. Ce qui semble différencier la crise plus grave de 1966 de
celle de 1981-1982, c'est la simultanéité de la pluie et de la fonte
en février, sur une courte période.
     Les événements hydrométéorologiques qui n'ont pas donné lieu à des
mouvements particuliers montrent des conditions hydrologiques
individuellement défavorables (surtout la pluviométrie), mais sans la
conjonction avec une situation critique des eaux souterraines.
     Le rôle des crues dans la Grande Eau est sans effet si la
conjonction avec les autres critères n'est pas remplie. Le cas de
crues isolées très violentes comme celle du 23 novembre 1944
(123 m^3/s) le démontre bien. Inversement, les débits de pointe durant
les crises de glissement n'étaient ni très élevés ni persistants.
Cela s'explique par le fait que les crues de la rivière jouent
surtout un rôle d'évacuation des matériaux en pied de glissement
après les mouvements et assurent ainsi la régénération progressive
des conditions d'instabilité. Elle ne sont donc pas un facteur
déclenchant des mouvements.

CONCLUSIONS

La présente étude contribue à mieux connaître les relations entre les
eaux et les glissements de terrain dans un cas de mouvement de grande
dimension de type alpin.
     La comparaison historique entre les événements hydrologiques et
l'évolution des déplacements montre la nécessité de choisir très
précautionneusement les paramètres caractéristiques. Chacun d'entre
eux doit être abordé selon différents pas de temps pour déterminer
quelles conditions ont les effets les plus sensibles sur la stabilité
du versant. La prise en compte globale des facteurs hydrologiques est
indispensable pour déterminer ces conditions.
     Dans le cas du glissement de la Frasse, nous avons pu comparer des
événements hydrologiques à première vue similaires, dont certains
avaient abouti à une accélération importante des mouvements, et
d'autres n'avaient eu aucun effet sur ceux-ci: l'analyse détaillée de
ces événements a montré que l'une des données hydrologiques les moins
apparentes, le régime des eaux souterraines, jouait un rôle
déterminant et permettait de distinguer les événements hydrologiques
de hautes eaux ayant effectivement conduit à une phase de crise du
glissement.

REFERENCES

Bersier, A. & Weidmann, M. (1970) Le glissement de terrain de
     Cergnat-La Frasse. Bull. Soc. Vaud. Sc. Nat., 334.

Bonnard, Ch. (1983) Nouvelles techniques de mesure au glissement de La Frasse (VD). <u>Route et trafic</u>, <u>1/83</u>.

Bonnard, Ch. & Noverraz, F. (1985) Projet d'Ecole DUTI, rapport final. EPFL, Lausanne.

Bonnard, Ch. & Noverraz, F. (1986) Le glissement de Cergnat-La Frasse, analyse pluridisciplinaire. DUTI-EPFL, Lausanne.

Engel, T. (1986) Nouvelles méthodes de mesures et d'analyse pour l'étude des mouvements du sol en terrains instables. Thèse EPFL, Lausanne.

Gabus, J.H. & Badoux, H. (1990) Atlas géologique de la Suisse, feuille 1985 Les Diablerets. Service hydrologique et géologique national, Berne, sous presse.

Lombard, A. et al. (1974) Atlas géologique de la Suisse, feuille 1267 Les Mosses. Service hydrologique et géologique national, Berne.

Lugeon, M., Paschoud, E. & Rothpletz, F. (1922) Le glissement de Cergnat-la Frasse, rapport d'expertise. Dép. des trav. publ. Vaud, Service des Routes, Lausanne.

Lutz, T., Parriaux, A. & Tissières, P. (1987) Traçage au Gouffre du Chevrier (Préalpes vaudoises) et méthodes d'identification de l'uranine à faible concentration. <u>Bull. Centre d'Hydrogéologie Univ. Neuchâtel</u>, <u>7</u>.

Miserez, A., Gabus, J.H., Koelbl, O., Stuby, J.J., Dupraz, H., Durussel, R. & Engel, T. (1982) Divers articles relatifs aux travaux de mensuration sur le glissement de la Frasse. <u>Mensuration, Photogrammétrie, Génie Rural</u>, <u>9/82</u>.

Hydrology in Mountainous Regions. II - Artificial Reservoirs; Water and Slopes
(Proceedings of two Lausanne Symposia, August 1990). IAHS Publ. no. 194, 1990.

Extreme floods and their morphological consequences: activities in Switzerland

A. PETRASCHECK,
Federal Office for Water Resources Management
Effingerstrasse 77, CH-3001 Bern, Switzerland

ABSTRACT Morphological changes induced by extreme floods
originate in mass movements in the upper catchments of
alpine rivers. Since the past century, river training
measures have been undertaken to prevent aggradation of
the alluvial planes of the large swiss rivers. These
measures have so far been successfull, aggradation has
been stopped and rivers are either stable or even ero-
ding. Not solved and only little investigated are the
erosion problems in the upper catchments. The 1987 floods
demonstrated that debris flows, river bed and bank erosion are even more dangerous than mere flooding. Research
on this subject has been started by an national investigation on the causes of the 1987 floods. This programme
is to be finished soon, but there must and will be a
follow up.

INTRODUCTION

The importance of geomorphological consequences of floods has been
recognized since the past century. Then, flood protection concentrated on the larger rivers and morphological problems restricted to
bed load transport, since rivers in the Prealps have generally been
in a status of aggradation, thus endangering the fertile planes by
frequent flooding. Bed load transport research in mountain rivers is
a main Swiss contribution to river morphology, calling into mind the
investigations of Meyer-Peter or Müller at the Hydraulic Laboratory
in Zürich.

Investigations on mountain torrents date back to 1864, when
Culmann listed the most dangerous torrents and estimated the costs
and means to solve the problem. Today, we may state that the problems
of larger rivers are solved - which does not mean that the necessary
maintainance and the adaption to the ever changing conditions can be
neglected - but, we still face the problem of flooding by torrents.
It is interesting to note that Culmann (1864), when describing the
torrents, hardly used the word "discharge", but was speaking of the
forces of the flowing water, thus recognizing that the problem is
less the discharge, but more the erosion and the sediment transport
within the floods. This knowledge has been forgotten for quite some
time. Floods, in particular floods of small catchments, have been
regarded as a hydrologic and hydraulic problem of peak discharges.
Just before the 1987 flood events some research programmes on
geomorphological problems have been started, but it has been the
extraordinary flood of 1987, which rembered ,that mass movements

caused by floods have severe economic consequences. The research on
debris flows, river bed and bank erosion has been intensified in the
last two years.

INVESTIGATIONS ON THE CAUSES OF THE 1987 FLOOD EVENTS

In 1987 large floods, causing a damage to property of about 1,200 Mio
sFr., ravaged Switzerland. The events may be classified extraordinary, not only because of their large discharges, but in particular because of the large number of debris flows, erosion and solid
matter transport phenomenons. The area affected was large enough to
cover different geologic formations and different land use with
varying amounts of extreme rainfall. Since extreme floods are rare
per definition, these events offered a unique change - from the
scientfic point of view - to collect data on extreme floods and
investigate causes and effects.

     Under the impression of the damages occured, the Federal
Goverment decided on a programm for immediate help and, in addition,
dedicated a sum of 2,5 Mio sFr. for a research programm on the causes
of these extreme floods. The questions to be answered are in
generalized form:
  - what have been the causes of the extreme events and the
    corresponding damage ?
  - Have men overused natural resources and, therefore, caused
    events of a magnitude not remembered so far ?
  - Has, induced by man made changes, the flood risk changed ?
  - Is, despite of the increased damage potential, the protection
    level still apropriate ?
  - Do we have the right knowleddge to design the protection works?

FIG.1 Simplified organization diagram of the programme
"Analysis of causes of 1987 flood".

The programme is soon to be finished. Objective of this paper is less to present results, since this is done in this session by five papers, which have been prepared in the scope of this programme, but to show the organization and aims of such an interdisciplinary programme.

Figure 1 shows the organization. The federal and cantonal offices formulated the questions to be answered in the scope of the programme. Their role was important in the first days and will be important again, when the findings must be transferred into measures. The lowest level is - as usual - the level, where the work has to be done, in this case by the most renomated research institutes and a number of consulting engineers. The project managment is in the responsibility of the National Flood Programme a joint coordination group of the Swiss National Hydrological and Geological Survey and the Federal Office for Water Resources Management. In addition to the general managment, which looks for the overall coordination, each project had a scientific advisor which followed the individual projects on behalf of the principal. This splitting was necessary since the investigations covered from meteorolgy to geology all fields of earth sciences. An important role for coordination is within the committee for the edition of final report. There the heads of the institutes of the major projects elaborate a synthesis of the findings of the different project

Figure 2 gives the list of the projects and the institutions carrying out the studies. There are three major groups. Aim of the first group is the investigation of the physical causes of the flood event. This group covers about 75% of the financial means, whereof 50% are dedicated to investigations concerning sediment transport and morphological changes. The second group of projects should answer on the question of likelihood of repeating of such events and the third group should check which measures must be improved. In total 18 different contracts have been issued. Cooperation between the different group was very good. It proved that an interdisciplinary project must have a certain size to allow the specialists (geologist, hydrologist, ect.) to work together for a longer time until real understanding is found.

Study of Causes of 1987 Floods   List of Projects

Project name	Responsible Institution	Project Name	Responsible Institution
ANALYSIS OF EVENTS		**ANALYSIS OF PROBABILITY**	
Impact of forests	WSL, Birmensdorf	Historic floods	University Bern, HI
Runoff simulation	EPFL Lausanne,IGR	Flood traces in sediments	EAWAG, Dübendorf
Precipitation	ETH Zürich, GI	Flood probability	University Bern, GI
Geology	ETH Zürich, IG	Climatic Change	PROCLIM, Bern
Sediment production	University Bern, GI		
Debris flows	ETH Zürich, VAW	**PROTECTION MEASURES**	
Impact of Reservoirs	BWW Bern		
Hydraulics of Reuss River	ETH Zürich, VAW	Vegetation in river courses	ETHZ Zürich, VAW
Bed load transport	EPFL Lausanne, LRH	Effect of river training	Different Consultants
Discharge determination	B+H Zürich, Consultants	Measures of public authorities	K+Z Bern, Consultants
Geomorphology	GEO7 Bern, Consultants		

FIG. 2 List of projects and executing agencies.

Some results may be sketched as follows:

- The peak discharges, even in the small catchments, are mainly due to the large sums of rainfall and only to a smaller extent to the intensities, meaning that runoff coefficients have been more important than short-term rainfall intensities. The same was observed in February 1990, when parts of the canton Valais have been struck by severe floods.
- Under saturated soil conditions the rainfall at the end of the event was transformed directly into runoff. Man made changes, like imprevious soil surfaces, have little impact in case of this extreme conditions, in particular, when the storage of water on soil surface is small owing to the steep slopes of the upper mountainous catchment.
- The high discharges combined with long duration caused severe river bed erosion. This process proved to be far more dangerous than the flooding by water only.
- Conditions for initiating debris flows could be better defined, thus enabling an outlining of endangered areas in the future. For more details on this subject reference is made to the papers of Zimmermann or Rösli & Schindler, presented in this session. We consider this as one of the most important results since the chance to compare 120 debris flow events of more than 1,000 m3 of volume is rare.
- Mobilisation of solid material in the different smaller catchments was substantial, but the potential of movable material was always higher, leaving speculations to a maximum event open.
- Erosion processes have been initiated by undercutting of slopes and only in very rare cases by direct surface erosion.
- Lake sediments of the Lake of Uri showed that the average sedimentation rate remained more or less constant for the last 1000 years, however the largest flood deposits are those of 1987, 1977 and 1868.
- Almost identical events with respect to area affected, occured in 1868 and 1834. While in the 19th century severe floods were frequent, the time from 1650 to 1750 was almost free of severe floods.
- The amount of damage on property is dependent on the activities of man in flood endangered areas. About 70% of the damages occured to roads and railways and flood protection works. Traffic lines cannot always avoid endangered areas and the tendency to build better roads to remote areas makes it likely that this damage potential will increase.

OTHER CURRENT RESEARCH ACTIVITIES IN SWITZERLAND

The above analysis of the causes of 1987 floods is perhaps the most comprehensive but not the only research activity on extreme floods and geomorphological developement. Other activities can be grouped according to the type of research and the source of financing as:

- project related research: As an example the study "Emme 2050" was recently terminated showing the past and a possible future development of the river Emme and its catchment. A study on the

discharge capacity of the Rhone River resulted in findings on
the effect of vegetation in flood plains. In the scope of the
flood protection concept for the valley of the Urner Reuss
intensive laboratory tests and mathematical modelling concerning
hydrology, hydraulics and river morphology was carried out. The
results will be incorporated in the analysis of the 1987 floods.

- Applied research which is frequently financed by offices of
  federal or cantonal governments. To improve the data base for
  extreme floods the Swiss National Hydrological and Geological
  Survey installed in addition to its regular observation network
  about 100 flood gauges, which register only the maximum flood
  level. The Federal Office for Water Resources Management initiated a programme on determination of PMP and PMF, which are
  important for the design of safe dams.
- Basic research which is financed the National Science Foundation
  or by funds of the universities. The sixth series of National
  Research Programmes, which is now in evaluation, includes a
  proposal on natural desasters in relation whith climatic
  changes.
- National programmes on special occasions are generally funded by
  the Federal Government. In March 1990 the Federal Government
  decided to contribute to the International Decade for Natural
  Desaster Prevention initiated by the UNO. The committee is
  formed now and the activities will soon be decided. Problems
  which concern extreme floods are closely related to climatic
  conditions. Therefore a close cooperation with the national
  programme PROCLIM, dealing with the expected climatic changes,
  is assured.

An other systematic approach to outline current research activities could be in enumerating the research centers and their main
fields of activities. This is rather dangerous, since certainly all
geological, geomorphological, hydrological, hydraulic and meteorological institutes are confronted once with floods and morphological
problems. A summary of swiss contributions to flood hydrology has
recently been published by R.Weingartner und M.Spreafico (1990). The
present enumeration therefore can be restricted to the most important
centers where flood induced morphological changes are investigated.

The Laboratory of Hydraulics, Hydrology and Glaciology at the
Federal Institute of Technology in Zürich (ETHZ) are known for its
long experience in river morphology and bed-load transport research.
The formula by Smart & Jäggi (1983) for bed load transport in steep
mountain channels and the recent studies on debris flows are
contributions to the better understanding of torrents. There are
close cooperations with other Institutes of the ETHZ.

The Federal Research Institute for Forest, Snow and Landscape in
Birmensdorf concentrates its investigations on the protective effects
of forests in case of rockfall avalanches and floods.

The Institute for Land and Water Management at the Federal
Institute of Technology in Lausanne (EPFL) investigates primarily on
flood and erosion formation in small rural catchments.

The Geographic Institute at the University of Bern has a hydrology and a geomorphology section. The latter is in particular concerned on erosion rates and sediment budgets. Studies of processes during flood events with the target on outlining endangered areas are carried out.

The work of several institutions is not mentioned for the sake of shortness of this paper.

Todays public oppinion demands high safety against natural desasters and Switzerland is in the lucky situation to be able to afford this safety. Therefore research on the extreme events will certainly intensify in the near future. Intensification is in particular necessary for the water related mass transports in mountain areas, since these problems have been neglected for long time in favour of hydrology and hydraulics.

REFERENCES

Culmann, (1864) Bericht an den hohen schweizerischen Bundesrat über die Untersuchungen der schweizer Wildbäche., Zürcher und Furrer, Zürich.

Smart, G., & Jäggi,M. (1983) Sediment transport on steep slopes. Mittl.der VAW 63, Zürich.

Weingartner, R.& Spreafico, M.(1990) Analyse und Abschätzung von Hochwasserabflüssen - Eine Uebersicht über neuere schweizerische Arbeiten. Deut. Gewässerkundl. Mittl. Jg 1990 (2), Koblenz.

Hydrology in Mountainous Regions.   II - Artificial Reservoirs; Water and Slopes
(Proceedings of two Lausanne Symposia, August 1990). IAHS Publ. no. 194, 1990.

Debris flows 1987 in Switzerland: modelling and fluvial sediment transport

D. RICKENMANN
Laboratory of hydraulics, hydrology and glaciology,
ETH - Zentrum, CH-8092 Zürich, Switzerland

ABSTRACT   An attempt is made to apply a simple avalanche model to some of the numerous debris flows that occurred in Switzerland in summer 1987. The model is based on two friction components. With observed runout distances and velocity estimates from field evidence, possible combinations of the two parameters are determined which best describe the actual field event. - A bed load transport formula is applied to the Münster creek flood event. The combination with an estimated flood hydrograph based on rainfall data leads to calculated fluvial sediment volumes, which are compared with field estimates.

INTRODUCTION

In mountain torrents there are two kinds of massive sediment transport processes which can lead to the deposition of huge amounts of gravel, sand and silt on alluvial fans: Debris flows and fluvial sediment transport. These processes occur during rainstorm events, and particularly the fast moving debris flow fronts may be destructive along the river course or in the fan area. Damage can also be caused by a damming of the main river due to a massive sediment input from a torrent. There are a number of theoretical approaches to treat these phenomena, but practical methods are still rather limited (Meunier, 1989; Takahashi, 1987).

During the summer 1987 two major rainstorm events occurred in Switzerland. Many debris flows were triggered in the Alps, and flooding caused problems in some of the main rivers. In an interdisciplinary study, the debris flow events were analysed in detail (Haeberli et al., 1990a). The geomorphological and meteorological aspects of these events are discussed by Zimmermann (1990), and the geological and hydrogeological situation is presented by Rösli & Schindler (1990). Here a simple avalanche model is applied to some of these debris flow events. The model allows to determine the velocities along the flow path and to estimate the runout distance. In the second part, bed load transport calculations are made to estimate sediment volumes which resulted from fluvial processes.

DEBRIS FLOW MODELLING

To estimate the runout distance of a debris flow, Takahashi (1981) proposed a theoretical approach based on energy or momentum conservation. A similar model had earlier been developed for snow avalanches (Salm, 1966). These models may be used when there is a fairly well defined change in slope from the transportation reach to the deposition zone.

Based on a similar approach, Körner (1980) presented a model to compute the velocity development along the whole avalanche path. As in earlier works on snow avalanches (Salm, 1966), it is assumed that the motion is mainly governed by two frictional components: A sliding friction coefficient and a turbulent friction coefficient that is determined by a Chezy-type relation. This allows to account for both solid-to-solid and fluid like shear stresses. The resulting equation gives the velocity v_{i+1} at the end of a segement of constant slope, if the input velocity v_i from the previous segement is known:

$$v_{i+1} = [v_{ei}^2 - (v_{ei}^2 - v_i^2)\ \exp(-2\ \frac{\Delta s_i}{k_2})]^{1/2} \qquad (1)$$

with
$$v_e = [H\ C^2\ (\sin\theta - \mu\cos\theta)]^{1/2} \qquad (2)$$

$$k_2 = \frac{H\ C^2}{g} \qquad (3)$$

where v_e: maximum velocity on a path of constant slope, Δs: length of the segement, H: flow depth, C: Chezy friction coefficient [$m^{1/2}$ /s], θ: slope angle, μ: sliding friction coefficient, g: gravitational acceleration, and the parameter k_2 [m] accounts for turbulent friction effects.

Theoretically, the two parameters μ and k_2 can assume different values for each segment. However, since there is not enough detailed data available, they are generally taken as constant over the whole flow path. Perla et al. (1980), using the same model, interpret the parameter k_2 as mass-to-drag ratio, and they discuss the effects of these two components on the value of k_2.

At concave transitions in slope, Perla et al. (1980) introduce a momentum correction, which is also applied in our case:

$$v_{i+1} = v_i\ \cos(\theta_i - \theta_{i+1}) \qquad (4)$$

The model is applied here to 8 debris flow events that occurred in the summmer 1987 in Switzerland. To determine possible combinations of the two friction parameters μ and k_2, two different criteria are used: Either there were velocity estimates at several cross sections, or the stopping point is well defined, if the flow deposited all the material without any major obstructions in the depositional area. From superelevation measurements in the field the velocity could be estimated for three events (cases no. 1, 3 and 4 in Table 1); in one case (no. 2) the velocity head was used to obtain velocity estimates. For all the other events (cases no. 5 to 8) the stopping point (where v = 0; known from the observed runout distance) was selected as criterion two compute the appropriate model parameters.

In principle, there are many possible combinations of μ and k_2 that satisfy the relatively poor field data. For given flow conditions, for example, the same runout distance can be obtained by different combinations of μ and k_2; the choice of a larger μ value generally requires an increase in k_2, resulting in higher flow velocities. An additional restriction is therefore introduced by limiting the maximum velocity to 30 m/s. Values for debris flows reported in the literature range up to about 20 m/s, but they were obtained at slopes below about 20° (Costa, 1984). The results of the model computations for the Swiss debris flow events are shown in Table 1.

DeLeon & Jeppson (1982) determined the Chezy-coefficient for some debris flows reported in the literature; all values lie within the range of 3 to 25. For the Swiss events the flow depths varied between about 1 and 5 m; using an average depth of 2 m, C values have been calculated in Table 1 (by equ. 3). It is seen that for μ values smaller than about 0.1, similar C values as given by DeLeon and Jeppson (1982) are obtained. This is not surprising since equ. (2) becomes identical with the Chezy formula for $\mu = 0$.

The resulting parameter combinations are also plotted in Fig.1, together with data from other events. Line A represents data for the 1970 ice/rock slide of Mount Huascaran (Peru), and line B gives possible parameter combinations for a snow avalanche with measured

TABLE 1   Model parameters μ and k_2 as computed for Swiss debris flow
events. Also given are mean slope f_p between starting and
end point, maximum velocity v_{max} corresponding to upper
value of k_2, and Chezy coefficient C for an assumed average
flow depth of 2 m.

No/event	f_p	μ	k_2 range [m]	k_2 [m]	v_{max} [m/s]	C [$m^{1/2}/s$]
1 Varuna	0.35	0.00	10 - 40	25	14	11
		0.05	10 - 50	30	15	12
		0.10	20 - 80	50	18	16
		0.15	130 - 170	150	23	27
2 Plaunca	0.33	0.00	40 - 50	45	19	15
		0.05	50 - 70	60	20	17
		0.10	70 - 130	100	25	22
3 Zavragia	0.24	0.00	40 - 100	70	21	19
		0.05	100 - 160	130	25	25
4 Münster	0.20	0.00	30 - 130	80	25	20
		0.05	40 - 200	120	29	24
5 Witenw.	0.35	0.10	10 - 60	35	17	13
		0.15	150 - 200	175	25	30
		0.20	300 - 400	350	28	42
		0.25	550 - 700	630	31	56
6 Lucendro	0.29	0.10	80 - 130	105	21	23
		0.15	160 - 200	180	24	30
		0.20	250 - 350	300	25	39
		0.25	400 - 600	500	25	50
7a Chüeboden	0.43	0.20	80 - 130	105	21	23
		0.25	160 - 260	210	26	32
		0.30	280 - 440	360	28	42
7b Gerental	0.24	0.05	1 - 20	10	10	7
		0.10	150 - 160	155	25	28
8 Saastal	0.28	0.05	1 - 50	25	16	11
		0.10	140 - 280	210	30	32

velocities (both lines taken from Körner, 1980). The lines K1 and K2
were determined from data of a japanese debris flow observation
station. In a study of Okuda et al. (1980) velocity measurements are
given together with the longitudinal profile for two debris flows of
Aug 14, 1976 (K1) and July 19, 1976 (K2). Using this information,
parameter combinations for K1 and K2 were "calibrated" with the
model.

It is interesting that the lines K1 and K2 plot within the same
region in Fig. 1 as is indicated by the lines representing the Swiss
data. With these events, the volumes involved in one single debris
surge was of the order of 1'000 to several 10'000 m³. The Huascaran
slide (line A) was much larger (volume of about 5·10⁷ m³) and had an
estimated flow depth of about 100 m (Körner, 1980); although the
debris stream contained some (melting) ice, the material composition
is in principle similar to a debris flow. The volume of the snow
avalanche (line B) was about 10'000 m³; in this case the different
material characteristics may be the reason, why the parameters lie
away from the region for the debris flow events.

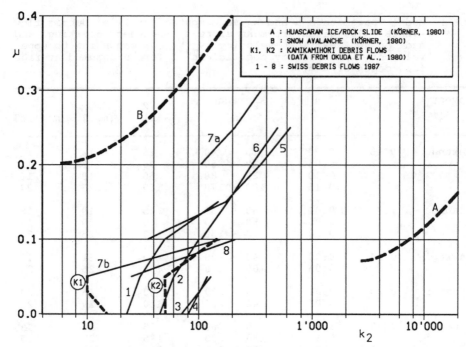

FIG. 1   Resulting combinations of the model parameters μ
and k_2,   for the Swiss events (no. 1 to 8) and other data.

Considering the Swiss events only, there is a tendency   for   flows
with a larger catchment area at the point of initiation (cases no. 1,
2, 3, 4, 7b and 8) to require smaller μ values than the   events   with
smaller catchment areas (no. 5, 6 and 7a). This fact may be explained
with larger amounts of water available in the main channel to   dilute
the   grain   mixture   of   the   debris   flow. A dilution will change the
rheological properties of the grain-water mixture, reducing its shear
strength   (Costa,   1984).   In   the above model, the parameter μ could
partly account for the shear strength characteristic of debris flows.

Alean (1984) determined possible parameter combinations for 19 ice
avalanches in the Alps. His best-fit parameters are generally   larger
(μ   up   to 0.7, k_2 up to 100'000) than for the debris flows. He found
that both μ and the mean slope (f_p) tend to decrease with   increasing
ice   volumes.   A   similar conclusion results from the analysis of the
numerous Swiss debris flow events (Zimmermann, 1990). Thus it appears
that   smaller   μ   values   are associated with smaller mean slopes and
probably with larger involved volumes.

It   should   be   pointed   out   that the runout distance can only be
modeled if the μ value is larger than the actual deposition slope. If
μ   approaches   this slope the computed runout distance is very sensitive to small changes in μ. With the events   no.   1   -   4,   the   main
objective   was   to   model   the velocity development; therefore also μ
values equal to zero were used.

SEDIMENT TRANSPORT

On August 24/25, 1987, a major rainstorm hit the central   area   of
Switzerland.   In the Münster creek, a debris flow occurred at about 1
p.m. of the 24th, several hours before the   peak   rainfall   intensity
during the following night. The debris flow was initiated in a steep

rocky couloir below the tongue of a glacier and flowed over a distance of about 5 km, stopping in the village of Münster. The catchment has an area of 15 km², and the mean creek gradient is 23%.

According to eyewitness accounts there was only one debris flow
surge which reached the alluvial fan, where large amounts of gravel
and sand were deposited between and in the houses of the village
Münster. Further deposition on the fan area due to fluvial sediment
transport is reported to have occurred mainly during the following
night. Numerous photographs document the situation during and after
the flood event. It was therefore possible to estimate the deposited
sediment volumes from both processes separately. The following
figures resulted from an analysis of deposition heights and involved
areas (Raetzo, 1989): 25'000 - 30'000 m³ of material deposited by the
debris flow event and 10'000 - 20'000 m³ of sediment resulting from
fluvial transport during the flood event.

Here an attempt is made to estimate the fluvial sediment volume by
combining sediment transport calculations with the flood hydrograph.
In a laboratory study Rickenmann (1990) determined bed load transport
rates in a steep flume, considering also the influence of high
suspended fine material concentrations. As long as the flow around
the grains is turbulent, this influence can be accounted for by an
appropriate exponent of the density factor (s-1). Data from similar
steep flume experiments of Smart & Jaeggi (1983) was also used in
developing the proposed formula:

$$q_B = \frac{12.6}{(s-1)^{1.6}} \left(\frac{d_{90}}{d_{30}}\right)^{0.2} (q - q_{cr}) \, J^{2.0} \tag{5}$$

where q_B is the bed load transport rate per unit width, $s = \rho_s/\rho_f$ is
the ratio of the grain to the fluid density, q is the specific
discharge per unit width, d_{90} and d_{30} are characteristic grain sizes,
at which 90% and 30% by weight of material are finer, and J is the
bed slope; q_{cr} is the critical discharge per unit width for beginning of transport:

$$q_{cr} = 0.065 \, (s-1)^{1.67} \, g^{0.5} \, d_m^{1.5} \, / \, J^{1.12} \tag{6}$$

where d_m is the mean grain size. Equation (6) represents a slight
modification of a formula proposed by Bathurst et al. (1987), and it
is partly based on the steep flume data leading to equ. (5). Whittaker and Jaeggi (1986) performed tests on the stability of block ramps
at slopes up to 25%; they developed a very similar equation, but with
a constant about a factor of two higher than the one in equ. (6).

For clear water one can put (s-1) = 1.65 and for a uniform grain
size distribution $(d_{90}/d_{30})^{0.2} = 1.05$ (Smart & Jaeggi, 1983). Then
equ. (5) can be simplified to:

$$q_B = 5.9 \, F \, (q - q_{cr}) \, J^2 \tag{7}$$

where F is a factor accounting for the combined effects of a changed
fluid density and a wide grain size distribution.

Information on the characteristic grain sizes in the Münster creek
was obtained from several frequency-by-number transect samples of the
armour layer. Subsequent transformation into a sieve-by-weight distribution of the whole grain mixture yielded the following values: d_m
= 0.16 m, d_{30} = 0.04 m, d_{90} = 0.42 m. This gives a ratio d_{90}/d_{30} of
10.5, resulting in a factor F of about 1.5.

According to the documents, an increased fine material concentration existed only for some hours immediately after the passage of the
debris flow, later the discharge appeared to be relatively clear. A
value of (s-1) = 1.65 was therefore used to determine q_{cr} from equ.
(6). The transport calculations were performed for an average cross

section at the head of the fan. The mean width there is 7 m and the bed slope 13 %. Flow resistance calculations resulted in flow depths of less than one meter, therefore a rectangular cross section was assumed and no sidewall correction was introduced.

In a first case (A), the critical discharge q_{cr} was determined with d_m, resulting in Q_{cr} = 2.1 m³/s (where Q_{cr} is equal to q_{cr} times the flow width). Since in this case the transport calculations yielded too high sediment volumes, a larger characteristic grain size was selected in equ. (6), i.e. d = 0.4 m ≈ d_{90}, giving Q_{cr} = 8.2 m³/s (case B). The laboratory tests leading to equ. (6) mainly involved relatively uniform sediments and rather flat beds. In a torrent, however, with a very wide grain size distribution and large boulders the bed surface is quite irregular both laterally and in the longitudinal direction (steps and pools). Therfore the critical discharge might in fact be higher. This is also indicated by the study of Whittaker and Jaeggi (1983) for flows with large relative roughnesses and steep slopes.

The flood hydrograph was constructed from given rainfall intensity data for three hour intervalls (based on interpolation from nearby raingauge stations). A runoff coefficient of 0.3 (at the beginning) up to 0.6 (at peak intensities and later) was selected; the resulting discharges for the afternoon period were slightly reduced, because hydraulic estimates based on photographs indicated smaller flow rates. The hydrograph is shown in Fig. 2.

In the sediment transport calculations it was assumed that no transport occurred before the passage of the debris flow. Probably a coarse armour layer had paved the creek bed before the event; in the main deposition zone of the debris flow numerous boulders with grain sizes from 0.5 to 1.5 m could be found. The eyewitnesses did not

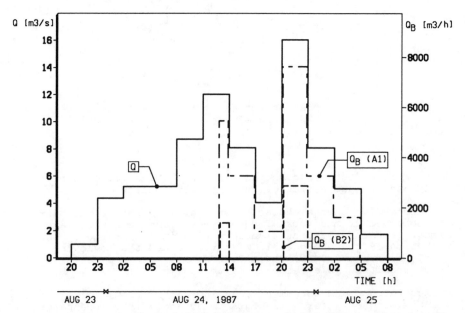

FIG. 2 Constructed flood hydrograph for Münster creek and two calculated sediment graphs. (See text and Table 2 for explanation of cases A1 and B2.)

report any significant transport on the morning of Aug 24. Bed load transport rates were computed with equ. (7), choosing a factor F = 1 and F = 1.5 for both cases A and B. Two sediment graphs (upper and lower extreme, cases A1 and B2) are also shown in Fig. 2. The resulting sediment volumes are presented in Table 2.

From the comparison of the observed fluvial deposits of the order of 10'000 to 20'000 m³ with the figures in Table 2 it can be concluded that the direct application of a sediment transport formula predicts too large sediment volumes; only if a higher critical discharge is introduced (case B), there is a better agreement with the observation. In case A, substantial amounts of sediment would have been transported in the afternoon, contrary to the observations.

TABLE 2 Calculated fluvial sediment volumes by combining the flood hydrograph with the bed load transport formula (7).

case	Q_{cr} [m³/s]	F	Volume [m³]
A1	2.1	1.5	57'000
A2	2.1	1.0	38'000
B1	8.2	1.5	15'000
B2	8.2	1.0	10'000

In the above example, full availability of sediment was assumed after the passage of the debris flow. During the receding part of the flood hydrograph, a new armour layer had been formed. With a wide grain size distribution, the critical shear stress for the breakup of the armour layer may be higher than the Shields stress for initiation of motion (Naef & Bezzola, 1990). This also indicates that the critical discharge for substantial sediment transport is higher than in the case of a relatively uniform grain size mixture. The above result seems to be confirmed in general from the calculations for other flood events where also a higher critical discharge than determined by equ. (6) had to be introduced to find better agreement between computed and estimated sediment volumes (Haeberli et al., 1990b).

CONCLUSIONS

A two parameter model originally developed for snow avalanches has been applied to some Swiss debris flow events. The resulting parameter combinations are in agreement with data from measured velocities of two japanese debris flows. A prediction of the runout distance is only possible if µ is larger than the deposition slope. For a practical application of the model more precise information on the values of the two parameters is needed. Hydraulic model tests could be performed to examine how the parameters depend on material characteristics and bed roughness.

Direct application of a bed load transport formula to a flood event in a torrent yielded much larger sediment volumes than those estimated from the deposited material. It appears that the effective transport rates are probably smaller in the field than in the laboratory because (a) the threshold discharge for beginning of substantial sediment transport is higher due to very irregular flow conditions (large relative roughness, wide grain size distribution, irregular bed profile) and (b) there is probably not a full availability of loose material even after the passage of a debris flow.

REFERENCES
Alean, J. (1984):
    Untersuchungen über Entstehungsbedingungen und Reichweiten von

Eislawinen. Mitt. der Versuchsanstalt für Wasserbau, Hydrologie und Glaziologie, ETH Zürich, Nr. 74.

Bathurst, J.C., Graf, W.H. and Cao, H.H. (1987):
Bed load discharge equations for steep mountain rivers. In Sediment transport in gravel bed rivers, eds. Thorne, Bathurst, Hey, John Wiley and Sons, 453–477.

Costa, J.E. (1984):
Physical geomorphology of debris flows. In Developments and applications of geomorphology, eds. Costa and Fleisher, Springer-Verlag, Berlin and Heidelberg.

Haeberli, W., Rickenmann, D., Rösli, U., Zimmermann, M. (1990a):
Investigation of 1987 debris flows in the Swiss Alps: General concept and geophysical soundings. Proc. Int. Conf. on Water Resources in Mountainous Regions, same issue.

Haeberli, W., Rickenmann, D., Rösli, U., Zimmermann, M. (1990b):
Murgänge 1987: Dokumentation und Analyse. Mitt. der Versuchsanstalt für Wasserbau, Hydrologie und Glaziologie, ETH Zürich, in preparation.

Körner, H.J. (1980):
Modelle zur Berechnung der Bergsturz- und Lawinenbewegung. Proc. Int. Symposium Interpraevent, Bad Ischl, A, 15–55.

Meunier, M. (1989):
Quelques éléments d'hydraulique torrentielle. Edition provisoire, CEMAGREF, Grenoble, France.

Naef, F., Bezzola, G.R. (1990):
Hydrology and morphological consequences of the 1987 flood event in the upper Reuss valley. Proc. Int. Conf. on Water Resources in Mountainous Regions, same issue.

Okuda, S., Suwa, H., Okunishi, K., Yokoyama, K., Nakano, M. (1980):
Observations on the motion of a debris flow and its geomorphological effects. Z. Geomorphol., Suppl. Bd. 35, 142–163.

Perla, R., Cheng, T.T., McClung, D.M. (1980):
A two-parameter-model of snow avalanche motion. J. Glaciol., 26 (94), 197–207.

Raetzo, H. (1989):
Zwischenbericht der Semesterarbeit über Münster, Universität Freiburg, Schweiz. Unpublished report.

Rickenmann, D. (1990):
Bedload transport capacity of slurry flows at steep slopes. Mitt. Nr. 103 der Versuchsanstalt für Wasserbau, Hydrologie und Glaziologie, ETH Zürich, in press.

Rösli, U., Schindler, C. (1990):
Debris flows 1987 in Switzerland: Geological and hydrogeological aspects. Proc. International Conference on Water Resources in Mountainous Regions, same issue.

Salm, B. (1966):
Contribution to avalanche dynamics. Proc. Int. Symp. on Scientific Aspects of Snow and Ice Avalanches, Christchurch, N.Z., IAHS Publ. No. 69, 199–214.

Smart, G.M., Jäggi, M.N.R. (1983):
Sediment transport on steep slopes. Mitt. Nr. 64 der Versuchsanstalt für Wasserbau, Hydrologie und Glaziologie, ETH Zürich.

Takahashi, T. (1981):
Estimation of potential debris flows and their hazardous zones; soft countermeasures for a disaster. J. Natural Disaster Science, 3(1), 57–89.

Takahashi, T. (1987):
High velocity flow in steep erodible channels. Proc. 22nd IAHR Congress, Lausanne, Switzerland, Tech. Session A, 42–53.

Whittaker, J., Jäggi, M.N.R. (1986):
Blockschwellen. Mitt. Nr. 91 der Versuchsanstalt für Wasserbau, Hydrologie und Glaziologie, ETH Zürich.

Zimmermann, M. (1990):
Debris flows 1987 in Switzerland: Geomorphological and hydrometeorological aspects. Proc. Int. Conf. on Water Resources in Mountainous Regions, same issue.

Hydrology in Mountainous Regions. II - Artificial Reservoirs; Water and Slopes
(Proceedings of two Lausanne Symposia, August 1990). IAHS Publ. no. 194, 1990.

Debris flows 1987 in Switzerland:
geological and hydrogeological aspects

U. ROESLI, C. SCHINDLER
Ingenieurgeologie, ETH Zürich, ETH Hönggerberg, CH-8093 Zürich

ABSTRACT A great number of debris flows occurred in the Swiss Alps during
catastrophic flood events in the summer of 1987. The geological and hydrogeological
aspects have been studied in detail. The regions affected mainly are located in
crystalline bedrock covered by massif to stratified and loose glacial or talus deposits
with poor sorting and with low clay and modest silt contents. Two main types of
failure mechanisms have been recognized: the slope type and the torrent bed type
debris flows. The main starting condition for the collapses observed is a high amount
of water, infiltrating the soils and creating a local saturation zone which may liquefy.
As failure mechanisms are complex, prediction of exact location and time of flow
initiation is difficult. However, in most investigated areas the potential for future
debris flows is still high.

INTRODUCTION

Alluvial fans in mountainous regions document both in geomorphological appearance as well as in
sedimentary texture the repeated occurrence of debris flows. In inhabited areas debris flows usually
cause damage to human work, to land resources and may even claim lives. During the flood events of
summer 1987 in the Swiss Alps a high number of debris flows of variable dimensions occurred,
covering pastures and destroying roads and railway tracks. The Federal Government initiated a research
programme to document and to understand the causes of such flood events. One project especially
investigated the debris flows. The general concept of the project and the results of geophysical soundings are described by Haeberli et al. (1990). The geomorphological aspects of the debris flows are
presented by Zimmermann (1990) and dynamic considerations are given by Rickenmann (1990). The
following discussion concentrates on the geological and hydrogeological aspects.

Debris flows have been described from all over the world (e.g. Hutchinson, 1988). Beside the
slope inclination and the vegetation, the availability of water and the physical properties of the debris
are most important for their initiation. During the 1987 events most slope failures to cause debris flows
occurred in surficial deposits. Bedrock failures, a further major potential for creating debris flows
(Eisbacher & Clague, 1984), were only subordinately involved in the primary initiation process, but
were a major element in secondary debris flows.

BEDROCK GEOLOGY

The main regions of 1987 debris flow occurrences with respect to the bedrock geology are given in Fig.
1. Most events happened in the area of crystalline rocks of the Aar and Gotthard massifs as well as of
the Penninic nappes in Central Switzerland (Fig. 1, III and I). The typical bedrocks are granites and
gneisses with a weak schistosity. The Vorderrheintal area (I) is situated in the borderzone between Aar
and Gotthard massifs. Here too, bedrock at the debris flow failure points is of crystalline and metamor-
phic origin. The lower parts of the catchment areas are composed of mica-rich schists of the Tavetsch

379

massif and of phyllites, metakonglomerates and dolomites with an alpine metamorphism in greenschist facies. The schists and phyllites show a distinct cleavage and are, therefore, rather susceptible to erosional processes. The marked cleavage planes in these rocks allow the formation of large slides. The permeability is very low.

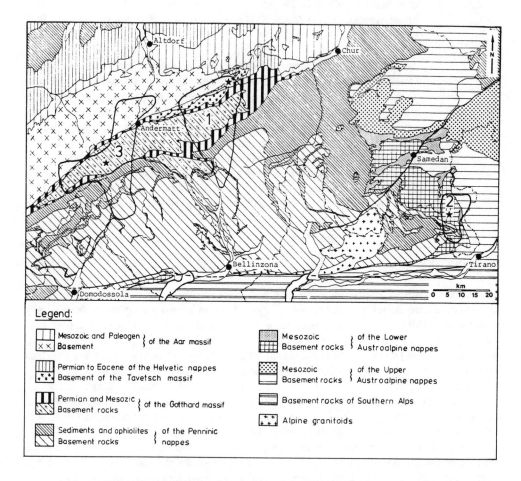

FIG. 1 Tectonic sketch map of Central Switzerland with the main regions showing debris flow activity during 1987. 1 = Vorderrheintal-Val Blenio (star = Plaunca Valley); 2 = Bernina-Poschiavo (star = Varuna Valley); 3 = Upper Goms-Gotthard-Val Bedretto-Val Bavona (star = Geren Valley).

Another badly hit region is the Varuna Valley near Poschiavo in Eastern Switzerland (Fig. 1, II). It is cut entirely in the mica-rich gneisses and schists with rare occurrences of graphitic phyllites of the Bernina nappe. The slopes around Varuna Valley are deeply disintegrated by ancient sagging of the bedrock (Naef et al., 1990). The lithological, structural and hydrogeological observations show that the Varunasch river follows the boundary between two major sagging masses. The bedrock resembles partly loose debris.

A few regions outside of the crystalline massifs, e.g. in the Prättigau Flysch, in the Molasse and in the Helvetic Alps, were affected by 1987 debris flow activity as well. However, because of the widely varying soil properties, as a function of bedrock lithologies, these regions will not be considered although debris flows occurred frequently in these regions during other flood events, as well.

SURFICIAL DEPOSITS IN REGIONS WITH CRYSTALLINE BEDROCK

Stiny (1910) has subdivided the surficial deposits into two main groups, i.e. the "Altschutt" deposits where debris accumulation has more or less stopped and the "Jungschutt" where accumulation processes are active. During 1987 the initiation of the huge debris flows frequently occurred in "Altschutt" deposits covering crystalline rocks, where large Little Ice-Age moraines and moraine slope accumulations occur at higher elevations. The vegetation cover is mostly negligible. The deposits are loose and display often stratification with alternating beds containing either large boulders or a higher sand and silt content. The pebbles are frequently platy and orientated. Fig. 2 shows the strata in a moraine slope in the Geren Valley where the beds are parallel to or even steeper than the present surface. Other localities display layers with an inclination parallel to or flatter than the slope (Fig. 3). The coarse grained beds may not be continuous but form lenses surrounded by finer material (Fig. 2). These beds may have been formed as mud and debris flows of till material in the forefields of small glaciers and by material from rockfalls and avalanches (Zimmermann & Haeberli, 1989).

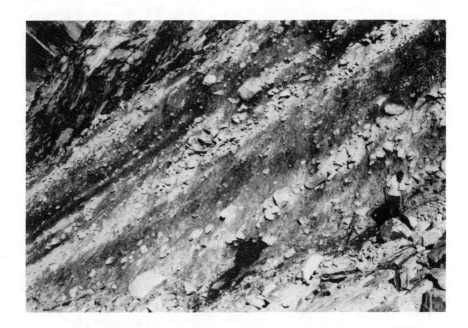

FIG. 2 Starting zone of the debris flow at the locality "Chiebode" in the Geren Valley at 2380 m a.s.l. (Swiss co-ordinates 675.93/150.53). The moraine slope is made up of stratified glacial deposits with lenses and strata of coarse grained material. Dark spot is a sample locality.

The geological situation at the initiation point of the debris flow in the Plaunca Valley is unique for the 1987 events. Fine-grained, loamy glacial deposits with a small amount of subangular and oriented pebbles, comparable to basal lodgement till, are overlain by coarser till flow sediments with a higher content of subangular to rounded pebbles.

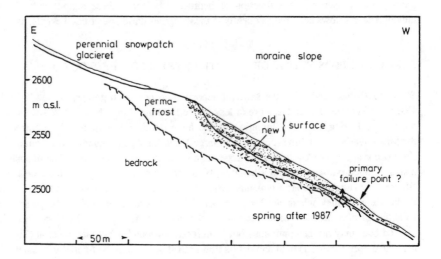

FIG. 3 Longitudinal section through the failure zone of the Witenwasseren debris flow (Swiss co-ordinates 682.33/155.11). The bedrock surface has been determined by seismic investigations. The strata in the upper part have a smaller, in the lower part the same inclination as the slope. The primary failure point may be at the border between these two slope sections at about 2490 m a.s.l.. Nowadays the water percolating in the debris drains to the slope surface where bedrock is nearest at 2490 m a.s.l..

Also "Jungschutt" deposits were often involved in debris flow initiation. This type of debris occurs in talus slopes, mostly at the bottom of steep cliffs, or as accumulations in mountain torrents. These deposits are often characterized by a weak stratification and by loose layering of angular, partially orientated components.

Debris properties

Grain size distribution as well as plasticity and mineralogy has been determined for the surficial deposits in the failure as well as in the major erosion zones of the debris flows. The grain size distribution of the particles <6 cm is given in Fig. 4. Discussing these analyses it has to be kept in mind that in reality most deposits contain a high fraction of material >6 cm, the influence of which on the geotechnical parameters is only poorly known (Takahashi, 1980).

The grain size distributions of the glacial deposits with crystalline bedrock are comparable to those of basal lodgement tills or of slightly sorted till-flow-sediments (Schlüchter, 1990). The medium clay content of 13 analyses is 1.5 ±1.0 wt%, the silt content is 11.7 ±5.6 wt%. The uniformity coefficient (Cu) is mostly high (17-341). The six talus deposits contain even smaller amounts of clay (1.0 ±0.5 wt%) and of silt fraction (8.9 ±2.8 wt%), with a uniformity coefficient up to 454. All these materials consist of 40-60 wt% quartz and of feldspar, mica and minor amounts of chlorite. This composition is typical for debris formed by disintegration of crystalline rock. The consistency limits could not be determined because of the very low plasticity index which is caused by the mineralogical composition without clay minerals. Sample PL3 1740 from the Plaunca Valley is in its grain size distribution (Fig. 4) comparable to a basal lodgement till (Schlüchter, 1980), with a high clay (8.5 wt%) and silt fraction (33.5 wt%), but, again, with no measurable plasticity.

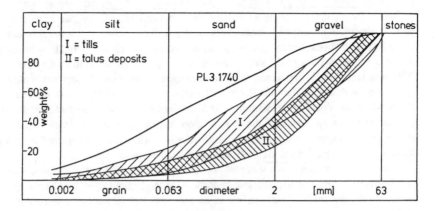

FIG. 4 Grain size distribution of the surficial deposits in the debris flow failure zones
and in the sectors with major erosion. Sample PL3 1740 is a basal lodgement till from
the Plaunca Valley (Vorderrheintal).

The investigated surficial deposits have no plasticity and, therefore, no effective cohesion. The
stability is mainly dependent of the angle of internal friction (φ'). This parameter can be estimated
roughly from the grain size distributions (Lang & Huder, 1984). Such an approach does not consider the
influence of the mineralogical composition, e.g. of the mica content, on the angle of internal friction.
This relationship is only poorly known and should be investigated further. However, Hohensinn (1979)
demonstrates that there is no obvious connection between the content of sheet silicates (micas, chlorite)
and the angle of internal friction.

The calculated values for φ' are between 31 and 37^0 for the sediments at the debris flow initiation
points in the glacial and talus deposits. The slope inclinations in the failure zones vary between 29 and
37^0. The medium deviation of the calculated φ' from the slope angles is -1^0. At some localities the
fraction >6 cm has been analysed in the field by counting the number of pebbles with the same
diameters. These analyses have been converted to weight% to complete the grain size distributions. The
resulting φ'-values are now 2^0 higher, on average and, thus, 1^0 higher than the slope angles. It can be
concluded that the angle of sedimentation for the deposits investigated seems to correspond in most
cases to the angle of internal friction.

The general grain size distribution pattern is comparable to that reported in the literature for slope
deposits originating from crystalline bedrocks where slope failures occurred (Hohensinn, 1979, Moser,
1980, Moser & Schoger, 1989). Furthermore, most debris flow materials as reported in the literature
have similar grain size distributions as our samples (Takahashi, 1980, Johnson, 1984, Hutchinson,
1988) with poor sorting and very low clay and silt contents.

Hydrogeology

The permeability (k) can be estimated roughly from the grain size distributions as well (Lang & Huder,
1984). The calculated values for the samples from the Plaunca Valley are very small ($6 \cdot 10^{-8}$ to
$6 \cdot 10^{-10}$ m/s), all the other samples are of higher permeabilities with k between $4 \cdot 10^{-5}$ and $2 \cdot 10^{-8}$
m/s. The latter range corresponds mainly to that obtained by field investigations in crystalline talus
deposits by Hohensinn (1979) ($3 \cdot 10^{-4}$ to $7 \cdot 10^{-8}$ m/s). The permeability of parts of the sediments may
even be higher in reality, because the influence of the fraction >6 cm is not known and the coarse layers
of the deposits (Fig. 2) could not be analysed properly.

In the slope deposits investigated water normally infiltrates into the sediment body from the surface or from channels, often beginning right at the foot of cliffs or glacierets, and then percolates down-sediment, as no surficial runoff can be observed. We conclude that water flow in the sediments is controlled by bedrock surface geometry and sometimes by ice and permafrost at higher elevations, where in the lower parts of the slope bedrock surface geometry seems to be the only main factor (e.g. Witenwasseren, Fig. 3). However, there are examples where bedrock does not control water flow. A typical case is described from the Geren Valley (Haeberli et al., 1990, Fig. 4), where a spring occurs in the middle of the slope. There, water flow is determined by local inhomogenities in the sediment. In the geoelectrical soundings parts of the moraine slope deposits are often characterized by high electrical resistivities combined with very low seismic velocities which can be explaned by a high amount of large pore spaces (Haeberli et al., 1990) implying a high permeability.

In the Vorderrheintal area water mainly flows in the fracture system at the surface of the crystal-line bedrock. In areas of impermeable bedrock or at the beginning of the steep slopes, spring levels occur. There, the surficial deposits are often saturated with water and consequently susceptible to sliding.

INITIATION OF DEBRIS FLOWS

Following Takahashi (1981) the most important debris flow failure mechanism is the slope type in the "Altschutt" materials. The detachment surfaces display often the shape of an inverted spoon, termed "Muschelanbruch" by Stini (1910). This shape is formed by rotational slides. There is no preformed sliding plane and, in addition, all material is transported away by the debris flows after initial collapse. This kind of failure has been termed "slope explosion" (Bunza, 1976). The main starting condition is a high amount of water, supplied by intense precipitation or snow melt (Zimmermann, 1990), infiltrating into the sediment. As the deposits are hydrogeologically inhomogeneous, water will flow mainly in levels of higher permeability such as coarser beds or large pore spaces. Where these zones of higher permeability end (Fig. 3), drainage is blocked and the water will be dammed and the debris becomes saturated locally. This will cause a pore water pressure to build up, reducing the effective internal shear strength. Compaction of loose zones in the sediment, formed by melt-out of underground ice or by internal erosion, might cause rapid loading and have the same effect (Sassa, 1984). As the slope inclinations are often close to the angle of internal friction and as the soil is very sensitive to variations in the water content, indicated by the low plasticity index, an increase of 3 to 4 weight% only in the water content will be sufficient to change the material from plastic to liquid (Moser, 1980) and, thus, cause failure. This type of event often causes the instability of the whole slope also leading to repeated failures, until the top of the steep slope or until the stabilizing permafrost or glacier is reached (Zimmermann & Haeberli, 1989).

Translational slides were of minor importance during the 1987 events and if they occurred, then mainly on channel banks. In the Varuna and in the Plaunca Valley, secondary debris flows formed from translational slides in the disintegrated sides of the gorges triggered by the undercutting of the slope. These two regions with disintegrated rocks in the lower course of the gullies also contributed a large amount of debris to the single events.

In the "Jungschutt" areas debris flow initiation mostly occurred at a distinct point at the bottom of the steep cliffs or in a channel which could be called the torrent bed type debris flow (Takahashi, 1981). If the debris is surficially saturated by an enhanced supply of water, liquefaction may happen, some-times triggered by the impact of a stream of water (the firehose effect by Johnson, 1984) or by the impact of a mass of debris (Sassa, 1984). This failure mechanism seems to have happened in the Plaunca Valley where the till flow deposits probably were saturated with water, due to the imper-meability of the underlying basal lodgement till. Flooding in the upper part of the catchment area, released by a small slide, lead to the initiation of the debris flow, there.

CONCLUSIONS

The initiation of debris flows depends greatly on the type of material, on the vegetation cover and on the topography of the slope. In 1987, most failures occurred in the Swiss Alps in glacial deposits of the Little Ice-Age, in talus deposits and in debris accumulations in mountain torrents. The deposits discussed originate from disintegrated crystalline bedrock and are characterized by typical grain size distributions as well as by mineralogy. In the steep moraine slopes, failures seem to have occurred due to local inhomogenities in the sediment such as lenses and beds of coarse material or large pore spaces. During the enhanced surficial infiltration of water, blockage of flow paths may have caused a local saturation zone and the liquefaction of the material. In the torrent bed type debris flows, often an additional impact of water or of a debris mass caused liquefaction of saturated debris. The prediction of the exact location and timing of failures is however quite difficult as the failure mechanism is rather complex (Moser, 1980, Moser & Schoger, 1989). Sometimes the debris is totally removed by one event. So the sediment has to accumulate again until debris flow failure may happen once more at the same point. This is the case in "Jungschutt" deposits. In the "Altschutt" deposits sediment accumulation is no more active. However, most accumulations contain still a large amount of material for innumerable debris flows to occur. This indicates that the next debris flow failure will happen certainly, at the same or at a neighbouring locality.

ACKNOWLEDGEMENTS The authors are indebted to the Bundesamt für Wasserwirtschaft, Bern, for the financial support and to Dr. Ch. Schlüchter, ETH Zürich, for helpful discussions and critically reading the manuscript.

REFERENCES

Bunza, G. (1976) Systematik und Analyse alpiner Massenbewegungen. Schriftenreihe der bayerischen Landesstelle für Gewässerkunde 11, 1-84.
Eisbacher, G.H. & Clague, J.J. (1984) Destructive mass movements in high mountains: Hazard and management. Geol Survey of Canada Paper 84-16.
Haeberli, W., Rickenmann, D., Zimmermann, M. & Rösli, U. (1990) Investigation of 1987 debris flows in the Swiss Alps: General concept and geophysical soundings. International Conference on Water Resources in Mountainous Regions, IAHS Publication, same volume.
Hohensinn, F. (1979) Bodenmechanische Analyse von Geländebrüchen bei Murenbildung in kristallinen Verwitterungsböden. Mitt. Inst. für Bodenmechanik, Felsmechanik und Grundbau, Univ. Innsbruck 2.
Hutchinson, J.N. (1988) Morphological and geotechnical parameters of landslides in relation to geology and hydrogeology. In: Proc. of the Fifth International Symp. on Landslides, Lausanne. Balkema, Rotterdam, 3-35.
Johnson, A.M. (1984) Debris flow. In: Slope Instability (Brunsden, D. & Prior, D.B., eds.), Wiley, Chichester.
Lang, H.-J. & Huder, J. (1984) Bodenmechanik und Grundbau. Springer, Berlin.
Moser, M. & Schoger, H. (1989) Die Analyse der Hangbewegungen im mittleren Inntal anlässlich der Unwetterkatastrophe 1985. Wildbach- und Lawinenverbau 110, 1-22.
Moser, M. (1980) Zur Analyse von Hangbewegungen in schwachbindigen bis rolligen Lockergesteinen im alpinen Raum anlässlich von Starkniederschlägen. Internationales Symp. INTERPRAEVENT 4 (1), 121-148.
Naef, F., Horat, P., Milnes, A.G., Hoehn, E. (1990) Anomalous hydrological behaviour of an alpine stream (Varuna, Poschiavo, Southern Switzerland) and its interpretation in terms of the geology

of the catchment. International Conference on Water Resources in Mountainous Regions, IAHS Publication, same volume.

Rickenmann, D. (1990) Debris flows 1987 in Switzerland: Modelling and fluvial sediment transport. International Conference on Water Resources in Mountainous Regions, IAHS Publication, same volume.

Sassa, K. (1984) The mechanism to initiate debris flows as undrained shear of loose sediments. Internationales Symp. INTERPRAEVENT 5 (2), 73-87.

Schlüchter, Ch. (1980) Bemerkungen zu einigen Grundmoränenvorkommen in den Schweizer Alpen. Zeitschr. für Gletscherkunde und Glazialgeologie 16, 203-212.

Schlüchter, Ch. (1990) Eiszeitliche Lockergesteine - Geologie, Genese und Eigenschaften. Habil.-Schrift, ETH - Zürich.

Stiny, J. (1910) Die Muren. Verlag der Wagner'schen Universitätsbuchhandlung, Innsbruck.

Takahashi, T. (1980) Evaluation of the factors relevant to the initiation of debris flow. Proc. of International Symp. on Landslides, New Delhi 3, 136-140.

Takahashi, T. (1981) Estimation of potential debris flows and their hazardous zones: soft countermeasures for a disaster. J. Natural Disaster Sci. 3, 57-89.

Zimmermann, M. (1990) Debris flows 1987 in Switzerland: Geomorphological and hydrometeorological aspects. International Conference on Water Resources in Mountainous Regions, IAHS Publication, same volume.

Zimmermann, M. & Haeberli, W. (1989) Climatic change and debris flow activity in high-mountain areas. Landscape-Ecological Impact of Climatic Change: Discussion Report on Alpine Regions, Universities of Wageningen/Utrecht/Amsterdam, 52-66.

Hydrology in Mountainous Regions. II - Artificial Reservoirs; Water and Slopes
(Proceedings of two Lausanne Symposia, August 1990). IAHS Publ. no. 194, 1990.

Debris flows 1987 in Switzerland:
geomorphological and meteorological aspects

M. ZIMMERMANN
Laboratory of Hydraulics, Hydrology and Glaciology,
ETH Zentrum, 8092 Zürich, Switzerland

ABSTRACT In the Swiss Alps three major regions with areas of 70 to 500 km^2 were heavily affected by numerous debris flows during two storm events in summer 1987. Based on a qualitative and quantitative interpretation of aerial photos and field investigations, the spatial distribution of the debris flow events was mapped and geomorphological properties were assessed. The analysis of rainfall amounts and intensities gave more or less similar behaviour in the three regions. The spatial distribution shows a distinct concentration of debris flows in the periglacial belt as well as several clusters of events in small tributary valleys. This distribution pattern could be only partly explained by the meteorological conditions.

INTRODUCTION

In the alpine and prealpine areas of Switzerland debris flows are a widespread geomorphological phenomenon. Within a single catchment however, the recurrence of such events is irregular and may take place after long intervals of inactivity. Therefore, systematic observation and investigation of debris flows is difficult. During the two major storm events in summer 1987 (17-19 July, 23-25 August 1987) a large number of debris flows occurred in several parts of the Alps (Switzerland, Italy, Austria; cf. Richter, 1987, Smiraglia, 1987, Zeller & Röthlisberger, 1988 or Naef et al., 1989). Damage to settlements, traffic routes and other infrastructures was severe. In the Swiss Alps the Puschlav, Lukmanier and Gotthard areas were badly hit. The simultaneous occurrence of many events provided the opportunity to investigate important aspects of alpine debris flows (Haeberli et al., 1990 a,b; Rickenmann 1990, Rösli & Schindler, 1990). In the present paper geomorphological characteristics and meteorological aspects are discussed.

DISTRIBUTION PATTERN OF 1987 DEBRIS FLOWS

About 600 debris flow events were systematically mapped in the three regions (see Table 1). This documentation is based on an interpretation of infrared and black-and-white airphotos and of oblique photos from helicopter flights. In order to confirm evidence of recent debris flow occurrence on slopes or in channels and to discern debris flows from other processes, such as rock slides or fluvial processes, several definite criteria were used (eg, Johnson & Rodine, 1984 or Costa, 1988): (1) u-shaped depth erosion with a width to depth ratio of less than about 5, (2) cleared gullies and polished rock, (3) marginal levees along the flow path built up with mainly coarse debris and boulders, and (4) unsorted debris lobes and debris cones with large boulders. The debris flow activity in the 3 investigated regions is summarized in Table 1 (all the figures are rough estimations):

TABLE 1 Areas affected by debris flows.

Date of occurrence	Area	Size km²	Debris flows number	Eroded vol. 10³ m³	Unit erosion m³/km²
18/7/87	Puschlav	60	70	400	6700
18/7/87	Lukmanier	300	90	500	1700
24/8/87	Gotthard	500	300	750	1500
	Bedretto[1]	140	140	500	3600

[1] Centre of Gotthard area

The spatial distribution of debris flow activity in these regions is very heterogenous. A dense pattern of debris flows with high values of specific erosion was found in the Puschlav area and between Bedretto and Urseren Valleys (part of Gotthard area). One of the largest events of 1987 in Val Varuna (Puschlav area) is estimated to have eroded more than 200'000 m³ of material. This explains the specific erosion of 6700 m³/km². The distribution patterns have the following characteristics (Fig. 1 shows the pattern in the Gotthard and Lukmanier areas):

- All altitudinal belts were affected by debris flow activity. However, a striking concentration of starting zones was observed in the periglacial belt (above about 2200 - 2400 m a.s.l.), especially in the Puschlav area (Zimmermann & Haeberli, 1989). The starting zone of about 70% of mainly large scale events is above 2300 m a.s.l.

FIG. 1 Distribution pattern of debris flow events in the Lukmanier and Gotthard areas. S: Val Soi, C: Val Carassina, G: Geren Valley, A: Aegenental. Each arrow indicates a large or a group of smaller debris flows.

- Some valleys have clusters of events (Val Soi; Geren Valley) whereas neighbouring catchments with similar conditions for debris flow initiation show only a small number of debris flows (Val Carassina; Aegenental).
- In many cases the boundary between heavily affected and unaffected areas is striking: For instance in the north face of Vorderrhein Valley the starting zones are at an altitude between 1600 m and 1900 m a.s.l.; steep talus slopes and moraines at higher altitudes are absolutely untouched.

Only in two cases (Val da Plaunca, Vorderrhein Valley and Spitzigrat near the village of Andermatt, Gotthard area) was the occurrence of debris flows not to be expected either on the basis of the geomorphological setting (silent witnesses, mainly on the cone) or the historical records. In most other cases there was clear evidence of events having occurred in the past. In all regions a large potential for future debris flows still exists.

GEOMORPHOLOGICAL CHARACTERISTICS

About 80 debris flows with an eroded volume of more than 1000 m^3 per event could be analysed on aerial photos and partly also by field reconnaissance. According to a classification by Takahashi (1981), the starting zones of the debris flows could be devided into two main categories:

Slope type starting zones

The starting mechanism consists of an oversaturation of loose debris with subsequent slide. Surface runoff is either not evident or is concentrated only in shallow channels:

1) The starting zone is on a steep and deep-seated slope of slightly consolidated debris (mainly holocene moraines). Slope angles are between 25° and 38°. In many cases the scars were enlarged by retrogressive erosion (eg, Witenwassern or Cristallina, both in the Gotthard area). In a few cases only (Geren Valley, Gotthard area), shallow slides occurred in the active layer of permafrost areas, similar to events in northern Sweden reported by Larsson (1982).
2) The starting zone is in the contact zone of a steep rock cliff with an adjacent talus slope. Slope angles varies in the same range as type 1). The water is concentrated in gullies on the rockcliff and seeps in to the scree (Palü or Varuna Valley, Puschlav area)

Valley type starting zones

The starting mechanism is a liquefaction of the torrent bed or the sudden outburst of a clogg mass of water and debris:

3) Moraine filled steep rock couloirs were eroded down to the bedrock basis (Minstiger Valley, Gotthard area or Cambrena, Puschlav area). Slope gradient was found to be 45% and about 70% (24° and 35°).
4) Parts of the debris-bed in a steep channel get suddenly mobilized and a debris flow forms (Val Zavragia or Val Luven, Lukmanier area). Slope gradient varies between 23% and 65% (13° and 33°).

The largest starting volumes were found in the type 1) starting zones. Maximum erosional cross sections were about 450 m^2 and maximum erosion depth about 15 m. These maximum values agree with values found for debris flows from small Alpine glacier floods (Haeberli, 1983). The contributing catchments above the starting point were in general very small: 90% smaller than 1 km^2, 40% smaller than 0.1 km^2. The correlation between the catchment area above the starting point and the slope gradient in the starting zone is shown in Fig. 2. Median catchment area of valley type starting zone (types 3 and 4) is about 60 ha, of slope type starting zone (types 1 and 2) only 9 ha. The steeper the slope the less important is the channelised surface flow. A clear trend have the valley type debris flows (open signs), whereas the slope type debris flows show only a weak correlation. This corresponds with data published by Takahashi (1981).

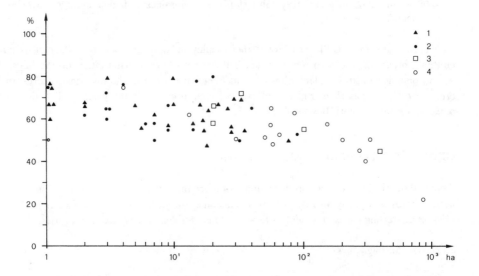

FIG. 2 Slope gradient of the starting zone as a function of the catchment area above the starting point.
1-4: Types of starting zones.

The runout distance (expressed by the mean slope) plotted as function of the catchment area at the cone and of the total volume is given in Fig. 3 a and b. In a large catchment there is, under equal rainfall conditions, in general a high runoff. This additional water influences the viscosity of the flowing mass and therefore the runout distance. In addition, a distinct channel from a large basin prevents the debris flow from spreading out and losing flow depth. Larger debris flows or pulses of debris flows have a longer travelling distance than smaller ones. Similar correlations are found for

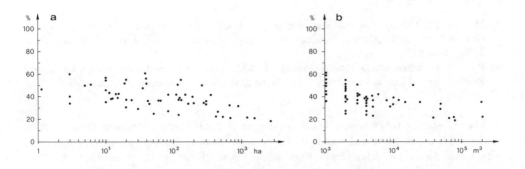

FIG. 3 Relation between mean slope of debris flows and catchment area at the cone (a) and total volume of debris flows (b).

ice avalanches (Alean 1984) or for rockfall events (Scheidegger 1973, Körner 1983). However, the deviation is much larger than from rockfalls, for example, and the mean slope is in no case less than 19% (11°). Losses along the flow path due to the building of levees were estimated to be 5 to 10 m^3/m. This loss is of great importance for small scale debris flows.

Cones, shaped by debris flows mainly have a very rugged surface. Large boulders are spread over the whole cone. The longitudinal profile compared to fluvial cones is steeper. These characteristics represent the distinct sedimentation processes. 80 to 90% of the total sediment load from 1987 events was deposited on the well developped debris flow cones. The sediment delivery to the river systems was relatively low. In the Urseren Valley, for example, total sediment transfer from 15 debris flows was about 50'000 m^3, the sediment input into the River Reuss was negligible. Control works on a cone, like deflection dams or river channelisation prevent the sedimentation. It is, therefore, important to enable the debris flow to spread out on the cone. This characteristic of natural sedimentation has to be taken into account for future land use or for technical measurments.

METEOROLOGICAL CONDITIONS

The hydrometeorological conditions for debris flow initiation may vary widely. Rainfall intensity, accumulated rain during the storm event as well as antecedent precipitation are important factors for triggering debris flows (Campell, 1975). Very small rainfall amounts are required, for exemple, in polar areas. Larsson (1982) describes a storm event in Spitsbergen of about 30 mm within 12 hours with heavy debris flow activity on slopes. The meteorological situation of summer 1987 was investigated by Grebner and Richter (1989). They produced maps with 3-h-isohyetes for the two rain storms in the Swiss Alps. These maps were used to estimate rainfall amount and intensity in the three mainly affected regions. In the Lukmanier area (17-19 July) the main part of the storm event lasted 30 to 40 hours. The time of occurrence of debris flows (reported by witnesses) was between 12 and 30 hours after the onset of the main storm. In this period the accumulated precipitation varied, therefore, from 90 to 170 mm. Medium rainfall intenisity was about 15 to 45 mm/3 h, not to mention the normal variability. Due to the synoptic weather situation no short time peaks were to be expected. The antecedent rainfall amount 20 days prior to the events was about 30 to 100 mm.

In the Gotthard area (23-25 August), after a 40-hour rainfall with medium intensities between 15 and 50 mm/3 h, an intense downpour of 40 mm/h followed at midnight of 24 August. A raingauge in Bedretto, in the centre of the intense rain cell, recorded this peak. Nearly all of the debris flows that reached the valley bottom with its settlements and roads, occurred around midnight. The accumulated rainfall reached between 150 and 200 mm in the north and upto 260 mm in the south of the Gotthard area. The conditions prior to the events were much drier than for the July storm: only 15 to 30 mm fell within the 20 days before.

A special case is the debris flow in the Minstiger Valley (Goms) which damaged Münster at noon, ie, about 12 hours before the extreme rainfall event. A water pocket rupture in Minstiger Glacier is assumed as the triggering mechanism of the debris flow originating in a rocky couloir filled with morainic material.

SPATIAL DISTRIBUTION AND RAINFALL

The spatial pattern of heavy debris flow occurrence in the Gotthard area coincides approximately with the 50 mm isohyete of the 3 hours around midnight, even if the accumulated precipitation varies by a factor of 2 within the whole region. In contrast, the debris flow events in the Lukmanier area lie not in the centre of the storm with high intensities (up to 150 mm/3 h) and very high total rainfall amounts (more than 400 mm in 36 hours). It is assumed that strong snowmelt in the first days of July had contributed a continuous input of moisture into the scree in the Lukmanier area. On the other hand, it is probable that earlier events (mainly in 1978) had emptied many channels in catchments susceptible to debris flows in the central areas of the July 1987 storm. It is assumed that the occurrence in clusters within all of these 3 regions is a result of local meteorological effects in narrow and deep-cut tributary valleys.

In both cases the striking concentration of debris flow activity in the periglacial area may be explained by the high air temperature during the events. Precipitation fell as rain in the highest catchments (over 3000 m a.s.l.) even at the end of the storm.

CONCLUSIONS

Most debris flows of the 1987 storm events occurred in gullies or on slopes where debris flow activity had to be expected on the basis of geomorphological signs and/or of past documented events. The extraordinary situation in 1987 is given by the simultaneous occurrence of numerous events in 3 large areas. For the triggering of debris flows, precipitation is an important but not the only critical factor. Hydrological conditions days and probably weeks before the event, as well as the chronology of events in the catchment, are essential for debris flow initiation. The events in 1987 made clear that debris flows are a great hazard and that they will be more important in future due to intesified use of alpine regions. The determination of areas susceptible to debris flow initiation is possible with the knowledge of the type and characteristics of the starting zone. The time of occurrence, however, can hardly be predicted. On the cone the sedimentation characteristics have to be taken into account: Large volumes of boulders, gravel and sand are trapped under natural sedimentation conditions. A massive channelisation may force a debris flow to travel over the whole cone and to cause greater damage in the main river.

REFERENCES

Alean, J. (1984) Untersuchungen über Entstehungsbedingungen und Reichweiten von Eislawinen. Mitt. VAW, Nr. 74. Zürich.

Campbell, R.H. (1975) Soil slips, debris flows, and rainstorms in the Santa Monica Mountains and vicinity, Southern California. U.S. Geol. Survey Prof. Paper 851, Washington.

Costa, J. (1988) Rheologic, geomorphic, and sedimentologic differentiation of water floods, hyperconcentrated flows, and debris flows. V.R. Baker, R.C. Kochel & P.C. Patton (ed), 1988: Flood Geomorphology: 113-122.

Grebner, D., K.G. Richter (1989) Ursachenanalyse Hochwasser 1987: Gebietsniederschlag. Internal report. Geogr. Inst. ETH, Zürich.

Haeberli, W. (1983) Frequency and characteristics of glacier floods in the Swiss Alps. Ann. Glaciol. Vol 4:85-90.

Haeberli, W., D. Rickenmann, U. Rösli & M. Zimmermann (1990a) Investigation of 1987 debris flows in the Swiss Alps: General concept and geophysic soundings. Int. Conf. on Water Resources in Mountainous Regions. IAHS Publ., same volume.

Haeberli, W., D. Rickenmann, U. Rösli & M. Zimmermann (1990b) Murgänge 1987: Dokumentation und Analyse. Mitt. VAW, ETH Zürich. In preparation.

Johnson, A.M., J.R. Rodine (1984) Debris flow. D. Brunsden & D.B. Prior (ed): Slope Instability: 257-361.

Koerner, H. (1983) Zur Mechanik der Bergsturzströme vom Huascaran, Peru. Hochgebirgsforschung, Vol 6. Innsbruck.

Larsson, S. (1982) Geomorphological effects on the slopes of Longyear Valley, Spitsbergen, after a heavy rainstorm in July 1972. Geogr. Ann. 64 A, 3/4:105-125.

Naef, F., W. Haeberli, M. Jäggi, D. Rickenmann (1989) Morphologische Veränderungen in den Schweizer Alpen als Folge der Unwetter vom Sommer 1987. Oe. Wasserwirtschaft, vol 40, no 5/6:134-138.

Richter M. (1987) Die Starkregen und Massenumlagerungen des Juli-Unwetters 1987 im Tessin und Veltlin. Erdkunde, 41 (4), 261-274.

Rickenmann, D. (1990) Debris flows 1987: flow behaviour and sediment transport. Int. Conf. on Water Resources in Mountainous Regions. IAHS Publ., same volume.

Rösli, U. and C. Schindler (1990) Debris flows 1987: geological and hydrogeological aspects. Int. Conf. on Water Resources in Mountainous Regions. IAHS Publ., same volume.

Scheidegger, A.E. (1973) On the prediction of the reach and velocity of catastrophic landslides. Rock Mechanics, Vol 5, 231-236.

Smiraglia, C. (1987) L'alluvione del Luglio 1987 in Valtellina. Boll. della Società Geografica Italiana. Ser. XI (IV), 509-542.

Takahashi, T. (1981) Estimation of potential debris flows and their hazardous zones: soft countermeasures for a disaster. J. Natural Disaster Science, 3 (1), 57-89.

Zeller J. and G. Röthlisberger (1988) Unwetterschäden in der Schweiz im Jahre 1987. Wasser-Energie-Luft, 80 (1/2), 29-42.

Zimmermann, M. and W. Haeberli (1989) Climatic change and debris flow activity in high-mountain areas. Landscape-Ecological Impact of Climatic Change: Discussion Report on Alpine Regions, Universities of Wageningen/Utrecht/ Amsterdam. 52-66

Topic C:
Influence of Anthropogenic Hydrological Modifications

Considerations on the instability risk of the historical centre of Urbino, Italy, in relation to the different hydrological conditions*

M. DIDERO, U. GORI, C. PALETTA & G. TONELLI
Institute of Applied Geology, University of Urbino, Italy

ABSTRACT. The historical centre of Urbino has recently undergone some instability phenomena due to anthropic interventions. The ground water surface is also subject to rises because of ceased aquifer exploitation and of probable leaks in the aqueduct and in the sewerage network. The practical aspects of this phenomenon have been evaluated in terms of safety factor in some representative sections. It has been proved that the expected variations of the water table levels may affect the stability of the built-up area. A ground water level monitoring network has been set up to control the stability of slopes in the town and provide information to build-up a drainage system in areas which proved to be dangerous.

INTRODUCTION

The water level rise due to the interruptions by anthropic causes of water drawing creates important problems, especially for its consequences on the slope stability degree.
A meaningful example is represented by the town of Urbino, in the Central Italy.
Interruption of the underground aquifer exploitation as a consequence of utilization of an aqueduct, has caused in the long run several changes in the flow of the underground water-table, which on its turn has endangered the stability of the built-up area.
The Medieval town-walls were built on a hill area (478 m above sea level) which is constituted by marls and marly limestones of the "Schlier" formations (Burdigalian-Tortonian period) and by those little cemented marls and sandstones of the "Marnoso-arenacea" formations dating back to the Tortonian-Messinian period.
These formations constitute the impermeable bed-rock of the aquifer. The aquifer itself flows within the surface cover (up to 23 m thick), which is formed by debris accumulation, talus, etc. The impermeable bed-rock top and the groundwater contours have been reconstructed through the collection of data referring to water points, along with the elaboration of 850 m of geognostic borings. The morphology of the geometrically complex bed-rock formations, play an important role in the aquifer flows. The above mentioned researches have led to the identification of flow directions of the aquifer recharge in the Northern and Southern parts of the built-up area, along with two main

---

(*) National Research Council G.N.D.C.I. Publication n. 249
    Responsible U.O. 2/47 U. Gori.

drainage axes with E-W direction.

On the basis of the acquired results, a network of observation wells has been built to keep under control the variations of the water-table levels.

Moreover some verification on the built-up area stability have been carried out (through back-analysis proceedings) introducing 3 variables, that is cohesion, internal friction angle and water level, whose values vary within the range indicated by the collected experimental data.

In conclusion this study has emphasized the importance of the water level fluctuation in the potential landslide hazard concerning the historical centre of Urbino.

GEOLOGICAL AND GEOMORPHOLOGICAL FEATURES

The historical centre of Urbino,is located on the top of two hills characterized by rather steep slopes.

Three main formations can be recognized in the examined area; that is, starting from the most ancient one: Bisciaro, Schlier and Marnoso-arenacea (Fig.1). The Bisciaro (Aquitanian pp - Burdigalian pp.) is set up by a varying sequence of beds, say limestone, grey marly limestones, marls, calcareous marls and grey shaley marls.

Nodular and bands of black chert can often be found in the lower calcareous levels. In addition several volcaniclastic levels (Guerrera F. & Veneri F. 1989) with thickness varying from 10 to approximately 50 cm have been discovered.

The whole formation is marked by numerous deep fractures due to the past tectonic stresses. The Bisciaro (thickness from 40 to 60 m) is not underlying the area of historical centre of the town.

The Schlier (Burdigalian pp. - Tortonian pp.) is mainly formed by marls, calcareous marls, grey shaley marls and secondarily by thin whitish marly-calcareous levels.

This bedding is not very evident due to the little difference among the lithological types, to the considerable fracturing and to the widespread cleavage characterizing the whole formation.

These conditions favour the degradation of the marls, which is frequently shown by the detrital deposits. The Schlier, whose assessed thickness is around 80 m, constitutes the substrate of the extreme Southern portion of the historical centre.

The Marnoso-arenacea (Tortonian pp. - Messinian pp.), is constituted by either finegrained and rough turbiditic sandstone structured in various tabular beds.

Interbedded to the sandstones there are some blue-grey pelites, mostly turbiditic whose thickness varies from a few centimeters to one meter. This formation, (thickness around 350 m) constitutes the unchanged substrate of the Northern and Central part of the historical centre of Urbino.

The above mentioned formations are generally outcropping outside the city walls. In fact they appear mainly covered not only by the urban structures and detrital layers originated by the past anthropic activities, but also by a detrital layer which is mainly produced by the alteration of the lithoid formation described above.

The thickness of the eluvial-colluvial cover range from a few centimeters to about 23 m.

FIG. 1 Geological map of the investigated area. 1) Marnoso-arenacea
formation (Tortonian pp. - Messinian pp.); 2) Schlier formation
(Burdigalian pp. - Tortonian pp.); 3) Bisciaro formation (Aquitanian
pp. - Burdigalian pp.); 4) Fault; 5) Back-thrust.

The structural setting is defined by three main structures having the
typical direction of the Appennines (NW-SE), composed from NE to SW of
an anticline followed by a syncline and again of an anticline.
The situation is actually much more complex due to the presence of a
series of folds, mainly with vertical flanks, sometimes overturned,
and of some faults.
The N-W side of the first anticline approaches only partially the
built-up area, just in its Northernmost part. This structure is
separated from the syncline by a fault contact following the pattern
NW-SE (see Fig. 1).
An anticlinal structure is following, the core of which is represented
by the "Bisciaro", which comes alongside the "Marnoso-arenacea"
through the shearing zone connected with the back-thrust of the
structure towards SW. The above described structures are also
characterized by faults with pattern NE-SW, which partially interrupt
the continuity.

HYDROGEOLOGICAL CONDITIONS

The presence of water in the Urbino subsoil has certainly favoured the development of the town. The exploitation of this water by dug wells, cisterns and drainage systems was particularly practiced in the past centuries. Recent studies stated that (Fabbri et. al. 1985), several complex underground hydraulic systems, which granted sufficient water supply to the "Corte" were in operation inside the "Palazzo Ducale" (fig. 2).

The surveys carried out during the present study proved that wells were regularly used for the water supply of individual houses, where in those areas where the underground resources were not sufficient, cisterns were used. The aquifer yield was undoubtedly poor and the wells were often dug trough the aquifer down to the unaltered and/or unfractured bed-rock, so that a sufficient water supply could be obtained also during periods of draught.

Although there are not historical documents available, there is no doubt that the introduction of a drainage system on one side, and, on the contrary, the aquifer no longer exploited by the inhabitants (because of the water supply trough the aqueduct), have altered the ground water conditions and the water table levels. Leaking of the oldest sections of the aqueduct may also contribute to alter said levels.

It appears of the utmost importance to verify consequently the possible effects of such variation on the stability of the slope condition.

From a methodological point of view, the study was carried out according to the usual procedures (Albani et al. 1973) including collection of data of all water points available, topographical levellings and setting up of a level and chemical-physical characteristics of the ground water monitoring network. (As far as the chemical phisical characteristics of the aquifer is concerned, only the parameters directly connected with the targets of present study will be measured (Didero et. al. 1990)).

Inventored data are synthesized in table n. 1. The general collection of data was carried out in August 1989 and two monitoring surveys out of the eight foreseen, were carried out in October and December 1989.

Up to now the general characteristics of the examined aquifer can be summarized as follows, although more detailed data should be provided by further borings:

- the aquifer levels are constituted by the deeper debris horizons, sand levels and the upper zone of the altered/fractured bed rock.
- recharge of the aquifer is caused by rainfall infiltrations, although urbanization processes as paving, may have reduced the direct flow of water into the subsoil and, on the other hand, probable leaks into the ground from aqueduct and sewerage network may have increased locally the flow;
- the ground water circulation patterns are made more complex by the heterogeneity, distribution and interconnections of the underground permeable levels;
- altough there are no experimental hydraulic conductivity (K) and transmissivity (T) data, it can be affirmed that the aquifer is poor and its yield is consequently low.

Elaboration of the collected data has led to the reconstruction of the aquifer geometry, through a creation of a map of the impermeable

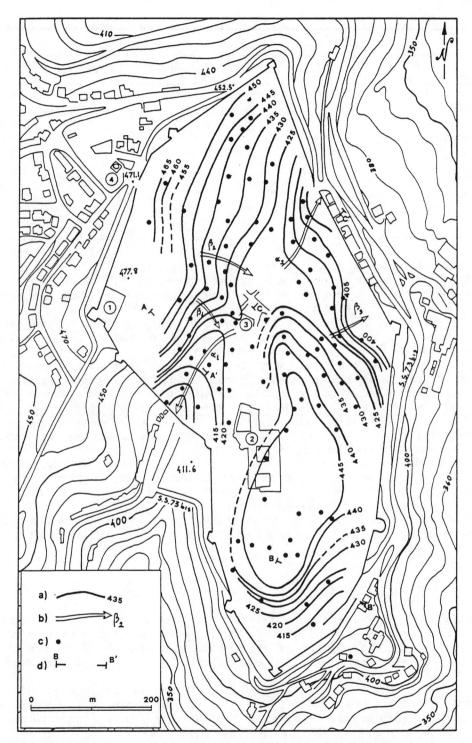

FIG. 2 Groundwater contour map of historical centre of Urbino.
a) Contour map of water levels m above s.l.; b) drainage axis;
c) wells of ground water monitoring network; d) section; 1) Albornoz
Fortress; 2) Ducale Palace; 3) Repubblica Square; 4) Roma Square.

TABLE 1 Situation of the hydrogeological data and monitoring network.

	WELLS	CISTERNS	SPRINGS	GEOGNOSTIC BORINGS
Inventored/Utilized	228/163	39/39	12/12	66/66
Monitoring network n. of water point	86	27	12	-
Monitoring network ratio <u>Monitored</u> Utilized	38	70	100	-

substrate and the groundwater contours map (Fig. 2).

The latter shows that in the extreme Northern hill chain (Fortress Albornoz - Roma Square) there is an underground stream whose direction is NW-S/SE, towards Repubblica Square.

The hydraulic gradient looks higher (4%) in the Bisciaro area and lower in the Marnoso-arenacea, North-Eastward from the zone of the verticalized bed of the latter formation.

An underground watershed connected to the verticalization/compression of the interbedded arenaceous and marly beds can be identified in the above mentioned zone were just on the sides of which two drainage axis β_1 and β_2 are barely notable. From the isophreatic 425 m a.s.l. the downward, the water table is altered by two main flows, α_1 and α_2 following respectively direction SW and NE and coinciding also with the main sewerage systems of the town.

In the Southernmost area of the town the water table mainly follows the topographical pattern and the influences of the Palace Ducale drainage system are no longer evident. A flow β_3 Eastward coincides with a branch of the sewerage system.

The data relative to the depth of the water table and of the bed-rock have been then used for those sections related with the evaluation of the stability conditions.

GEOTECHNICAL LABORATORY RESULTS.

More than 60 borings with relevant sampling have been carried out within the city walls of Urbino pursuing several and different aims.

Consequently the wide range of information allows the description of the average geotechnical characteristics of the most important lithological types.

As far as the subsoil of Urbino is concerned we can indicate three main lithotechnical units, the first of which can on its turn be splitted into three sub-units, following perculiar classification criteria, grouping heterogeneous lithological situations:

```
                  ┌ A'  : Anthropic accumulation soil
A - Cover         │ A'' : silt - clay soil with debris
                  └ A''': sand - silt soil with debris
B - Schlier  formation              C - Marnoso-arenacea formation
```

The recognized facies are characterized by the following average geotechnical parameters obtained from 85 samples analyses: (table 2)

TABLE 2 Geotechnicals data.

	γ kN $(m^3)^{-1}$	W %	LL %	LP %	A %	θ' x°	C' kPa	Cu kPa	K cm s^{-1}	θr x°	Cr kPa
A ⌐ A'	18	28	46	25	0,9	22	18	27	10^{-2}	–	–
A ⎮ A''	19,5	33	55	30	1,1	25	40	60	10^{-5}	20	12
A ⌙ A'''	18	26	35	18	0,8	30	21	100	10^{-3}	24	4
B	20,5	18	58	30	1,0	28	85	450	10^{-8}	20	16
C	20	23	40	26	0,7	34	68	450	10^{-6}	24	10

the Cu value derives from Vane tests; the K value, from 100 to 200 kPa of consolidation, by means of the oedometer in laboratory, the ø and C' values result from CD tests at the direct shear apparatus with effective tension among 100 and 200 kPa and speed of 0,005 mm/min; the residual data have been obtained after 10 shear cycles.

ANALYSIS PROCEEDINGS AND BACK PROCESS.

Some stability analyses have been carried out along three planimetric sections (Fig. 3) in order to verify relationship existing among

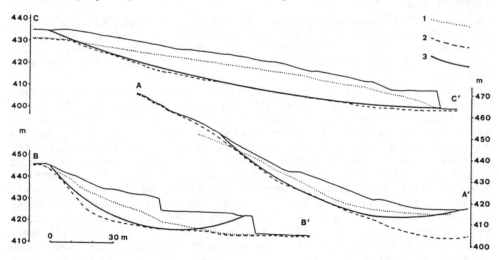

FIG. 3   Profile of hypothetical slide movements. 1) Water table; 2) Bed-rock/cover boundary; 3) slip surface.

geotechnical characteristics, morphology, anthropic influence and ground water variation (Gori U. 1987). This study has been carried out with the limit equilibrium method using back analysis procedures with a safety factor respectively equal to 1 and 1,5 as required by the Italian law. In the tests the values related to the internal friction angle, cohesion and ground water level have been indicated within a defined range in order to draw a comparison between the experimental data and those effectively required by the imposed equilibrium (Gori U. 1989). According to the stratigraphic data of the tests it has been assumed that the slip surface follows the discontinuity existing between cover and bed rock. In all cases the ground water flow resulted to be parallel to the topographical surface as previously indicated by the experimental tests. The ground water level consequent to a period of scarce rainfall (August/December 1989), is represented by such a low value, that in the long run it cannot but increase.

The anthropic effect due to the charges exerted by the buildings on the foundations can be considered balanced by the remarkable soil removal carried out for the foundation excavations, and the depth assumed for the slip surfaces.

The examination of the analytical data shown in Fig. 4, suggests the following remarks:

SECTION C-C':

during the observation, the ground water level (hw) from the top surface ranged from 3 to 5 m. Assuming a minimum value of the residual cohesion equal to $0 \div 4$ kPa (Krahn et al. 1987), and adopting a safety factor of respectively 1 and 1,5 the mobilized frictional values on the failure zone are equal to $10° \div 14°$ and $16° \div 20°$.

SECTION B-B':

in this case the depth of hw remained between 4 and 6 m from the top surface. Assuming a cohesion value of $0 \div 4$ kPa the requested internal frictional values are $14° \div 19°$ and $22° \div 27°$ being the safety factor equal to 1 and 1,5.

SECTION A-A':

it was observed that the position of the ground water was higher and its depth varied between 2 and 4 m from the top surface. Fixing the cohesion value to $0 \div 4$ kPa some internal frictional values of $20° \div 30°$ and $32° \div 39°$ are mobilized, again referring to a safety factor of 1 and 1,5.

From the analysis results it can be stated that the theorical shearing values which can occur along the slip sufaces chosen for the three test sections reflect the laboratory experimental values shown in the table 2 (A''' values). The only exception was section A-A', as its shearing demand exceeded the magnitudo of the laboratory tests. For example with a safety factor of 1,5 the internal frictional values should be higher than the peak data. Thus the mentioned hypothesis does not seem very probable because the slow developing displacements processes revealed along section A-A' require the consideration of residual data (Ishihara & Hsu 1986). The condition of limit equilibrium being the safety factor equal to 1 is feasible only through the introduction of the maximum residual resistance value obtained in laboratory and only if is hw $\geq$ 4m. Obviously the above described statements do not concern the reconsolidation phenomena due to the gravitational deformation of the upper covers, which can modify the natural water content and the cohesion values. However section A-A' certainly shows a state of unstable equilibrium, depending on the superficial ground water position. Controlling the aquifer drainage which is anyway to be pulled down at least to 8 m below the top surface by means of adequate draining processes, the equilibrium conditions would be more compatible with the data relative to the shear resistance obtained in laboratory.

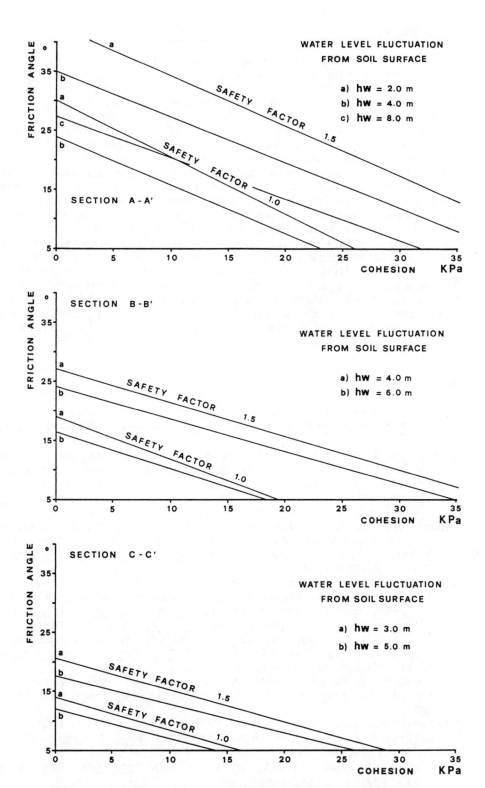

FIG. 4   Back analysis response.

CONCLUSIONS

The situation of the acquifer laying under the built-up area of Urbino has undergone substantial changes.
The main cause of this phenomenon can be brought back to the lack of direct groundwater withdrawal for people consumption. Other causes may be consequent to local faults in the aqueduct and in the old sewerage systems and the related dispersion of water. These conditions determined a rise of the average ground water level and this situation endangers the stability of some areas.
Some stability tests were carried out in back analysis on sample sections in order to identify the risks connected to the present hydrogeological situation; the result show very low safety factors values considering the geotechnical parameters of the slip surfaces. Being the ground water depth observed in a period of scarce rainfall, (as that of the surveys carried out in August and December 1989) very low, just considering a rise of only 1 m in the water level, the calculated stability conditions are significantly reduced.
The monitoring of this phenomenon and the long-term control of the ground water variations will enable experts to identify slides risks. Therefore it will be possible to point out the most adequate operational drainage systems and stability factors to ensure slope stability in the endangered area.

REFERENCES

Albani, R., Lombardi, L. & Vicinanza, P. (1973) Idrogeologia della città di Roma. 2nd Intern. Symp. ou groundwater 329-339. Palermo (Italy)
Didero, M. & Paletta, C. (1990) Ricerca ed individuazione di risorse idriche ancora adatte ad uso acquedottistico esistenti in acquiferi alluvionali ad alto indice di inquinamento. Strumenti programmatici utilizzabili per la loro conservazione. Acque Sotterranee n. 3 1990. (In press).
Fabbri, M., Forti, P., Moretti, E. & Wezel, C. (1985) Esplorazione e rilevamento dei cunicoli drenanti e di alcuni vani sotterranei del Palazzo Ducale di Urbino. II Conv. Naz. di Speleologia Urbana. Castel dell'Ovo (Napoli) 1985.
Gori, U. (1987) Analisi di impatto ambientale nei riguardi dei fenomeni di stabilità su terreni pliocenici e su argille scagliose in provincia di Pesaro-Urbino. Int. Congr. Geoidrologia: Antropizzazione e degradazione dell'ambiente fisico. Firenze.
Gori, U. (1989) Back-analysis and laboratory tests relationships in clay shale slopes of Appennines. I Int. Symp. on landslide, Vol. 1, 342-351. Paipa Colombia.
Guerrera, F. & Veneri, F.(1989) Neogene and Pleistocene volcaniclastites of the Apennines (Italy). Geologie and Mijnbouw vol. 68: 381-390.
Ishihara, K., Hsu, H.L. (1986) Consideration for landslides in natural slopes triggered by earthquakes. Proc.of Jsce n. 376/III-6
Krahn, J., Fredlund, D.G. & Klassen, M. J.(1987) The effect of soil suction on slope stability at notch hill. Proc. 40th Can Geotech. Conf., Regina, Saskatchewan.

Hydrology in Mountainous Regions. II - Artificial Reservoirs; Water and Slopes
(Proceedings of two Lausanne Symposia, August 1990). IAHS Publ. no. 194, 1990.

Gully erosion resulting from anthropogenic-hydrological modifications: case of the Opi-Ugwogo-Abakpa Nike Road, Anambra State, Nigeria

C.O. OKOGBUE & J. U. AGBO
Department of Geology, University of Nigeria, Nsukka
Nigeria

ABSTRACT This paper discusses the gully erosion at the Opi end of the Opi-Ugwogo-Abakpa Nike Road in Anambra State, Nigeria. The gully was initiated following the construction of this road which cuts across an escarpment - the Udi Nsukka escarpment. The study reveals that the gully erosion is the result of the blocking of natural drainage courses along the highway path during construction, heightened by the topography and vulnerable geologic formation exposed in the area. Provision of adequate and well constructed drainage paths may ameliorate the situation although a complete relocation/realignment of the affected road section, slightly to the south and away from the river flood plain, may be a better cost-saving alternative.

INTRODUCTION

In the desire to better life, man has continued to interfere with natural drainage courses. Such interference often is beneficial in the long run, e.g. benefits from the construction of dams. However, the interference is not always beneficial but may infact be very detrimental to the environment. The indiscriminate dumping of refuse along drainage courses (a form of refuse disposal in many developing countries) has been known to cause flooding due to drainage blockage. Opening up of new highways also has caused the blocking of several natural drainage ways thus leading to flooding and erosion. In addition to engineering construction agricultural practices also expose the landscape to the devastating effects of erosion.

In this present paper the role of man as an agent of erosion/gullying at the Opi-end of the Opi-Ugwogo-Abakpa Nike road section in Anambra State, Nigeria is discussed. This road, still under construction for over ten years, is facing serious problems of abandonment due to erosion/gullying at the Opi end of the road stretch.

GENERAL CAUSES OF GULLY EROSION

The causes of soil/gully erosion have often been traced to several factors like geology/soil type, topography, climate, vegetation and human action. In southeastern Nigeria, the problem has been highlighted by such workers as Ofomata (1965), Floyd (1965), Nwajide & Hoque (1979), Egboka & Okpoko (1984), Okagbue (1986), Uma & Onuoha (1987), Onuoha & Uma (1988) and Okagbue &

Ezechi (1988). All workers seem to agree that soil/gully erosion is more severe in areas of rugged terrain underlain by friable and unconsolidated sandy bedrock. Onuoha & Uma (1988), on the basis of intensity have, for example, sub-divided erosion menance in Nigeria into three zones namely, zone of incipient to slight erosion, zone of slight to moderate erosion, and zone of intense erosion within which are found areas of active gullying. This sub-division could be traced to two major causes - geology and topography. Areas of flat terrain show moderate to low intensity erosion, whereas areas of rugged terrain show potentially high erosion intensity. The potential is highly manifested when the rugged terrain is underlain by unconsolidated sand deposits. This is typical of the scarp slopes of the two major cuestas in southeastern Nigeria - the 250km long north-south trending Arochukwu-Ohafia-Awgu-Udi-Nsukka cuesta and the 75km long north-west-southeast trending Awka-Orlu uplands, which are dissected by numerous rills, ravines and gullies of all sizes and shapes.

PHYSIOGRAPHY OF STUDY AREA

FIG. 1 Map of Nigeria showing southeastern Nigeria and study area.

The study area (Fig.1) is located within the scarp slope of the northern extension of the 250km long north-south trending Arochu-kwu-Ohafia-Awgu-Udi-Nsukka cuesta. Locally the cuesta is winding consisting of several ridges and valleys, with the underlying geologic formations exposed along the scarp-face that eventually flattens eastwards into the Cross River Plain. Several rivers take their rise from the cuesta and flow almost in an easterly

direction through the Cross River Plain (Fig.2).   The Ora River
of the study area (see Fig.2) is one of such rivers; it takes
its rise from the cuesta and flows eastwards into the Abonyi
River which eventually empties into the Cross River.

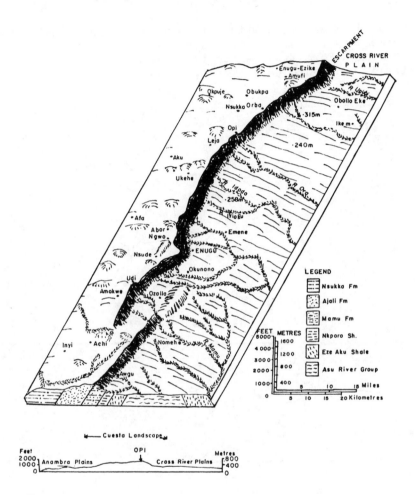

FIG. 2 Block diagram showing the Awgu-Nsukka cuesta.
Note the positions of Opi, Ora River and Enugu.
Abakpa Nike is in Enugu. (Modified from Ofomata,
1975).

     The area is characterised by heavy rainfall typical of the
rainforest regions of the tropics.   The annual rainfall ranges
from 1500 to 1800mm, accompanied by frequent storms of high
intensity.   There are two seasons, the rainy season spanning a
period of about eight months (March to October), and the dry season which lasts for four months (November to February), with the
characteristic dry winds of the hamattan period dominating   most
of December and January.   During the dry season average monthly
maximum temperatures of up to 34°C are recorded whereas the

lowest average monthly minimum temperatures of 19°C are obtaina-
ble especially during the peak rainy season and the harmattan.

GEOLOGY

The study area falls within the southeastern Nigeria
sedimentary basin. It is underlain by rocks of the Mamu, Ajali
and Nsukka Formations which form the north-south trending cuesta
already mentioned (see Figs 2, 3 and 4).

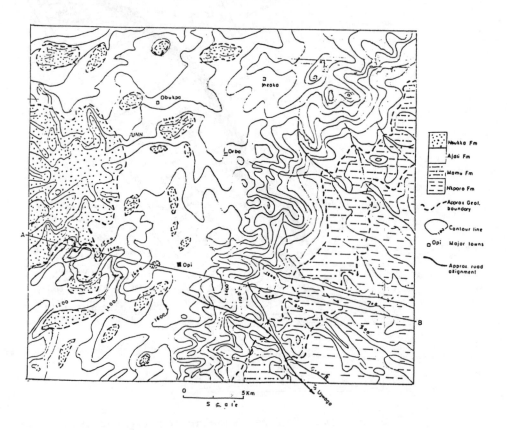

FIG. 3 Surface geology of the Opi area and environs.

        Capping the cuesta to the west is the iron-stained Nsukka
Formation which locally forms lateritic resistant caps over the
ridges.   This Formation generally consists of shales, coals, and
fine to coarse grained sandstone units which are ferrugenized and
lateritized locally.   The Ajali Sandstone Formation conformably
underlies the Nsukka Formation and consists of friable, poorly
consolidated, whitish, medium to coarse grained sandstones.   The
upper part is locally iron-stained due to laterization.   It is very
well exposed along the scarp face of the cuesta and is the sole
formation underlying the erosion sites as well as the valleys that
adjoin the ridges of the cuesta.   It is a prolific aquifer yield-
ing large quantities of water to wells as well as sustaining many

perenial streams e.g. the Ora River of the study area, during
the dry season. Underlying the Ajali Formation is the Mamu
Formation, a paralic sequence consisting of coals, shales and
sandstone units. The upper part of the Formation consists of
sandstone units. The Formation is exposed farther down the
escarpment before the slope flattens into that portion of the
Cross River Plain (see Fig.2) underlain by the Nkporo/Asata Shale
Formation, a lateral equivalent of the Enugu Shale. Fig. 3 is a
sketch of the surface geologic layout of the Opi area, while
Fig. 4 is a section through the surface geology.

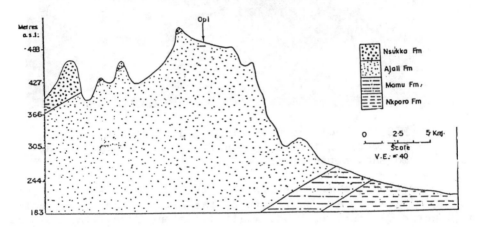

FIG. 4   Cross section through Fig. 3 showing disposition of geologic units.

GENESIS OF PRESENT PROBLEMS

In 1975 a road link between Opi and Abakpa Nike through Ugwogo was
planned. This road was to cut accross the 250km long north-south
trending Arochukwu-Ohafia-Awgu-Udi-Nsukka cuesta, near Opi. There
were fillings of depressions and cuts of elevated areas. The
alignment of the road near Opi was very close to the Ora River and
in the same direction as the main river flow. A section of the
road which is now badly gullied (Fig.5) actually lies almost
within the flood plains of the river.

     Because of the rugged topography, several small tributaries,
especially intermittent ones that are very active only during
storms, empty into the Ora River. Such tributaries as would be
expected do not necessarily drain in the same direction as the
main river. Many of their drainage paths were therefore interfered
with, some completely blocked during the road construction.

     The result of the interference was that during heavy rain-
storms characteristic of the area, the runoff, that would hitherto
have been naturally channelled into the river through the drainage
courses, sought alternative ways of discharge. And since no
artificial drainages were provided during the road construction,
the unchannelled runoff carved discharge channels for itself.
Erosion was thus initiated.

FIG. 5 Photograph showing road stretch being
seriously attacked by runoff. Man standing is used
to show depth of erosion.

The erosion was most severe near the toes of the cut slopes
which unfortunately are underlain by the friable and easily gullied (Okagbue & Ezechi, 1988) Ajali Sandstone Formation. Because
the Formation also forms the grade on which the road was constructed, the erosion led to not only cut slope undermining but also
to the undermining of the pavement (see Fig. 6). Such undermin-

FIG. 6 Photograph showing undermining of cut-slope as
well as pavement. Note the slump features on the
cut slope as well as the collapsing of the pavement.

ing led to lots of slumping/sliding along the cut slopes as well
as the collapse of the undermined sections of the pavement. In
these sections, the entire pavement has been completely washed
away (See Figs 7 and 8) such that the road has now become a
drainage way during storms.

The fill sections of the road have been similarly attacked
as the embankment toes become undermined by runoff. In these
sections, gullies as deep as the height of the cut slopes have
been generated. This investigation also revealed that the grading or levelling of the ground created landslide susceptible
conditions. In the fill sections, for example, failure planes
develop on the former ground surface where vegetation was not
properly cleared prior to regrading. During the rainy season,
increased soil saturation results where surface and subsurface
drainage was destroyed by regrading. The fills, though compacted, lose strength during these rainy periods and become subject
to mass movement.

FIG. 7 Photograph showing a section of pavement that
collapsed recently. The debris are yet to be carried
away by runoff.

SUGGESTIONS FOR MITIGATION

The erosion menace in the study area is quite alarming that urgent
attention is needed, if the road construction must continue. The
menance is so complex that on a face value it would appear the
problem is insolvable. However, if this road is to still retain
its original alignment then a lot of work has to be done.

FIG. 8 Photograph showing a completely washed away
section of pavement.

It is conceived that if wide re-inforced concrete drainages
are provided on both sides of the road from Opi town, straight
down into the banks of the Ora River, and if at the same time the
slopes of the cuts and embankments are considerably flattened,
the menance could be brought under control. This, however is
likely to be very expensive as the present gullies have to be first
filled before any constructions can be undertaken.

To minimize cost and possibly the re-generation of the gullies,
a complete re-alignment/relocation of this section of the road,
slightly to the south, away from the flood plains of the Ora River
might be a better alternative solution. This, however, would still
require the provision of drainages as the cuesta would still be cut
accross, but this time not very close to the river.

CONCLUSIONS

The following conclusions can be drawn from the above study:

1. Serious gullying can be generated by human activities, albeit
    inadvertently. The gully erosion discussed herein is linked to
    engineering construction.
2. Adequate geological and hydrological investigations must
    precede road constructions if man-made hazards must be minimised
    or averted. It is most likely that such investigations were
    not done prior to the construction of the Opi-Ugwogo-Abakpa
    Nike Road.
3. Because of the topography and the nature of the geological
    formations exposed in the study area, a complete re-alignment/
    relocation of the road section seriously affected by gullying
    is advocated, coupled with the provision of adequate drainages
    on both sides of the road.

REFERENCES

Egboka, B.C.E., & Okpoko, E.I.   (1984)   Gully erosion in the
    Agulu-Nanka region of Anambra State, Nigeria. In: Challe-
    nges in African Hydrology and Water Resources,(Proc. Harare
    Symp., August 1984) 335-344. International Association of
    Hydrological Sciences Publ.no. 144.
Floyd, B. (1965) Soil erosion and deterioration in Eastern
    Nigeria. Nigerian Geogr. J. 8, 33-43.
Nwajide, C.S. & Hoque, M. (1979) Gullying processes in Eastern
    Nigeria. The Nigerian Field. 54(2), 64-74
Ofomata, G.E.K. (1965) Factors of soil erosion in Enugu area of
    Nigeria. Nigerian Geogr J. 8 45-59
Ofomata, G.E.K. (1975) Nigeria in Maps: Eastern States. Ethiope
    Publishing House, Benin, Nigeria.
Okagbue, C.O. (1986). Gully development and advance in a rain
    forest zone of Nigeria. Proc. 5th Int. Congr. Int. Assoc.
    Engng. Geol. Buenes Aires, Argentina, 1990-2010.
Okagbue, C.O. & Ezechi, J.I. (1988) Geotechnical characteristics
    of soils susceptible to severe gullying in Eastern Nigeria.
    Bull. Int. Assoc. Engng. Geol. 38, 111-419.
Onuoha, K.M., & Uma, K.O. (1988) An appraisal of recent
    geologic and hydrologic hazards in Nigeria. In: Natural
    and man made Hazards, Kluwer Academic Publishers, The Nether-
    lands.
Uma, K.O. & Onuoha, K.M. (1987) Groundwater fluxes and gully
    development in southeastern Nigeria. In: Groundwater and
    Mineral Resources of Nigeria, Earth Evolution Science
    Monograph Series, Friedr. Vieweg & John Wiesbaden.

TOPIC D:

ASSESSMENT AND MAPPING OF FLOOD AND LANDSLIDE HAZARDS WITH RESPECT TO LAND-USE PLANNING

Hydrology in Mountainous Regions. II - Artificial Reservoirs; Water and Slopes
(Proceedings of two Lausanne Symposia, August 1990). IAHS Publ. no. 194, 1990.

Relationships between land use and morphological phenomena due to stream erosion and denudation: an example

V. CHIANTORE, F. CHIARAVALLI
ISMES S.p.A., Via dei Crociferi 44, 00187 Rome, Italy.
D. DOTTI
Studio Dotti - Ambiente e Territorio
Via P. Sterbini 10, 00153 Rome, Italy

ABSTRACT   Land use influences the morphological evolution
of an area in central Italy. This paper investigates some
factors responsible for the interaction between the
erosion phenomena, due to surficial waters, and land use.
In the analysis phase, couples of thematic maps
(geomorphological - land use) derived from
photointerpretation, have been compared. In the synthesis
phase, a map illustrating the origin, the intensity and
the acceleration of the territorial transformation
phenomena has been plotted.

INTRODUCTION

Land use influences the morphology of a hill area in central Italy.
This work outlines the relationships between the morphological
evolution of this area and its agricultural use.

The study area is a part of the coast of the Abruzzo region, in
the province of Pescara. The main land use is agriculture. The
climate of the area is typically mediterranean with rains
concentrated in autumn and winter. In this area marine pliocenic and
quaternary deposits, represented by clays, marls, sands and
conglomerates, outcrop.

ANALYSIS

A photointerpretative analysis of two aerial photographs series of
August 1974 and March 1989 has been carried out. After that, two land
use maps and two geomorphological maps (for both years 1974 and 1989)
1:10.000 scale have been drawn and compared.

The sediments outcropping in the study area, covered by less
erosible deposits, originated wide valleys characterized by
morphological features like "calanchi" (bad lands) and landslides.
These valleys are bordered by narrow subplain ridges on which the
most ancient villages were founded (i.e. Mutignano).

Agriculture is the basic anthropic activity in this area. Along
the narrow coastal plain there are only few factories and some

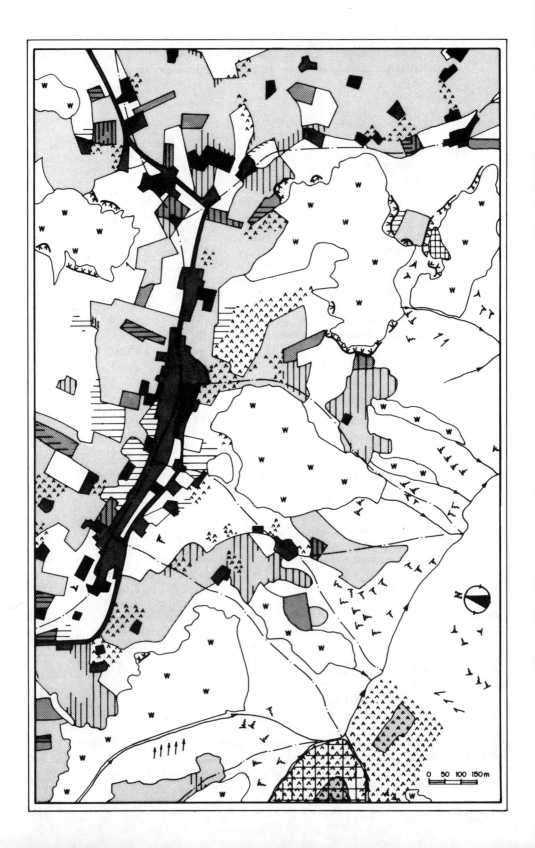

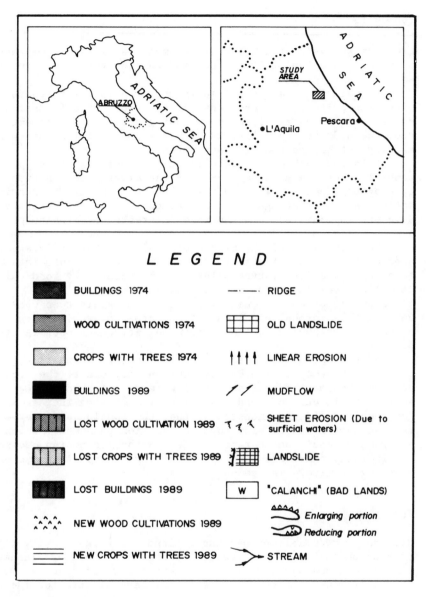

FIG. 1 The study area.

important transport infrastructures (roads and railway).
Main cultures are seed crops, often cultivated together with olive
trees. Olive trees are rarely cultivated alone and are localized;
vineyards are widespread, while natural woods are absent.
The area is characterised by the presence of small artificial basins,
by isolated trees in the seed crops, while hedges and steps have been
often removed. These are the techniques adopted to optimize
agriculture in a land which, due to lithology, morphology and
erosion, is quite unfavourable to it.

SYNTHESIS

From the analysis of the elaborated maps, a synthetic map has been
plotted. A section of it is enclosed to show the evolution of the
study area (Fig. 1).

The main feature recognized in the area is the increase of
vineyards cultures; however, new vine fields, of different sizes, do
not seem to have been planted following criteria to protect the soil
from the hydrogeological risks. In 1974 wood cultivations were
already not homogeneously distributed.

It is reasonable to relate the differences of the slope
conditions of the Mutignano hill to the diverse cultivation
typologies. In fact, wood cultivations near the urban area increased,
acting as a barrier against the "calanchi" regressive erosion.
However, in 1989 the total surface interested by erosion phenomena is
almost the same of 1974.

The withdrawal of the margin of "calanchi" areas interested only
seed crops or uncultivated terrains. The tendency to maintain the
existing agricultural typologies and an increase of wood cultivations
to protect the land from erosion has also been noticed.

Signs of decades of bad agricultural management on weak soils and
unfavourable morphological conditions are, however, evident; they can
be mainly attributed to land overexploitation and poor territorial
planning.

The total "calanchi" extension in the area shows that the
constant presence of man constitutes an obstacle to the evolution of
erosion phenomena due to surficial waters. These phenomena could
accelerate in case of land desertion. The missing increase of
"calanchi" surfaces demonstrates that the continuous intervention of
man can contribute to slow down the erosion phenomena, which, on the
other hand, could degenerate when the anthropic action ceased.

In Italy there are many areas showing the consequences of decades
of wrong territory management.

FUTURE WORK

Studies on remedial engineering actions for areas heavily affected by
erosion phenomena and not easily recoverable could be planned. In the
future the same areas could constitute a sort of "natural monument"
in the framework of the resources of a naturalistic tourism.

REFERENCES

Benedini M., Gisotti G. (1987) Il dissesto idrogeologico. Ed. La
    Nuova Italia Scientifica.
Bucci M., Cautilli F. et al. (1988) L'analisi geologico ambientale
    nell'area della miniera di Pasquasia (Enna, Sicilia); un
    contributo alla definizione del rischio globale ed un tentativo
    di recupero ambientale. Enea tecn. rep.
Canuti P., Garzonio C.A., Rodolfi G. (1979) Attivita' agricola e
    franosita' nell'area rappresentativa di Montespertoli (Toscana).
    Geol. Appl. e Idrogeol 14, 437.
Chisci G. (1979) Considerazioni sulle trasformazioni di sistemi di

agricoltura collinare in relazione al regime idrologico e al
   dissesto dei versanti. <u>Geol. Appl. e Idrogeol 14</u>, 225.
Gisotti G. (1988) Principi di geopedologia. <u>Ed. Calderini</u>.
Panizza M. (1988) Geomorfologia applicata. <u>Ed. La Nuova Italia
   Scientifica</u>.

Hydrology in Mountainous Regions. II - Artificial Reservoirs; Water and Slopes
(Proceedings of two Lausanne Symposia, August 1990). IAHS Publ. no. 194, 1990.

Risk mapping in the Pyrenees area: a case study

J. COROMINAS, J. ESGLEAS & C. BAEZA
Geotechnical Engineering Department, Technical
University of Catalunya, Jordi Girona Salgado 31
08034 Barcelona, E- Spain

ABSTRACT A risk map of Andorra at 1:25 000 scale
is discussed. The map has been carried out based
on geomorphological criteria. The risk assessment
is considered through risk localization,
intensity and reach of phenomena and activity.
Four risk classes are defined based on magnitude
and activity of processes. The latter are
represented as symbols on the zoning map.

INTRODUCTION

A geological risk map of a 100 km^2 area in Andorra
Principality has been carried out at 1:25 000 scale. The
area surveyed corresponds to the Gran Valira and the Valira
d'Orient valleys. The main part of the area is over 1000 m
above the mean sea level and was covered by glaciers until
holocene period. Valley bedrock is composed of schists,
phyllites, sandstones and limestones from Paleozoic ages
which are overlaid by quaternary deposits : till and
colluvium. These surficial deposits show signs of recent
instability. For instance, a debris avalanche detached from
a till destroyed the small village of Fener in 1865 (Thos y
Codina 1884) and recently several movements have been
triggered by heavy rain periods. The purpose of the map was
the analysis of both landslide and flood risks.

METHODOLOGICAL PRINCIPLES

The map is geomorphologically based. The basic criteria was
to apply the principle of the actualism as used by Varnes
(1984).Only natural phenomena have been considered, that
is, no evaluation has been done concerning excavated slopes
or foundations. The reason is that stability of cut slopes
depends on geometrical characteristics of final slope and
on the excavation method. Nevertheless the geological
structure of the bedrock and the location of unfavourable
joints for cut slopes have been indicated.

RISK ASSESSMENT

Risk assessment it has been considered in four different
ways:

(a) risk localization, by means of geomorphological
     reconnaisance using photointerpretation and field
     techniques. Ancient scarps, developed scars, landslide
     deposits and other geomorphological features are used
     together with historical information.
     A landslide inventory was carried out in the study area.
     From it, threshold stability slope angles have been
     derived. Using Varnes (1978) terminology :
     (i) translational slides (in colluvial soils) occur in
          slopes over 27º, usually from 32 to 40º.
     (ii) rotational slides (in tills) occur in slopes from
           35 to 40º
     (iii) debris flows occcur in slopes over 27º in
           colluvium and over 35º in tills.
     (iv) rock falls occur in rock slopes normally steeper
           than 40º
(b) Intensity.For landslides, intensity has been related to
     mobilized volume. For floods, intensity has been derived
     from main historical floods recorded in the area.

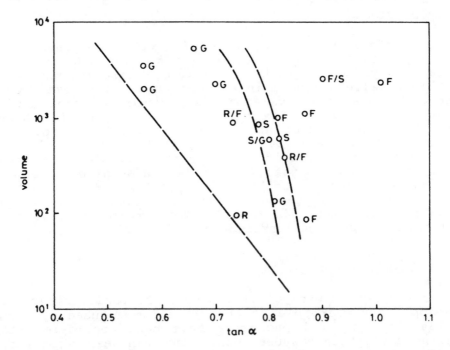

FIG. 1 Rockfall mobility. Plot of mobilized volume versus
apparent coefficient of friction (tan α) derived from the
path of the fallen debris, for several rock falls from
Andorra   and   neighbouring   Pyrenean   area.   Slope
characteristics below the rock fall source : (G) grass (R)
rock (S) scree deposits (F) Forest (see explanation in the
text).

(c) Assessment   of   areas subjected to hazard .Different
    landslide types show variations in runout distances

covered by them. The mobility of a landslide may be
expressed as the ratio between the maximum vertical drop
and the maximum horizontal distance travelled
(equivalent coefficient of friction or tan α, where α is
the angle of the line linking the highest point of the
landslide scar and the farthest point of the slided
mass). Hsü (1975) in very large rockfalls observed a
decrease of tan α with the rockfall volume. We have also
found a friction reduction with volume for small shallow
landslides. Nevertheless, the mobility is also dependent
on the type of failure mechanism : rockfall, debris flow
or translational slide(Corominas et al 1988).
These kind of relationship are useful in assessing
landslide prone areas. For example, Fig. 1 shows
different rockfalls inventoried in the Pyrenees area.No
rockfall paths have been found below the dashed line on
the left. Above this line, the effect of the slope
characteristics below the rockfall source is observable.
Rockfalls propagate more easily in bedrock or grass
covered slopes (tan α lesser than 0.75-0.8)than in scree
and forested slopes. Central dashed line delimitate
rockfalls paths through grass and bedrock slopes from
scree slopes(tan α lesser than 0.8-0.85) and these ones
from forested slopes.Given a rockfall source site and an
expected volume to be mobilized, the downslope area
between the source and the arrival point (intersection
of a straight line with angle α and the slope surface)
has been designed as a risk area.
(d) Activity. Due to the lack of historical information
    (only present century floods are known with a minimum
    data) the activity has been inferred from the last
    experience of November 1982 floods and landslides and
    from field geomorphological criteria (open scars, tilted
    trees, open cracks in buildings).

RISK ZONING

Varnes (1984) distinguished betwen hazard and risk. A low
risk area may be attributed either to a populated area
without a threatening hazard or to an important hazard in a
non urban area. In order to avoid possible
misinterpretations on land use potentiallity, an urban use
is assumed in the whole studied area. Four risk levels have
been defined (Fig. 2) considering the magnitude and
activity of phenomena. In each zone the hazardous phenomena
are represented by means of symbols which have been
overlaid on it.

CONCLUSIONS

This methodology has allowed to develop the risk map in a
very short period of time (only five months) with a
reasonable degree of accuracy. The data extracted from

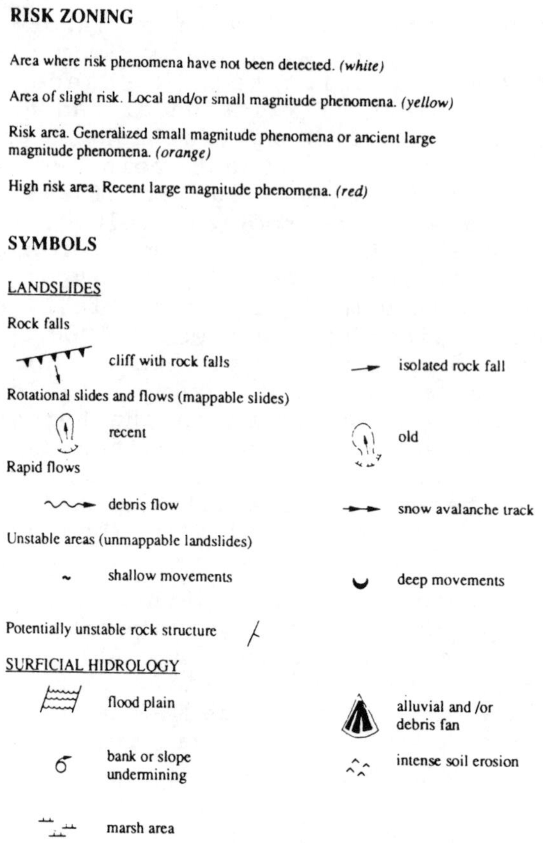

RISK ZONING

Area where risk phenomena have not been detected. *(white)*

Area of slight risk. Local and/or small magnitude phenomena. *(yellow)*

Risk area. Generalized small magnitude phenomena or ancient large magnitude phenomena. *(orange)*

High risk area. Recent large magnitude phenomena. *(red)*

SYMBOLS

LANDSLIDES

Rock falls

cliff with rock falls   isolated rock fall

Rotational slides and flows (mappable slides)

recent   old

Rapid flows

debris flow   snow avalanche track

Unstable areas (unmappable landslides)

shallow movements   deep movements

Potentially unstable rock structure

SURFICIAL HIDROLOGY

flood plain   alluvial and /or debris fan

bank or slope undermining   intense soil erosion

marsh area

FIG. 2 Legend of the risk map of Andorra.

landslide inventory referring to the landslide reach may be extrapolated to other risk areas because they are independent from the climate and in a lesser measure from the geological context as well.

REFERENCES

Corominas, J., Peñaranda, R & Baeza, C. (1988) Identificación de factores que condicionan la formación de movimientos superficiales en los valles altos del Llobregat y Cardener. In : II Simposio sobre taludes y laderas inestables, Andorra la Vella, 195-207.

Hsü, K.J. (1975) Catastrophic debris stream (sturzstroms) generated by rockfalls. Geol. Soc. Am. Bull 86, 129-140.

Thos y Codina, S (1884) Reconocimiento físico, geológico y minero de los valles de Andorra, Bol. Com. Mapa Geol. Esp. 11, 183-207, Madrid.

Varnes, D.J. (1978) Slope movement: types and processes. In :R.L. Schuster & R.J. Krizek Landslides : analysis and control, Trans. Res. Board Spec. Rep. 176, 11-33.

Varnes, D.J. (1984) Landslide hazard zonation : a review of principles and practice, Natural Hazards 3, UNESCO, Paris.

Hydrology in Mountainous Regions. II - Artificial Reservoirs; Water and Slopes
(Proceedings of two Lausanne Symposia, August 1990). IAHS Publ. no. 194, 1990.

Essai de recensement cartographique des glissements de terrain et écroulements rocheux sur le territoire Suisse

F. NOVERRAZ
Centre interdépartemental d'Etude des Terrains Instables
(CETI), Ecole Polytechnique Fédérale de Lausanne,
1015 Lausanne, Suisse

RESUME   La détection et la cartographie systématique des
glissements de terrains et écroulements rocheux qui
affectent en très grand nombre le territoire suisse a pu
être réalisée par interprétation géomorphologique des 232
cartes topographiques au 1:25'000 de l'atlas national. Ce
travail a été rendu possible par la qualité excellente
des cartes en question, ainsi que par la pratique répétée
de cette démarche en prélude à des levés complets sur le
terrain, et par une longue habitude des glissements de
terrain en contexte alpin. Cette méthode présente
l'avantage d'un coût minime et d'un délai de réalisation
très court.

Le document obtenu peut servir de base à des levés
détaillés tels que ceux requis pour l'aménagement du
territoire, par exemple dans le cadre des plans
directeurs cantonaux pour la Suisse. Il sert aussi de
carte de risque d'instabilité pour des phénomènes
secondaires tels que glissements rapide, coulées de boue,
laves torrentielles, débâcles torrentielles, souvent liés
aux grandes zones glissées.

INTRODUCTION

La Suisse, pays dont le territoire est dans une large proportion
dominé par le relief alpin, est très concernée par les problèmes
d'instabilité de versant, qui n'en épargnent pratiquement aucune des
grandes unités géographiques.

Ces phénomènes sont parfois connus en raison des dégâts qu'ils
occasionnent aux habitations et aux infrastructures de manière
épisodique ou permanente, parfois à la suite d'études spécifiques à
un projet; certains ont été cartographiés sur les cartes géologiques
1:25'000 de l'atlas géologique suisse, mais ces cartes - surtout les
feuilles antérieures aux vingt dernières années - sont souvent
lacunaires ou incorrectes sur la question des glissements de terrain;
elles ne couvrent de surcroît qu'un tiers du pays environ; certains
cas de glissement enfin ont fait l'objet d'études sous forme de
monographies.

ETUDES GENERALES

De 1980 à 1984, le projet d'Ecole pluridisciplinaire DUTI (Détection
et Utilisation des Terrains Instables) de l'Ecole Polytechnique
Fédérale de Lausanne a consacré une partie de ses activités à lever
environ 200 km^2 de territoire, sous forme de cartes d'instabilité au
1:5'000 et 1:10'000 (DUTI, 1985, Noverraz, 1985). Ces levés,

entièrement effectués sur le terrain, constituaient un recensement complet de tous les types d'instabilité de terrain déclarés. Ils ont été effectués sur la base d'une préinterprétation géomorphologique sur cartes topographiques 1:5'000 et photos aériennes.

Un travail semblable, un peu simplifié, a été appliqué depuis 1985 à la cartographie complète du canton de Vaud (3'200 km²) au 1:10'000 pour le compte du Service de l'Aménagement du Territoire; 2'000 km² ont ainsi déjà été levés.

En 1986, un recensement des glissements de terrain à l'échelle suisse a été tenté par voie d'enquête auprès des divers services administratifs de chaque canton; il a été complété par un report de tous les glissements connus ou cartographiés sur les cartes de l'atlas géologique suisse au 1:25'000. Ce mandat de l'Office Fédéral des Mensurations cadastrales est repris dans le cadre de la Réforme de la Mensuration Officielle (REMO) qui vise notamment à tenir compte des effets des mouvements de terrain sur la triangulation et les plans cadastraux. Ces travaux ont été menés dans le cadre du CETI, Centre interdépartemental d'Etude des Terrains Instables de l'EPFL, créé dans le prolongement du projet DUTI (CETI, 1985). Le recensement s'est révélé en partie décevant, en ce qui concerne les renseignements obtenus par voie d'enquête: ces derniers furent très inégaux selon les cantons, le plus souvent très lacunaires selon toute évidence, voire inexistants. La carte ainsi publiée (fig. 1 et 3) fut néanmoins la première du genre élaborée à l'échelle du pays. Ce travail eut le mérite de faire apparaître qu'un recensement beaucoup plus complet, et en même temps plus homogène, pouvait être tenté par la seule interprétation géomorphologique des cartes topographiques de l'atlas national au 1:25'000: en effet, les renseignements obtenus par voie d'enquête nous sont souvent parvenus sous forme de zones désignées sans limites précises, alors que la confrontation avec la carte 1:25'000 suffisait à établir avec une évidence plus ou moins grande les limites morphologiques réelles de la zone instable en question. Le procédé a donc déjà été utilisé localement dans le cadre de l'élaboration de ce premier recensement.

CARTOGRAPHIE DES PHENOMENES D'INSTABILITE DE VERSANT PAR ANALYSE GEOMORPHOLOGIQUE SUR CARTES TOPOGRAPHIQUES

Il était donc tentant d'étendre l'application de cette démarche à l'ensemble du pays, puisqu'elle ne pouvait que conduire à une amélioration considérable de la cartographie élaborée pour la REMO d'une part, puisqu'aucune cartographie des glissements de terrain à l'échelle suisse n'était à attendre dans un proche avenir d'autre part.

La méthode se justifie en outre par son seul coût relatif: en effet, le même travail effectué sur la base d'une analyse stéréographique de photographies aériennes, toutes autres conditions étant identiques (même opérateur, pas de contrôle sur le terrain), offrirait une précision et une fiabilité un peu supérieures, l'accroissement de la précision étant d'ailleurs d'intérêt limité du fait de l'échelle à laquelle est faite le travail; en revanche, une photo-interprétation systématique demanderait un temps - donc un coût - cinq à dix fois supérieur. Enfin, un recensement à partir de levés systématiques sur le terrain, le seul à pouvoir prétendre à une fiabilité sensiblement plus élevée - du moins dans les limites de compétence des auteurs du travail - demanderait dix à vingt fois plus de temps que la seule photo-interprétation.

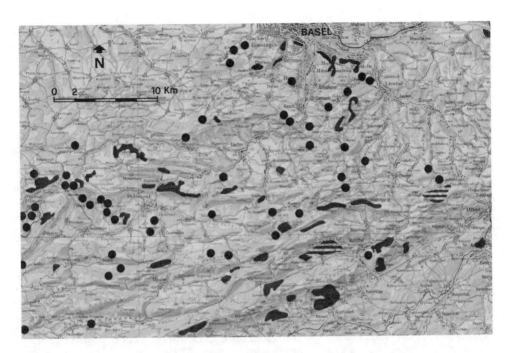

FIG. 1 Extrait du recensement des glissements obtenu par voie d'enquête (REMO, 1985): Jura septentrional.

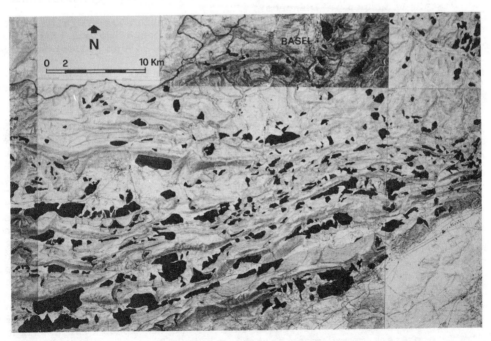

FIG. 2 Extrait de la carte des glissements de terrain de la Suisse inventoriés par analyse géomorphologique sur cartes: Jura septentrional (même région que fig. 1).

Par expérience, un levé géologique des seuls phénomènes d'instabilité de terrain demande une journée pour 4 à 5 km², moyenne Alpes-Plateau, pour le contexte suisse, c'est-à-dire de 8'000 à 10'000 journées de terrain pour l'ensemble de la Suisse. Par comparaison, le recensement effectué sur cartes 1:25'000 a demandé en moyenne 3 heures par feuille de 215 km², soit 600 heures de travail ou 70 journées seulement! L'entreprise est donc justifiée largement par son seul rapport prix-résultat; mais elle l'est aussi par le fait que les fonds disponibles pour financer un travail de terrain complet, soit un budget de l'ordre de 10 millions de francs suisses, n'existent pas faute de motivation, tant au niveau politique qu'économique et même scientifique. Peut-être cette constatation ne sera-t-elle bientôt plus tout à fait d'actualité grâce aux efforts entrepris par le Service hydrologique et géologique national dans le cadre de la décennie "pour la réduction des catastrophes naturelles", qui débute en 1990.

Ce travail d'interprétation cartographique (fig. 2 et 4) a donc été effectué de 1988 à 1989; l'identification des zones instables a été faite sur la base des modifications bien connues que glissements et affaissements rocheux impriment aux versants, des crêtes aux cours d'eau de thalweg en passant par le modelé même des pentes, leur adoucissement et le ramollissement du relief, les doubles crêtes, les arcs de déchirure et l'allure du réseau hydrographique, etc.

La nature même de cette procédure implique que les phénomènes d'instabilité déclarés qui ne marquent pas de manière significative la morphologie du terrain ne peuvent pas être identifiés par cette méthode; de tels cas sont cependant rarissimes pour des glissements de dimensions importantes: ils peuvent se produire dans trois circonstances:

- glissements sur des pentes très faibles (courbes de niveau trop distantes et peu influencées),
- glissements à peine amorcés, avec transport très faible des matériaux, donc sans atteinte au contexte morphologique en-dehors de la zone de cisaillement amont, qui n'est pas toujours identifiable au 1:25'000,
- glissements fossiles ou occultes, remodelés par l'érosion normale jusqu'à disparition plus ou moins complète de leurs caractères morphologiques.

Il est évident d'autre part que des glissements de petites dimensions (moins de dix hectares par exemple) peuvent échapper totalement à une identification à l'échelle du 1:25'000, surtout lorsqu'ils sont peu profonds et affectent des pentes faibles. Mais ces glissements d'intérêt très local sont hors du propos du présent document.

Ces restrictions aux possibilités de la méthode ayant été énumérées, il est temps d'en évaluer l'impact quantitatif: l'expérience accumulée avec le levé sur le terrain de plus de 2'000 km² de cartes d'instabilité permet d'admettre que les terrains en glissement non identifiés par la méthode décrite ici représentent en superficie environ 10% des zones instables existantes. Cette proportion doit en fait encore être minimisée par le fait de l'intégration à la carte présentée de l'ensemble des cas tirés des cartes et études publiées ainsi que du recensement pour la REMO.

En conclusion, on peut raisonnablement estimer à plus de 90% du total réel la surface des zones instables effectivement reportées sur la carte présentée ici. Le risque inverse que des zones stables aient été interprétées comme zones instables existe également, mais à titre vraisemblablement exceptionnel et dans des proportions bien inférieures aux omissions.

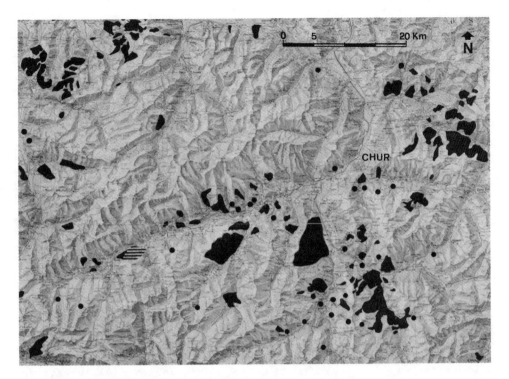

FIG. 3 Extrait du recensement des glissements obtenu par voie
d'enquête (REMO, 1985): Bassin du Rhin, Grisons.

FIG. 4 Extrait de la carte des glissements de terrain de la Suisse
inventoriés par analyse géomorphologique sur cartes: Bassin du Rhin,
Grisons (même région que fig. 3).

BUTS ET LIMITES D'UTILISATION DU DOCUMENT PRESENTE

L'absence d'une cartographie spécifique des phénomènes d'instabilité en Suisse justifie à elle seule la réalisation de la présente cartographie, dans l'optique limitée de donner une évaluation de l'ampleur réelle du problème à l'échelle du pays. Ce recensement se prête à une confrontation de nature purement académique avec les différents ensembles géologiques et lithologiques en présence, dans la perspective de décrire la sensibilité effective des différentes formations rocheuses aux phénomènes d'instabilité, travail qui a été exécuté[1]. Elle présente une utilité évidente dans un cadre comme celui de l'Office Fédéral des Mensurations Cadastrales, en vue du contrôle de la triangulation de 4e ordre et de l'explication de certains désordres subis par celle-ci. Elle permet d'évaluer l'ampleur du problème selon les régions et notamment selon les cantons, et devrait permettre de désigner les régions où des études plus poussées se justifient. Elle pourrait être comparée avec profit aux cartes cantonales de risques naturels lorsque celles-ci ont été élaborées dans le cadre des plans directeurs, conformément à la loi fédérale sur l'aménagement du territoire de 1979.

Cette cartographie ne peut en revanche, bien entendu, pas faire l'objet d'un usage direct comme carte de risques, carte d'aménagement, ou simplement comme inventaire exhaustif des glissements de terrain, en raison de la part de lacunes qu'elle contient assurément et du fait du très faible risque local d'erreur "par excès". Pour accéder à un tel usage, elle devrait au moins être vérifiée à peu près systématiquement sur photos aériennes au stéréoscope, et faire l'objet de vérifications sur le terrain des cas les plus incertains. Cette amélioration, qui nécessiterait déjà un investissement financier supplémentaire très important, amènerait en principe la cartographie au moins au niveau d'élaboration de ce qu'ont fait les quelques cantons les plus avancés dans ce domaine, dans l'élaboration de leurs plans directeurs. Cette égalité de principe est toutefois beaucoup plus théorique qu'effective, car à ce niveau apparaît un autre problème très singulier: il s'agit de la compétence des personnes concernées par cette tâche pourtant facile à premier vue que représente le levé systématique des zones instables. Le fait est que les résultats sont assez chroniquement lacunaires voire très décevants, et ce sont presque toujours les très grandes zones glissées qui font prioritairement les frais de ces lacunes.

Etant donné que le document présenté ici est au contraire incomplet au niveau des petits glissements, on peut aisément conclure que sa confrontation avec les documents en mains des Services d'Aménagement du Territoire cantonaux, par exemple, ne peut être que profitable, et cela dans les deux sens.

Il faut cependant relever que le but et l'intérêt de recenser et cartographier systématiquement des grandes zones instables telles que les glissements de retrait glaciaire échappe le plus souvent aux administrations et aux utilisateurs potentiels, même directement concernés: en effet ces glissements invisibles pour la plupart, jamais spectaculaires, n'engendrent à première vue pas de destructions ni surtout de dommages physiques aux personnes, du fait de leurs vitesses très lentes (souvent guère plus de quelques cm/an) et pas immédiatement décelables. Pourtant l'importance de ces phénomènes dans la vie économique va croissant avec l'ouverture de la plupart des vallées alpines au tourisme de masse et à un intense trafic motorisé, avec la construction de stations de tourisme hivernal

---

[1] Répartition géographique, origine et contexte géologique des glissements de terrain latents en Suisse, Symposium 4, thème 4D du présent congrès.

tentaculaires: en effet, pour peu spectaculaires qu'ils soient le plus souvent, les dégâts aux infrastructures et aux constructions, et les litiges consécutifs, finissent par coûter des sommes considérables à la communauté. D'autre part, et c'est là un aspect secondaire peu connu de ces grands glissements, ils sont souvent à l'origine des dégâts beaucoup plus spectaculaires que provoquent coulées de boues, laves torrentielles et débâcles torrentielles, ces dernières constituant de surcroît des dégâts et des conséquences "exportés". Les causes de cette relations résident dans le peu de résistance à l'érosion torrentielle et au ruissellement qu'offrent ces surfaces glissées vastes de plusieurs km^2 (et même de 10 à 45 km^2 pour une bonne centaine de cas en Suisse): glissements secondaires et coulées boueuses s'y produisent et viennent obstruer les cours d'eau en crue, accroître leur débit solide et en conséquence leur pouvoir d'érosion. Cet enchaînement de processus est susceptible de prendre des proportions dévastatrices en cas de crues événementielles telles celles de l'été 1987 (Aschwanden et al., 1988, Haeberli et al., 1988); et pourtant celles-ci ne se sont pas produites, en ce qui concerne la Suisse, sur une région particulièrement sensible à cet égard.

REPARTITION DES ZONES INSTABLES

Ce sujet n'est que brièvement résumé ci-après; il est traité plus en détail dans un deuxième article paru dans le même symposium, qui traite également des relations entre cette répartition et le contexte géologique (Noverraz, 1990).

   Les régions les plus riches en phénomènes d'instabilité et qui sont de surcroît plus particulièrement menacées par les phénomènes secondaires venant d'être évoqués, sont principalement le canton des Grisons (bassin du Rhin, fig. 4, val Müstair et région de Poschiavo surtout) et la bordure nord des Alpes entre le lac de Thoune et le Walensee. Le canton du Valais est très riche en vastes glissements de retrait glaciaire, mais son climat très sec et pratiquement dépourvu de pointes de pluviométrie extrêmes (sauf sa partie orientale) limite les effets événementiels sur ces instabilités. A l'inverse, c'est le caractère fréquemment extrême des pointes de pluviométrie qui rend très dangereux les quelques glissements très vastes de certaines vallées du canton du Tessin, au sud des Alpes (Val Leventina, Val Maggia, Val Blenio). Les Préalpes vaudoises, fribourgeoises et bernoises, de même que le Jura septentrional (fig. 2), sont très riches en glissements de terrain, mais le relief plus modéré et plus doux en limite souvent les conséquences, de même que le caractère très argileux et peu perméable des formations incriminées (Flysch et unités ultra-helvétiques riches en schistes argileux).

CONCLUSIONS

La méthode cartographique exposée dans le présent article donne une image globale de la répartition des phénomènes d'instabilité en Suisse qui n'existait pas jusqu'à présent. Elle ne prétend pas donner une image absolument exacte ni surtout complète de la réalité. En revanche, elle devrait pouvoir servir de "tremplin" à des études plus poussées incluant un travail de terrain. On peut penser qu'elle est de nature à permettre de combler une bonne partie des lacunes dans les informations dont disposent certains services cantonaux d'aménagement du territoire dans le cadre de l'élaboration imposée par la loi fédérale des plans directeurs. Le procédé utilisé, par son caractère peu coûteux et rapide, devrait aider à persuader politiques et aménagistes qu'un recensement des risques liés aux terrains instables n'est pas nécessairement une opération très longue et très coûteuse, au moins au niveau préliminaire. Le gain de temps que permettrait ultérieurement cette opération, en cas d'un véritable recensement sur le terrain, est à nouveau plus que suffisant pour le justifier économiquement.

REFERENCES

Aschwanden, H. & Schaedler, B. (1988) Hochwasserereignisse im Jahre 1987 in der Schweiz. <u>Mitt. 10</u>, Lndeshydrologie und -geologie, Bern.

Centre interdépartemental d'Etude des Terrains Instables (CETI) (1985) Mensuration parcellaire et conservation en zones d'instabilité naturelle du terrain (REMO). Ecole Polytechnique Fédérale de Lausanne.

Détection et Utilisation des Terrains Instables (DUTI) (1985) Rapport final du projet d'Ecole. Ecole Polytechnique Fédérale de Lausanne.

Haeberli, W. & Naef, F. (1988) Murgänge im Hochgebirge. <u>Die Alpen</u>, <u>64/4</u>, Schweiz. Alpen-Club, Bern.

Noverraz, F. (1985) Etudes régionales - cartes d'instabilités. DUTI, Ecole Polytechnique Fédérale de Lausanne.

Noverraz, F. (1990) Mapping Methodology of Landslides and Rockfalls in Switzerland. <u>Proc. ALPS 90-Alpine Landslide Practical Seminar</u>, 6th Int. Conf. and Field Workshop on Landslides.

Noverraz, F. (1990) Répartition géographique, origine et contexte géologique des glissements de terrain latents en Suisse. <u>Proc. Conf. Int. sur les ressources en eau en régions montagneuses</u> (AISH).

Hydrology in Mountainous Regions. II - Artificial Reservoirs; Water and Slopes
(Proceedings of two Lausanne Svmposia, August 1990). IAHS Publ. no. 194, 1990.

Répartition géographique, origine et contexte géologique des glissements de terrain latents en Suisse

F. NOVERRAZ
Centre interdépartemental d'Etude des Terrains Instables
(CETI), Ecole Polytechnique Fédérale de Lausanne,
1015 Lausanne, Suisse

RESUME   Un recensement systématique des phénomènes
d'instabilité de versants affectant le territoire suisse
a été effectué par l'auteur dans le cadre de son activité
au sein du CETI à l'EPFL. Les méthodes utilisées sont
décrites dans un autre article publié dans le cadre du
même symposium[1].
    Ce recensement fait apparaître une répartition très
inhomogène des zones instables, sans relations directes
avec l'ampleur du relief, les unités géographiques et le
climat. La densité, les dimensions moyennes et la typologie des zones instables dépendant en revanche étroitement
du contexte géologique et de l'histoire géomorphologique
récente de la région considérée.
    L'article proposé résume donc les relations entre
grands ensembles géologiques et lithologiques caractéri-
sant le territoire suisse, et typologie et importance du
développement des zones instables recensées. Il met en
évidence l'extraordinaire tendance au glissement de
certaines formations rocheuses.
    Ce travail n'avait pas pour but de parvenir à une
conclusion particulière; on peut néanmoins en tirer comme
enseignement l'illustration donnée de la relation très
étroite qui lie la géologie et les phénomènes
d'instabilité, relation qui devrait aider à motiver un peu
plus sérieusement les géologues et l'enseignement de la
géologie pour ce sujet encore étonnamment mal connu.

INTRODUCTION

La méthode utilisée pour le recensement des glissements de terrain
déclarés et des écroulements rocheux sur lequel se base le présent
travail a consisté principalement en une identification sur carte
topographique 1:25'000 recourant à l'analyse géomorphologique. Cette
méthode a été préalablement utilisée couramment par l'auteur dans le
cadre de travaux de recensement sur le terrain, qui ont permis d'en
tester et confirmer l'efficacité (DUTI 1985, Noverraz 1985).
    Tous les glissements connus par les cartes et travaux publiés en
Suisse, par les travaux du CETI, ainsi que les cas d'instabilité
recensés dans le cadre d'un mandat confié au CETI par l'Office
fédéral des mensurations cadastrales pour la REMO (Réforme de la
Mensuration officielle), ont été en outre intégrés au présent
travail. Précisons que le recensement effectué dans le cadre de la

---

[1] Problèmes de recensement et de cartographie des glissements de terrain,
incidence sur l'aménagement du territoire.

REMO a été basé principalement sur le résultat d'une enquête auprès
des différents offices cantonaux susceptibles de détenir des informations relatives aux terrains instables (CETI 1985).

REPARTITION GEOGRAPHIQUE DES INSTABILITES DE VERSANT

Sur l'ensemble du territoire suisse, la répartition des instabilités
frappe d'emblée par son hétérogénéité, sans relation aucune avec
l'ampleur du relief ou toute autre considération de nature géographique. Certaines régions du pays apparaissent extraordinairement
riches en zones instables, celles-ci pouvant couvrir jusqu'à 30 à 40%
du territoire sur des secteurs de plusieurs centaines de kilomètres
carrés. Ces secteurs sont parfois très bien délimités, et ils corres-
pondent souvent à des zones à relief modéré, peu nerveux, voire mou;
la raison tient évidemment au contexte géologique.
    Parmi les grandes régions les plus riches en instabilités de
pente, on peut citer notamment le nord et le centre du canton des
Grisons (haute vallée du Rhin et vallées latérales, Prättigau, figure
1), le Valais central, les Préalpes fribourgeoises et bernoises (fig.
3), la région située entre Interlaken et Lucerne, celle entre Schwytz
et la Linth (Lac de Zurich) (fig. 5), et enfin le Jura septentrional.
D'une manière générale, la bordure externe ou nord des Alpes est très
riche en phénomènes d'instabilité, tant en ce qui concerne les
glissements que les écroulements et les éboulements.
    D'autres régions apparaissent, au contraire, très pauvres en
instabilités de pente, et cela encore une fois indépendamment du
relief: ce sont notamment la partie centrale et méridionale du canton
du Tessin, les hautes Alpes centrales, le bassin de l'Inn aux
Grisons, certaines parties du plateau molassique, ainsi que le Jura
méridional - soit la partie la plus élevée de la chaîne.

RELATIONS CONSTATEES ENTRE LA REPARTITION DES INSTABILITES ET LE
CONTEXTE GEOLOGIQUE

Il faut d'abord préciser que l'on entend par contexte géologique la
nature du soubassement rocheux, soit le type de formations rocheuses
qui le constituent et sa structure tectonique interne. La couverture
meuble quaternaire est fréquemment le siège de glissements de
terrain, mais dans des proportions insignifiantes relativement au
nombre, au volume et à la surface des glissements impliquant le
soubassement rocheux. Par ailleurs, on peut admettre que les glissements inventoriés par la méthode utilisée ici sont pratiquement tous
des glissements affectant le rocher, de par leurs dimensions.
    On peut constater d'une manière très générale que le sud des Alpes
suisses est relativement pauvre en phénomènes d'instabilité: c'est le
domaine des unités métamorphiques penniques, simplo-tessinoises et
austro-alpines. Parmi ces unités, celles qui ont subi un métamorphisme relativement léger (faciès schistes verts et amphibolique)
telles les nappes penniques supérieures, sont les plus riches en
phénomènes d'instabilité, généralement hérités du retrait glaciaire
(canton du Valais méridional).
    Les massifs centraux granitiques sont presque dépourvus de phéno-
mènes d'instabilité autres que des éboulements de taille modérée, et
cela malgré les reliefs très accentués et élevés auxquels ils sont
liés (Alpes centrales valaisannes, bernoises et uranaises).
    La couverture permo-carbonifère, généralement décollée, des nappes
penniques et austro-alpines, constituée de roches gréso-phylliteuses

à métamorphisme léger, peut donner lieu à une très grande abondance de phénomènes de glissements de taille parfois considérable, hérités également des retraits glaciaires würmien ou antérieurs. Ces glissements coïncident avec les formations à prédominance phylliteuse (Valais, vallée du Rhin antérieur aux Grisons), tandis que les formations gréso-conglomératiques (faciès Verrucano) sont stables.

La couverture triasique peu épaisse des nappes penniques et austro-alpine de nature phylliteuse, évaporitique (gypse-anhydrite), calcaro-dolomitique, bréchique (cornieules) est très souvent associée à de grands glissements, à l'origine desquels elle semble même se trouver parfois (Valais). Elle est parfois seule impliquée dans des glissements de taille plus modérée, mais souvent très actifs (Valais central, au sud du Rhône).

Les schistes lustrés crétacés (calcschistes sériciteux) sont à l'origine de très grands glissements dans le canton des Grisons, où ils sont particulièrement développés (Bündnerschiefer). On peut citer le glissement de Heinzenberg près de Coire, qui, avec 45 km^2, est le plus grand glissement du pays (Jäckli 1953), lui aussi consécutif au retrait glaciaire, mais toujours actif. Que ce soit dans la région Coire-Splügen-Prättigau ou dans la basse Engadine (rive gauche de l'Inn), soit les deux principaux domaines qu'occupent les schistes lustrés, les glissements couvrant plusieurs km^2 se comptent par dizaines.

Les Flyschs penniques, qui atteignent un grand développement dans la région à l'est de Coire (Flysch du Prättigau, Grisons, fig. 1 et 2), donnent lieu à une très grande concentration de glissements de grande taille, généralement liés à l'érosion et au retrait glaciaire (glissement de Conters, 22 km^2). Il en va de même pour le Flysch du Niesen plus à l'ouest. Ces formations alternativement grésoconglomératiques et schisto-marneuses peuvent former d'importants reliefs relativement stables ou au contraire s'avérer très instables, selon les relations entre la topographie et la tectonique.

Les sédiments ultra-helvétiques, avec lesquels on retrouve les séries triasiques (gypse et cornieules surtout), et surtout les schistes argileux aaléniens et les Flyschs crétacés, sont extraordinairement propices aux glissements de terrain. Ces dépôts sont cependant assez éparpillés géographiquement, formant principalement une bande étroite entre le Valais central (glissements de la région Montana-Sierre) et Coire aux Grisons d'une part (glissement géant de Lumnez, 35 km^2, fig. 1 et 2), et des domaines plus importants à la bordure nord des Alpes (zones des cols en Suisse romande, Préalpes externes fribourgeoises et bernoises). Dans ces régions, les surfaces en glissement peuvent couvrir jusqu'à 40% du territoire.

Les formations sédimentaires constituant les nappes helvétiques, dans lesquelles sont taillés les hauts reliefs des Alpes septentrionales, présentent des relations variables avec les phénomènes d'instabilité, quantitativement et du point de vue de la nature de ceux-ci, entre le sud-ouest de la chaîne et le nord-est. On constate en effet que dans la partie méridionale de la chaîne (nappes de Morcles et des Diablerets, nappe du Wildhorn jusqu'à Interlaken et parautochtone, la stabilité est généralement excellente, grâce à la puissante ossature qu'offrent les calcaires massifs du Malm et, subsidiairement, de l'Urgonien. Cette stabilité tient aussi à un facteur de nature topographique: l'absence de vallée importante transversale à la chaîne. Avec le grand développement à l'affleurement des roches marno-calcaires du Dogger et surtout des schistes argileux de l'Aalénien, dès Lauterbrunnen, apparaissent de très vastes zones de glissement (Grindelwald) (Kienholz 1977).

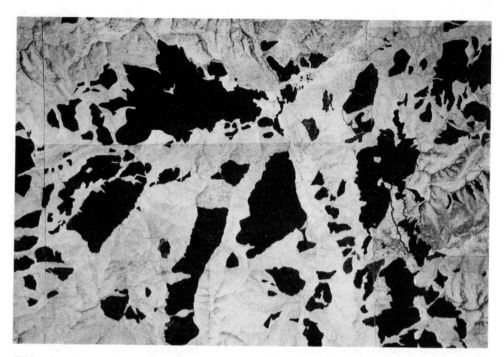

FIG. 1 Inventaire des glissements et écroulements rocheux de Suisse (surfaces noires), extrait (Région de Coire, Rhin antérieur; canton des Grisons); voir aussi figure 2.

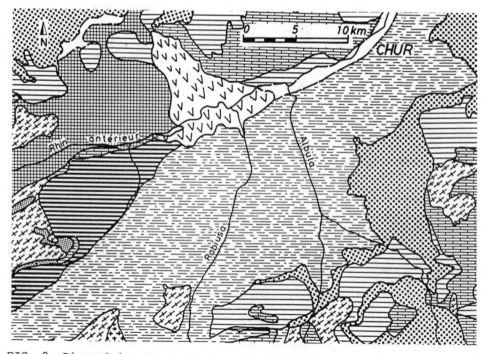

FIG. 2 Répartition des principaux ensembles lithologiques (Région de Coire, Rhin antérieur; canton des Grisons).

LEGENDE FIGURE 2 ET 4:

 Calcaires, dolomies

 Roches sédimentaires marno-calcaires

 Roches sédimentaires marno-argileuses

 Roches sédimentaires à léger métamorphisme, phyllito-gréseuses schisteuses (p.ex. Permo-Trias)

 Schistes lustrés penniques (calaschistes sériciteux)

 Formations de Flysch schisto-gréseux, argilo-conglomératique

 Formations molassiques à prédominance gréso-conglomératique

 Formations molassiques à prédominance marneuse

 Gneiss para-, faciès schistes verts, à amphibolites, lité

 Granites, gneiss granitiques massifs, non lités

La couverture sédimentaire mésozoïque des massifs cristallins centraux, autochtone, parautochtone, nappe du Doldenhorn, est dans l'ensemble très stable, grâce notamment aux puissantes séries calcaires du Malm. Elle a pourtant été le théâtre, au dernier retrait glaciaire, de deux gigantesques glissements couche sur couche, l'un à son extrémité SW ("éboulement" de Salquenen/Sierre), l'autre près de son extrémité NE (le célèbre "éboulement" de Flims, qui, avec 11 km3, est le plus grand glissement d'Europe) (fig. 1 et 2). Les séries tertiaires parautochtones sont en revanche très instables comme tous les Flysch, et ont produit de très grands glissements dans le Schächental (Altdorf) et le canton de Glaris (région de Linthal et d'Elm). Dans la partie nord-est de la chaîne, la nappe de l'Axen (Lias-Dogger-Malm) se caractérise par la présence de très grands glissements au niveau des roches marno-calcaires et schisto-argileuses du Dogger et de l'Aalénien à nouveau (Braunwald, Glaris). De très nombreux glissements et écroulements rocheux de grande taille caractérisent le domaine de la nappe du Säntis, constituée par les séries marno-calcaires et calcaires litées du Crétacé. Les Flyschs tertiaires du domaine helvétique et ultra-helvétique constituent sans doute, en Suisse, les formations rocheuses les plus propices aux glissements de tous types, de toutes tailles, de tous âges et de toutes origines: des grands glissements de retrait glaciaire des vallées alpines tels ceux du Schächental et de Glaris, déjà évoqués pour les flyschs parautochtone, aux glissements superficiels de la couverture éluviale, qui caractérisent les pentes plus modérées des Préalpes externes fribourgeoises et bernoises (fig. 3 et 4), ce peut être jusqu'à 40-50% du territoire qui présente un état d'instabilité latent (Inst. géol. Univ. Fribourg 1976). C'est probablement dans ces zones que le pourcentage de glissements non identifiables par la méthode utilisée pour le présent recensement est le plus grand. La Molasse charriée oligocène (Rupélien, Chattien, Aquitanien dans le nord-est), qui borde au nord toute la chaîne alpine, est très propice aux glissements de par sa nature alternativement gréseuse et argilo-marneuse. On constate cependant qu'elle a donné lieu à un nombre plutôt limité de glissements; la raison est à chercher dans les relations entre les contextes structuraux et topographiques (voir chapitre suivant). De très grandes densités de glissements sont cependant observables dans certaines régions, telles la cuvette lémanique (région à l'est de Lausanne) (Noverraz & Weidmann 1983, Noverraz 1985), le nord du lac de Thoune et la région d'Einsiedeln (Schwytz) (fig. 5).

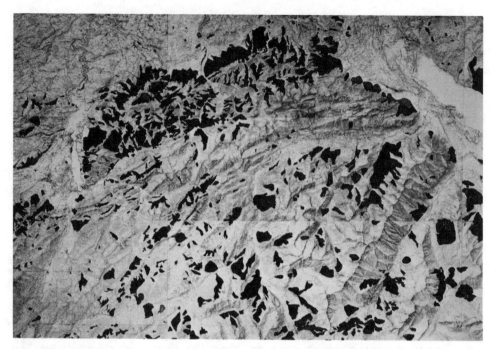

FIG. 3 Inventaire des glissements et écroulements rocheux de Suisse, extrait (région des Préalpes fribourgeoises et bernoises); voir aussi figure 2.

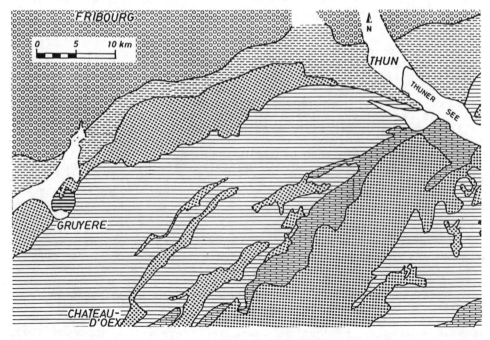

FIG. 4 Répartition des principaux ensembles lithologiques (région des Préalpes fribourgeoises et bernoises) (légende voir fig. 2)

La <u>Molasse du Plateau</u> est d'autant plus sensible aux glissements que le rapport marnes/grès est plus élevé d'une part, que l'épaisseur moyenne des bancs de grès et de conglomérats est plus faible d'autre part. La <u>Molasse lacustre de l'Aquitanien</u> et surtout la <u>Molasse marine du Burdigalien et de l'Helvétien</u>, riches en puissantes assises gréseuses, confèrent une bonne stabilité aux versants des vallées recoupant le SW du Plateau entre Lausanne et le lac de Sempach. Le processus d'instabilité dominant dans ces versants consiste en écroulements de falaises de volume limité. Dans la partie NE du Plateau, du lac de Sempach au lac de Constance, avec la présence de la Molasse lacustre tortonienne (Miocène supérieur), la stabilité est à nouveau plus précaire, cela d'autant plus que le relief est plus accentué dans cette région. La <u>Molasse</u> marno-gréseuse et conglomératique du <u>Tortonien</u> donne lieu aux plus grands glissements recensés sur le Plateau molassique. Le long du pied du Jura et dans le fond des principales vallées synclinales du Jura septentrional, la Molasse lacustre chattienne affleure à nouveau avec des faciès silto-marneux voire exclusivement marneux; cette forte prédominance marneuse explique les phénomènes d'instabilité par glissement systématiques auxquels la Molasse donne naissance dans cette région, et cela même sur des pentes très faibles.

La chaîne du Jura se caractérise, du point de vue des phénomènes d'instabilité, par un accroissement progressif du caractère instable et de la densité de glissements du SW vers le NE. Au SW, le Jura genevois et vaudois se caractérise par une quasi-absence de phéno

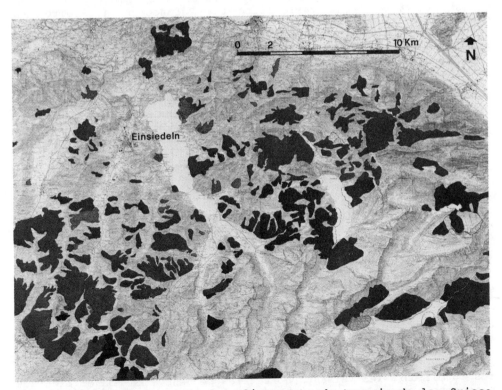

FIG. 5 Extrait de la carte des glissements de terrain de la Suisse inventoriés par analyse géomorphologique sur cartes topographiques 1:25:000: région Einsiedeln-Schwytz.

mènes d'instabilité, bien que l'amplitude des plissements et la
hauteur de la chaîne y soient à leur maximum: cette situation tient à
la puissante série calcaire du Malm, qui forme la carapace stable et
résistante des chaînes anticlinales, ainsi qu'au caractère essentiellement calcaire également des séries crétaciques. Avec la diminution
progressive de puissance des séries sédimentaires vers le NE, la
solidité et la continuité de la carapace du Malm diminue, les vallées
anticlinales apparaissent et avec elles les séries plus profondes et
plus marneuses de l'Argovien, puis du Dogger et du Lias, et enfin du
Trias (argilites du Keuper). La très grande densité de glissements
recensée dans le Jura suisse alémanique est due à la présence à
l'affleurement des marnes et calcaires marneux de l'Argovien (couches
d'Effingen) des marnes oxfordiennes dans le NE, du Bajocien et du
Bathonien qui deviennent marneux au NE de Baden, des marnes argi-
leuses de l'Aalénien (Opalinustone), des schistes bitumineux et
marnes à silex du Toarcien et enfin, dans la région Bâloise, des
argilites bigarrées du Keuper (marnes irisées); à ces différents
faciès mésozoïques s'ajoute encore la sédimentation molassique
chattienne des fonds de vallées dont il a déjà été question.

RELATIONS ENTRE LES INSTABILITES DE VERSANT ET LA TECTONIQUE

Ces relations sont d'importance presque comparable à celles liant les
instabilités à la nature géologique des roches. Elles ne se prêtent
cependant pas à une analyse à échelle aussi vaste que le territoire
suisse, du fait de la variabilité très grande et aléatoire des
données tectoniques, variabilité encore accrue par l'interaction
entre celles-ci et le contexte topographique pour ce qui est de leurs
relations avec la stabilité d'un massif. De ce fait, ces relations
relèvent plus de l'étude de détail, cas par cas, que d'une analyse
globale autre que théorique.

On peut cependant se livrer à quelques constatations générales
concernant les relations entre grandes structures géologiques d'une
part, types et ampleur des instabilités occurrentes d'autre part.

La constatation la plus générale et la plus importante - ce n'est
pas une surprise - est que les versants conformes (avec couches stra-
tigraphiques ou schistosité principale subparallèle à la pente) sont
beaucoup plus riches en instabilités que les versants contraires.
D'une manière générale les formations rocheuses peu litées, résis-
tantes, ou à forte ossature de puissants horizons massifs, sont peu
ou non sujettes au glissement sur versants contraires, voire même en
cas de pendage neutre (horizontal ou perpendiculaire au versant),
mais peuvent donner lieu à de gigantesques glissements sur versants
conformes: les exemples abondent et l'on peut citer Flims et Sierre
dans la couverture sédimentaire parautochtone des massifs cristallins, Val Maggia (Tessin) dans les gneiss penniques, Bettmeralp dans
la couverture métamorphique du massif de l'Aar (Steck 198…), les
glissements de la vallée du Rhin dans la nappe du Säntis, de très
nombreux glissements de moindre ampleur en Molasse, etc.

D'une manière tout aussi générale, on relève que cette différence
de stabilité entre versants conformes et contraires va décroissant
avec la diminution d'importance, en proportion et dimension, des
horizons massifs d'une part, avec l'accroissement du caractère
schisteux, argileux ou phylliteux des formations d'autre part. Dans
ces formations, les versants contraires peuvent même donner lieu aux
glissements les plus profonds et les plus volumineux, avec ou sans
relations avec le fauchage des couches (ex.: glissement d'Hérémence-
Mayens de Sion, de Loye, de Glis et de Mörel en Valais, du

Gotschnahang à Klosters). Toutefois, même pour les formations très litées ou schisteuses, les glissements et les écroulements alpins les plus notoires et les plus nombreux se sont produits sur des versants conformes ou assimilables (Heinzenberg, Safiental, Lumnez aux Grisons, Goldau, Hergiswil en Suisse centrale, Montana, Produit-Leytron en Valais, tous les grands glissements du Plateau molassique, etc…).

Les discontinuités liées à la tectonique cassante (chevauchements, décrochements, failles, fractures, diaclases) jouent presque toujours un rôle très important également, mais celui-ci n'apparaît bien sûr que rarement avec le mode de détection utilisé et décrit ici.

ORIGINE DES GLISSEMENTS DE TERRAIN DECLARES EN SUISSE

Une très large proportion des surfaces couvertes par les glissements inventoriés, que l'on peut estimer à plus de 5% du territoire national, est constituée par les vastes glissements et écroulements des versants des grandes vallées alpines; ceux-ci sont le plus souvent situés dans une tranche d'altitude comprise entre 2'000 à 2'300 m et le fond des vallées. Cette localisation montre, si besoin était, que ces phénomènes sont tous des instabilités consécutives aux retraits glaciaires würmien ou antérieurs. Font principalement exception la plupart des glissements du Jura, les glissements des lunatak (régions préservées de l'englacement des périodes glaciaires), la plupart des glissements du Plateau molassique (sauf les grands glissements de la cuvette lémanique), et enfin les nombreux petits glissements liés directement à l'érosion fluviatile.

La particularité marquante des grands glissements de retrait glaciaire est qu'ils se sont produits dans pratiquement tous les types de formations géologiques et de lithologies, à l'exception des granites des massifs centraux; de fait, seul le processus d'érosion très particulier propre à l'érosion glaciaire a pu rendre possible le déclenchement de glissements atteignant de plusieurs kilomètres carrés à plusieurs dizaines de kilomètres carrés dans des formations apparemment peu sujettes au glissement, comme notamment les gneiss du domaine pennique (Valais, Tessin).

TRAVAUX FUTURS

L'inventaire présenté des glissements de terrain en Suisse fait actuellement l'objet d'un travail de représentation à l'échelle du 1:200'000 avec l'aide de l'Office Fédéral de Topographie, à Wabern. Une carte de synthèse des grandes unités géologiques citées, regroupées par ensembles de faciès lithologique équivalent lorsque cela se justifiait (extrait sous figure 2 et 4), fera également l'objet d'un travail de représentation graphique à la même échelle du 1:200'000. Ces documents graphiques seront publiés ultérieurement par les soins du CETI.

REFERENCES

Centre interdépartemental d'Etude des Terrains Instables (CETI) (1985) Mensuration parcellaire et conservation en zones d'instabilité naturelle du terrain (REMO). Ecole Polytechnique Fédérale de Lausanne.

Détection et Utilisation des Terrains Instables (DUTI) (1985) Rapport final du projet d'Ecole. Ecole Polytechnique Fédérale de Lausanne.

Institut de géologie de l'Université de Fribourg & Alii (1976) Carte préliminaire des glissements de terrain. Direction des Travaux Publics du canton de Fribourg.

Jaeckli, H. (1953) Geologische Eigentümlichkeiten der Geschiebeherde des Bündnerischen Rheingebietes. <u>Wasser- und Energiewirtschaft</u>, <u>8-9</u>, Zurich.

Kienholz, H. (1977) Kombinierte geomorphologische Gefahrenkarte 1:10'000 von Grindelwald. Geographisches Institut der Universität Bern.

Noverraz, F. & Weidmann, M. (1983) Le glissement de terrain de Converney-Taillepied (Belmont et Lutry, Vaud, Suisse). <u>Bull. de géol. Uni. de Lausanne</u>, <u>269</u>.

Noverraz, F. (1985) Etudes régionales - cartes d'instabilités. DUTI, Ecole Polytechnique Fédérale de Lausanne.

Noverraz, F. (1990) Problèmes de recensement et de cartographie des glissements de terrain; incidence sur l'aménagement du territoire. <u>Proc. Conf. Int. sur les ressources en eau en régions montagneuses</u> (AISH).

Noverraz, F. (1990) Mapping Methodology of Landslides and Rockfalls in Switzerland. <u>Proc. ALPS 90-Alpine Landslide Practical Seminar</u>, 6th Int. Conf. and Field Workshop on Landslides.

Steck, A. (1983) Geologie der Aletsch Region (VS). <u>Bull. Murithanienne</u>, <u>101</u>, 135-154.

International Association of Hydrological Sciences

Large scale effects of seasonal snow cover

Edited by B. E. Goodison,
R. G. Barry & J. Dozier

IAHS Publication no. 166 (published August 1987); ISBN 0-947571-16-7; 26 + xii pages; price $42

Large Scale Effects of Seasonal Snow Cover is the proceedings of a symposium held during the XIXth General Assembly of the International Union of Geodesy and Geophysics at Vancouver, August 1987. The symposium was convened under the auspices of the International Commission on Snow and Ice of the International Association of Hydrological Sciences and was co-sponsored by the Commission on Polar Meteorology of the the International Association of Meteorology and Atmospheric Physics.

There were three main themes:

role of snow cover in climate dynamics (polar and mid-latitute regions)

large scale hydrological effects of snow cover

remote sensing of snow cover

Aspects of particular interest for snow-climate interactions included snow cover as a climate indicator and for climate system monitoring, and snow cover parameterization for climate modelling. For hydrological effects, the focus was on inter-relationships between snow cover, snowmelt, flooding, spring soil moisture and runoff in large basins (>2500 km^{-2}), as well as the effect of spatial variability of inputs and model parameters and the appropriate scale of modelling. In remote sensing, the emphasis was on properties measurable by remote sensing, the mapping of snow cover in polar, mid-latitude and mountain regions, and the use of remotely sensed data in hydrological/climatological models and the integration of remotely sensed and ground based snow measurements.

This publication contains 35 papers divided between the three themes.

Please send orders and enquiries to:

Office of the Treasurer IAHS
(Attn: Meredith Compton)
2000 Florida Avenue NW
Washington, DC 20009, USA

IAHS Press
Institute of Hydrology
Wallingford, Oxfordshire
OX10 8BB, UK

INTERNATIONAL ASSOCIATION OF HYDROLOGICAL SCIENCES

The Proceedings of the following eight symposia held during the Third Scientific Assembly of IAHS at Baltimore, Maryland, May 1989, are now available:

Atmospheric Deposition
Publ.no.179, price $45

SYSTEMS ANALYSIS FOR WATER RESOURCES MANAGEMENT:
Closing the Gap Between Theory and Practice
Publ.no.180, price $45

Surface Water Modeling: New Directions for Hydrologic Prediction
Publ.no.181, price $50

Regional Characterization of Water Quality
Publ.no.182, price $45

Snow Cover and Glacier Variations
Publ.no.183, price $30

Sediment and the Environment
Publ.no.184, price $40

Groundwater Contamination
Publ.no.185, price $40

Remote Sensing and Large-Scale Global Processes
Publ.no.186, price $40

The following addresses will be pleased to deal with orders and enquiries:

Office of the Treasurer IAHS, 2000 Florida Avenue NW, Washington, DC 20009, USA
Bureau des Publications de l'UGGI, 140 Rue de Grenelle, 75700 Paris, France
IAHS Press, Institute of Hydrology, Wallingford, Oxfordshire OX10 8BB, UK

INTERNATIONAL ASSOCIATION OF HYDROLOGICAL SCIENCES

In 1987 IAHS Press published the following nine titles:

Water for the Future: Hydrology in Perspective
Proceedings of the Rome Symposium, April 1987
Publ.no.164, price $50

Erosion and Sedimentation in the Pacific Rim
Proceedings of the Corvallis Symposium, August 1987
Publ.no.165 (1987), price $55

Avalanche Formation, Movement and Effects
Proceedings of the Davos Symposium, September 1986
Publ.no.162, provisional price $50

Hydrology 2000
IAHS Working Group Report
Publ.no.171, provisional price $20

Proceedings of the five symposia held during the IUGG Assembly, Vancouver, August 1987:

Large Scale Effects of Seasonal Snow Cover
Publ.no.166, price $42

Forest Hydrology and Watershed Management
Publ.no.167, price $55

The Influence of Climate Change and Climatic Variability on the Hydrologic Regime and Water Resources
Publ.no.168, price $55

Irrigation and Water Allocation
Publ.no.169, price $32

The Physical Basis of Ice Sheet Modelling
Publ.no.170, price $40

The following addresses will be pleased to deal with orders and enquiries
Office of the Treasurer IAHS (Attn: Meredith Compton), 2000 Florida Avenue NW, Washington, DC 20009, USA
Bureau des Publications de l'UGGI, 140 Rue de Grenelle, 75700 Paris, France
IAHS Press, Institute of Hydrology, Wallingford, Oxfordshire OX10 8BB, UK